1.00

THE NEW BUSINESS
ENCYCLOPEDIA

THE EMPIRE STATE BUILDING

situated at the corner of 34th Street and 5th Avenue, New York, N.Y. This building is the tallest in the world; at its top is a 217-foot television antenna.

Courtesy Empire State, Inc.

THE NEW BUSINESS ENCYCLOPEDIA

Edited by

HENRY MARSHALL

Editor of THE BOOK OF BUSINESS ETIQUETTE
THE BUSINESS MAN'S DICTIONARY *and*
GUIDE TO ENGLISH

Revised, Up-to-date Edition

1951

GARDEN CITY BOOKS
Garden City, N.Y.

PARTIAL LIST OF CONTRIBUTORS

Ivan A. Booker, Assistant Director, Research Division, National Education Association of the United States, Washington, D.C.

Melvin Dean, Assistant Editor, *Engineering News Record*, New York, N.Y.

Carl F. Distelhorst, Vice President and Director of Education, American Savings and Loan Institute, Chicago, Ill.

William Favel, Vocational Editor, *Scholastic Magazines*, New York, N.Y.

Arnold Fischer, member M. Margolin, Winer & Evans, Accountants, New York, N.Y.

Alfred Gross, Assistant Professor of Marketing, School of Commerce, Accounts and Finance, New York University, New York, N.Y.

Leonard F. Howard, Secretary, General American Investors Company, New York, N.Y.

C. F. Hughitt, Chief, Small Business Division, Office of Industry and Commerce, United States Department of Commerce, Washington, D.C.

J. Harold Janis, Professor of Business English, School of Commerce, Accounts and Finance, New York University, New York, N.Y.

Ernest Kurnow, School of Commerce, Accounts and Finance, New York University, New York, N.Y.

George N. Lockwood, Assistant to the Editor, New York *World-Telegram and Sun's* "First Aid to the Ailing House," New York, N.Y.

George J. Malinsky, attorney, lecturer, and contributor to *New York Law Journal*, and *Law Reviews*, New York, N.Y.

Frances Maule, Editor, *Independent Woman*, official magazine of the National Federation of Business and Professional Women's Clubs, and author of "Your Next Job," New York, N.Y.

Julian Roth, member Emery Roth and Sons, Architects, New York, N.Y.

Sidney G. Roth, Administrative Assistant in Charge of the Academic Department, Division of General Education, New York University, New York, N.Y.

Michael Schiff, Associate Professor of Accounting, Graduate School of Business Administration, New York University, New York, N.Y.

Grace G. Shaw, Associate Editor, C. L. Barnhart, Inc., Reference Books, New York, N.Y.

Earl G Shields, author of "Making Money at Home," Chicago, Ill.

W. W. Sproul, Treasurer, Clark and Gibby, Inc., New York, N.Y.

Hubert Francis Teitman, Certified Public Accountant, New York, N.Y.

Stanley W. Warren, Professor of Farm Management, New York State College of Agriculture, Cornell University, Ithaca, N.Y.

Albert B. Wagner, Head, Business Management Unit, College of the City of New York, N.Y.

Sidney Witaskin. Certified Public Accountant, Brooklyn, N.Y.

1951 GARDEN CITY BOOKS

Originally published under the title
THE BUSINESS ENCYCLOPEDIA

PRINTED AT THE *Country Life Press*, GARDEN CITY, N. Y., U. S. A.

Alphabetical Table of Contents

CONTENTS   vii

CONTRACTS

A contract is the expression of an intention by two or more persons to effect their legal relationship; in other words, a contract is an agreement whereby one party acquires a legal right to an act or a forbearance on the part of another.

There are two kinds of obligations: those resulting from *contract,* and those resulting from *operation of law.* Contractual obligations are voluntarily assumed after mutual agreement; no person can be placed under contractual obligation without his consent. Other forms of obligations occur without consent. These are known as *quasi contracts,* and are imposed by law. A quasi contract rests upon the equitable principle that a person shall not be allowed to enrich himself unjustly at the expense of another. It is an obligation which the law creates, in the absence of any agreement, when and because the acts of one party have placed in the possession of another money, or its equivalent, under such circumstances that in equity and good conscience he ought not to retain it. For example, if a doctor renders services to an unconscious person injured in an accident, the doctor is legally entitled to payment, even though the consent of the unconscious person was not obtained. The liability rests on a legal fiction created in the interest of justice. Other illustrations are found in the obligation to repay money received from another by mistake or through fraud, undue influence, or coercion.

Elements of a Contract

There are four elements to every contract. These are:

1. An *offer* by one party, duly accepted by the other. There is no contract until there is a definite meeting of the minds of the contracting parties upon all essential terms. This agreement occurs only when a definite and unconditional offer has been made by one party and unqualifiedly accepted by the other. A mere expression of intention is not an offer. An offer imports a willingness to incur a legal obligation. If one says to another, "I will sell my tennis racket for $10," it is an offer. If he says, "I intend to sell my tennis racket for $10," it is merely a declaration of intention. The acceptance of the former results in a binding and enforceable contract, whereas the latter is incapable of acceptance. An offer need not be in any particular form, but it must clearly import a willingness to be bound to the person to whom it is made. There is a vital distinction between an offer which, if accepted, creates a contract, and a *proposal* which is intended merely to open negotiations which may eventually result in a contract. Newspaper advertisements, letters, circulars, price lists, or catalogues distributed to prospective buyers, stating terms upon which goods are to be sold, are proposals, not offers.

1

To create a binding contract, there must be an unambiguous acceptance, showing a clear intention to accept the offer precisely as made. An intended acceptance which changes the terms of the offer is inoperative as an acceptance; it constitutes a new offer. A proposal to accept an offer if modified, or an acceptance subject to other terms and conditions than those stated in the offer, is equivalent to an absolute rejection. Such a proposal is a counter offer, which, if it is to ripen into a contract, must be accepted by the party making the original offer.

An offer transmitted by mail is deemed accepted when the letter of acceptance is posted, even though it never reaches the party who made the offer, unless the latter party imposed the express condition that no contract should be made until the acceptance was received by him. If the language of the offer clearly indicates an intention to impose this condition, the contract is incomplete until the acceptance has been received. However, when an acceptance is transmitted by a different agency from that used or requested by the party who made the offer, the acceptance is not effective until it is received. To illustrate, when an offer which did not specify any particular mode of acceptance is sent by mail and accepted by telegraph, no contract results until the telegram is received by the party who made the offer.

The consent of the contracting parties must be free and voluntary. Consent may be affected by mistake of intention, misrepresentation, fraud, duress, or undue influence.

A party who signs a contract without reading it is bound by it. But, if his failure to read was induced by the other party's fraud, coercion, or undue influence, the signer's negligence will not bar relief and he can escape liability.

2. *Legal capacity* (as distinguished from physical or mental capacity) of all contracting parties is essential. By statute the age of legal capacity is 21. *Infants* are those under 21; contracts of such persons are not void, merely voidable. This means that such contracts may be disaffirmed or ratified at the option of the infant. The other party to the contract, if adult, is bound by it. The defense of infancy is solely for the protection of the infant. When the infant ratifies the contract he assumes all liabilities and rights arising therefrom. When he disaffirms, he thereby avoids any liability. He can ratify the contract only after becoming 21. He can disaffirm all contracts, except deeds to real estate, either during infancy or within a reasonable time after becoming 21. Deeds to real estate can be disaffirmed only after he reaches 21.

Disaffirmance may be by express notice or by conduct which is manifestly inconsistent with the existence of the contract. Ratification requires affirmative action evidencing an intention to affirm the contract. The infant cannot ratify the beneficial parts and repudiate the detrimental parts. Once a contract is disaffirmed it cannot thereafter be ratified.

If a statute expressly permits an infant to enter into certain kinds of contracts, there is no right of disaffirmance. Marriage is such a contract.

Contracts made by a person after he has been adjudged *insane* are void; but contracts made by an insane person before such judicial declaration are voidable, not void. Insanity is a complete defense when performance of some contractual provision is still required, even though the other party made the contract without knowledge of the insanity, and before judicial declaration of insanity. But, if the contract is completely performed, the contract can be avoided by the incompetent, provided he returns all that he received under the contract. When such person is no longer insane he may affirm his contract.

A contract made by a person who was so *intoxicated* at the time that he did not know what he was doing is voidable by him but may be ratified when he becomes sober.

Formerly, *married women* had no right to enter into contracts. This restriction has been largely removed by statute; in most states married women may now make contracts as if they were single.

Aliens, although they are subjects of and owe sole allegiance to a foreign country, have the right to enter into contracts. Contracts between subjects of belligerent countries made after the commencement of war are void. If such contracts are made before war, they will be suspended during war, unless, from their nature, they are incapable of suspension, in which case they are not enforceable at the end of the war.

3. *Legality.* Contracts must have lawful purposes. Contracts contrary to statutory law or public policy are illegal. Illegality may affect only part of a contract. If the illegal part is severable from the legal part, the latter is enforceable by judicial action.

4. *Consideration.* No contract is valid without consideration. A valid consideration may consist of some right, profit, or benefit accruing to the party, or some forbearance, detriment, loss, responsibility, or some act or service given, suffered, or undertaken by the other party.

Formal and Informal Contracts

Contracts are either formal or informal. Most contracts are informal and may be oral; but, by statute, certain types of contracts must be in writing. They are:

1. Contracts which by their terms are not to be performed within one year from the time they are made
2. Contracts which provide for the payment of debts, defaults, or wrongs of another
3. Contracts by an executor or administrator of an estate to pay debts of the deceased out of his property
4. Contracts made in consideration of marriage, except promises to marry
5. Contracts for the sale of land, or a lease for more than one year
6. Contracts for the sale of goods above a certain value. (This varies in the different states. In New York the amount is fixed at $50. However, when the value exceeds $50, if: (a) the buyer accepts and receives a part of the goods; (b) pays part of the purchase price; or (c) the sale is by auction and the auctioneer makes a written memorandum of the sale, the contract is enforceable, even if it is not in writing)
7. A promise to pay a debt when recovery has become barred by a statute of limitations
8. A promise to pay a debt discharged in bankruptcy

9. A promise to convey or assign a trust in personal property
10. A contract to bequeath property or make a will
11. A contract to establish a trust
12. An assignment of an interest in the estate of a deceased person
13. An authorization of an agent to sell land or create an interest therein or to lease land for more than one year
14. A contract to assign, or an assignment of, a life or health or accident insurance policy, or a promise to name a beneficiary of such policy
15. A contract to pay a fee for services rendered in negotiating the purchase, sale, exchange, or lease of land or of a business.

Oral contracts to pay compensation to an auctioneer, lawyer, or duly licensed real estate broker or salesman are valid.

Since contracts reflect the intention of the contracting parties, they should be in clear and unambiguous language. Pencil, chalk, ink, print, or typewriting may be used. The entire contract need not be on one piece of paper; an exchange of letters, telegrams, or other form of communication will suffice.

A contract is regarded as made at the place of acceptance and is interpreted according to the law of that place, unless it is to be performed elsewhere, in which case it is interpreted according to the law of the place where it is to be performed.

Generally, contracts are to be performed in the time specified in the contract. If no time is specified, the implication is that the contract is to be performed within a reasonable time.

A contract may provide that a certain amount in damages shall be paid for nonperformance. The enforcement of such a provision depends upon whether that amount is a penalty or liquidated damages. If it is a penalty, courts will not enforce it, and the aggrieved party can recover the actual damages only. It is not easy to determine when such an agreed amount will be considered to be a penalty. It is fairly safe to assume that if the amount is grossly in excess of the actual damages, the court will consider it a penalty. If the actual damages are uncertain and difficult to ascertain, the court will consider it to be stipulated damages.

Parties are bound to perform what they contracted to do. An act of God will excuse nonperformance of a duty imposed by law, but it will not excuse a duty imposed by contract. A contract for personal services is discharged by death or incapacitating illness.

Liability

There are three different kinds of liability: (1) several, (2) joint, (3) joint and several. When a several obligation is entered into by two or more persons in one instrument, it is the same as if each had signed separate instruments, although they may all relate to the same subject matter. Each is liable for his several promise, and cannot be held liable for the others. A joint contract is one in which two or more persons jointly bind themselves to fulfill its obligations; either of them may be held responsible for the whole debt. When one joint promisor pays more than his pro rate share, he is entitled to contributions from the others. Several persons may also bind themselves jointly as one party, and also severally as separate individuals; in such case all the promisors may be joined in one action, or may be sued separately. By statute, in many states joint liabilities are treated as joint and several liabilities.

Contract of Agency

An agent is a person authorized to act for another party, called the *principal*. A *general agent* is one who represents his principal in a particular line of business, for example, the manager of a store.

A *special agent* is one authorized to do some particular act, or to act upon some particular occasion. He acts usually in accordance with specific instructions, or under certain limitations necessarily implied by the nature of the act to be done.

A *factor* is a commission merchant. He has possession of the goods and usually sells them in his own name. He has a lien on the goods consigned to him while they are in his possession, or on the proceeds of sale, for his commissions, advances, and expenditures properly incurred.

A *broker* is one who is engaged for others, on a commission basis, to negotiate contracts relative to property. A broker is usually not entrusted with the possession of the property, and is not authorized to buy and sell it in his own name.

A principal may expressly authorize the appointment of *subagents;* by so doing, he confers authority in advance. Sometimes authority to appoint subagents will be implied by the nature of the act to be performed or by the nature of the agency. When an agent has determined upon the propriety of a certain course of action, he has implied authority to entrust the performance of any purely mechanical act to another. For example, an agent employed to sell land may employ a subagent to exhibit it, and an insurance agent may employ clerks to collect premiums and deliver policies. A subagent, appointed by express or implied authority of a principal, is, as far as third parties are concerned, the agent of the principal, and the acts of the subagent within the scope of his agency are binding upon the principal. If the agent has undertaken to transact certain business for the principal, and appoints a subagent to assist him, even though the principal assents to this appointment the relation of principal and agent does not exist between the principal and subagent, although such relation does exist as far as third parties are concerned.

Appointment of Agents

Agents may be appointed orally, but an agency to buy and sell land or make leases for more than one year is required to be in writing. The usual way to appoint an agent is by means of a power of attorney.

Generally, agents are appointed by the principal, orally or in writing. However, if a person, by his affirmative conduct or silence, knowingly and without dissent permits another to act for him in a particular transaction, he will be estopped from repudiating the agency as against one who in good faith, and exercising reasonable prudence, has dealt with such apparent agent relying on such apparent authority. The acts of an unauthorized person on behalf of another may be subsequently adopted and affirmed. Such ratification is equivalent to prior authorization, and binds the principal as effectively as though prior authority had been given.

Termination of Agency

A contract of agency may be terminated in three ways: (1) by the language of the agency agreement, (2) by acts of the parties, (3) by operation of law.

If the agency is a general and continuing one, persons who deal in good faith with the agent are protected unless notice of revocation of the agent's authority is given. For example, a debtor is justified in paying an agent until notified by the creditor that the authority of the agent to receive payments has been revoked.

Some agencies are irrevocable by the principal. If an agent is authorized to collect a debt, and out of the proceeds reimburse himself for advances made to the principal, his authority may not be revoked by the principal; or if an agent is engaged to perform an act which entails personal liability and has actually incurred such liability, his authority to act may not be withdrawn by the principal; and if the agent has an interest in the subject matter of the agency, the principal may not revoke the power.

Death, insanity, or bankruptcy of either the principal or agent terminates the contract of agency. War or statutory law may also terminate the agency.

Obligation of Principal and Agent

A principal is liable for the torts of the agent committed in the performance of the agency. For example, when a manager affirms the act of a salesman who caused the arrest of a customer, the owner of the business will be held responsible. A principal is liable for the authorized frauds of his agent, and he may be liable in instances in which the agent was acting within the scope of his actual or apparent authority when the fraud was practiced.

An agent must exercise skill, care, and diligence in the performance of his duties. He must act in good faith and always be loyal to his principal. He may not acquire an interest adverse to that of his principal.

As a general rule, the agency agreement specifies how much and when the agent is to be paid for his services. If no amount is fixed the agent will be entitled to the reasonable value of the services rendered. He must have fully performed his duties before he is entitled to his compensation.

Patents for inventions made by an agent during an agency are considered the property of the agent, not of the principal, even though the invention is a direct outcome of information gained during the exercises of the agency. Generally, as a matter of business expediency, when it is known in advance that the agent is likely to make an invention (for example, if he is employed in a shop where mechanical appliances are designed or manufactured) it is customary for the company to provide by contract that all inventions made and discovered by their agents or employees shall belong to the company. Sometimes the employee is given additional compensation for such discoveries.

Unrestricted Power of Attorney[1]

Know all men, that I, John Doe, residing at ————, do hereby constitute and appoint Richard Roe, residing at ————, my true and lawful attorney for me, and in my name,

1. To enter upon and take possession of any lands, buildings, tenements, or other structures, or any part or parts thereof, that may belong to me, or to the possession whereof I may be entitled;

2. To ask, collect and receive any rents, profits, issues, or income, of any and all of such lands, buildings, tenements, or other structures, or/of any part, or parts, thereof;

3. To make, execute and deliver any deed, mortgage, or lease, whether with or without covenants and warranties, in respect of any such lands, buildings, tenements, or other structures, or of any part or parts thereof, and to manage any such lands, and to manage, repair, alter, rebuild, or reconstruct, any buildings, houses, or other structures, or any part or parts thereof, that may now or hereafter be erected upon any such lands;

4. To demand, sue for, collect, recover, and receive all goods, claims, debts, moneys, interest, and demands whatsoever now due, or that may hereafter be due, or belong to me (including the right to institute any action, suit, or legal proceeding, for the recovery of any land, buildings, tenements, or other structures, or any part or parts thereof, to the possession whereof I may be entitled), and to make, execute, and deliver receipts, releases, or other discharges therefor, under seal or otherwise;

5. To make, execute, endorse, accept, and deliver any and all bills of exchange, checks, drafts, notes, and trade acceptances;

6. To pay all sums of money, at any time or times, that may hereafter be owing by me upon any bill of exchange, check, draft, note, or trade acceptance, made, executed, endorsed, accepted, and delivered by me, or for me, and in my name by my said attorney;

7. To sell any and all shares of stocks, bonds, or other securities now or hereafter belonging to me, that may be issued by any association, trust, or corporation, whether private or public, and to make, execute, and deliver an assignment or assignments of any such shares of stocks, bonds, or other securities;

8. To defend, settle, adjust, compound, submit to arbitration and compromise all actions, suits, accounts, reckonings, claims, and demands whatsoever that now are or hereafter shall be pending between me and any person, firm, or corporation, in such manner and in all respects as my said attorney shall think fit;

9. To hire accountants, attorneys at law, clerks, workmen, and others, and to remove them, and appoint others in their place, and to pay and allow to the persons to be so employed such salaries, wages, or other remuneration as my said attorney shall think fit;

10. To enter into, make, sign, execute, deliver, acknowledge, and perform any contract, agreement, writing, or thing that may, in the opinion of my said attorney, be necessary or proper to be entered into, made, or signed, sealed, executed, delivered, acknowledged, or performed;

11. To constitute and appoint, in his place and stead and as his substitute, one attorney or more for me, with full power of revocation; and

12. Without in any wise limiting the foregoing, generally to do, execute, and perform any other act, deed, matter, or thing whatsoever that ought to be done, executed, and performed or that, in the opinion of my said attorney, ought to be done, executed, or

---

[1]This is only a suggested form. The reader is advised to obtain a blank form, valid in his state, from a lawyer or legal stationer for use in specific transactions.

performed, in and about the premises, of every nature and kind whatsoever as fully and effectually as I could do if personally present.

And I, the said John Doe, do hereby ratify and confirm all whatsoever my said attorney, or his substitute, or substitutes, shall do or cause to be done in or about the premises, by virtue of this power of attorney.

In witness whereof, I have hereunto set my hand and seal, in (city), state of ————, on this ———— day of ————, 19—.

                                                    John Doe (L.S.)

In the presence of
  John Doe, Jr.,
  Richard Roe, Jr.

Revocation of Power of Attorney[1]

Know all men, that—

Whereas, I, John Doe, residing at ————, (city), (state), did, in writing, under date of ————, 19—, appoint Richard Roe, residing at (city), my true and lawful attorney, to demand, receive, sue for and collect all claims, debts, moneys, and demands whatsoever due, or to become due, to me, all as in the said written power of attorney more particularly set forth; and .

Whereas, I, the said John Doe, desire to terminate the said written power of attorney:

Now, therefore, I, the said John Doe, do hereby annul, cancel, revoke, and terminate the said written power of attorney, dated ————, 19—, and do hereby annul, cancel, revoke, and terminate all rights, powers, authorities, privileges, and immunities therein and thereby vested in, or given to, the said Richard Roe.

In witness whereof, in (city), state of ————, I have hereunto set my hand and seal, on the ———— day of ————, 19—.

                                                    John Doe (L.S.)

In the presence of
  John Doe, Jr.,
  Richard Roe, Jr.

Contracts of Sale

Most states have enacted statutes covering the entire subject of sales. A sale of goods is a contract whereby the seller transfers title to the goods to a buyer for a consideration called the price. The sale may be absolute or conditional. Mutual assent is necessary. The parties must have legal capacity to contract.

A contract to sell or a sale may be in writing (either with or without a seal), or by word of mouth, or partly in writing and partly by word of mouth, or may be inferred from the conduct of the parties.

The sale may consist of goods which the seller owns or possesses at the time of the contract, or of goods to be manufactured or acquired by the seller after the making of the contract. The former are called "existing goods," the latter "future goods."

If the seller did not know that the goods were wholly perished at the time the agreement to sell was made, the agreement is void. If the goods have only partly perished or have wholly or partly deteriorated, the buyer may at his option treat the sales as avoided or take the remaining part, or as much as has not deteriorated, in which case he must pay the purchase price for such goods. If the property is destroyed or damaged before the time agreed upon for title to pass, the buyer cannot be com-

---

[1]This is only a suggested form. The reader is advised to obtain a blank form, valid in his state, from a lawyer or legal stationer for use in specific transactions.

pelled to pay the price; if he has paid the price in advance it may be recovered.

The *price* for the goods is usually fixed in the contract, if it is not, the buyer must pay a reasonable price, usually the market price at the time and place fixed by the contract for the delivery of the goods.

If the contract contains no specific contrary provision, the seller warrants by implication that he has a right to sell and that the buyer shall enjoy *possession* of the goods as against the legal claim of others. This has no application to sales by sheriffs or auctioneers. If the sale is by description or sample, the goods must correspond to the description or sample. If they do not, the buyer may refuse to accept the goods; if he has taken them he may promptly return them. He may also bring an action against the seller for failing to deliver the goods agreed upon.

There is generally no implied warranty of *quality* nor of fitness for any particular purpose. The buyer makes the purchase at his risk. However, when the buyer expressly or by implication notifies the seller of the particular purpose for which the goods are required, and the buyer relies on the seller's skill or judgment, there is an implied warranty that the goods shall be reasonably fit for such purpose. When the goods are purchased by description from a seller who generally deals in such goods, there is an implied warranty that the goods are of merchantable quality. There is no implied warranty of fitness for any particular purpose if the goods are sold under a patent or trade name. If the buyer has examined the goods, there is no implied warranty as to obvious defects which the examination ought to have revealed. The warranty survives inspection when the defect is latent and not discoverable by reasonable care.

Generally, and in the absence of contrary provisions, *payment* is due at the time of delivery. The unpaid seller has a lien for the purchase price on goods while he has possession of them. If the buyer becomes insolvent while the goods are in transit, the seller can stop shipment, resell the goods, and recover from the buyer the amount of his loss. But if the resale price is greater than the original contract price, the seller must refund the surplus to the buyer. The seller may also rescind the contract.

If the buyer has received the goods and wrongfully refuses to pay according to the terms of the contract, the seller may sue for the purchase price. The price may be recovered when it is payable on a certain day, irrespective of delivery, although title to the goods has not passed to the buyer. When the buyer wrongfully neglects or refuses to accept and pay for the goods, the seller may sue the buyer for nonacceptance. Generally, the measure of those damages will be a sum of money which puts the seller in as good a position as he would have been had the buyer accepted the goods. This loss can be ascertained if there is a market for the goods; then the loss to the seller would be the difference between the contract price and the market price at the time and place fixed in the contract. If there is no available market for the goods the seller is entitled to receive the full amount of the damage which he sustained as a result of the breach of the contract.

The seller must *deliver* the goods in accordance with the terms of the contract. In the absence of contractual provisions or custom in the particular trade, it is generally presumed that the place of delivery is the seller's place of business. It is the buyer's duty to call for the goods, rather than the seller's duty to deliver. If the seller is required by the contract to deliver the goods, but no time is specified, the delivery must be made within a reasonable time. Since "a reasonable time" is somewhat indefinite, the buyer should give notice to the seller as to when he wishes delivery.

If the seller delivers a smaller quantity than is required by the contract, the buyer may reject the goods; but if he accepts the part delivered, knowing that the seller will not deliver the balance, the buyer must pay for what he accepts at the agreed contract price. If the buyer uses the goods before he knows that the seller is not going to deliver the balance required by the terms of the contract, the buyer will be liable only for the fair value of the goods to him and not for the contract price. If more is delivered and the buyer accepts the goods, he must pay for them all at the contract price. Unless it is otherwise agreed, a buyer need not accept delivery in installments. If the contract provides for delivery in installments which are to be separately paid for, and the seller makes defective deliveries, or the buyer neglects or refuses to take delivery of, or to pay for, the installment, the remedies that the parties have against each other will in each case depend upon the terms of the contract; if no provision is made for such contingency, the circumstances of each case will determine whether the injured party may refuse to proceed further with the contract and sue for damages, or whether he can only sue for damages and not treat the whole contract as broken.

When the seller wrongfully neglects or refuses to deliver the goods, the buyer may sue for such nondelivery and recover his direct loss, which is the difference between the contract price and the market price at the time and place the contract is broken. If the seller repudiates the contract, the buyer may rescind the contract and recover the price paid.

Bill of Sale[1]

Know all men by these presents,
that John Doe, residing at ———, (city), party of the first part, for and in consideration of the sum of ——— to him in hand, paid at or before the ensealing and delivery of these presents by Richard Roe, residing at ———, (city), party of the second part, the receipt whereof is hereby acknowledged, has bargained and sold, and by these presents does grant and convey unto the said party of the second part, his executors, administrators, successors and assigns the following:

The shoe store located at ———, (city), including stock and merchandise, fixtures, chattels, and equipment, that are described in "Schedule A" hereto annexed and made part hereof, together with the good will and trade name of "The Bootery," heretofore used by the seller in the conduct of the said business.

To have and to hold the same unto the said party of the second part, his executors, administrators, successors, and assigns forever. And I do for myself, and my heirs, executors and administrators, covenant and agree, to and with said party of the second

---

[1]This is only a suggested form. The reader is advised to obtain a blank form, valid in his state, from a lawyer or legal stationer for use in specific transactions.

part, to warrant and defend the sale of the aforesaid shoe store business hereby sold to the party of the second part, his executors, administrators, successors, and assigns against all and every person and persons.

And I do further covenant and agree, to and with the said party of the second part, that I will not re-establish, reopen, be engaged in, nor in any manner whatsoever become interested in, directly or indirectly, either as employee, as owner, as partner, as agent, or as stockholder, director, or officer of a corporation, or otherwise, in any business, trade, or occupation similar to the one hereby sold within a radius of five (5) square blocks from the address of the business hereby sold to the party of the second part, for a term of ten (10) years from the date of these presents.

In witness whereof, the party of the first part has set his hand and seal this ————— day of —————, 19—.

———————————
Seller

(Annex a schedule of fixtures, chattels, etc.)

STATE OF ————— } ss:.
COUNTY OF —————

John Doe, being duly sworn, deposes and says; that he resides at —————, (city). That he is the same person who executed the within bill of sale. That he is the sole and absolute owner of the property described in said bill of sale and has full right to sell and transfer the same. That the said property and each and every part thereof is free and clear of any liens, mortgages, debts, or other encumbrances of whatsoever kind or nature.

That he is not indebted to anyone and has no creditors.

That there are no judgments existing against him, in any court, nor are there any replevins, attachments, or executions against him, now in force, nor has any petition in bankruptcy been filed by or against him.

Warranty

Warranties may be implied or expressed. An *express warranty* is an affirmative statement of fact made by the seller relating to the goods which induces the buyer to make the purchase. A statement of value or of opinion is not warranty.

The buyer has many remedies for a seller's breach of warranty. He may: (1) accept the goods and, when sued for the purchase price, apply the damages he suffered on either diminution or extinction of the price; (2) accept the goods and sue for damages; (3) refuse to accept the goods and sue for damages; (4) rescind the contract and refuse to accept the goods, or, if the goods have been received, return them and recover the price paid.

In the absence of any express or implied agreement, the buyer's acceptance of the goods does not discharge the seller from liability for breach of warranty. But if, after accepting the goods, the buyer fails to give notice to the seller of the breach within a reasonable time after the buyer knows of such breach, the seller is not liable.

Option

An option is a privilege granted to a party to accept an offer within a stated time. If no consideration is given, the offer may be withdrawn at any time before acceptance, but if the offer is accepted prior to such withdrawal it ripens into a binding contract. If any consideration is paid the offer is irrevocable for the stated period of time and may not be withdrawn before the expiration of such period.

Assignment

An assignment is a transference of all right, title, or interest in the property or thing assigned from one person to another. It arises from contract or by operation of law, as when title to property passes to an executor or administrator of an estate, a trustee in bankruptcy, or a guardian.

TORTS

A tort is a violation of a legal right or duty. Moral wrongs are not torts. Torts do not arise from contract. Libel, slander, false arrest, malicious prosecution, deceit, fraud, assault, and conversion of personal property are torts.

SEALS

At common law, seals had great importance; without them certain contracts were not legal. By statute, it is now generally provided that the presence or absence of a seal upon a written instrument shall be without legal effect, except in specific cases that are governed by special statute.

BANKS AND BANKING

Banks are generally regarded as our most important financial institutions. It has been estimated that over 90 per cent of the business of the country is conducted by means of checks drawn by depositors against accounts they have in the banks. Banking functions are so important to the public interest that traditionally banks in the United States have been subject to broader regulation than any other type of business. This regulation begins with the organization of the bank and is continued through regular supervision and examination by Government authorities.

Organization of the Banking Structure

In this country there are two classes of banks, based on the authority from which they receive their charters. The Federal Government charters *national banks,* while *state banks* are chartered under the authority of the legislatures and constitutions of each of the 48 states. The Comptroller of the Currency is the officer of the Federal Government charged with the responsibility of granting charters for the establishment of *national banks.* The law sets down strict requirements which must be met. These include the amount of capital to be supplied by the organizing stockholders, proof of need for the bank in the community, its future prospects for success, and the general character of the proposed management. It is compulsory for national banks to be members of the Federal Reserve System, which is the central banking system or system of "banks for the banks," and of the Federal Deposit Insurance Corporation, another agency of the Federal Government which protects depositors against loss by insuring their accounts up to $10,000 per depositor.

The charters of *state banks,* granted under authority of the individual state legislatures, are obtained through the offices of the bank superintendents or commissioners, or banking boards, depending upon the method of incorporation adopted by the state. There is a reasonable degree of uniformity in the principles of incorporation among the various states. Differences lie in the specific application of the principles. For example, in some states the amount of capital required for organization is smaller than that prescribed in the Federal statute for national banks, while in other states the requirement is greater.

State banks may be classified into three different groups, according to the type of business they perform: *commercial banks, trust companies,* and *mutual savings banks.* On the other hand, all national banks are classified as commercial banks, although they may do a combined commercial, trust, and savings business. Similarly, some state commercial banks and trust companies may perform all three functions.

13

Mutual savings banks are chartered only by states. They differ from commercial banks and trust companies in several important respects. Whereas the latter are organized by stockholders who buy stock and receive dividends from the profits earned, mutual savings banks do not have stock ownership; part of their profits is distributed to their depositors and part is retained to provide a protective cushion against losses, for the benefit of the depositors. Mutual savings banks do not offer a checking service, and the methods by which they invest their money are usually more closely supervised by law. Mutual savings banks exist only in Connecticut, Delaware, Indiana, Maine, Maryland, Massachusetts, Minnesota, New Hampshire, New Jersey, New York, Ohio, Oregon, Pennsylvania, Rhode Island, Vermont, Washington, and Wisconsin.

Banks chartered by the states have the *option* of membership in the Federal Reserve System. If they decide to join, they are also required to become members of the Federal Deposit Insurance Corporation. State banks which do not join the Federal Reserve System still may have their deposits insured by the FDIC, provided they meet prescribed tests for admission similar to those required for the organization of a national bank. In becoming members of either of these Federal instrumentalities, state banks subject themselves to Federal supervision, in addition to that already exercised over them by the banking departments of the states in which they are chartered.

Banking Services

The following is a brief description of the principal banks:
Each bank does not necessarily perform all these services.

There are two types of deposits, commercial (or *demand*) and time (mostly *savings*). Commercial banks usually accept both types, while mutual savings banks confine their activities to savings deposits. Demand deposits are the basis for the check payment system by which most business transactions are conducted. When you open a checking account at the bank, you fill out a card with your signature and other information which later will help the bank to identify you. The bank will provide you with a book of blank checks and a passbook. In making a deposit, you fill out a deposit slip which shows how much money, whether currency or checks from others, you wish to place in the bank. The teller enters the amount in your passbook and retains the deposit slip for the bank's records. (Some banks no longer issue passbooks for checking accounts, but use instead Burroughs Tellers Machines. The depositor is given a receipt showing the amount deposited, the number on the receipt corresponding to the number on the bank's records.) After the account has been opened, you may draw checks on demand against the deposit. However, if you deposit checks you may not draw against them until the bank has cashed them at the banks upon which they were drawn.

Checking accounts are adapted to the needs of the customer. If you draw only a few checks a month and desire to keep only a small amount of money on deposit, you may open a "special" checking account, on which you pay a nominal fee for each check drawn. Practices of banks differ. Some charge for deposit items as well. Some banks require that a balance be maintained, while others do not, although it is necessary, of course, for funds to be on deposit at the time a check is presented for collection against the account. Sometimes the bank will charge a small flat fee for the account, in addition to the charges for individual checks.

Other checking accounts are available for those who draw a relatively large number of checks each month and who are able to maintain a larger average balance. In determining whether you are to pay any service charge on these accounts, the bank considers how many checks and deposits you have had during the month, as well as your average deposit balance. Your balance provides a source of income for the bank, against which the expenses for the checks and deposits are offset. If the credit earned on the balance is sufficient to cover the charges, you will not be required to pay anything for the services rendered. Otherwise a charge will be made in the following month.

The Checkbook

A check is an order upon a bank to pay from the depositor's account according to the instructions therein contained. It is payable on demand. A postdated check is one containing a later date than that of delivery. A postdated check is a mere promise to discharge a present obligation at a future date. The presumption is that the maker has an inadequate fund in the bank at the time of giving the check, but will have enough at the date of presentation.

By statute a person who, with intent to defraud, shall make or draw or utter or deliver any check, draft, or order for the payment of money upon any bank or other depository, knowing at the time of such making that the maker or drawer has not sufficient funds with such bank for the payment of such check, although no express representation is made in reference thereto, shall be guilty of a misdemeanor. The making, drawing, uttering, or delivering of a check, payment of which is refused by the bank because of lack of funds, shall be prima-facie evidence of intent to defraud and of knowledge of insufficient funds. This statute has no application to a postdated check, since the implication of giving a postdated check is that the maker presently has not sufficient funds on deposit.

Checks are not only a convenient means of payment but are also an excellent method of preserving permanent evidence and record of payment.

The following rules should be observed in making out your checks and in the use of the stub which remains permanently in your checkbook.

1. Know your balance. Banks are prohibited from paying an overdraft. Embarrassment, annoyance, and criminal prosecution will be avoided if you keep proper record of your bank balances and verify your bank statements.

2. Always write your checks in ink; if possible avoid the use of a "ball point" pen; the ink sometimes fades. Never use pencil. If possible use a mechanical check writer to write the amount of the check.

3. Fill out the stub first; make complete entries.

4. Number the checks consecutively; be sure the numbers on the check and the stub correspond.

5. Be sure to date your check; write out or abbreviate the month. A check made out on a Sunday or a legal holiday should be dated the following day.

6. Write distinctly; avoid flourishes. If you make a mistake do not cross out or rewrite the mistaken part. Tear the check up completely. Mark the check stub "Void."

7. Do not cross out the name of the bank on a check and write in the name of your own bank. Most banks, hotels, and department stores have a printed form of a blank check for use by people who have forgotten their checkbooks. Use this form but make a note of the amount and the name of the payee and enter it in your checkbook as soon as possible by filling out the stub; destroy the check in your book for which this is the substitute.

8. Write out the full name of the payee. It is unwise to make checks payable to "Cash" or "Bearer." Such checks can be cashed by anyone who holds them and may be cashed by one not entitled to the money. Never sign completely or partially blank checks. If the payee's name does not fill up the space then draw a line from the end of the name to the dollar sign. Begin writing the name as close as possible to the left of the line. This will prevent the insertion of additional names as payees. A check payable to more than one payee can be cashed by either payee unless the word "and" is used. Obviously, any person harboring the intent to wrongfully cash the check will insert the "or." Leave no empty space on the line and it will be difficult for anyone to tamper with the check.

9. Be sure that the amount written in words corresponds to the amount in figures. If there is a difference, the amount in words will be considered the proper amount by the bank. Do not leave any blank space; begin as close as possible to the dollar sign and to the left on the line where you write out the amount. Fill up the balance of the space by running a line to the word "Dollars."

Care and prudence must be exercised in drawing checks and in verifying accounts. The legal relationship between a bank and a depositor is that of debtor and creditor, and the bank can justify a payment on the customer's account only upon the actual direction of the depositor. The questions arising between the maker and the bank concerning checks, therefore, always relate to what the one has authorized the other to do. The question of the depositor's negligence, however, may arise in disputes between depositors and the bank. Such questions of negligence arise when the depositor, in drawing his check, has left blanks unfilled, or by some affirmative act of negligence has facilitated the commission of a fraud by those into whose hands the check may come. Now, while the drawer of a check may be liable when he draws the instrument so incompletely that it facilitates or invites fraudulent alterations, it is not the law that he is bound so to prepare the check that nobody else can successfully tamper with it. What affirmative acts of negligence will be legally attributable to the depositor cannot be categorically enumerated, but if the rules given above are followed in making out checks, the depositor will avoid the imputation of negligence.

The law casts a duty upon the depositor to exercise diligence in examining his returned canceled vouchers and in notifying the bank within a reasonable time that forged checks were wrongfully paid by the bank. A failure to give such notice to the bank will absolve it from liability to the depositor. By statute it is now provided that no bank shall be liable to a depositor for the payment by it of a forged or raised check, unless within one year after the return to the depositor of the voucher of such payment such depositor shall notify the bank that the check so paid was forged or raised.

Request for Stop Payment

Date _August 21_ 19___

Garden City Bank and Trust Company
Garden City, N. Y.

GENTLEMEN:

Please stop payment on check No. _462_

dated _August 15_, 19___ for $ _25 00_

to the order of _Richard Rae_

for the following reasons: _lost in mail_

_____

_____

_____

The undersigned hereby agrees to hold you harmless for said amount and from all expenses, costs, attorney's fees incurred by you on account of your refusing to pay the said check and not to make any claim against you on account of payment if same occur through accident. I will endeavor to get this matter adjusted and make a release of this check within thirty days or make a new request for this stop payment to continue in force.

Remarks: _____

_____

_____

Signed: _John Doe_

Request for Stop Payment on a Check

Endorsements

Before it can be cashed or deposited a check must be endorsed by the person to whom it is payable.

To endorse a check, turn it over and write your name near the top on the end farthest from the signature on the face of the check:

John Brown

Spell your name as it is spelled by the person who made out the check. If this name is different from your regular signature, write your regular signature beneath it:

B. John Brown
John Brown

If you wish to pass a check on to someone else the endorsement should be as follows:

Pay to the order of Henry Smith
John Brown

Then Henry Smith, upon presenting the check at the bank, must add his endorsement below the one already given:

Pay to the order of Henry Smith
John Brown
Henry Smith

If the check is to be deposited the endorsement may read:

For deposit
John Brown

or:

For deposit only
John Brown

A check endorsed:

Pay to the order of the First National Bank
John Brown

will be deposited unless John Brown owes the bank money, in which case it may be applied on the loan.

People who for one reason or another find it difficult to go to the bank in person, perhaps because their business keeps them on the road, often mail their checks to the bank with this form of endorsement.

If you are given a check on a bank where you are not known and are likely to have some difficulty in collecting, the best procedure is to get the one who made out the check to guarantee your signature. For instance, if Sam Jones made out such a check to Henry Smith, Henry Smith should endorse it in the regular way. Then Sam Jones should write just below this endorsement "Signature Guaranteed, *Sam Jones*," or "Signature O.K., *Sam Jones*."

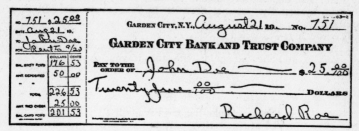

A Check and Stub, Properly Filled Out

Certified Checks

A certified check is the equivalent of cash, since the bank on which it is drawn certifies that it will pay the check upon presentation. You fill out the check in the usual manner, and take it to your bank, where the amount is immediately deducted from your balance, the check becoming a liability of the bank. As such, the check is acceptable, whereas your personal check might not be. Certification consists in stamping or marking the check "Certified," together with the signature of the bank.

Cashier's Checks

A cashier's check is a check drawn by the bank upon itself, and signed by an authorized officer. It is used to pay the bank's own bills and expenses.

Bad and Postdated Checks

Nearly all the states have laws which provide that a person who issues a check or a person (whether he issued it in the beginning or not) who negotiates a check knowing that there are not funds enough to back it up, is guilty of a crime. The degree of crime varies in the several states; in some it is a misdemeanor, in others, a felony or larceny.

Postdated checks, that is, checks dated ahead of the day on which they are issued, are not considered bad checks unless there is behind them intent to defraud.

All checks should be presented promptly for payment.

No check is good when the maker is dead. The creditor can get his money only by filing a claim against the estate.

The Monthly Statement

At certain regular periods usually on the first of every month, you receive from the bank an exact record of your transactions with and through the bank during the past month.

The statement should be carefully compared with your checkbook, item by item. The deposits are in one column. These should be added and checked against the deposits recorded in your checkbook and in your passbook.

The vouchers—canceled checks, drafts, promissory notes, etc., which the bank returns with the statement—should be arranged by date, then by numbers, and checked against the stubs in your checkbook.

If you find that a mistake has been made, go at once to the bank.

Mistakes

Don't assume that a mistake has been made if all your checks are not there. The chances are that they have not yet been returned. You may find one or two items that you did not expect, like a small collection fee on out of town checks or a service charge against you because your average account has been below the minimum amount required by the bank. These should be noted in your checkbook in order to bring about the proper balance.

Joint Accounts

Joint bank accounts, which may be either checking or savings accounts, are payable to either of the two (or more parties) who enter into them. Another way in which a second person can be given access to an account is through a power of attorney. Sometimes men who are going away on long trips leave a power of attorney (see page 7) over their bank accounts with a trustworthy friend. Husbands and wives sometimes find this an easier way to handle their funds than the joint account. This makes it possible for both to have separate accounts and yet, in case of emergency, for each to draw upon the other.

Savings Accounts

A savings account is opened in about the same way that a checking account is opened, but the passbook is much more important in the savings bank. In the checking account the passbook is simply a memorandum of deposits; in the savings account it contains a complete record of deposits and withdrawals and must be presented every time a transaction is made, whether the money is put into the account or taken out. If the deposit is made by mail the passbook should be mailed with it and the envelope registered. The book is balanced at the end of each transaction; there is no periodic statement of deposits and withdrawals as in the case of the checking account. The passbook is the statement. On savings accounts, interest is paid to the depositor. There are many ways of computing this interest. The amount is entered the first time the depositor presents the passbook after the computation period is ended.

The depositor cannot issue a check against a savings account to be cashed by another person, but most savings banks furnish cashiers' or treasurers' checks by means of which the depositor can draw out money to his own order.

Other Banking Services

Trust Services: A trust company or the trust department of a commercial bank may perform a variety of fiduciary services, such as acting as executor under a will, serving as trustee under trust agreements, managing property for others, investing funds, acting as corporate trustee under bond issues, and carrying out other services concerned with the management and protection of the financial assets of the community.

Foreign Departments: Some banks have foreign departments or specialists to facilitate transactions in international trade. They may secure and transfer foreign exchange, provide information concerning such trade, and afford a means for financing the import or export of goods and facilitating their actual movement through commerce.

Safe Deposit Facilities: Banks will rent, at a small annual fee, special safekeeping vaults for the storage of valuables, such as jewels, securities, deeds, insurance policies, etc.

Miscellaneous Services: In meeting the financial needs of the community, a bank may perform a collection service on out-of-town items, bond coupons, public utility bills, matured bonds, and the like. It may provide business advisory service; some banks have established business or industrial development departments which afford information and advice regarding the community's property values, labor supply, plant locations, market data, and incorporation procedure. Banks act as agents for the United States Treasury in the sale and cashing of War and Savings Bonds. They sell travelers' checks, and some even provide travel services. They may have an investment counsel service or may assist in the purchase or sale of securities. In agricultural communities, they may offer the farmer assistance in such matters as soil conservation, flood control, and scientific crop production. They help customers to secure technical advice in the financing and construction of homes. Banks are also an excellent source of credit information.

Bank Loans

The bank uses funds invested by stockholders and deposits which have been made by its customers to lend to others having a wide variety of credit needs. In some banks, loan departments may be separated into, for example, commercial, industrial, mortgage, and personal divisions. The principal types of bank loans are as follows:

Personal loans, made to individuals to help them meet emergency financial needs, such as payment of doctor's bills. Loans may be repaid on installments or in a lump sum.

Installment purchase loans, made to individuals to finance the purchase of an automobile or other durable goods; loans are secured by a chattel mortgage on the article.

Repair and modernization loans, made to individuals to finance home repairs and improvements.

Real estate loans, secured by real estate mortgages, and made to enable purchase of new or existing homes, farm land, or other property, under certain restrictions.

Commercial and industrial loans, which vary considerably, depending upon the type of business, the financial position of the borrower, the purpose of the loan, the security involved, etc. Such loans might include: (1) *unsecured loans* which are based on the bank's faith in the ability of the borrower to repay without specific security; (2) *loans on warehouse receipts* for goods in storage; (3) *loans on other paper* covering the movement of goods from seller to buyer; (4) *loans on accounts or notes receivable* by the borrower from his own customers; (5) *agricultural loans* to farmers for the production and storage of crops or the purchase of machinery; (6) *term loans,* repayable over a period of years, usually for capital purposes; (7) *chattel mortgage loans,* for example, on autos owned by a dealer pending their sale to the public; (8) *co-maker loans,* in which a second party agrees to repay in the event that the borrower defaults; (9) *business loans* on other assets, such as plant and equipment.

Security loans, made to investment dealers and others for the purpose of carrying or purchasing securities. For example, when a corporation decides to issue new securities, an investment house may agree to sell them for the corporation. The bank will lend money to the investment firm to carry the securities until they are sold.

Clearing Houses

In order to avoid the cumbersome process of actually interchanging money, banks send their checks to central places of exchange known as clearing houses. Here the amounts the banks owe and the amounts due the banks are set against each other and the accounts balanced, the balance being either received or paid off, as the case may be. Some clearing houses are also collecting agencies. The Federal Reserve banks act as clearing houses for their customers.

A Short Outline of Banking History

"A million in the hands of a single banker is a great power; he can at once lend it where he will, and borrowers can come to him because they know or believe that he has it. But the same sum scattered in tens and fifties through a whole nation is no power at all: no one knows where to find it or whom to ask for it."

" 'The distinctive function of the banker,' says Ricardo, 'begins as soon as he uses the money of others'; as long as he uses his own money he is only a capitalist."

The first bank of any importance in the world was the Bank of Venice, which was established in 1171. The next most famous, historically speaking, was the Bank of Barcelona, established in 1401; it was the first to make use of the system of negotiating bills of exchange. In England banks grew out of the custom of merchants who, to protect themselves from theft, deposited their surplus funds with goldsmiths. The goldsmiths began to pay six per cent interest on the deposits, and banking as we know it today began. There are still in existence banks which owe their origin to these goldsmiths' establishments.

The first bank in the United States grew out of a patriotic desire to relieve the distress of Washington's troops. This was the Bank of Pennsylvania, organized in 1780 and destined to live only a very short time. The Bank of North America was established in 1781, the Bank of New York and the Bank of Boston in 1784.

The First Bank of the United States was established in 1791, the Second in 1816, Congress providing one-fifth of the capital of each. Until after the Civil War these two were the only banks in the United States which operated under the national law. All others were organized according to the laws of the states in which they were established. It was in the period of depreciated currency and financial distress during and following the Civil War that the National Banking Act was passed. The Act itself was passed in 1863. It was amended in 1864 and has been amended since.

FEDERAL RESERVE SYSTEM

BOUNDARIES OF FEDERAL RESERVE DISTRICTS AND THEIR BRANCH TERRITORIES

BOUNDARIES OF FEDERAL RESERVE DISTRICTS
BOUNDARIES OF FEDERAL RESERVE BRANCH TERRITORIES
★ BOARD OF GOVERNORS OF THE FEDERAL RESERVE SYSTEM
● FEDERAL RESERVE BANK CITIES
● FEDERAL RESERVE BRANCH CITIES

It was the panic of 1907 that brought about a widespread desire to do something to improve our banking methods. Following an investigation by the National Monetary Commission, which went quite thoroughly into banking methods and needs, the Federal Reserve Act became a law in 1913.

The United States was divided into 12 districts, as indicated by the above map. These districts, which were carefully planned and marked out on a commercial rather than a geographic basis, can, if the authorities wish, be split into a number of branch territories.

The Federal Reserve Board in Washington, which is the center of the system, is composed of seven members appointed by the President with the approval of the Senate. The full term is 14 years.

Each of the 12 Reserve Banks has a board of nine directors. Six of these —three bankers and three business men (not bankers)—are elected by the member banks of the District, and three are appointed by the Reserve Board in Washington. One of the last three acts as chairman of the Reserve Bank board of directors and Federal Reserve Agent.

All national banks are members of the system. State institutions may become members without losing their rights under their state charters.

All the capital stock of the Federal Reserve Banks is owned by member banks, each of which subscribe six per cent of its paid-up capital and surplus. Only half of this, however, or three per cent, has had to be paid in. If at any time a member bank increases its capital or surplus, it must at the same time increase its subscription. Similarly, when a bank reduces either or withdraws from the system, it receives a corresponding refund. On paid-in stock member banks receive annually a six per cent cumulative dividend.

The capital requirements of national banks are as follows:

In cities of 6,000 and under	$ 50,000
In cities of more than 6,000 but not more than 50,000	$100,000
In cities of more than 50,000	$200,000

While state laws vary with respect to capital requirements, state banks admitted to membership in the Federal Reserve System must have the same capital as that required of national banks in the same place, except that, in certain circumstances, a state bank in a town of 3,000 or under may be admitted to membership with a capital of not less than $25,000.

The 12 Federal Reserve Banks are fiscal agents of the United States; they issue Federal Reserve notes, they hold the required reserves of member banks of the Federal Reserve System, and they are empowered to discount for member banks and to buy and sell Government obligations in the open market for the purpose of stabilizing credit conditions.

FEDERAL DEPOSIT INSURANCE CORPORATION

The Corporation was created by the **Banking Act of 1933,** also known as the *Glass-Steagall Act,* which as well as the **Banking Act of 1935** strongly affected the organization of banks.

The purpose of these Acts and of the Emergency Acts of March and June, 1933, was:[1] to meet emergency conditions in 1933, while the Act of

---

[1] Passages taken out of the statement by Mr. M. S. Eccles of the Federal Reserve Board before the Committee on Banking and Currency of the House of Representatives (March 4, 1935).

1935 incorporated into permanent legislation the features of the emergency laws that had proved valuable; in addition the legislation aimed to prevent the recurrence of speculative excesses which preceded the breakdown of the country's banking machine at that time.

The Corporation was designed to insure depositors against loss in insured banks. With enactment of the Banking Act of 1935, insurance was established on a permanent basis and the individual coverage determined at $5,000 per depositor, later extended to $10,000 per depositor.

All national and state banks which are members of the Federal Reserve System are insured by the Corporation. Banks which are not members of the Federal Reserve System are admitted to insurance upon application and subsequent examination and approval by the Corporation.

The major functions of the Corporation are to pay off the depositors of insured banks closed without adequate provision having been made to pay claims of their depositors, and to act as receiver for all suspended national banks and for suspended state banks when appointed by state authorities. The Corporation prevents the continuance or development of unsafe and unsound banking practices by periodical examinations of all insured banks which are not examined by other agencies of the Federal Government, and by its supervisory powers over such banks.

The three members of the board of directors of the Corporation are appointed by the President, one of these being the Comptroller of the Currency.

The income of the Corporation is obtained from assessments upon banks and interest upon its investments. Each insured bank is assessed annually $\frac{1}{12}$ of one per cent of its average total deposits.

NEGOTIABLE INSTRUMENTS

Broadly defined, negotiable instruments are written promises or requests for the payment of money. A certain degree of uniformity in the law dealing with all forms of commercial paper was obtained by established custom and usage which, however, soon became inadequate to the needs of modern commerce. Consequently, uniformity was sought by statute. There is now a uniform Negotiable Instruments Law, which codifies the applicable legal principles; but one of the provisions of this uniform law expressly states that if a case is not covered thereby, the rules of the *law merchant*, *i.e.*, custom and usage, shall govern.

The term "negotiable" applies to any written instrument given as security for the payment of money, which may be transferred either by delivery or endorsement, vesting legal title in the party to whom it is so transferred. To be negotiable the instrument (1) must be in writing and signed by the maker, or drawer; no particular form of writing or signature is necessary; an authorized agent may sign his principal's name; (2) must contain an unconditional promise to pay a definite amount of money; (3) must be payable on demand, or at a fixed or ascertainable future time; (4) must be payable to order or to bearer; (5) if addressed to a drawee, must name or otherwise indicate that person with reasonable certainty.

If the instrument conforms to these requirements it is negotiable, even if (1) it is not dated; (2) does not specify the value given; (3) does not specify the place where it is made or payable; (4) does not designate a particular kind of currency in which payment is to be made.

Antedating or postdating an instrument does not invalidate it, provided neither is done for an illegal or fraudulent purpose. Title to an instrument so dated vests in the person to whom it is delivered on the date of delivery.

When the signature is forged or made without authorization it is wholly inoperative, unless the party against whom it is sought to enforce payment is precluded from setting up forgery or lack of authority. No hard-and-fast rule can be given as to when and under what circumstances a forged or unauthorizedly-signed instrument can be enforced. This depends upon the particular facts of each case. Subsequent endorsers are not liable on a negotiable instrument if it is materially altered without their consent; those who do assent to the material alteration, however, remain liable. But when an instrument has been materially altered and is owned by a *holder in due course,* not a party to the alteration, he may enforce payment according to its original terms.

A holder in due course is a person who acquires the instrument, complete and regular on its face, in good faith and for value before it became overdue, and without prior notice that it had been previously dishonored (if such was the fact) and had no notice at the time it was endorsed or delivered to him that there was any infirmity in it, or that there was a defect in title of the person who negotiated it.

An alteration is material if it changes the date, the amount payable, the time or place of payment, or the currency in which payment is to be made, or if it in any other way alters the effect of the instrument.

The following are negotiable instruments: bills of exchange; trade acceptances; drafts; clearinghouse certificates; United States Treasury notes; bearer bonds and letters of credit. Any other form of instrument may be negotiable provided the previously mentioned minimum legal requirements are met.

Drafts

A draft is a written order by one person, called the *drawer,* upon another called the *drawee,* for the payment of a specified sum of money to a third person, the *payee.* The terms "draft" and "check" are sometimes used interchangeably. A draft, however, is distinguishable from a check by the fact that the drawer of a draft is a bank, while the drawer of an ordinary check is an individual. There is also a difference between a cashier's check and a draft. A cashier's check is the primary obligation of the bank, which issues it, constituting a written promise to pay upon demand, whereas a draft is an order upon a third party drawn upon a deposit of funds. Drafts are payable at sight, on demand, or on a specified date.

The drawer by drawing the instrument admits the existence of the payee and agrees with the drawee and payee and the subsequent holders that on due presentment the draft will be accepted and paid according to its terms, and that if it be dishonored the drawer will pay the amount to the holder, or to any subsequent endorser who may be compelled to pay it.

The drawee's liability begins with his acceptance, which is an agreement on his part that he will pay. This is generally accomplished by writing the

Various Kinds of Drafts

Various Kinds of Drafts (Cont.)

word "Accepted" and the date across the face of the instrument and signing his name below it.

Nonpayment means that the instrument has been dishonored, and all persons secondarily liable may be sued after notice of dishonor has been given to the drawer and each endorser, and any drawer or endorser to whom such notice is not given is discharged from liability. The notice may be given in writing or orally, either personally or by mail, within 24 hours. The form of notice should properly identify the instrument, and indicate that it has been dishonored by nonacceptance or nonpayment.

Trade Acceptance

A trade acceptance is a draft or bill of exchange drawn by the seller on the purchaser of goods sold, and accepted by such purchaser. Upon acceptance by the drawee it becomes in effect a promissory note. The acceptance makes the drawee primarily liable, and notice of presentment and demand for payment are not necessary.

The seller draws the draft and forwards it to the buyer with the invoice or mails it separately. The buyer signifies his acceptance by writing "Accepted" and filling in the date of acceptance, designating the bank at which it is to be paid, and signing it. He then returns it to the seller, who may hold it until it is payable, or may discount it. Trade acceptances are negotiable.

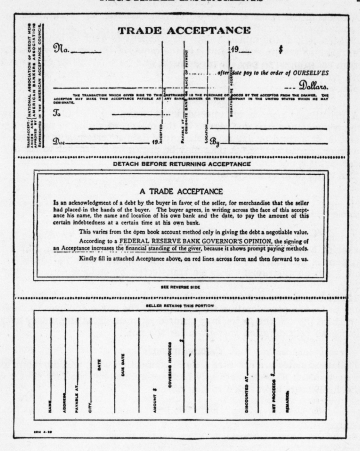

Bills of Exchange

A bill of exchange is an unconditional written order drawn by one person on another to pay a third person a certain sum of money, absolutely and in all events. It is distinguishable from a check in that a check is always drawn on a bank. There are two kinds of bills of exchange, (1) an *inland bill of exchange*, which is drawn and payable within the state, and (2) *foreign bills* (all others). Unless notice to the contrary appears on the face of the bill the holder may treat it as an inland bill. A foreign bill of exchange must be protested before the drawer can be held liable, but inland bills need no protest, notice of dishonor being sufficient.

All bills of exchange are payable (1) on demand, (2) at sight, or (3) at some future fixed date. A bill of exchange bears two dates, the date on which it is made and the date on which it is paid. A bill does not operate as an assignment of funds in the hands of the drawee, who is the person called upon to pay the instrument, and he is not liable unless and until he accepts it in writing, although it is negotiable even before acceptance.

Promissory Notes

A promissory note is an unconditional promise in writing made by one person to another, and signed by the maker, engaging to pay on demand or at a fixed or determinable future date a certain sum of money "to order" or "to bearer." A note may be drawn by the maker to his own order, but it is not complete until endorsed by him.

The usual form of a note is:

New York, N.Y., ———, 19—

Six months after date I promise to pay to Mr. John Doe or order the sum of one hundred dollars ($100) for value received.

(Signed) *Richard Doe*

A note may be valid as a *nonnegotiable* instrument. To charge the maker of a nonnegotiable demand note, a personal demand on him for payment is necessary. A nonnegotiable note should recite its consideration. Such an instrument may be transferred by endorsement and delivery.

If the payee sues the maker of the note to collect payment the payee must prove the consideration for the note. If the payee endorses the note to a third person, the latter may enforce payment from the maker even though no consideration was given for the note.

Collateral Notes

Collateral notes are executed *only* in connection with, and pursuant to, an agreement; this stipulation is best exemplified by the fact that the note itself bears a provision to that effect.

Collateral Note[1]

(city) ———

$———

On demand, for value received, John Doe promises to pay to Richard Roe or order, at his office, ———, (city), ——— dollars, with interest at the rate of six (6) per cent per annum, the said sum to be secured by the assignment to Richard Roe or order as collateral security for the payment of this and of all previous and subsequent obligations of John Doe, due or to become due, of certain accounts receivable, debts, claims, and demands created in favor of and belonging to John Doe, at the time of such assignment, and all moneys due, or to grow due thereon, together with all the right, title, and interest of John Doe in and to the merchandise, for the sale and delivery of which the said accounts arose; with the right on the part of the said Richard Roe and his assigns, from time to time to demand such additional security as he or they may deem necessary; and, on failure to comply with any such demand, this obligation shall be deemed to be due and payable forthwith, without notice or demand; and with the further right to accept and substitute other assigned accounts subsequent to the date hereof, in lieu of accounts this day assigned, and to hold such other accounts as collateral on this loan,

[1]This is only a suggested form. The reader is advised to secure a form, valid in his state, from a lawyer or legal stationer for use in specific transactions.

with the same rights and powers and under the same conditions as the accounts, and each of them, assigned and delivered herewith; with full power and authority to the said Richard Roe and his assigns to sell and deliver any and all of the said collateral security, at public or private sale, at the option of the said Richard Roe and his assigns, without demand, advertisement, or notice, and with the right on the part of the said Richard Roe and his assigns to be the purchaser thereof at such sale, free and discharged of any equity of redemption; and, after deducting all costs and expenses incident to the said sale and delivery, to apply the net proceeds to the payment of such just claims and obligations as may at the time of said sale be owing from John Doe to said Richard Roe or his assigns, whether due or to become due; and the undersigned agrees to remain and continue liable for any unpaid balance remaining.

This note is given in connection with a certain agreement between John Doe and Richard Roe, dated ————, 19—, and is to be interpreted in harmony with the said agreement.

RECEIPTS

A receipt is an acknowledgment in writing, signed by the person who gives it, that he has received certain personal property, which may be money or goods or both. If it is a receipt for property (see Warehouse Receipt, page 183), the property should be described sufficiently to be identified, the terms under which it is to be stored or otherwise looked after should be stated. All receipts should be dated and signed. If an agent signs he should first write his principal's name, then his own beneath it, thus:

Robert Compton
By George Smith

If the receipt is for money, it should indicate whether the money is paid "on account" or "in full of account." If there is more than one account between the payer and the payee, the receipt should state which account the money has been applied to.

Many receipts are given simply by stamping "Paid in full" with initials or other identifying mark in ink on the face of a due bill. The returned voucher of a check is also considered a valid receipt, but most firms will give an additional receipt if it is requested.

A receipt is not necessary when a note is paid up, since the instrument itself then becomes a receipt.

If it can be proved that a receipt was given through mistake or fraud, it can be voided.

Receipts should be kept until after the time for action prescribed by the Statute of Limitation has passed. This varies in the different states and must be determined by consulting local statute books.

CARRYING MONEY
Letters of Credit

A letter of credit is a letter from a bank or business house addressed to one or more of its agents elsewhere requesting the payment of a certain sum of money to the person named in the letter. Letters of credit are much in use by people traveling abroad, especially when large sums of money are needed. Usually the person carrying a letter of credit has deposited with the firm which issued it an amount equal to the sum mentioned in

Letter of Credit

the letter. A small commission fee is charged by the concern issuing the letter.

The letter bears the signature of the holder. For further identification the bank or person issuing the letter, especially when the amount involved is a large one, often sends a letter through the mail to the agent or correspondent upon whom the letter of credit is drawn, giving a description of the holder and any other information which he may think helpful.

Letters of credit carry an expiration limit. This may consist of a notation, such as "Available until ————", or "Drafts must be drawn before ————", or any one of a number of other forms.

AMERICAN EXPRESS COMPANY
CIRCULAR LETTER OF CREDIT.

Nº 00000

New York, June fifth 19___

Gentlemen

We beg to introduce to you

_____

whom we hereby authorize to draw at sight on the
AMERICAN EXPRESS COMPANY, *New York to an aggregate amount of* ___ *One Thousand Dollars* ___
($1000. ___

We engage that such drafts shall be met with due honor in New York, if negotiated on or before December fifth 19___

Each draft must bear the number of this Letter of Credit, be signed in your presence, and the signature compared with the one below.

THE AMOUNT OF EACH DRAFT MUST BE ENDORSED ON THIS LETTER OF CREDIT.

Your negotiation of a draft drawn against this Letter will be considered a guarantee to the American Express Company that you have complied with these requirements.

Yours very respectfully,
AMERICAN EXPRESS COMPANY.

_____   _____
Treasurer   *President*

To our Correspondents   *The signature of bearer*

_____

Letter of Credit issued by The American Express Company

Letter of Indication to Accompany Letter of Credit

Travelers' Checks

Travelers' checks are issued by banks, express companies, and some of the tourist agencies. They are either sight drafts or promissory notes. The person buying them signs when he buys and again when he presents them for payment, the signature establishing his identity. A small commission is charged. The minimum fee is one dollar, the usual rate being about one dollar for every $100 worth of checks. The usual denominations of travelers' checks are $10, $20, $50, and $100.

Travelers' Check

SENDING MONEY

Money may safely be sent in the following ways:

Bank Check or Draft

This is the cheapest and nearly always (except for very small sums) the most convenient way to send money. An additional advantage of sending money this way is that there is no limit to the amount that can be sent.

Post Office Money Order

Domestic money orders are issued for any amount up to $100. A good way to send small sums. (For fees, see Postal Information, page 173.)

Express Money Order

Such orders are as secure as a bank draft. They are sold by many thousands of druggists and others throughout the country and can be negotiated as freely as personal checks.

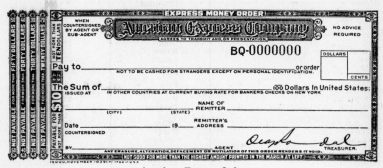

American Express Order

Registered Letter

Registered letters receive special handling and are therefore safer than ordinary letters. (For fees, see Postal Information, page 171.)

Stamps

Stamps should be sent to cover only very small amounts.

Coin

When it is not possible to send stamps, coins may be used. They should first be slipped inside a pasteboard card or otherwise protected so that they will not wear through the envelope nor be recognized in transit.

Telegraph

Telegraph offices furnish blanks. (See page 181.)

VALUES OF THE PRINCIPAL FOREIGN MONETARY UNITS

Principal countries	Monetary unit	U.S. cents per currency unit
Australia	Pound	224.000
Austria	Schilling	6.863
Belgium	Franc	2.000
Bolivia	Boliviano	2.380
Brazil	Cruzeiro	5.405
Canada	Dollar	90.909
Chile	Peso	3.225
Colombia	Peso	51.282
Costa Rica	Colon	17.809
Cuba	Peso	100.000
Czechoslovakia	Koruna	2.000
Denmark	Krone	14.477
Dominican Republic	Peso	100.000
Ecuador	Sucre	7.407
Egypt	Pound	287.156
El Salvador	Colon	40.000
Ethiopia	Dollar	40.250
Finland	Markka	.400
France	Franc	29.000
Germany (West)	Mark	23.800
Greece	Drachma	.020
Guatemala	Quetzal	100.000
Honduras	Lempira	50.000
India	Rupee	21.000
Iran	Rial	3.100
Iraq	Dinar	280.000
Ireland	Pound	280.000
Israel	Pound	280.000
Italy	Lira	16.000
Japan	Yen	.279
Mexico	Peso	11.560
Netherlands	Guilder	26.315
New Zealand	Pound	280.000
Nicaragua	Cordoba	20.000
Norway	Krone	14.000
Panama	Balboa	100.000
Pakistan	Rupee	30.300
Paraguay	Guarani	32.362
Peru	Sol	15.300
Philippine Republic	Peso	50.000
Poland	Zloty	1.000
Portugal	Escudo	3.480
Spain	Peseta	10.140
Sweden	Krona	19.300
Switzerland	Franc	23.000
Turkey	Lira	35.714
Union of South Africa	Pound	280.000
Union of Soviet Socialist Republics	Ruble	25.000
United Kingdom	Pound	280.000
Uruguay	Peso	52.631
Venezuela	Bolivar	29.850
Yugoslavia	Dinar	2.000

HOW TO PLAN A BUDGET

In order to live safely within an income and to get the most value out of money spent it is necessary to formulate a careful plan of spending and saving. This is known as budgeting. There are no set rules for the use of income, since the needs and requirements of people in various communities and income groups differ greatly. There are, however, certain general rules that should be followed if a budget is to be successful.

First, it is essential to plan on spending less than you earn in order that some portion of your income will be saved. Second, you must consider your fixed expenses such as food, shelter, clothing, and operating costs. These expenses are *musts* on your list, and the amounts spent on them should be carefully apportioned. Third, a certain part of your income should be set aside for miscellaneous expenses beyond those necessary for living. Careful judgment should be given to the allotment of expenses in this group. It is important, for example, to choose carefully between pleasures of a temporary nature and those that are more enduring. Money allotted for fixed expenses must, to some extent, be governed by the cost-of-living standard of your particular community. Money allotted for the miscellaneous group is naturally more flexible. You can do without one thing in order to buy another. It is within this group that you must watch expenses that add up before you know it!

Budgeting

In order to plan a good budget, the whole family should cooperate in a definite program. It is an excellent idea to keep a list of all the family expenses over a period of time to see where your money is going. Thus you will have prepared the necessary groundwork for a successful budget.

Although there are various methods of budgeting, the following general practice may be helpful. First, deduct taxes from your monthly income. The remaining figure is your total expendable income for the month. Next, write down the main categories of your expenses in column form, placing each subject at the top of a column: Savings, Food, Shelter, Clothing, Operating Costs (insurance, transportation, medicine, telephone, electricity, laundry, etc.), and Advancement (church, charity, books and magazines, education, recreation, etc.). Under each of these columns list the amount of money that you can safely allot to each category, making certain that the separate figures add up to original total figure.

This first apportionment of your income will probably not be satisfactory. After the first month you may find that you allotted more for food than you needed, or that you spent much more on operating costs than you expected. On the other hand you may find that you allotted more money for advancement than you actually needed, and that this extra

SALARY AND WAGES TABLE[1]

Showing amounts earned per year, per month, per week (on a 48 weeks to the year and a 52 weeks to the year basis) and per day.

Per year	Per month	Per week 48 pmt.	Per week 52 pmt.	Per day
400.00	33.33	8.33	7.69	1.28
416.00	34.67	8.67	8.00	1.33
420.00	35.00	8.75	8.08	1.34
425.00	35.42	8.85	8.17	1.36
450.00	37.50	9.38	8.65	1.44
468.00	39.00	9.75	9.00	1.50
475.00	39.58	9.90	9.13	1.52
480.00	40.00	10.00	9.23	1.53
500.00	41.67	10.42	9.61	1.60
520.00	43.33	10.83	10.00	1.66
525.00	43.75	10.94	10.10	1.68
540.00	45.00	11.25	10.38	1.73
550.00	45.83	11.46	10.58	1.76
572.00	47.67	11.92	11.00	1.83
575.00	47.92	11.98	11.06	1.84
600.00	50.00	12.50	11.54	1.92
624.00	52.00	13.00	12.00	2.00
625.00	52.08	13.02	12.02	2.00
650.00	54.17	13.54	12.50	2.08
660.00	55.00	13.75	12.69	2.11
675.00	56.25	14.06	12.98	2.16
676.00	56.33	14.08	13.00	2.16
700.00	58.33	14.58	13.46	2.24
720.00	60.00	15.00	13.84	2.30
725.00	60.42	15.10	13.94	2.32
728.00	60.67	15.17	14.00	2.33
750.00	62.50	15.63	14.42	2.40
775.00	64.58	16.15	14.90	2.48
780.00	65.00	16.25	15.00	2.50
800.00	66.67	16.67	15.38	2.56
825.00	68.75	17.19	15.87	2.64
832.00	69.33	17.33	16.00	2.66

Per year	Per month	Per week 48 pmt.	Per week 52 pmt.	Per day
840.00	70.00	17.50	16.15	2.69
850.00	70.83	17.71	16.35	2.73
875.00	72.92	18.23	16.83	2.81
884.00	73.67	18.42	17.00	2.83
900.00	75.00	18.75	17.31	2.89
925.00	77.08	19.27	17.79	2.97
936.00	78.00	19.50	18.00	3.00
950.00	79.17	19.79	18.27	3.05
960.00	80.00	20.00	18.46	3.07
975.00	81.25	20.31	18.75	3.13
988.00	82.33	20.58	19.00	3.16
1000.00	83.33	20.83	19.23	3.21
1020.00	85.00	21.25	19.61	3.26
1025.00	85.42	21.35	19.71	3.29
1040.00	86.67	21.67	20.00	3.33
1050.00	87.50	21.88	20.19	3.37
1075.00	89.58	22.40	20.67	3.45
1080.00	90.00	22.50	20.76	3.46
1092.00	91.00	22.75	21.00	3.50
1100.00	91.67	22.92	21.15	3.53
1125.00	93.75	23.44	21.63	3.61
1140.00	95.00	23.75	21.92	3.65
1144.00	95.33	23.83	22.00	3.66
1150.00	95.83	23.96	22.12	3.69
1175.00	97.92	24.48	22.60	3.77
1196.00	99.67	24.92	23.00	3.83
1200.00	100.00	25.00	23.08	3.85
1225.00	102.08	25.52	23.56	3.93
1248.00	104.00	26.00	24.00	4.00
1250.00	104.17	26.04	24.04	4.01
1260.00	105.00	26.25	24.23	4.03
1275.00	106.25	26.56	24.52	4.09

Per year	Per month	Per week 48 pmt.	Per week 52 pmt.	Per day
1300.00	108.33	27.08	25.00	4.17
1320.00	110.00	27.50	25.38	4.23
1325.00	110.42	27.60	25.48	4.25
1350.00	112.50	28.13	25.96	4.33
1352.00	112.67	28.17	26.00	4.33
1375.00	114.58	28.65	26.44	4.41
1380.00	115.00	28.75	26.53	4.42
1400.00	116.67	29.17	26.92	4.49
1404.00	117.00	29.25	27.00	4.50
1425.00	118.75	29.69	27.40	4.57
1440.00	120.00	30.00	27.69	4.61
1450.00	120.83	30.21	27.88	4.65
1456.00	121.33	30.33	28.00	4.66
1475.00	122.92	30.73	28.37	4.73
1500.00	125.00	31.25	28.85	4.81
1508.00	125.67	31.42	29.00	4.83
1525.00	127.08	31.77	29.32	4.89
1550.00	129.17	32.29	29.81	4.97
1560.00	130.00	32.50	30.00	5.00
1575.00	131.25	32.81	30.29	5.05
1600.00	133.33	33.33	30.77	5.13
1612.00	134.33	33.58	31.00	5.16
1620.00	135.00	33.75	31.15	5.19
1625.00	135.42	33.85	31.25	5.21
1650.00	137.50	34.38	31.73	5.29
1664.00	138.67	34.67	32.00	5.33
1675.00	139.58	34.90	32.21	5.37
1680.00	140.00	35.00	32.30	5.38
1700.00	141.67	35.42	32.69	5.45
1716.00	143.00	35.75	33.00	5.50
1725.00	143.75	35.94	33.17	5.53
1740.00	145.00	36.25	33.46	5.57

Per year	Per month	Per week 48 pmt.	Per week 52 pmt.	Per day
1750.00	145.83	36.46	33.65	5.61
1768.00	147.33	36.83	34.00	5.66
1775.00	147.92	36.98	34.13	5.69
1800.00	150.00	37.50	34.62	5.77
1820.00	151.67	37.92	35.00	5.83
1825.00	152.08	38.02	35.10	5.85
1850.00	154.17	38.54	35.58	5.93
1860.00	155.00	38.75	35.76	5.96
1872.00	156.00	39.00	36.00	6.00
1875.00	156.25	39.06	36.06	6.01
1900.00	158.33	39.57	36.54	6.09
1920.00	160.00	40.00	36.92	6.15
1924.00	160.33	40.08	37.00	6.16
1925.00	160.42	40.11	37.02	6.17
1950.00	162.50	40.63	37.50	6.25
1975.00	164.58	41.14	37.98	6.33
1976.00	164.67	41.17	38.00	6.33
1980.00	165.00	41.25	38.07	6.34
2000.00	166.67	41.67	38.46	6.42
2025.00	168.75	42.19	38.94	6.49
2028.00	169.00	42.25	39.00	6.50
2040.00	170.00	42.50	39.23	6.53
2050.00	170.83	42.71	39.42	6.57
2075.00	172.92	43.23	39.90	6.65
2080.00	173.33	43.33	40.00	6.66
2100.00	175.00	43.75	40.38	6.73
2125.00	177.08	44.27	40.86	6.81
2132.00	177.67	44.42	41.00	6.83
2150.00	179.17	44.79	41.35	6.89
2160.00	180.00	45.00	41.53	6.92
2175.00	181.25	45.31	41.83	6.97
2184.00	182.00	45.50	42.00	7.00

[1]By courteous permission of the Lefax Corporation, Philadelphia.

Per year	Per month	Per week 48 pmt.	Per week 52 pmt.	Per day
2200.00	183.33	45.83	42.31	7.05
2220.00	185.00	46.25	42.69	7.11
2225.00	185.42	46.35	42.79	7.13
2236.00	186.33	46.58	43.00	7.16
2250.00	187.50	46.87	43.27	7.21
2275.00	189.58	47.40	43.75	7.29
2280.00	190.00	47.50	43.84	7.30
2288.00	190.67	47.67	44.00	7.33
2300.00	191.67	47.92	44.23	7.37
2325.00	193.75	48.44	44.71	7.45
2340.00	195.00	48.75	45.00	7.50
2350.00	195.83	48.96	45.19	7.53
2375.00	197.91	49.48	45.67	7.61
2392.00	199.33	49.83	46.00	7.66
2400.00	200.00	50.00	46.15	7.69
2425.00	202.08	50.52	46.63	7.77
2444.00	203.67	50.92	47.00	7.83
2450.00	204.17	51.04	47.12	7.85
2460.00	205.00	51.25	47.30	7.88
2475.00	206.25	51.56	47.59	7.93
2496.00	208.00	52.00	48.00	8.00
2500.00	208.33	52.08	48.08	8.01
2520.00	210.00	52.50	48.46	8.07
2525.00	210.42	52.60	48.56	8.09
2548.00	212.33	53.08	49.00	8.16
2550.00	212.50	53.13	49.04	8.18
2575.00	214.58	53.65	49.52	8.25
2580.00	215.00	53.75	49.61	8.26
2600.00	216.67	54.17	50.00	8.33
2625.00	218.75	54.69	50.48	8.41
2640.00	220.00	55.00	50.76	8.46
2650.00	220.83	55.21	50.96	8.49

Per year	Per month	Per week 48 pmt.	Per week 52 pmt.	Per day
2652.00	221.00	55.25	51.00	8.50
2675.00	222.92	55.73	51.44	8.57
2700.00	225.00	56.25	51.92	8.65
2704.00	225.33	56.33	52.00	8.67
2725.00	227.08	56.77	52.40	8.73
2750.00	229.17	57.29	52.88	8.81
2756.00	229.67	57.42	53.00	8.83
2760.00	230.00	57.50	53.07	8.84
2775.00	231.25	57.81	53.36	8.89
2800.00	233.33	58.33	53.85	8.97
2808.00	234.00	58.50	54.00	9.00
2820.00	235.00	58.75	54.23	9.03
2825.00	235.42	58.85	54.33	9.06
2850.00	237.50	59.38	54.81	9.14
2860.00	238.33	59.58	55.00	9.14
2875.00	239.58	59.90	55.29	9.22
2880.00	240.00	60.00	55.38	9.23
2900.00	241.67	60.42	55.77	9.30
2912.00	242.67	60.67	56.00	9.33
2925.00	243.75	60.94	56.25	9.38
2940.00	245.00	61.25	56.53	9.42
2950.00	245.83	61.46	56.73	9.46
2964.00	247.00	61.75	57.00	9.50
2975.00	247.92	61.98	57.21	9.54
3000.00	250.00	62.50	57.69	9.62
3016.00	251.33	62.83	58.00	9.67
3025.00	252.08	63.02	58.17	9.70
3050.00	254.17	63.54	58.65	9.78
3068.00	255.67	63.75	59.00	9.81
3075.00	256.25	64.06	59.13	9.86
3100.00	258.33	64.58	59.62	9.94

Per year	Per month	Per week 48 pmt.	Per week 52 pmt.	Per day
3120.00	260.00	65.00	60.00	10.00
3125.00	260.42	65.11	60.10	10.02
3150.00	262.50	65.63	60.58	10.10
3172.00	264.33	66.08	61.00	10.17
3175.00	264.58	66.15	61.06	10.18
3180.00	265.00	66.25	61.15	10.19
3200.00	266.67	66.67	61.54	10.26
3224.00	268.67	67.16	62.00	10.33
3225.00	268.75	67.19	62.02	10.34
3240.00	270.00	67.50	62.31	10.39
3250.00	270.83	67.71	62.50	10.42
3275.00	272.92	68.23	62.98	10.50
3276.00	273.00	68.25	63.00	10.50
3300.00	275.00	68.75	63.46	10.58
3325.00	277.08	69.27	63.94	10.66
3328.00	277.33	69.33	64.00	10.67
3350.00	279.17	69.79	64.42	10.74
3360.00	280.00	70.00	64.62	10.77
3375.00	281.25	70.31	64.90	10.82
3380.00	281.67	70.42	65.00	10.83
3400.00	283.33	70.83	65.38	10.90
3420.00	285.00	71.25	65.77	10.96
3425.00	285.42	71.36	65.87	10.98
3432.00	286.00	71.50	66.00	11.00
3450.00	287.50	71.88	66.35	11.06
3475.00	289.33	72.40	66.83	11.14
3484.00	290.33	72.58	67.00	11.17
3500.00	291.67	72.92	67.31	11.22
3525.00	293.75	73.44	67.79	11.30
3536.00	294.67	73.67	68.00	11.33
3540.00	295.00	73.75	68.08	11.35
3550.00	295.83	73.96	68.27	11.38

Per year	Per month	Per week 48 pmt.	Per week 52 pmt.	Per day
3575.00	297.92	74.48	68.75	11.46
3588.00	299.00	74.75	69.00	11.50
3600.00	300.00	75.00	69.23	11.54
3625.00	302.08	75.52	69.71	11.62
3640.00	303.33	75.83	70.00	11.67
3650.00	304.17	76.04	70.19	11.70
3660.00	305.00	76.25	70.38	11.73
3675.00	306.25	76.56	70.67	11.78
3692.00	307.67	76.92	71.00	11.83
3700.00	308.33	77.08	71.15	11.86
3720.00	310.00	77.50	71.54	11.92
3725.00	310.42	77.60	71.63	11.94
3744.00	312.00	78.00	72.00	12.00
3750.00	312.50	78.13	72.12	12.02
3775.00	314.58	78.65	72.60	12.10
3780.00	315.00	78.75	72.69	12.12
3796.00	316.33	79.08	73.00	12.18
3800.00	316.67	79.17	73.08	12.18
3825.00	318.75	79.69	73.56	12.26
3843.00	320.25	80.17	74.00	12.33
3850.00	320.83	80.21	74.03	12.34
3875.00	322.92	80.73	74.52	12.42
3900.00	325.00	81.25	75.00	12.50
3925.00	327.08	81.77	75.48	12.58
3950.00	329.17	82.29	75.96	12.66
3952.00	329.33	82.33	76.00	12.66
3960.00	330.00	82.50	76.15	12.69
3975.00	331.25	82.81	76.44	12.74
4000.00	333.33	83.33	76.92	12.82

sum should have been entered under savings. By making adjustments from time to time, you will see where your money actually goes, and how you can get the most for it.

Suggested Distribution of Income

The following table[1] gives a suggested distribution of income for various income groups, after taxes have been deducted. Adjustments should be made for higher living expenses in large metropolitan areas.

Monthly income	No. in family	Savings	Food	Clothing	Shelter	Operating costs	Advancement
$150	2	$15	$60	$15	$30	$12	$18
	3	10	65	16	30	12	17
	4	5	70	17	30	13	15
$200	2	$30	$65	$18	$40	$17	$30
	3	22	75	19	40	17	27
	4	15	80	20	40	20	25
$250	2	$40	$70	$22	$50	$23	$45
	3	35	85	22	50	24	34
	4	25	90	25	50	25	35
$300	2	$55	$75	$30	$55	$25	$60
	3	47	95	32	55	26	45
	4	40	100	35	55	30	40
$350	2	$68	$80	$32	$65	$35	$70
	3	60	97	37	65	35	56
	4	50	105	45	65	35	50
$400	2	$90	$88	$40	$70	$37	$75
	3	86	100	42	70	38	64
	4	70	112	50	70	38	60
$450	2	$120	$90	$45	$75	$40	$80
	3	105	105	50	75	40	75
	4	90	120	55	75	40	70
$500	2	$145	$95	$50	$80	$45	$85
	3	120	120	55	80	45	80
	4	110	125	65	80	45	75

[1]Source *Personal Money Management*, issued by the American Bankers Association.

Various factors make it necessary that each individual family plan its own distribution of income. Some groups will have to spend more for clothing than others. Professional people are likely to have greater expenses for social requirements. The cost of living in various communities is another factor of consequence. The above figures serve only as examples of how an income can be distributed over the main categories. The actual amount allotted in each case depends upon the requirements of the individual family.

Wise Buying and Planning

Other factors are important in a well-planned budget. Once you have established your monthly expenditures in the various categories, you can see where savings can be made. Food, for example, must be selected to provide the best diet possible, but this need not be the most expensive.

Consideration of food values and a careful allotment of money for basic types of food require wise buying. This does not mean that the cheapest product is necessarily the best bargain. It does mean finding the most nutritious food products at the most economical prices. There are a number of things to watch for. For example, foods should be bought in season, when prices are likely to be lowest. Comparison shopping is a good idea. If storage is possible, bulk shopping, particularly for staple foods, will result in savings. Carefully planned meals will make it possible to avoid wasted food.

The choice of clothing also requires wise buying. A basic wardrobe, carefully planned, will make it possible for everyone in the family to be well dressed at a reasonable cost. Bargains in clothing are not a saving unless the garments fit into a well-planned wardrobe and can be worn frequently. Clothes and accessories should be considered in terms of the complete wardrobe. For example, a man's tie that looks well with only one of his suits is not a bargain at any price. Color schemes should be planned carefully. Above all, simplicity in design is important. You and your friends will tire quickly of a too "dressy" outfit. On the other hand, a simple outfit of good quality can be given variety by well-chosen accessories and will always look well.

The household operating expenses can be another source of considerable savings. Fuel, telephone, laundry, cleaning, electricity and gas, are just a few of the numerous expenses that come under this category. These will naturally vary greatly under different living conditions, but thrifty management can result in worth-while savings. Planned housekeeping and careful economy will be profitable.

Similar factors must be considered in all the expense categories if a budget plan is to be successful. Whether you are buying a complete living room suite or a can opener for your kitchen, watch for the value, consider the quality and durability of the product. Compare the cost of similar products at other stores before buying. In the long run a slightly more expensive product may be the most economical. The careful buyer will get the greatest value for his money.

INVESTING MONEY

In selecting your investment objectives, serious consideration should be given to your earned income and annual savings; your age and health; your family responsibilities; the requirements in time and money, as well as the prospects, of your own business; maturing obligations such as mortgages; installment debt; educational expenses for children; and your own retirement objectives. These questions, of course, are tied into an insurance program and a liquid savings account for emergencies of illness, unemployment, disability, or general disaster, which in all well-run investment programs demand precedence.

Important guiding principles for an investor are: (1) secure adequate insurance and a savings account apart from any investible funds; (2)

establish and maintain your investment objectives, whether for safety of principal, for income, for gradual growth of capital, or for speculative appreciation; (3) consult your bank or lawyer, and through them, a reputable investment or brokerage firm for advice on attaining your objectives; and (4) keep informed on your investments.

For the investor's protection, a great body of laws, both Federal and state, has been built up, particularly over the past 20 years. In part, such laws prohibit the fraudulent or deceptive schemes which lure the unwary on the promise of huge or "sure" profits; but most investors are concerned more with mistakes of judgment than with fraud in investments. The laws, especially the Federal securities acts,[1] emphasize in the main that full information be made available to investors, but no attempt is made by governmental authorities to render an opinion on investments. The investor, then, must be sure to get and use information intelligently and not rely solely on the laws. After all, there are traffic laws for our protection but one does not, therefore, blindly cross the street.

Among the pitfalls to avoid are: (1) "playing the market" for short-term gains, following "tips" or advice from dabblers, being impressed or swayed by mere masses of figures, or rushing to buy securities on impulse, or because they are popular; (2) retaining investments not on their basic merit but for sentimental reasons, or because they are still paying dividends, or because you have a loss; (3) entertaining or acting on vague ideas about the soundness of an industry or a company without bothering to learn the available facts; (4) being misled by the high or low price of a security, without relating it to earnings, dividends, assets, and other determinants of value (a $500 stock in one company, for example, may be a sounder and cheaper investment than a $5 stock in another company); and (5) forgetting that the past record and present data on an investment must be supplemented by an appraisal of its future.

The positive steps to take as an investor include acting on the four guiding principles outlined at the beginning of this section. Where investment is considered in a company's securities, obtain information on the company's assets, its products or services, its debts, the amount of stock outstanding, what it earns, and how it compares with other companies in the same line of business.

Generally speaking, the higher a yield or return promised on an investment, the greater the risk to the investor's capital. The expert investment adviser should be able to appraise the risks and possibilities in a speculative investment; but even the expert can give no guaranty on his appraisal. However, the amateur or occasional investor will serve his own ends well if he secures the help and counsel of a conscientious and reputable adviser.

There is no exact formula for solving the problems of investing money; but there is need to weigh all the factors, to consult an expert in whom you can repose confidence, to settle on a choice of alternatives, and then to exercise that most elusive of qualities, patience.

[1]See also page 108

BUYING A HOME[1]

Most homes which people buy or build to order are acquired on credit. If the owner is careful of his investment and keeps the property in good condition, in addition to the various amenities of home ownership, he can figure a return in the form of rent "paid" to himself. The sensible and safe approach is to buy or build a house properly located and of a design suitable to the family's way of life; at a cost consistent with the income of the head of the family; and under financing terms that are reasonable and considerate of the family's needs and ability to pay.

Whether you are buying or building, consideration should be given to schools, churches, shopping facilities, recreational facilities, and convenience to work, including transportation costs. The general appearance of the neighborhood and whether it is developing, static, or deteriorating (if developing, consideration should be given to probable type of new development in relation to the house you have selected or plan to build); drainage of the lot and whether the area is subject to flooding; the type of people living in the neighborhood with respect to their incomes, types of work, and general living standards in relation to your own; zoning ordinances pertaining to apartments, business and industrial development; the condition of the streets; and public utility services. The tax rate must also be seriously considered.

In purchasing an existing house, inquire into the age of the house, its structural qualities, heating and ventilation, insulation, plumbing, electric wiring, closets and storage space, room arrangements, and adaptability to the family. Examine the many little details such as hardware, doors, drawers, and the like which, if not satisfactory, could be irritating.

Since most houses are acquired through the services of a realtor it is important to select one whom others regard as reliable. It is also advisable to double check information with friends who know house construction or the neighborhood. In building a new house one should give consideration to the employment of an architect. Changes during process of construction, even though they seem to be minor, are quite expensive in relation to the results. Supervision of construction is also desirable. You should find your local home-financing institution helpful on these matters.

Two families with the same monthly income may reasonably spend entirely different amounts for housing, depending on how they prefer to spend and save, and depending, too, on the long-run outlook for the family income. There are two rules of thumb that may serve as a guide. One is that the amount invested in the house and lot should not exceed two or two and a half times the annual stable income, after income taxes. Thus, with a $3,600 income the maximum recommended investment in a

---

[1]For technical information concerning home design and construction see page 351.

house and lot would be $9,000. The other is that monthly expenditures for acquiring and owning one's home, including monthly payments of principal and interest on the mortgage, real estate taxes, insurance, and maintenance should not exceed 25 per cent of the monthly income. In the previous illustration this monthly expenditure would be $75 per month and would be sufficient to retire a $6,000 mortgage in 15 to 20 years, depending on local property taxes and insurance rates and the proportion of maintenance work taken care of by the owner.

In financing the purchase of a home it is important to make advance inquiry into the preliminary costs, the down payment, and the terms of the mortgage. Preliminary costs, generally paid by the borrower, include: the appraisal fee; revenue stamps and notary fees; a mortgage tax (in a few states) ; cost of recording the mortgage; legal fees for obtaining a clear title and for the drawing of legal papers; pro rata portion of prepaid taxes and insurance; survey; repair costs; and a service fee which may be as high as 2 per cent or 3 per cent of the amount of the loan. (This is not charged by all lenders.) When you are building a home, additional preliminary costs may include: architect's fee; inspection fees; insurance and interest during construction; and the cost of basic household equipment not included in the cost of the house.

It is impossible to generalize on a cash down payment except on houses whose construction started after August 3, 1950. Under the Defense Production Act of 1950, government agencies have received authority to set minimum down payments when these houses are purchased. The down payment may be changed from time to time in order to get the desired control over the building of new houses. Down payments have ranged from 10 per cent on houses selling for $5000 or less to 50 per cent on houses selling for $24,250 and more. Legally, most savings and loan associations and cooperative banks can lend up to 80 per cent of appraised value which would mean a minimum $1,500 down payment (or lot value) on a property appraised at $7,500. Savings banks, depending on state laws, can lend from 66⅔ per cent to 80 per cent of appraised value; insurance companies, usually 66⅔ per cent; and, commercial banks, 60 per cent of appraised value. Exceptions are loans insured by the FHA (Federal Housing Administration), and guaranteed or insured loans to veterans. These exceptions are discussed later. As a practical matter the down payment required may often exceed the minimum provided by law and will vary with economic conditions, the property itself, the borrower, and the judgment of the lender. Second mortgage funds may be available to assist those who have insufficient funds to meet the down payment requirements. However, the cost of such funds is often prohibitive and usually they must be repaid within a few years. The borrower must take care not to commit himself for obligations he will be unable to meet.

With regard to manner of repayment, mortgage loans may be classified as *straight mortgages* and *amortized* or *direct reduction* loans. A straight mortgage loan requires that interest be paid quarterly or semiannually with the amount of the debt falling due generally in three, five or ten years.

The amortized or direct reduction mortgage loan is repaid by monthly payments of interest and principal. The amount of the monthly payment depends primarily on the number of years to pay and the monthly payment required remains the same until the loan is paid off. From each month's payment there is first deducted an amount for interest; the remainder of the payment is applied toward the debt. Each month the amount of interest declines and the balance applied to debt reduction increases. This plan is most suitable for those receiving regular wages or salaries. Usually under this plan, too, the borrower pays in each month one-twelfth of the annual property taxes and insurance and when these amounts fall due they are paid by the lender out of the fund accumulated.

The FHA does not grant loans. It is a Government agency which insures the lender (not the borrower) against loss on mortgage loans. The borrower (not the lender) pays the insurance premium of ½ per cent per year, calculated on the balance of the loan, in addition to the interest charge. Created primarily to assist small-home owners, FHA-insured loans are available on new construction with as little as 7 per cent down and 25 years to pay on new homes when the mortgage is for $5,800 or less, and the selling price is for not more than $7,000.

On higher priced houses, the FHA will insure loans only if the principal amount involved is not in excess of $14,000 if a down payment ranging from 17 per cent to 28 per cent of selling price is made by the purchaser. Twenty years is the maximum period within which to repay these loans.

The minimum down payments may be changed from time to time by the government officials as part of the government's campaign to control inflation.

The borrower under an FHA mortgage loan should recognize that the lender is required to report arrearages and also to foreclose promptly on delinquent loans in order to benefit from the insurance. Thus the borrower cannot expect as much consideration in a financial emergency as he can with certain other loans. He should also remember that FHA loans are often sold to another financial institution in another locality. There is an added charge for paying off an FHA loan before it matures.

The borrower must determine for himself how important the lower down payment and longer term are in relation to these other factors. Certainly there are advantages in dealing wholly with local lenders who know your standing in the community and who are willing to grant special consideration in times of temporary financial difficulty. There is also some question of the desirability of stretching the mortgage payments over too many years, especially when a 20-year plan results in monthly payments almost comparable to rent. Interest charges pile up rapidly when the loan is extended beyond 20 years. For example interest on a $5,000, 20-year loan at 5 per cent would total $2,920, compared with $4,663 for a 30-year loan. Thus, by paying $33.00 per month on a $5,000 loan instead of $26.85, an interest saving of $1,743 can be realized. As soon as the home is owned debt-free the over-all housing costs decline substantially.

If possible, the borrower should secure a mortgage contract which permits prepayment in whole or in part (preferably without penalty); which permits making advance payments that can be applied to offset future delinquencies; and which provides that the borrower may secure additional loans at a later date, under the mortgage, for modernization or repairs. Since savings and loan associations typically finance homes only in their locality and do not sell them, the prospective home owner is more apt to find these and other favorable features in the mortgage from them.

The following tables show how payments are applied to both principal and interest on a $1000 loan for 15 years at 5%:[1]

HOW PAYMENTS ON A 15-YEAR $1,000 LOAN REDUCE MONTHLY BALANCE DURING THE FIRST YEAR

Month	Payment	Interest	Principal Reduction	Balance
1	7.91	4.17	3.74	996.26
2	7.91	4.15	3.76	992.50
3	7.91	4.14	3.77	988.73
4	7.91	4.12	3.79	984.94
5	7.91	4.10	3.81	981.13
6	7.91	4.09	3.82	977.31
7	7.91	4.07	3.84	973.47
8	7.91	4.06	3.85	969.62
9	7.91	4.04	3.87	965.75
10	7.91	4.02	3.89	961.86
11	7.91	4.01	3.90	957.96
12	7.91	3.99	3.92	954.04

HOW INTEREST PAYMENTS ON A 15-YEAR $1,000 LOAN DECREASE FROM YEAR TO YEAR

At end of	Total Yearly Payments	Interest	Principal Reduction	Balance
1st year	94.92	48.96	45.96	954.04
3rd year	94.92	44.13	50.79	854.95
5th year	94.92	38.80	56.12	745.45
7th year	94.92	32.92	62.00	624.47
9th year	94.92	26.41	68.51	490.79
11th year	94.92	19.22	75.70	343.08
13th year	94.92	11.28	83.64	179.87
15th year	0.00	0.00	0.00	0.00

[1]Tables courtesy of Gardner Taylor, President, First Federal Savings and Loan Association, New York, N. Y.

Home loans to veterans are made by local financial institutions; the Veterans Administration will guarantee up to 60 per cent of the loan but not more than $7,500 provided the veteran had not used any of his guaranty prior to April 20, 1950. If the veteran had used a part of his guaranty prior to this date, his remaining guaranty is determined by subtracting the amount used from $4,000. This guarantee of the Government to assume a substantial amount of the loss on a loan to a veteran was granted to encourage lenders to make 100 per cent or very low down payment loans to veterans of World War II on homes at a preferred rate of interest. The loan guarantee is only available to veterans for loans on their own homes and the maximum guarantee credit available to a veteran for a home loan is $7,500, or $4,000 less any part used prior to April 20, 1950. Business loans and loans to finance farming operations are limited to a $2,000 guarantee. Eligible veterans of World War II have up to July 25, 1957 to avail themselves of this benefit.

The special features of home loans to eligible veterans of World War II are: the possibility of securing a loan with a very small or no down payment; a lower rate of interest (a 4 per cent rate was provided in the Servicemen's Readjustment Act of 1944); up to 30 years to pay; some protection against paying an unreasonable price, since the Veterans Administration will not guarantee the loan unless the sales price is found by one of its designated appraisers to be reasonable in the current market; and, a mortgage which permits prepayments without penalty.

As a part of the government's program to control inflation, veterans can be required to make certain minimum down payments when purchasing houses if the loans are to be insured or guaranteed by the Veterans Administration. The minimum down payments may be changed from time to time as government officials try to control the demand for real estate by controlling terms under which it is financed.

DEEDS

A deed is a written instrument transferring title to real property. The person conveying the property is called the *grantor* and the person to whom title is transferred is called the *grantee*. Apart from statutory provisions, a deed requires: (1) competent parties, *i.e.*, the grantor and the grantee must have the legal capacity to transfer and acquire real property; (2) an adequate description of the real estate (in terms of monuments, metes and bounds, maps, lot and block numbers); (3) a valid or good consideration, *i.e.*, money, or love and affection, etc.; (4) proper and adequate language, indicating an intent to transfer legal title; and (5) a formal signing, execution, and delivery to the grantee.

Deeds are recorded in public offices designated by statute.

The two most common forms of deed are *warranty deeds* and *quit-claim deeds*.

Warranty Deed

A warranty deed contains five specific provisions for the benefit of the grantee:

1. Seizin—a covenant meaning that the grantor at the time of execution and delivery of the deed has legal title to the property and lawful authority to sell.

2. Quiet enjoyment—a covenant meaning that the grantee and his heirs may at all times thereafter peaceably hold, use, and occupy the property free from claims of any other persons.

3. Freedom from encumbrances—a covenant meaning that the property is free from all liens and encumbrances such as judgments, assessments, taxes, etc.

4. Further assurance—a covenant meaning that the grantor will thereafter, upon request and at his own expense, execute and obtain any and all other instruments to more effectively validate the title.

5. Warranty of title—a covenant meaning that the grantor will forever warrant the title to the grantee and defend it against the claims of all other persons.

Quit-Claim Deed

A quit-claim deed is one which purports to convey nothing more than the *interest* of the grantor, rather than the property itself. The title to real property may be as effectually transferred by such a deed as by another form of conveyance. Such a deed conveys whatever title or interest the grantor may have, and only such title or interest. Except in so far as the grantee's rights may be enlarged by statute, he takes the property subject to existing encumbrances and the rights of others.

Deed in Escrow

A deed delivered in escrow is a deed *entrusted to a third person* until some stipulated condition has been fulfilled or some specified particular event has occurred. If the condition is not fulfilled or if the event does not occur, the grantor is entitled to a return of the deed.

Deed in Trust

A deed in trust is essentially a mortgage. It is a conveyance of the property intended to be pledged, to one or more trustees, who are to hold it for the benefit of a lawful holder of a note, bond, or other obligation of the grantor, permitting the latter to retain possession of the property and collect the rents thereof until default is made in the payment of the obligation, and with a power in the trustee or trustees, on such default, to sell the property and pay the obligation out of the net proceeds, returning the surplus, if any, to the grantor.

Acknowledgment

The acknowledgment of a deed is a *formal declaration* before a duly authorized public officer, generally a notary public, by the grantor that he is the person described in the instrument and the person who executed it.

Deed with Full Covenants[1]

This indenture, made the ———— day of ———— between JOHN DOE, of No. ————
———— Street, (City), (State) and RICHARD ROE, of No. ———— ———— Street, (City),
(State)

————, party of the second part: *witnesseth,* that the party of the first part, in
consideration of ———— dollars lawful money of the United States, paid by the party of
the second part, does hereby grant and release unto the party of the second part, his
heirs, executors, administators, (if a corporation, "successors" instead of foregoing) and
assigns forever, all that piece and parcel of land, known and described as No. ————
———— Street, (City), (State) and noted on the land map of ———— County as being
Section No. ————, Block No. ————, more particularly described as follows: (Here
insert description from prior deeds. Also what mortgages the conveyance is subject to if
any. Describe mortgage by giving its amount, due date, interest, mortgagee, liber and
page numbers in register's office where recorded.)

together with the appurtenances and all the estate and rights of the party of the first
part in and to said premises.
To have and to hold the premises herein granted unto the party of the second part
———— and assigns forever.

And the said JOHN DOE covenants as follows:

First: That said JOHN DOE is seized of the said premises in fee simple, and has good
right to convey the same.

Second: That the party of the second part shall quietly enjoy the said premises.

Third: That the said premises are free from incumbrances; except as hereinbefore set
forth.

Fourth: That the party of the first part will execute or procure any further necessary
assurance of the title to said premises.

Fifth: That said JOHN DOE will forever warrant the title to said premises.
In witness whereof, the party of the first part has hereunto set his hand and seal the
day and year first above written.
In presence of

(Signed) *John Doe* (seal)

(Acknowledgment)

Quit-Claim Deed[1]

This indenture, made the ———— day of ————, nineteen hundred and ————
between JOHN DOE, of No. ———— ———— Street, (City), (State) and RICHARD ROE, of
No. ————, ———— Street, (City), (State), party of the first part,

————, party of the second part, *witnesseth,* that the party of the first part, in
consideration of ———— dollars, lawful money of the United States, and other good and
valuable considerations to the party of the first part in hand paid by the party of the
second part, does hereby remise, release and quit-claim unto the party of the second
part, his heirs, executors, administrators (if a corporation "successors" instead of
foregoing) and assigns forever. *All* that piece and parcel of land known and described as
No. ————, ———— Street, (City), (State) and noted upon the land map of ————
County, as being Section No. ————, Block No. ———— and more particularly described as follows: (Here insert description from prior deed.)

---

[1]This is only a suggested form. The reader is advised to obtain a blank form, valid in his
state, from a lawyer or a legal stationer for use in specific transactions.

Together with the appurtenances and all the estate and rights of the party of the first part in and to said premises.

To have and to hold the premises herein granted unto the party of the second part, his heirs, administrators, executors and assigns forever.

In witness whereof, the party of the first part has hereunto set his hand and seal the day and year first above written.
In the presence of

(Signed) *John Doe* (seal)

(Acknowledgment)

Trust Deed[1]

This indenture, made this ——— day of ———, 19—, between JOHN DOE of No. ———, ——— Street, (City), (State) (hereinafter called the "grantor") party of the first part, and ——— TRUST COMPANY, a corporation organized and existing under the laws of the state of ——— (hereinafter called the "trustee"), party of the second part, *witnesseth:* that the grantor in consideration of the sum of One Dollar ($1) to him in hand paid by the trustee, the receipt whereof is hereby acknowledged, and of the covenants hereinafter contained, hath sold, assigned, transferred and set over, and by these presents does sell, assign, transfer and set over unto the trustee the securities and property specified and described in a schedule hereto annexed and marked "Schedule A," the receipt of which securities and property is hereby acknowledged by the trustee.

To have and to hold the said securities and property to the said trustee, its successors or assigns upon the following express trust and conditions and with the powers and limitations hereinafter conferred and set forth, that is to say:

1. To collect and receive the rents, income, interest and dividends therefrom (hereinafter referred to as "income") and to pay the net income therefrom after deducting all proper charges and expenses to the grantor during his lifetime.

2. Upon the death of the grantor to pay over the principal of the said trust fund as he, the said grantor, may by his last will and testament appoint, and in default of such appointment, the same shall constitute and be disposed of as a part of his estate.

3. The trustee is expressly authorized and empowered (here insert whatever investment powers, with limitations or discretion, it is desired that the trustee shall have).

4. The grantor hereby expressly reserves the right at any time by a notice in writing, signed and acknowledged by him, and filed with the trustee, to revoke, cancel and annul this indenture and the trust hereby created, either in whole or in part, and he also reserves the right at any time, and from time to time, by a notice in writing, signed and acknowledged by him and filed with the trustee, to alter, amend and modify this agreement in any and every respect.

5. The trustee shall be entitled to the following compensation: (herein insert schedule for compensation).

6. The trustee shall have the right to resign at any time by giving written notice to the grantor.

7. The trustee by joining in this indenture signifies its acceptance of the trust.

In witness whereof the said parties have hereunto set their hands and seals the day and year first above written.

John Doe (seal)
——— TRUST COMPANY,
By Vice President.

Attest:
   Asst. Secretary (seal of company)
    (Acknowledgments)

---

[1]This is only a suggested form. The reader is advised to obtain a blank form, valid in his state, from a lawyer or a legal stationer for use in specific transactions.

REAL ESTATE MORTGAGES

A real estate mortgage is an interest in real property given to secure payment for a debt. The person who executes a mortgage is called a *mortgagor*, the person whose debt is secured is called a *mortgagee*. A mortgage does not transfer title but only creates a lien upon the land. The mortgagor retains title to the land.

By statute, a binding and valid mortgage on real property must be *in writing*. Apart from express statutory requirements, no particular form is necessary, nor is any particular language required; it is only necessary that the instrument manifest a present purpose of the grantor or mortgagor to convey title of specified real estate to a designated person as the mortgagee, the instrument to be held by the latter as security for the payment of a certain sum of money. The instrument must be executed or acknowledged before a public officer, generally a notary public, and recorded in a public office. The purpose of recording it is to give notice to others, who can then only acquire an interest in the mortgaged property subject to the mortgage. A mortgage, to be valid, must be delivered by the mortgagor.

The debt for which a mortgage is given is always evidenced by a bond or note of the mortgagor.

Ordinarily the mortgagee has no right of possession prior to default. By statute, in some states, it is provided that after default in payment of the secured debt or other breach of the mortgage, the mortgagee is entitled to possession of the property, and may enter, peaceably or by appropriate legal proceeding.

In the absence of statute or agreement providing otherwise, the creditor may bring an action on the bond or note without first foreclosing the mortgage.

Since the last depression many states have enacted moratorium laws suspending the right to sue for a debt secured by a mortgage if the interest and taxes on the mortgaged premises are paid; but such a statute does prevent the mortgagee from suing for the principal even if the taxes and interest are paid.

A valid judgment obtained in an action on a mortgage debt exists until the judgment is paid, and the mortgage remains a valid lien. The judgment does not discharge nor release the mortgage.

A mortgage can be assigned; the assignment must be in writing. Although the recording of an assignment of a mortgage is not prerequisite to its validity between the parties, under some statutes an assignee, *i.e.*, the person to whom it is assigned, must record his assignment to give constructive notice to third persons unless they are otherwise chargeable with notice.

In some states, by statute, a transfer of the debt secured by a mortgage carries with it the mortgage security and such an assignee succeeds to all the rights of the assignor.

The owner of mortgaged property may sell the property to a third party, without prejudice to the rights of the mortgagee. By selling the mortgaged property, the mortgagor does not relieve himself from his personal obligation on the secured debt.

If the purchaser does not agree to pay the mortgage, he is not liable to the mortgagor for its payment. He may, of course, expressly agree to pay the mortgage. When the land is sold subject to a mortgage, the mortgagee's lien continues, and the land is the primary fund for the satisfaction of the mortgage, as though the purchaser had expressly assumed the payment of the debt.

The lien of a mortgage continues until the debt is paid or the lien is extinguished by release or operation of law.

Foreclosure is a remedy by which the property may be subjected to sale for the payment of the debt for which the mortgage is security. This remedy is ordinarily necessary to cut off the mortgagor's equity of redemption, which is the right of the mortgagor to pay the full amount of the indebtedness with interest, in order to redeem the property. Once the mortgage is foreclosed, the mortgagor's title to the property vests in the mortgagee and amounts to a satisfaction of the mortgaged debt to the extent of the value of the mortgaged property, or, in the case of a sale thereof, to the extent of the amount realized therefrom.

Form of Real Estate Mortgage[1]

This mortgage, made the ———— day of ———— nineteen hundred and ————, between ———— the mortgagor, and ————, the mortgagee,

Witnesseth, that to secure the payment of an indebtedness in the sum of ———— Dollars lawful money of the United States, to be paid ———— with interest thereon, to be computed from the date hereof at the rate of ———— per centum per annum, and to be paid on the ———— day of ———— next ensuing and ———— thereafter, ———— according to a certain bond or obligation bearing even date herewith, the mortgagor hereby mortgages to the mortgagee *all* that certain plot, piece or parcel of land, with the buildings and improvements thereon erected, situate, lying and being in the

(Here follows description of property.)

Together with all right, title and interest of the mortgagor in and to the land lying in the streets and roads in front of and adjoining said premises, and

Together with all fixtures, chattels and articles of personal property attached to or used in connection with said premises or which may hereafter be attached to or used in connection with said premises, including but not limited to furnaces, boilers, oil burners, radiators and piping, coal stokers, plumbing and bathroom fixtures, refrigeration, air conditioning and sprinkler systems, wash tubs, sinks, gas and electric fixtures, stoves, ranges, awnings, screens, window shades, elevators, motors, dynamos, refrigerators, kitchen cabinets, incinerators, and all other equipment and machinery, appliances, fittings, and fixtures of every kind in or used in the operation of the buildings standing on said premises, together with any and all replacements thereof and additions thereto, and the whole of said principal sum secured by said bond and this mortgage shall become due and payable, at the option of the mortgagee in the event of the removal, demolition or destruction in whole or in part of any of said fixtures, chattels or articles

---

[1]Because of differences in practice in the various states, it is suggested that forms in common use in the state where the property is located be procured from a lawyer or a legal stationer and used for specific transactions. This form is only a suggested one; it is in current use in New York.

of personal property, unless the same are promptly replaced by similar fixtures, chattels and articles of personal property at least equal in quality and condition to those replaced, provided, however, that such substituted fixtures, chattels or articles of personal property be purchased free from any encumbrance and without reservation of title thereto in the seller.

Together also with any and all awards heretofore made and hereafter to be made to the present and all subsequent owners of said premises, including any award and awards for change of grade of any street affecting said premises, which said award and awards are hereby assigned to the mortgagee, who is hereby authorized and empowered to collect and receive such award and awards and to give proper receipts and acquittances therefor, and to apply the same toward the payment of the amount owing on this mortgage, notwithstanding the fact that the amount owing on this mortgage may not then be due and payable; and the mortgagor for himself, his heirs and all subsequent owners of said premises, hereby covenants and agrees with the mortgagee and the successors and assigns of the mortgagee, upon request by the holder of this mortgage to make, execute and deliver any and all assignments and other instruments sufficient for the purpose of assigning said award and awards to the holder of this mortgage, free, clear and discharged of any encumbrances of any kind or nature whatsoever.

and the mortgagor covenants with the mortgagee as follows:

1. That the mortgagor will pay the indebtedness as hereinbefore provided.

2. That no building on the premises shall be altered, removed or demolished without the consent of the mortgagee.

3. That the mortgagor will pay all taxes, assessments or water rates and in default thereof the mortgagee may pay the same.

4. That the mortgagor warrants the title to the premises.

5. That the mortgagor will keep the buildings on the premises insured against loss by fire for the benefit of the mortgagee; that he will assign and deliver the policies to the mortgagee; and that he will reimburse the mortgagee for any premiums paid for insurance made by the mortgagee on the mortgagor's default in so insuring the buildings or in so assigning and delivering the policies. The mortgagee is authorized, at its option, to collect, adjust and compromise any loss under any policies on said property and to apply the net proceeds, at its option, either as a credit on the mortgage debt or to restoring the improvements, or to deliver the same to the owner of said mortgaged premises.

6. That the mortgagor will, upon ten days' written demand by the mortgagee, deliver to the mortgagee receipted bills showing the payment of all taxes, assessments and water rates, and if such receipted bills are not delivered within said ten days, then all taxes, assessments and water rates appearing to be unpaid on the books of any officer for the collection of any such items shall be conclusively deemed to be unpaid, and all defenses of payment of any such items are hereby waived.

7. That the whole of said principal sum and interest shall become due, at the option of the mortgagee, after default in the payment of any instalment of principal for ten days, or after default in the payment of interest for fifteen days, or after default in the payment of any tax, assessment or water rate (including future instalments of assessments confirmed, whether said future instalments are liens or not) for thirty days after the same become payable, anything hereinbefore contained to the contrary notwithstanding, or immediately upon the actual or threatened alteration, removal or demolition of any building standing on the mortgaged premises, or after default after notice and demand either in assigning and delivering the policies insuring the buildings against loss by fire or in reimbursing the mortgagee for premiums paid on such insurance, as hereinbefore provided; or after default upon request in furnishing a statement of the amount due on the mortgage and whether any offsets or defenses exist against the mortgage debt, as hereinafter provided.

8. That in the event of a foreclosure of this mortgage said premises may be sold in one parcel, any provision of law to the contrary notwithstanding.

9. The rents, issues and profits of said mortgaged premises are hereby transferred and assigned to the mortgagee as further security for the payment of said indebtedness, and the mortgagor, for himself, his heirs and all subsequent owners of said premises, grants to the mortgagee license to enter upon said premises for the purpose of collecting the same and to let said premises or any part thereof, and to apply the

rents, issues and profits, after payment of all necessary charges and expenses, on account of said indebtedness. This assignment and grant shall continue in effect until this mortgage is paid. The mortgagee hereby waives the right to enter upon said premises for the purpose of collecting said rents, issues and profits, and the mortgagor and any subsequent owner of said premises shall be entitled to collect and receive said rents, issues and profits until default under the covenants, conditions and agreements contained in this mortgage or the bond hereby secured, and the mortgagor for himself, his heirs, and all subsequent owners of said premises, covenants to use such rents, issues and profits in payment of principal and interest becoming due on this mortgage and in payment of taxes and carrying charges becoming due against said premises, but such right of the mortgagor and any subsequent owner to collect said rents, issues and profits may be revoked by the mortgagee upon any default, on five days' written notice. The mortgagor for himself, his heirs, and all subsequent owners of said premises, covenants that he will not, without the written consent of the mortgagee, receive or collect rent from any tenant of said premises or any part thereof for a period of more than one month in advance, and in the event of any default under this mortgage or the bond hereby secured, will pay monthly in advance to the mortgagee, or to any receiver appointed to collect said rents, issues and profits, the fair and reasonable rental value for the use and occupation of said premises or of such part thereof as may be in the possession of the mortgagor, his heirs, or any subsequent owner of said premises, and upon default in any such payment will vacate and surrender the possession of said premises to the mortgagee. The covenants contained in this paragraph shall run with the land and bind the mortgagor, his heirs and all subsequent owners, tenants, sub-tenants and assigns of said premises or any part thereof.

10. That neither the value of the mortgaged premises nor the lien of this mortgage will be diminished or impaired in any way by any act or omission of the mortgagor, and that said mortgagor will not do or permit to be done to, in, upon or about said premises or any part thereof, anything that may in any wise substantially impair the value thereof, or substantially weaken, diminish or impair the security of this mortgage. This covenant shall run with the land and bind the mortgagor, his heirs and all subsequent owners of said premises.

11. That the whole of said principal sum shall become due at the option of the mortgagee if the buildings on said premises are not maintained in reasonably good repair, after notice of the condition of the building is given to the mortgagor, or upon the failure of any owner of said premises to comply with the requirements of any governmental department claiming jurisdiction within three months after an order making such requirements has been issued by any such department, or upon the failure of any owner of said premises or any person holding under said owner as tenant, lessee, or otherwise, to comply with all statutes, orders, requirements or decrees relating to said premises by any Federal, State or Municipal authority.

12. That the mortgagee in any action to foreclose this mortgage shall be entitled, without regard to the adequacy of any security for the debt and without notice, to the appointment of a receiver.

13. That in the event of the passage of any law changing in any way the laws for the taxation of mortgages or debts secured by mortgage for State or local purposes, this mortgage shall, at the option of the mortgagee, become due and payable after thirty days' written notice to the mortgagor.

14. If any action or proceeding be commenced (except an action to foreclose this mortgage or to collect the debt secured thereby), to which action or proceeding the holder of this mortgage is made a party, or in which it becomes necessary to defend or uphold the lien of this mortgage, all sums paid by the holder of this mortgage for the expense of any litigation to prosecute or defend the rights and lien created by this mortgage (including reasonable counsel fees), shall be paid by the mortgagor, together with interest thereon at the rate of six per centum per annum, and any such sum and the interest thereon shall be a lien on said premises, prior to any right, or title to, interest in or claim upon said premises attaching or accruing subsequent to the lien of this mortgage, and shall be deemed to be secured by this mortgage and by the bond which it secures. In any action or proceeding to foreclose this mortgage, or to recover or collect the debt secured thereby, the provisions of law respecting the recovery of costs, disbursements and allowances shall prevail unaffected by this covenant.

15. That the mortgagor will receive the advances secured by this mortgage and will hold the right to receive such advances as a trust fund to be applied first for the purpose of paying the cost of improvement, and that he will apply the same first to the payment of the cost of improvement before using any part of the total of the same for any other purpose.

16. That the mortgagor within five days upon request in person or within ten days upon request by mail will furnish a written statement duly acknowledged of the amount due on this mortgage and whether any offsets or defenses exist against the mortgage debt.

17. That notice and demand or request may be in writing and may be served in person or by mail.

If more than one person joins in the execution of this mortgage, and if any be of the feminine sex, or if this mortgage is executed by a corporation, the relative words herein shall be read as if written in the plural, or in the feminine or neuter gender, as the case may be, and the words "mortgagor" and "mortgagee" where used herein shall be construed to include their and each of their heirs, executors, administrators, successors and assigns.

In witness whereof, this mortgage has been duly executed by the mortgagor.

(Signed) *John Doe* (seal)

In presence of:

(2 witnesses)
(Acknowledgment)

Bond Secured By Mortgage[1]

Know all men by these presents, that

hereinafter designated as the obligor ——— do ——— hereby acknowledge ——— to be ——— justly indebted to ——— hereinafter designated as the obligee, in the sum of ——— Dollars, lawful money of the United States, which sum ——— said obligor ——— do ——— hereby ——— covenant to pay to said obligee, ——— or assigns, ——— with interest thereon to be computed from the date hereof, at the rate of ——— per centum per annum, and to be paid on the ——— day of ——— next ensuing, and

It is hereby expressly agreed that the whole of said principal sum and interest shall become due, at the option of said obligee, after default in the payment of any instalment of principal for ten days, or after default in the payment of interest for fifteen days, or after default in the payment of any tax, assessment or water rate (including future instalments of assessments confirmed, whether said future instalments are liens or not) for thirty days after same become payable, or immediately upon the actual or threatened alteration, demolition or removal of any building standing on the mortgaged premises or after default after notice and demand either in assigning and delivering policies insuring the buildings against loss by fire or in reimbursing the mortgagee for premiums paid on such insurance; or after default upon request in furnishing a statement of the amount due on the mortgage and whether any offsets or defenses exist against the mortgage debt.

And it is further expressly agreed that the obligation of this bond shall continue until said indebtedness shall be fully paid notwithstanding any waiver by the obligee of any breach of any condition or covenant of this bond or of the mortgage accompanying the same and notwithstanding any action to foreclose said mortgage and/or the settlement and/or discontinuance of such action and regardless of whether the due date of this bond shall have been extended or the terms modified by such settlement and/or discontinuance.

---

[1]Because of differences of practice in the various states, it is suggested that forms in common use in the state where the property is located be procured from a lawyer or a legal stationer and used for specific transactions. This form is only a suggested one; it is in current use in New York.

All the covenants and agreements contained in the mortgage covering the premises therein described and collateral hereto, are hereby made part of this instrument. Signed and sealed this ———— day of ————

In Presence of

John Doe (seal)

(Acknowledgment)

CHATTEL MORTGAGES

A chattel mortgage is a *conveyance of a legal or equitable right in personal property,* as security for the payment of money. In some states it operates to pass legal title of the property to the mortgagee, but in other states it merely creates a lien.

All kinds of personal property can be the subject of a chattel mortgage. There must be consideration for a chattel mortgage.

Unless required by statute, no particular form of words is necessary to create a chattel mortgage, and any language is sufficient if it indicates an intention to create a lien on personal property to secure payment of a debt.

The chattel mortgage must (1) describe the property and its location (2) state the amount of indebtedness, and when and how it is payable. The instrument must be executed and filed in accordance with statutory provisions to be valid and effective against third persons, but not between the mortgagor and mortgagee.

The generally accepted rule is that legal title to the mortgaged property is vested in the mortgagee on default by the mortgagor.

Prior to default, in the absence of statute or agreement between the parties, the general rule is that the mortgagee has the right to possession, but in some states the courts have decided that the right of possession is vested in the mortgagor. A mortgagor in possession must not impair the rights of the mortgagee.

When the mortgagor complies with the terms of the chattel mortgage, it is discharged and, generally, a satisfaction is signed by the mortgagee and filed in the same office in which the chattel mortgage was filed. If the debt is not paid, the mortgagee may foreclose the chattel mortgage and out of the net proceeds of the sale of the mortgaged goods satisfy the debt; he must remit the surplus, if any, to the mortgagor. Generally, the procedure to foreclose is regulated by statute, which also provides in what manner the sale is to be conducted.

Mortgage on Goods or Chattels[1]

To all to whom these presents shall come, know ye that, I, JOHN DOE, of No. ————, ———— Street, (city), (state), party of the first part, for securing the payment of the money hereinafter mentioned, and in consideration of the sum of one dollar to me duly paid by RICHARD ROE, of No. ———— ———— Street, (city), (state), party of the second part, at or before the ensealing and delivery of these presents, the receipt whereof is

---

[1]This is only a suggested form. The reader is advised to obtain a blank form, valid in his state, from a lawyer or a legal stationer for use in specific transactions.

hereby acknowledged, have bargained and sold, and by these presents do grant, bargain and sell unto the said party of the second part, (here insert goods sold) and all other goods and chattels mentioned in the schedule hereunto annexed, and now in the (here insert location of goods) to have and to hold, all and singular the goods and chattels above bargained and sold, or intended so to be, unto the said party of the second part, his executors, administrators and assigns for ever. And JOHN DOE the said party of the first part, for his heirs, executors and administrators, all and singular the said goods and chattels above bargained and sold unto the said party of the second part, his heirs, executors, administrators and assigns, against JOHN DOE the said party of the first part and against all and every person or persons whomsoever, shall and will warrant, and for ever defend. Upon condition, that if JOHN DOE the said party of the first part, shall and do well and truly pay unto the said party of the second part, his executors, administrators or assigns, (here insert the sum of money owing, the time of payment, rate of interest, interest dates, etc.), then these presents shall be void. And JOHN DOE the said party of the first part, for his executors, administrators and assigns, does covenant and agree to and with the said party of the second part, his executors, administrators and assigns, that in case default shall be made in the payment of the said sum above mentioned, or any part thereof then it shall and may be lawful for, and JOHN DOE the said party of the first part, does hereby authorize and empower the said party of the second part, his executors, administrators and assigns, with the aid and assistance of any person or persons, to enter his dwelling-house, store, and other premises, and such other place or places as the said goods or chattels are or may be placed, and take and carry away the said goods or chattels, and to sell and dispose of the same for the best price they can obtain; and out of the money arising therefrom, to retain and pay the said sum above mentioned, including interest, cost of sale, etc., and all charges touching the same; rendering the overplus (if any) unto JOHN DOE or to his executors, administrators or assigns. And until default be made in the payment of the said sum of money it is understood and agreed that JOHN DOE is to remain and continue in the quiet and peaceable possession of the said goods and chattels, and the full and free enjoyment of the same. If from any cause said property shall fail to satisfy said debt, interest, costs and charges, the said JOHN DOE, party of the first part, covenants and agrees to pay the deficiency.

In witness whereof, JOHN DOE, the said party of the first part, has hereunto set his hand and seal the ———— day of ———— one thousand nine hundred ————.
Sealed and delivered in the presence of

(Signed) *John Doe* (seal)

(Acknowledgment)

(Here follows the schedule referred to in the contract.)

LEASES

A lease is a *contract for the use and possession of real estate* for a specified period of time; it requires the *lessee,* or tenant, to pay the *lessor,* or landlord, an agreed rental. A lease for more than one year is void unless the contract, or some note or memorandum thereof, expressing the consideration, is in writing subscribed and not merely signed by the party to be charged, or by his lawful agent, whose authority must be in writing. In some states leases for more than a specified number of years must be recorded.

Generally the rights, duties, and obligations of the party are fixed by the terms of the lease after preliminary negotiations.

In the absence of agreement, the landlord does not warrant that the leased premises are fit for use and occupancy. This is a matter to be determined by the tenant after inspection.

If there is no express prohibition against assignment or subleasing the tenant may do so without the landlord's consent. Most leases, however, prohibit that this be done; when it is permitted, the lease generally provides that the original tenant shall remain liable for the payment of rent and the other terms of the lease, notwithstanding the assignment or subletting.

The shortage of space for housing and business purposes prevalent since World War II has led Congress and most states to pass statutes regulating and controlling the rights of owners and occupants of such space. The state statutes are not uniform. The primary purposes of all these statutes are (1) to prevent landlords from evicting tenants after the expiration of their leases, (2) to fix maximum rentals, and (3) to establish procedures for procuring increases or decreases in rent.

These statutes, as originally passed or later amended, have been held constitutional.

Lease of an Office or Loft Building[1]

Agreement, made this ———— day of ———— nineteen hundred and ———— be-*tween* ———— hereinafter designated as the Landlord, and ———— hereinafter designated as the Tenant, *Witnesseth,* that the said Landlord does hereby let unto the said Tenant, and the said Tenant does hereby hire from the said Landlord ———— Borough of ———— New York City, to be used and occupied for the business of ———— for the term of ———— to commence on the ———— day of ———— and to end at nine o'clock in the forenoon on the ———— day of ———— at the yearly rent of ———— lawful money of the United States, payable as follows: ————.

The above letting is upon the following conditions, all and every one of which said Tenant covenants and agrees to and with said Landlord to keep and perform.

First: Neither the Tenant nor his heirs, executors or administrators shall assign or encumber this lease, and the said premises, or any part thereof, shall not be let or underlet, nor used or permitted to be used, for any purpose other than above-mentioned, nor by any other person without the written consent of said Landlord.

Second: The Tenant shall take good care of the premises and fixtures, make good any injury or breakage done by such Tenant or any agents, clerks, servants, or visitors, and shall quit and surrender said premises, at the end of said term, in as good condition as the reasonable use thereof will permit; and shall not make any additions, alterations, or improvements in said premises, nor permit any additional lock or fastening on any door, without the written consent of the Landlord; and all alterations, partitions, additions, or improvements which may be made by either of the parties hereto upon the premises, except movable office furniture other than partitions, put in at the expense of the Tenant, shall be the property of the Landlord, and shall remain upon and be surrendered with the premises, as a part thereof, at the termination of this lease, without disturbance, molestation, or injury, but injury caused by moving said movable furniture in or out shall be repaired at the expense of the Tenant.

Third: In case of damage, by fire, or other action of the elements, to the demised premises, the Landlord shall repair the same with all reasonable despatch, after notice of the damage. But in case the building generally throughout (though the herein demised premises may not be affected) be so injured or destroyed that the Landlord shall decide, within a reasonable time, to rebuild or reconstruct the said building, then this agreement shall cease and come to an end, and the rent be apportioned and paid up to the time of such injury or destruction, provided, however, that such damage or destruction as hereinbefore mentioned be not caused by the carelessness, negligence,

---

[1]This is only a suggested form. The reader is advised to obtain a blank form, valid in his state, from a lawyer or legal stationer for use in specific transactions.

or improper conduct of the Tenant, agents, or servants. No claim for compensation shall be made by the Tenant by reason of inconvenience, damage, or annoyance arising from the necessity of repairing any portion of the building, however the necessity may occur.

Fourth: The Landlord agrees to use due diligence in operating the elevators in said building, and in furnishing steam for heating the premises between October 15 and April 15 in each year, during the hours between 8 o'clock A.M. and 6 o'clock P.M., Sundays and Holidays excepted; but it is expressly agreed that if the operation of the elevators, or the furnishing of steam heat ———— shall cease by reason of accident, strike, repairs, cleaning out boilers, alterations or improvements to be made or done to any part of the apparatus or appurtenances belonging thereto, or any cause beyond the control of the Landlord, the obligations of the Tenant under the terms of this lease shall not be affected thereby, nor shall any claim accrue to the Tenant by reason thereof.

Fifth: The Landlord shall not be liable for any damage or injury to the demised premises, for goods, wares, merchandise, or property of the Tenant contained therein, by reason of any damage done or occasioned by or from electric wiring, plumbing, water, gas, steam or other pipes, or sewage or the breaking of any electric wire, the bursting, leaking or running of water from any cistern, tank, washstand, water closet or waste pipe, radiator or any other pipe, in, above, upon, or about said building or premises; nor for any damage occasioned by electricity, or water, snow, or ice being upon or coming through the roof, skylight, trap door, or otherwise, or for any damages or injuries arising from acts or neglect of the cotenants, or occupants of the same building, or of any owners or occupants of adjacent or contiguous property, or any other cause.

Sixth: The following RULES AND REGULATIONS shall be faithfully observed and performed by the Tenant and the clerks, servants, and agents of such Tenant, to wit:

(a) The sidewalks, entry, halls, passages, staircases, and elevators shall not be obstructed, nor used for any other purpose than for ingress and egress, nor shall any property of any kind be moved in or out of the building between 9 o'clock A.M., and 5 o'clock P.M.

(b) The toilet rooms, water closets, urinals, and other water apparatus shall not be used for any purposes other than those for which they were constructed, and no improper substance or articles shall be thrown therein, nor shall any faucet be left open nor any water wasted.

(c) The sashes, sash doors, windows, glass doors, and any skylights that reflect or admit light in to the halls or other places of said building shall not be covered or obstructed.

(d) No one shall mark, paint, or drill into, or in any way deface the walls, ceilings, partitions, floors, wood, stone or iron work; and no nails, hooks, or screws shall be driven or inserted in any part of the walls or woodwork of said building.

(e) If Tenants desire telegraphic or telephone connections, the Landlord will direct the electricians as to where and how the wires are to be introduced; and without such direction no boring or cutting for wires will be permitted.

(f) No sign, advertisement, notice, or device shall be inscribed, painted or affixed on any part of the outside or inside of said building, except of such color, size, and style or in such places upon or in said building, as shall be first designated by said Landlord.

(g) All lettering on doors or windows shall be ordered and done by the Landlord's painter at the expense of the lessee.

(h) No machinery of any kind will be allowed to be operated on the premises without the written consent of the Landlord.

(i) No Tenant shall do or permit anything to be done in said premises, or bring or keep anything therein, or permit anything to be brought or kept therein, which shall in any way increase the rate of fire insurance on said building, or on the property kept therein; nor use the demised premises, or any part thereof, nor suffer or permit their use in any business of such a character as to increase the rate of fire insurance on said building or on the property kept therein.

(j) The Tenant covenants and agrees not to do or permit anything to be done in or about said premises, or bring or keep anything therein, or permit anything to be brought or kept therein, which shall in any way conflict with the orders, ordinances, regulations, or rules of the state or any department thereof, the municipality of the

City of New York, or any department thereof, or of any public or municipal authority, or of the New York Board of Fire Underwriters, or the requirements of any policy of fire insurance upon said building, or upon any property contained therein.

(k) The Landlord shall have the power to prescribe the weight and position of iron safes; and they shall, in all cases, stand on two-inch-thick strips to distribute the weight; and all damage done to the building by taking in or putting out a safe, or during the time it is in or on the premises, shall be repaired at the expense of the Tenant. Safes shall be moved only after 5 o'clock P.M.; and no safe will be allowed to be moved upon the elevators; and safes shall only be moved by competent persons acceptable to the Landlord.

(l) The Landlord shall not be responsible to any Tenant or other person for any loss of property from said leased premises, or damage done to furniture or effects, however occurring, whether said loss or damage occur or be done through or by any employees, or by any other person whatsoever.

(m) The Landlord shall have the right to enter any of the leased rooms, at reasonable hours in the day, to exhibit the same to applicants to hire, and to put up upon them the usual notice "To Let," which said notice shall not be removed by any Tenant during the six months next preceding the time of expiration of the lease of the premises.

(n) Nothing shall be thrown by the Tenants, their clerks or servants, out of the windows or doors, or down the passages of the buildings, and Tenants shall not make or permit any improper noises in the building, or interfere in any way with other Tenants, or those having business with them. Nor shall any animals or birds be brought or kept in or about the building.

(o) The lessee shall not use the premises, or any part thereof, nor permit the same to be used for the business of stenography, typewriting, or other copying or similar occupation, nor permit any employee to carry on such business in or from the premises.

(p) The use of the elevator for moving purposes is subject to the consent of the Landlord and first to be obtained therefor.

(q) No illuminating oil or fluid shall be used or kept on the premises, and no stove or other heating apparatus employed in the rooms; nor shall any shades be used other than those supplied by the lessor, or awning permitted, unless first approved by the lessor.

(r) The Landlord reserves the right to make such further rules and regulations as, in the judgment of the landlord, may from time to time be needful for the safety and protection of the premises and its care and cleanliness, and for the preservation of good order therein, which rules and regulations when so made shall have the same force and effect as if originally made a part of this lease.

Seventh: The Tenant agrees that the Landlord and representatives shall have the right, during the term, to enter into and upon said premises, or any part thereof, or any part of said building, at all reasonable hours, for the purpose of inspecting the same, to see that the covenants on the part of the Tenant are being kept and performed; and of examining the same, or making such repairs, alterations, additions, or improvements therein as may be necessary for the safety, preservation, or improvement thereof, or which the Landlord may for any reason deem desirable. But the Tenant shall not be entitled to any damages or rebate on account of the making of any repairs, alterations, improvements or enlargements of said building, nor shall the Tenant be relieved from liability under this lease in consequence thereof.

Eighth: The Tenant having deposited with the Landlord the sum of ———— dollars, as security for the payment of the rent and performance of the covenants herein contained on the part of the Tenant, and as an inducement to the Landlord to enter this lease upon the terms and covenants herein contained, it is expressly understood and agreed that for special and peculiar reasons applicable to this lease, the Landlord shall be entitled to hold and retain the said deposit in the event of any breach on the part of the Tenant in respect to any of the covenants herein contained, without regard to the amount of damage suffered by the Landlord in consequence of such breach; but that if the Tenant shall carry out and perform all the covenants and agreements required to be carried out and performed by the Tenant, then at the expiration of the time herein limited for the term of this lease the said deposit shall be returned to the said Tenant.

Ninth: It is further agreed that, in case the said demised premises shall be deserted or vacated, or in the event of the insolvency of the Tenant, either before or after the commencement of the term, or if default shall be made in the payment of rent, or any part thereof, at the time specified herein, or if default shall be made in the performance of any of the covenants and agreements, conditions, rules, and regulations herein contained or hereafter established, as herein provided, on the part of the Tenant, this lease shall (if the Landlord so elect) become null and void thereupon, and the Landlord shall have the right to re-enter or repossess the said premises, either by force, summary proceedings, surrender, or otherwise, and dispossess and remove therefrom the Tenant, or other occupants thereof, and their effects, without being liable to any prosecution therefor, and to hold the same as if this lease had not been made; and, in such case, the Landlord may, at his option, relet the premises, or any part thereof, as the agent of the Tenant; and the Tenant agrees to pay the Landlord the difference, as ascertained, from time to time, between the rents and sums hereby reserved and agreed to be paid by the Tenant and those otherwise received, on account of rents of the demised premises, during the residue of the term remaining at the time of re-entry or repossession. The Tenant hereby expressly waives the service of notice of intention to re-enter, or of instituting legal proceedings to that end. The Tenant waives and will waive all right to trial by jury in any summary proceeding hereafter instituted by the Landlord against the Tenant in respect to the demised premises. The Tenant waives all rights to redeem under §1437 of the Civil Practice Act.

Tenth: In addition to any other legal remedies, for violation, or attempted or threatened violation, by or on the part of the Tenant or any one holding or claiming under him, of any of the covenants herein contained, the same shall, in addition to all other legal remedies, be restrainable by injunction.

Eleventh: The said Landlord covenants that the said Tenant, on paying the said yearly rent, and performing the covenants aforesaid, shall and may peaceably and quietly have, hold, and enjoy the said demised premises for the term aforesaid.

Twelfth: The consent of the Landlord, in any instance, to any variation of the terms of this lease, or the receipt of rent with knowledge of any breach, shall not be deemed to be a waiver as to any breach of any covenant or condition herein contained, nor shall any waiver be claimed as to any provision of this lease unless the same be in writing, signed by the Landlord or his authorized agent. This instrument may not be changed orally.

Thirteenth: This lease shall be subordinate to any mortgage or mortgages which shall, at any time, or from time to time, be placed upon said premises, or any part thereof.

Fourteenth: The covenants herein contained shall bind and inure to the benefit of the parties hereto, and their respective successors, heirs, executors, and administrators.

In witness whereof, the parties have interchangeably set their hands and seals or caused these presents to be signed by their proper corporate officers and caused their proper corporate seals to be hereto affixed the day and year first above written.
Signed, sealed, and delivered in
   the presence of
    (Acknowledgments)

Lease of an Unfurnished House[1]

This indenture, made the ———— day of ———— in the year one thousand nine hundred and ———— between ———— hereinafter known as Landlord and ———— residing at ———— hereinafter known as Tenant, *Witnesseth,* that the said Landlord has letten, and by these presents does grant, demise and to farm let, unto the said Tenant and the said Tenant has agreed to take and hereby does take from the said Landlord ———— with the appurtenances for the term of ———— to commence at noon on the ———— day of ————, 19— and to end at noon on the ———— day of ————, 19—

And the said Tenant hereby covenants and agrees that he will pay unto the said Landlord, the ———— rent of ———— dollars payable as follows, viz: ———— dollars on signing of lease, receipt of which is hereby acknowledged.

And that at the expiration of the said term the said Tenant will quit and surrender the premises hereby demised in as good state and condition as they were in at the commencement of the term, reasonable use and wear thereof and damages by the elements excepted.

---

[1]This is only a suggested form. The reader is advised to obtain blank forms, valid in his state, from a lawyer or legal stationer for use in specific transactions.

And the Landlord does covenant that the said Tenant on paying the said rent, and performing the covenants herein contained shall and may peaceably and quietly have, hold, and enjoy the said demised premises for the term aforesaid.

And the said Tenant covenants that if the said premises, or any part thereof, shall become vacant during the said term, the said Landlord or agents may re-enter the same, either by force or otherwise, without being liable for any prosecution therefor; and relet said premises as the agent of the said Tenant, and receive the rent thereof, applying the same first to the payment of such expenses as the Landlord will be put to in re-entering, and then to the payment of the rent due by these presents; the balance (if any) to be paid over to said Tenant, who shall remain liable for any deficiency.

And the said Tenant hereby further covenants that if any default be made in the payment of said rent, or any part thereof, at the time above specified, or if any default be made in the performance of any other covenants or agreements herein contained, the said hiring, and the relation of Landlord and Tenant, at the option of said Landlord shall wholly cease and determine; and the said Landlord shall and may re-enter said premises, and remove all persons therefrom; and the said Tenant hereby expressly waives the service of any notice in writing of intention to re-enter, as provided for in the third section of an act entitled "An Act to Abolish Distress for Rent, and for Other Purposes," passed May 31, 1846.

It is understood and agreed, between the parties hereto:

First: That the Tenant will pay all charges for water, electricity, telephone, and gas used during the term of this lease or any renewal thereof.

Second: That during the last three months of this lease or any renewal thereof, the Landlord or his agent, shall have the privilege of displaying the usual "For Sale" and "To Let" signs on the premises and to show the property to prospective purchasers or tenants.

Third: That in case the Tenant has the privilege of renewing this lease, the Tenant shall give notice in writing to the broker or Landlord of his intention at least three months prior to the expiration hereof.

Fourth: That the Tenant shall use the premises hereby leased exclusively for a private residence, and that the Tenant will not, without the consent of the Landlord, assign this lease, nor let or underlet the whole or any part of the said premises, nor make any alterations therein or thereupon under the penalty of forfeiture and damage.

Fifth: That if the said premises or any part thereof shall, during said term or previous thereto, be slightly damaged by fire, the premises shall be promptly repaired by the Landlord and an abatement will be made for the rent corresponding with the time during which and the extent to which said premises may have been untenantable; but if the building or buildings should be so damaged that the Landlord shall decide to rebuild, the term of this lease shall cease and the aggregate rent be paid up to the time of the fire.

Sixth: The Tenant agrees that the Landlord or broker shall have the right to enter into and upon said premises, or any part thereof, at all reasonable hours for the purpose of examining the same, or making such repairs or alterations as may be necessary for the safety and preservation thereof.

Seventh: That the Tenant shall keep the fixtures in said house or on said pemises in good order and repair; shall keep the faucets in repair; the furnace, smoke pipe, and flues clean and the electric bells in order, and shall at the Tenant's expense make all required repairs to the plumbing work, range, heating apparatus, and electric light or gas fixtures whenever damage shall have resulted from misuse, waste, or neglect, it being understood that the Landlord is to have same in good order when giving possession.

Eighth: That the Tenant is to comply with all the sanitary laws, ordinances and rules and all orders of the Board of Health or other authorities affecting the cleanliness, occupancy, and preservation thereof for the demised premises and the sidewalks connected to the said premises, during said term of this lease.

Ninth: That the Landlord agrees that the Tenant shall have the free use of all fruit, vegetables, and other products of the premises during the term of this lease, and the Tenant agrees that the Tenant will permit no waste or injury to the trees, shrubbery, or vines or remove same from the premises and that the grounds shall be kept at all times in neat order and condition.

Tenth: That the Landlord agrees that the oil burner shall be clean and in good working condition on giving possession to the Tenant and said Tenant agrees to pay for the annual servicing of the oil burner by a servicing company acceptable to the Landlord.

Eleventh: The Tenant agrees that this lease shall be subject and subordinate to any mortgage or mortgages now on said premises or which any owner of said premises may hereafter at any time elect to place on said premises, and to all advances already made or which may be hereafter made on account of said mortgages, to the full extent of the principal sums secured thereby and interest thereon; and the Tenant agrees upon request to hereafter execute any paper or papers which the counsel for the said Landlord may deem necessary to accomplish that end; and that in default of the Tenant so doing the Landlord is hereby empowered to execute such paper or papers in the name of the Tenant and as the act and deed of the Tenant; and this authority is hereby declared to be coupled with an interest and not revocable.

Twelfth: That the Landlord agrees to deliver the premises to the Tenant in a broom-clean condition, with all rubbish removed, and the Tenant agrees to leave the premises in the same condition upon the termination of this lease.

The covenants and conditions herein contained shall apply to and bind the heirs, executors, and legal representatives of the parties hereto. This instrument may not be changed orally.

In witness whereof, the parties to these presents have hereunto set their hands and seals, the day and year first above written.

In the presence of

....

....

....

Lease of an Apartment[1]

This indenture, made the ———— day of ———— in the year one thousand nine hundred and ———— between ———— as Landlord, and ———— as Tenant.

Witnesseth, that the said Landlord has let unto the said Tenant, and the said Tenant has hired from the said Landlord, apartment No. ———— on the ———— floor of the premises known as No. ———— City of ———— County of ————, for the term of ————, commencing on the ———— day of ————, nineteen hundred and ————, and ending on the ———— day of ————, nineteen hundred and ————, at noon, to be used and occupied as a strictly private dwelling apartment for the said Tenant and members of his family only and for no other purpose, at the yearly rental or sum of ———— dollars, payable in equal monthly payments of ———— dollars, in advance on the first day of each and every month during the said term.

First: This lease is granted upon the express condition, however, that in case said Landlord, his agents or assigns, shall deem objectionable or improper any conduct on the part of said Tenant or occupant of said apartment, said Landlord, his agents or assigns may give the Tenant five (5) days notice of said Landlord's intention to terminate this lease and tender return of the rent paid on account of the unexpired term; and upon the expiration of said notice this lease shall terminate as effectually as if such date of expiration were the date fixed herein for its termination; and thereupon said Landlord, his agents or assigns shall have full license and authority to re-enter and have full possession of said premises, either with or without legal process, by means of summary proceedings or any other method prescribed by law; and in consideration of the above letting said Tenant consents that said Landlord, his agents and assigns, shall not be liable to prosecution for damages for so resuming possession of said premises.

Second: The said premises are also leased upon the further covenants and conditions between the parties hereto.

Third: Said Tenant shall take good care of the premises and fixtures, make good any

---

[1]This is only a suggested form. The reader is advised to obtain a blank form, valid in his state, from a lawyer or a legal stationer for use in specific transactions.

injury or breakage done by the Tenant, servants, or visitors of the Tenant, and any damage caused by the overflow or escape of water, steam, or gas resulting from the negligence of the Tenant, or visitors or servants of the Tenant. The Tenant shall quit and surrender said premises at the end of said term in as good condition as the reasonable use thereof will permit; and shall not make any alterations, additions, or improvements in said premises without the written consent of the said Landlord; and all alterations, additions, or improvements which may be made by either of the parties hereto upon the premises, except movable furniture put in at the expense of the Tenant, shall be the property of the Landlord, and shall remain upon and be surrendered with the premises, as a part thereof, at the termination of this lease, without disturbance, molestation, or injury; but injury caused by moving said movable furniture in and out shall be repaired by the Tenant. That any and all shelves, locks, plumbing fixtures, or any other improvements that the Tenant may place or cause to be placed in the said apartment shall immediately become a part of the house and the property of the Landlord.

Fourth: That the Tenant shall not expose any sign, advertisement, illumination, or projection in or out of the windows or exteriors, or from the said building, or upon or in any place, except such as shall be approved and permitted in writing by the Landlord or his duly authorized agent. Tenant shall only use such shades in the front windows as may be approved by the Landlord; and the Tenant shall not keep or maintain any dogs in or about said premises nor permit any other party to keep or maintain therein any dog or domestic animals without the written consent of the Landlord.

Fifth: The Tenant hereby agrees not to assign this agreement, or underlet the premises or any part thereof, or make any alterations in the apartment or premises without the Landlord's or agent's consent in writing, and will not use the said premises, or any part thereof, or permit the same to be used for any other purpose than that of private dwelling apartment for the Tenant and the Tenant's immediate family, or for any purposes deemed extra hazardous on account of fire, under penalty of damages and forfeiture of this lease.

Sixth: That the Tenant shall, in case of fire, give immediate notice thereof to the Landlord, who shall thereupon cause the damage to be repaired as soon as reasonably convenient, and no claim for compensation shall be made by reason of inconvenience, annoyance from loss arising from necessity of repairing any portion of the building; but if the premises be so damaged that the Landlord shall decide to rebuild, the accrued rent shall be paid by the Tenant up to the time of the fire, and the term shall then cease and the Tenant shall immediately surrender said premises and all interest therein to the Landlord.

Seventh: The Tenant agrees to conform to the rules and regulations governing said house, which are printed on this lease and which are made part of this lease, and to any reasonable alterations thereto or new rule or regulation that may be deemed necessary for the protection of the building and the general comfort and welfare of the occupants of the same; and also shall comply with all rules, orders, ordinances, and regulations of the city government, and of any and all its departments and Bureaus applicable to the said premises, and with the requirements of the Board of Fire Underwriters and the Fire Insurance Exchange, which may in anywise relate to or affect the premises hereby leased; and upon default in any of the covenants contained in this paragraph this lease may at the option of the Landlord terminate and the Tenant after five days' written notice shall vacate the premises; and in default thereof the Landlord shall have the right to proceed against the Tenant as a holdover after expiration of the term of the Tenant.

Eighth: That the Landlord is exempt from any and all liability for any damage or injury to person or property caused by or resulting from steam, electricity, gas, water, rain, ice, or snow, or any leak or flow from or into any part of said building, or from any damage or injury resulting or arising from any other cause or happening whatsoever, unless said damage or injury be caused by or be due to the negligence of the Landlord. Said Tenant shall give to said Landlord or agents, prompt written notice of any accident to or defects in the water pipes, gas pipes, or warming apparatus, to be remedied by the Landlord with due diligence.

Ninth: That in case of default in any of the covenants or if the premises become vacant, the Landlord may re-enter by means of summary proceedings or any other method prescribed by law, with or without notice of an intention so to do, and resume possession and relet the premises in his own name, without terminating this lease or in any manner affecting the obligation of the Tenant to pay the rent herein covenanted to be paid; in which event, however, there shall be credited to the account of the Tenant the amount received from reletting after deducting the expenses of such summary or other proceedings as may be necessary in order to regain possession under this provision, as well as the cost of reletting the premises, and repairing and redecorating if any; and the execution of a new lease for the same premises shall not terminate the Tenant's liability or obligations hereunder, which shall in any event remain in full force and effect for the full term of this lease; and a Tenant, who has once vacated may not re-enter without the consent of the Landlord or his agents, and no act or thing done by the Landlord or his agents during the term hereby granted, shall be deemed an acceptance or a surrender of said premises, and no agreement to accept a surrender of said premises shall be valid, unless the same be made in writing and personally subscribed by the Landlord. And the Landlord further reserves the right to rent the premises for a longer period of time than fixed in the original lease without releasing the original Tenant from any liability. The Tenant hereby expressly waives any and all right of redemption in the event the Tenant shall be dispossessed by judgment or warrant, of any court or judge, and the Tenant waives and will waive all right to trial by jury in any summary proceeding hereafter instituted by the Landlord against the Tenant in respect of the demised premises or in any action brought to recover rent or damages hereunder.

Tenth: That the Tenant shall exhibit the premises to prospective tenants daily at reasonable hours during four months prior to the expiration of the lease, and in the event of the Tenant's absence hereby agrees to arrange for such exhibiting of the premises. The Tenant agrees not to interfere with the Landlord's renting to a new Tenant. That the Landlord or his agent shall also be permitted at any time during the term to visit and examine the premises at any reasonable hour of the day, and workmen may enter at any time, when authorized by the Landlord or his agents to make or facilitate repairs in any part of the building; and if the Tenant shall not be personally present to open and permit an entry into said premises, at any time, when for any reason an entry therein shall be in the judgment of the Landlord or his agents necessary or permissible hereunder, for the protection of the building or property therein, or to make such repairs, or to show such apartment to prospective tenants, the Landlord or his agents may forcibly enter the same without rendering himself or them liable to any claim or cause for action for damages by reason thereof without in any manner affecting the obligations and covenants of this lease; it is, however, expressly understood that the right and privilege hereby reserved does not impose, nor does the Landlord assume by reason thereof, any responsibility or liability whatsoever for the care and supervision of said premises, or any of the pipes, fixtures, appliances, or appurtenances therein contained or therewith in any manner connected.

Eleventh: No claim shall be made by, or compensation paid to, the Tenant, family, or servants by reason of inconvenience, annoyance, loss, or damage arising from the necessity of repairing any portion whatsoever of the building, its machinery or appliances, however the necessity may occur.

Twelfth: The Landlord is in no event, liable for any loss of, or damage to, the property of the Tenant, family, servants, or guests, howsoever such damage or loss may arise, and whether such property be contained in the demised premises, in the storage room, or in any other portion of said building or any place appurtenant thereto.

Thirteenth: The Tenant hereby agrees to pay to the Landlord as often as is demanded all charges for telephone service and telephone tolls used by the Tenant; and all such charges shall be added to and considered a part of the rent. If such charges are not immediately paid by the Tenant when the same shall fall due as herein set forth, the Landlord may, at his option, without any notice to said Tenant discontinue such telephone service, and such discontinuance by said Landlord shall in no way affect the obligation of the Tenant under this lease, and the Landlord shall be under no obligation to install telephone service.

Fourteenth: The Landlord will furnish to the Tenant without additional charge, steam heat during the winter months, and hot and cold water; and it is further mutually understood and agreed upon by and between the parties hereto, that in case it shall become necessary or proper at any time, from accident, or for improving the condition or operation of the heating apparatus, plumbing, boilers, machinery, electric plant, or anything appertaining thereto, to omit the operating of said light or heating apparatus or other service, until all necessary repairs or improvements shall have been made and completed, the Landlord shall be at liberty to do the same without in any manner or respect affecting or modifying the obligations or covenants of the said Tenant herein contained, or rendering the Landlord liable for any damage or offset by reason thereof.

Fifteenth: The Tenant agrees that this lease shall be subject and subordinate to any renewal of any mortgage or mortgages now on said premises or any new mortgage or mortgages which any owner of said premises may hereafter at any time elect to place on said premises; and the Tenant agrees, upon request, to hereafter execute any paper or papers which the Landlord may deem necessary to accomplish that end, and in default of the Tenant so doing, that said Landlord be and is hereby empowered to execute such paper or papers in the name of the Tenant, and as the act and deed of said Tenant, and this authority is hereby declared to be coupled with an interest and not revocable.

Sixteenth: That this agreement shall be binding on the heirs, executors, administrators, and assigns of both parties.

Seventeenth: The Landlord acknowledges the receipt of the sum of ———— dollars from the Tenant to be retained by the Landlord as security for the performance by the Tenant of each term, covenant, and condition of this lease on the part of the Tenant to be performed, which said sum of money the Landlord agrees to return to the Tenant at the termination of this lease provided the Tenant has fully complied with all the terms, covenants, and conditions herein contained.

Eighteenth: The Tenant hires said premises after examination, and without any representation on the part of the Landlord, and no representative or agent of said Landlord is authorized to make any representations in reference thereto or to vary or modify this agreement in any way. This instrument contains all the agreements and conditions made between the parties hereto. Any additions thereto, or alterations or changes in this contract, or other agreements hereafter made or conditions created, to be binding, must be in writing signed by both parties; and it is agreed that this provision cannot be waived except by writing, duly signed by the parties hereto.

Nineteenth: It is understood and agreed that the space on the roof is provided by the Landlord of this building to accommodate the Tenants in the airing and drying of clothing, with the express understanding that the space is furnished gratuitously by the Landlord, and the Tenants using the same for any purpose do so at their risk, and with the express stipulation and agreement that the Landlord shall not be liable for any loss of property thereon, nor for any damage or injury whatever.

Twentieth: The obligation of the Tenant to pay the full rent herein reserved shall not be affected by, and the Tenant agrees and hereby does waive the legal effect of any future act or omission on the part of the Landlord with respect to, the tenantability of the premises hereby let, or the building of which they are a part, unless the Tenant shall give to the Landlord or Landlord's agents at his principal place of business immediate written notice of said act or omission and a reasonable time to perform his legal duty with respect to the condition complained of.

Twenty-first: The failure of the Landlord to insist upon strict performance of any of the covenants or conditions of this lease, or to exercise any option herein conferred in any one or more instances, shall not be construed as a waiver or relinquishment for the future of any such covenants, conditions, or options; the same shall be and remain in full force and effect.

Twenty-second: That in the event of a bona fide sale, subject to this lease, the Landlord, or Landlord's assigns, shall have the right to transfer the aforementioned security to the vendee for the benefit of the Tenant, and the Landlord, or Landlord's assigns, shall be considered released by the Tenant from all liability for the return of such security.

Twenty-third: It is further mutually understood and agreed upon by and between the parties hereto, that if the operation of the elevators shall cease by reason of accident, strikes, repairs, alterations, or improvements to be made or done to any part of same or appurtenances thereto, or any cause beyond the control of the Landlord, the obligation of the Tenant under the terms of this lease shall not be affected thereby, nor shall any claim accrue to the Tenant by reason thereof.

Twenty-fourth: That this letting and hiring shall be extended and renewed by and against the parties hereto for the further term of ———— years from the expiration of the term granted hereby, at the same rental without any deduction or concession, and upon all the above terms, conditions, and covenants, unless either party on or before the first day of ———— next preceding the termination of any term granted hereby shall give notice to the other of an intention to surrender or have possession of the premises, as the case may be. Notice by the Landlord to the Tenant must be given by sending the same by United States Registered Mail. Notice by the Tenant to the Landlord must be given by sending the same by United States Registered Mail. This clause shall be and continue operative likewise with respect to any renewals or extensions hereof.

Twenty-fifth: This lease and the obligations of the Tenant to pay rent hereunder and perform all of the other covenants and agreements hereunder on part of the Tenant to be performed shall in nowise be affected, impaired, or excused because the Landlord is unable to supply or is delayed in supplying any service expressly or impliedly to be supplied or is unable to make, or is delayed in making any repairs, additions, alterations, or decorations or is unable to supply or is delayed in supplying any equipment or fixtures if the Landlord is prevented or delayed from so doing by reason of governmental preemption in connection with a national emergency declared by the President of the United States, or in connection with any rule, order, or regulation of any department or subdivision thereof of any governmental agency, or by reason of the conditions of supply and demand which have been or are affected by war.

In witness whereof, the parties have interchangeably set their hands and seals or caused these presents to be signed by their proper corporate officers and caused their proper corporate seal to be hereto affixed the day and year first above written.

Signed, sealed, and delivered
in the presence of

RULES AND REGULATIONS

1. The front stoop, entries, passages, halls, corridors, or stairways shall not be obstructed by any of the tenants, nor be used by them for any purposes except ingress or egress to their respective apartments, and the sidewalks shall not be in any manner obstructed.

2. Tenants shall not incumber the fire escapes or dumb-waiters or place flowerpots or any other articles on the window sills or doorcaps of the building, nor shall they waste nor unreasonably use water supply.

3. All garbage and refuse shall be sent down to the basement from apartments and kitchens at the time called for by the janitor.

4. The water closet and other water apparatus shall not be used for any other purposes than those for which they are constructed, and no sweepings, rubbish, rags, ashes, or other substances shall be thrown therein. Any damage resulting to them from misuse shall be borne by the tenant causing the same.

5. No tenant shall do anything, nor permit anything to be done in the premises, nor bring or keep anything therein, which will in any way increase the rate of fire insurance on the building or on the property kept therein, or conflict with the laws relating to fire.

6. Tenants, or their servants shall not make or permit any unseemly or disturbing noises, nor interfere in any way with other tenants, or those having business with them; nor throw anything out of the windows or doors, or down the dumb-waiter, passages, or skylights of the building; nor mark or defile the water closets, or the walls, windows, and doors of the building.

7. It is understood and agreed that the owner shall be in nowise responsible to any tenant for any loss of property, however occurring, or for any damage done to furniture or other effects by the janitor or any of his employees.

8. No animal shall be kept in or about the premises without the written consent of the landlord or agent.

9. The window shades and awnings for the building are to be kept in good order by the tenants.

10. Servants, except nurses accompanying children, shall have ingress and egress through the basement only, and are not to make entrance or exit by main entrance.

11. Tenant shall give immediate notice to the superintendent of any accident or injury to the water pipes, gas pipes, gas fixtures, or dumb-waiters in the building.

12. Bicycles and baby carriages shall not be taken in or out of the building through main entrance.

13. Hall boys shall not be sent on private messages during hours they are on duty.

14. Hours for closing entrances at night will be fixed and noticed in agent's office, and are to be complied with.

15. No peddlers shall be allowed on the premises.

16. Each tenant must, upon the termination of the within lease, return all keys of the apartments and appurtenances or pay for same.

17. No tenant shall make or permit any disturbing noises in the building by himself, his family, friends, or servants; nor do or permit anything by such person that will interfere with the rights, comforts, or conveniences of other tenants. No tenants shall play upon, or suffer to be played upon, any musical instrument, or operate a radio in the demised premises between the hours of ten o'clock P.M. and the following eight o'clock A.M. if the same shall disturb or annoy other occupants of the building. No tenant shall operate a phonograph or a radio loud-speaker between the hours of ten o'clock P.M. and the following nine o'clock A.M.

LIENS

Liens, or charges upon real or personal property, are of different types. A *common law lien* is the right that a party has to retain possession of personal property of another until a debt secured by such property is paid. A *statutory lien* is created by statute. *Mechanic's liens, garagekeeper's liens, factor's liens, hospital liens,* etc. are statutory. An equitable lien is a right recognized in equity, although not at law, to have property applied in payment of a particular debt. For example, a purchaser of real property who has paid either the whole or part of the purchase price and sues to rescind the contract because of fraud may have a lien declared upon the property in the action brought to recover the money paid, in order that if the judgment is not paid he can enforce the equitable lien against the property.

Liens are also classified as *general* and *special.* A general lien is the right to retain the property of another to secure a balance due from the owner. A special lien is a charge on a particular piece of property, which is held for the payment of a particular debt, in priority to the general debts of the owner.

Lienholders may enforce their liens by sale of the property only after fully complying with the applicable statutes; until then they only have the right to possession.

A lien may be lost by *operation of law,* such as by destruction of the property on which it exists, or if the lien is created by law, by the *death or bankruptcy* of the owner of the property. In some states the lien is discharged if a legal proceeding to enforce it is not instituted within the statutory time. A lien is discharged by payment of the secured debt.

LICENSES

A license is a permission granted by a governmental agency to carry on a business or occupation which, without such license, would be illegal. It is not a contract between the authority (be it Federal, state, or municipal) and the person to whom it is granted; it creates no vested right. Generally, a license fee must be paid to the granting authority. Such licenses are granted for two primary reasons: (1) to protect the public interest through governmental supervision and regulation; (2) to collect taxes.

Some typical businesses and practitioners that must be licensed are: automobile driving schools; banks; businesses of salvage; businesses charging storage fees; liquor businesses; collection agencies; drug stores; bailbonding companies; insurance companies; theater ticket agencies; engineers; certified accountants; lawyers; dentists; doctors, etc.

A *real estate license* is an authorization by the owner permitting another to do something to the property or to use land for a particular purpose without, however, giving such person an interest in the property. It is merely a personal privilege, and is always revocable. A typical license is the privilege granted by a landlord to a tenant to install a television aerial on the roof of the building or to erect a sign. If such privilege is granted for a consideration it is not a license. These informal licenses may be written or oral. Such licenses are not assignable.

A licensing agreement with respect to copyrights and patents is a right to make, use, or sell the patented or copyrighted article.

ASSIGNMENT

An assignment is a transfer of property or of any interest from one party to another. Assignments of copyrights (see page 152) or patents (see page 155) are governed by Acts of Congress.

Assignment of Patent[1]

Whereas, JOHN DOE, of (city), County of ———— and State of, ———— did obtain Letters Patent of the United States, for an improvement in ———— which Letters Patent are numbered ———— and bear date the ———— day of ———— 19—; and *whereas* JOHN DOE is ———— now the sole owner of said patent and of all rights under the same; and *whereas* RICHARD ROE, of (city) ————, County of ———— and State of ————, is desirous of acquiring

    an
       interest in the same;
the entire

Now, therefore, to all whom it may concern, be it known that, for and in consideration of the sum of ———— dollars to me the said JOHN DOE in hand paid, the receipt whereof is hereby acknowledged. I, the said JOHN DOE, have sold, assigned, transferred and by these presents do sell, assign and transfer unto the said RICHARD ROE, his executors, administrators and assigns the ———— whole right, title, and interest in and to the said invention, described as an improvement in ———— and in and to the Letters Patent therefor aforesaid; the same ———— to be held and enjoyed by the said RICHARD ROE for his own use and behoof and for the use and behoof of his legal representatives, to the full end of the term for which the said Letters Patent are or may be granted, as fully and entirely as the same would have been held and enjoyed by me had this assignment and sale not been made.

In testimony whereof, I have hereunto set my hand and affixed my seal at (City) in the County of ———— and State of ———— this ———— day of ———— 19—.
In presence of: *John Doe* (seal)

ATTACHMENTS

Writ of Attachment

Attachment is a proceeding for the seizure of property before judgment. It is not a common law right, but is a *statutory* remedy and can be used only as part of a pending action. It does not initiate a law suit. The purpose of this remedy is to enable the creditor to obtain possession of and hold the debtor's property until the recovery of judgment, and thereby prevent him from disposing of it to frustrate the purpose of the action.

---

[1]This is only a suggested form. The reader is advised to secure a form from a legal stationer for use in specific transactions.

Since it is a statutory remedy, it is within the legislative power to determine the actions in which, and the conditions under which, it may be resorted to. It is generally limited to actions brought to recover sums of money arising out of contract. It is ordinarily given to creditors and is available against all debtors, whether corporate or individual.

Statutes generally permit an attachment to issue on the property of a debtor on the ground that he has absconded, or absents himself, or keeps himself concealed for the purpose of defrauding his creditors or of avoiding service of process.

The procedure to obtain a writ of attachment is regulated by statute; and all statutory requirements must be strictly followed. Generally the statutes require the creditor-plaintiff to submit an affidavit setting forth the facts to justify the issuance of the writ; and he must furnish a bond to indemnify the debtor for any loss or injury the latter may suffer as a result of the attachment if it proves wrongful.

Generally, all property of the debtor except such property as is exempted by statute is subject to attachment for his debts. Bank deposits, shares of stock, money, fixtures, goods, merchandise, and other personal property may be attached, as well as real property.

Property Exemptions

Most states have specifically exempted certain property from attachment by creditors. The underlying reason for such exemptions is to protect debtors from destitution, which would make them and their families public charges. These exemption statutes are founded on public policy.

In most states certain amounts of wearing apparel, food, household goods and furniture, a mechanic's tools, burial grounds, and a limited amount of life insurance and of wages are exempt.

Garnishment

Garnishment is a statutory proceeding whereby the creditor seeks to obtain payment of his claim from money or property of the debtor which is in the possession of a third person.

A valid and final judgment against the debtor is the basis for the remedy.

In some states the proceeding may not be instituted until an execution on the judgment against the debtor's nonexempt property has been returned unsatisfied.

Wages and salary due the judgment debtor over a certain amount may be garnished, as well as any other property in the hands of third persons which belongs to the judgment debtor.

Body Attachment

A body attachment is an execution against the person of the judgment debtor. This remedy permits the sheriff to arrest the debtor and imprison him until he pays the judgment or it is discharged by law. The proceeding is strictly regulated by statute. It can only issue in certain types of actions, such as those involving embezzlement, misappropriation, fraud, and the like. It is a very drastic remedy and is permissible only as a last resort, when all other remedies have failed to obtain payment.

In some states various classes of persons such as idiots, lunatics, infants, members of the legislature while performing their legislative duties, persons in military service, and females are exempt from arrest on execution.

BAIL

An arrested person prior to trial and a convicted person prior to sentence may, in the court's discretion, obtain his liberty from jail until his trial or until sentence is imposed, by posting bail in an amount fixed by the court.

The object of requiring bail is to compel the defendant to appear in court for trial or sentence. If cash is not available a bail bond may be furnished. If he fails to appear at the required time the bail is forfeited. The United States Constitution provides that excessive bail shall not be demanded.

BAILMENT

A bailment is the delivery of personal property for a special purpose, the property to be returned to the owner after the purpose has been fulfilled. The person who delivers the property is called a *bailor* and the person to whom it is delivered is called the *bailee*.

There are several kinds of bailment: (1) bailments for the benefit of both parties, as when jewelry is left with another to be exhibited and sold for a commission; (2) bailments for the sole benefit of the bailor, as when goods are temporarily left by the purchaser with the seller and no storage fee is to be paid; (3) bailments for the sole benefit of the bailee, as when a neighbor borrows a lawn mower for a short period of time and pays nothing for the privilege of using it.

The essence of a bailment is the delivery and acceptance of the subject matter of the bailment. To be valid it must be for a legal purpose. The title to the property always remains with the bailor; the bailee merely has a temporary possessory right.

The *rights, duties,* and *liabilities* of the parties are determined from the express or implied terms of the bailment contract.

When a bailment is for mutual benefit, the bailee, in the absence of special contract, must exercise ordinary care and is responsible for ordinary negligence. Ordinary care is that care and attention which, under the circumstances, a man of ordinary prudence would use if he were dealing with his own property; the want of such care is ordinary negligence. Such a bailee is not an insurer. He is not responsible for losses necessarily incident to the property's use, nor for losses caused by infirmities in the thing itself nor by natural causes, such as fire, storm, or other acts of God.

When a bailment is for the sole benefit of the bailor, the bailee is liable only for gross negligence or bad faith, which is the failure to exercise slight care and caution.

All bailees are responsible for affirmative acts of negligence and fraud. The subject matter of the bailment must be returned to the bailor, and if the bailee refuses to do so after demand, or otherwise misappropriates or converts the property, he is liable to the bailor.

The bailee is not entitled to compensation if the bailment is for the sole benefit of either the bailor or the bailee; he is entitled to reasonable payment in the absence of express or implied agreement in all other cases. All bailees are entitled to repayment of any disbursements necessarily incurred by them in preserving or protecting the subject matter of the bailment.

Bailees who by their skill or labor confer some benefit on the bailed property have a lien thereon for the reasonable value of their services.

The duration of the bailment depends upon the intention of the parties; or, if the bailment is for a limited time, the lapse of such time terminates the bailment.

The liability of certain bailees is regulated and limited by statute. An example is that of hotel keepers. Generally, they are absolutely responsible for property delivered to their care; but by providing a safe and posting a certain form of notice they may limit their liability to a certain amount of money for a loss if it is not due to their own affirmative negligence.

NEGLIGENCE

Negligence is the failure to exercise the degree of care required by the circumstances of a particular situation. It is measured by the conduct of a reasonable and prudent person. *Actionable negligence, i.e.,* negligence for which legal redress can be obtained, arises only from a violation of duty. It is doing something which duty to another requires not to be done, or failing to do something which duty requires to be done.

There are three *degrees* of negligence: ordinary, slight, and gross. They have been previously defined in the subject matter of bailments.

DEMURRAGE

It is usual to insert a clause in an agreement between the owner of a vessel and a charterer or shipper of merchandise to the effect that a specified number of days shall be allowed for loading or unloading cargo.

Demurrage is the money paid by the owner of a vessel to the charterer or shipper of merchandise by boat for an improper and unreasonable delay in unloading cargo after the expiration of such specified time.

GUARANTY AND SURETY

Guaranty and surety are closely related, guaranty being a form of surety. There are, however, one or two essential differences. A surety is part of a principal contract. It is a direct assumption of responsibility and the surety is liable from the moment the contract is made. If the principal fails the surety must pay, and is not entitled to demand or notice. A guaranty is a collateral contract, separate and distinct from the main contract. The guarantor agrees to pay if the principal cannot, and the creditor cannot approach the guarantor until he has made all reasonable effort to collect from the principal. The guarantor is entitled to demand and notice.

A surety or a guarantor is relieved of his obligations if he was persuaded to assume them through misrepresentation or through concealment of material facts. (For warranty see Contracts, page 11.)

INSURANCE

Insurance has been defined as "a provision, or contract, by which the risk of pecuniary loss arising from death or personal injury, or from destruction of, or damage to, property owing to perils of any kind to which an individual, the insured, may be exposed, is undertaken by a group of persons or a corporation, called the insurers. As consideration an appropriate premium is paid to the insurers, either in a single sum or by periodical payments."

The contract is called the policy.
The events insured against are called risks or perils
The thing insured is called the insurable interest.

Marine Insurance

The oldest known form of insurance is marine insurance, which, as its name implies, was originally insurance against perils at sea.

There are two forms of marine insurance: that by which the *owner's interests,* including the body of the ship, etc., are protected, and that by which the *cargo* is protected. Limits are imposed upon the kind of trading that can be done; when these limits are overstepped additional premiums are required.

The ordinary cargo insurance policy protects against perils of the sea, pirates, thieves, jettison, and barratry (breach of trust on the part of the master of the ship resulting in injury to the owner or the cargo of the ship). Further protection must be had through special clauses. In some policies the cargo is protected only after it is actually on the ship; in others it is protected from shipper's to consignee's warehouse. This is partly regulated by custom, the custom varying in different kinds of shipments, and partly by special arrangements of the one holding the insurance policy. Policies may be valued. The value includes freight and insurance charges plus a reasonable profit. For unvalued policies the value must be determined at the time of the loss. A number of policies contain an average clause by which the person taking out the insurance agrees to pay a certain percentage of loss, usually, in American policies, five per cent. Other policies are f.p.a. (free from particular average).

Inland marine risks are divided into three groups: (1) domestic shipments; (2) bridges, tunnels, and other instrumentalities of transportation and communication; and (3) personal property floater risks.

The Personal Property Floater is the latest policy issued under the marine insurance group and covers in one policy loss from fire, windstorm, tornado, smoke, smudge, falling aircraft, vehicular damage, burglary, robbery, larceny, and theft. It covers not only the domicile of the assured, but also his personal property and that of members of his family anywhere in the world.

75

Fire Insurance

An owner of property, real or personal, or anyone with an insurable interest in property may insure to the extent of his interest. Insurable interest requires that the insured stand in such relation to the property as to be pecuniarily interested in its preservation and directly injured by its destruction. Generally, the standard fire insurance policy in use in the several states insures against direct loss by fire and lightning. It does not cover the risk of fire caused by war, invasion, insurrection, rebellion, revolution, civil war, or usurped power.

By endorsement, known as "Extended Coverage Endorsement," the policy may be extended to include direct loss or damage from the perils of windstorm, hail, explosion, riot, riot attending a strike, civil commotion, aircraft, vehicles, and smoke—that is, smoke due to a sudden, unusual, and faulty operation of any heating unit when such unit is connected to a chimney by a smokepipe and is on the premises of the insured. Smoke from fireplaces or industrial apparatus is excluded.

Life Insurance

Life insurance is a means whereby a person may have a portion of his income continued to his dependents after his death, or to himself in his old age. Life insurance premiums are based upon three factors: (1) the expected mortality experience among the individuals insured; (2) the rate of interest which the life insurance company expects to earn on its invested funds; and (3) the costs of operating the insurance company. Premiums are payable in advance, and are paid on an annual, semi-annual, quarterly, or sometimes a monthly basis in ordinary insurance. Industrial insurance premiums are generally collected weekly, or sometimes monthly, at the home of the insured. Industrial insurance is insurance for amounts less than $500.

Three types of ordinary insurance are available: (1) Whole Life, with protection being provided throughout life. This may be accomplished by either a *straight life policy* for which premiums are paid throughout life, or by a *limited-payment policy* for which the premium payment period is limited to a certain number of years, such as 20 or 30 years; (2) Term Insurance, which provides *temporary protection* for a designated period; the term policy may be *convertible* without medical examination within a specified number of years to either whole life or endowment insurance, or it may be *renewable* without a medical examination at the end of the term, the premium for the renewed policy being higher than that for the original one, since the policyholder is older, hence his chance of death greater; (3) Endowment Insurance, which provides life insurance protection for a stated period in combination with an increasing savings element so that the face amount of the policy is paid to the policyholder at the end of the endowment period.

Life insurance contracts may be terminated: (1) by death, at which time the proceeds are paid to the person the insured designated to receive them (the beneficiary) ; (2) by maturity as an endowment, when the proceeds are paid to the insured person; (3) by lapse for nonpayment of premium; or (4) within the contestable period, by company proof that the insured committed fraud in procuring the contract. If the insured is unable to continue paying premiums, he may surrender his policy and receive a stipulated cash surrender value.

Instead of surrendering his policy for cash, the insured may apply his cash value to purchase a paid-up policy for a reduced amount of protection, or he may choose an extended term insurance policy which provides protection for the same amount as the original contract, but for a limited period. The policyholder who wishes to keep his insurance in force but who needs funds, may borrow from the accumulated cash value of his policy, the policy itself being the security for the loan.

Upon termination of a policy by death or maturity, the proceeds may be paid in a lump sum or under an optional mode of settlement. The settlement options generally available are those which pay the face value of the contract: (1) periodically for a designated number of years; (2) as a specific amount periodically until the proceeds are exhausted; (3) as a life annuity to the beneficiary. A fourth option specifies that the proceeds are to be held by the company for later disposition, the interest earnings being paid to the beneficiary or added to the fund. Where it is intended to provide for the beneficiary's continued support after the insured dies, it is generally wise to avoid payment of the proceeds in a lump sum, choosing instead an option which will assure the beneficiary an adequate, well administered, and certain income.

The primary purpose of life insurance is to provide a family with income after the breadwinner's death. Life insurance also provides an excellent medium for saving toward particular goals, such as the accumulation of funds for education of children, for retirement, etc., and is also much used to provide for payment of a debt in case of death. Life insurance is also quite commonly used to replace the loss to a business caused by the death of one of its key men; it may be used to provide surviving business associates with sufficient funds for buying out the interest of a deceased partner or stockholder, thereby assuring continuity of the business. Employers interested in improving employee morale often purchase group insurance for their workers, freeing the workers' families from the financial burdens created by the breadwinners' deaths.

Accident, Health, and Compensation Insurance

Accident and health insurance provides a weekly income to the insured in the event of disability by accident or sickness and a fund to the beneficiary in case of death by accident. Such insurance is closely related to compensation insurance, which covers accidents which occur to employees while at work. The various types of policies include:

1. *Ticket policies,* which are sold at the ticket offices of airports and railroad stations, and provide for the payment of certain sums if injury by accident occurs within a specified time—a day, a week, a month, 90 days, etc.

2. *Limited policies,* which cover particular kinds of accidents.

3. *General policies,* which more or less cover all types of accidents.

4. *The newest form of health insurance,* which provides for hospitalization and medical expenses, as well as weekly payments during disability.

Casualty Insurance and Suretyship

Casualty insurance is written to protect the insured from loss due to injury to his person or property (except losses covered exclusively by life, fire, or marine companies) and from liability for damages for death or injury to the person or property of others. Casualty insurance covers public liability, property damage liability, workmen's compensation, employers' liability, accident and health liability; automobile and aircraft collision; water damage, plate glass damage; burglary, robbery, and theft; damage to boilers and machinery, and to elevators; animals; check alteration and forgery, and credit insurance.

The surety branch of the business provides: fidelity and surety bonds indemnifying against dishonesty of employees, breach of contract, certain bank losses, the failure of public officials to faithfully perform their duties; also, license bonds, court and fiduciary bonds, and many other types of bonds required by law or used in business transactions.

Automobile Insurance

The most common types of policies covering automobiles are: Liability, Property Damage, and Fire and Theft. Complete protection is assured when Collision insurance is added to these basic coverages.

The Liability policy insures against legal liability "for damages on account of bodily injuries sustained by any person or persons other than the owner or his employees engaged in operating or caring for the automobile, as a result of the ownership, maintenance, use of the automobile covered." The rates for this policy and for the property damage policy depend upon the type of car (private, taxicab, truck, etc.), the territory in which it is to be used, (the hazards and therefore the rates, being much higher in large cities where there are more people and more cars), the motive power and price of the automobile, and the driver, the cost being less where the owner is the driver.

The usual policy provides a payment of $5,000 for injuries to one person in one accident, and $10,000 for injuries to more than one person in one accident, but there are many arguments in favor of larger policies. The company generally agrees to make investigations and settle claims, to pay for immediate surgical relief to the injured, to defend the insured in suits, and to pay legal costs, the total liability of the company being limited to the amount on the face of the policy. The policy generally runs for the period of a year. Accidents occurring when the car is subjected to extraordinary use, as in speed contests, or, in the case of private automobiles, when they are being operated for hire, are not covered by the ordinary policy and must be made the subject of special arrangements.

The Property Damage policy provides for the payment of damage to the property of others not carried in the car covered by the insurance policy. The company's liability is limited to the amount on the face of the policy. The usual policy is for $5,000.

Collision insurance covers damages to the owner's car through collision with a moving or stationary object. Damages are based on either the value of the car or the cost of repair.

There are two kinds of fire insurance policies, valued and unvalued, the first being one in which the value of the automobile is agreed upon in advance, the second being one in which the value is determined at the time of the loss.

Under the Comprehensive Fire and Theft policy, the company makes full payment in the case of theft, or damage not caused by collision or upset, such as scratching and marring by hail, windstorm, flying objects, etc.

Theft insurance covers only the automobile itself, not its contents.

Aviation Insurance

During recent years aviation risks of every description have been insured under standard forms of policies and at published rates.

Planes are classified in accordance with the use to which they are put, as (1) private business and pleasure; (2) commercial, including or excluding instruction, and (3) scheduled air lines.

Miscellaneous Insurance

There are many other kinds of insurance. Public events may be insured against rain; certain broadcasts are insured against S O S calls. Protection may be had against hail, windstorms, tornadoes, earthquakes, theft, forgery, riots, explosions, and so on through a long list. Descriptions of Workmen's Compensation and the Social Security Act may be found on pages 317 and 318.

ANNUITIES

The ends served by annuities and by life insurance are directly opposite. Whereas life insurance is bought in order to create an estate, protecting the insured against the hazard of not living long enough to accumulate an estate through his earnings, annuities are purchased in order to liquidate an already accumulated estate, providing the purchaser with protection against the hazard of outliving his income.

An annuity is, strictly speaking, an annual payment of a definite sum of money. Many annuities, however, are payable semiannually, quarterly, monthly, or even weekly, notwithstanding the definition of *annuity*.

The person receiving an annuity is called the *annuitant,* and the period during which payments are made is called the *term of the annuity*. In purchasing an annuity, one must pay the present value of all future annuity payments, the present value being the amount which, placed at interest now, will be sufficient to provide the periodic payments when they fall due.

Two general kinds of annuities are most common. One, the *life annuity,* pays a guaranteed income to the annuitant throughout his life, no matter how long he or she lives. If he dies before the annuity payments have equaled the cost of the annuity, the sum which has not been returned to him is used to provide continued life payments to the annuitants who live to collect much more than the cost of the annuity.

The other most common kind of annuity is an *annuity certain*. An annuity certain provides payments for a specified period. At the end of that period, all payments cease.

One of the most popular forms of annuities sold by life insurance companies is a combination of a life annuity and an annuity certain. This type of annuity provides payments for the life of the annuitant. If the annuitant dies within a specified period, payments continue to a beneficiary until the end of that period.

Deferred annuities are also available. The purpose of these is to permit a person to make deposits with the life insurance company while he is young and still working, the deposits being returned to him as an annuity after he has retired. Either life annuities or annuities certain may be purchased on a deferred basis.

Annuities are frequently purchased by retired persons. They provide an excellent investment for old people because an annuity is much safer than most stocks and bonds and involves no managerial expense, worry, or care to the investor, because the rate of return is the highest commensurate with safety, and because an annuity provides an income which cannot be outlived.

Joint and survivor annuities may be purchased by two persons wishing to provide themselves with an income that neither can outlive. The advantage of this type of contract is that the income payments do not cease at the death of the first person, but continue until the death of the second joint annuitant.

Since each annuity payment to the annuitant consists of a portion of the annuity principal, as well as interest earned on the remaining fund, whereas other investments can provide a life income safely only by restricting payments to interest, the monthly income from annuities is generally much greater than that from other investments. Because of this, a person may invest a portion of his savings in an annuity, devote the balance of the savings to some other use, and still realize as great a return from the annuity portion as he would receive from investing his total savings elsewhere. Thus, people frequently purchase annuities from which they receive a large, regular income, and use the balance of their savings to provide advanced education for their children, to help them get started in business, or for presenting a sizeable gift to a philanthropic, charitable, or educational institution.

Premiums for life annuities are computed on the basis of mortality tables. The table most commonly used today is the 1937 Standard Annuity Table, based on annuity mortality experience in the United States.

1937 Standard Annuity Table

	Value of an annuity of $1.00 a year at 2½% interest		Amount of annual annuity purchased by $1,000	
Age	Male	Female[1]	Male	Female[1]
35	22.8870	24.6023	$43.69	$40.65
45	19.1212	21.0540	52.30	47.50
55	15.0647	17.1137	66.38	58.43
65	11.0134	13.0157	90.80	76.83
75	7.3436	9.1072	136.17	109.80

[1]Because women on the average live five years longer than men of the same age, the premium for a life annuity to a woman is higher than for a man.

There are many kinds of annuity tables; a book thicker than this one would be necessary to hold all of them. In addition to the one above, the one on page 82 is one of the most useful. It shows the amount of an annuity certain of $1.00 at the end of each period. To find the amount of an annuity of $15,000, simply multiply the amount of $1.00 for a given period at a given rate. For instance, find the amount of an annuity of $15,000 at 5 per cent for 10 years. Looking at the table, you see that the amount of $1.00 at 5 per cent for 10 years is 12.577893. For practical purposes, let us call it $12.58. Multiplying this by 15,000 we have $188,700, which is the answer. There is no way to calculate the amount of an annuity in perpetuity, since there is no end point from which to work.

In large organizations annuity calculations are done by machines.

TABLE SHOWING AMOUNT OF ANNUITY OF $1.00 AT END OF EACH PERIOD

No. of years	Annual Rates of Interest				
	3 per cent	4 per cent	4-1/2 per cent	5 per cent	6 per cent
1	1.	1.	1.	1.	1.
2	2.03	2.04	2.045	2.05	2.06
3	3.0909	3.1216	3.137025	3.1525	3.1836
4	4.183627	4.246464	4.278191	4.310125	4.374616
5	5.309136	5.416323	5.470710	5.525631	5.637093
6	6.468410	6.632975	6.716892	6.801913	6.975319
7	7.662462	7.898294	8.019152	8.142008	8.393838
8	8.892336	9.214226	9.380014	9.549109	9.897468
9	10.159106	10.582795	10.802114	11.026564	11.491316
10	11.463879	12.006107	12.288209	12.577893	13.180795
11	12.807796	13.486351	13.841179	14.206787	14.971643
12	14.192030	15.025805	15.464032	15.917127	16.869941
13	15.617790	16.626838	17.159913	17.712983	18.882138
14	17.086324	18.291911	18.932109	19.598632	21.015066
15	18.598914	20.023588	20.784054	21.578564	23.275970
16	20.156881	21.824531	22.719337	23.657492	25.672528
17	21.761588	23.697512	24.741707	25.840366	28.212880
18	23.414435	25.645413	26.855084	28.132385	30.905653
19	25.116868	27.671229	29.063562	30.539004	33.759992
20	26.870374	29.778079	31.371423	33.065954	36.785591

EXPECTATION OF LIFE IN THE UNITED STATES*

AGE	Total Population	WHITE		NON-WHITE	
		Males	Females	Males	Females
0	67.2	65.5	71.0	58.1	62.5
1	68.4	66.8	71.9	60.2	64.2
5	64.9	63.2	68.3	56.9	60.8
10	60.1	58.4	63.5	52.1	56.1
15	55.2	53.6	58.6	47.4	51.3
20	50.6	49.0	53.8	42.9	46.8
25	46.0	44.4	49.0	38.7	42.5
30	41.3	39.8	44.3	34.6	38.3
35	36.8	35.2	39.6	30.5	34.2
40	32.3	30.7	35.0	26.8	30.3
45	28.0	26.5	30.5	23.3	26.7
50	24.0	22.4	26.2	20.1	23.4
55	20.2	18.8	22.0	17.5	20.5
60	16.6	15.4	18.1	15.2	17.8
65	13.4	12.4	14.4	13.1	15.7
70	10.6	9.8	11.2	11.5	14.5
75	8.1	7.5	8.3	10.3	13.2

*Based on 1948 statistics. Figures denote years.

AVERAGE WEIGHT
OF MEN AND WOMEN[1]

The weights are for persons with shoes on, and without coat and vest, which weigh from 3 to 7 pounds, depending on the height of the individual and the season of the year.

	MEN								WOMEN						
Age Group	Hgt. and Wgt.	Hgt. and Wgt.	Hgt. and Wgt.	Hgt. and Wgt.	Hgt. and Wgt.	Hgt. and Wgt.	Hgt. and Wgt.	Hgt. and Wgt.	Hgt. and Wgt.	Hgt. and Wgt.	Hgt. and Wgt.	Hgt. and Wgt.	Hgt. and Wgt.	Hgt. and Wgt.	Hgt. and Wgt.
	5'	5'1"	5'2"	5'3"	5'4"	5'5"	5'6"	5'7"	4'11"	5'	5'1"	5'2"	5'3"	5'4"	5'5"
15–19	108	111	114	118	122	126	130	134	105	107	110	113	116	119	123
20–24	119	121	124	127	131	135	139	142	113	115	117	120	123	126	129
25–29	124	126	128	131	134	138	142	146	116	118	120	122	125	129	132
30–34	127	129	131	134	137	141	145	149	119	121	123	125	128	132	136
35–39	129	131	133	136	140	144	148	152	122	124	126	129	132	136	140
40–44	132	134	136	139	142	146	150	154	126	128	130	133	136	139	143
45–49	134	136	138	141	144	148	152	156	129	131	133	136	139	142	146
50–54	135	137	139	142	145	149	153	157	131	133	135	138	141	144	148
	5'8"	5'9"	5'10"	5'11"	6'	6'1"	6'2"	6'3"	5'6"	5'7"	5'8"	5'9"	5'10"	5'11"	6'
15–19	138	142	146	151	156	161	166	171	127	131	135	139	143	147	151
20–24	146	150	154	158	163	168	173	178	133	137	141	145	149	153	157
25–29	150	154	158	163	169	175	181	187	136	140	144	148	152	155	159
30–34	154	158	163	168	174	180	186	192	140	144	148	152	155	158	162
35–39	157	162	167	172	178	184	191	197	144	148	152	156	159	162	165
40–44	159	164	169	175	181	187	194	201	147	151	155	159	162	166	169
45–49	161	166	171	177	183	190	197	204	151	157	162	166	170	170	173
50–54	162	167	172	178	184	191	198	205	152	157	162	166	170	174	177

[1]Compiled by the Association of Life Insurance Medical Directors and the Actuarial Society of America.

DIET TABLE

Foods may be divided into proteins, fats, carbohydrates, and the mineral matter of ash. *Proteins* are very complex substances consisting approximately of 16 per cent of nitrogen. They are found in all living cells, both animal and vegetable, and are present in large quantities in the white of egg, in milk curd, lean meat, and the gluten of grains. *Fats* are stored as such in the fat of meats, in butter, olive oil, and other oils. *Carbohydrates* (sugar, starch, etc.) are converted into fat before they are assimilated. All these foods give energy in the form of heat and muscle. The *mineral matter of ash* helps in the digestive processes and in the formation of bone.

Food values are measured in calories. Calories may be large or small. The small calorie is equal to the amount of heat required to raise the temperature of one gram of water one degree centigrade. The large or great calorie is equal to the amount of heat required to raise one kilogram of water one degree centigrade. In other words, the large calorie is equal to 1,000 small calories.

WEEKLY QUANTITIES OF FOOD FOR EACH MEMBER OF FAMILY*

Family members	Leafy, green, yellow vegetables (Lb. Oz.)	Citrus fruit, tomatoes (Lb. Oz.)	Potatoes, sweet potatoes (Lb. Oz.)	Other vegetables and fruit (Lb. Oz.)	Milk† (Qt.)	Meat, poultry, fish (Lb. Oz.)	Eggs (No.)	Dry beans and peas, nuts (Lb. Oz.)	Flour, cereals‡ (Lb. Oz.)	Fats and oils§ (Lb. Oz.)	Sugar, sirups, preserves (Lb. Oz.)
Children under 12 years:											
9-12 months	1 — 8	1 — 12	0 — 8	1 — 12	6	0 — 4	5	0	0 — 10	0 — 1	0 — 1
1-3 years	2 — 0	2 — 0	0 — 0	1 — 8	6	¶ 1 — 12	6	0	1 — 4	0 — 0	0 — 2
4-6 years	2 — 4	2 — 4	0 — 0	2 — 0	6	1 — 4	7	0	1 — 8	0 — 6	0 — 8
7-9 years	2 — 8	2 — 8	1 — 12	2 — 8	6-1/2	1 — 12	7	0	2 — 0	0 — 8	0 — 12
10-12 years	3 — 0	2 — 12	1 — 4	2 — 8	7	2 — 4	7	0	2 — 12	0 — 12	0 — 14
Girls:											
13-15 years	3 — 8	2 — 12	2 — 8	3 — 8	7	¶ 2 — 12	7	0	2 — 8	0 — 14	0 — 14
16-20 years	3 — 8	2 — 12	2 — 8	3 — 8	6	¶ 2 — 12	7	0	2 — 8	0 — 12	0 — 12
Boys:											
13-15 years	3 — 8	3 — 0	3 — 8	3 — 0	7	3 — 0	7	0	4 — 4	1 — 0	1 — 2
16-20 years	4 — 0	3 — 8	4 — 8	3 — 8	7	3 — 4	7	0	5 — 0	1 — 6	1 — 4
Women:											
Sedentary	3 — 4	2 — 8	1 — 12	3 — 4	5	2 — 8	7	0	1 — 12	0 — 10	0 — 12
Moderately active	3 — 8	2 — 8	2 — 8	3 — 8	5	2 — 12	7	0	2 — 8	0 — 14	0 — 14
Very active	3 — 12	3 — 8	2 — 4	4 — 8	5	¶ 3 — 0	7	0	3 — 12	0 — 12	1 — 2
Pregnant	4 — 0	4 — 0	3 — 0	3 — 0	7-1/2	¶ 3 — 0	7	0	2 — 8	0 — 10	1 — 0
Nursing	4 — 0	4 — 8	3 — 0	3 — 0	10-1/2	¶ 3 — 0	7	0	2 — 8	0 — 12	1 — 0
60 years or over#	3 — 8	2 — 12	2 — 0	3 — 8	5-1/2	2 — 8	6	0 — 1	1 — 12	0 — 8	1 — 0
Men:											
Sedentary	3 — 8	2 — 8	2 — 8	3 — 8	5	2 — 12	7	0	2 — 8	0 — 14	0 — 14
Physically active	3 — 12	3 — 0	3 — 4	4 — 0	5	3 — 0	7	0	3 — 8	1 — 2	1 — 4
With heavy work	4 — 0	3 — 8	5 — 0	4 — 0	5	3 — 8	7	0	7 — 0	2 — 0	1 — 4
60 years or over#	3 — 8	2 — 12	2 — 12	4 — 0	5-1/2	2 — 12	6	0	2 — 8	0 — 12	0 — 12

† Or its equivalent in cheese, evaporated milk, or dry milk.

‡ Count 1-1/2 pounds of bread as 1 pound of flour. Use as much as possible in the form of whole grain, enriched or restored products.

§ For small children and pregnant and nursing women, cod liver oil or some other source of vitamin D is also needed. For elderly persons and for persons who have no opportunity for exposure to clear sunshine a small amount of vitamin D is also desirable.

¶ To meet iron allowance, one large or two small servings of liver or other organ meats should be served each week.

The nutritive content of the weekly food quantities for a man and woman 60 years or over was based on the National Research Council's recommended daily allowances for the sedentary man and woman.

* Prepared by the Bureau of Human Nutrition and Home Economics, U. S. Department of Agriculture.

CANNING, QUICK-FREEZING, AND STORING FOOD AT HOME

In the home, as in business, long-range planning frequently results in added efficiency and economy. Many homemakers find it thrifty and labor-saving to can or quick-freeze certain foods when they are in season or low in price, and to serve them later, in season or out.

The housewife who decides to preserve foods by these methods must always remember three important rules: (1) In order to stop the action of enzymes in foods and prevent spoilage by organisms (bacteria, molds, and yeasts) present at all times in air, water, and soil, follow all directions with utmost care; (2) insure success by purchasing only top-quality material and equipment; (3) use sanitary precautions. Hands, food, containers, equipment, and work surfaces should be scrupulously cleaned.

The general directions given below should be supplemented by booklets available from the United States Department of Agriculture and state agricultural colleges or extension services; these booklets contain scientifically tested, step-by-step directions, and timetables adaptable to all home food-preservation.

Canning Equipment

You will need a steam-pressure canner for poultry, meats, and low-acid vegetables, such as beans and corn; a water-bath canner (any deep vessel of tin, aluminum, enamelware, or galvanized iron, at least 12 in. deep) with a tight-fitting cover for processing tomatoes, fruits, and pickled vegetables; a rack on which to place jars in canner so that they do not touch bottom; glass jars (tins may be used but require a special sealer) and lids; new rubber rings (unless self-sealing type of closure is used); large pan or kettle for hot water; tongs for lifting hot jars; long-handled spoons (wooden, if possible) for stirring; colander; jar funnel; spatula or knife; measuring cups; measuring spoons.

Preliminary Steps

1. Figure yield of canned food from fresh, in order that you may prepare sufficient number of jars.
2. Examine jars and lids. Discard any with chips, dents, or cracks which would cause breakage. Wash glass jars and lids (except those with sealing compound) in hot, soapy water. Rinse well in hot water. Then keep hot until time to fill jars. Jars should be hot when packing hot foods.

Methods

Two canning methods are used today, each suited to specific groups of food. They are (1) boiling-water bath, for processing tomatoes, fruits, and pickled vegetables; (2) steam-pressure canner, absolutely essential for processing poultry and meats, corn, beans, and other common vegetables. For safety's sake these foods require processing at a temperature above that of boiling water, to insure killing heat-resistant bacterial spores which may spoil, or produce toxins in low-acid canned foods.

Do not try to process foods in your oven. This method is not only inefficient in destroying bacteria but may cause jars to explode.

Do not use open-kettle cooking for canning. The United States Department of Agriculture warns that cooking food in an ordinary kettle, removing it to hot jars, and sealing without processing may permit entry of spoilage organisms. This method is reserved for processing jellies and jams, with which the cooking-down process and concentration of sugar help in preventing spoilage.

Boiling-Water Bath—Steps to Take

Prepare ¾ to 1 cup syrup for each quart jar of fruit. In general, the three types of syrup used are: thin syrup—1 cup sugar to 3 cups water or fruit juice; medium syrup—1 cup sugar to 2 cups water or juice; heavy syrup—1 cup sugar to 1 cup water or juice. Syrup is prepared by boiling for 5 minutes over low flame until sugar dissolves. If fruits are juicy merely add sugar directly to fruit and heat without adding liquid—in this case use about ½ cup sugar to 1 quart fruit. When sugar is scarce replace with mild honey or corn syrup for up to half the sugar required. Sweetening helps preserve color, shape, and flavor but is not needed to prevent spoilage; food may be processed in boiling water and sweetened just before serving.

Sort fruit for size and ripeness; use only firm, fresh fruits, neither too ripe nor too green. Handle only as much as can be processed at one time. Wash carefully, in small quantities, in wire basket or colander. Lift fruit from water; avoid bruising. Repeat, washing several times, rinsing container each time. Dip peaches or tomatoes briefly in boiling water to loosen skins, then dip for a moment in cold water, using wire basket. Peel and prepare fruits or tomatoes as required (coring, pitting, slicing). At this point drop apples, peaches, and apricots into water containing 2 tbs. each of salt and vinegar to the gallon—they should be drained just before heating—to prevent discoloration.

Peaches and tomatoes may be heated or not, as you prefer, before packing and processing. Soft berries, such as red raspberries, are best packed without preheating. Firm berries are best preheated.

For a *hot pack,* place fruit in boiling sugar syrup or boiling water and heat so that fruit is cooked through but not soft. Quarter tomatoes, and bring to boil, stirring often. While food is heating lift clean jars from water; set in shallow, cloth-lined pan; put hot, wet rubber ring on jars requiring ring. Now fill jars. Pack food in loosely, leaving ½ in. space at top of jar. Cover fruit with boiling liquid, filling within ½ in. of jar top. Tomatoes should be packed to ½ in. of top, with ½ tsp. salt for pints, 1 tsp. for quarts. Remove air bubbles by running spatula down sides of jar. As each jar is filled wipe rim and rubber ring with clean, damp cloth and adjust closure.

When all jars are filled place on rack in canner. Fill canner with enough boiling water to reach 1 in. to 2 in. above jars, adding boiling water, if necessary, to maintain this level. Jars should not touch each other. When processing time required is up, remove jars and complete sealing when required. Never open a jar to replace any liquid which may have been lost in processing. To do so would permit entry of bacteria.

Strawberries require a slightly different procedure. To these berries add ½ cup sugar to each quart fruit and bring slowly to a boil; remove from stove and allow to stand overnight. Next day bring quickly to boil, then pack in jars for canning in a boiling-water bath.

For a *cold pack* of peaches, tomatoes, or red raspberries pack the raw food into jars as for hot pack. Add salt but no water to tomatoes. Add boiling syrup to cover fruits.

Steam-Pressure Canner—Steps to Take

Poultry, meats, and all garden vegetables (*except* tomatoes) should be canned this way. The time required for processing varies with each food. Follow manufacturer's directions for care of canner, use, and timing, and make use of supplementary bulletins.

Beef, veal, mutton, lamb, pork, poultry, and game can be canned successfully at home. Do not can mixtures such as hashes and stews, chile con carne, pork and beans, scrapple, cereal or vegetable soups, etc., unless tested home-canning procedures are available.

Follow these general steps:

Fill canner with 2 to 3 in. of water. Place hot, filled jars on rack, permitting steam to flow freely about each jar. Always fasten canner cover securely so that steam escapes only at open petcock or weighted gauge opening.

When steam begins to escape steadily from opening, permit it to escape for 7 to 10 minutes so that air is forced from canner. Then close petcock and watch pressure gauge until desired number of pounds is reached. Begin specific timing the instant desired pressure is reached. Maintain constant pressure level by regulating stove heat—do not try to regulate pressure by opening petcock.

When processing required for individual food is completed remove canner from heat. Permit canner to stand 1 minute to 2 minutes after pressure has reached zero point. Never hasten cooling by applying cold water or cloths. Open petcock gradually or remove weighted gauge. Unfasten canner cover with extreme care, tilting it far side up, so that steam escapes away from face and hands.

Remove jars. Complete sealing immediately if jars are not self-sealing. As with boiling-water bath, never reopen jars to add liquid which may have been lost during processing.

Canning in High Altitudes

Because the boiling point of water decreases with increasing altitude, those living in elevated regions must allow longer processing time in the water bath, or increased pressures, to reach the temperature (240 F.) which insures the destruction of spoilage organisms in low-acid foods. *Boiling-water bath:* If you live at an altitude of 1,000 ft. or more, for each 1,000 ft. above sea level add 1 minute to processing time for fruits and tomatoes, if time needed is 20 minutes or less. If time needed is 20 minutes or more, add 2 minutes for each 1,000 ft. *Steam-pressure canner:* For meats and low-acid vegetables, increase pressure by 1 lb. for each 2,000 ft. of altitude. You may need to have a weighted gauge regulated for altitude by the manufacturer.

To Close Jars

Several types of glass jars are used for canning, each having a different type of closure. Sealing of the various types is carried out as follows: (1) *Porcelain-lined screw cap with rubber ring,* suitable for standard Mason jar. When rubber-ringed jar is ready for closing, screw cap on tightly, then turn back ¼ in. After jar is taken from canner turn cap back and screw tightly. (2) *Wire bail with glass lid and rubber ring.* When rubber-ringed jar is ready for closing, cover with glass lid. Leaving short wire up, snap long wire over into groove on top of lid. After jar is taken from canner push short wire down. (3) *Flat metal lid edged with sealing compound,* held in place by metal screw band; fits standard Mason jar. When jar is ready for closing place lid on it with sealing compound resting on jar. Fasten metal band down tightly with hand—never use implement for this. After canning do not tighten further or you may break seal. (4) *Glass lid and rubber ring,* held in place by metal screw band; suitable for standard Mason jar. When jar is ready for closing fit wet rubber ring on glass lid. Place lid on jar with rubber side down. Screw metal band on tightly, then turn back about ¼ turn, making certain that band and jar mesh. Do not make too tight. After canning screw tightly.

Cooling and Testing Jars

Cool jars overnight, top side up, on thick cloth or paper surface. Keep out of draft. Next day turn jars partly over to test for leaks. To test self-sealing jars tap with spoon, listening for clear, ringing sound denoting complete seal.

Wipe jars. Label with name of contents, date, and, if more than one lot is canned in a day, lot number. Store in cool, dry place where food can neither freeze nor become too warm.

Examine carefully for spoilage before using. Do not use any canned food showing such spoilage signs as bulging can ends, rings, or jar lids; gas bubbles or leakage; spurting liquid, bad odor, or mold when opened. For safety, before tasting *boil* vegetables and meat for 10 minutes. *Warming is not enough.* Destroy any spoiled food by burning or burying deep in the ground to insure that neither man nor animal will eat it.

FREEZING AND STORAGE

Home Freezing Units

Freezing is a highly modern technique of preserving foods which has won many advocates among homemakers. The numerous types of zero storage cabinets available include individual units as little as 3 or 4 cu. ft. in size. Thus, even the small city or town family without access to home-grown produce can save time as well as money by purchasing a supply of commercially frozen food (all-food, with no waste in bone, hulls, etc.) and storing it in the freezer (thereby reducing marketing trips to a minimum), or by purchasing items when plentiful and freezing them at one time. The infinite variety of foods adaptable to home freezing includes cakes, rolls, breads, cooked dishes, and desserts. Ice cream storage is one of the most popular features.

Among the types of freezers on the market are: (1) *Walk-in freezer,* usually a built-in room, although sometimes prefabricated—a large home freezer suited to small farms or estates where quantity storage is called for; (2) *Two-temperature units*—contain ordinary refrigerator space plus a separate freezing compartment of from 1 cu. ft. to 4 cu. ft. The frozen-food compartment here is not to be confused with the ice-cube compartment of the regular automatic refrigerator. The latter is suitable for storing small amounts of frozen food for little more than a week or two; (3) *Top-opening chest*—square, oblong, or cylindrical in shape; and (4) *Upright freezer*—has either front- or side-opening doors.

If your unit is not equipped with a warning device indicating power failure, it is wise to purchase such an alarm and adapt it to your freezer.

The *locker plant* is a commercial plant affording freezing and storage facilities. Many families maintain a small zero storage compartment at home for freezing small quantities of food and for keeping foods between trips to their commercial lockers.

Best results with freezers are gained by following manufacturers' directions and using supplementary literature. General directions are given below.

Foods Suitable for Freezing

Most fruits, vegetables, poultry, meats, and fish can be successfully frozen. As in canning, use best-quality food. Cucumbers, endive, lettuce, uncooked celery, radishes, whole tomatoes, and a few others are unsuited to freezing. Work with chilled food—even vegetables which require heating should be chilled before packaging and freezing.

How to Preheat Vegetables

Preheating vegetables for freezing is accomplished by scalding with boiling water or by steaming. This step is necessary to destroy enzymes which would cause food deterioration. Time needed for preheating varies with individual foods.

Wash vegetables thoroughly and peel or cut as if readying for ordinary cooking.

To preheat with boiling water, place vegetables in colander or wire basket with handle, and immerse in large kettle of boiling water. Use 1 gal. of water for each pound of vegetables. Preheat no more than 1 lb. at a time. Start counting time when vegetable is immersed in boiling water. Agitate (to insure even heating) by moving colander or basket to and fro. The boiling-water method is practicable for most vegetables. Broccoli has better flavor when preheated with steam.

To preheat with steam, use a 6- to 12-qt. kettle with a rack placed on bottom. Again, work with no more than 1 lb. of produce at a time. Pour slightly more than 1 in. of water on bottom of kettle. When water reaches rolling boil place colander or basket with vegetables on rack and cover steamer tightly. Begin timing immediately. This method of blanching is especially suited to cut-up vegetables and cut sweet corn.

At 5,000 ft. or more above sea level 1 minute should be added to scalding time.

How to Cool Vegetables After Preheating

Remove container immediately after scalding and plunge it under cold running water or into pan of ice water. Cool vegetables thoroughly before proceeding with packaging.

How to Prepare Fruits

Wash fruits thoroughly. Remove stems or skins and slice if necessary. Peaches and apricots may be peeled as described for canning. Fruits do not require blanching, except in the case of apples, which must be heated by either of the methods described or may be treated with an antidarkening agent.

For protection during storage and thawing most fruits need the addition of dry sugar or cold syrup. In general it is recommended that sugar alone be used on juicy fruits, such as strawberries, which will form their own syrup. The specified proportion of sugar should be sprinkled over fruit and stirred in, preferably with a fork, until berries are covered with juice. Sugar syrup is prepared by mixing sugar and water, or white corn syrup and water, in proportions specified for each fruit. In order to prevent discoloration of peaches, apricots, cherries, plums, and pears, add ½ tsp. ascorbic acid (vitamin C) to syrup for every quart of syrup just before adding to fruit.

Packaging Materials

Numerous packaging materials are available in department stores, hardware stores, and at locker plants. Among the types offered are heavily waxed paperboard cartons; re-usable rigid containers of tin, glass, or plastic; tin cans (some foods require special lacquer linings in tin cans); special round or square glass containers; lightweight aluminum boxes with aluminum lids that can be sealed to the box with a small tool supplied with the box; and moistureproof, vaporproof wrappings. Make your choice on the basis of price, size, convenience, etc.; most freezer containers and packaging materials available today give satisfactory results when used correctly.

Meat and Fish

Any good fresh meat or fish can be frozen satisfactorily. Duration of top quality and flavor under storage varies with individual meats. Locker plants will often slaughter, age, cut up, pack, freeze, and store meat and poultry you may raise or buy from farms. Some meat shops are equipped to cut up, package, wrap, and label their meats for your home freezer at no extra cost.

Meats for freezing should be prepared in fairly small packages, since these freeze more rapidly than large packages. All meats should be chilled before freezing. In general they should be cleaned as for service at the table. They require no precooking—are frozen raw.

Meat requires extremely careful packaging to protect it from drying out and becoming rancid. Smoked meats demand extra-careful wrapping to prevent escape of their odors to other items.

Fish and shellfish should be frozen on the same day they are caught, if possible, otherwise they must be under constant refrigeration until freezing time. Fish should be scaled, beheaded, eviscerated, and otherwise cleaned, just as for table service. Large fish should be cut into fillets and steaks. Some home economists recommend immersing fillets and steaks of cod and haddock (never fatty fish such as mackerel and salmon) for 20 seconds to 1 minute in brine of 1 lb. salt to 4½ qts. water before packing.

Clams, scallops, and oysters must be shucked before freezing. The raw meats may be washed under a spray of clean cold water, or in a 2½-percent brine, and drained. Fruit and vegetable containers may be used here with inner liner of moistureproof vaporproof cellophane and with space allowed for expansion.

Crab and lobster must be cooked as for table service. Cooked, picked crab meat and lobster meat should be packed in jars with 2½-per-cent brine, allowing space for expansion during freezing.

Shrimps should have heads and appendages removed and discarded. Some authorities advise freezing it uncooked (cooked shrimp toughens during storage) in shells; others advise shelling before packing.

Whole meats and fish are wrapped tightly in moistureproof, waterproof material especially prepared for freezer storage. Among these materials are cellophane, Philofilm, aluminum foil, and coated paper. Always protect your foods with good quality material. Special sealing tape is used. Large irregular-shaped pieces, such as roasts, are usually further protected by overwrapping in stockinette or heavy paper. Small cuts of meat and fish may be wrapped in lined cartons. To give whole fish extra protection some people freeze it in the regular manner, then dip it in thoroughly chilled ice water, drain, and repeat the process until an ice glaze forms. Fish is then rewrapped in moistureproof, vaporproof material, sealed, and returned to freezer.

Sandwiches for Lunch Box or Parties

The home freezer enables you to make and store a two-weeks' supply of sandwiches at one time, avoiding morning hustle, and economizing by using left-overs. Use day-old bread. Spread softened (not melted) butter or margarine on entire surface of each slice—it will prevent fillings from soaking bread. Fillings suitable for freezing include cheese, sliced or ground poultry or meat, peanut butter, and hard-cooked egg yolk (hard-cooked egg white is not suitable). In fact, almost any filling except salad greens, tomatoes, jellies, mayonnaise, and salad dressing may be used. Wrap sandwiches individually in moistureproof, vaporproof material, and pack several in a carton, taking care not to mash them. Sandwiches can go directly from freezer to lunch box, will be thawed by noon. *Canapés* and party sandwiches are usually wrapped and placed in cartons in layers. Each layer is separated from the others by a double thickness of wrapping material. Fancy loaves for ribbon sandwiches should be frozen whole and cut after thawing.

Thawing

Most frozen vegetables may be cooked without thawing. Meats and fish may be cooked while frozen, but even cooking and a saving in cooking time result from two-thirds thawing.

Labeling

Because different foods have different lasting capacities it is important to label each package with the date of packing and freezing and a description of contents. A china-marking pencil may be used. Take inventory of stored foods at regular intervals.

Other Storage Suggestions

Families living in the suburbs or the country sometimes have a basement room suitable for storing food. A good storage cellar should have at least one window and should not be near a furnace. Outdoor storage cellars, or caves, pits, and trenches may also be used. Apples and pears may be stored in a storage cellar, pit, or basement; storage period varies in relation to variety of fruit, temperature of storage, and maturity of fruit. Grapes and plums may be stored in a cool and moderately moist basement or storage cellar, the former for 1 month to 2 months, the latter for 4 to 6 weeks. Dry beans and peas may be kept in any cool dry place for several months, or until needed, if protected from weevils or rodents; potatoes in a pit, basement, or storage cellar, through fall and winter; sweet potatoes in a moderately dry, rather cool (55° to 60° F.) cellar or basement, through fall and winter.

TAXES

A tax is a compulsory sum of money paid to a government.

Taxes are of two kinds, direct and indirect.

A *direct tax* is one levied on a person, *e.g.*, the poll tax, or on his property, or on his business. The tax on a person's business is called a *license fee*.

An *indirect tax* is a tax on imported goods, when it is called a duty, or a tax on certain kinds of manufactures, when it is called an *excise tax* (internal revenue).

Taxes are *Federal* when they are levied by the United States.

Taxes for local benefits, such as street paving, sidewalks, sewers, etc., are sometimes called *assessments*.

Tax assessors are persons appointed to estimate the value of each person's property and to apportion the taxes equitably according to the value.

The *assessment roll* is a list of property owners, with a brief description of their properties, the assessed valuation of each, and the taxes levied.

The *assessed valuation* is the base upon which the tax is figured.

Taxes must be levied legally; that is, they must be announced to the taxpayer far enough ahead of their due dates for him to be heard if he thinks his tax unjust.

Real estate taxes become liens on the property the day they are due; if they are unpaid, the property may eventually be sold to satisfy the tax claim. A tax lien is prior to a mortgage lien. All mortgages and all purchasers of real estate should have tax searches made.

Inheritance taxes also must be paid before a real estate title is clear. There is a Federal inheritance tax and a state tax in most of the states. Florida is an exception, and there are others.

The income tax is of comparatively recent origin. The first income tax laws were repealed; the present law began with the ratification of the Sixteenth Amendment to the Constitution in 1913. It has been changed and revised many times since. What its current provisions are may be learned through application to the local collector of internal revenue, who will furnish the proper blanks and the necessary information. The Bureau of Internal Revenue has made available to the public a very readable booklet called *Your Federal Income Tax*. It is issued each year, with up-to-date changes in the tax laws explained, particularly for the average taxpayer.

Taxpayers should keep records, inventories, etc., to help the collector determine the income. If the taxpayer keeps his books on a fiscal basis his return must be made out on that basis; if he keeps them on a calendar basis he must follow that form. A new taxpayer can begin on any basis he likes, but if he wishes to change from one to the other or to change the dates of his fiscal year he must apply to the tax commissioner 30 days before the end of the period for which the return is to be filed. The fiscal year basis is not allowed unless books are kept. If the accounting method of the taxpayer is not clear the commissioner has a right to require an inventory or a new accounting, taken upon whatever basis he thinks best.

Federal personal income taxes are payable under the "pay-as-you-go" plan in two ways: (1) by *withholding* the amount due from wages or salaries, and (2) by quarterly *declaration and payment of estimated tax* for incomes not subject to the withholding tax. The balance of the tax is payable on March 15, after the close of the calendar year upon which the tax is reckoned; or if it is reckoned on a fiscal year, on the 15th day of the third month following the end of the year. If the taxpayer has overpaid his taxes, a refund will be made on the basis of the taxpayer's return filed at the end of the year.

All citizens and residents of the United States with a gross income of $600 or more during the taxable year, or as much as $11.54 per week, must file a Federal income tax return. This includes minors (under 21) and all foreigners who meet the minimum earnings requirement. Parents or guardians are responsible for filing a minor's tax return and for its payment.

Exemptions are those portions of gross income specifically excluded by law from tax. These include: (1) personal exemption of $600, and additional exemption of $600 each for those 65 years of age or over before the close of the taxable year, and for those who are blind at the close of the year, and the same exemption for a spouse in a joint return; (2) a $600 exemption for a spouse with the additional allowances for age and blindness, provided the taxpayer makes a separate return and the spouse does not have any gross income; and (3) an allowance of $600 for each closely related dependent who is a United States citizen or a resident of the United States, Canada, or Mexico classified as receiving more than half his support from the taxpayer but not having $500 or more of gross income.

In addition, the principal items of income exempt from tax are: (1) proceeds of a life insurance policy which has been paid on the decease of the insured, and the *cost* of endowment policies; (2) the value of gifts, bequests, or inheritances (this value is not taxable to the recipient, unless the items involve receipt of income at intervals—for example, if items of a gift of real estate specify that the recipient will get the income from the gift at intervals, such income is taxable); (3) certain interest income, including interest on any obligation of a political subdivision of the United States, interest on United States Government obligations issued before March 1, 1941, to the extent provided in the particular obligations; (4) sickness and injury benefits, as a general rule; (5) war veteran pensions, mustering-out pay, and other armed forces benefits, except retirement pay; (6) social security benefits; (7) railroad retirement pensions; and (8) annuities and pensions to the extent of the "cost" of the annuity, the cost representing the total of the actual payments made for the annuity or pension.

Income that must be reported for tax purposes always includes: (1)

salaries and wages; (2) competitive prizes and awards; (3) bonuses and tips; (4) alimony and separate maintenance payments; (5) rents and royalties; (6) interest on United States savings bonds, series A to G; (7) regular dividends and interest on investments and tax refunds; (8) gambling winnings; (9) real estate profits; (10) rewards; and (11) income in forms other than money (meals, lodging, capital stock, etc.).

Capital gains and losses refer to results of the sale or exchange of stocks, bonds, and personal residence or other personal property; they must be reported in accordance with a special set of income tax rules. The period of time the capital asset is held is important in determining whether a profit or loss is long-term or short-term. If the asset is held for six months or less, the gain or loss on the disposal of the asset is short-term; an asset held longer than six months may only incur a long-term gain or loss.

In the income tax return, the short-term gain must be reported in full; and full credit is also given for short-term losses within certain limitations. However, only one-half of long-term gains or losses are taken into account. Any net balance of loss from the combination of such foregoing profits and losses is deductible from taxable income to the extent of such income or $1,000, whichever is smaller. Any excess loss may be carried over to be applied against income to the same extent for five succeeding years. An important exception to the above treatment of losses is that any loss on a personal residence or other property not purchased for profit purposes is not allowed, even though a profit on such a transaction is taxable, either as a long-term or short-term gain.

There are other items of expense or loss which are properly deductible from gross income before the income tax is figured. The basic principle governing deductions is that the taxpayer must be able to point to some specific provision of law or regulations which authorizes that deduction, and that he must be able to prove he is entitled to such deduction.

In the broad category of deductions, not necessarily applicable to everybody, are business and professional expenses; bad debts which become worthless in the tax year and will remain worthless; depreciation; charitable and other similar contributions (up to 15 per cent of the adjusted gross income); casualty and burglary losses and medical expenses of over 5 per cent of adjusted gross income, not reimbursed by insurance; interest expense; state income and other state taxes, except estate and gift taxes; union initiation fees and dues.

A recent feature of the Federal Revenue Act (since 1948) allows married taxpayers who file joint returns to "split" their income in computing their income tax; this possibility generally, but not always, results in a lower income tax than under the older methods. Thus, a husband with $10,000 gross income, whose wife has $2,000 income, would pay, under the old separate tax return, a combined tax of as much as $2,060, or over 17 per cent on both incomes.

However, if a joint return is filed, the husband-wife taxpayers, by dividing their combined income, figure their tax at a lower scale of rates. The tax on half their income would be no more than $925; this tax is then multiplied by two, to arrive at the joint return tax of $1,850, or 15½ per cent of the gross income.

Penalties for neglect or fraud in connection with income tax returns vary. Understatement of the amount of the tax through negligence or disregard of rules is penalized five per cent of the total tax due. The penalty for delay without reasonable cause is five per cent to 25 per cent of the tax. The penalty for understatement with fraudulent intent to evade tax, or wilful failure to pay a tax or file a return, is up to 50 per cent of the tax due plus costs; in addition a prison sentence may be imposed. For aiding in a false return the same penalty is imposed. An interest penalty of one per cent a month is charged when a tax is due and not paid, except on the estate of an incompetent, deceased, or bankrupt person, in which case the interest is six per cent a year.

Tax returns may be inspected by the Government only under orders issued by the President of the United States. The returns of an individual may be inspected by that individual, his attorney, or, if he is deceased, his executor, heirs, or next of kin. The joint return of a husband and wife may be inspected by either. Corporate returns may be inspected by the president, vice president, secretary, or treasurer of the company, or by bona fide stockholders who own one per cent or more of the outstanding stock. Certain Congressional committees may inspect income tax returns, and copies of returns may be furnished in court cases in which the United States is an interested party or to a United States grand jury. The unofficial disclosure of information is severely penalized.

CORPORATIONS

A corporation is created pursuant to state law and has a legal entity entirely separate and distinct from the individuals who compose it, with the capacity of continuous existence, notwithstanding changes in its membership. It has the right to buy, hold, and convey property, make contracts, sue and be sued, and to exercise such other powers and privileges as are conferred on it by law. The stockholders are not liable for corporate debts, except under certain circumstances and only by reason of specific statutory provision.

A corporation should be organized by a lawyer familiar with the law of the state in which the corporation is to function.

A corporation can be organized only for legal purposes, which must be set forth in the certificate of incorporation. This corporate charter is in essence a contract between the state and the corporation. Unless there is statutory right or unless such power is specified in the certificate, the state has no power to withdraw or change the certificate after acceptance. The certificate is filed in a state office upon payment of a statutory fee.

Every corporation must have a name; this name is set forth in the certificate of incorporation. The name must not conflict with that of another corporation, nor be so similar to it that the new name will deceive the public and result in confusion or unfair competition; and no corporation can appropriate to its exclusive use geographical or generic terms.

The business policies of the corporation are controlled by the directors, who are elected by the stockholders.

The internal affairs of a corporation are regulated and defined in its bylaws. These bylaws are binding upon the directors, officers, and stockholders. They are adopted by the stockholders or board of directors. No bylaw can conflict with or be contrary to what is set forth in the certificate nor be in violation of any statute.

The *capital stock* of a corporation is the sum fixed by the certificate as the amount with which the corporation is to do business. Capital is the fund contributed by the stockholders to the corporation.

The power of a corporation to issue stock depends on its certificate and the state laws under which it is organized. A *share* of capital stock is the interest that a stockholder has in the corporation. The shares of stock are represented by a certificate, which he may transfer by sale or otherwise to another person. At times, such right is restricted by an agreement between stockholders, called stockholders' agreement.

Kinds of Stock

Common stock entitles the owner thereof to pro rata dividends without any priority or preference over any other shareholder but equally with all other stockholders, except preferred stockholders. A common stockholder is an owner of the corporate business in the proportion that his stock bears to the entire stock; he is ordinarily entitled to participate in the management, profits, and assets of the corporation.

Preferred stock entitles the owner to dividends in priority to the holders of common stock. Sometimes the owners of such stock are preferred as to assets; when the corporation is dissolved they receive their share of the assets before the holders of common stock.

Dividends are payable only out of profits, never out of capital. No corporation may guarantee that it will pay dividends, but a corporation may guarantee that the stockholders of another corporation will receive dividends.

Dividends on preferred stock may be *cumulative* or *noncumulative*. A cumulative dividend carries over from year to year; if the corporation has no profits and declares no dividend in any one year the deficit is paid as soon thereafter as dividends are earned and declared. Holders of common stock receive no dividends until all cumulative dividends are paid. Noncumulative dividends do not carry over from year to year; if not paid in any year they are never thereafter payable. Payment of dividends on preferred stock may be assured by means of a sinking fund.

Preferred stockholders usually have no right to vote except on certain questions, for instance, as to whether more preferred stock shall be issued. Nonvoting stock may be issued; but a stockholder with the right to vote his stock may not thereafter be deprived of such right.

There are several types of preferred stock: (1) nonparticipating preferred stock, which entitles the owner to receive a certain dividend, usually six per cent, then nothing more; (2) simple participating preferred stock, which entitles the owner to receive the specified dividend, after which assignment what is left is shared equally by the holders of common stock; (3) participating immediately preferred stock, which entitles the owner to receive the specified dividend, the balance to be shared immediately by owners of the common stock; (4) special participating stock, which may be arranged according to any scheme which the directors of the corporation may devise, with the stipulation that the arrangement must be provided for in the certificate of incorporation.

Redeemable stock is stock which a corporation has the right to buy back from its holders upon the terms fixed in the certificate of incorporation. The right to do so is optional with the corporation.

Convertible stock is stock of one class which may be exchanged for stock of another class, usually preferred stock which may be exchanged for common stock. The right to do so is optional with the stockholder.

Holding Companies

A holding company is a company formed to own and control the stock of other corporations. The holding company's income is derived from the interest or dividends upon the stock and securities which it holds of the other corporations. Such companies are legal as long as they do not operate in restraint of trade or in violation of the antitrust laws. Such corporations engaged in interstate commerce are regulated by Federal statutes.

Subsidiary Companies

A subsidiary company is a company whose entire or whose controlling stock is owned by another corporation, called the parent corporation.

PARTNERSHIP

The statutory law of partnerships varies in the different states. In essence, a partnership is a legal relation arising from contract beween two or more persons who agree to pool their money and labor to engage in a lawful business or trade and share profits and losses equally or in specified proportions.

All property brought into the partnership or acquired by partnership funds becomes partnership property. Land may be acquired in the partnership name, and can be sold only in the partnership name.

A *secret partner* actually shares the profits and losses of the business, but the fact that he does is not generally known by outsiders. A *dormant partner* is one who takes no active part in the business and whose association with it is also unknown. Such a partner is liable for contracts made by the active and known partners in the partnership name, as well as for implied contracts of the firm. A *nominal partner* is one who is designated a partner, but who in fact is not a partner. He is, however, liable for partnership debts.

Every partner is an agent of the partnership for all business purposes. The acts of each partner bind the partnership as well as all the other partners, unless the partner so acting has no authority to act for the partnership in the particular matter, and the person with whom he is dealing knows that he has no such authority. An act by the partner which is not apparently for the partnership business will not bind the partnership unless it is authorized by the other partners. All partners are required to act in (1) assigning the partnership property for the benefit of creditors; (2) disposing of the good will of the business, or doing anything which would make it impossible to carry on the ordinary business of the partnership; (3) confessing a judgment or submitting a partnership claim to arbitration. No act of any partner in contravention of a restriction on his authority will bind the partnership to persons who have knowledge of the restriction.

Whereas the liability of a stockholder in a corporation is limited to the extent of his interest in the corporation as represented by the amount of his stock, the *liability of a partner* is not limited to the extent of his investment, except in those states which provide for the formation of limited partnerships or joint stock companies.

Generally, partners are *fiduciaries* to each other and must act equitably; no partner may obtain any personal interest adverse to his partners' interest or that of the partnership. A partner may be entitled to an accounting whenever he is wrongfully excluded from the partnership or whenever circumstances render it just and reasonable.

A partnership is *dissolved* by the expiration of the time fixed in the agreement for its duration, or by the completion of the purpose for which it was formed, or by the will of all partners, either before or after the time fixed for its duration; and any partner can bring about a dissolution if no term has been fixed nor particular purpose has been specified in their agreement. It may also be dissolved by operation of law, for instance, if any event occurs which makes the enterprise unlawful or if one or more partners are inducted into military service. The court can also decree dissolution if any partner becomes incapable of performing his partnership duties or has been judicially declared an incompetent. There are many other statutory causes for dissolution by the court; these vary in the different states.

Death dissolves a partnership; and the heirs do not succeed to membership in the firm unless it was expressly so provided in the agreement.

Regardless of the cause of the dissolution, the partnership continues to function until all partnership affairs are completely wound up. Dissolution does not put an end to partnership contracts nor change the liability of partners to third persons.

In the absence of an express agreement between the partners and a partnership creditor, a retiring partner continues to remain liable for partnership contracts made before dissolution. The person to whom the retiring partner transfers his interest in the partnership does not thereby become a member of the firm unless the other partners consent thereto. A retiring partner should give public notice of his retirement, and personal notice to all those with whom he personally dealt on behalf of the firm.

The liability of a partner in a limited partnership is limited to his capital investment. Such partnerships must be drawn up in strict accord with the statutory law of the state in which they are formed.

A *joint stock association* has some of the attributes of a corporation as well as of a partnership; but it is based on a written agreement between the parties and not on a state charter.

Article of Co-Partnership[1]

Article of agreement, made the ———— day of ———— nineteen hundred and ———— between JOHN DOE, of No. ———— ———— Street, (city), (state) and RICHARD ROE of No. ———— ———— Street, (city), (state), as follows: The said parties above named have agreed to become co-partners in business, to sell peanuts and by these presents do agree to be co-partners together under and by the name or firm of DOE AND ROE in the buying, selling and vending all sorts of goods, wares and merchandise to the said business belonging, and to occupy the suite of offices (here describe the firm

---

[1]This is only a suggested form. The reader is advised to obtain a form, valid in his state, from a lawyer or legal stationer for use in specific transactions.

property), their co-partnership to commence on the ———— day of ————, 19—, and to continue for the term of ———— years, that is to say until the ———— day of ————, 19—, and to that end and purpose the said JOHN DOE agrees to deposit in the ———— bank ———— dollars in the firm name by the ———— day of ———— 19—, and the said RICHARD ROE agrees to deposit in the ———— bank, ———— dollars in the firm name by the ———— day of ———— 19— (or any property that each is to contribute), to be used and employed in common between them for the support and management of the said business, to their mutual benefit and advantage.

And it is agreed by and between the parties to these presents, that at all times during the continuance of their co-partnership, they and each of them will give their attendance, and do their and each of their best endeavors, and to the utmost of their skill and power, exert themselves for their joint interest, profit, benefit and advantage, and truly employ, buy, sell, and merchandise with their joint stock, and the increase thereof, in the business aforesaid.

And also, that they shall and will at all times during the said co-partnership, bear, pay, and discharge equally between them, all rents, and other expenses that may be required for the support and management of the said business; and that all gains, profit and increase that shall come, grow or arise from or by means of their said business, shall be divided between them, in the following proportions:— to the said JOHN DOE—50%; to the said RICHARD ROE—50%, and all loss that shall happen to their joint business by ill commodities, bad debts or otherwise, shall be borne and paid between them.

And it is agreed by and between the said parties, that there shall be had and kept at all times during the continuance of their co-partnership, perfect, just, and true books of account, wherein each of the said co-partners shall enter and set down, as well all money by them or either of them received, paid, laid out and expended in and about the said business, as also all goods, wares, commodities and merchandise, by them or either of them bought or sold, by reason or on account of the said business, and all other matters and things whatsoever, to the said business and the management thereof in anywise belonging; which said books shall be used in common between the said co-partners, so that either of them may have access thereto, without any interruption or hindrance of the other.

And also, the said co-partners, once in (here insert stated periods when accounts shall be made) or oftener if necessary, shall make, yield and render, each to the other, a true, just and perfect inventory and account of all profits and increase by them, or either of them made, and all losses by them, or either of them, sustained; and also all payments, receipts, disbursements and all other things by them made, received, disbursed, acted, done, or suffered in this said co-partnership and business; and the same account so made shall and will clear, adjust, pay and deliver, each to the other, at the time their just share of the profits so made as aforesaid.

And the said parties hereby mutually covenant and agree, to and with each other, that during the continuance of the said co-partnership, neither of them shall nor will endorse any note, or otherwise become surety for any person or persons whomsoever, without the consent of the other of the said co-partners. And at the end or other sooner termination of their co-partnership the said co-partners, each to the other, shall and will make a true, just and final account of all things relating to their said business, and in all things truly adjust the same; and all and every the stock and the stocks, as well as the gains and increase thereof, which shall appear to be remaining, either in money, goods, wares, fixtures, debts or otherwise, shall be divided between them.

In witness whereof the parties have on the day first above written, affixed their hands and seals.

Sealed and delivered in the presence of:

John Doe (seal)

Richard Roe (seal)

(Acknowledgment)

Dissolution of Partnership[1]

This agreement made the ——— day of ——— one thousand nine hundred ———
between JOHN DOE, of No. ——— ——— Street, (city), (state) party of the first
part and RICHARD ROE, of No. ——— ——— Street, (city), (state) party of the
second part,

Witnesseth: whereas the parties hereto have formed a co-partnership for the purpose of selling peanuts under the firm name of DOE AND ROE and have maintained and
continued said partnership up to the present time, and

Whereas the parties hereto have agreed that the partnership existing between them
should be dissolved and at an end, and

Whereas an accounting of the assets and liabilities of the said firm has been duly
had by the parties hereto, for the purpose of ascertaining the condition of said co-
partnership business, and on said accounting it was found that a true statement of the
conditions and of the affairs of such co-partnership are as set forth in the schedule of
assets and liabilities hereto annexed, and made part hereof, and

Whereas the parties hereto have agreed to distribute said assets in the following
manner: To JOHN DOE—50% of all the assets, to RICHARD ROE—50% of all the assets.

Now in consideration of the sum of One Dollar each to the other in hand paid, the
receipt whereof is hereby acknowledged, and in consideration of the foregoing premises
the parties hereto agree to terminate and dissolve said co-partnership and each of the
parties hereto hereby severally releases the other of and from any and all manner of
obligations growing out of the said partnership, and it is further

Agreed that the party of the first part, in consideration of the sum of ——— dollars
paid to him by the party of the second part the receipt whereof is hereby acknowledged,
has transferred, assigned and set over and by these presents does assign, transfer and
set over unto said party of the second part, his executors, administrators and assigns,
all right, title, interest and share of, in and into the assets and property of every kind,
nature and description of said partnership, together with the good will of the business
thereof, and it is further

Agreed that none of said partners has signed or endorsed the firm name to any commercial paper, nor other evidence of debt, nor incurred any obligation nor liability,
contingent or actual, in behalf of said co-partnership, except as mentioned or included
in the accounting herein set forth, and it is further

Agreed by the parties hereto that the party of the first part shall and will pay and
discharge all the firm obligations and liabilities referred to and mentioned in the
accounting hereinbefore set forth, without contribution by the party of the second part
thereto; and that the said party of the first part does hereby agree to save, indemnify
and keep harmless the said party of the second part of and from any and all such firm
obligations and liabilities and of and from all damage, cost, charge and expense occurring through the default or failure of the party of the first part to promptly and fully
pay and discharge the same.

In witness thereof, the parties hereto have hereunto set their hands and seals, the
day and year first above written.
Witness:

(Signed)   *John Doe*   (seal)
Richard Roe   (seal)

(Acknowledgment)

SCHEDULE

ASSETS

Cash on hand and in bank	$....................
Outstanding accounts as per schedule hereunto annexed	....
Stock on hand	....
Fixtures, machinery and fittings	....
Miscellaneous property as per schedule annexed	....
Total assets	$....................

[1]This is only a suggested form. The reader is advised to obtain a form, valid in his state,
from a lawyer or legal stationer for use in specific transactions.

For merchandise as per annexed schedule .... $......................
Money loaned as per annexed schedule ....
Notes or other obligations as per annexed schedule ....
Miscellaneous liabilities as per schedule annexed ....
Total liabilities $.....................

STOCK EXCHANGES

A stock exchange is a place where securities are bought and sold. The three leading stock exchanges in the world are the London Stock Exchange, the Paris Bourse, and the New York Stock Exchange. The largest in the United States is the New York Stock Exchange, though there are others of considerable importance, among which the New York Curb Exchange may especially be mentioned. New issues and other issues which, for one reason or another, are either not willing or not able to meet the requirements of the New York Stock Exchange may still be listed on the New York Curb or some other exchange.

The investing public is now protected by the Securities and Exchange Commission (SEC) which was established in 1934 to administer the Securities Act of 1933 and the Securities Exchange Act of 1934. Under the provisions of these two Acts issuers of securities to be sold in interstate commerce or through the mails are required to file with the Commission and furnish to prospective buyers all basic information concerning the securities offered. Neither the Commission nor the Exchange passes on the soundness of the securities; its aim is to give the public the truth. Penalties are imposed for fraudulent or misleading statements. On the flotation of foreign securities the domestic fiscal agent of the issuer is held responsible. The Commission is empowered in various ways to prevent the manipulation of stocks and unreasonable speculation on the exchanges.

The 1,375 members of the New York Stock Exchange may be roughly divided into five different groups; commission house brokers, floor brokers, specialists, odd-lot dealers, traders. Commission brokers represent, on the trading floor, firms which primarily do business with the public. Floor brokers execute orders for other brokers. Specialists, as the name implies, undertake to make markets in securities, acting as dealers, besides executing orders entrusted to them for execution in such securities. Odd-lot dealers accommodate buy-and-sell orders for less than the customary 100-share round lot. Traders deal primarily for their own account. The brokers' minimum commissions are fixed by the rules of the exchange.

All orders given to brokers are considered canceled at the end of the day upon which they were entered, unless express provisions are made to the contrary. Orders may be given to buy or sell at the market price or at a specified price. In buying stock the broker is required to buy, if possible, at a lower price than the one specified. In selling stock he must sell either at the specified price or a higher one. One of the most common specified-price orders is the stop-loss order. This is used when a customer buys on

ANNUAL RATE OF RETURN ON DIVIDEND-PAYING STOCKS AT VARIOUS PRICES[1]

Based on Par Value of $100

Price	1%	2%	2½%	3%	3¼%	3½%	3¾%	4%	4¼%	4½%	4¾%
20	5.00	10.00	12.50	15.00	16.25	17.50	18.75	20.00	21.25	22.50	23.75
21	4.76	9.52	11.90	14.28	15.47	16.66	17.85	19.04	20.23	21.42	22.61
22	4.54	9.08	11.35	13.62	14.75	15.89	17.02	18.16	19.29	20.43	21.56
23	4.34	8.68	10.85	13.02	14.10	15.19	16.27	17.36	18.44	19.53	20.61
24	4.16	8.32	10.40	12.48	13.52	14.56	15.60	16.64	17.70	18.72	19.76
25	4.00	8.00	10.00	12.00	13.00	14.00	15.00	16.00	17.00	18.00	19.00
27½	3.64	7.27	9.09	10.91	11.82	12.73	13.64	14.55	15.46	16.37	17.28
30	3.33	6.67	8.33	10.00	10.83	11.66	12.49	13.33	14.16	14.99	15.82
32½	3.08	6.15	7.69	9.23	10.00	10.77	11.54	12.31	13.08	13.85	14.62
35	2.86	5.71	7.14	8.57	9.28	10.00	10.71	11.43	12.14	12.86	13.57
37½	2.67	5.33	6.66	8.00	8.67	9.33	10.00	10.67	11.34	12.00	12.67
40	2.50	5.00	6.25	7.50	8.12	8.75	9.37	10.00	10.62	11.25	11.87
42½	2.35	4.71	5.88	7.06	7.65	8.23	8.82	9.41	10.00	10.58	11.17
45	2.22	4.44	5.55	6.67	7.22	7.78	8.33	8.89	9.44	10.00	10.55
47½	2.11	4.21	5.26	6.32	6.85	7.37	7.90	8.42	8.95	9.47	10.00
50	2.00	4.00	5.00	6.00	6.50	7.00	7.50	8.00	8.50	9.00	9.50
52½	1.90	3.81	4.76	5.71	6.18	.6.66	7.13	7.62	8.09	8.57	9.04
55	1.82	3.64	4.55	5.45	5.90	6.36	6.81	7.27	7.72	8.18	8.63
57½	1.74	3.48	4.35	5.22	5.65	6.09	6.52	6.96	7.39	7.83	8.26
60	1.67	3.33	4.16	5.00	5.42	5.83	6.25	6.67	7.09	7.50	7.92
62½	1.60	3.20	4.00	4.80	5.20	5.60	6.00	6.40	6.80	7.20	7.60
65	1.54	3.08	3.85	4.62	5.00	5.39	5.77	6.15	6.53	6.92	7.30
67½	1.48	2.96	3.70	4.44	4.81	5.18	5.55	5.93	6.30	6.67	7.04
70	1.43	2.86	3.57	4.29	4.65	5.00	5.36	5.71	6.07	6.42	6.78
72½	1.38	2.76	3.45	4.14	4.48	4.83	5.17	5.52	5.85	6.21	6.55
75	1.33	2.67	3.33	4.00	4.33	4.66	4.99	5 33	5.66	5.99	6.32
77½	1.29	2.58	3.22	3.87	4.19	4.51	4.83	5.16	5.48	5.80	6.12
80	1.25	2.50	3.12	3.75	4.06	4.37	4.68	5.00	5.31	5.62	5.93
82½	1.21	2.42	3.02	3.64	3.94	4.24	4.54	4.85	5.15	5.45	5.75
85	1.18	2.35	2.94	3.53	3.82	4.12	4.41	4.71	5.00	5.30	5.59
87½	1.14	2.29	2.86	3.43	3.71	4.00	4.28	4.57	4.85	5.14	5.42
90	1.11	2 22	2.77	3.33	3.61	3.88	4.16	4.44	4.72	4.99	5.27
92½	1.08	2.16	2.70	3.24	3.51	3.78	4.05	4.32	4.59	4.86	5.13
95	1.05	2.11	2.63	3.16	3.42	3.68	3.94	4.21	4.47	4.73	4.99
97½	1.03	2.05	2.56	3.08	3.34	3.59	3.85	4.10	4.36	4.61	4.87
100	1.00	2.00	2.50	3.00	3.25	3.50	3.75	4.00	4.25	4.50	4.75
105	.95	1.90	2.37	2.86	3.10	3.33	3.57	3.81	4.05	4.28	4.52
110	.91	1.82	2.27	2.73	2.96	3.18	3.41	3.64	3.87	4.09	4.32
115	.87	1.74	2.17	2.61	2.83	3.04	3.26	3.48	3.70	3.91	4.13
120	.83	1.67	2.08	2.50	2.71	2.91	3.12	3.33	3.54	3.74	3.95
125	.80	1.60	2.00	2.40	2.60	2.80	3.00	3.20	3.40	3.60	3.80
130	.77	1.54	1.92	2 31	2.50	2.69	2.88	3.08	3.27	3.46	3.65
135	.74	1.48	1.85	2.22	2.40	2.59	2.77	2.96	3.14	3.33	3.51
140	.71	1.43	1.78	2.14	2.32	2.49	2.67	2.86	3.04	3.21	3.39
145	.69	1.38	1.72	2.07	2.24	2.41	2.58	2.76	2.93	3.10	3.27
150	.67	1.33	1.66	2.00	2.17	2.33	2.50	2.67	2.84	3.00	3.17
155	.65	1.29	1.61	1.94	2.10	2.26	2.42	2.58	2.74	2.90	3.06
160	.63	1.25	1.56	1.87	2.03	2.18	2.34	2.50	2.66	2.81	2.97
165	.61	1.21	1.51	1.82	1.97	2.12	2.27	2.42	2.57	2.72	2.87
170	.59	1.18	1.47	1.76	1.91	2.05	2.20	2.35	2.50	2.64	2.79
175	.57	1.14	1.42	1.71	1.85	1.99	2.13	2.29	2.43	2.57	2.71
180	.56	1.11	1.39	1.67	1.81	1.95	2.09	2.22	2.36	2.50	2.64
185	.54	1.08	1.35	1.62	1.75	1.89	2.02	2.16	2.29	2.43	2.56
190	.53	1.05	1.31	1.58	1.71	1.84	1.97	2.11	2.24	2.37	2.50
195	.51	1.03	1.28	1.54	1.67	1.79	1.92	2.05	2.18	2.30	2.43
200	.50	1.00	1.25	1.50	1.62	1.75	1.87	2.00	2.12	2.25	2.37
210	.48	.95	1.19	1.43	1.55	1.67	1.79	1.90	2.02	2.14	2.26
220	.45	.91	1.13	1.36	1.47	1.58	1.69	1.82	1.93	2.04	2.15
230	.43	.87	1.08	1.30	1.41	1.51	1.63	1.74	1.85	1.95	2.07
240	.41	.83	1.03	1.25	1.35	1.45	1.55	1.67	1.77	1.87	1.97
250	.40	.80	1.00	1.20	1.30	1.40	1.50	1.60	1.70	1.80	1.90
260	.38	.77	.96	1.15	1.24	1.34	1.43	1.54	1.63	1.73	1.82
270	.37	.74	.92	1.11	1.20	1.29	1.38	1.48	1.57	1.66	1.75
280	.36	.71	.89	1.07	1.16	1.25	1.34	1.43	1.52	1.61	1.70
290	.34	.69	.86	1.03	1.11	1.20	1.28	1.38	1.46	1.55	1.63
300	.33	.67	.83	1.00	1.08	1.16	1.24	1.33	1.41	1.49	1.53

[1]By courteous permission of the Lefax Corporation, Philadelphia.

Price	5%	5¼%	5½%	5¾%	6%	6½%	7%	8%	9%	10%	12%
20	25.00	26.25	27.50	28.75	30.00	32.50	35.00	40.00	45.00	50.00	60.00
21	23.80	24.99	26.18	27.37	28.56	31.94	33.32	38.08	42.84	47.60	57.12
22	22.70	23.83	24.97	26.10	27.24	29.51	31.78	36.32	40.86	45.40	54.48
23	21.70	22.78	23.87	24.95	26.04	28.21	30.38	34.72	39.06	43.40	52.08
24	20.80	21.84	22.88	23.92	24.96	27.04	29.12	33.28	37.44	41.60	49.92
25	20.00	21.00	22.00	23.00	24.00	26.00	28.00	32.00	36.00	40.00	48.04
27½	18.18	19.09	20.00	20.91	21.82	23.64	25.45	29.09	32.73	36.36	43.60
30	16.67	17.50	18.33	19.16	20.00	21.66	23.33	26.67	30.00	33.33	40.00
32½	15.38	16.15	16.92	17.69	18.46	20.00	21.54	24.62	27.69	30.77	36.92
35	14.29	15.00	15.72	16.43	17.14	18.57	20.00	22.86	25.71	28.57	34.29
37½	13.33	14.00	14.66	15.33	16.00	17.33	18.67	21.33	24.00	26.67	32.00
40	12.50	13.12	13.75	14.37	15.00	16.25	17.50	20.00	22.50	25.00	30.00
42½	11.76	12.35	12.93	13.52	14.12	15.29	16.47	18.82	21.18	23.53	28.23
45	11.11	11.66	12.22	12.77	13.33	14.44	15.56	17.78	20.00	22.22	26.67
47½	10.53	11.06	11.58	12.11	12.63	13.68	14.74	16.84	18.95	21.05	25.26
50	10.00	10.50	11.00	11.50	12.00	13.00	14.00	16.00	18.00	20.00	24.00
52½	9.52	9.99	10.47	10.97	11.43	12.38	13.33	15.24	17.14	19.05	22.86
55	9.09	9.54	10.00	10.45	10.91	11.82	12.73	14.55	16.36	18.18	21.82
57½	8.70	9.13	9.57	10.00	10.43	11.30	12.17	13.91	15.65	17.39	20.87
60	8.33	8.75	9.16	9.58	10.00	10.83	11.67	13.33	15.00	16.67	20.00
62½	8.00	8.40	8.80	9.20	9.60	10.40	11.20	12.80	14.40	16.00	19.20
65	7.69	8.07	8.46	8.84	9.23	10.00	10.77	12.31	13.85	15.38	18.46
67½	7.41	7.78	8.15	8.52	8.89	9.63	10.37	11.85	13.33	14.81	17.78
70	7.14	7.50	7.85	8.21	8.57	9.23	10.00	11.43	12.86	14.29	17.14
72½	6.90	7.24	7.59	7.93	8.28	8.97	9.66	11.03	12.41	13.79	16.55
75	6.67	7.00	7.33	7.66	8.00	8.66	9.33	10.67	12.00	13.33	16.00
77½	6.45	6.77	7.09	7.41	7.74	8.38	9.03	10.32	11.61	12.90	15.48
80	6.25	6.56	6.87	7.18	7.50	8.12	8.75	10.00	11.25	12.50	15.00
82½	6.06	6.36	6.66	6.96	7.27	7.87	8.48	9.70	10.91	12.12	14.55
85	5.88	6.17	6.47	6.76	7.06	7.65	8.24	9.41	10.59	11.76	14.12
87½	5.76	6.04	6.33	6.61	6.86	7.43	8.00	9.14	10.29	11.43	13.71
90	5.51	5.79	6.06	6.34	6.67	7.12	7.78	8.89	10.00	11.11	13.33
92½	5.41	5.68	5.95	6.25	6.49	7.03	7.57	8.65	9.73	10.81	12.97
95	5.26	5.52	5.78	6.04	6.32	6.84	7.37	8.42	9.47	10.53	12.63
97½	5.13	5.39	5.64	5.90	6.15	6.66	7.18	8.21	9.23	10.26	12.31
100	5.00	5.25	5.50	5.75	6.00	6.50	7.00	8.00	9.00	10.00	12.00
105	4.76	5.00	5.23	5.47	5.71	6.18	6.67	7.62	8.57	9.52	11.43
110	4.55	4.78	5.00	5.23	5.45	5.90	6.36	7.27	8.18	9.09	10.91
115	4.35	4.57	4.78	5.00	5.22	5.65	6.09	6.96	7.83	8.70	10.43
120	4.17	4.38	4.58	4.79	5.00	5.41	5.83	6.67	7.50	8.33	10.00
125	4.00	4.20	4.40	4.60	4.80	5.20	5.60	6.40	7.20	8.00	9.60
130	3.85	4.04	4.23	4.42	4.62	5.00	5.38	6.15	6.92	7.69	9.23
135	3.70	3.88	4.07	4.25	4.44	4.81	5.19	5.93	6.67	7.41	8.89
140	3.57	3.75	3.92	4.10	4.29	4.64	5.00	5.71	6.43	7.14	8.57
145	3.45	3.62	3.79	3.96	4.14	4.48	4.83	5.52	6.21	6.90	8.28
150	3.33	3.50	3.66	3.83	4.00	4.33	4.67	5.33	6.00	6.67	8.00
155	3.23	3.39	3.55	3.71	3.87	4.19	4.52	5.16	5.81	6.45	7.74
160	3.12	3.28	3.43	3.59	3.75	4.06	4.38	5.00	5.63	6.25	7.50
165	3.03	3.18	3.33	3.48	3.64	3.94	4.24	4.85	5.45	6.06	7.27
170	2.94	3.09	3.23	3.38	3.53	3.82	4.12	4.71	5.29	5.88	7.06
175	2.86	3.00	3.14	3.28	3.34	3.71	4.00	4.57	5.14	5.71	6.86
180	2.78	2.92	3.06	3.20	3.33	3.61	3.89	4.44	5.00	5.56	6.67
185	2.70	2.83	2.97	3.10	3.24	3.51	3.78	4.32	4.86	5.41	6.49
190	2.63	2.76	2.89	3.02	3.16	3.42	3.68	4.21	4.74	5.26	6.32
195	2.56	2.69	2.81	2.94	3.08	3.33	3.59	4.10	4.62	5.13	6.15
200	2.50	2.62	2.75	2.87	3.00	3.25	3.50	4.00	4.50	5.00	6.00
210	2.38	2.50	2.62	2.74	2.86	3.10	3.33	3.81	4.29	4.76	5.71
220	2.27	2.38	2.49	2.60	2.73	2.95	3.18	3.64	4.09	4.55	5.45
230	2.17	2.28	2.38	2.50	2.61	2.82	3.04	3.48	3.91	4.35	5.22
240	2.08	2.18	2.28	2.38	2.50	2.70	2.92	3.33	3.75	4.17	5.00
250	2.00	2.10	2.20	2.30	2.40	2.60	2.80	3.20	3.60	4.00	4.80
260	1.92	2.01	2.11	2.20	2.31	2.50	2.69	3.08	3.46	3.85	4.62
270	1.85	1.94	2.03	2.12	2.22	2.40	2.59	2.96	3.33	3.70	4.44
280	1.79	1.88	1.97	2.06	2.14	2.32	2.50	2.86	3.21	3.57	4.29
290	1.72	1.80	1.89	1.97	2.07	2.24	2.41	2.76	3.10	3.45	4.14
300	1.67	1.75	1.83	1.91	2.00	2.16	2.33	2.67	3.00	3.33	4.00

Example.—A $100 par value stock paying 1 per cent and purchased at $20 gives a return of 5 per cent. Similarly, a $100 par value stock paying 3½ per cent purchased at $70 gives a return of 5 per cent. For par values less or greater than $100, multiply the "rate of return" figures by $\frac{P}{100}$, where P is the par value.

margin. He names a certain price below the market price at which he wishes his broker to sell, should the market value of the security decline, so as to "stop" his losses. Many orders are given to brokers with instructions that they are "good till canceled." These are commonly known as G. T. C. orders. Before placing an order, the prospective buyer or seller can ascertain the approximate price of a stock by asking his broker for quotations. This is the current highest bid to buy, and lowest offer to sell, the stock in question.

Prices of stocks are designated in various ways according to the kinds of transactions that are taking place.

The *bid price* is the price offered by a prospective purchaser of stock. The *asked price* is the price asked by the seller of a stock.

The *actual price* is the price at which the transaction is finally concluded.

The *market price* is the price at which a security is selling at a specified time. If no transactions are taking place at the time, the bid and ask prices are given.

The *nominal price* is an estimated price when there are no bid and ask prices.

A *firm price* is one which is quoted and held to for a certain period. It is generally used between brokers when stocks are not active.

The *exhaust price* is the price at which the holder's margin will be exhausted.

Buying on margin is buying partly on credit. The buyer advances a percentage of the money required for the entire number of stocks bought, the percentage varying with different stocks and with different brokers. The following estimate has been made, but the variations between the amounts listed here and actual conditions may be very wide indeed:

The initial maximum credit value of a registered security for margin purposes, as prescribed by the Federal Reserve System pursuant to the Securities Exchange Act (1947), is 50 per cent of its current market value. The general maintenance margin, prescribed by the New York Stock Exchange, is 25 per cent of the security's market value.

The holder may be called upon to put up more margin and more and more and more, if the value of the stock decreases. It is through marginal trading that big sums of money are made in the market, but big sums are lost in the same way. Margin buying is no game for a man who has not money enough to cover his account if there is a sudden drop in market prices.

Selling short is a term used to describe the operation of selling securities one does not own. The seller is betting that the price will go down. He asks his broker to sell short, at, say, 90, and cover at 85. The broker sells the stock and then, since the exchange rules demand delivery the third full business day following the date of the transaction, borrows the stock to make the delivery. The stock is loaned in return for payment of the market price. This is returned, with interest, if there is interest, or premium, when the broker buys the stock, for delivery to the lender, at 85. The seller has made the difference between 90 and 85 minus broker's commission, transfer taxes, and interest fees. Selling short is as a rule confined to professional operators of the market and should have little practical interest for readers of this book.

Much of the trading in the stock exchange is done on borrowed money. There are two kinds of loans, *time loans* and *call loans*. The first is for a definite period, say for 60 days or a year. The rate of interest is agreed upon and does not change, although if the value of the securities placed for collateral falls below the required margin, more securities or money may be demanded. The second, or call, loan, is not for a stated time, but is renewed every day. The interest is subject to change from day to day and the day's activities depend largely upon whether call money is high or low.

All stock exchange transactions are given immediate publicity through the *ticker tape*. As soon as a sale is made it is recorded on the stock ticker. Each stock has a certain symbol, and the symbols and the prices are recorded on the tape. A strip of tape is reproduced below with a translation of the symbols.

TICKER TAPE

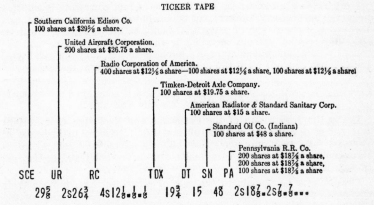

When the tumult and shouting have died the buyer of a share or a group of shares of stock has a small piece of paper known as a *stock certificate* to show for it, which represents, in effect, a partnership in the business of that company. He should not put it away and forget it. Stocks fluctuate too much to make this wise. If he loses it he should at once notify the corporation and the broker from whom he bought it.

As time goes on the company which issued the stock may float another issue. In this case the original stockholders will have the privilege of buying a certain number of the new shares (allotted according to the number of old shares they held). This privilege is called a *right*. Rights may be extremely valuable or they may be almost worthless, depending upon the subscription price and the market price of the issue. Rights are negotiable and may be bought and sold.

The same general principles set forth above with regard to stocks apply to transactions in bonds.

Stockholders are part owners in a corporation; *bondholders* have loaned it money at interest, and they are the creditors. The usual principal amount on the face of a bond is $1,000 but the delivery of two $500 bonds instead of one $1,000 bond is considered a good delivery. And there are a number of $100 bonds ("baby bonds") on the market.

On coupon bonds the contracts for the payment of interest are on the coupons, which, as they mature, are detached from the bond and may be presented at the bank for payment like a check or draft.

Those who hold registered bonds have their names registered with the agent or maker of the bond. Fully registered bonds are registered as to both principal and interest, and the interest payments are made by check or draft mailed to the owner of the bond. Bonds which are registered as to principal only carry coupons, which are like the ones on regular coupon bonds.

Most bonds are secured by actual property and constitute in effect a mortgage on property. Government bonds, however, are not secured, and there is a certain type of unsecured bond, called debenture, which is sometimes issued, without security, by firms of long standing and excellent reputation. A debenture is a promise to pay, and the validity of the promise depends upon the amount of profit the firm makes.

SECURITIES ACTS OF 1933 AND 1934

Under the jurisdiction of the Securities and Exchange Commission[1] this Act is designed to compel full and fair disclosure to investors of material facts regarding securities[2] publicly offered and sold in interstate commerce, or through the mails, and to prevent fraud in the sale of securities.

Dealers who participate in the sale of securities must provide their customers with a prospectus. This prospectus is a condensation of the data contained in the registration statement which the issuer must place on file with the Commission before an issue of securities may be offered for public sale.

The Commission has prescribed special forms for filing this information. Each form is designed to record for investors the pertinent information about the securities, the company, the management, the purpose of issue, together with financial statements, options, salaries, contracts, etc.

---

[1] The Commission also administers the Public Utility Holding Company Act of 1935, the Investment Company Act of 1940, and the Investment Advisers Act of 1940.

[2] There are certain exceptions, including domestic Government securities and limited intrastate offerings (under certain conditions).

A registration statement must become effective before the securities may be offered for sale. A registration statement and prospectuses are available for public inspection and must undergo an examination by the Registration Division, which is composed of a staff of accountants, security analysts, examiners, and attorneys. If the statement appears to be misleading, inaccurate, or incomplete on its face, the issuer is advised and may file amendments to meet these deficiencies. The Commission is empowered to refuse registration in cases in which the issuer fails to supply required data, or to suspend registration if it develops after registration has become effective that information is lacking or misleading. Registration may be refused or suspended only after public hearing.

The examination of a registration statement is concerned only with the completeness and accuracy of the information. It is not to be considered as a finding by the Commission that the registration statement is true, accurate, or complete, or that the security has investment merit.

The Act provides for civil and criminal liability on the part of issuers and others for the fraudulent sale of securities and protects investors against such outright frauds as bucket shops and "sell-and-switch" devices. Prior to the enactment of this law, stock swindlers could escape justice merely by stepping across a state line.

There is also the **Securities Exchange Act of 1934.** Its aims are threefold: to prevent unfair practices in the securities markets; to regulate the use of credit to finance trading in securities; and to provide the investor with information through the filing of periodic reports with the Commission and the exchanges on which the securities are listed.

Under this Act stock exchanges must be registered with the Commission, as must brokers and dealers who transact business in the over-the-counter market; and provisions are made for civil remedies for injured investors and criminal penalties for violations.

The Trust Indenture Act of 1939 is applicable to certain bonds, debentures, notes, and similar debt securities. It requires that any debentures under which such securities are issued conform to prescribed standards designed to safeguard the rights and interests of the purchasers of such securities. Among other things, the indenture trustee must be "independent" and free of any conflicting interests which might interfere with the full performance of duties in behalf of the investor.

BLUE SKY LAWS

"Blue sky" laws are the securities acts by which the states exercise control over the sale of stocks, bonds, and other securities within their borders. The first of these laws was passed in Kansas in 1911. Its purpose was to stop the sale of securities based upon worthless or nonexistent oil wells in Oklahoma. The name is said by some authorities to have come about because the corporations were capitalized out of the blue sky; by others equally competent it is said to be because the blue sky was the limit to what the corporations offered. Today all states with the exception of Nevada have laws in the nature of blue sky laws.

The provisions of the present-day laws vary, but most of them require a sworn statement listing the securities, together with definite and accurate information as to the basis upon which they were issued.

Many securities which it is lawful to issue in one state are not within the law in another state. Anyone contemplating an issue should consult a competent attorney.

BANKRUPTCY[1]

A person in bankruptcy is one who has been declared by a court of law unable to pay his debts. The purpose of the bankruptcy law is twofold: (1) to bring about an equitable distribution of the bankrupt's property among his creditors; and (2) to discharge the honest bankrupt from his obligations and enable him to start anew unencumbered.

The Federal Constitution gives to Congress the power to pass a bankruptcy law which shall have authority throughout the country. The several states may enact statutes to cover points which have not been covered by Federal legislation but they may not pass laws to complement or to provide additional or auxiliary regulations to a Federal Bankruptcy Act when in force.

The Bankruptcy Act now in force is the Act of 1898 as amended by the Act of 1938. This latter amendatory Act is known popularly as the **Chandler Act.**

In addition there are several specific Acts affecting the situation: the Corporate Reorganization Act of 1934; the Frazier-Lemke Farm Mortgage Act of 1935; the Debtors' Relief Act of 1933, supplemented 1935; the Railroad Reorganization Act of 1933, amended 1935; the Municipal Debt Adjustment Act of 1937; and the Chandler Railroad Adjustment Act of 1939.

Municipalities, farmers, railroads, and wage earners especially have profited by the new laws. Banks and insurance companies are still excluded from the benefits of the Acts. The bankruptcy of a corporation does not release its officers, directors, or stockholders, as such, from any liability under the laws of a state or territory in the United States.

Candidates for Bankruptcy

Any person owing debts, no matter how small in amount or number, may file a petition in voluntary bankruptcy. A debtor with but one small debt and no assets may therefore file such a petition, or a petition in bankruptcy may be filed for the purpose of obtaining a discharge from a particular debt. Generally, provable debts are dischargeable.

Minors, aliens, and, in all states where they can contract debts, married women, may be entitled to the benefits of the Act.

---

[1]The subject of bankruptcy is a highly technical field. This article is designed as a brief summary of the fundamentals. Any specific situation must be considered individually with careful attention to the provision of the Bankruptcy Act (available through the Superintendent of Documents, Washington, D.C.), the General Orders and Forms in Bankruptcy prescribed by the United States Supreme Court, the rules of the local District Court, the exemptions provided for under state laws, and the pertinent court decisions.

The estate of a deceased debtor cannot be declared bankrupt, but if a debtor dies after bankruptcy proceedings have been instituted, they shall proceed just as if he were alive, in so far as this is possible.

Involuntary bankruptcy proceedings are instituted by a creditor or group of creditors filing a petition to have the debtor adjudicated a bankrupt and his assets taken into custody for distribution to his creditors. The alleged bankrupt has the opportunity of contesting the claim asserted against him.

An involuntary petition may be filed against any natural person, excepting a wage-earner or a farmer, and may be filed against any corporation except municipal, railroad, insurance, or banking corporations or a building and loan association.

When the debtor's creditors are 12 or more in number, at least three of the creditors are required to join in filing the petition for involuntary bankruptcy. If there are less than 12 creditors, one creditor may file. A petition may be filed by such creditors only if:

1. The debtor owes $1,000 or more;
2. The creditors who file the petition have provable claims against the debtor totalling $500 or more in excess of any securities which they may hold;
3. The debtor has committed an act of bankruptcy within four months of the filing of the involuntary petition. The Act defines six acts of bankruptcy, namely (a) conveyances in fraud of creditors; (b) voluntary transfers of property to give preferences to certain creditors while insolvent; (c) permitting any creditor to obtain a lien upon the debtor's property through legal proceedings while the debtor is insolvent which has not been vacated or discharged; (d) making a general assignment for the benefit of creditors; (e) permitting while insolvent the appointment of a receiver or trustee to take charge of the debtor's property; (f) admitting in writing inability to pay debts and willingness to be adjudged a bankrupt.

In either a voluntary or an involuntary petition, application may be made for the appointment of a receiver if it is deemed that the interest of the creditors requires protection against loss of assets.

Property Exemptions

Property exemptions are prescribed by the laws of the state in which the proceedings are held and vary from one state to another. In most states the tools and implements of the bankrupt's trade, his household furniture and wearing apparel (within limits), and his homestead are exempt. Pension money is exempt.

Duties of a Bankrupt

The bankrupt shall:
1. Attend the first meeting of his creditors, if directed by the court or a judge thereof to do so, and the hearing upon his application for a discharge, if filed;

2. Comply with all lawful orders of the court;

3. Examine the correctness of all proofs of claims filed against his estate;

4. Execute and deliver such papers as shall be ordered by the court;

5. Execute to his trustee transfers of all his property in foreign countries;

6. Immediately inform his trustee of any attempt, by his creditors or other persons, to evade the provisions of this act, coming to his knowledge;

7. In case of any person having to his knowledge proved a false claim against his estate, disclose that fact immediately to his trustee;

8. Prepare, make oath to, and file in court within ten days after adjudication if an involuntary bankrupt, and within ten days after the filing of a petition if a voluntary bankrupt, unless in either case further time is granted, a schedule of his property, showing the amount and kind of property, the location thereof, its money value, in detail, and a list of his creditors, showing their residences, if known (if unknown that fact to be stated), the amount due each of them, the consideration thereof, the security held by them, if any, and a claim for such exemptions as he may be entitled to, all in triplicate—one copy of each for the clerk, one for the referee, and one for the trustee; and

9. When present at the first meeting of his creditors, and at such other times as the court shall order, submit to an examination concerning the conducting of his business, the cause of his bankruptcy, his dealings with his creditors and other persons, the amount, kind, and whereabouts of his property, and, in addition, all matters which may affect the administration and settlement of his estate; but no testimony given by him shall be offered in evidence against him in any criminal proceedings.

Provable Claims

All claims against the estate of a bankrupt must be filed within six months of the date first set for the first meeting of creditors or they will not be allowed, and must be under oath signed by the creditor containing a statement of the claim, consideration therefor, the securities held, if any, and the payments made on the claim, if any, and that the claim is justly owing. An unliquidated claim is not allowed until liquidated. Unliquidated claims against the bankrupt may, pursuant to applications to the court, be liquidated in such manner as it shall direct, and may thereafter be proved and allowed against his estate. Claims of secured creditors are allowed to the extent of the difference between the value of their security and the amount owed.

Debts which may be proved and allowed against the estate of a bankrupt:

1. A fixed liability as evidenced by a judgment or an instrument in writing, absolutely owing at the time of the filing of the petition against

him, whether then payable or not, with any interest thereon which would have been recoverable at that date, or with a rebate of interest upon such as were not then payable and did not bear interest;

2. Due as costs taxable against an involuntary bankrupt who was at the time of the filing of the petition against him plaintiff in a cause of action which would pass to the trustee and which the trustee declines to prosecute after notice;

3. Founded upon a claim for taxable costs incurred in good faith by a creditor before the filing of the petition in an action to recover a provable debt;

4. Founded upon an open account, or upon a contract express or implied;

5. Founded upon provable debts reduced to judgments after the filing of the petition and before the consideration of the bankrupt's application for a discharge, less costs incurred and interest accrued after the filing of the petition and up to the time of the entry of such judgments;

6. Founded upon an award of industrial accident commissions having jurisdiction of workmen's compensation cases when the injuries occurred prior to adjudication;

7. Founded upon claims for damages in a negligence action instituted prior to and pending at the time of the filing of a petition in bankruptcy;

8. Founded upon contingent debts and contingent contractual liabilities;

9. Founded upon claims for anticipatory breach of contract, including unexpired leases of real or personal property, with the exception that landlords' claims are limited to one year's rent for the year following the date of surrender of the premises or the re-entry plus unpaid accrued rent.

Bankruptcy Courts and Referees

The United States District Courts are the "Courts of Bankruptcy" or bankruptcy courts. As all questions of both law and fact in relation to the rights of various parties must be decided in the bankruptcy proceedings, it is provided that the judges in each district may appoint *referees* who are charged with the duty of hearing the testimony of all parties and deciding all such questions as may arise. Referees are appointed for terms of two years and take the same oath of office as that prescribed for judges of the United States Courts. The Bankruptcy Act is in effect administered by the referees, subject to review by the judges. Each case as it comes up is assigned to a referee, whose duty it is to adjudicate and pass upon all such questions arising therein in the first instance.

Trustees

The *trustee* is an officer of the court. Trustees are appointed by the creditors, at their first meeting after the adjudication, or if they fail to do so, by the court. It is the duty of the trustee to collect assets, reduce them to money, and close up the estate as soon as it can be done, with due regard for the interests of those concerned. Except in matters which are more or less routine the trustee should consult the wishes of the creditors. The power of removing a trustee rests solely with the judge, though creditors may institute proceedings for his removal. A trustee may resign, but the resignation is ineffectual unless the judge or the referee consents. If a trustee dies or is removed his place may be filled in the same way that he was appointed, or the decision may be to have his joint trustees carry on without the addition of another person. A trustee designates the attorney to handle the estate. Creditors must therefore be particularly concerned as to the competence of both the trustee and the attorney designated by him, since great care is often necessary to uncover bankruptcy fraud, to trace concealments, or to recover preferences or transfers which have been made.

Compositions

The National Bankruptcy Act provides that debtors may settle with their creditors by means of a compromise. If the bankrupt and a majority of his creditors can come to an agreement about the settlement basis and can get the agreement approved by the court, the agreement becomes binding on all the creditors. This agreement is known as a *composition*. If it is not approved, bankruptcy proceedings continue in the regular way.

Assignments

It is also possible for debtors to make *assignments* in trust whereby they turn all their assets over to a trustee to sell and distribute the profits among the creditors. There is much less publicity attached to this procedure than to regular bankruptcy proceedings, since it is a private matter between the debtor and his creditors, but in most states the assignment must be recorded. If the creditors are not satisfied they can have the assignments set aside by filing petition of bankruptcy.

Debts Not Affected by a Discharge in Bankruptcy

A *discharge in bankruptcy* releases a bankrupt from all of his provable debts, except such as:

1. Are due as a tax levied by the United States, the state, county, district, or municipality in which he resides, except real estate taxes where the liability for the tax is on the land rather than on the owner;

2. Are liabilities for obtaining property by false pretenses or false representation, or for wilful and malicious injuries to the person or property of another, or for alimony due or to become due, or for maintenance or support of wife or child, or for seduction of an unmarried female, or for

breach of promise of marriage accompanied by seduction, or for criminal conversation;

3. Have not been duly scheduled in time for proof and allowance, with the name of the creditor, if known to the bankrupt, unless such creditor had notice or actual knowledge of the proceedings in bankruptcy; or

4. Were created by his fraud, embezzlement, misappropriation, or defalcation while acting as an officer or in any fiduciary capacity; or

5. Are for wages due to workmen, clerks, traveling or city salesmen, or servants, which have been earned within three months before the date of commencement of the proceedings in bankruptcy; or

6. Are due for moneys of an employee received or retained by his employer to secure the faithful performance by such employee of the terms of a contract of employment.

Debts Which Have Priority

The following claims are entitled to priority in the order listed:

1. Administration costs which are the actual and necessary costs of preserving the estate subsequent to filing the petition;

2. Wage claims not exceeding $600 to each claimant which have been earned within three months before the date of the beginning of the bankruptcy proceeding. Wage-earners' claims exceeding $600 or wages earned outside the three months' period participate as general claims;

3. Creditors' expenses in successfully opposing a bankrupt's discharge or confirmation of an arrangement or wage-earner's plan or in discovering evidence resulting in the conviction of any person under the Act;

4. Taxes due to the United States or any state or subdivision thereof;

5. Debts owing to any person who by the laws of the United States is entitled to priority, and rent owing to a landlord who by state law is entitled to priority.

Conduct of Bankrupt Preventing Discharge

A bankrupt may be denied a discharge not only from undischargeable debts but from all his debts if any of the following circumstances or situations has occurred. The circumstances prior to the proceeding which will result in the denial of a discharge to the bankrupt are:

1. The destruction of his books by the bankrupt or his failure to keep books of account or records unless the court considers such acts or failure to have been justified;

2. The making or publishing of a materially false written financial statement by means of which credit or an extension of credit was obtained;

3. The transfer or concealment of any of the bankrupt's property within one year of the filing of the petition with intent to hinder, delay, or defraud his creditors; or

4. The obtaining of a previous discharge in bankruptcy or the confirmation of a composition, arrangement, or wage-earners' plan under the Act within six months prior to the present bankruptcy proceeding.

The circumstances occurring subsequent to the filing of the petition which may result in the denial of a discharge are:

An offense punishable by imprisonment under the Act, such as: (a) fraudulent appropriation of property belonging to a bankrupt estate by a trustee, receiver, marshal, or other officer of the court; (b) the concealment of any property of a bankrupt estate or transfer of property in contemplation of the bankruptcy proceeding or the concealment or falsification of a document relating to the affairs of the bankrupt; and (c) during the course of a proceeding under the Act, by the bankrupt's refusal to obey a lawful order or answer a material question asked by the court.

Dividends

Dividends of an equal per cent shall be declared and paid on all allowed claims, except such as have priority or are secured.

The first dividend shall be declared within 30 days after the adjudication, if the money of the estate in excess of the amount necessary to pay the debts which have priority and such claims as have not been, but probably will be, allowed equals five per cent or more of such allowed claims. Dividends subsequent to the first shall be declared upon like terms as the first and as often as the amount shall equal ten per cent or more and upon closing the estate. Dividends may be declared oftener and in smaller proportions if the judge shall so order: *Provided,* That the first dividend shall not include more than 50 per cent of the money of the estate in excess of the amount necessary to pay the debts which have priority and such claims as probably will be allowed: and provided further, That the final dividend shall not be declared within three months after the first dividend shall be declared.

The rights of creditors who have received dividends, or in whose favor final dividends have been declared, shall not be affected by the proof and allowance of claims subsequent to the date of such payment or declarations of dividends; but the creditors proving and securing the allowance of such claims shall be paid dividends equal in amount to those already received by the other creditors if the estate equals so much before such other 'creditors are paid any further dividends.

Whenever a person shall have been adjudged a bankrupt by a court without the United States and also by a court of bankruptcy, creditors residing within the United States shall first be paid a dividend equal to that received in the court without the United States by other creditors before creditors who have received a dividend in such court shall be paid any amounts.

A claimant shall not be entitled to collect from a bankrupt estate any greater amount than shall accrue pursuant to the provisions of this Act.

If dividends remain unclaimed for six months after the final dividend has been declared the trustee must pay them into the court. If they remain unclaimed for a year the court shall distribute them among the creditors whose claims have been allowed but not fully paid. What is left is paid to the bankrupt. Minors have a year after coming of age to claim such dividends.

STATUTES OF LIMITATION

Statutes of limitation fix an arbitrary time within which every form of action shall be brought. The statutes vary in the different states.

The primary purpose of such statutes is to prevent the enforcement of stale or fraudulent claims after proper vouchers and evidence may have been lost, or when it may be impossible to establish the facts because of faulty memory, death, or unavailability of witnesses.

Such statutes will not ordinarily have a retroactive effect. However, within constitutional limitations, a statute of limitation may apply to causes of action which accrued before the enactment of the statute, as well as to causes of action which accrued thereafter.

The statute of limitation may be waived under certain circumstances, for example, when a person borrows money and the lender agrees that he will not enforce payment for a period of ten years. While the statute of limitation applicable to such cause of action is six years, suit can be brought before six years after expiration of the ten years. In some states a claim outlawed by the statute of limitation may be revised through the execution of a formal acknowledgment of the indebtedness by the debtor.

In the absence of statute, criminal prosecutions are not barred by the lapse of time. However, some states have statutes specifying the time within which criminal prosecutions must be commenced. Such statutes are regarded as acts of grace or amnesty. The period of limitation applicable to particular crimes is determined by the statutory provision in the jurisdiction in which the offender is prosecuted.

Under the Federal statutes, an indictment or information for an offense punishable by death may be found at any time without regard to any statute of limitation. As to crimes arising under the internal revenue laws the limitation is three years, except as to offenses involving the defrauding or attempting to defraud the United States, or the offense of willfully attempting in any manner to evade or defeat any tax or the payment thereof; or offenses with respect to the preparation or presentation of false or fraudulent returns, affidavits, claims, or documents, and conspiracies to evade any tax or payment thereof. In these cases the limitation is six years. Under the Bankruptcy Act, an indictment or information must be filed within three years after the commission of any offense arising under the Act.

THE GOVERNMENT OF THE UNITED STATES

Men must either govern or be governed; they must take part in the control of their own lives, or they must lead subject lives, helplessly dependent in the little things and great things of life upon the will and power of others.—ELIHU ROOT.

The President

The President of the United States is chosen by the electoral college, the membership of which is selected by the various states according to whatever method they choose. Each state has as many members in the electoral college as it has members in both houses of Congress. In case of a tie, the House decides by a majority of states, each state having one vote.

The candidate for the Presidency must be a natural born citizen of the United States, at least 35 years old, and must have lived within the United States for 14 years.

The President receives a salary of $75,000 a year. Since 1907 there has been an additional annual appropriation of $25,000 for traveling and official entertainment expenses.

The Constitution of the United States directs that the President, before he enters on the execution of his office, shall take the following oath or affirmation:

"I do solemnly swear (or affirm) that I will faithfully execute the office of President of the United States, and will, to the best of my ability, preserve, protect, and defend the Constitution of the United States."

It is the duty of the President as the head of the Government to see that the provisions of the Constitution are carried out, that laws are enforced, treaties respected, and decisions of the Federal courts strictly observed.

In the administration of his duty he is greatly aided by a cabinet of ten members. These ten members, each the head of an important department, are appointed by the President subject to the approval of the Senate. They meet regularly twice a week (on Tuesdays and Fridays at ten-thirty o'clock) and the President has the privilege of summoning them at any time for a special meeting. The meetings are informal, no formal record of the proceedings is kept, and the discussions are, as a rule, kept secret. In case of the removal, death, resignation, or inability of both the President and the Vice President, the Speaker of the House of Representatives, upon his resignation as Speaker and Representative, shall act as President. Should there be no Speaker, or should he fail to qualify, the president pro tempore of the Senate becomes the President. In the absence of both a

118

Speaker and president pro tempore of the Senate, the cabinet officers succeed to the Presidency in the following order:

Secretary of State	Postmaster General
Secretary of the Treasury	Secretary of the Interior
Secretary of Defense	Secretary of Agriculture
Attorney General	Secretary of Commerce
	Secretary of Labor

Members of the cabinet are not allowed to sit in either the Senate or the House of Representatives.

They receive salaries of $15,000 a year, and have under secretaries and assistants with salaries ranging from $10,000 down.

The President has great influence throughout the judicial department of the Government through his power of appointing Federal judges, even though these appointments must have the approval of the Senate. Federal judges are appointed for life or during good behavior and can be removed only by impeachment.

The President is by virtue of his office Commander in Chief of the Army and Navy, and in time of war has almost absolute control of the economic resources and man power of the country.

The President theoretically determines our foreign policy, but is constantly held in check by the Senate. He may negotiate treaties, but the Senate must confirm them. He appoints diplomats and consuls, but these, too, are subject to the approval of the Senate.

The President receives the ambassadors and other ministers from foreign countries and may dismiss them, no matter how serious the consequences which may follow.

The President has unlimited power to grant pardons or reprieves for offenses against the United States.

The President is required by the Constitution[1] to send or deliver from time to time a message to Congress on the state of the country, with recommendations for such legislation as he may think desirable. The Presidential message may have great influence, especially when his party is in control, but the President has no power to enforce his desires; he can merely state them.

The only direct control he has over legislation is through the fact that he can veto any Act of Congress that does not win his approval, and even this is not unlimited. Every Act or resolution must be presented to the President after it has been passed by Congress. If he signs it or fails to return it within ten days, it becomes a law. If he returns it with a statement of his reasons for disapproving it, this constitutes a veto, and the measure is killed unless it goes again before both Houses and wins a two-thirds vote, in which case it becomes a law in spite of the veto.

If the President retains a bill without signing it for more than ten days (Sunday excepted) it automatically becomes a law unless it was passed within ten days of the adjournment of Congress, in which case the President may retain or "pocket" the bill, which does not then become a law but

---

[1]The Constitution is reprinted in this book, and if you are really interested in what your Government can and cannot do you might turn to page 122 and read this excellent and famous document.

is killed without a direct veto and without the risk of being passed over a veto. This veto is provided for in the Constitution, Article I, Section 7, Clause 2.

The Cabinet

The duties of the nine departments headed by cabinet members are indicated by the titles of the departments.

The *Department of State* has charge of foreign affairs. It issues passports and in general looks after our relationships with other countries. The Secretary of State is custodian of the national archives and keeper of the Great Seal of the United States. The Department of State is older than the Constitution. Before the Declaration of Independence was issued the Continental Congress had found it necessary to establish a Department of Foreign Affairs, a Treasury Department, a War Department, and a Post Office Department. All these departments were immediately reestablished by the first Congress which met under the Constitution, and, although their duties have been modified and enlarged in various ways, all four have continued active until the present day.

The *Department of the Treasury* acts as the financial agent of the Government. Its duties include the collection of Federal taxes, customs duties, and internal revenue; the minting of coin and printing of paper money, stamps, etc.; the supervision of the national banks; the detection of counterfeiters and smugglers; the maintenance of the coast guard, the enforcement of prohibition, and the construction and maintenance of United States Government buildings throughout the country.

This department also prepares an annual budget, which, however, is mainly suggestive, since the department has not the authority to determine expenditures and appropriations, this authority resting in the hands of Congress.

The *Departments of War, Navy, and Air Force* were reorganized in 1947 under the *Secretary of Defense.* The secretaries of these departments do not have cabinet status, but are represented in the cabinet by the *Secretary of Defense,* who coordinates the functions of all three departments. The *Secretary of the Army* is in charge of organizing, training, and maintaining the Army. His responsibilities include control of Army appropriations and expenditures; development of improved weapons and matériel; defense of coastal cities and harbors of the United States, and of the Panama Canal. The *Department of the Navy* has charge of the construction and maintenance of vessels, the maintenance of Navy yards, and the administration of the personnei and equipment of the Navy. The *Department of the Air Force* was created from the Army Air Forces in 1947 and includes all military aviation forces, combat and service, and otherwise assigned. It is organized and trained for prompt and sustained air offensive and defensive operations.

The *Attorney General,* who is head of the Department of Justice, is the chief law counselor of the United States. Upon request he is required by statute to render advice to the President or to any one of the executive departments. The Department of Justice passes upon the validity of titles to public lands bought by the United States for the erection of public buildings and acts in all litigation where the United States is concerned. The Attorney General appears sometimes in the Supreme Court but seldom in the lower courts.

The *Post Office Department* has a much greater number of employees than any other department. Besides carrying the mails, the department operates the postal savings banks and handles a great deal of currency through money orders.

The *Department of the Interior* has charge of pensions, public lands, education, Indian affairs, national parks, reclamation service, and a variety of other matters which do not fit directly into any other department.

Few of the departments render so direct and personal a service as the *Department of Agriculture*. For its duties, see pages 343 to 346.

The *Department of Commerce* has charge of the development of foreign and domestic trade. The Bureau of Standards functions under the supervision of this department which also has charge of the licensing and inspection of steamboats, the regulation of fisheries, the regulation and maintenance of the lighthouse service, the making of coastal and geodetic surveys, the taking of the census, issuing of patents, and the publication of commercial statistics.

The *Department of Labor* has charge of the administration and enforcement of statutes designed to advance the welfare of wage earners in the United States, to improve their working conditions, and to advance their opportunities for profitable employment. The department is directed by the Secretary of Labor, assisted by the Under Secretary and several Assistant Secretaries. The department is composed of several major units including the Bureau of Apprenticeship, the Office of International Labor Affairs, the Bureau of Labor Standards, the Bureau of Labor Statistics, the Bureau of Veterans' Reemployment Rights, the Wage and Hour and Public Contracts Divisions and the Women's Bureau.

Congress

The legislative department of the United States Government is known as Congress and consists of two houses, the Senate and the House of Representatives. Each state has two Senators who are elected by popular vote for a period of six years. Senators may serve as many terms as their followers will allow. A Senator must be 30 years old and, if he is an alien, he must have been a citizen of the United States for nine years and must be a resident of the state in which he is elected. His salary is $12,500 a year, with an additional expense allowance of $2,500 which is nontaxable. In addition to its lawmaking power, the Senate confirms the appointments of the President, ratifies treaties, and tries impeachments.

Members of the House of Representatives are elected by the people for a period of two years and may be reelected. The number of Representatives from each state is based upon the population figures from that state at the last official census. (It was to determine the number of Representatives, as a matter of fact, that the census was instituted.) The census is taken every ten years. A Representative must be 25 years old, and, if he is an alien, he must have been a citizen of the United States for seven years and must be a resident of the state which elects him. His salary is $12,500 a year, with an additional expense allowance of $2,500 which is non-taxable. The House of Representatives has the sole power of presenting impeachments, just as the Senate has the sole power of trying them.

The Federal Courts

At the head of the Federal courts stands, of course, the Supreme Court. The Supreme Court has nine members, a Chief Justice who receives a salary of $25,500 a year, and eight associate justices with salaries of $25,000 each. This court is the highest judicial authority in the United States. From its decisions there is no appeal.

The Supreme Court has jurisdiction over cases in which foreign ambassadors, public ministers, consuls, *et al.*, are involved and over cases governed by admiralty and maritime laws; over cases in which the United States is a party; cases between a citizen of the United States and of a foreign state; between citizens of different states, or citizens of the same state claiming land granted by another state, or between a state and its citizens, etc. Its greatest power is the one which gives it the right to declare any Federal or state statute null and void if a majority of the justices find it unconstitutional.

There are ten circuits in the United States in each of which there are circuit judges, the number depending upon the amount of judicial work that has to be done. The circuit judges sit with the district judges, thus forming the Circuit Courts of Appeal.

Below the Circuit Court is the District Court, which is the lowest Federal court. If a district is large it may be subdivided, and each subdivision may be presided over by one or more judges.

Circuit judges receive $17,500 and district judges $15,000 a year.

The Court of Claims hears all citizen claims against the Federal Government. It consists of a chief justice, who receives $17,500 a year, and four associate judges, who receive the same salary as their chief.

The Court of Customs and Patent Appeals consists of a presiding judge and four associate judges. Formerly this court was called the Court of Customs Appeals and acted as the final court of appeal in matters connected with the administration of the tariff laws. In 1929 the title was changed to the United States Court of Customs and Patent Appeals. In addition to tariff questions it now handles all matters connected with appeals from the Patent Office in patent and trademark cases which were formerly under the jurisdiction of the Court of Appeals in the District of Columbia.

THE CONSTITUTION OF THE UNITED STATES[1]

Preamble

We, the people of the United States, in order to form a more perfect Union, establish justice, insure domestic tranquillity, provide for the common defence, promote the general welfare, and secure the blessings of liberty to ourselves and our posterity, do ordain and establish this Constitution for the United States of America.

---

[1] The Amendments I-X are commonly known as the *Bill of Rights*.

ARTICLE I.

Section 1—(Legislative powers; in whom vested:)

All legislative powers herein granted shall be vested in a Congress of the United States, which shall consist of a Senate and House of Representatives.

Section 2—(House of Representatives, how and by whom chosen. Qualifications of a Representative. Representatives and direct taxes, how apportioned. Enumeration. Vacancies to be filled. Power of choosing officers, and of impeachment.)

1. The House of Representatives shall be composed of members chosen every second year by the people of the several States, and the electors in each State shall have the qualifications requisite for electors of the most numerous branch of the State Legislature.

2. No person shall be a Representative who shall not have attained to the age of twenty-five years and been seven years a citizen of the United States, and who shall not, when elected, be an inhabitant of that State in which he shall be chosen.

3. Representatives and direct taxes shall be apportioned among the several States which may be included within this Union according to their respective numbers, which shall be determined by adding to the whole number of free persons, including those bound to service for a term of years, and excluding Indians not taxed, three-fifths of all other persons. The actual enumeration shall be made within three years after the first meeting of the Congress of the United States, and within every subsequent term of ten years, in such manner as they shall by law direct. The number of Representatives shall not exceed one for every thirty thousand, but each State shall have at least one Representative; and until such enumeration shall be made, the State of New Hampshire shall be entitled to choose 3; Massachusetts, 8; Rhode Island and Providence Plantations, 1; Connecticut, 5; New York, 6; New Jersey, 4; Pennsylvania, 8; Delaware, 1; Maryland, 6; Virginia, 10; North Carolina, 5; South Carolina, 5, and Georgia, 3.[1]

4. When vacancies happen in the representation from any State, the Executive Authority thereof shall issue writs of election to fill such vacancies.

5. The House of Representatives shall choose their Speaker and other officers, and shall have the sole power of impeachment.

Section 3—(Senators, how and by whom chosen. How classified. State Executive, when to make temporary appointments, in case, etc. Qualifications of a Senator. President of the Senate, his right to vote. President pro tem., and other officers of the Senate, how chosen. Power to try impeachments. When President is tried, Chief Justice to preside. Sentence.)

1. The Senate of the United States shall be composed of two Senators from each State, chosen by the Legislature thereof, for six years; and each Senator shall have one vote.

2. Immediately after they shall be assembled in consequence of the first election, they shall be divided as equally as may be into three classes. The seats of the Senators of the first class shall be vacated at the expiration of the second year, of the second class at the expiration of the fourth year, and of the third class at the expiration of the sixth year, so that one-third may be chosen every second year; and if vacancies happen by resignation, or otherwise, during the recess of the Legislature of any State, the Executive thereof may make temporary appointment until the next meeting of the Legislature, which shall then fill such vacancies.

3. No person shall be a Senator who shall not have attained to the age of thirty years, and been nine years a citizen of the United States, and who shall not, when elected, be an inhabitant of that State for which he shall be chosen.

4. The Vice President of the United States shall be President of the Senate, but shall have no vote unless they be equally divided.

5. The Senate shall choose their other officers, and also a President pro tempore, in the absence of the Vice President, or when he shall exercise the office of President of the United States.

---

[1]See Article XIV, Amendments.

6. The Senate shall have the sole power to try all impeachments. When sitting for that purpose, they shall be on oath or affirmation. When the President of the United States is tried, the Chief Justice shall preside; and no person shall be convicted without the concurrence of two thirds of the members present.

7. Judgment of cases of impeachment shall not extend further than to removal from office, and disqualification to hold and enjoy any office of honor, trust, or profit under the United States; but the party convicted shall nevertheless be liable and subject to indictment, trial, judgment, and punishment, according to law.

Section 4—(Times, etc., of holding elections, how prescribed. One session in each year.)

1. The times, places, and manner of holding elections for Senators and Representatives shall be prescribed in each State by the Legislature thereof; but the Congress may at any time by law make or alter such regulations, except as to places of choosing Senators.

2. The Congress shall assemble at least once in every year, and such meeting shall be on the first Monday in December, unless they shall by law appoint a different day.

Section 5—(Membership, Quorum, Adjournments. Rules. Power to punish or expel. Journal. Time of adjournments, how limited, etc.)

1. Each House shall be the judge of the elections, returns, and qualifications of its own members, and a majority of each shall constitute a quorum to do business; but a smaller number may adjourn from day to day, and may be authorized to compel the attendance of absent members in such manner and under such penalties as each House may provide.

2. Each House may determine the rules of its proceedings, punish its members for disorderly behavior, and with the concurrence of two-thirds expel a member.

3. Each House shall keep a journal of its proceedings, and from time to time publish the same, excepting such parts as may in their judgment require secrecy; and the yeas and nays of the members of either House or any question shall, at the desire of one fifth of those present, be entered on the journal.

4. Neither House, during the session of Congress shall, without the consent of the other, adjourn for more than three days, nor to any other place than that in which the two Houses shall be sitting.

Section 6—(Compensation. Privileges. Disqualification in certain cases.)

1. The Senators and Representatives shall receive a compensation for their services to be ascertained by law, and paid out of the Treasury of the United States. They shall in all cases, except treason, felony, and breach of the peace, be privileged from arrest during their attendance at the session of their respective Houses, and in going to and returning from the same; and for any speech or debate in either House they shall not be questioned in any other place.

2. No Senator or Representative shall, during the time for which he was elected, be appointed to any civil office under the authority of the United States which shall have been created, or the emoluments whereof shall have been increased during such time; and no person holding any office under the United States shall be a member of either House during his continuance in office.

Section 7—(House to originate all revenue bills. Veto. Bill may be passed by two-thirds of each House, notwithstanding, etc. Bill, not returned in ten days, to become a law. Provisions as to orders, concurrent resolutions, etc.)

1. All bills for raising revenue shall originate in the House of Representatives, but the Senate may propose or concur with amendments, as on other bills.

2. Every bill which shall have passed the House of Representatives and the Senate shall, before it becomes a law, be presented to the President of the United States; if he approve, he shall sign it, but if not, he shall return it, with his objections, to that House in which it shall have originated, who shall enter the objections at large on their journal, and proceed to reconsider it. If after such reconsideration two-thirds of that

House shall agree to pass the bill, it shall be sent, together with the objections, to the other House, by which it shall likewise be reconsidered; and if approved by two-thirds of that House it shall become a law. But in all such cases the votes of both Houses shall be determined by yeas and nays and the names of the persons voting for and against the bill shall be entered on the journal of each House respectively. If any bill shall not be returned by the President within ten days (Sundays excepted) after it shall have been presented to him, the same shall be a law in like manner as if he had signed it, unless the Congress by their adjournment prevent its return; in which case it shall not be a law.

3. Every order, resolution, or vote to which the concurrence of the Senate and House of Representatives may be necessary (except on a question of adjournment) shall be presented to the President of the United States; and before the same shall take effect shall be approved by him, or being disapproved by him, shall be repassed by two-thirds of the Senate and the House of Representatives, according to the rules and limitations prescribed in the case of a bill.

Section 8—(Powers of Congress.)

The Congress shall have power:

1. To lay and collect taxes, duties, imposts, and excises, to pay the debts, and provide for the common defence and general welfare of the United States; but all duties, imposts, and excises shall be uniform throughout the United States.

2. To borrow money on the credit of the United States.

3. To regulate commerce with foreign nations, and among the several States, and with the Indian tribes.

4. To establish an uniform rule of naturalization and uniform laws on the subject of bankruptcies throughout the United States.

5. To coin money, regulate the value thereof, and of foreign coin, and fix the standard of weights and measures.

6. To provide for the punishment of counterfeiting the securities and current coin of the United States.

7. To establish post-offices and post-roads.

8. To promote the progress of science and useful arts by securing for limited times to authors and inventors the exclusive rights to their respective writings and discoveries.

9. To constitute tribunals inferior to the Supreme Court.

10. To define and punish piracies and felonies committed on the high seas, and offences against the law of nations.

11. To declare war, grant letters of marque and reprisal, and make rules concerning captures on land and water.

12. To raise and support armies, but no appropriation of money to that use shall be for a longer term than two years.

13. To provide and maintain a navy.

14. To make rules for the government and regulation of the land and naval forces.

15. To provide for calling forth the militia to execute the laws of the Union, suppress insurrections, and repel invasions.

16. To provide for organizing, arming, and disciplining the militia, and for governing such part of them as may be employed in the service of the United States, reserving to the States respectively the appointment of the officers, and the authority of training the militia according to the discipline prescribed by Congress.

17. To exercise exclusive legislation in all cases whatsoever over such district (not exceeding ten miles square) as may, by cession of particular States and the acceptance of Congress, become the seat of Government of the United States, and to exercise like authority over all places purchased by the consent of the Legislature of the State in which the same shall be, for the erection of forts, magazines, arsenals, dry-docks, and other needful buildings.

18. To make all laws which shall be necessary and proper for carrying into execution

the foregoing powers and all other powers vested by this Constitution in the Government of the United States, or in any department or officer thereof.

Section 9—(Provision as to migration or importation of certain persons. Habeas Corpus. Bills of attainder, etc. Taxes, how apportioned. No export duty. No commercial preference. Money, how drawn from Treasury, etc. No titular nobility. Officers not to receive presents, etc.)

1. The migration or importation of such persons as any of the States now existing shall think proper to admit shall not be prohibited by the Congress prior to the year one thousand eight hundred and eight, but a tax or duty may be imposed on such importation, not exceeding ten dollars for each person.

2. The privilege of the writ of habeas corpus shall not be suspended, unless when in cases of rebellion or invasion the public safety may require it.

3. No bill of attainder or ex post facto law shall be passed.

4. No capitation or other direct tax shall be laid, unless in proportion to the census or enumeration hereinbefore directed to be taken.

5. No tax or duty shall be laid on articles exported from any State.

6. No preference shall be given by any regulation of commerce or revenue to the ports of one State over those of another, nor shall vessels bound to or from one State be obliged to enter, clear, or pay duties in another.

7. No money shall be drawn from the Treasury but in consequence of appropriations made by law; and a regular statement and account of the receipts and expenditures of all public money shall be published from time to time.

8. No title of nobility shall be granted by the United States. And no person holding any office of profit or trust under them shall, without the consent of the Congress, accept of any present, emolument, office or title of any kind whatever from any king, prince, or foreign state.

Section 10—(States prohibited from the exercise of certain powers.)

1. No State shall enter into any treaty, alliance, or confederation, grant letters of marque and reprisal, coin money, emit bills of credit, make anything but gold and silver coin a tender in payment of debts, pass any bill of attainder, ex post facto law, or law impairing the obligation of contracts, or grant any title of nobility.

2. No State shall, without the consent of the Congress, lay any impost or duties on imports or exports, except what may be absolutely necessary for executing its inspection laws, and the net produce of all duties and imposts, laid by any State on imports or exports, shall be for the use of the Treasury of the United States; and all such laws shall be subject to the revision and control of the Congress.

3. No State shall, without the consent of Congress, lay any duty of tonnage, keep troops or ships of war in time of peace, enter into agreement or compact with another State, or with a foreign power, or engage in war, unless actually invaded, or in such imminent danger as will not admit of delay.

ARTICLE II.

Section 1—(President; his term of office. Electors of President; number and how appointed. Electors to vote on same day. Qualification of President. On whom his duties devolve in case of his removal, death, etc. President's compensation. His oath of office.)

1. The Executive power shall be vested in a President of the United States of America. He shall hold his office during the term of four years, and, together with the Vice-President, chosen for the same term, be elected as follows:

2. Each State shall appoint, in such manner as the Legislature thereof may direct, a number of electors equal to the whole number of Senators and Representatives to which the State may be entitled in the Congress; but no Senator or Representative or person holding an office of trust or profit under the United States shall be appointed an elector.

3. The electors shall meet in their respective States and vote by ballot for two persons, of whom one at least shall not be an inhabitant of the same State with themselves. And they shall make a list of all the persons voted for, and of the number of votes for each, which list they shall sign and certify and transmit, sealed, to the seat of the Government of the United States, directed to the President of the Senate. The President of the Senate shall, in the presence of the Senate and House of Representatives, open all the certificates, and the votes shall then be counted. The person having the greatest number of votes shall be the President, if such number be a majority of the whole number of electors appointed, and if there be more than one who have such a majority, and have an equal number of votes, then the House of Representatives shall immediately choose by ballot one of them for President; and if no person have a majority, then from the five highest on the list the said House shall in like manner choose the President. But in choosing the President, the vote shall be taken by States, the representation from each State having one vote. A quorum, for this purpose, shall consist of a member or members from two-thirds of the States, and a majority of all the States shall be necessary to a choice. In every case, after the choice of the President, the person having the greatest number of votes of the electors shall be the Vice President. But if there should remain two or more who have equal votes, the Senate shall choose from them by ballot the Vice President.[1]

4. The Congress may determine the time of choosing the electors and the day on which they shall give their votes, which day shall be the same throughout the United States.

5. No person except a natural born citizen, or a citizen of the United States, at the time of the adoption of this Constitution, shall be eligible to the office of President; neither shall any person be eligible to that office who shall not have attained to the age of thirty-five years and been fourteen years a resident within the United States.

6. In case of the removal of the President from office, or of his death, resignation, or inability to discharge the powers and duties of the said office, the same shall devolve on the Vice President, and the Congress may by law provide for the case of removal, death, resignation, or inability, both of the President and Vice President, declaring what officer shall then act as President, and such officer shall act accordingly until the disability be removed or a President shall be elected.

7. The President shall, at stated times, receive for his services a compensation which shall neither be increased nor diminished during the period for which he shall have been elected, and he shall not receive within that period any other emolument from the United States, or any of them.

8. Before he enter on the execution of his office he shall take the following oath or affirmation:
"I do solemnly swear (or affirm) that I will faithfully execute the office of President of the United States, and will, to the best of my ability, preserve, protect, and defend the Constitution of the United States."

Section 2—(President to be Commander-in-Chief. He may require opinions of Cabinet officers, etc., may pardon. Treaty-making power. Nomination of certain officers. When President may fill vacancies.)

1. The President shall be Commander-in-Chief of the Army and Navy of the United States, and of the militia of the several States when called into the actual service of the United States; he may require the opinion, in writing, of the principal officer in each of the executive departments upon any subject relating to the duties of their respective offices, and he shall have power to grant reprieves and pardons for offences against the United States except in cases of impeachment.

2. He shall have power, by and with the advice and consent of the Senate, to make treaties, provided two-thirds of the Senators present concur, and he shall nominate and by and with the advice and consent of the Senate shall appoint ambassadors, other public ministers and consuls, judges of the Supreme Court, and all other officers of the United States whose appointments are not herein otherwise provided for, and which shall be established by law: but the Congress may by law vest the appointment of such

---

[1]This clause is superseded by Article XII, Amendments.

inferior officers as they think proper in the President alone, in the courts of law, or in the heads of departments.

3. The President shall have power to fill up all vacancies that may happen during the recess of the Senate by granting commissions, which shall expire at the end of their next session.

Section 3—(President shall communicate to Congress. He may convene and adjourn Congress, in case of disagreement, etc. Shall receive Ambassadors, execute laws, and commission officers.)

He shall from time to time give to the Congress information of the state of the Union, and recommend to their consideration such measures as he shall judge necessary and expedient; he may, on extraordinary occasions, convene both Houses, or either of them, and in case of disagreement between them with respect to the time of adjournment, he may adjourn them to such time as he shall think proper; he shall receive ambassadors and other public ministers; he shall take care that the laws be faithfully executed, and shall commission all the officers of the United States.

Section 4—(All civil offices forfeited for certain crimes.)

The President, Vice President, and all civil officers of the United States shall be removed from office on impeachment for and conviction of treason, bribery, or other high crimes and misdemeanors.

ARTICLE III.

Section 1—(Judicial powers. Tenure. Compensation.)

The judicial power of the United States shall be vested in one Supreme Court, and in such inferior courts as the Congress may from time to time ordain and establish. The judges, both of the Supreme and inferior courts, shall hold their offices during good behavior, and shall at stated times receive for their services a compensation which shall not be diminished during their continuance in office.

Section 2—(Judicial power; to what cases it extends. Original jurisdiction of Supreme Court. Appellate. Trial by jury, etc. Trial, where.)

1. The judicial power shall extend to all cases in law and equity arising under this Constitution, the laws of the United States, and treaties made, or which shall be made, under their authority; to all cases affecting ambassadors, other public ministers and consuls; to all cases of admiralty and maritime jurisdiction; to controversies to which the United States shall be a party; to controversies between two or more States, between a State and citizens of another State, between citizens of different States, between citizens of the same State claiming lands under grants of different States, and between a State, or the citizens thereof, and foreign states, citizens, or subjects.

2. In all cases affecting ambassadors, other public ministers, and consuls, and those in which a State shall be party, the Supreme Court shall have original jurisdiction. In all the other cases, before mentioned, the Supreme Court shall have appellate jurisdiction both as to law and fact, with such exceptions and under such regulations as the Congress shall make.

3. The trial of all crimes, except in cases of impeachment, shall be by jury, and such trial shall be held in the State where the said crimes shall have been committed; but when not committed within any State the trial shall be at such place or places as the Congress may by law have directed.

Section 3—(Treason defined. Proof of. Punishment of.)

1. Treason against the United States shall consist only in levying war against them, or in adhering to their enemies, giving them aid and comfort. No person shall be convicted of treason unless on the testimony of two witnesses to the same overt act, or on confession in open court.

2. The Congress shall have power to declare the punishment of treason, but no

attainder of treason shall work corruption of blood or forfeiture except during the life of the person attained.

ARTICLE IV.

Section 1—(Each State to give credit to the public acts, etc., of every other State.)

Full faith and credit shall be given in each State to the public acts, records, and judicial proceedings of every other State. And the Congress may by general laws prescribe the manner in which such acts, records, and proceedings shall be proved, and the effect thereof.

Section 2—(Privileges of citizens of each State. Fugitives from justice to be delivered up. Persons held to service having escaped, to be delivered up.)

1. The citizens of each State shall be entitled to all privileges and immunities of citizens in the several States.

2. A person charged in any State with treason, felony, or other crime, who shall flee from justice, and be found in another State, shall, on demand of the Executive authority of the State from which he fled, be delivered up, to be removed to the State having jurisdiction of the crime.

3. No person held to service or labor in one State, under the laws thereof, escaping into another shall in consequence of any law or regulation therein, be discharged from such service or labor, but shall be delivered up on claim of the party to whom such service or labor may be due.

Section 3—(Admission of new States. Power of Congress over territory and other property.)

1. New States may be admitted by the Congress into this Union; but no new State shall be formed or erected within the jurisdiction of any other State, nor any State be formed by the junction of two or more States, or parts of States, without the consent of the Legislatures of the States concerned, as well as of the Congress.

2. The Congress shall have power to dispose of and make all needful rules and regulations respecting the territory or other property belonging to the United States; and nothing in this Constitution shall be so construed as to prejudice any claims of the United States, or of any particular State.

Section 4—(Republican form of government guaranteed. Each State to be protected.)

The United States shall guarantee to every State in this Union a Republican form of government, and shall protect each of them against invasion, and, on application of the Legislature, or of the Executive (when the Legislature cannot be convened), against domestic violence.

ARTICLE V.

(Constitution; how amended. Proviso.)

The Congress, whenever two-thirds of both Houses shall deem it necessary, shall propose amendments to this Constitution, or, on the application of the Legislatures of two-thirds of the several States, shall call a convention for proposing amendments, which in either case, shall be valid to all intents and purposes, as part of this Constitution, when ratified by the Legislatures of three-fourths of the several States, or by conventions in three-fourths thereof, as the one or the other mode of ratification may be proposed by the Congress; provided that no amendment which may be made prior to the year one thousand eight hundred and eight shall in any manner affect the first and fourth clauses in the Ninth Section of the First Article; and that no State, without its consent, shall be deprived of its equal suffrage in the Senate.

ARTICLE VI.

(Certain debts, etc., declared valid. Supremacy of Constitution, treaties, and laws of the United States. Oath to support Constitution, by whom taken. No religious test.)

1. All debts contracted and engagements entered into before the adoption of this Constitution shall be as valid against the United States under this Constitution as under the Confederation.

2. This Constitution and the laws of the United States which shall be made in pursuance thereof and all treaties made, or which shall be made, under the authority of the United States, shall be the supreme law of the land, and the judges in every State shall be bound thereby, anything in the Constitution or laws of any State to the contrary notwithstanding.

3. The Senators and Representatives before mentioned, and the members of the several State Legislatures, and all executive and judicial officers, both of the United States and of the several States, shall be bound by oath or affirmation to support this Constitution; but no religious test shall ever be required as a qualification to any office or public trust under the United States.

ARTICLE VII.

(What ratification shall establish Constitution.)

The ratification of the Conventions of nine States shall be sufficient for the establishment of this Constitution between the States so ratifying the same.

Amendments to the Constitution of the United States

ARTICLE I.
Religious Establishment Prohibited, Freedom of Speech, of the Press, and Right to Petition.

Congress shall make no law respecting an establishment of religion, or prohibiting the free exercise thereof; or abridging the freedom of speech or of the press; or the right of the people peaceably to assemble and to petition the Government for a redress of grievances.

ARTICLE II.
Right to Keep and Bear Arms.

A well-regulated militia being necessary to the security of a free State, the right of the people to keep and bear arms shall not be infringed.

ARTICLE III.
No Soldier to Be Quartered in Any House, Unless, Etc.

No soldier shall, in time of peace, be quartered in any house without the consent of the owner, nor in time of war but in a manner to be prescribed by law.

ARTICLE IV.
Right of Search and Seizure Regulated.

The right of the people to be secure in their persons, houses, papers, and effects, against unreasonable searches and seizures, shall not be violated, and no warrants shall issue but upon probable cause, supported by oath or affirmation, and particularly describing the place to be searched, and the persons or things to be seized.

ARTICLE V.

Provisions Concerning Prosecution, Trial, and Punishment.—Private Property Not to Be Taken for Public Use, Without Compensation.

No person shall be held to answer for a capital or other infamous crime unless on a presentment or indictment of a Grand Jury, except in cases arising in the land or naval forces, or in the militia, when in actual service, in time of war or public danger; nor shall any person be subject for the same offence to be twice put in jeopardy of life or limb; nor shall be compelled in any criminal case to be a witness against himself, nor be deprived of life, liberty, or property, without due process of law; nor shall private property be taken for public use without just compensation.

ARTICLE VI.

Right to Speedy Trial, Witnesses, Etc.

In all criminal prosecutions, the accused shall enjoy the right to a speedy and public trial by an impartial jury of the State and district wherein the crime shall have been committed, which districts shall have been previously ascertained by law, and to be informed of the nature and cause of the accusation; to be confronted with the witnesses against him; to have compulsory process for obtaining witnesses in his favor, and to have the assistance of counsel for his defense.

ARTICLE VII.

Right of Trial by Jury.

In suits at common law, where the value in controversy shall exceed twenty dollars, the right of trial by jury shall be preserved, and no fact tried by a jury shall be otherwise re-examined in any court of the United States than according to the rules of the common law.

ARTICLE VIII.

Excessive Bail or Fines and Cruel Punishment Prohibited.

Excessive bail shall not be required, nor excessive fines imposed, nor cruel and unusual punishments inflicted.

ARTICLE IX.

Rule of Construction of Constitution.

The enumeration in the Constitution of certain rights shall not be construed to deny or disparage others retained by the people.

ARTICLE X.

Rights of States Under Constitution.

The powers not delegated to the United States by the Constitution, nor prohibited by it to the States, are reserved to the States respectively, or to the people.

ARTICLE XI.

Judicial Powers Construed.

The following amendment was proposed to the Legislatures of the several states by the Third Congress on March 5, 1794, and was declared to have been ratified in a message from the President to Congress, dated January 8, 1798.

The judicial power of the United States shall not be construed to extend to any suit in law or equity, commenced or prosecuted against one of the United States, by citizens of another State, or by citizens or subjects of any foreign state.

ARTICLE XII.
Manner of Choosing President and Vice-President.

The following amendment was proposed to the Legislatures of the several states by the Eighth Congress on December 12, 1803, and was declared to have been ratified in a proclamation by the Secretary of State, dated September 25, 1804. It was ratified by all the states except Connecticut, Delaware, Massachusetts, and New Hampshire.

The Electors shall meet in their respective States, and vote by ballot for President and Vice-President, one of whom at least shall not be an inhabitant of the same State with themselves; they shall name in their ballots the person voted for as President, and in distinct ballots the person voted for as Vice-President; and they shall make distinct list of all persons voted for as President, and of all persons voted for as Vice-President, and of the number of votes for each, which list they shall sign and certify, and transmit, sealed to the seat of the Government of the United States, directed to the President of the Senate; the President of the Senate shall, in the presence of the Senate and House of Representatives, open all the certificates and the votes shall then be counted; the person having the greatest number of votes for President shall be the President, if such number be a majority of the whole number of Electors appointed; and if no person have such majority, then from the persons having the highest number, not exceeding three, on the list of those voted for as President, the House of Representatives shall choose immediately, by ballot, the President. But in choosing the President, the votes shall be taken by States, the representation from each State having one vote; a quorum for this purpose shall consist of a member or members from two-thirds of the States, and a majority of all the States shall be necessary to a choice. And if the House of Representatives shall not choose a President, whenever the right of choice shall devolve upon them, before the fourth day of March next following, then the Vice-President shall act as President, as in the case of the death or other constitutional disability of the President. The person having the greatest number of votes as Vice-President shall be the Vice-President if such number be a majority of the whole number of Electors appointed, and if no person have a majority then from the two highest numbers on the list the Senate shall choose the Vice-President; a quorum for the purpose shall consist of two-thirds of the whole number of Senators, and a majority of the whole number shall be necessary to a choice. But no person constitutionally ineligible to the office of President shall be eligible to that of Vice-President of the United States.

ARTICLE XIII.
Slavery Abolished.

The following amendment was proposed to the Legislatures of the several states by the Thirty-eighth Congress on February 1, 1865, and was declared to have been ratified in a proclamation by the Secretary of State dated December 18, 1865. It was rejected by Delaware and Kentucky; was conditionally ratified by Alabama and Mississippi; and Texas took no action.

1. Neither slavery nor involuntary servitude, except as a punishment for crime whereof the party shall have been duly convicted, shall exist within the United States, or any place subject to their jurisdiction.

2. Congress shall have power to enforce this article by appropriate legislation.

ARTICLE XIV.
Citizenship Rights Not to Be Abridged.

The following, popularly known as the Reconstruction Amendment, was proposed to the Legislatures of the several states, by the Thirty-ninth Congress on June 16, 1866, and was declared to have been ratified in a proclamation by the Secretary of State, dated July 23, 1868. The amendment got the support of 23 Northern states; it was rejected by Delaware, Kentucky, Maryland, and ten Southern states; California took no action. Subsequently it was ratified by the ten Southern states.

1. All persons born or naturalized in the United States, and subject to the jurisdiction thereof, are citizens of the United States and of the State wherein they reside. No State shall make or enforce any law which shall abridge the privileges or immunities of

citizens of the United States; nor shall any State deprive any person of life, liberty, or property without due process of law, nor deny to any person within its jurisdiction the equal protection of the laws.

Apportionment of Representatives in Congress.

2. Representatives shall be apportioned among the several States according to their respective numbers, counting the whole number of persons in each State excluding Indians not taxed. But when the right to vote at any election for the choice of Electors for President and Vice-President of the United States, Representatives in Congress, the executive and judicial officers of a State, or the members of the Legislature thereof, is denied to any of the male inhabitants of such State, being twenty-one years of age, and citizens of the United States, or in any way abridged, except for participation in rebellion, or other crime, the basis of representation therein shall be reduced in the proportion which the number of such male citizens shall bear to the whole number of male citizens twenty-one years of age in such State.

Power of Congress to Remove Disabilities of United States Officials for Rebellion.

3. No person shall be a Senator or Representative in Congress, or Elector of President and Vice-President or holding any office, civil or military, under the United States, or under any State, who, having previously taken an oath, as a member of Congress, or as an officer of the United States, or as a member of any State Legislature or as an executive or judicial officer of any State, to support the Constitution of the United States, shall have engaged in insurrection or rebellion against the same, or given aid and comfort to the enemies thereof. But Congress may, by a vote of two-thirds of each House, remove such disability.

What Public Debts Are Valid.

4. The validity of the public debt of the United States, authorized by law, including debts incurred for payment of pensions and bounties for services in suppressing insurrection and rebellion, shall not be questioned. But neither the United States nor any State shall assume or pay any debt or obligation incurred in aid of insurrection or rebellion against the United States, or any claim for the loss or emancipation of any slave; but all such debts, obligations, and claims shall be held illegal and void.

5. The Congress shall have power to enforce by appropriate legislation the provisions of this article.

ARTICLE XV.
Equal Rights for White and Colored Citizens.

The following amendment was proposed to the Legislatures of the several states by the Fortieth Congress on February 27, 1869, and was declared to have been ratified in a proclamation by the Secretary of State, dated March 30, 1870. It was not acted on by Tennessee; it was rejected by California, Delaware, Kentucky, Maryland, and Oregon: ratified by the remaining 30 states; New York rescinded its ratification, January 5, 1870. New Jersey rejected it in 1870, but ratified it in 1871.

1. The right of the citizens of the United States to vote shall not be denied or abridged by the United States or by any State on account of race, color, or previous condition of servitude.

2. The Congress shall have power to enforce the provisions of this article by appropriate legislation.

ARTICLE XVI.
Income Taxes Authorized.

The following amendment was proposed to the Legislatures of the several states by the Sixty-first Congress on July 12, 1909, and was declared to have been ratified in a proclamation by the Secretary of State, dated February 25, 1913. The income tax amendment was ratified by all the states except Connecticut, Florida, Pennsylvania, Rhode Island, Utah, and Virginia.

The Congress shall have power to lay and collect taxes on incomes from whatever sources derived, without apportionment among the several States, and without regard to any census or enumeration.

ARTICLE XVII.
United States Senators to Be Elected by Direct Popular Vote.

The following amendment was proposed to the Legislatures of the several states by the Sixty-second Congress on May 16, 1912, and was declared to have been ratified in a proclamation by the Secretary of State, dated May 31, 1913. It got the vote of all the states except Alabama, Delaware, Florida, Georgia, Kentucky, Louisiana, Maryland, Mississippi, Rhode Island, South Carolina, Utah, and Virginia.

1. The Senate of the United States shall be composed of two Senators from each State, elected by the people thereof, for six years; and each Senator shall have one vote. The Electors in each State shall have the qualifications requisite for Electors of the most numerous branch of the State Legislatures.

Vacancies in Senatorships, When Governor May Fill by Appointment.

2. When vacancies happen in the representation of any State in the Senate, the executive authority of such State shall issue writs of election to fill such vacancies: Provided, That the Legislature of any State may empower the Executive thereof to make temporary appointment until the people fill the vacancies by election as the Legislature may direct.

3. This amendment shall not be so construed as to affect the election or term of any Senator chosen before it becomes valid as part of the Constitution.

ARTICLE XVIII.
Liquor Prohibition Amendment.

The following amendment was proposed to the Legislatures of the several states by the Sixty-fifth Congress, December 18, 1917; and on January 29, 1919, the United States Secretary of State proclaimed its adoption by 36 states, and declared it in effect on January 16, 1920.

1. After one year from the ratification of this article the manufacture, sale, or transportation of intoxicating liquors within, the importation thereof into, or the exportation thereof from the United States and all territory subject to the jurisdiction thereof for beverage purposes is hereby prohibited.

2. The Congress and the several States shall have concurrent power to enforce this article by appropriate legislation.

3. This article shall be inoperative unless it shall have been ratified as an amendment to the Constitution by the Legislatures of the several States, as provided in the Constitution, within seven years from the date of the submission hereof to the States by the Congress.

ARTICLE XIX.
Giving Nation-Wide Suffrage to Women.

The following amendment was proposed to the Legislatures of the several states by the Sixty-fifth Congress, having been adopted by the House of Representatives, May 21, 1919, and by the Senate, June 4, 1919. On August, 26, 1920, the United States Secretary of State proclaimed it in effect, it having been adopted (June 10, 1919–August 18, 1920), by three-quarters of the states.

1. The right of citizens of the United States to vote shall not be denied or abridged by the United States or by any State on account of sex.

2. Congress shall have power, by appropriate legislation, to enforce the provisions of this article.

ARTICLE XX.
Terms of President and Vice-President to Begin on Jan. 20; Those of Senators and Representatives on Jan. 3.

The following amendment was proposed to the Legislatures of the several states by the Seventy-second Congress, in March, 1932, a joint resolution to that effect having been adopted, first by the House, and then, on March 2, by the Senate. On February 6, 1933, the Secretary of State proclaimed it in effect, 39 of the 48 states having ratified.

Section 1. The terms of the President and Vice-President shall end at noon on the 20th day of January, and the terms of Senators and Representatives at noon on the 3rd day of January, of the years in which such terms would have ended if this article had not been ratified; and the terms of their successors shall then begin.

Section 2. The Congress shall assemble at least once in every year, and such meeting shall begin at noon on the 3rd day of January, unless they shall by law appoint a different day.

Section 3. If, at the time fixed for the beginning of the term of the President, the President-elect shall have died, the Vice-President-elect shall become President. If a President shall not have been chosen before the time fixed for the beginning of his term, or if the President-elect shall have failed to qualify, then the Vice-President-elect shall act as President until a President shall have qualified; and the Congress may by law provide for the case wherein neither a President-elect nor a Vice-President-elect shall have qualified, declaring who shall then act as President, or the manner in which one who is to act shall be selected, and such person shall act accordingly until a President or Vice-President shall have qualified.

Section 4. The Congress may by law provide for the case of the death of any of the persons from whom the House of Representatives may choose a President whenever the right of choice shall have devolved upon them, and for the case of the death of any of the persons from whom the Senate may choose a Vice-President whenever the right of choice shall have devolved upon them.

Section 5. Sections 1 and 2 shall take effect on the 15th day of October following the ratification of this article (Oct. 1933).

Section 6. This article shall be inoperative unless it shall have been ratified as an amendment to the Constitution by the legislatures of three-fourths of the several States within seven years from the date of its submission.

ARTICLE XXI.
Repeal of the Eighteenth (Prohibition) Amendment by Conventions in the States.

The following amendment, embodied in a joint resolution of the Seventy-second Congress (Senate, February 16, 1933, by 63 to 23; House, February 20, 1933, by 289 to 121), was transmitted to the Secretary of State on February 21 and he at once sent copies to the governors of the states. The amendment went into effect December 5, 1933, having been adopted by 36 of the 48 states.

Section 1. The eighteenth article of amendment to the Constitution of the United States is hereby repealed.

Section 2. The transportation or importation into any State, Territory, or Possession of the United States for delivery or use therein of intoxicating liquors, in violation of the laws thereof, is hereby prohibited.

Section 3. This article shall be inoperative unless it shall have been ratified as an amendment to the Constitution by conventions in the several States, as provided in the Constitution, within seven years from the date of the submission hereof to the States by the Congress.

PROPOSED AMENDMENTS

The Constitution of the United States may be amended according to the procedure and requirements established in Article V. Various amendments have been proposed in recent years, including a restriction of child-labor practices, the limitation of the office of President to two terms, a change in the present organization of the Electoral College, and equal rights for women.

THE CIVIL SERVICE

All branches of the public service that are not military, legislative, or judicial belong to the civil service. Civil service positions exist in the Federal Government, and in state, county, and municipal governments.

The Federal civil service consists of about 2,000,000 positions, and offers practically every form of employment. Most positions are in the competitive service; when vacancies occur, they are filled through open competitive examinations, announced by the United States Civil Service Commission, or by other procedures provided for under the system, such as promotion, transfer, and reinstatement.

When examinations are announced, they are publicized through such means as (1) notices posted on bulletin boards in first- and second-class post offices and in other Federal buildings, and (2) notices distributed to schools, public libraries, organizations, periodicals, and newspapers.

Examinations vary in nature according to the types of positions for which they are held. Each one is designed to test the ability of the applicant to perform the duties of the position applied for, or to test his ability to learn how to perform them. Some examinations consist in, or include, a written test; others consist in an appraisal of applicants' experience or training, which they describe in their application forms.

For complete information about an examination, the examination announcement (a printed or processed bulletin) should be consulted. Announcements are furnished, upon request, by whatever office of the Civil Service Commission is announcing a particular examination: (1) Examinations for filling positions in Washington, D.C., and, in some cases, throughout the country, are announced by the Commission's central office, Washington, D.C.; (2) examinations for filling positions in a civil service region (a state or group of states), and certain local examinations (for example, those held for filling positions in post offices), are announced by the Commission's regional offices, of which there are 14; (3) examinations for filling many types of positions in Federal establishments such as navy yards, arsenals, and veterans' hospitals are announced by boards of United States civil service examiners located at those establishments.

Anyone planning to enter the Federal service and in need of more information should write to the United States Civil Service Commission, Washington 25, D.C.

RANK OF GOVERNMENT OFFICIALS OF THE UNITED STATES

Even in a democratic country like ours, a strict order of precedence is followed by Government officials. Protocol in ranking Government officials varies, but the following is the most generally accepted order:

The President
The Vice President
President of the Senate
Foreign Ambassadors
Chief Justice of the Supreme Court
United States Senators
Speaker of the House
Representatives
Associate Justices of the Supreme Court
Secretary of State
Diplomatic Corps (other than ambassadors)

Secretary of the Treasury
Secretary of Defense
The Attorney General
The Postmaster General
Secretary of the Interior
Secretary of Agriculture
Secretary of Commerce
Secretary of Labor
Secretaries of the Army, Navy, and Air Force
Governors of the states

RANK IN THE ARMY AND NAVY OF THE UNITED STATES

In the United States the Army outranks the Navy because it was established first. In England the opposite is true, the Navy there being the older service. The President of the United States is Commander in Chief of both the Army and the Navy. Below him, in order, are the following:

Army and Air Force	*Navy*
General of the Army[1]	Fleet Admiral
General	Admiral
Lieutenant General	Vice Admiral
Major General	Rear Admiral
Brigadier General	Commodore
Colonel	Captain
Lieutenant Colonel	Commander
Major	Lieutenant Commander
Captain	Lieutenant
First Lieutenant	Lieutenant (Junior Grade)
Second Lieutenant	Ensign

Enlisted men's ratings are, in the *Army:* recruit, private, private first class, corporal, sergeant, sergeant first class, master sergeant, warrant officer (3rd, 2nd, and 1st class), chief warrant officer; in the *Navy:* seaman recruit, seaman apprentice, seaman, petty officer (3rd, 2nd, and 1st class), chief petty officer, warrant officer, chief warrant officer; in the *Air Force:* private, private first class, corporal, sergeant, staff sergeant, technical sergeant, first sergeant, master sergeant, warrant officer junior grade, chief warrant officer.

In the Army, all holding the rank of second lieutenant or higher are addressed in writing and speech by their titles. Below the rank of second lieutenant they are introduced by their titles and addressed by them in writing, but in speech they are addressed or referred to as "Mr."

In the Navy all holding the rank of commander or higher are addressed by their titles in writing and speech. Those below the grade of commander are introduced by their titles, and so addressed in letters, but in ordinary speech they are addressed and referred to as "Mr."

The President, in this capacity, and indeed in all others, is addressed as "Mr. President" and "Sir." His wife (as are all other wives of American officials) is addressed simply as "Mrs."

---

[1]The Air Force, as this is written, does not have a five-star general ranking with "General of the Army."

STATE NICKNAMES, FLOWERS, MOTTOES, AND OTHER DATA

State	Nickname	Capital	Date admitted to Union
ALABAMA	Cotton State	Montgomery	Dec. 14, 1819
ARIZONA	Grand Canyon State	Phoenix	Feb. 14, 1912
ARKANSAS	Wonder State	Little Rock	June 15, 1836
CALIFORNIA	Golden State	Sacramento	Sept. 9, 1850
COLORADO	Centennial State	Denver	Aug. 1, 1876
CONNECTICUT	Constitution State	Hartford	Jan. 9, 1788
DELAWARE	Diamond State	Dover	Dec. 7, 1787
FLORIDA	Peninsula State	Tallahassee	March 3, 1845
GEORGIA	Cracker State	Atlanta	Jan. 2, 1788
IDAHO	Gem State	Boise	July 3, 1890
ILLINOIS	Prairie State	Springfield	Dec. 3, 1818
INDIANA	Hoosier State	Indianapolis	Dec. 11, 1816
IOWA	Hawkeye State	Des Moines	Dec. 28, 1846
KANSAS	Sunflower State	Topeka	Jan. 29, 1861
KENTUCKY	Bluegrass State	Frankfort	June 1, 1792
LOUISIANA	Pelican State	Baton Rouge	April 8, 1812
MAINE	Pine Tree State	Augusta	March 15, 1820
MARYLAND	Old Line State	Annapolis	April 28, 1788
MASSACHUSETTS	Bay State	Boston	Feb. 6, 1788
MICHIGAN	Wolverine State	Lansing	Jan. 26, 1837
MINNESOTA	Gopher State	St. Paul	May 11, 1858
MISSISSIPPI	Magnolia State	Jackson	Dec. 10, 1817
MISSOURI	Show-Me State	Jefferson City	Aug. 10, 1821
MONTANA	Treasure State	Helena	Nov. 8, 1889
NEBRASKA	Cornhusker State	Lincoln	March 1, 1867
NEVADA	Sagebrush State	Carson City	Oct. 31, 1864
NEW HAMPSHIRE	Granite State	Concord	June 21, 1788
NEW JERSEY	Garden State	Trenton	Dec. 18, 1787
NEW MEXICO	Sunshine State	Santa Fe	Jan. 6, 1912
NEW YORK	Empire State	Albany	July 26, 1788

Flower	Motto	Origin of state name
ldenrod	We Dare Defend Our Rights	From Indian tribe name, Alabama
guaro Cactus	*Ditat Deus* (God Enriches)	From Indian word "Arizonac," meaning "small spring"
ple Blossom	*Regnat Populus* (The People Rule)	Algonquin name of the Quapaw Indians
lden Poppy	*Eureka* (I Have Found It)	An imaginary island named in a 16th-century Spanish romance
cky Mountain lumbine	*Nil Sine Numine* (Nothing Without the Deity)	Spanish word for "red"
untain Laurel	*Qui Transtulit Sustinet* (He Who Transplanted Continues to Sustain)	Indian, "Quonecktacut," meaning "long river" or "river of pines"
ach Blossom	Liberty and Independence	From Lord De La Warr, of England, Governor of Virginia
ange Blossom	In God We Trust	Spanish words, "Pascua Florida," or Feast of Flowers
erokee Rose	Wisdom, Justice, and Moderation	From King George II, of England
ringa	*Esto Perpetua* (Mayest Thou Endure Forever)	Indian words "Edah hoe," meaning "light on the mountains"
tive Violet	State Sovereignty—National Union	Indian word meaning "The River of Men"
nia	The Crossroads of America	State of Indians
ld Rose	Our Liberties We Prize and Our Rights We Will Maintain	A Sioux tribe, the Ioways or Aiouez, meaning "sleepy ones"
tive Sunflower	*Ad Astra per Aspera* (To the Stars Through Difficulties)	Name of a Sioux tribe
ldenrod	United We Stand, Divided We Fall	From Wyandot name, "Ken-tah-teh," meaning "tomorrow"
agnolia	Union, Justice and Confidence	From King Louis XIV, of France
ne Cone and Tassel	*Dirigo* (I Guide)	From ancient province in France
ack-eyed Susan	*Scuto Bonae Voluntatis Tuae Coronasti Nos* (With the Shield of Thy Good-will Thou Hast Covered Us)	From Queen Henrietta Maria, of England
ayflower	*Ense Petit Placidam Sub Libertate Quietem* (By the Sword We Seek Peace, but Peace Only Under Liberty)	Algonquin name, "Massadchu-es-et," meaning "great-hill-small-place"
ple Blossom	*Si Quaeris Peninsulam Amoenam Circumspice* (If You Seek a Pleasant Peninsula, Look Around You)	From the Mishigamaw or Mishawiguma Indians
occasin Flower	*L'Étoile du Nord* (The Star of the North)	From Sioux words meaning "sky-colored water"
agnolia	*Virtute et Armis* (By Valor and Arms)	Indian words, "Maesi"—"fish," "Sipu"—"river": Fish River
awthorn	*Salus Populi Suprema Lex Esto* (Let The Welfare of the People Be the Supreme Law)	Name of a Sioux tribe
tterroot	*Oro y Plata* (Gold and Silver)	Spanish for "mountainous"
ldenrod	Equality Before the Law	An Omaha Indian name for the "wide river" Platte
gebrush	All for Our Country	A Spanish word, meaning "snow-clad"
rple Lilac	Live Free or Die	From the County of Hampshire, in England
olet	Liberty and Prosperity	From the Island of Jersey
cca Flower	*Crescit Eundo* (It Grows As It Goes)	From "mexitli," Aztec war god
se	*Excelsior* (Higher)	From the Duke of York (1664)

STATE NICKNAMES, FLOWERS, MOTTOES, AND OTHER DATA

State	Nickname	Capital	Date admitted to Union
NORTH CAROLINA	Tarheel State	Raleigh	Nov. 21, 1789
NORTH DAKOTA	Flickertail State	Bismarck	Nov. 2, 1889
OHIO	Buckeye State	Columbus	Feb. 19, 1803
OKLAHOMA	Sooner State	Oklahoma City	Nov. 16, 1907
OREGON	Beaver State	Salem	Feb. 14, 1859
PENNSYLVANIA	Keystone State	Harrisburg	Dec. 12, 1787
RHODE ISLAND	Little Rhody	Providence	May 29, 1790
SOUTH CAROLINA	Palmetto State	Columbia	May 23, 1788
SOUTH DAKOTA	Coyote State	Pierre	Nov. 2, 1889
TENNESSEE	Volunteer State	Nashville	June 1, 1796
TEXAS	Lone Star State	Austin	Dec. 29, 1845
UTAH	Beehive State	Salt Lake City	Jan. 4, 1896
VERMONT	Green Mountain State	Montpelier	March 4, 1791
VIRGINIA	The Old Dominion	Richmond	June 25, 1788
WASHINGTON	Evergreen State	Olympia	Nov. 11, 1889
WEST VIRGINIA	Panhandle State	Charleston	June 20, 1863
WISCONSIN	Badger State	Madison	May 29, 1848
WYOMING	Equality State	Cheyenne	July 10, 1890

Flower	Motto	Origin of state name
wood	*Esse Quam Videri* (To Be Rather Than To Seem)	From Charles II, of England
d Prairie Rose	Liberty and Union, Now and Forever, One and Inseparable	From Sioux word meaning, "alliance with friends"
rlet Carnation	(None)	Iroquois name, meaning "great"
tletoe	*Labor Omnia Vincit* (Labor Conquers All Things)	Choctaw, meaning "red people"
gon Grape	The Union	Probably from Spanish word "Orejon," meaning "big-eared men"
untain Laurel	Virtue, Liberty and Independence	Named in honor of William Penn, father of the founder
let	Hope	"Isles of Rhodes," name chosen by colony General Court in 1644
low Jessamine	*Animus Opibusque Parati* (Ready in Soul and Resource)	(See North Carolina)
que Flower	Under God the People Rule	(See North Dakota)
	Agriculture and Commerce	From "Tennese," name of chief Cherokee town
ebonnet	Friendship	From an Indian word meaning "friends" or "allies"
o Lily	Industry	From an Indian tribe, named the Utes
Clover	Freedom and Unity	From the French words "vert" and "mont," meaning "green mountain"
wood	*Sic Semper Tyrannis* (Thus Ever to Tyrants)	In honor of Elizabeth, the "Virgin Queen" of England
stern Rhododron	*Alki* (By and By)	In honor of George Washington
Rhododendron	*Montani Semper Liberi* (Mountaineers Are Always Freemen)	(See Virginia)
od Violet	Forward	From an Indian name
ian Paintbrush	*Cedant Arma Togae* (Let Arms Yield to the Gown)	From Wyoming Valley, Pa. Word means "alternating mountains and valleys"

VOTING QUALIFICATIONS IN THE DIFFERENT STATES

Alabama.—Previous residence required two years in the state, one year in the county, three months in the town or city, district, precinct, or ward. The voter must pay all poll taxes owed, if any, since 1901. Members of the armed forces are exempt from poll taxes. Registration is permanent unless removed for cause. No absentee registration, but absentee voting permitted.

Arizona.—Previous residence required, one year in the state, 30 days in the county, town or city, district, precinct, or ward. Voter must be able to read and write. Registration is required. Absentee registration and voting permitted.

Arkansas.—Previous residence required, one year in the state, six months in the county, one month in the town or city, district, precinct, or ward. Poll tax is required. Registration of any kind is prohibited by the state constitution. Absentee voting is permitted.

California.—Previous residence required, one year in the state, 90 days in the county, 40 days in the district, precinct, or ward. Voter must be able to read the Constitution and to write his name, and must have been a citizen for 90 days. Absentee registration and voting permitted.

Colorado.—Previous residence required, one year in the state, 90 days in the county, 30 days in the town or city, 15 days in the district, precinct, or ward. Registration is required for all except certain minor elections. Absentee registration and voting permitted.

Connecticut.—Previous residence required, one year in the state, six months in the district, town or city. Voter must pass a literacy test, and must be registered. The voter must have been a citizen for five years. No absentee registration, but absentee voting permitted.

Delaware.—Previous residence required, one year in the state, three months in the county, 30 days in the district, precinct, or ward. Voter must be able to read the Constitution and write name. Registration is required. No absentee registration, but absentee voting permitted.

Florida.—Previous residence required, one year in the state, six months in the county. Registration is required for all elections. There is no literacy test, but there is a poll tax. No absentee registration, but absentee voting permitted.

Georgia.—Previous residence required, one year in the state, six months in the county. Under 1949 law, all voters must pass a literacy test or qualify by answering ten to 30 prescribed oral questions. Voter must be registered. No absentee registration, but absentee voting permitted.

Idaho.—Previous residence required, six months in the state, 30 days in the county. Voter must be registered. No absentee registration, but absentee voting permitted.

Illinois.—Previous residence required, one year in the state, 90 days in the county, 30 days in the town or city, and 30 days in the district, precinct, or ward. Voter must be registered for state and Federal elections. No absentee registration, but absentee voting permitted.

Indiana.—Previous residence required, six months in the state, 60 days in the county, 30 days in the town or city, district, precinct, or ward. Voter must be registered for all except certain minor elections. Absentee registration and absentee voting permitted.

Iowa.—Previous residence required, six months in the state, 60 days in the county, ten days in the town or city, district, precinct, or ward. Voter must be registered. No literacy test is required. Absentee registration permitted only in permanent system. Absentee voting permitted.

Kansas.—Previous residence required, six months in the state, 30 days in the county, town or city, district, precinct, or ward. Voter must be registered. No literacy test is required. No absentee registration, but absentee voting permitted.

Kentucky.—Previous residence required, one year in the state, six months in the county, 60 days in the town or city, district, precinct, or ward. Voter must be registered. No literacy test is required. Absentee registration and voting permitted.

Louisiana.—Previous residence required, two years in the state, one year in the parish, four months in the municipality, three months in the district, precinct, or ward.

Under 1949 law, all voters must pass a literacy test or qualify by answering ten to 30 prescribed oral questions. Voter must be registered. No absentee registration, but absentee voting permitted.

Maine.—Previous residence required, six months in the state, three months in the county, three months in the town or city, district, precinct, or ward. Voter must pass a literacy test and must be registered. No absentee registration, but absentee voting permitted.

Maryland.—Previous residence required, one year in the state, six months in the county, town or city, and six months in the district, precinct, or ward. Voter must be able to read and must be registered. Absentee registration and voting for armed services only.

Massachusetts.—Previous residence required, one year in the state, six months in the town or city, district, precinct, or ward. Voter must be able to read the Constitution and write his name, and must be registered. Absentee registration for armed services only. Absentee voting for armed services and those unable to appear in person because of physical disability.

Michigan.—Previous residence required, six months in the state, 20 days in the town or city, district, precinct, or ward. Registration is required. Payment of property tax is required for vote on bond issue or special assessments only. Absentee registration and voting permitted.

Minnesota.—Previous residence required, six months in the state, 30 days in the town or city, district, precinct, or ward. Voter must have been citizen for 90 days. Registration is required. Absentee registration and voting permitted.

Mississippi.—Previous residence required, two years in the state, one year in the town or city, district, precinct, or ward. Voter must pay poll tax and must owe no past-due taxes. A literacy test is required. Registration is required for all state and county elections. A separate registration is required for municipal elections. No absentee registration and voting permitted.

Missouri.—Previous residence required, one year in the state, 60 days in the county, town or city, district, precinct, or ward. Registration is required. No absentee registration, but absentee voting permitted.

Montana.—Previous residence required, one year in the state, 30 days in the county, town or city, district, precinct, or ward. Registration is required for all except certain minor elections. Payment of property tax is required for vote on bond issues or special assessments only. Absentee registration and voting permitted.

Nebraska.—Previous residence required, six months in the state, 40 days in the county, ten days in the town or city, district, precinct, or ward. Registration required for all except certain minor elections. Absentee registration and voting permitted.

Nevada.—Previous residence required, six months in the state, 30 days in the county, ten days in the town or city, district, precinct, or ward. Voters must be registered. Payment of property tax is required for vote on bond issues or special assessments only. No absentee registration, but absentee voting permitted.

New Hampshire.—Previous residence required, six months in the state, county, the town or city, district, precinct, or ward. Voters must be registered, and must pass a literacy test. Absentee registration and voting permitted.

New Jersey.—Previous residence required, one year in the state, five months in the county. Registration is required. No absentee registration. Absentee voting for armed forces only.

New Mexico.—Previous residence required, one year in the state, 90 days in the county, 30 days in the town or city, district, precinct, or ward. Registration is required. No absentee registration. Absentee voting for armed forces only.

New York.—Previous residence required, one year in the state, four months in the county, 30 days in the town or city, district, precinct, or ward. There is a literacy test. Voter must have been a citizen for 90 days. Registration is required. Absentee registration and voting permitted.

North Carolina.—Previous residence required, one year in the state, four months in the district, precinct, or ward. Voter must be registered and must be able to read and write. Absentee registration for armed forces and persons holding citizenship for more than five years. Absentee voting permitted.

North Dakota.—Previous residence required, one year in the state, 90 days in the county, 30 days in the district, precinct, or ward. Registration is required. Absentee registration and voting permitted.

Ohio.—Previous residence required, one year in the state, 30 days in the county, 20 days in the town or city, district, precinct, or ward. Registration is required. No absentee registration, but absentee voting permitted.

Oklahoma.—Previous residence required, one year in the state, six months in the county, 30 days in the town or city, precinct, or ward. Voters must be registered. Absentee registration permitted under certain conditions. Absentee voting permitted.

Oregon.—Previous residence required, six months in the state. Voters must be able to read and write English. Registration is required. Absentee registration and voting permitted.

Pennsylvania.—Previous residence required, one year in the state, two months in the district, precinct, or ward. Registration is required. No absentee registration or voting permitted.

Rhode Island.—Previous residence required, two years in the state, six months in the district, town or city. Voter must be registered. Absentee registration for armed forces only. Absentee voting permitted.

South Carolina.—Previous residence required, two years in the state (six months for ministers), one year in the county, four months in the town or city, district, precinct, or ward. Voter must be able to read and write or must own and pay taxes on property. Voter must pay poll tax unless specifically exempted. Registration is required. No absentee registration or voting permitted.

South Dakota.—Previous residence required, one year in the state, 90 days in the county, 30 days in the town or city, district, precinct, or ward. Absentee registration and voting permitted.

Tennessee.—Previous residence required, one year in the state, six months in the county. A poll tax is required from all except veterans, women, and blind persons. Registration is required. Absentee registration and voting permitted.

Texas.—Previous residence required, one year in the state, six months in the county, town or city, district, precinct, or ward. Poll tax is required unless voter is specifically exempted. Payment of property tax is required for vote on bond issues or special assessments only. Registration is required by the state constitution, but no system exists. Eligibility of the voter is determined by poll tax receipt. No absentee registration, but absentee voting permitted.

Utah.—Previous residence required, one year in the state, four months in the county, 60 days in the district, precinct, or ward. Voter must be registered. Payment of property tax is required for vote on bond issues or special assessments only. Voter must have been a citizen for 90 days. Absentee registration and absentee voting permitted.

Vermont.—Previous residence required, one year in the state, three months in the town or city, district, precinct, or ward. Voter must be registered. No absentee registration, but absentee voting permitted.

Virginia.—Previous residence required, one year in the state, six months in the county, town or city, 30 days in the district, precinct, or ward. Voter must be able to read and understand the Constitution, must pay poll tax, and must not owe past-due taxes. Registration is required. No absentee registration, but absentee voting permitted.

Washington.—Previous residence required, one year in the state, 90 days in the county, 30 days in the town or city, district, precinct, or ward. Voter must be able to read and write English. Registration is required. Absentee registration and voting permitted.

West Virginia.—Previous residence required, one year in the state, 60 days in the county. Registration is required in all except special elections. No absentee registration, but absentee voting permitted.

Wisconsin.—Previous residence required, one year in the state, ten days in the town or city, district, precinct, or ward. Registration is required. Absentee registration and voting permitted.

Wyoming.—Previous residence required, one year in the state, 60 days in the county, ten days in the town or city, district, precinct, or ward. Registration and a literacy test are required. No absentee registration, but absentee voting permitted.

In all states voters must, of course, be citizens. Voters in all states must be 21 years of age or over, with the exception of Georgia, where the minimum age is 18.

Residents of the District of Columbia, as such, have no votes either in national or local matters. The government is directly under Congress with executive commissioners appointed by the President and confirmed by the Senate. Persons holding civil service positions in the District of Columbia have the privilege of retaining their voting residence in their own states. The vote is controlled by the voting laws of the state in question.

In 1924 Congress passed a law giving citizenship to all native-born Indians.

LEGAL AND PUBLIC HOLIDAYS IN THE UNITED STATES

January	1.	New Year's Day: In all the states, territories, and possessions.
January	8.	Anniversary of the battle of New Orleans: In Louisiana.
January	19.	Lee's Birthday: In Ala., Ark., Fla., Ga., Ky., La., Miss., N.C., S.C., Tenn., and Va.
January	20.	Inauguration Day: Observed every fourth year since 1937, in the District of Columbia only.
January	30.	Franklin D. Roosevelt Day: In Kentucky and West Virginia.
February	12.	Lincoln's Birthday: Alaska, Ariz., Ark., Calif., Colo., Conn., Del., Ill., Ind., Ia., Kan., Ky., Md., Mich., Minn., Mo., Mont., Neb., Nev., N.J., N.Y., N. Dak., Ohio, Ore., Pa., S. Dak., Tenn., Texas, Utah, Vt., Wash., W.Va., Wyo., and, by Governor's proclamation, in Mass.
February	12.	Georgia Day: In Ga., date of Oglethorpe's landing in 1733.
February	14.	Admission Day: In Arizona.
February	22.	Washington's Birthday: In all the states, territories, and possessions.
March	2.	Texas Flag Day: In Texas.
March	15.	Andrew Jackson's Birthday: In Tennessee.
March	17.	Evacuation Day: In Boston and Suffolk County, Mass.
March	22.	Emancipation Day: In Puerto Rico.
March	25.	Maryland Day: In Maryland.
March	30.	Seward Day: In Alaska.
April	12.	Date of passage of Halifax Independence Resolutions: In North Carolina.
April	13.	Birthday of Thomas Jefferson: In Ala., Mo., Okla., and Va.
April	16.	De Diego's Birthday: In Puerto Rico.
April	19.	Patriots' Day: In Me. and Mass.
April	21.	San Jacinto Day: In Texas.
April	22.	Oklahoma Day: In Oklahoma. Arbor Day: In Nebraska.
April	26.	Confederate Memorial Day: In Ala., Fla., Ga., and Miss.
May	1.	Child Health Day (by annual Presidential proclamation).
May	4.	Rhode Island Independence Day and Arbor Day: In Rhode Island.
May	10.	Confederate Memorial Day: In S.C. and N.C.
May	20.	Anniversary of the signing of the Mecklenburg Declaration of Independence: In North Carolina.
May	30.	Decoration or Memorial Day: In all states and possessions except Ala., Ga., Miss., S.C., and W.Va. In Va., known as Confederate Memorial Day. In N.C., for state and national banks only. In Fla. for veterans of all wars.
June	3.	Jefferson Davis's Birthday: In Ala., Fla., Ga., Miss., S.C., Texas, and Va. In Ky., La., and Tenn., known as Confederate Memorial Day.
June	11.	Kamehameha Day: In Hawaii.
June	14.	Flag Day: In Pennsylvania.
June	15.	Pioneer Day: In Idaho.
July	4.	Independence Day: In all states, territories, and possessions.
July	13.	Birthday of Gen. Forest: In Tennessee.
July	17.	Munoz Rivera Day: In Puerto Rico.
July	24.	Pioneer Day: In Utah.
July	25.	Occupation Day: In Puerto Rico.
July	27.	Dr. Barbosa's Birthday: In Puerto Rico.
August	1.	Colorado Day: In Colorado.
August	14.	Victory Day: In Rhode Island.

August	*16.*	Battle of Bennington Day: In Vermont.
August	*30.*	Huey P. Long's Birthday: In Louisiana.
September		(First Monday.) Labor Day: In all states and territories.
September	*9.*	Admission Day: In California.
September	*12.*	Defenders' Day: In Maryland.
October	*10.*	Oklahoma Historical Day: In Oklahoma.
October	*12.*	Columbus Day: In Ark., Ariz., Calif., Colo., Conn., Del., Fla., Ga., Ill., Kan., Ky., La., Md., Mass., Mich., Minn., Mo., Mont., Neb., Nev., N.H., N.J., N.M., N.Y., Ohio, Okla., Ore., Pa., R.I., Texas, Utah, Vt., Va., Wash., W.V., and Puerto Rico. Fraternal Day: In Ala. Discovery Day: In Ind. and N.D. Landing Day: In Wis.
October	*31.*	Admission Day: In Nevada.
November		General Election Day. First Tuesday after the first Monday in November. In every state except Ala., Conn., District of Columbia, Ga., Kan., Ky., Me., Mass., Miss., Mo., Neb., N.M., Utah, and Vt. In some of the states it is a half holiday or a bank holiday.
November	*11.*	Armistice Day: In all states, Alaska, Hawaii, and Puerto Rico.
November	*19.*	Discovery Day: In Puerto Rico.
November		Thanksgiving Day (by proclamation of the President, traditionally the last Thursday in November): In all states, territories, and possessions.
December	*25.*	Christmas Day: In all states, territories, and possessions.

Mother's Day is the second Sunday in May. Armed Forces Day is the third Saturday in May. Father's Day is the third Sunday in June.

Shrove Tuesday is celebrated in Ala., in some Fla. cities, some La. parishes, and the Canal Zone. Good Friday is a public holiday in Ark., Calif., Conn., Del., Fla., Ill., Ind., La., Md., Minn., N. J., N. D., Pa., Tenn., Canal Zone, Hawaii, Puerto Rico, and the Virgin Islands.

COUNTY GOVERNMENT IN THE UNITED STATES

Every state in the United States is divided into counties except Louisiana, where the divisions are known as parishes. In all there are about 3,000 counties. There is no uniformity as to the number in each state. Texas, for instance, has 254 while Delaware has only three.

County administration is a local matter for each state to decide, not a national one. Consequently, there is a great variety of systems throughout the country. The county has in all cases comparatively little legislative authority; it is for the most part an agent of administration under the state government. In most states the county is the district of record for deeds, administration of estates, probate of wills, etc. Roads, bridges, education, etc., are usually county concerns. Poor relief is sometimes a county job, and in many states the county is the school district. City and county government sometimes merge to a certain extent, as in the case of New York City, which includes five counties. In most states the principal county offices are elective. The county seat is the town or village selected for the headquarters of the county administration. It is often the most important settlement in the county.

MUNICIPAL GOVERNMENT IN THE UNITED STATES

Essentially, municipal government provides those public services which people living together in urban places need for their community existence. Most commonly these services are police protection, fire prevention and fire fighting, sanitation, construction of city streets and recreation facilities, and maintenance of public service enterprises, such as water supply and electric power. The municipality is recognized as the government "closest to the people" because of the fundamental character of these services, as well as because of the local nature of municipal government. The suspension of vital municipal services would present an immediate threat to the life and property of the community. The larger the city, the more profound is this dependence on municipal functions.

In Colonial times, municipal governments were characterized by colonial governors. Of course, cities as they now exist were unimaginable and local government was rudimentary. One of the first municipal officials was the "town crier." He often served as a kind of constable for the city fathers. Early municipal functions were keeping a curfew, making and enforcing simple sanitary regulations, and maintaining law and order in the community. Since then, the United States has evolved from an agricultural into an industrial nation, and the majority of the population has moved from farms to cities and towns. Now about two-thirds of the population lives in urban places. This has heightened tremendously the need for new and expanded municipal services.

The burgeoning of cities and towns has brought into existence municipal services unheard of in the 19th century—planning and zoning, municipally-owned rapid transit lines, air-pollution control, a variety of health services, and many others. Traffic engineering and regulation have become prime concerns of city governments throughout the nation, and hundreds of municipalities now provide offstreet parking facilities.

Municipal and industrial growth have been parallel and interdependent in the United States. The services of a modern municipality now enable people to live together comfortably in large urban communities; this situation provides the necessary working force for industrial mass production.

Yet during this tremendous urban growth and flux, the legal relationship of municipalities to their state governments has not changed greatly. In some states new municipal charters must still be approved by the state legislature. In many states rurally-minded legislatures tend to dominate municipal affairs. Gradually, however, states are adjusting to the increasing importance of municipal governments by granting them "home rule"— broad powers of local self-government. Basically, home rule authorizes municipal voters to adopt the kind of city or town charter they desire, within broad limits, or to amend the charter in existence. At present more than 20 states have some kind of constitutional or statutory provisions for home rule, although not all of them are in effect.

As municipal voters acquired greater freedom to choose and manage their local governments, municipal fiscal structures were strengthened. At one time the property tax on real estate was almost the sole source of municipal income. Today, to enable them to meet increased demands for services, many municipalities are permitted to tax local sales, tobacco, theater admissions, wages, etc. In some states cities have broad powers to levy such nonproperty taxes; in other states these powers are virtually non-existent. Cities and towns are also adding to their revenues by fees and service charges, such as for sewer rental. Municipal income is augmented further by shares of state-collected taxes and other forms of state aid.

There are four major forms of municipal government in the United States: the *weak mayor* form, the *strong mayor* form, the *commission* form, and the *council-manager* form. The growth of cities and the complexity of municipal services has caused a healthy ferment of controversy about the relative strengths and weaknesses of these forms. The weak mayor form is gradually becoming extinct except in small towns. The commission form, first adopted as an emergency plan in Galveston, Texas, after the flood of 1900, enjoyed a vogue for several decades but is being gradually abandoned. The strong mayor form predominates in big cities. The council-manager form is a 20th-century development designed to cope with modern problems of municipal management. It has become increasingly popular, and though not a panacea, will unquestionably continue to grow. The basic characteristics of each form are as follows:

Commission Form.—Commissioners (usually five) elected at large by a majority vote. They serve both as municipal legislators and as administrative heads of municipal departments. The plan fails to focus responsibility and authority in a single executive and can easily lead to "buck-passing" unless an almost divine cooperation prevails among commissioners. Especially in big cities, the plan tends toward administrative ambiguity. Since the commissioners both vote municipal funds and spend them, there is no adequate control of spending.

Weak Mayor Form.—Councilmen elected by wards. Most administrative heads elected also—at least the treasurer, the city attorney, and usually some others. The mayor is elected, usually by direct popular vote, sometimes by the council. Administrative boards are elected to enact council policies. A basic disadvantage of this type of administration is that too many officials are elected, thus causing a high turnover of top administrators and failing to attract competent career men. This pattern scatters responsibility and action so widely that it is virtually unworkable in a city of any size.

Strong Mayor Form.—The mayor elected at large. Councilmen elected by wards. The mayor may veto acts of the council, and has authority to hire and fire department heads. He is the chief executive of the municipality, and is responsible also for preparing the budget and submitting it to the council. The strong mayor form fixes responsibility adequately but does not separate the policy-making and administrative functions. This form can be very effective, but only if the mayor combines exceptional political acumen with keen executive abilities.

Council-Manager Plan.—A small council elected at large. The council hires a city manager as chief administrator. The council decides all policy matters; the manager is responsible for all municipal administration. He has the power to hire and fire department heads and others. The manager is also responsible for drafting the budget and presenting it to the council. The plan adequately separates the policy-making and administrative functions, and focuses responsibility for each. This form of municipal government was first adopted by Sumter, S.C., in 1912. Today the number of United States municipalities with this kind of charter is nearly 1,000.

JUSTICE OF THE PEACE

A justice of the peace holds a judicial office of ancient origin. His election or appointment, term of office, and jurisdiction are governed by constitutional or statutory provisions. To be eligible for such office the candidate must have certain qualifications: he must be over 21 years old, a citizen of the United States, and of the state in which he seeks office. In some states the candidate must be a male, in others females are eligible; in some states only lawyers can qualify.

The Justice's Court is an inferior tribunal having civil jurisdiction in particular cases generally limited to $200. The proceedings in civil matters are less formal and technical here than in other courts, but a justice of the peace is bound by the general rules of evidence applicable to other courts; he is not merely an arbitrator, but must decide cases according to the weight of evidence and established principles of law. Generally, either plaintiff or defendant may have a trial by jury. This jury may consist of either six or twelve persons.

The justice of the peace also has some criminal jurisdiction. Under most statutes it does not cover felonies, but is limited to the trial of specified misdemeanors and minor offenses for which the punishment on conviction is fixed by statute. In some states justices of the peace have inquisitorial power; like grand juries, they may inquire into crimes committed or believed to have been committed within their territorial jurisdiction. They may also act as committing magistrates, with the power to conduct preliminary hearings, to remand the accused to jail, to discharge the accused, or to admit him to bail on all charges except murder, pending the outcome of the action of the grand jury; or to hold him for trial in a higher court having jurisdiction over the particular crime. However, such committing magistrate has no power to try the case.

JURIES

A jury is a group of selected persons sworn to render a fair and just verdict on the evidence presented to them and in accordance with the presiding judge's charge citing the applicable principles of law.

Trial by jury is constitutionally guaranteed to litigants, but there is not a mandatory right to a jury trial in all classes of cases. The right exists only in cases for which it existed at common law or as it was granted by statute at the time of the adoption of the Constitution. In some states the right may be waived in all cases, both civil and criminal; in others it cannot be waived in criminal cases of a specified character, such as felonies, nor in a capital case, *i.e.*, murder. The right to waive depends upon constitutional or statutory provision.

A *special jury* is a jury ordered by the court on due application in cases for which a fair and impartial trial cannot otherwise be had, or in cases of unusual importance or intricacy. Such juries are sometimes called "blue ribbon" juries. The United States Supreme Court has held trial by these juries to be constitutional.

A *grand jury* is a body of men selected and summoned according to statutory provision. After being impaneled and sworn a grand jury is charged by the court to inquire into a crime alleged to have been committed within its jurisdiction. Its duty is to ascertain whether prima facie grounds for a criminal prosecution have been made out, sufficient to warrant the accused to stand trial. If sufficient evidence is presented an indictment is returned charging the accused with the commission of a particular crime. No presumption of guilt arises from such indictment; it is merely an accusation. The guilt or innocence of the accused is determined after a trial, which is based on the indictment. Ordinarily, the accused and his witnesses are not entitled to appear before the grand jury, unless such right is granted by statute. The proceedings are secret.

The qualifications, composition, sex, number, and selection of all juries in civil and criminal proceedings is governed by constitutional or statutory provisions. At common law a grand jury must be composed of not less than 12 nor more than 23 people, but the number is now generally fixed by constitutional or statutory provision. A unanimous opinion of the grand jury is not necessary before an indictment may be returned; nor is a unanimous opinion of the jury necessary for a verdict in civil or criminal cases. The statutes specify how many grand jurors must agree to return an indictment, and how many jurors must be in accord as to what the verdict shall be in civil or criminal cases.

A *coroner's jury,* composed of a specified number of people, fixed by statute, conducts an inquest to determine the cause of death when there is reason to believe that it was not due to natural causes, and in cases of death by clearly non-natural causes, to obtain evidence of possible criminality.

The coroner is a public officer who summons the jurors. The office is ancient; it has been abolished by statute in some states.

AFFIDAVITS

An affidavit is a written statement under oath taken before an officer authorized by statute to administer an oath, for instance, a judge, a notary public, or a commissioner of deeds. It must specify the venue, *i.e.,* the state and county in which the affidavit is made, and must state facts within the personal knowledge of the person making the affidavit; or, if it contains statements not within the personal knowledge of such person, the source of such facts must be stated. The affidavit must be signed. An illiterate person can sign by making a cross or other symbol. The person making the affidavit is called the *affiant* or *deponent.* At the end of the affidavit is the statement, "Sworn to before me this   day of 1950," under which the person before whom the affidavit is made signs his name and writes his title. This statement is called a *jurat.* Under proper circumstances an affirmation may replace the oath.

An affidavit differs from a *deposition* in that the former is voluntary and made without notice to the adverse party in the litigation; the latter, however, is generally made in answer to specific questions propounded under a court order or other legal notice.

LAW

Constitutional Law

Constitutional law is that branch of jurisprudence which deals with the formation, adoption, construction, and interpretation of state constitutions and the Federal constitution. In its respective domain each is the supreme law; but no state constitution or statute is constitutional if it is in conflict with that of the United States, and no state statute is constitutional if it is in conflict with the constitution of its state.

Statutory Law

Statutory law is law found in the various statutes enacted by the legislative bodies of the states or by Congress. Federal statutes prevail over state statutes whenever there is conflict between the two.

Common Law

Common law originated and developed in England, where it was administered by secular as distinguished from ecclesiastical tribunals. It is a flexible body of jurisprudence based upon decisional law designed to serve the interests of society, and is susceptible of adaptation to new conditions. It does not depend on positive legislative enactment, although many statutes are a codification of common-law principles, and in the absence of statutory law common-law principles prevail.

Other Legal Classifications

Maritime law has reference to the legal principles that apply to ship owners, seamen, shipping, and other maritime matters.

Commercial law has reference to the legal principles that apply to commercial paper, such as notes, bills of exchange, drafts, etc.

International law has reference to the legal principles which govern the interrelations of sovereign states.

THE COPYRIGHT LAW OF THE UNITED STATES[1]

The author's, designer's, composer's, engraver's, printer's, draftsman's, photographer's, sculptor's, or artist's exclusive right to reproduce, publish, sell, etc., the products of his intellect or genius is called a copyright.

The purpose of the copyright law is "to promote the progress of science and useful arts by securing for a limited time to authors and inventors the exclusive right to their respective writings and discoveries."

Those who are entitled to copyright protection in the United States are:

1. The *author* of a work, if he is a citizen of the United States, if he is an alien living here at the time of the first publication of his work, or if he is a citizen of a country which grants to citizens of the United States the benefit of copyright on substantially the same basis as to its own citizens. (For a list of our copyright relations with various countries, see page 154.)

2. The *proprietor* of a work, that is, the person who derives his title to the work from the author. If the author is not entitled to copyright protection the proprietor cannot claim it.

3. The *executors, administrators,* or *assigns* of the author or the proprietor of a work.

Generally speaking, the copyright of material in magazines, newspapers, dictionaries, encyclopedias, and other compilations, is held in the name of the proprietor, but the author may, if he wishes, retain the right to his contribution if it is published separately also, or if he applies for a separate registration for it. Because of income tax regulations an increasing number of authors are having copyrights taken out in their own names, but where authors wish to retain their copyright and yet have their publishers named as copyright claimants it is provided that "the legal title to a copyright vests in the person in whose name it is taken out, but it may be held in trust for the true owners."

Title 17 of the United States Code provides that the application for registration of any work "shall specify to which of the following classes the work in which copyright is claimed belongs."

Class A. — Books published in the United States (Application Form A)
  Books or periodicals first published in a foreign language outside the United States (Application Form AB Foreign)
  Books or periodicals in the English language first published outside the United States (Application Form Ad Interim)
Class B. — Periodicals (Application Form B)
  Contributions to periodicals (Application Form B5)
Class C. — Lectures, sermons, addresses, prepared for oral delivery (Application Form C)
Class D. — Dramatic or dramatico-musical compositions (Application Form D)
Class E. — Musical compositions (Application Form E)
Class F. — Maps (Application Form F)
Class G. — Works of art; models or designs for works of art (Application Form G)
Class H. — Reproductions of a work of art (Application Form H)
Class I. — Drawings or plastic works of a scientific or technical character (Application Form I)
Class J. — Photographs (Application Form J)
Class K. — Prints and pictorial illustrations (Application Form K)
  Prints or labels used for articles of merchandise (Application Form KK)

[1]Subject to amendment or change.

Class L. — Motion-picture photoplays (Application Form L)
Class M. — Motion pictures other than photoplays (Application Form M)

The first term of copyright is 28 years, which is computed, in the case of a work published in the first instance, from the date of publication; and, in the case of an unpublished work, from the date of registration. In the 28th year a renewal application (Form R) may be made to secure a second term of 28 years. Form RR is to be used for renewal of copyright of a print or label used for articles of merchandise.

Copyright may be secured for:

Unpublished Works.—These include lectures, sermons, addresses, or similar productions for oral delivery; dramatic, musical, and dramatico-musical compositions; photographs; works of art (drawings, paintings, and sculptures); plastic works; motion-picture photoplays; and motion pictures other than photoplays.

The copyright procedure for such works is to file a claim of copyright with registration fee, to be accompanied as follows:

In the case of lectures, sermons, addresses, and dramatic, musical, and dramatico-musical compositions, one *complete* copy of the work, which may be written by hand or typewritten but must be clean and legible, with the sheets fastened securely together, should be deposited.

In the case of unpublished photographs, one copy of the work should be deposited.

In the case of works of art, models, designs, etc., a photograph or other identifying reproduction should be deposited.

In the case of motion-picture plays, the title and a description and one print from each scene or act should be deposited.

In the case of motion pictures other than photoplays, the title and a description, with not less than two prints taken from different sections of the motion picture, should be deposited.

Any work in this group, if published, that is, if reproduced in copies for sale, must be deposited a second time and registered as a published work.

Published Works.—Published works are those which are printed or otherwise produced and "placed on sale, sold, or publicly distributed."

The fee for copyright registration is $4.00 except that in the case of a commercial print or label it is $6.00. The fee for renewal registration is $2.00, except for renewal of a print or label which fee is $6.00.

New versions of a work must be copyrighted on their own account. This does not mean that mere corrections or additions need an extra copyright. The dramatization of a story, the photoplay version of a drama, etc., must have independent copyrights.

Foreign books and periodicals first published abroad can be copyrighted in the United States for ad interim copyright by registering and depositing the book or periodical in the United States Copyright Office within six months from the date of foreign publication. The copyright thus secured lasts for five years from the date of publication. The Copyright Office issues import statements for 1,500 copies of books or periodicals of foreign origin which have been registered for ad interim copyright. These imported copies must bear copyright notices. Whenever during the existence of the five-year ad interim copyright the book or periodical is manufactured, published, and registered in the United States, the copyright is extended for the usual copyright term with the regular opportunity available for renewal.

The usual form of copyright notice for books, periodicals, dramatic and musical compositions is "Copyright, 19 — (Fill out with the year of publication), by —— —— (Fill out with the name of the claimant)."

In the case of books and dramatic compositions the notice should be on the title page or the page immediately following; in the case of a periodical, on the title page or first page of the text. The notice in the case of a musical composition should be on the title page or the first page of music.

On maps, works of art, drawings, photographs, and prints the notice may consist of the letter C, inclosed within a circle, thus, ©, accompanied by the initials, monogram, mark, or symbol of the holder of the copyright, but somewhere on the work should appear the name of the copyright holder himself. The prescribed notice must be affixed to each copy of the work published or offered for sale in the United States.

Promptly upon publication two complete copies of the best edition of the work should be sent to the copyright office, with a proper application for registration (such application may be had free upon request from the Copyright Office at Washington, D.C.) and a money order for the amount of the legal registration fee ($4.00). "Promptly" means "without unnecessary delay."

In the United States copyrights are good for 28 years. Application for renewal should be filed by the author (or some person legally entitled to do so) one year before the expiration of the existing term. The copyright is then good for another 28 years. The registration fee for renewal of copyright is $2.00. Failure to renew within the specified time terminates the copyright.

Copyright is not automatically secured in foreign countries in the absence of a treaty or convention, but only through complying with the legislation of such countries. Conversely, copyright in foreign countries has no effect in the United States, but must be secured through compliance with the United States copyright law.

Nearly all the civilized nations of the world were represented at the Berne Copyright Convention, held in 1885–86. Through this and later conventions arrangements were made by which a copyright issued in one country was to be respected in all countries which were parties to the Berne Convention. In general, the term of copyright was to last for 50 years after the death of the author. The United States was not a party to these deliberations, but a number of foreign countries have agreed to give protection to American authors under reciprocal copyright agreements with the United States Government.

Copyright relations have been established by proclamation of the President with Argentina, Austria, Belgium, Canada, Chile, Costa Rica,

Cuba, Czechoslovakia, Denmark, Finland, France, Germany, Great Britain and the British possessions, Greece, Hungary, the Irish Free State, Italy, Japan, Luxemburg, Mexico, The Netherlands and possessions, Norway, Poland, Portugal, Rumania, Spain, Sweden, Switzerland, Tunis, and the Union of South Africa.

Copyright proclamations have been issued, securing copyright control of mechanical musical reproduction in the United States to citizens or subjects of Argentina, Australia, Austria, Belgium, Canada, Chile, Cuba, Czechoslovakia, Denmark, Finland, France, Germany, Great Britain, Greece, Hungary, the Irish Free State, Italy, Luxemburg, The Netherlands, New Zealand, Norway, Poland, Rumania, South Africa, Spain, Sweden, and Switzerland.

Copyright treaties have also been entered into with China, Japan, and Hungary. The Copyright Convention of Mexico of 1902 was ratified by the United States and became effective from July 1, 1908, and is now in force between the United States and Salvador. The Pan-American Copyright Convention signed at Buenos Aires in 1910 was proclaimed July 16, 1914, and is effective between the United States and Bolivia, Brazil, Colombia, Costa Rica, Dominican Republic, Ecuador, Guatemala, Haiti, Honduras, Nicaragua, Panama, Paraguay, Peru, and Uruguay.

Upon application to the Register of Copyrights a search will be made of the records, indexes, or deposits for such information as they may contain relative to specific copyright claims. The applicant for a search should state clearly the nature of the work under consideration, its title, the name of the claimant of copyright, and the probable date of its entry. The fee for such searches is $3.00 an hour for each hour of time consumed in making the search.

A copyright owner may bring suit for infringement and receive damages covering his loss and whatever profit the infringer may have made. Suits for infringement cannot be maintained in court until copies of the work have been deposited in the Copyright Office and registration made. The owner of a copyright has a certificate of registration which is prima facie evidence.

The Copyright Office, Library of Congress, Washington, D.C., will give further information.

THE PATENT LAW OF THE UNITED STATES

A *patent* grant gives an inventor the exclusive right to make, use, or sell his invention for a period of 17 years.

Under the laws of the United States any one may apply for a patent, even minors, aliens, and convicts, but the applicant must be the inventor himself. Joint inventors may receive a joint patent, but no one who has not actually had a part in creating the invention can be considered a joint inventor. A person whose only contribution is in the nature of financial aid cannot be considered a joint inventor, but a patent can be assigned to him. All patents are assignable in whole or in part. Assignments should be printed or written and duly signed in the presence of a notary public or someone with similar authority. When an inventor dies, the application may be made by his executor or administrator, in which case the patent will be issued to the one making the application.

The following paragraph is quoted from a bulletin issued by the United States Department of Commerce:

A patent may be obtained by any person who has invented any new and useful art, machine, manufacture, or composition of matter, or any new and useful improvement thereof, not known or used by others in this country before his invention and not patented or described in any printed publication in this or any foreign country before his invention, or more than one year prior to his application and not patented in a country foreign to the United States on an application filed by him or his legal representatives or assigns more than twelve months before his application, and not in public use or on sale in the United States for more than one year prior to his application, unless the same is proved to have been abandoned, upon payment of the fees required by law and other due proceedings had.

Applications for letters patent must be addressed to the Commissioner of Patents at Washington, D. C. The patent office does not furnish blanks for petitions, oaths, etc., but it issues a bulletin (General Information Concerning Patents, United States Government Printing Office) in which forms are shown. The application should be written in the English language and should be permanent and legible. It should contain a clear, exact description of the invention, or if it is an improvement on a former invention, an exact description of its relation to that invention. The specification should contain the name and address of the inventor, the name of the invention, its general object, a detailed description, the claim or claims of the inventor as to just what part the applicant considers his invention. It must be signed by the applicant. The applicant must swear (and there is a special form the oath must take) that he believes that he is the original inventor of the device in question. He must also state whether he is a sole or joint inventor.

If the invention is such that it can be shown in a drawing or a series of drawings, these drawings should be made by a skilled draftsman according to specifications laid down by the Patent Office. (These specifications will be found in the bulletin mentioned above.) The Patent Office will furnish the drawings at cost, if material from which they can be made is provided. The Patent Office will not accept a model unless it asks for it.

The fee for filing a patent is $30 payable in advance plus $1.00 for each claim in excess of 20. If no reason is found against granting the patent, it is allowed and issued on payment of an additional fee of $30.

The most important step in getting a patent is selecting an attorney. The patent business is not one for amateurs. The Patent Office in Washington has issued about two million patents already. The technicalities are such that only one skilled in such matters is competent to handle them. Just "any attorney" will not do. He should be one versed in this particular line and in whom the inventor has confidence. Only by working closely and frankly with his lawyer can he secure a strong patent.

Inventors, from the very first conception of the invention, should keep dated notes. Many times in court the evidence which these afford has been the determining factor in deciding to whom a patent belongs.

A patent issued by the United States is good throughout the United States and its territorial possessions.

The question of foreign patents is very complicated. Whether or not such patents should be applied for depends largely upon the nature of the invention and its probable use abroad. If the inventor plans to make application in foreign countries he should do so within a year after he has filed his application in the United States to obtain certain advantages.

The United States courts only can handle questions of patent infringement, but the Government, as well as the private individual, may be sued.

The term for which patents for inventions are issued in the United States is 17 years. Only Congress can extend the term of the patent.

THE TRADEMARK LAW OF THE UNITED STATES[1]

A *trademark* is an arbitrary word or symbol used on articles of merchandise to indicate who manufactures them or who deals in them. Most often words are chosen for their popular appeal and advertising value. Such a word or symbol may be registered in the Patent Office at Washington, D.C., by the person, firm, or corporation to whom it belongs. The fee for registration is $25.

Trademarks may be protected in the United States in the following ways: *Common law rights,* acquired by priority of adoption, ensure protection against infringement and unfair competition in the use of the trademark, even in the absence of registration. Registration on the so-called "principal register" of the **Federal Trade Mark Act** or **Lanham Act**[2] (effective July 5, 1947) affords numerous benefits not otherwise available. Such registration provides that, after five years of continuous use, a trademark so registered becomes "incontestable" (subject to certain limitations and exceptions), thus conclusively establishing the registrant's exclusive right and title to the trademark.

Requirements for registration on the principal register of the Lanham Act are: The trademark must be used "in commerce," that is, commerce within the control of Congress. Trademarks used on a local basis only may be protected by state laws, but they do not come under Federal control. The trademark must actually be in use at the time of application, either on merchandise or on displays associated with merchandise. Use in advertising alone is not enough. The trademark must not violate certain enumerated statutory prohibitions: It must not contain immoral or scandalous matter; it must not be primarily merely geographical or primarily merely a surname; it must not be descriptive or misdescriptive of the goods of the applicant. The name or portrait of a living individual may be registered

---

[1]Compiled from material supplied by the U. S. Patent Office, Dept. of Commerce.
[2]The text of the Act and Rules and Regulations of the Patent Office concerning the Act may be obtained from the Patent Office or the Government Printing Office upon request.

only if the written consent of such person is given. Registration of national insignia or emblems such as the Red Cross emblem is not permitted.

However, the Lanham Act permits the registration of geographical or descriptive words or surnames on the principal register, if they have acquired distinctiveness or a so-called "secondary meaning." The Act also provides for registration of so-called "service marks," *i.e.*, trademarks used by dry cleaners, railroads, insurance companies, etc., to indicate their services rather than merchandise made by them. Under the new Act, so-called "certification marks" and "collective marks" may also be registered.

Registration not available on the principal register of the Lanham Act may be secured on the "supplemental register," which is a continuation of a register first created by an Act of 1920. This register is intended to serve as a basis for registration abroad and has little domestic value. The Lanham Act provides for the registration of labels, packages, and configurations of goods on the supplemental register. Commercial labels and advertisements may also be copyrighted as such at the Library of Congress. Supplementing Federal registration laws are trademark registration statutes in almost all of the 48 states. These laws cover a wide variety of business devices and usually provide for criminal remedies of willful infringement. Many of these state laws permit registration of trademarks before they are actually in use. State registration is necessarily limited to business activities carried on exclusively within the boundaries of the state.

The United States is a party to two international conventions: The Paris Convention for the Protection of Industrial Property as last revised in London in 1934, and the Washington Pan-American Convention of 1929. Both afford protection against unfair competition and trademark infringement for citizens and residents of the contracting countries. The Lanham Act enlarges the protection of trademarks and trade names.

CUSTOMS REGULATIONS OF THE UNITED STATES

Taxes levied on certain classes of imported goods are called *customs*. Regulations vary from country to country, and travelers and traders need to familiarize themselves with the laws of the countries which they are visiting or with which they are trading. In general, personal effects are admitted free in all countries. Alcohol and tobacco are nearly always subject to limitation, prohibition, or tax. Perfumes frequently come under restrictions. Foreign reprints of English copyrighted books are not allowed in England and may be confiscated if taken there. It is often wise to declare typewriters and cameras so as to have no difficulty in getting them out when the time comes. Almost all countries have currency regulations, and travelers are advised to check with customs officers at the border for specific rulings.

Baggage is usually examined at the pier, but if it is destined for a capital city may be forwarded thither under bond and examined at the railroad station upon arrival. At frontier stations on land trunks are examined in the customs room. Hand baggage is often examined on the train itself.

The laws of the United States require, generally speaking, that the baggage of persons arriving here from foreign countries shall be examined by customs officers. Before examination is made the traveler must declare, orally or in writing, the articles he is importing. When a written declaration is required, a form will be provided by a customs officer or the purser of the ship. The completed form must be returned to the customs officer, or to the purser if the traveler received the form from him. In the latter event, the traveler should retain the coupon on the bottom of the form for surrender to the customs officer when his baggage is about to be examined.

One member of a family group may make one declaration for the entire group.

Residents of the United States returning through any port, except ports on the Mexican border, may bring in $200 worth of articles acquired abroad as an incident of the trip for their personal or household use or as souvenirs or gifts, but not purchased on commission for others, or for sale, provided they have been abroad for 48 hours or longer and have not claimed this exemption within the preceding 30 days. Residents returning across the Mexican border are entitled to the same exemption subject to the same conditions, except that if they return through a port on the Mexico-California border they must have been abroad not more than 24 hours, but if they return through a port elsewhere on the Mexican border, there is no specified time during which they must have stayed abroad.

A returning resident may bring in an additional $300 worth of articles of the character described in the preceding paragraph, if he has been abroad not less than 12 days and has not claimed this exemption within the preceding six months. If articles passed free under this exemption are sold within three years, they will be subject to double duty.

Not more than one gallon of distilled spirits, wines, and malt liquors and not more than 100 cigars may be included under the $200 exemption, but none of these articles may be included under the $300 exemption. Neither exemption covers gifts sent from abroad to the donee.

All articles to be claimed free of duty under one of the exemptions must be declared upon arrival in the United States, whether or not the resident has them with him; otherwise, an exemption will not be applied.

The exemptions of residents who are members of a family residing in one household and who are returning to the United States together may be grouped and allowed without regard to which member owns the articles concerned. However, a grouped exemption may not be allowed to an article of a person not entitled to the exemption.

A resident of the United States may bring back to the United States free of duty personal and household effects, professional books, and instruments or tools of his trade or profession which he took abroad. However, if the articles are repaired otherwise than as an incident of the use abroad, or altered, the cost of the repairs and alterations will be dutiable. The cost of the repairs and alterations should be declared; not the cost of the article concerned.

UNITED STATES FOREIGN TRADE BY CONTINENTS, LEADING COUNTRIES, AND AREAS

Note: Data for the war and postwar years include lend-lease and aid and relief shipments as well as the usual commercial trade.

(Five-year Average—Thousands of Dollars)

Continent and country	1936-1940 average		1941-1945 average		1946-1949 average	
	Exports[1]	Imports[2]	Exports[1]	Imports[2,3]	Exports[1]	Imports[2,3]
Grand Total	3,219,581	2,482,030	10,051,075	3,514,080	12,433,257	6,109,555
North America	812,972	614,660	1,872,369	1,542,113	3,263,670	2,204,938
Canada, incl. Newf. and Lab.	521,482	367,683	1,296,058	950,622	1,869,559	1,295,013
Mexico	85,525	58,027	212,910	170,032	529,628	242,453
Central American Republics, total[4]	35,238	33,619	75,877	53,241	240,658	117,308
Cuba	80,471	118,313	151,213	271,704	396,295	398,799
Netherlands Antilles (Curaçao)	30,236	18,867	29,325	54,153	66,358	87,397
South America	317,400	337,703	500,039	801,021	1,744,098	1,358,419
Colombia	42,152	48,282	58,177	87,337	184,438	210,028
Venezuela	50,796	26,853	76,765	46,955	418,363	210,651
Chile	26,912	41,249	49,039	136,365	112,568	134,426
Brazil	74,108	106,596	169,213	236,305	469,716	479,883
Argentina	83,141	78,149	56,162	161,403	345,731	156,582
Europe[5]	1,332,708	627,085	5,673,543	287,826	4,547,115	917,066
Sweden	61,722	42,312	19,511	10,418	201,827	71,411
United Kingdom	602,744	165,156	3,221,368	110,031	825,852	219,416
Netherlands	74,990	34,441	16,431	1,229	299,727	38,009
Belgium and Luxemburg	64,135	53,638	27,032	5,644	357,289	83,575
France	172,433	58,766	98,670	4,015	654,395	60,934
Germany	76,412	58,912	451	1,072	[6]587,634	21,652
Switzerland	13,811	25,684	40,813	50,521	154,221	95,181
U.S.S.R. (Russia)	57,917	24,223	1,967,502	38,598	135,372	75,888
Italy[7]	60,819	38,655	135,821	1,815	448,324	69,426
Asia	535,283	784,989	799,063	478,314	2,004,896	1,130,744
Turkey	10,189	16,070	27,456	36,374	85,025	57,805
India[8]	43,047	78,648	457,151	132,107	283,369	248,857
Pakistan[8]	n.s.s.*	n.s.s.*	n.s.s.*	n.s.s.*	[9]31,273	[9]26,913
British Malaya	9,663	188,088	10,782	79,429	49,995	218,924
Indonesia (Netherlands Indies)	31,104	103,158	38,916	68,355	98,380	69,405
Philippines, Republic of	85,020	100,716	30,239	21,852	410,943	158,860
China	52,965	75,975	77,525	26,512	293,679	109,045
Japan	238,390	164,459	12,570	15,736	[6]327,146	65,883
Australia and Oceania	89,150	36,372	363,562	187,281	196,075	157,030
Australia	67,604	23,140	299,092	153,643	143,960	124,428
New Zealand	20,308	11,916	60,340	24,327	45,359	29,299
Africa	132,068	81,220	842,499	217,524	677,405	341,359
Egypt[10]	14,297	8,583	480,079	14,097	47,779	25,723
French Africa	10,950	9,084	143,808	11,480	127,556	18,655
British West Africa	6,405	21,301	30,657	23,397	19,682	77,543
Belgian Congo	2,411	6,569	19,259	41,879	42,796	30,228
Union of South Africa	80,386	22,472	139,782	88,743	349,878	128,433
20 Amer. Republics[4,11]	537,091	552,828	950,377	1,310,437	2,958,938	2,151,494
ERP countries[12]	1,211,278	545,684	3,655,211	253,291	4,207,238	798,420

[1]Exports including re-exports. [2]General imports. [3]Data for 1942–48 include adjustments made in 1949 in the value of tin ore. [4]Includes Canal Zone in 1936 and 1937. [5]Includes Iceland for all years shown. [6]Includes supplies sent to occupied areas through United States armed forces beginning in 1947. [7]Includes Free Territory of Trieste; exports to Free Territory of Trieste, available separately only after 1947, amounted to $11,517,000 in 1948 and $11,897,000 in 1949 and imports amounted to $5,000 and $17,000, respectively. [8]Pakistan included with India prior to 1948; Burma also included prior to 1938. [9]Average for 1948 and 1949. [10]Including Anglo-Egyptian Sudan. [11]Mexico, Guatemala, El Salvador, Honduras, Nicaragua, Costa Rica, Republic of Panama, Cuba, Haiti, Dominican Republic, Colombia, Venezuela, Ecuador, Peru, Bolivia, Chile, Brazil, Paraguay, Uruguay, and Argentina. [12]Includes Iceland, Sweden, Norway, Denmark, United Kingdom, Ireland, Netherlands, Belgium and Luxemburg, France, Germany, Austria, Switzerland and Portugal, Italy, Free Territory of Trieste, Greece, and Turkey. *n.s.s.—Not shown separately.

Prepared in the Department of Commerce, by Division of International Economic Analysis, Office of Foreign Commerce, from basic data of the Bureau of the Census, June 1950

It saves trouble if receipted bills for purchases, repairs, and alterations are kept. Frankness on the part of the traveler will speed up passage through customs.

The wearing apparel and similar personal effects owned abroad by nonresidents arriving in the United States are free of duty. Adult nonresidents may bring in for their own use free of duty 50 cigars or 300 cigarettes, or three pounds of manufactured tobacco, and not more than one quart of alcoholic beverages. If they are immigrating to the United States, they may bring with them, without duty payment, professional books, instruments, and tools which they owned and used abroad.

Persons coming to the United States, whether residents or nonresidents, may import free of duty for their own use household effects which have been used abroad by them for not less than one year.

EXPORTS AND IMPORTS

Goods taken into a country are called imports; those sent out of a country are called exports. Both imports and exports are valued at the customhouse or in some other authorized place. In this way it is possible for all countries to issue periodical returns showing the relation between imports and exports. The difference between the imports and the exports is known as the "balance of trade." The basis of United States official statistics are export declarations and import entries filed with United States Customs officials at the time of exportation of the merchandise and at the time of importation of the merchandise, or preceding its arrival. Charges incidental to the transportation of the goods from country to country are not included in the value of merchandise shown on these declarations. These charges are not included in the reported values of merchandise exports and imports; they are taken into account, however, in calculations of "balance of payments" between the United States and foreign countries. Practices among countries vary greatly and the subject of valuation is extremely complex.

Export values in the facing table are "f.a.s. (free alongside ship) values" as shown on United States Shippers' declarations; import values are, in general, "f.a.s. values" at the foreign port of shipment as shown on importers' entries. Ocean freight, insurance, and other charges on goods from port of deportation to port of arrival are excluded from both export and import values.

NATURALIZATION[1]

A foreigner born outside the jurisdiction of the United States is considered an alien until he is naturalized. An alien is entitled to all the privileges of a citizen, except political rights. He can buy and sell, make contracts, and sue and be sued; and he is entitled to the full protection of the Government in his person and his property.

---

[1]The *Immigration and Naturalization Service* is part of the United States Department of Justice, Washington, D.C. Specific questions should be addressed to that office.

The first step toward naturalization is the filing of a declaration of intention in the office of the Clerk of Court. No person under 18 can file such a declaration. Children of naturalized persons, if under 21 years of age at the time of the naturalization of their parents and residing in the United States, are considered citizens of the United States. Children of citizens of the United States, though born in a foreign country, are still considered citizens of the United States.

The citizenship of a married woman is not the same as that of her husband. If she is or was married to a United States citizen, she may be admitted to citizenship without having previously made a declaration of intention. Such a person may file a petition for naturalization after having resided in the United States for only one, two, or three years, depending upon the date of the marriage and other facts applicable to the individual case. These rights are also enjoyed by a male alien who is or was married to a citizen.

Generally, no alien shall be admitted to citizenship unless (1) immediately preceding the date of his petition the alien has resided continuously within the United States for at least five years and within the state where the petitioner resided at the time of filing his petition for at least six months; (2) he has resided continuously within the United States from the date of his petition up to the time of his admission to citizenship; and (3) during all the periods referred to he has been and still is a person of good moral character, attached to the principles of the Constitution of the United States, and well disposed to the good order and happiness of the United States.

At the hearing of the petition, residence in the state where the petitioner resides at the time of filing his petition, and the other qualifications required during such residence, shall be proved by the oral testimony of at least two credible witnesses, citizens of the United States, in addition to the affidavits required to be included in the petition.

If the petitioner has resided in two or more places in such state and for this reason two witnesses cannot be procured to testify as to all such residence, they may be proved by the oral testimony of two such witnesses for each such place of residence, in addition to the affidavits required to be included in the petition.

At the hearing, residence within the United States but outside the state, and the other qualifications required during such residence shall be proved either by depositions or by the oral testimony of at least two such witnesses for each place of residence.

Absence from the United States for a continuous period of more than six months and less than one year during the period immediately preceding the date of filing the petition for citizenship for which continuous residence is required as a condition precedent to admission to citizenship shall cause the continuity of such residence to be presumed to be broken, but such presumption may be overcome by the presentation of satisfactory evidence that such individual had a reasonable cause for not returning to the United States sooner.

Absence from the United States for a continuous period of one year or more during the period immediately preceding the date of filing the petition for citizenship for which continuous residence is required as a condition precedent to admission to citizenship, shall break the continuity of such residence.

A petition generally may not be heard until at least 30 days after it is filed.

The Commissioner of Immigration and Naturalization is given authority to designate naturalization examiners to conduct preliminary hearings on petitions for naturalization and make recommendations to the court.

The **Alien Registration Act of 1940** is designed to prohibit certain subversive activities; to amend certain provisions of law with respect to the admission and deportation of aliens; to require the fingerprinting and registration of certain aliens in the United States. Aliens must register within 30 days, if they intend to remain longer than that period, and if they have not been already registered and fingerprinted at consular offices. Children who have reached their 14th birthday must register in person; prior to that date they must be registered by their parents or guardians. Aliens who are residents of the United States shall notify the Commissioner of Immigration and Naturalization in writing of each change of residence and new address within five days after the date of such change. Any other alien required to be registered shall notify the Commissioner in writing of his address at the end of each three months' period of residence in the United States.

NATIONAL FLAG CODE[1]

1. The flag should be displayed only from sunrise to sunset, or between such hours as may be designated by proper authority. It should be displayed on national and state holidays and on historic and special occasions.

2. When carried in a procession with another flag or flags, the flag of the United States should be either on the marching right, *i.e.*, the flag's own right, or when there is a line of other flags the flag of the United States may be in front of the center.

3. When displayed with another flag against a wall from crossed staffs, the flag of the United States should be on the right, the flag's own right, and its staff should be in front of the other flag.

4. When a number of flags are grouped and displayed from staffs, the flag of the United States should be in the center or at the highest point.

5. When flags of states or cities or pennants of societies are flown on the same halyard with the flag of the United States, the national flag should always be at the peak. When they are flown from adjacent staffs the flag of the United States should be hoisted first. No flag or pennant should be placed above or to the right.

---

[1]Rules, as adopted by the National Flag Conference.

6. When flags of two or more nations are displayed they should be flown from separate staffs of the same height and the flags should be of approximately equal size.

7. When the flag is displayed from a staff projecting horizontally or at an angle from the window sill, balcony, or front of building, the union of the flag should go clear to the head of the staff unless the flag is at half mast.

8. When the flag of the United States is displayed in a manner other than by being flown from a staff it should be displayed flat, whether indoors or out. When displayed either horizontally or vertically against a wall, the union should be uppermost and to the flag's own right, *i.e.*, to the observer's left. When displayed in a window it should be displayed the same way, that is, with the union or blue field to the left of the observer in the street.

9. When displayed over the middle of the street, as between buildings, the flag of the United States should be suspended vertically with the union to the north in an east-and-west street or to the east in a north-and-south street.

10. When used on a speaker's platform, the flag should be displayed above and behind the speaker. It should never be used to cover the speaker's desk nor to drape over the front of the platform. If flown from a staff it should be on the speaker's right.

11. When used in unveiling a statue or monument, the flag should not be allowed to fall to the ground but should be carried aloft to wave out, forming a distinctive feature.

12. When flown at half staff, the flag is hoisted to the peak for an instant, and then lowered to the half-staff position, but before lowering the flag for the day it is raised again to the peak. By "half staff" is meant hauling the flag down to one-half the distance between the top and bottom of the staff. If local conditions require, divergence from this position is permissible. On Memorial Day, May 30, the flag is displayed at half staff from sunrise until noon and at full staff from noon until sunset.

13. Flags flown from fixed staffs are placed at half staff to indicate mourning. When the flag is displayed on a small staff, as when carried in parade, mourning is indicated by attaching two streamers of black crepe to the spearhead, allowing the streamers to fall naturally.

14. When used to cover a casket the flag should be placed so that the union is at the head and over the left shoulder. The flag should not be lowered into the grave nor allowed to touch the ground.

15. When the flag is displayed in the body of a church it should be from a staff placed on the congregation's right as the members face the clergyman. The service flag, the state flag, or other flag should be at the left of the congregation. If it is in the chancel, or on the platform, the flag of the United States should be placed on the clergyman's right as he faces the congregation, and other flags on his left.

THE PLEDGE TO THE FLAG[1]

I pledge allegiance to the Flag of the United States of America
And to the Republic for which it stands;
One nation indivisible,
With liberty and justice for all.

MONETARY SYSTEM OF THE UNITED STATES

Gold Coin

Weight, 15�5/21 grains to the dollar
Fineness, 900–1000, or ⅟₃₅ ounce of pure gold
Denominations, $2.50, $5, $10, $20

The United States Government does not issue any gold coin, nor permit hoarding of gold; and Section 5 of the Gold Reserve Act of 1934 provided that no gold should thereafter be coined for domestic use and that all gold coins should be withdrawn from circulation.

Silver Coin

Standard Dollar

Weight, 412.5 grains
Fineness, 900–1000
Ratio to gold, 15.988 to 1

Unlimited as to use for legal tender. Receivable for all public dues; exchangeable for silver certificates and other forms of money.

Other Silver Coins

Weight 385.8 grains to the dollar
Fineness, 900–1000
Ratio to gold, 14.953 to 1
Denominations, 10 cents, 25 cents, 50 cents

Legal tender. Receivable for all public dues; exchangeable. for minor coin, *i.e.,* five-cent pieces or one-cent pieces.

Minor Coin

Weight, five-cent piece, 77.16 grains (75% copper, 25% nickel)
Weight, one-cent piece, 48 grains (95% copper, 5% tin and zinc)

---

[1]Adopted by the National Education Association and taught in most of the public schools, where it is daily repeated by the pupils.

Paper Currency

On July 10, 1929, the Treasury began to issue a small-size paper currency to replace the old larger-size currency. In less than a year this was practically accomplished. The new currency is 6⅛ in. × 2⅝ in. The back designs are uniform for each denomination, regardless of the kind of currency it may be; the face designs, too, are essentially the same, but with small characteristic variations.

The portraits assigned to the faces and the embellishments for the backs of the several denominations are as follows:

Denomination	Portrait on face	Embellishment on back
$1	Washington	Ornate One
$2	Jefferson	Monticello
$5	Lincoln	Lincoln Memorial
$10	Hamilton	U. S. Treasury
$20	Jackson	White House
$50	Grant	U. S. Capitol
$100	Franklin	Independence Hall
$500	McKinley	Ornate Five Hundred
$1,000	Cleveland	Ornate One Thousand
$5,000	Madison	Ornate Five Thousand
$10,000	Chase	Ornate Ten Thousand

The United States issues the following kinds of paper currency:

Gold Certificates.—These were issued against gold coin and against gold bullion for greater convenience in handling. Denominations, $10, $20, $50, $100, $500, $1,000, $5,000, $10,000. The United States Government issues gold certificates only to Federal Reserve Banks.

Silver Certificates.—These are issued against deposits of silver or against silver coins. They are legal tender and are receivable for all public dues and are redeemable in silver dollars at the Treasury. Denominations, $1, $2, $5, $10, $20, $50, $100.

United States Notes.—These are notes guaranteed by the United States Government. They are legal tender for all debts, customs and interest on the public debt.

Federal Reserve Notes.—These are a first lien upon all the assets of the Federal Reserve Banks by which they are issued. They are full legal tender. They constitute the principal part of the circulating medium.

National Bank Notes.—These notes were issued by the national banks and guaranteed by the national Government, the bank in question depositing whatever security was required; said security not exceeding the capital of the bank. In 1935 the Treasury called for redemption the only Government securities on which national banks might issue notes and their issue thereupon ceased.

United States Mints are at Philadelphia, San Francisco, and Denver. Assay offices are at New York and Seattle.

United States Bullion Depositories are at Fort Knox, Ky. (*gold*) and West Point, N. Y. (*silver*).

HANDLING MAIL

Saving Money on Postage

There are many ways in which an alert businessman can save money on postage. Letters with advertising matter enclosed often weigh more than 2 oz., thereby requiring 3 cents postage, when the message they carry might just as effectively be presented on material weighing less than 2 oz. Three cents is a small amount, but if there are 10,000 circulars to be sent out there will be a saving of $100 on the lot if the less-than-two-ounce rule is observed. In the same way post cards can be kept within the 1-cent limit. Business reply cards now make it possible for commercial organizations to pay only for the return postage that will mean something to them, instead of broadcasting actual stamps. And there are special mailing permits, about which any post office can give information, which are well worth investigation when a large volume of mail is handled.

No business house should guess at mailing costs. Letters sent out without sufficient postage are held until it is paid, thus causing, in some instances, serious delays. One company which handled a great deal of incoming and outgoing mail discovered that between $15 and $20 a month was spent on incoming mail which had been started on its way without sufficient postage. This company sent an excess postage report to each offender. But it is very doubtful whether this was a wise thing to do. The irritation at having to pay the postage was simply transferred to the person who sent the letter. He was at least equally irritated at being "called down" on so small a point. It is much better to keep one's self regulated than to try to regulate someone else.

Business Reply Cards and Envelopes

It is now possible, instead of sending a post card or a stamped envelope with a circular for the return order, to send a card or an envelope on which postage need not be paid until it has returned to the office where it originated. Persons wishing this privilege must make application to the postmaster and must conform with the established rules and regulations.

Business reply envelopes and cards must be printed like one of the forms shown on the permit issued by the post office. They may be distributed by mail or otherwise, in any quantity, for return through the domestic mails to the permit holder. They may not be sent to foreign countries, for they cannot be returned therefrom. The permit holder pays the regular rate of postage, plus 1 cent for each card or envelope returned to him. Collection of postage is made in the regular manner by the letter carrier or other postal employee at time of delivery.

Keeping Mailing Lists Up-to-Date

The best way to keep a mailing list up-to-date is to keep a careful check on the responses which it brings in, but sometimes other methods also are necessary. One of the most valuable of these is to ask the post office to check the list. The post office will eliminate dead names and correct all addresses. The cost amounts to 1 cent an address (minimum charge 25 cents) plus postage for mailing and return of the list.

Another valuable method for use in keeping up-to-date lists is the "Form 3547" procedure, whereby the mailer of advertising matter may request notice to be sent to him on a card in the event the mail is undeliverable as addressed. This particular service is restricted to matter sent as third- or fourth-class mail and for a purpose other than to obtain the address of an individual. Your local post office will furnish details.

Recalling Mail

It is possible to recall mail after it has been deposited in the mail box or post office up to the time of its delivery. A form to be filled out is provided and may be obtained at any post office. The expense of the recall, which may include telegraphing if the mail has already been dispatched, is borne by the recaller and must be deposited with the postmaster at the time the application for withdrawal is filled out. There is no expense if the mail has not left the office at which it was first deposited. Mail cannot, of course, be recalled once it has been delivered.

The Law of Post Cards

It is unlawful to write upon a post card or an envelope anything which reflects injuriously upon the character or conduct of another; the writer may be held liable for damages. No one should ever threaten another on a post card. The statement of an account on a post card, with no threatening words added, is not considered illegal, but it is safer to send all bills in sealed envelopes. Then the writer runs no danger, although, of course, threats can be carried too far, even in letters. Most of the states have laws against threatening letters, especially designed to prevent blackmail. It is always legal to threaten to sue a person for an unpaid account by letter, but not by post card.

Since 1898 it has been lawful to send private post cards by mail. The size of the cards is regulated by statute. Each card must be an unfolded piece of cardboard not larger than 9 × 14 centimeters (about 3⁹⁄₁₆ × 5⁹⁄₁₆ in.) nor smaller than 7 × 10 centimeters (about 2¾ in. × 4 in.). The quality must be substantially the same as that of the Government post card. The card may be any color and may have a picture on its face. The back may be divided into two parts, that to the right for the address, that to the left for a message.

DOMESTIC POSTAGE RATES

First-Class. Letters and written and sealed matter, 3 cents for each ounce.

Post cards and private mailing cards, 1 cent each.

Second-Class. Newspapers, magazines, and other periodicals containing notice of second-class entry, 1 cent for each 2 oz. or fraction thereof, or the fourth-class rate, whichever is lower.

Third-Class (limit 8 oz.). Circulars and other miscellaneous printed matter, also merchandise, 2 cents for the first 2 oz. and 1 cent for each additional ounce.

Books (including catalogs) of 24 pages or more, seeds, cuttings, bulbs, roots, scions, and plants, 1½ cents for each 2 oz.

Bulk lots of identical pieces may be mailed under permit in quantities of not less than either 20 lb. or 200 pieces, at the rate of 14 cents a pound, or fraction thereof, in case of circulars, miscellaneous printed matter, and merchandise, and 10 cents a pound, or fraction thereof, in the case of books or catalogs having 24 pages or more, seeds, plants, etc., with a minimum charge of 1 cent a piece in either case. The bulk mailing fee is $10 per calendar year.

Special Rates for Books (limit 70 lb.). Books containing no advertising matter other than incidental announcements of books may be mailed at the rate of 8 cents for first pound, 4 cents each additional pound.

Fourth-Class or Parcel Post (over 8 oz.). Merchandise, books, printed matter, and all other mailable matter not in first or second class. The limit of size is 100 in. in girth and length combined. Weight limit 70 lb.

The rate on fourth-class matter between any point in the United States or its possessions and any point in the Hawaiian Islands, the Canal Zone, and Tutuila, Manua, and other islands of the Samoan group is the same as for Zone 8.

Special Handling. The special handling postage charge on fourth-class matter is graduated according to the weights of the parcels, namely, 15 cents for parcels weighing not more than 2 lb.; 20 cents for parcels weighing more than 2 lb., but not exceeding 10 lb.; 25 cents for parcels weighing more than 10 lb.

Payment of the special handling postage charge entitles the parcel to receive the most expeditious handling, transportation, and delivery practicable, but does not include special delivery at the office of address.

Special Delivery. Fees for all classes of mail, including air mail: (first-class) 15 cents up to 2 lb.; 25 cents over 2 lb. up to 10 lb.; 35 cents over 10 lb. (second-, third-, and fourth-class) 25 cents up to 2 lb.; 35 cents over 2 lb. up to 10 lb.; 45 cents over 10 lb.

Air Mail. Detailed information can be found on pages 171 and 177.

PARCEL-POST RATES (Amounts in dollars)

Weight in pounds	Local	Zones						
		1–2 Up to 150 miles	3 150 to 300 miles	4 300 to 600 miles	5 600 to 1,000 miles	6 1,000 to 1,400 miles	7 1,400 to 1,800 miles	8 Over 1,800 miles
1	$0.10	$0.12	$0.13	$0.14	$0.15	$0.16	$0.17	$0.18
2	.11	.15	.16	.19	.21	.24	.27	.30
3	.12	.17	.19	.23	.27	.31	.36	.41
4	.13	.19	.22	.28	.33	.39	.46	.53
5	.14	.21	.25	.32	.39	.46	.55	.64
6	.15	.23	.28	.37	.45	.54	.65	.76
7	.16	.25	.31	.41	.51	.61	.74	.87
8	.17	.27	.34	.46	.57	.69	.84	.99
9	.18	.29	.37	.50	.63	.76	.93	1.10
10	.19	.31	.40	.55	.69	.84	1.03	1.22
11	.20	.33	.43	.59	.75	.91	1.12	1.33
12	.21	.35	.46	.63	.80	.98	1.21	1.44
13	.22	.37	.49	.68	.86	1.06	1.31	1.56
14	.22	.39	.52	.72	.91	1.13	1.40	1.67
15	.23	.41	.54	.76	.97	1.20	1.49	1.78
16	.24	.43	.57	.80	1.02	1.27	1.58	1.89
17	.25	.45	.60	.85	1.08	1.35	1.68	2.01
18	.25	.47	.63	.89	1.13	1.42	1.77	2.12
19	.26	.49	.66	.93	1.19	1.49	1.86	2.23
20	.27	.51	.68	.97	1.24	1.56	1.95	2.34
21	.28	.53	.71	1.02	1.30	1.64	2.05	2.46
22	.28	.55	.74	1.06	1.35	1.71	2.14	2.57
23	.29	.57	.77	1.10	1.41	1.78	2.23	2.68
24	.30	.59	.80	1.14	1.46	1.85	2.32	2.79
25	.31	.61	.82	1.19	1.52	1.93	2.42	2.91
26	.31	.63	.85	1.23	1.57	2.00	2.51	3.02
27	.32	.65	.88	1.27	1.63	2.07	2.60	3.13
28	.33	.67	.91	1.31	1.68	2.14	2.69	3.24
29	.34	.69	.94	1.36	1.74	2.22	2.79	3.36
30	.34	.71	.96	1.40	1.79	2.29	2.88	3.47
31	.35	.73	.99	1.44	1.85	2.36	2.97	3.58
32	.36	.75	1.02	1.48	1.90	2.43	3.06	3.69
33	.37	.77	1.05	1.53	1.96	2.51	3.16	3.81
34	.37	.79	1.08	1.57	2.01	2.58	3.25	3.92
35	.38	.81	1.10	1.61	2.07	2.65	3.34	4.03
36	.39	.83	1.13	1.65	2.12	2.72	3.43	4.14
37	.40	.85	1.16	1.70	2.18	2.80	3.53	4.26
38	.40	.87	1.19	1.74	2.23	2.87	3.62	4.37
39	.41	.89	1.22	1.78	2.29	2.94	3.71	4.48
40	.42	.91	1.24	1.82	2.34	3.01	3.80	4.59
41	.43	.93	1.27	1.87	2.40	3.09	3.90	4.71
42	.43	.95	1.30	1.91	2.45	3.16	3.99	4.82
43	.44	.97	1.33	1.95	2.51	3.23	4.08	4.93
44	.45	.99	1.36	1.99	2.56	3.30	4.17	5.04
45	.46	1.01	1.38	2.04	2.62	3.38	4.27	5.16
46	.46	1.03	1.41	2.08	2.67	3.45	4.36	5.27
47	.47	1.05	1.44	2.12	2.73	3.52	4.45	5.38
48	.48	1.07	1.47	2.16	2.78	3.59	4.54	5.49
49	.49	1.09	1.50	2.21	2.84	3.67	4.64	5.61
50	.49	1.11	1.52	2.25	2.89	3.74	4.73	5.72
51	.50	1.13	1.55	2.29	2.95	3.81	4.82	5.83
52	.51	1.15	1.58	2.33	3.00	3.88	4.91	5.94
53	.52	1.17	1.61	2.38	3.06	3.96	5.01	6.06
54	.52	1.19	1.64	2.42	3.11	4.03	5.10	6.17
55	.53	1.21	1.66	2.46	3.17	4.10	5.19	6.28
56	.54	1.23	1.69	2.50	3.22	4.17	5.28	6.39
57	.55	1.25	1.72	2.55	3.28	4.25	5.38	6.51
58	.55	1.27	1.75	2.59	3.33	4.32	5.47	6.62
59	.56	1.29	1.78	2.63	3.39	4.39	5.56	6.73
60	.57	1.31	1.80	2.67	3.44	4.46	5.65	6.84
61	.58	1.33	1.83	2.72	3.50	4.54	5.75	6.96
62	.58	1.35	1.86	2.76	3.55	4.61	5.84	7.07
63	.59	1.37	1.89	2.80	3.61	4.68	5.93	7.18
64	.60	1.39	1.92	2.84	3.66	4.75	6.02	7.29
65	.61	1.41	1.94	2.89	3.72	4.83	6.12	7.41
66	.61	1.43	1.97	2.93	3.77	4.90	6.21	7.52
67	.62	1.45	2.00	2.97	3.83	4.97	6.30	7.63
68	.63	1.47	2.03	3.01	3.88	5.04	6.39	7.74
69	.64	1.49	2.06	3.06	3.94	5.12	6.49	7.86
70	.64	1.51	2.08	3.10	3.99	5.19	6.58	7.97

ADDITIONAL POSTAL INFORMATION

Air Mail. Matter weighing 8 oz. or less, except for Canada (weight limit 60 lb.) and Mexico (weight limit 4 lb. 6 oz.), 6 cents for each ounce or fraction thereof in the United States, Alaska, Canada, Canal Zone, Canton Island, Guam, Hawaii, Mexico, Midway Island, Puerto Rico, United States Virgin Islands, and Wake Island.

Air Parcel Post. Matter weighing over 8 oz. up to 70 lb. and measuring up to 100 in. in length and girth combined may be mailed anywhere in the United States, its possessions, or territories. For further information see page 177.

Registry, Insurance, and C. O. D. Services for Airplane Mail. Any matter may be sent by air mail service upon payment of the prescribed fee and the required air mail postage.

Special Delivery. The use of special delivery stamps in addition to the air mail postage will insure prompt delivery at office of address.

Registered Mail. The registry fees on both domestic and foreign mail must be prepaid by stamps affixed in addition to the regular postage.

The registry fees for domestic registered mail are: when contents are valued at $5.00, 25 cents; $5.01 to $25, 35 cents; $25.01 to $50, 40 cents; $50.01 to $75, 45 cents; $75.01 to $100, 50 cents; $100.01 to $200, 60 cents; $200.01 to $300, 70 cents; $300.01 to $400, 85 cents; $400.01 to $500, $1.00; $500.01 to $600, $1.10; $600.01 to $700, $1.20; $700.01 to $800, $1.30; $800.01 to $900, $1.40; $900.01 to $1000, $1.50.

A registry surcharge is collectible in addition to registry fee when value of registered article exceeds limit of indemnity prescribed for the fee paid. Consult post office for particulars.

Mail matter without intrinsic value for which no indemnity is provided may be registered at the minimum fee of 25 cents.

For all articles of whatever class addressed to foreign countries 25 cents, except registered parcel post packages for certain countries, concerning which consult postmaster. International indemnity for the total loss (cover and contents) of a *Postal Union* registered article ranges from $3.27 to $8.17, except for registered mail exchanged with Canada, which is limited to $25.

A charge of 5 cents is collected from the sender, in addition to the postage and registry fee, for a return receipt for a *Postal Union* registered article, if requested at the time of mailing. When the request for a return receipt is made *after* mailing, the charge is 10 cents. Consult postmaster as to fees chargeable for return receipts for registered international *parcel post* packages.

A charge of 10 cents is made for an inquiry as to the disposal of any registered article addressed to a foreign country, unless the sender has failed to receive a return receipt for which he paid the required fee, is able to show that a prima facie loss or other irregularity has occurred through fault of the Postal Service, or has definite word of nonreceipt from addressee.

Any mailable articles, except unsealed fourth-class matter (parcel post) for domestic destinations, may be registered.

Mailable second- and third-class matter valued at over $100, upon which a registry fee providing indemnity in excess of $100 is paid, must be sealed and first-class postage paid thereon.

Domestic parcels containing fourth-class matter may also be registered, if sealed, and the required fee and postage at the first-class rate is paid.

Return receipts for domestic registered mail, showing delivery, may be obtained at time of mailing, 5 cents; after mailing, 10 cents; at time of mailing to show address of delivery, 31 cents.

An additional charge of 20 cents is made when registered mail is restricted in delivery to addressee only, or to the addressee or order.

Letters, prints, samples of merchandise, and commercial papers may be registered to practically all foreign countries.

International parcel post mail may be registered to some, but not all, foreign countries. In the case of a few foreign countries only indemnity ranging from $3.27 to $50 is paid for the loss, rifling, or damage of international parcel post articles.

Insured Mail. Domestic third- and fourth-class matter, mailed at or addressed to any post office in the United States or its possessions or on or to United States naval vessels, may be insured against loss, rifling, or damage in an amount equivalent to its value or the cost of repairs, upon payment of the following fees: $0.01 to $5.00, 5 cents; $5.01 to $10, 10 cents; $10.01 to $25, 15 cents; $25.01 to $50, 20 cents; $50.01 to $100, 25 cents; $100.01 to $200, 30 cents. The fee is in addition to the postage, both fee and postage to be prepaid.

Return receipts for domestic insured parcels, showing delivery, may be obtained at time of mailing, 5 cents; after mailing, 10 cents; at time of mailing to show address of delivery, 31 cents.

An additional charge of 20 cents is made when insured mail is restricted in delivery to addressee only, or to the addressee or order.

Insured International Mail. International insurance service is provided for Argentina, Bahamas, Barbados, British Guiana, Canada, Cape Verde Islands, Colombia, Denmark, Ecuador, Finland, Great Britain and Northern Ireland, Guatemala, Iceland, Ireland, Leeward Islands, New Zealand, Norway, Portugal (including Madeira and the Azores), Portuguese East Africa (Mozambique), Portuguese West Africa, Surinam, Sweden, Western Samoa (British), and Windward Islands.

Canada. Mailable merchandise and printed matter designated as third- and fourth-class matter addressed to Canada may be insured for the same fees and under the same conditions, in so far as applicable, including payment of indemnity, as apply to domestic mail of these classes. Third-class or "printed matter" may be registered, if desired, but fourth-class parcels of general merchandise may be registered only when sealed and postage is paid at letter rate.

A charge of 10 cents is made for an inquiry as to the disposal of an insured article addressed to Canada.

Certain articles of considerable intrinsic value, usually of small size, such as jewelry, coins, precious stones, etc., cannot be insured, but may be registered when sealed and prepaid at the letter rate of postage in addition to the registry fee.

Return receipts for insured parcels addressed to foreign countries except Canada will be furnished only upon request therefor by the sender and upon payment of a fee of 5 cents for each receipt. A fee of 10 cents is charged for return receipts requested subsequent to mailing.

Collect-on-Delivery International Mail. Registered international parcel post packages, registered Postal Union samples of merchandise, and all matter of the third class mailed under domestic classification and all international "Prints" within the prescribed limits of weight may be sent collect on delivery between any money order post office in the United States (including Alaska, Canada, Canal Zone, Canton Island, Guam, Hawaii, Midway Island, Puerto Rico, United States Virgin Islands, and Wake Island, and any money order post office in Mexico or Colombia.)

Domestic C. O. D. Mail. Unregistered (third and fourth classes and sealed matter of any class bearing first-class postage). Fees for collection and indemnity limited to:

$2.50	20¢	$ 50	45¢
5	25¢	100	55¢
25	35¢	150	60¢
	$200	65¢	

Domestic C. O. D. Mail. Registered (sealed matter of any class bearing first-class postage). Fees for collections and indemnity limited to:

$10	55¢	$100	90¢
50	70¢	200	$1.15

C. O. D. charges not exceeding $200, but indemnity up to:

$300	$1.20	$600	$1.35	$ 800	$1.45
400	1.25	700	1.40	1,000	1.55

Surcharges are collectible on registered C. O. D. mail—see postmaster.

Parcels sent C. O. D. shall in all cases be based upon bona fide orders or be in conformity with agreements between senders and addressees.

An additional charge of 20 cents is made when C. O. D. mail is restricted in delivery to addressee only, or to the addressee or order.

A demurrage charge of 5 cents a day is collected on each C. O. D. article which the addressee fails to accept within 15 days after the first attempt to deliver or the first notice of arrival at the office of the address is given.

A fee of 5 cents is charged for notifying sender of nondelivery of C. O. D. mail.

Money Orders. The maximum is $100, but there is no limit to the number that can be issued in one day to the same remitter. The fees for domestic money orders are: $0.01 to $5.00, 10 cents; $5.01 to $10, 15 cents; $10.01 to $50, 25 cents; $50.01 to $100, 35 cents.

International money orders cost 10 cents for $10 or less, and 10 cents extra on each additional $10 up to $1.00 for $100. Domestic money orders are payable within 30 days at any United States post office (continental); after that, only at the office designated.

Postal Notes. The maximum amount of each postal note is $10 with a fee of 8 cents a note. Postal notes are valid for two calendar months from last day of month of issue and are payable thereafter only by means of a duplicate note, application for which may be filed at any post office.

Unmailable Matter. Includes not only all legitimate matter not conforming to the rules as to legibility of address, size of package, or certificates of inspection, but also pistols, revolvers, or other firearms that can be concealed on the person; game, etc., killed out of season; poisons; explosive, inflammable, or bad-smelling articles; all spirituous and malt liquors; all liquor advertisements to or from Prohibition localities; indecent matter, written or otherwise; dunning post cards, and lottery, endless chain, and fraud matter. In addition, sealed mail to a *foreign country,* except it be obviously letters, cannot be sent, nor can publications in violation of the copyright laws of the country of destination.

Postal Savings. One dollar will open an interest-bearing account. Any person ten years old or over may start an account. A married woman may deposit in her own name. Any number of dollars may be deposited, and at any time, until the balance to the credit of a depositor amounts to $2,500.

FOREIGN POSTAGE RATES

Letter Rates. 3 cents an ounce or fraction thereof, to the following countries:

Argentina, Bolivia, Brazil, Canada, Chile, Colombia, Costa Rica, Cuba, Dominican Republic, Ecuador, Guatemala, Haiti, Republic of Honduras, Mexico, Morocco (Spanish zone), Nicaragua, Panama, Paraguay, Peru, Philippines, Rio de Oro, El Salvador, Spain and its colonies. Spanish Guinea, Uruguay, Venezuela.

The rate to other foreign countries and places in foreign countries for letters is 5 cents for the first ounce or fraction thereof, and 3 cents for each additional ounce or fraction thereof.

Weight Limit. 4 lb. 6 oz., except that to Canada it is 60 lb.

Maximum Dimensions. Length, breadth, and thickness combined, 36 in.; maximum length, 24 in. When in the form of a roll the length (maximum 32 in.), plus twice the diameter, limited to 40 in.; however, in the case of indivisible objects for the countries having a 3-cent letter rate (see above) the length (40 in. maximum) plus twice the diameter may be as much as 48 in.

Post Cards. Single post cards for any of the countries having a 3-cent letter rate (see above), 2 cents. Single post cards for all other foreign destinations, 3 cents. *Maximum dimensions:* 6 in. × 4¼ in. *Minimum dimensions:* 4 in. × 2¾ in. Each half of a double or reply-paid post card must be fully prepaid at the rate applicable to a single card.

Printed Matter (including second-class matter, except when mailed by publishers or registered news agents to the countries having a 3-cent letter rate; see above). For all foreign destinations, 1½ cents each 2 oz. or fraction. *Limit of weight:* 6 lb. 9 oz. in general and 11 lb. for single volumes of printed books, except in the case of certain countries. *Dimensions:* same as for letters (see above).

Samples of Merchandise. For all foreign destinations, 1½ cents each 2 oz. or fraction with a minimum charge of 3 cents. *Limit of weight:* 18 oz. *Dimensions:* same as for letters (see above).

Commercial Papers. For all foreign destinations 1½ cents each 2 oz. or fraction, with a minimum charge of 5 cents. *Limit of weight:* 4 lb. 6 oz. *Dimensions:* same as for letters (see above).

Eight-Ounce Merchandise Packages. Packages of merchandise weighing 8 oz. or less, for Argentina, Bolivia, Brazil, Canada, Chile, Colombia, Costa Rica, Cuba, Dominican Republic, Ecuador, Guatemala, Haiti, Republic of Honduras, Mexico, Morocco (Spanish zone), Nicaragua, Panama, Paraguay, Peru, Rio de Oro, El Salvador, Spain, Spanish Guinea, Uruguay, and Venezuela, 2 cents for each 2 oz. or fraction thereof, except that when the contents consists of seeds, scions, plants, cuttings, bulbs, or roots, the rate is 1½ cents for each 2 oz. (This is not parcel post and must not have a customs declaration attached or be sealed except when addressed for delivery in Canada or Mexico.)

Small Packets. Limit of weight: 2 lb. 3 oz. *Dimensions:* same as for letters (see above). The rate is 3 cents for each 2 oz., with a minimum charge of 15 cents per packet.

Registration Fee. For all foreign destinations, 25 cents in addition to postage. When a return receipt is requested at the time of mailing, there is an additional charge of 5 cents therefor, and a charge of 10 cents when requested after mailing.

The Dead-Letter Office

"Every man knows his own address, if not that of his correspondent. Put it in the upper left-hand corner!"

The dead-letter office is anything but dead; it is one of the most active of all the post office departments, receiving more than 18,000,000 undeliverable letters a year. All of these are without return address on the outside. They are opened and those with addresses inside are returned to the senders. The fee for this service is 5 cents. Only about 17 per cent can be returned; all the others are destroyed. More than 3,500,000 of the 18,000,000-odd items are Christmas cards.

Parcels which find their way to the dead-letter office are treated in the same way, except that instead of returning them and collecting the fee at the other end the department notifies the sender (when his address can be found) that the parcel is being held for a certain amount of postage and names the postage. Insured parcels are held for six months, ordinary parcels for 60 days. Parcels sales are held periodically at each dead-letter branch post office from two to six times a year, depending upon the amount of dead mail on hand.

Most of the mail that goes to the dead-letter office goes there because the sender failed to wrap it securely or to address it correctly or to put his return address on the outside. It is some comfort, however, to know that the dead-letter office is in some degree self-supporting. The fees from return postage from unclaimed packages (packages are held for a year and then sold at public auction) along with the money which was inclosed in some of the letters amounts to about $250,000, which is only about $20,000 less than the entire operating expenses.

Surface Mail Time from New York to Foreign Countries

In the following table the average time is given from New York to the chief port in the country named. If there is no port in the country the time is reckoned to the principal city. Where there are two or more important ports the time is given to the nearest, and allowance should be made accordingly. It is possible for a letter to go to England, for instance, in considerably less than eight days if it is on a fast ship, but eight days is the time that under ordinary circumstances should be allowed. Sailing dates, and in some instances, as with Trinidad, the number of steamers per month, should be checked.

Europe

	Days		Days
Albania	11	Italy	10
Austria	11	Latvia	11
Belgium	9	Lithuania	10
Bulgaria	12	Netherlands	9
Czechoslovakia	10	Norway	11
Denmark	11	Poland	11
England	8	Portugal	9
Estonia	12	Rumania	12
Finland	12	Russia	12
France	8	Spain	9
Germany	9	Sweden	12
Greece	13	Switzerland	9
Hungary	11	Turkey	12
Ireland	8	Yugoslavia	11

South America

	Days		Days
Argentina	17–20	Ecuador	9–11
Bolivia	10–12	Paraguay	19–22
Brazil	13–15	Peru	11–13
Chile	16–21	Uruguay	18–21
Colombia	8–12	Venezuela	5–9

Bahamas, West Indies, and Central America

	Days		Days
Bahamas	3	Jamaica	6
Bermuda	2	Mexico	5
Costa Rica	9	Nicaragua—E. coast	8
Cuba	3	W. coast	11–12
Dominican Republic	7	Panama	6–8
Guatemala	7	Puerto Rico	5
Haiti	6	Trinidad	8–12
Honduras	7–8	Virgin Islands	6

The Orient

	Days		Days
China	23	Israel	18
Hongkong	27	Japan	17
India	25	Malaya	30
Indo-China	27	Pakistan	28
Indonesia	35	Philippines (Republic of)	25
		Thailand	30

Australia, New Zealand, and South Seas

	Days		Days
Australia	27	Hawaii	12
Fiji Islands	21	New Zealand	24

Africa

	Days		Days
Algeria	11	South Africa	20-25
Egypt	14		

AIR MAIL SCHEDULE FOR QUICK REFERENCE

Any mailable matter except that liable to damage from freezing will be carried by airplane, including sealed parcels.

Air mail postage stamps and special air mail envelopes are available. Ordinary postage stamps may be used. All mail should be conspicuously endorsed VIA AIR MAIL.

Mail intended for dispatch by air mail service may be registered, insured and sent C. O. D. and special delivery; the parcels are sealed upon prepayment of the proper fees in addition to the air mail postage (for rates see p. 171).

The domestic postage is 6 cents for each ounce or fraction thereof, anywhere in the United States, including Alaska. The rate for the transpacific air-mail service is 6 cents to *Hawaii*, 6 cents to *Guam*, and 25 cents to the *Philippine Islands* for each half-ounce; 6 cents for each half-ounce or fraction thereof to *Puerto Rico* and *United States Virgin Islands;* and 10 cents to *Canal Zone.*

Approximate Transit Time for Air Mail[1]

Argentina (2); Australia (4–5); Azores (1); Bahamas (2 hr.); Bermuda (5 hr.); Bolivia (2); Brazil (2); Canal Zone (1); Chile (2); China (5–7); Colombia (1); Costa Rica (1); Cuba (2–4 hr.); Dominican Republic (8 hr.); Ecuador (1–2); Europe (1–3); Formosa (3); Guatemala (1); Haiti (6 hr.); Honduras (1); India (4); Indochina (6); Japan (3); Martinique (1); Mexico (3–8 hr.); Netherlands Indies (6); Nicaragua (1); Panama (1); Paraguay (2); Peru (1); Portugal (1); Puerto Rico (1); Salvador, El (1); Siam (5); Venezuela (1); Virgin Islands (1).

---

[1]Time is given in days; time differences (*e.g.*, 8–10) depend on the distance of the particular city.

Any mailable matter (ask your postmaster about merchandise) may be sent to foreign countries at the postage rate shown below. The weight limit is 4 lb. 6 oz. The dimensions are 36 in. for length, breadth, and thickness combined, the length being limited to 24 in. (ask your postmaster about articles in the form of rolls).

Combined postage and air mail fee to foreign countries must be fully prepaid.

Air fee per ½ ounce for principal countries
(including ordinary postage)

Afghanistan ....25¢	Germany ....15¢	Nicaragua ....10¢
Albania ....15¢	Great Britain and	Norway ....15¢
Argentina ....10¢	Northern Ireland ..15¢	Pakistan ....25¢
Australia ....25¢	Greece (inc. Crete) ..15¢	Panama ....10¢
Austria ....15¢	Guatemala ....10¢	Paraguay ....10¢
Belgium ....15¢	Hashemite-Jordan	Peru ....10¢
Bolivia ....10¢	Kingdom ....25¢	Philippines ....25¢
Brazil ....10¢	Honduras (Rep.) ....10¢	Poland ....15¢
Bulgaria ....15¢	Hungary ....15¢	Portugal ....15¢
Burma ....25¢	India ....25¢	Rumania ....15¢
Canada .... 6¢	Iran ....25¢	Salvador, El ....10¢
(per each oz.)	Iraq ....25¢	Saudi Arabia ....25¢
Chile ....10¢	Ireland ....15¢	Siam ....25¢
China ....25¢	Israel ....25¢	Spain ....15¢
Colombia ....10¢	Italy ....15¢	Sweden ....15¢
Costa Rica ....10¢	Japan ....25¢	Switzerland ....15¢
Cuba .... 8¢	Korea ....25¢	Syria ....25¢
Czechoslovakia .....15¢	Lebanon ....25¢	Turkey ....15¢
Denmark ....15¢	Liberia ....25¢	U.S.S.R. ....15¢
Dominican Republic ..10¢	Luxemburg ....15¢	Union of South
Ecuador ....10¢	Mexico .... 6¢	Africa ....25¢
Egypt ....15¢	(per each oz.)	Uruguay ....10¢
Ethiopia ....25¢	Netherlands ....15¢	Venezuela ....10¢
Finland ....15¢	New Zealand ....25¢	Yugoslavia ....15¢
France ....15¢		

TELEGRAMS, CABLES, ETC.

When people say there is nothing new under the sun they forget the modern systems of communication which are so intertwined and interlaced that it is possible for almost anyone at any time to be in almost instantaneous touch with any part of the world. Cables have been sent from New York to London and answers received in less than a minute and telephone conversations between New York and Paris are a daily commonplace.

The services which the various communication systems have to offer have been classified and the alert business man needs to be familiar with the classifications and the advantages they have to offer.

Domestic Service

The regular *telegram* is accepted at any hour of the day or night for immediate delivery. It has the right of way over all other traffic. The minimum charge is for ten words, low extra-word rate charges being reckoned on words in excess of ten. It should be used when quick service is needed.

Serial service is used when it is necessary to send a series of short telegrams to the same addressee in the course of one day. Rates are charged on the basis of a minimum of 15 words per telegram and 50 words for the whole day.

The *day letter* is subordinate to messages in full-rate and serial service classifications. The delay in transmission is usually slight, and the cost is reckoned on a minimum basis of 50 instead of ten words. Fifty words can be sent for about the same cost as a 17-word telegram. Code language may be used.

The *night letter* is accepted any time during the day and at night up until two A.M. for delivery the following morning. The cost of a 25-word night letter varies according to the distance it is to be sent. The cost of additional words, over 25, decreases as the length of the message increases. This is the cheapest service of all for long messages and is much used by businessmen in place of letters when speed is essential. Code language may be used.

How to Write a Telegram

All telegrams should be as brief as they can be and yet state their messages clearly. Punctuation marks, including the period (or decimal point), comma, colon, semicolon, dash or hyphen, parentheses, quotation marks, and apostrophe are free, but words such as "stop," "quote," "comma," and

179

"semicolon," when written out, are charged as one word each. Abbreviations, figures, letters, and other signs such as $, %, &, /, ' (for feet), and " (for inches), are counted at the rate of one word for each five characters in messages between points within the United States and between the United States and Mexico or Alaska.[1] For example, each of the following is counted as one word: AM or A.M., PM or P.M., NY or N.Y., B.&O., COD or C.O.D., 1st, 2nd, $25.05, 12345, and AB175. A group of letters, figures, or signs containing more than five characters is counted as two or more words; for example, #78694 (two words). If abbreviations are separated by spaces (A. M., N. Y., B. & O.), they are counted as one word for each character. Proper and personal names in the message are charged for according to the way they are normally written: for example, New York City (three words), Du Pont (two words), Vandewater (one word). Initials, if not spaced, count as one word (R.L.S.). If spaced, they count as one word for each letter; for example, R. L. S. (three words).

Any dictionary word from any one of the following languages may be used and counted as one word: English, German, French, Italian, Dutch, Portuguese, Spanish, and Latin. All groups of letters which do not form dictionary words from one of the languages mentioned above are counted at the rate of five letters to a word.

On a domestic telegram the address and signature are free. The address should be as full as possible to facilitate prompt delivery to the addressee. Code addresses cannot be used in domestic messages. Messages addressed to two people are charged for as two telegrams, and a separate copy is delivered to each person. If a telegram is addressed to John Brown *or James Smith,* the italicized words are charged for.

If the message is not to be signed the word "Unsigned" should be written in place of the signature. When there is more than one signature, all except the last are counted and charged for. In *"John Brown and* James Smith", the italicized words are charged for, but in a family signature like "John and Mary", no extra charge is made.

The sender can have a report made as to whether his message is delivered by writing "Report delivery" immediately following the addressee's name. These words are charged for and the reply, wired back collect to the sender, will state when and to whom the message was delivered.

If the sender desires to have his message repeated back (and this is a good way to insure accuracy in important messages) he should write "Repeat back" at the top of the message. The repetition will cost one half as much as the regular rate, and, in addition, the sender has to pay for the words, "Repeat back."

Messages to be sent collect will be accepted from holders of Western Union collect cards, which may be obtained through application from members of reputable social or commercial organizations, and from any responsible person or business firm.

---

[1] In telegrams between points in the United States and Canada, and St. Pierre and Miquelon Islands, these signs are counted as one word each.

Principal Miscellaneous Services

Telegraph money orders provide a rapid, accurate service for transferring money quickly and safely from one point to another. Charges are based on the amount of money telegraphed plus the distance involved. Supplementary messages may be sent with the money.

Another business service is the *leased-wire* service, which provides direct private telegraphic communication between two offices of one firm, or between two regular correspondents, or between the main office and branches of the same firm.

Social uses of telegraph services include congratulatory telegrams, condolence telegrams, invitations, etc. The telegraph company will suggest suitable texts, and charges are made at regular full rates.

Messengers are provided to do personal errands, to serve advertising and sales promotion purposes, to deliver professional samples, pick up newspaper "copy," deliver tickets, etc.

International Service

International cable and radio messages are constructed similarly to domestic telegrams, except that registered (abbreviated) code addresses may be used to save tolls, and code words (secret language) are permitted in the full-rate classification. Each word in the address, text, and signature is counted and charged for.

The *full-rate* classification of international service, which is the standard fast service for messages in plain language, in secret (code or cipher) language, or in a combination of plain and secret languages, is subject to a minimum charge for five words.

The *letter telegram* classification of international service, which is for messages in plain language *only,* is charged for at one-half the per-word rates applicable to full-rate messages, with a minimum charge for 22 words. This is an overnight service with delivery generally being made the day after the filing date; but in certain countries delivery may be made in the morning of the second day after the filing date. Letter Telegram messages are designated by the indicator "LT," which is placed before the address, and counted and charged for as one word. Secret language is *not* admitted but registered (abbreviated) code addresses may be used in the address or signature of such LT messages.

In the address of an international cable or radio message, the name of the country of destination is seldom necessary. Unregistered addresses should not be unduly shortened, since senders are responsible for incorrect or insufficient addresses and corrections or amplifications can be made only by sending a paid-service message at the full rate.

Each plain language (dictionary) word appearing in messages in the full-rate and letter telegram (LT) classifications is counted at the rate of 15, or fraction of 15 letters to the word and any figures or figure-groups appearing in such messages are counted at the rate of five, or fraction of five, figures to the word. Punctuation marks (period, comma, colon, question mark, apostrophe, hyphen or dash, parentheses or brackets, fraction bar or stroke, and quotation marks) are counted and charged for as one word each when used in their normal sense. However, when such punctuation marks appear in a group of figures or in a group of letters, they are each counted as one figure or one letter in the group and not as a separate word. The dollar sign and the pound sterling mark are each counted and charged for as separate words. Secret language, consisting of non-dictionary words, which is admitted only in messages in the full-rate classification, is counted at the rate of five, or fraction of five, characters to the word.

Cable money orders provide a quick way to send funds to many foreign countries. The money is deposited at the telegraph office and a fast cable money order is sent abroad. Payment is made through a foreign representative. A message can be sent at a slight additional cost.

Ship radiograms. Communication with ships at sea in all parts of the world is provided by radiomarine-telegraph companies. Only the full-rate message classification is available.

TRANSPORTATION

"If our industrial progress is to continue, there is nothing more important to industry, whether on the farm or in the city, than the proper organization and operation of an adequate system for the distribution of our products. Everyone who lives in the United States should be interested in distribution. It is the necessary link between production and selling, and neither can function properly unless this third partner is efficient."—IRVING T. BUSH, Founder and President of the Bush Terminal Company.

Common Carriers

A person or organization which transports goods or people or both from one place to another for a price is called a *common carrier*. The fact that the common carrier announces himself in business becomes a standing offer to the public which turns into a contract as soon as it is accepted. The carrier cannot refuse anyone or anybody without good reason. He is not required to transport dangerous commodities like dynamite or nitroglycerin, and he is not required to carry goods when his means of transport are already fully occupied. The rules by which the carrier regulates his business are usually announced. (See post office regulations or the terms on the back of a receipt from the express company.) While the goods are in his hands the carrier must exercise due care as to their safety, for which, as a matter of fact, he is responsible unless the loss or damage is caused by an act of God or of the public enemy. The bill of lading is evidence of the contract between the sender and the carrier. The carrier is not legally responsible for the safety of human passengers if it can be proved that he has taken due care toward insuring their safety.

Common carriers are of many kinds—trains, motor buses, automobiles, airplanes, steamships, etc. Telephone and telegraph companies are also common carriers, though not quite in the same sense that carriers of actual property are. They do not, for instance, insure the correctness of the messages that they transmit. An operator must send the message exactly as it is given to him. It may not make sense to him but it is possible that it will mean something to the person for whom it is intended. An operator can refuse to accept a message if it is illegible but once he has accepted it he must send it as best he can. The message is not considered delivered until it is received by the person to whom it is addressed. Mere delivery to a messenger boy is not real delivery. The employees of telephone and telegraph companies are strictly bound to secrecy, and even if they are summoned into court they are protected against having to repeat dispatches or make testimony with regard to their contents.

WAREHOUSES

Warehouses are of several different types, but broadly speaking may be divided into those used for general merchandise storage and those used

183

for the storage of perishable commodities requiring refrigeration. Merchandise warehouses serve manufacturers and distributors of nonperishable commodities while refrigerated warehouses provide scientific refrigeration and controlled humidity for the storage of perishable foods, certain drugs, florists' stocks, etc. In addition to storage these warehouses usually provide such other services as pool car distribution, repacking and coopering, distribution, and in the case of refrigerated warehouses, quick freezing, refrigerator-car icing, pipeline refrigeration, etc.

Warehouses may be distinguished as public (which store goods for others) or private (which store only their own goods). All public warehouses issue warehouse receipts which may be used as collateral for loans against the commodities represented by the receipt.

Some warehouses specialize in the handling and storage of one commodity such as household goods, tobacco, cotton, grain, etc.

Bonded Warehouses

The term bonded warehouse is one which implies various types of protection to the storer. State-bonded or state-licensed warehouses cover fidelity or personal security aspects of the storage problem. Federal-bonded warehouses are those in which the Government has permitted the approved warehouse to set aside for storage imported merchandise not yet released from the Government's custody. There are also *Internal Revenue Bonded Warehouses* which set aside space for storage of alcohol, liquor, cigarettes, etc.; *United States Warehouse Act Bonded Warehouses*, wherein certain agricultural commodities are stored at Government expense; and warehouses bonded under the Quarantine Acts which are permitted to store plant and animal products prior to inspection. There are in addition several Government departments which require performance bonds from warehousemen contracting Government-owned, or Government-controlled, goods.

ANTITRUST DIVISION OF THE DEPARTMENT OF JUSTICE

The Antitrust Division of the Department of Justice, with the F. B. I., has the power to investigate complaints and prosecute violations of laws which make illegal all contracts, combinations, trusts, and conspiracies in restraint of interstate or international trade. The Small Business Section of the Division receives anti-trust complaints from small concerns and represents them before other Government agencies.

THE INTERSTATE COMMERCE COMMISSION

It is a fundamental part of our Constitution that there shall be complete freedom of trade among the several states of the Union. The provisions of the Constitution were supplemented in 1887 by the Interstate

Commerce Act, which declared that common carriers between the states were subject to regulation, that their charges should be reasonable, and that there should be no special rates, rebates, preferences, etc. The Interstate Commerce Commission was established to execute the provisions of this act. The members are appointed by the President.

By the **Transportation Act of 1940** changes were made to the Interstate Commerce Act, including the addition of a part dealing with the *Regulation of Water Carriers in Interstate and Foreign Commerce*. The commission also has jurisdiction over common carriers engaged in interstate commerce by railroad, by highway, by water, and by pipeline of oil and other commodities (except water and gas), and over freight forwarders.

THE FEDERAL TRADE COMMISSION

The purpose of the Commission, which was created in 1914, is to promote in the interest of the public free, fair competition in interstate trade through prevention of price-fixing agreements, boycotts, combinations in restraint of trade, unlawful price discriminations, and other unfair methods of competition and unfair and deceptive acts and practices. It also promotes and safeguards the health and life of the consuming public by preventing the dissemination of false advertisements of foods, drugs, cosmetics, and devices which may be injurious to health.

Under the jurisdiction of the Commission are: The Wheeler-Lea Act of 1938; the Clayton Antitrust Act of 1914 (together with the Interstate Commerce Commission); the Robinson-Patman Act of 1936; the Webb-Pomerene Export Trade Act of 1918; the Wool Labeling Act of 1939; and the Lanham Trade Mark Act of 1946.

THE ROBINSON-PATMAN ACT OF 1936

The Act under the jurisdiction of the Federal Trade Commission forbids in Section 2 (a), price discrimination in interstate commerce between purchasers of goods of like grade and quality, where the effect of such discrimination substantially lessens competition or tends to create a monopoly in any line of commerce.

Other subsections forbid the payment of brokerage in any guise by one party to the other, or the other's agent, or to any intermediary acting for the other party. Also forbidden are payments and allowances commonly referred to as for advertising and promotional work if not available on proportionally equal terms to all customers competing in the distribution of such commodities.

Section 3 of the Act provides penalties of fines and imprisonment for persons who are parties to or assist in sales which discriminate, to their knowledge, against competitors of the purchaser and also makes unlawful discriminatory prices made for the purpose of destroying competition or eliminating a competitor.

CHAMBERS OF COMMERCE

A chamber of commerce is a voluntary association of merchants and business leaders for the protection and development of commercial interests, the improvement of business opportunities, and civic betterment in the city, county, or state which it is intended to serve. First in the United States was the New York Chamber of Commerce, founded in 1768 by 20 merchants. It received a royal charter from London in 1770, and was reincorporated by act of the state legislature in 1784 as the Chamber of Commerce of the State of New York.

Meanwhile, Charleston, S.C. and Boston, Mass., each founded a chamber of commerce in 1773. Today there is a chamber of commerce or board of trade in every city of commercial importance in the United States, and a similar organization on a broader area level in most of the states. Some of the larger chambers, in cooperation with the Chamber of Commerce of the United States, provide courses of commercial training for young men.

The Chamber of Commerce of the United States, a national business organization, is a federation of 2,550 local chambers of commerce and more than 500 trade associations, with an underlying membership of 1,319,000. It was established in 1912 for the purpose of doing in a national way what the local chambers do in their communities.

The national chamber performs the continuous task of collecting statistical information and sending it to its members. Its official organs are *Nation's Business,* published monthly in Washington, and *Business Action,* published weekly.

BETTER BUSINESS BUREAUS

A Better Business Bureau is an agency maintained by business to protect consumers and businessmen alike from fraud, misrepresentation, and chicanery in commercial transactions through the promotion of advertising and selling practices which are fair to both.

Better Business Bureaus have published the "Guide for Retail Advertising and Selling"—a 138-page consolidation of the various standards and recommendations which they have adopted. Some of these recommendations are based on laws, others on legal decisions and rulings by Government agencies. Business usually cooperates with the bureaus on a voluntary basis; moreover, public exposition of violation of bureau standards is often very effective in stopping unfair practices.

The National Better Business Bureau fosters a program of consumer education in collaboration with high school principals through the National Association of Secondary School Principals. Through the Solicitations Division of the national bureau, local groups keep members informed about organizations which approach business firms in order to solicit funds or offer services.

The first Better Business Bureaus were organized on a local level in 1912; there are now some 100 groups in the United States and Canada.

DISHONEST SALESMANSHIP

Unscrupulous companies swindle unsuspecting housewives by selling them cheap or inferior products at exorbitant prices. The technique most frequently employed is as follows:

The salesman, usually claiming to be a representative of a nationally known business, poll, or survey organization, gains access to the home. By skillful questions he determines the customer's preference for a particular product. He then offers her a "bargain." These bargains are household articles which can be paid for on the installment plan. The customer is asked to sign a simple order blank, which does not contain any claims, representations, or warrantees and does not provide for return or refund if the customer is dissatisfied. Sales are final. The order blank is a legally binding and enforceable contract. When the ordered product is delivered the housewife signs a receipt. The "bargain," upon inspection, is found to be of poor quality, sometimes even defective. The customer has no legal redress no matter how false the claim and how bad the article. Swindles and "rackets" that are fairly common are listed as follows:

Baby Contests

Photograph salesmen do not find it difficult to persuade mothers into ordering baby pictures by representing that their studios are conducting baby contests for national advertisers.

Electric Appliance Repair

The "fake" repair man claims that for a small charge he will repair vacuum cleaners or other appliances at his shop. He may try to collect for unauthorized work or may not return your appliance.

Light Bulbs and Fixtures

Some inferior foreign electric light bulbs are so marked that when they are assembled the name of the country of origin is concealed. They may be falsely labeled on the outside as made in the U.S.A. Sometimes they are mislabeled as to the number of watts.

Sometimes the salesman obtains the signature to an order for fixtures by representing that they are on trial. His representation that the fixtures give better light at less cost may prove to be false. Frequently it will be found that they are ordinary fixtures with expensive, inefficient, and misbranded bulbs.

Vacuum Cleaners and Sewing Machines

Unscrupulous salesmen of vacuum cleaners and sewing machines often obtain signatures to purchase-contracts by inducing the belief that their products are on trial. The tricky sewing machine salesman may claim that his company will supply sewing work to help pay for the machine.

Hosiery

"Fake" stocking salesmen offer low prices, take orders for future delivery, collect deposits, and then disappear with the money.

Magazines

Subscriptions are obtained by the "college boy gag." Boys and girls are employed in organized crews and instructed to represent that they are working their way through school. There are legitimate subscription agencies; they do not permit such misrepresentations.

Permanent Waves

A certificate purporting to entitle the recipient to a "free" permanent wave is sometimes sold for a small sum. A complete permanent wave includes a shampoo (oil or plain) before the wave; permanent waving; and "setting" hair after the wave. The holder of the "free" certificate later learns that it refers to the permanent waving only, and that she is required to pay for the other essential operations—at a price more than adequate to cover the complete process.

Cosmetic and Health Schemes

No hair dye is "permanent." There is no known preparation or process which will "restore" the "original" color to hair.

There is nothing that, put in bath water, will reduce weight. Soaps, creams, bath salts, and other external applications can have no possible value in permanently reducing obesity. Care should be exercised in using obesity remedies. Certain ingredients are potentially dangerous.

Some creams have been advertised as "skin foods," "tissue builders," etc., but these terms are misnomers. Creams sold to develop the bust or other parts of the body are also useless.

Businessmen sometimes fall prey to the schemes of unscrupulous salesmen, who resort to trickery. Some such common schemes are:

Stimulating Business

Small merchants are induced to buy business-stimulating plans from promotors who sell display advertisements and premium coupons. The merchant's customers then have to pay exorbitant sums to redeem the coupons, and the merchants lose the good will of their customers.

Collection Agencies

Small merchants in order to recover delinquent accounts use collection agencies. Some collection-agency contracts make it possible for the agency to charge fees exceeding those of a reliable lawyer.

Convention Reporting

Merchants should not order stenographic reports of convention records at a given rate per page without first finding out the total number of pages. Such reports may be lengthy; if so, the contract will obligate the merchant to pay a large sum.

Directories

Circulation figures and the publisher's reputation should be ascertained before buying advertising or listings in a directory. The directory exhibited by a crooked salesman may prove to be the only copy in existence.

Adjusters

Insurance companies furnish forms without cost; it is not necessary to hire adjusters to complete these forms. Some "fake" insurance adjusters seek to obtain advance fees for rendering such service.

Listing Fees

When a business broker requests an advance fee to list a business for sale, obtain a clear written understanding as to the precise services he agrees to render. Unscrupulous brokers often charge listing fees and then render no services.

PASSPORT REGULATIONS OF THE UNITED STATES[1]

A passport is an official document, issued under authority of the State Department, declaring its holder a citizen of the United States, and requesting all whom it may concern to permit him safely and freely to pass, and, in case of need, to give him all lawful aid and protection. Every American citizen traveling abroad should have a passport; in fact, in most countries he is required to have one.

A person in the United States who wishes a passport must submit a written application to a clerk of a Federal court or a state court authorized to naturalize aliens. If, however, there is a passport agent in the place where he lives, the application should be presented to the agent. Passport agents are in New York City, San Francisco, Boston, Chicago, and New Orleans.

The senior member of a family may include members of his immediate family in his passport. This means that a husband may include his wife and minor children in his passport, or that a woman may include her minor children in her passport. Children who are over 21 must have separate passports. It is not necessary for a wife or children to appear in court when they are included in a husband's application, but children who need individual passports must apply in person. Regardless of the rules stated here, members of a family who wish to travel in separate countries or to return to the United States at different times should have separate passports.

A native American citizen applying for a passport must submit a birth certificate or a baptismal certificate showing the date and place of the birth of the applicant. If neither of these is obtainable there must be an affidavit, sworn to before a notary, by either parent, by a brother, a sister, or other relative, preferably one older than the applicant, or by the physician who attended at his birth. If none of these is obtainable an affidavit by some reputable person not related to the applicant will serve. The person making the affidavit must make a brief statement as to how he has acquired the information needed.

An identifying witness must appear in person with the applicant. A witness will not be accepted if he has not known the applicant two years or more, and he will not be accepted if he has received or expects to receive money for his testimony.

A naturalized citizen applying for a passport must submit his naturalization certificate. A person who is a citizen through the naturalization of a parent must present proof of the naturalization of the parent.

---

[1] Passport applications may be accepted from persons of military age. Such persons, however, should keep their draft boards advised of their whereabouts.

Passport and Visa Information for Tourist and Business Travel

Country	Passport required[1]	Visa required[1]	Tourist card (t.c.) obtainable[2]	Visa or t.c. fee
Albania	Yes	Yes	No	$10
Argentina	Yes	Yes	No	none
Australia	Yes	Yes	No	none
Austria	Yes	No[3]	No	none
Bahamas	No	No	No	none
Belgium	Yes	No[4]	No	none
Belgian Congo	Yes	Yes	No	$10
Bermuda	No	No	No	none
Bolivia	Yes	Yes	No	$7.50[5]
Brazil	Yes	Yes	No	none
Bulgaria	Yes	Yes	No	$10
Canada	No	No	No	none
Chile	Yes	Yes	No	$1.75
China	Yes	Yes	No	ea. $2.50
Colombia	Yes	Yes	No	none
Costa Rica	Yes	Yes	Yes[6]	none
Cuba	No	No	No	none
Czechoslovakia	Yes	Yes	No	$10
Denmark	Yes	No	No	none
Dominican Republic	Yes	Yes	Yes[6]	none
Ecuador	Yes	Yes	Yes[6]	$1.00 (t.c.)
Egypt	Yes	Yes	No	$2.00
El Salvador	Yes	Yes	Yes[6]	none
Ethiopia	Yes	Yes	No	$3.50
Finland	Yes	Yes	No	none
France	Yes	No	No	none
Great Britain and Northern Ireland	Yes	No	No	none
British Possessions	Yes	Yes[7]	No	$2.00
Greece	Yes	Yes	No	$5.00
Guatemala	Yes	Yes[8]	Yes[6]	none
Haiti	Yes[8]	Yes[8]	No[9]	none
Honduras	Yes	Yes	Yes[6]	none
Hungary	Yes	Yes	No	$10
Iceland	Yes	Yes	No	none
India	Yes	Yes	No	$2.00
Indonesia	Yes	Yes	No	$2.00
Iran	Yes	Yes	No	none
Iraq	Yes	Yes	No	none
Ireland	Yes	No	No	$2.00
Israel	Yes	Yes	No	$10
Italy	Yes	No	No	none

Country	Passport required[1]	Visa required[1]	Tourist card (t.c.) obtainable[2]	Visa or t.c. fee
Japan[10]	Yes	Yes	No	none
Korea	Yes	Yes	No	none
Lebanon	Yes	Yes	No	$4.75
Liberia	Yes	Yes	No	none
Liechtenstein	Yes	No	No	none
Luxemburg	Yes	No	No	none
Mexico	Yes[11]	No	Yes[12]	[12]
Monaco	Yes	Yes[11]	No	$.90
Netherlands and Netherlands West Indies	Yes	No	No	none
New Zealand	Yes	Yes	No	$2.00
Nicaragua	Yes	Yes	Yes[6]	none
Norway	Yes	No	No	$2.00
Pakistan	Yes	Yes	No	$2.00
Panama	Yes[13]	Yes	Yes[13]	none
Paraguay	Yes	Yes	No	$4.00
Peru	Yes	Yes	No	none
Philippine Republic	Yes	Yes	No	$5.00
Poland	Yes	No	No	$10
Portugal	Yes	Yes	No	none
Rumania	Yes	Yes	No	$10
Saudi Arabia	Yes	Yes	No	$10
Siam	Yes	No	No	none
Spain	Yes	Yes	No	$10
Sweden	Yes	No[14]	No	none
Switzerland	Yes	No	No	none
Syria	Yes	Yes	No	$4.75
Thailand (see Siam)				
Turkey	Yes	Yes	No	$1.56
Union of South Africa	Yes	Yes	No	none
U.S.S.R.	Yes	Yes	No	$11[15]
Uruguay	Yes	No	No	none
Venezuela[16]	Yes	Yes	Yes[6]	$2.00
Yugoslavia	Yes	Yes	No	$2.00

[1]Requirements listed below do not apply to persons who go as immigrants to foreign countries. [2]Tourist cards may be obtained from consuls or from transportation companies. Usually the cards are all that are necessary for tourist travel; businessmen may not substitute such cards for passports and visas. [3]Military permit is required. [4]Unless staying for more than two months. [5]Special visa fee for tourists, $2.00. [6]Tourist cards are valid for specified period; usually may be extended for another specified period. [7]Tourists do not need visa for less than two-month stay. [8]Unless staying for less than one month. [9]Identity card issued to tourists on arrival by officials in Haiti. [10]Tourist travel permissible in approved areas only. [11]Passports and visas required of American citizens entering Mexico in any category except: tourists; summer school and similar students; and American legal residents of Mexico. Where passport and visa are required, an identification certificate is also necessary. Passports not required of American legal residents of Mexico who depart and return in possession of Mexican immigration card No. 14. [12]Tourist and Visitante cards (the latter for businessmen only) available: fee $3.00. Valid for six months. [13]Entry permit also obtainable for non-tourists in lieu of passport. [14]Unless staying for more than three months. [15]Temporary residence visa fee $2.00, permanent residence visa fee $10. [16]Tourists who intend to stay less than six months will not need passports, and following special facilities will be granted: (a) for less than 48-hour visit, no documents are necessary; (b) for 12-hour to eight-day visit, tourist cards issued by transportation company are sufficient; (c) for eight-day to six-month visit, a tourist card must be obtained from Venezuelan consul.

If the applicant has an old passport, issued since 1918, it should be presented for cancellation. This passport, if properly issued, will be accepted as evidence of citizenship.

Two duplicate photographs of each person named in the application on thin paper unmounted, and not more than 3 × 3 inches nor less than 2½ × 2½ inches in size must be submitted with the application. A group photograph should be used when more than one person is named in the application. Photographs in uniform will not be accepted unless the applicant is in active military service and is going abroad on official business.

A fee of ten dollars is collected for every passport issued unless the applicant is the widow, child, parent, brother, or sister, of an American soldier, sailor, or marine buried abroad, and the purpose of the trip is to visit the country of burial.

Even after the United States has issued the passport, the traveler must obtain permission to enter the country he intends to visit. To do this he presents himself to the consul of that country for a visa. The consul examines the passport and indorses it as valid. Visas should be obtained in this country before sailing unless the plans of the traveler are uncertain, in which case they can be obtained abroad as required. A visa is usually good for 12 months. Visa terms and fees are subject to change without notice.

Only countries of chief interest are listed below. Entry into Austria and Germany is subject to the issuance of a military permit.

The *original period of possible validity of a passport* is restricted to two years: *Provided,* that the passport may be renewed for a period of not more than two additional years under regulations prescribed by the Secretary of State: *provided further,* that the Secretary of State may restrict the original or renewal period of a passport to less than two years. The Secretary of State may in his discretion require an applicant for the renewal of a passport to submit satisfactory documentary evidence of the object of his journey abroad.

Resident aliens intending to return to the United States should apply to the Department of Justice for a return permit or a non-quota visa from an American consul abroad. Return permits can be issued only in the United States.

Travelers by air are subject to the same general regulations that govern travelers by other means of transport.

Anyone wishing further information should write to the Passport Division of the Department of State at Washington, D.C.

CUSTOMS REGULATIONS CONCERNING AUTOMOBILES ENTERING CANADA AND RETURNING TO THE UNITED STATES

Automobiles may be brought into Canada under Traveler's Vehicle Permit by nonresidents for their personal transportation, whether for pleasure or business purposes, for a period up to six months without the payment of duty or deposit thereon.

An automobile is admissible only when brought in for the use of the owner or a member of his immediate family; except that a tourist may bring in for touring purposes an automobile which is not his own property, provided he is a nonresident of Canada and produces to the satisfaction of the customs officer a letter or other evidence from the owner of the automobile identifying the vehicle by motor or license numbers and stating that the person so bringing it has the owner's permission to use the automobile for touring in Canada.

No tourist need pay any fees for an automobile entry permit or its extension; Canadian customs officers will, without charge, assist in filling out the form. The following information is required:

1. Name of manufacturer of car
2. Manufacturer's serial number
3. Style and value of car
4. State license number
5. A list of extra auto equipment and other articles such as guns, cameras, and outboard motors
6. Signature and street address of owner
7. City or town and state of which owner is resident

This form is also available at the touring bureaus of the American Automobile Association clubs; members going to Canada will save time if the document is properly executed before their arrival. The form should be made out in duplicate, one copy to be kept on file by the Canadian customs officials, the other to be retained by the tourist and surrendered upon his leaving Canada. Permits are valid for periods up to six months; the usual permit is for 60 days, with extensions available for periods up to six months. After this period, the Department of National Revenue, Ottawa, Canada, should be consulted.

Special customs regulations apply to Alaska Highway travel. Consult the Canadian Government Travel Bureau in Ottawa for further information.

American tourists are not required to register their cars with the United States customs when entering Canada. On his return to the United States, the tourist's state registration card is accepted as establishing American ownership and origin of the car.

A point to be remembered by motorists from the United States, when purchasing gasoline or oil, is that the Imperial measure is used in Canada. This measure is one-fifth larger than the corresponding United States measure. Thus five gallons Canadian measure are equal to six gallons United States measure and, therefore, fewer gallons are required to fill the gas tank.

DRIVER'S SAFETY INFORMATION
100 Questions and Answers[1]

QUESTIONS

1. Is driving an automobile in New York State a right to which one is entitled or is it a privilege?
2. For how long is this privilege granted?
3. Why is carefulness so important?
4. Can a person legally drive an automobile after his license has been suspended or revoked?
5. Can one drive for hire with an operator's license?
6. What must a driver do who changes his address?
7. Should one, in case of an emergency, lend his operator's license?
8. Should one permit an unlicensed operator to drive his automobile?
9. What happens to an operator when he disregards traffic laws and rules for safety?
10. What is the difference between suspension and revocation?
11. What must be the condition of car when appearing for test?
12. How far ahead should one's headlights show an object the size of a child?
13. How far must one's tail-light be discernible from the rear?
14. In what distance must four-wheel brakes stop one's car when traveling at 20 miles per hour? And two-wheel brakes?
15. If one were traveling at 40 miles per hour and a child ran into the road 50 feet in front of him, would one be able to stop his car in time?
16. If one has to stop when driving on wet or icy pavement, how should he put on his brakes?
17. Is skidding sometimes caused by putting on the brakes suddenly when the road is slippery?
18. When the car starts to skid what should one do?
19. Does speed entering curves cause skidding?
20. How far must one park from a fire hydrant?
21. How far must one stop behind a street car discharging passengers where there is no safety zone?
22. Why is it dangerous to park on a blind curve?
23. How should one park a car on a steep incline?
24. Is one permitted to park on a highway?
25. Is it permissible to park in front of a driveway?
26. May one park close to a street intersection?
27. Which three vehicles have the right of way?
28. What must one do if he is involved in an accident resulting in injury or death?
29. What must an operator do if he has an accident resulting in property damage only?
30. What is the purpose of the accident report?
31. When two vehicles approach an intersection not controlled by a traffic light, at approximately the same time, which vehicle has the right of way?
32. How should one make a right hand turn?
33. How should one make a left hand turn?
34. How should one operate a car when approaching an intersection without a traffic signal?
35. If a pedestrian is crossing a street into which one is about to turn, who has the right of way?

---

[1]Compiled and reprinted from *Drivers Manual*, formerly issued by the Bureau of Motor Vehicles of the State of New York. (Answers on page 196.) It includes the 30 questions which license applicants in N. Y. State must be able to answer.

36. What is the meaning of these traffic lights: (a) Red; (b) Green; (c) Amber?
37. Should one follow a car closely?
38. What must one do when an emergency vehicle approaches?
39. When an operator signals he wishes to pass, what must one do?
40. How should one enter a highway from a driveway?
41. Should one pass a vehicle going in the same direction when approaching a curve, or on a hill?
42. May a vehicle overtake and pass another vehicle when approaching a railroad grade crossing?
43. What must an operator do when approaching a school bus receiving or discharging passengers?
44. Is it legal to pass a vehicle on the right?
45. May one pass the left of a street car proceeding in the same direction?
46. How should a vehicle be operated in the vicinity of playgrounds and schools?
47. Should the operator heed all traffic signs or only a few outstanding signs?
48. When must one deflect his lights?
49. What is the maximum legal speed permitted?
50. Should one come to a complete standstill on approaching an intersection controlled by a stop sign?
51. May one over-crowd the front seat of a car?
52. What should one do when a tire blows out?
53. Are tires worn smooth, safe?
54. How should one drive through a fog?
55. Is it advisable to carry the certificate of registration of the vehicle you are operating?
56. How must a license plate be placed on a vehicle?
57. If one sells or destroys his car, what does he do with his license plates?
58. When leaving curb, how should one proceed?
59. How should one back a car safely?
60. When driving past a line of parked cars, is it good judgment to drive at a fast rate of speed?
61. Is it good judgment to let any person ride on the side of one's car?
62. While operating a car, should one's attention be distracted by conversation or scenery?
63. What is the purpose of the center lane of a three strip highway?
64. What is the meaning of a solid white line painted down the center of a two lane road?
65. May one drive through a safety zone?
66. Why is speed so dangerous?
67. Should one reduce his speed at night?
68. When should one's headlights be lighted?
69. What is the reason for discouraging the use of stickers on one's rear window?
70. What should one do when he sees a child playing on the sidewalk as he drives along the street?
71. What can one expect when a car parks?
72. What can one expect when a bus stops?
73. What can one expect when he sees a ball roll into the roadway?
74. What are the three most grievous faults of the operator that cause accidents?
75. What is the most serious type of accident?
76. Why is the show-off driver dangerous?
77. What is meant by defensive driving?
78. What is a cooperative driver?
79. What are common faults of pedestrians?
80. How often should a car be inspected by a competent mechanic?
81. Should one drive while fatigued?
82. Does a car stop quicker with the clutch out?
83. Will a car stop quicker on a hard road than on a loose gravel one?
84. Are intoxicants dangerous for the driver?
85. Can one avoid monoxide gas while driving?
86. Is it ever permissible to cross the double solid line in the center of a highway?

87. When, if at all, is it permissible to cross the broken white line separating traffic lanes?

88. May the single solid line on the highway be crossed when conditions are favorable?

89. If one were driving on a highway where a solid and broken line appeared together and the solid line was on his side, could he cross this line?

90. If one were driving on a highway where a solid and broken line appeared together and the broken line was on his side, could he cross the line?

91. What is a safety zone?

92. How should one hand signal for stopping?

93. How should one hand signal for a right turn?

94. What is the recommended hand signal for making a left turn?

95. What is the meaning of a flashing red light?

96. What is the meaning of a flashing amber light?

97. What does a square traffic sign mean?

98. What does a round traffic sign mean?

99. What does the diamond shaped sign mean?

100. What does the eight-sided sign mean?

ANSWERS

1. A license to operate is a privilege granted by the state and not a right to which one is entitled.

2. The holder of a driver's license may keep it as long as he drives safely, provided he renews it within the time prescribed by law.

3. Because most automobile accidents result from ignorance or carelessness.

4. Driving after a license has been suspended or revoked constitutes a misdemeanor.

5. No, the chauffeur's license is required of any person who is employed for the principal purpose of operating a motor vehicle, or who drives a motor vehicle while in use as a public or common carrier of persons or property.

6. The nearest branch office of the Motor Vehicle Bureau must be notified by letter of any change of address.

7. A driver's license may not be lent to another person.

8. No, an unlicensed person is not permitted to drive a car.

9. Disregard of traffic laws may result in cancellation of the license; conviction for certain violations must be accompanied by its revocation.

10. When a license is revoked, the permission to drive an automobile is cancelled; a new license will not be granted within 30 days. The applicant must pass a new examination. When a license is suspended, the permission to drive an automobile is withheld for a limited period (not more than six months); at its expiration the license will be automatically returned.

11. The car must be properly registered, and all mechanical equipment must be in good condition. Windshield and rear window must be free from all obstructions, including stickers (except those authorized by the Commissioner of Motor Vehicles).

12. 350 feet ahead.

13. 500 feet from the rear of the car.

14. Four-wheel: within 30 feet; two-wheel: within 45 feet.

15. No. At 40 miles per hour, the stopping distance with four-wheel brakes is 120 feet.

16. When stopping on a wet or icy pavement, brakes should be touched gently, almost patting them, and the car kept in gear.

17. The tendency to skid is increased very materially by applying the brakes, or accelerating, suddenly.

18. If the car starts to skid, the wheels should be turned in direction of skid; brakes should not be applied but motor gently accelerated until car responds to your direction.

19. Yes. Speed should be brought down before entering a curve.

20. A car may not be parked within ten feet of a fire hydrant (15 feet in New York City).

21. A car should be stopped seven feet (eight feet in New York City) from the nearest door of a standing street car.

22. The driver of an approaching automobile may not be able to see the parked car quickly enough to avoid an accident.

23. The emergency brake should be applied, the wheels cramped to the curb and the car left in gear.

24. Parking on the pavement of a main highway is prohibited.

25. A parked car may not block a driveway.

26. Do not park within a car-length of an intersection.

27. Fire apparatus, ambulances, police cars, emergency repair vehicles of a public utility or bureau of buildings, and any vehicle legally equipped with a gong or siren have the right of way over other vehicles.

28. (a) The car is to be stopped immediately; (b) it should be moved off the highway immediately, if accident occurred at night or in heavy traffic or where the car cannot be seen easily by approaching vehicles; (c) otherwise it should be left where it is until an officer requests it to be moved; (d) medical help should be sought; (e) the operators of the cars involved should exchange name, address, license and registration number (and make them known to a policeman or judicial officer); (f) every accident involving death or injury to a person or property damage of more than $50 must be reported forthwith to the Bureau of Motor Vehicles on the Bureau's printed form; if the operator is unable to do so, some other person should send in a report for him.

29. The driver who collides with an unattended vehicle or other property must find the owner and give his name and address, or report to the nearest police or judicial official. Failure to comply with these requirements may result in the loss of the license.

30. To give a word picture of the accident so that conditions which might have contributed to the cause of the accident can be corrected.

31. The vehicle at the right hand side has the right of way if approaching at right angles.

32. Place your car as far to the right as possible for a right turn, then signal your intent to turn and keep as close as possible to the right hand curb while turning.

33. Place your car as near the center of the highway as possible, indicate your intention to turn by proper signal and keep to right of center of intersection when turning.

34. Use extreme caution when approaching or turning at intersections not controlled by a signal light. Do not pass other cars and stop for pedestrians.

35. Operators must watch for pedestrians crossing the street they are entering. The pedestrians have the right of way at all times.

36. Red light requires traffic to stop and remain standing. Green light requires traffic to move. Amber light is a warning that lights are about to change.

37. Another car should not be followed too closely.

38. Drive your vehicle to the curb and stop. If this is prevented by parked vehicles or other obstruction, proceed as close to the right hand side of the highway as possible, giving the emergency vehicle opportunity to pass.

39. Never increase speed. Pull over to the right.

40. When entering a highway from a driveway or alley, car should be stopped and traffic observed in both directions.

41. No, passing on hills and curves is always dangerous.

42. No vehicle should be overtaken and passed within 200 feet of a railroad grade crossing unless the crossing is controlled by signals.

43. A car must be stopped when overtaking or meeting a standing school bus which is taking on or discharging passengers. The car must remain stopped until the school bus resumes motion or until signalled by the bus driver to proceed, providing the bus is equipped with the required flashing red signal light, and a sign at least four inches in height designating the bus as a school bus and displayed on the front and rear of such bus.

44. Cars going in the same direction should always be passed on the left, except in New York City, where a driver may pass on the right provided that, in passing, the vehicle being overtaken shall not be forced out of his right of way.

45. A street car proceeding in the same direction may never be passed on the left, except on a one-way street or where tracks are so located as to prevent compliance with this rule.

46. Operators should drive especially carefully and at low speed in the vicinity of schools or playgrounds.

47. The competent driver heeds all traffic signs and signals.

48. When approaching another car and while driving in lighted areas.

49. Not to exceed 50 miles per hour for a distance of one-quarter of a mile except where a greater speed is permitted by the State Traffic Commission.

50. Yes. Stop, look both ways, then proceed cautiously.

51. No, there may not be more than three people in the front seat, or any luggage or equipment so placed as to hamper the driver.

52. The foot should be taken off the accelerator and the steering wheel held as rigidly as possible; clutch should not be disengaged or brakes applied until speed is reduced materially.

53. It is dangerous especially if driving at more than 35 m.p.h.

54. Under foggy conditions one should drive very slowly on the extreme right with bright lights deflected.

55. The registration certificate should always be carried and shown on request.

56. License plates must be securely fastened to the vehicle at a distance of not less than 12 in. from the ground, nor higher than 48 in.

57. The license plates should be retained; they may be used on another vehicle of the same class.

58. When leaving the curb, the operator should observe traffic conditions both front and rear, give proper signal and proceed slowly.

59. An operator backing up his car should make certain that he has a clear space to the rear and use the horn.

60. No, as there is a danger of cars pulling from the curb or pedestrians stepping out from between these parked vehicles.

61. No one should ride on the exterior of any vehicle.

62. The driver's attention should never be distracted by unnecessary conversation or looking at scenery.

63. On a three-lane road the center lane is for passing only.

64. A solid white line separates opposing traffic lanes.

65. Only if directed to do so by a police officer.

66. Because, the greater the speed, the less control one has of the vehicle.

67. Yes.

68. From a half hour after sundown to a half hour before sunrise.

69. Stickers obstruct the driver's view.

70. The competent driver drives carefully because he knows the child may dart into the street.

71. To see that the driver of a parking car does not step into his path.

72. To see passengers crossing in front of the bus.

73. To see a child trying to retrieve it.

74. The most grievous faults causing accidents are excess speed; driving on the wrong side; and against the right of way.

75. Head-on collisions are directly chargeable to dangerous drivers.

76. Because the show-off driver believes himself to be a superior driver and does not regard the rights of others.

77. Defensive driving is driving a car in such a manner as to make allowances for the weaknesses of other drivers and to anticipate all emergencies.

78. A cooperative driver, the direct opposite of a dangerous driver, cooperates with other drivers and officials, obeys all traffic signs and markings, and does his utmost to make driving safe and pleasurable.

79. Common faults of pedestrians are crossing between intersections, crossing intersections diagonally, crossing against signals, jaywalking, coming from behind or between parked cars, children playing in the roadway.

80. Brakes, lights and steering should be checked at least two or three times a year.

81. When fatigued, one should drive completely off the highway and rest until the sleepy feeling leaves.

82. No, a car stops faster with the clutch engaged, for the motor will aid in retarding speed.

83. A car will not stop as quickly on a loose gravel or dirt road as it will on a hard surface road.

84. One should refrain from driving after drinking as the ability to carry on several activities at once and the ability to judge distances are affected for the worse with a relatively small amount of alcohol.

85. An open window will prevent the collection of poisonous monoxide gas in the car

86. Crossing of the double solid line is prohibited from either side at any time.
87. The broken line may be crossed if crossing will not interfere with traffic.
88. The single solid line may be crossed when conditions are favorable.
89. One may not cross from the solid line side of the road.
90. One may cross from the broken line side, exercising extreme caution.
91. The safety zone is the space set aside within a roadway for the use of pedestrians.
92. By extending the left arm straight out, showing the back of the whole hand.
93. By beckoning to another driver to pass.
94. By extending the left arm out straight and pointing with the index finger.
95. Flashing red light means to stop and proceed with caution.
96. Flashing amber light means to slow down and proceed with caution.
97. Caution. Be prepared to meet a possible operating hazard such as a crossroad.
98. Round signs mean railroad crossings.
99. Diamond signs mean reduce speed for permanent physical hazards, such as curves, steep hills, and narrow bridges.
100. Octagonal (eight-sided) signs mean stop and then proceed with caution when traffic is clear.

GASOLINE TAX RATES BY STATES

Federal, county, and municipal taxes are not included

(Figures are cents per gallon)

State	1920	1940*	1950*	State	1920	1940*	1950*
Alabama	...	6	6	Nevada	...	4	4-1/2
Arizona	...	5	5	New Hampshire	...	4	4
Arkansas	...	6-1/2	6-1/2	New Jersey	...	3	3
California	...	3	4-1/2	New Mexico	...	5	7
Colorado	1	4	6	New York	...	4	4
Connecticut	...	3	4	North Carolina	...	6	6
Delaware	...	4	5	North Dakota	1	4	4
Florida	...	7	7	Ohio	...	4	4
Georgia	...	6	7	Oklahoma	...	4	6-1/2
Idaho	...	5	6	Oregon	1	5	6
Illinois	...	3	3	Pennsylvania	...	4	5
Indiana	...	4	4	Rhode Island	...	3	4
Iowa	...	3	4	South Carolina	...	6	6
Kansas	...	3	5	South Dakota	...	4	4
Kentucky	1	5	7	Tennessee	...	7	7
Louisiana	...	7	9	Texas	...	4	4
Maine	...	4	6	Utah	...	4	4
Maryland	...	4	5	Vermont	...	4	5
Massachusetts	...	3	3	Virginia	...	5	6
Michigan	...	3	3	Washington	...	5	6-1/2
Minnesota	...	3	5	West Virginia	...	5	5
Mississippi	...	6	7	Wisconsin	...	4	4
Missouri	...	2	2	Wyoming	...	4	4
Montana	...	5	6	Dist. of Columbia	...	2	4
Nebraska	...	5	6				

* Source American Automobile Association

States	Maximum speed limits	Minimum age regular permit	Dimming of headlights required	Must use hand signals	Passing stopped street car prohibited
Alabama	(A)	16	No Law	Yes	Yes
Arizona	60 (B)	18†	No†	Yes	Yes
Arkansas	55	18§	Yes	Yes	Yes
California	55 p.f.	16†	Yes	Yes	Yes
Colorado	60	16	Yes	Yes	Yes
Connecticut	45 (J)	16	Yes	Yes	Yes
Delaware	50 (C)	16	Yes	Yes	Yes
District of Columbia	25	16	Yes	Yes	Yes
Florida	60 p.f. (D)	16§	Yes	Yes	Yes
Georgia	55	16	Yes	Yes	Yes
Idaho	(A)	16†	Yes	Yes	Yes
Illinois	(A)	15§	Yes	Yes	Yes
Indiana	(A)	16	Yes	Yes	Yes
Iowa	(A)	16†	Yes	Yes	No†
Kansas	(A)	16†	Yes	Yes	Yes
Kentucky	45 p.f. (A)	16	Yes	Yes	Yes
Louisiana	60	15	Yes	Yes	Yes
Maine	45	15	Yes	†	Yes
Maryland	50 (E)	16	Yes	Yes	Yes
Massachusetts	40 p.f. (A)	16	Yes	Yes	Yes
Michigan	(A)	16†	Yes	Yes	Yes
Minnesota	60 p.f. (D)	15§	Yes	Yes	Yes
Mississippi	55	17†	Yes	Yes	Yes
Missouri	(A)	16	Yes	Yes	Yes
Montana	50	15	Yes	Yes	Yes
Nebraska	60 (F)	15-1/2	Yes	Yes	Yes
Nevada	(A)	16†	Yes	Yes	No Law
New Hampshire	50	16	Yes	Yes	Yes
New Jersey	40 (G)	17	Yes	Yes	Yes
New Mexico	(A)	14	Yes	Yes	Yes
New York	50	18†	Yes	Yes	No†
North Carolina	55	16§	Yes	Yes	Yes
North Dakota	60	16†	Yes	Yes	Yes
Ohio	50 p.f.	16†	Yes	Yes	Yes
Oklahoma	65 (I)	16†	Yes	Yes	No Law
Oregon	55	16†	Yes	Yes	Yes
Pennsylvania	50	18†§	Yes	Yes	Yes
Rhode Island	35 p.f. (H)	16	No	No	Yes
South Carolina	55	14	Yes	Yes	No Law
South Dakota	60 (F)	15	Yes	Yes	Yes
Tennessee	(A)	16†	Yes	Yes	Yes
Texas	60 (I)	16†	Yes	Yes	Yes
Utah	60 (F)	16	Yes	Yes	Yes
Vermont	50	18†	Yes	Yes	Yes
Virginia	50 (E)	15	Yes	Yes	Yes
Washington	50	16	Yes	Yes	Yes
West Virginia	50	16	Yes	Yes	Yes
Wisconsin	65 (I)	16†	Yes	Yes	Yes
Wyoming	60 p.f.	15	Yes	Yes	No Law

(A) Reasonable and proper.
(B) Lower speed at night and on old highways.
(C) 55 mph on four-lane roads.
(D) 50 mph p.f. at night.
(E) 55 mph on dual-lane roads.
(F) 50 mph at night.
(G) Certain highways 45 mph.
(H) Highways zoned to 50 mph.
(I) 55 mph at night.
(J) Parkways to 55 mph where marked.
p.f.—prima facie limit

†Junior permits issued. §License issued under age of 18 must be signed by parent or guardian.

†But requested by safety authorities.

†Recommended.

†Permitted with restrictions.

* Source: American Automobile Association

AUTOMOBILE TOURING MILEAGE IN THE UNITED STATES*

Cities in the South	Asheville, N. C.	Atlanta, Ga.	Birmingham, Ala.	Charleston, S. C.	Columbia, S. C.	Jacksonville, Fla.	Knoxville, Tenn.	Memphis, Tenn.	Miami, Fla.	Nashville, Tenn.	New Orleans, La.	Richmond, Va.	Savannah, Ga.	Tampa, Fla.	Washington, D. C.	W.Palm Beach,Fla.
Asheville, N.C....		209	365	281	166	436	112	531	791	306	736	389	300	621	487	724
Atlanta, Ga.	209		161	306	225	327	194	408	678	258	527	564	273	482	655	611
Birmingham, Ala. ..	365	161		467	386	465	269	251	796	214	404	719	434	566	796	729
Charleston, S. C. ..	281	306	467		122	267	407	730	618	601	776	425	109	508	479	551
Columbia, S. C. ...	166	225	386	122		309	285	649	660	479	749	371	151	508	479	593
Jacksonville, Fla. ..	436	327	465	267	309		528	728	351	585	589	664	158	199	763	284
Knoxville, Tenn....	112	194	269	407	285	528		419	879	194	518	450	418	683	509	812
Memphis, Tenn.....	531	408	251	730	649	728	419		1059	225	406	869	730	829	928	992
Miami, Fla.	791	678	796	618	660	351	879	1059		929	944	1015	509	272	1123	67
Nashville, Tenn....	306	258	214	601	479	585	194	225	929		576	644	531	780	703	869
New Orleans, La....	736	527	404	776	749	589	518	406	944	576		1100	667	672	1203	855
Richmond, Va.....	389	564	719	425	371	664	450	869	1015	644	1100		506	357	108	948
Savannah, Ga.....	300	273	434	109	151	158	418	730	509	531	667	506		357	614	442
Tampa, Fla.	621	482	566	508	508	199	683	829	272	780	672	863	357		971	232
Washington, D. C. .	487	655	796	479	479	763	509	928	1123	703	1203	108	614	971		1056
W. Palm Beach, Fla..	724	611	729	551	593	284	812	992	67	869	855	948	442	232	1056	

MILEAGE ON IMPORTANT AUTOMOBILE ROUTES*

New York — San Francisco

Miles		Miles	Miles		Miles	Miles		Miles
0	New York, N. Y.	3,173	653	Van Wert, Ohio	2,520	1,675	North Platte	1,498
11	Newark, N. J.	3,162	688	Fort Wayne, Ind.	2,485	1,750	Big Spring	1,423
18	Elizabeth	3,155	756	Plymouth	2,417	1,800	Sidney, Neb.	1,373
62	Trenton, N. J.	3,111	798	Valparaiso	2,375	1,901	Cheyenne, Wyo.	1,272
94	Philadelphia, Pa.	3,079	822	Dyer, Ind.	2,351	1,953	Laramie	1,220
159	Lancaster	3,014	828	Chicago Heights, Ill.	2,345	2,073	Rawlins	1,100
183	York	2,990	852	Joliet	2,321	2,184	Rock Springs	989
212	Gettysburg	2,961	873	Aurora	2,300	2,199	Green River	974
258	McConnellsburg	2,915	882	Geneva	2,291	2,299	Evanston, Wyo.	874
293	Bedford	2,880	923	Rochelle	2,250	2,384	Salt Lake City, Utah	789
360	Greensburg	2,813	950	Dixon	2,223	2,579	Wells, Nev.	594
392	Pittsburgh, Pa.	2,781	964	Sterling	2,209	2,633	Elko	540
427	Chester, W. Va.	2,746	991	Fulton, Ill.	2,182	2,762	Winnemucca	411
428	E. Liverpool, Ohio	2,745	994	Clinton, Iowa	2,179	2,895	Wadsworth	278
445	Lisbon	2,728	1,077	Cedar Rapids	2,096	2,933	Reno, Nev.	240
481	Canton	2,692	1,153	Marshalltown	2,020	2,967	Truckee, Calif.	206
488	Massillon	2,685	1,191	Ames	1,982	3,040	Auburn	133
511	Wooster	2,662	1,235	Jefferson	1,938	3,075	Sacramento	98
543	Mansfield	2,630	1,360	Council Bluffs, Iowa	1,813	3,144	Vallejo	29
568	Bucyrus	2,605	1,365	Omaha, Neb.	1,808	3,171	Oakland	2
585	Upper Sandusky	2,588	1,453	Columbus	1,720	3,173	San Francisco, Calif.	0
640	Delphos	2,533	1,567	Kearney	1,606			

New York — Buffalo

Miles		Miles	Miles		Miles	Miles		Miles
0	New York, N. Y.	398	101	Liberty	297	285	Bath	113
6	Ridgefield, N. J.	392	117	Roscoe	281	310	Wayland	88
11	Hackensack	387	144	Hancock	254	317	Dansville	81
20	Hohokus, N. J.	378	158	Deposit	240	332	Mt. Morris	66
28	Suffern, N. Y.	370	189	Binghamton	209	337	Leicester	61
35	Tuxedo	363	211	Oswego	187	350	Warsaw	48
43	Harriman	355	230	Waverly	168	360	Varysburg	38
56	Goshen	342	246	Elmira	152	377	East Aurora	21
64	Middletown	334	264	Corning	134	398	Buffalo, N. Y.	0
89	Monticello	309	267	Painted Post	131			

Boston — Miami

Miles		Miles	Miles		Miles	Miles		Miles
0	Boston, Mass.	1,639	463	Washington, D. C.	1,176	1,513	Ft. Pierce	136
45	Providence, R. I.	1,594	517	Fredericksburg, Va.	1,122	1,571	W. Palm Beach	68
87	Westerly, R. I.	1,552	573	Richmond	1,066	1,639	Miami, Fla.	0
107	New London, Conn.	1,532	595	Petersburg	1,044			
160	New Haven	1,479	651	South Hill, Va.	988		(Alternate, Petersburg to Jacksonville via Charleston)	
177	Bridgeport, Conn.	1,462	733	Raleigh, N. C.	905			
234	New York, N. Y.	1,405	836	Rockingham, N. C.	803	595	Petersburg, Va.	756
245	Newark, N. J.	1,394	946	Columbia, S. C.	693	698	Rocky Mount, N. C.	653
296	Trenton, N. J.	1,343	1,005	Aiken, S. C.	634	836	Wilmington, S. C.	515
327	Philadelphia, Pa.	1,312	1,021	Augusta, Ga.	618	955	Florence	398
340	Chester, Pa.	1,299	1,205	Waycross, Ga.	434	1,067	Charleston, S. C.	284
353	Wilmington, Del.	1,286	1,282	Jacksonville, Fla.	367	1,193	Savannah, Ga.	158
374	Elkton, Md.	1,265	1,323	St. Augustine	316	1,273	Brunswick, Ga.	78
390	Havre de Grace	1,249	1,377	Daytona Beach	262	1,351	Jacksonville, Fla.	0
426	Baltimore, Md.	1,213	1,465	Melbourne	174			

*Source American Automobile Association

Cities in the East	Albany, N.Y.	Atlantic City, N.J.	Baltimore, Md.	Boston, Mass.	Buffalo, N.Y.	Burlington, Vt.	Charleston, W.Va.	Chicago, Ill.	Cincinnati, Ohio	Cleveland, Ohio	Columbus, Ohio	Detroit, Mich.	Evansville, Ind.	Gettysburg, Pa.	Hagerstown, Md.	Harrisburg, Pa.
Albany, N.Y.		262	336	175	282	154	694	806	716	467	607	534	947	314	351	278
Atlantic City, N.J.	262		135	345	437	426	555	809	640	489	532	658	874	176	210	160
Baltimore, Md.	336	135		412	375	493	420	697	505	363	397	532	739	54	75	74
Boston, Mass.	175	345	412		464	259	832	990	880	651	772	718	1114	416	452	394
Buffalo, N.Y.	282	437	375	464		386	458	526	435	190	327	254	667	321	306	301
Burlington, Vt.	154	426	493	259	386		844	912	821	573	713	640	1053	468	504	432
Charleston, W.Va.	694	555	420	832	458	844		494	200	271	179	367	393	382	346	418
Chicago, Ill.	806	809	697	990	526	912	494		294	354	315	272	297	639	700	689
Cincinnati, Ohio	716	640	505	880	435	821	200	294		248	108	254	234	459	429	487
Cleveland, Ohio	467	489	363	651	190	573	271	354	248		140	165	480	309	301	335
Columbus, Ohio	607	532	397	772	327	713	179	315	108	140		188	342	347	320	382
Detroit, Mich.	534	658	532	718	254	640	367	272	254	165	188		452	478	470	504
Evansville, Ind.	947	874	739	1114	667	1053	393	297	234	480	342	452		705	662	724
Gettysburg, Pa.	314	176	54	416	321	468	382	639	459	309	347	478	705		36	36
Hagerstown, Md.	351	210	75	452	306	504	346	700	429	301	320	470	662	36		72
Harrisburg, Pa.	278	160	74	394	301	432	418	689	487	335	382	504	724	36	72	
Indianapolis, Ind.	775	707	572	947		881	308	186	108	308	175	280	172	522	495	557
Lake George, N.Y.	60	334	401	219	328	94	765	869	778	529	669	596	1009	376	413	340
Louisville, Ky.	822	749	614	989	544	930	268	300	109	357	217	363	125	568	538	596
Montreal, Que.	234	506	573	353	387	93	845	865	822	574	714	593	1045	545	585	509
New York, N.Y.	143	124	191	221	377	301	597	831	660	508	555	631	897	211	236	173
Norfolk, Va.	465	273	228	618	606	721	405	889	605	559	584	728	798	269	261	305
Philadelphia, Pa.	241	62	98	314	369	394	518	757	586	427	481	596	823	118	144	103
Pittsburgh, Pa.	476	357	235	590	222	628	228	462	291	132	186	301	528	177	162	196
Portland, Me.	242	452	519	107	522	203	939	1047	957	708	848	775	1188	523	559	501
Quebec, Que.	399	671	738	387	552	258	1010	1030	987	739	879	758	1210	710	750	674
Richmond, Va.	480	280	145	557	523	638	318	802	518	474	497	643	711	186	178	222
St. Louis, Mo.	1018	953	818	1193	741	1127	533	294	343	554	421	526	172	768	741	803
Toledo, Ohio	579	601	475	763	299	685	310	242	197	112	131	57	395	421	413	438
Toronto, Ont.	382	570	484	573	109	479	567	511	493	296	436	239	691	430	415	410
Washington, D.C.	373	172	37	449	376	530	383	698	497	368	395	537	737	78	70	114
White Mts., N.H.	220	451	518	167	493	107	921	1019	928	680	820	747	1160	532	569	496

Cities in the West	Bismarck, N.D.	Boise, Idaho	Calgary, Alta.	Cheyenne, Wyo.	Chicago, Ill.	Dallas, Texas	Denver, Colo.	Duluth, Minn.	El Paso, Texas	Gd. Canyon, Ariz.	Helena, Mont.	Houston, Texas	Kansas City, Mo.	Los Angeles, Calif.	Memphis, Tenn.	Mexico City, Mex.
Bismarck, N.D.		1053	884	723	884	1333	827	454	1510	1699	668	1579	863	1849	1387	2534
Boise, Idaho	1053		914	797	1784	1686	860	1507	1407	771	582	1932	1505	1086	2080	2784
Calgary, Alta.	886	914		1066	1800	2001	1184	1270	1927	1312	422	2247	1750	1657	2274	3106
Cheyenne, Wyo.	723	797	1066		994	921	104	1028	847	866	681	1167	692	1211	1190	2026
Chicago, Ill.	884	1784	1800	994		968	1052	495	1522	1813	1596	1107	517	2219	542	2168
Dallas, Texas	1333	1686	2001	921	968		817	1182	632	1104	1619	246	540	1446	478	1200
Denver, Colo.	827	860	1184	104	1052	817		1086	743	872	785	1063	645	1268	1164	1789
Duluth, Minn.	454	1507	1270	1028	495	1182	1086		1814	1831	1122	1428	642	2176	999	2382
El Paso, Texas	1570	1407	1927	847	1522	632	743	1814		636	1526	757	1094	814	1110	1377
Grand Canyon, Ariz.	1699	771	1312	866	1813	1104	872	1831	636		890	1350	1336	526	1459	2013
Helena, Mont.	668	582	422	681	1596	1619	785	1122	1526	890		1865	1331	1235	1935	2707
Houston, Texas	1579	1932	2247	1167	1107	246	1063	1428	757	1350	1865		786	1571	588	1130
Kansas City, Mo.	863	1505	1750	692	517	540	645	642	1094	1336	1331	786		1742	478	1740
Los Angeles, Calif.	1849	1086	1657	1211	2219	1446	1268	2176	814	526	1235	1571	1742		1865	2191
Memphis, Tenn.	1387	2080	2274	1190	542	478	1164	999	1110	1459	1935	588	478	1865		1657
Mexico City, Mexico	2534	2784	3106	2026	2168	1200	1789	2382	1377	2013	2707	1130	1740	2191	1657	
Milwaukee, Wis.	795	1793	1685	1003	91	1057	1061	467	1611	1869	1505	1196	563	2214	631	2257
Minneapolis, Minn.	449	1532	1339	874	435	1028	932	154	1569	1677	1159	1274	488	2210	886	2228
New Orleans, La.	1820	2237	2505	1425	998	504	1321	1405	1124	1600	2123	367	892	1938	406	1497
Omaha, Neb.	658	1297	1545	507	487	705	556	521	1202	1373	1146	951	205	1718	683	1905
Portland, Ore.	1382	478	859	1275	2262	2164	1338	1836	1885	1249	714	2410	1983	1026	2558	3262
Reno, Nev.	1502	606	1390	1007	2001	1885	1064	1972	1294	659	912	2009	1709	480	2228	2671
Salt Lake City, Utah	970	380	921	475	1469	1353	514	1440	1027	391	499	1595	1177	736	1696	2321
St. Louis, Mo.	1129	1758	2016	945	294	674	898	692	1228	1589	1677	813	253	1925	307	1882
San Antonio, Texas	1608	1884	2181	1101	1243	275	864	1457	566	1202	1782	205	815	1380	732	925
San Francisco, Calif.	1736	840	1571	1241	2235	1850	1298	2206	1252	897	1146	2009	1943	404	2182	2629
Santa Fe, N.M.	1237	1322	1594	514	1369	661	410	1494	333	484	1195	907	856	890	1043	1710
Seattle, Wash.	1302	547	779	1307	2232	2280	1407	1756	1954	1318	634	2479	1957	1217	2627	3331
Spokane, Wash.	993	444	470	998	1923	1939	1102	1451	1215		325	2190	1648	1415	2260	3032
Vancouver, B.C.	1418	690	791	1423	2348	2364	1527	1872	2097	1461	750	2615	2073	1360	2685	3457
Winnipeg, Man.	448	1751	917	1128	934	1410	1252	430	1907	1809	1116	1656	910	2154	1385	2610
Yellowstone Nat'l Pk.	613	440	575	498	1461	1419	602	1067	1345	748	183	1665	1148	1093	1708	2524

Indianapolis, Ind.	Lake George, N.Y.	Louisville, Ky.	Montreal, Que.	New York, N. Y.	Norfolk, Va.	Philadelphia, Pa.	Pittsburgh, Pa.	Portland, Me.	Quebec, Que.	Richmond, Va.	St. Louis, Mo.	Toledo, Ohio	Toronto, Ont.	Washington, D. C.	White Mts., N. H.	Cities in the East
775	60	822	234	143	465	241	476	242	399	480	1018	579	382	373	220	Albany, N.Y.
707	334	749	506	124	273	62	357	452	671	280	953	601	570	172	451	Atlantic City, N. J.
572	401	614	573	191	228	98	235	519	738	145	818	475	484	37	518	Baltimore, Md.
947	219	989	353	221	618	314	590	107	387	557	1193	763	573	449	167	Boston, Mass.
495	328	544	387	377	606	369	222	522	552	523	741	299	109	376	493	Buffalo, N.Y.
881	94	930	93	301	721	394	628	203	258	638	1127	685	479	530	107	Burlington, Vt.
308	765	268	845	597	405	518	228	939	1010	318	533	310	567	383	921	Charleston, W. Va.
186	868	300	865	831	889	757	462	1047	1030	802	294	242	511	698	1019	Chicago, Ill.
108	778	109	822	660	605	586	291	957	987	518	343	197	493	497	928	Cincinnati, Ohio
308	529	357	574	508	559	427	132	708	739	474	554	112	296	368	680	Cleveland, Ohio
175	669	217	714	555	584	481	186	848	879	497	421	131	436	395	820	Columbus, Ohio
280	596	363	593	631	728	596	301	775	758	643	526	57	239	537	747	Detroit, Mich.
172	1009	125	1045	897	798	823	528	1188	1210	711	172	395	691	737	1160	Evansville, Ind.
522	376	568	545	211	269	118	177	523	710	186	768	421	430	78	532	Gettysburg, Pa.
495	413	538	585	228	261	144	162	559	750	178	741	413	415	70	569	Hagerstown, Md.
557	340	596	509	173	305	103	196	501	674	222	803	438	410	114	496	Harrisburg, Pa.
	837	114	873	730	713	656	361	1016	1038	626	246	223	519	570	993	Indianapolis, Ind.
837		887	174	209	540	303	538	265	339	546	1083	641	440	438	201	Lake George, N. Y.
114	887		956	769	673	695	403	1096	1121	586	265	306	602	606	1043	Louisville, Ky.
873	174	956		381	699	475	609	282	165	718	1119	650	354	610	186	Montreal, Que.
730	209	769	381		329	93	369	329	546	336	976	620	228	237	656	New York, N. Y.
713	540	673	699	329		237	427	725	864	87	938	671	715	191	656	Norfolk, Va.
656	303	695	475	93	237		295	421	640	243	902	539	478	135	430	Philadelphia, Pa.
361	538	403	609	369	427	295		697	774	344	607	244	331	236	694	Pittsburgh, Pa.
1016	265	1096	282	328	725	421	697		280	664	1262	820	624	556	96	Portland, Me.
1038	339	1121	165	546	864	640	774	280		883	1248	815	519	775	242	Quebec, Que.
626	546	586	718	336	87	243	344	664	883		851	586	632	108	663	Richmond, Va.
246	1083	265	1119	976	938	902	607	1262	1248	851		469	765	816	1239	St. Louis, Mo.
223	641	306	650	620	671	539	244	820	815	586	469		296	480	792	Toledo, Ohio
519	440	602	354	228	715	478	331	624	519	632	765	296		488	586	Toronto, Ont.
570	438	606	610	237	191	135	236	556	775	108	816	480	488		560	Washington, D. C.
993	201	1043	186	656	656	430	694	96	242	663	1239	792	586	560		White Mts., N. H.

Milwaukee, Wis.	Minneapolis, Minn.	New Orleans, La.	Omaha, Neb.	Portland, Ore.	Reno, Nev.	Salt Lake City, Utah	St. Louis, Mo.	San Antonio, Tex.	San Francisco, Calif.	Santa Fe, N. M.	Seattle, Wash.	Spokane, Wash.	Vancouver, B. C.	Winnipeg, Man.	Yellowstone National Park	Cities in the West
795	449	1820	658	1382	1502	970	1129	1608	1736	1237	1302	993	1418	448	613	Bismarck, N. D.
1793	1532	2237	1297	478	606	380	1578	1884	840	1322	547	444	690	1751	440	Boise, Idaho
1685	1339	2505	1545	859	1390	921	2016	2181	1571	1594	779	470	791	917	575	Calgary, Alta.
1003	874	1425	507	1275	1007	475	945	1101	1241	514	1307	998	1423	1128	498	Cheyenne, Wyo.
91	435	998	487	2262	2001	1469	294	1243	2235	1369	2232	1923	2348	934	1461	Chicago, Ill.
1057	1028	504	705	2164	1885	1353	674	275	1850	661	2280	1939	2364	1410	1419	Dallas, Texas
1061	932	1321	556	1338	1064	514	898	864	1298	410	1947	1102	1527	1252	602	Denver, Colo.
467	154	1405	521	1836	1972	1440	692	1457	2206	1494	1756	1447	1872	430	1067	Duluth, Minn.
1611	1569	1124	1202	1885	1294	1027	1228	566	1252	333	1954	1851	2097	1907	1345	El Paso, Texas
1869	1677	1608	1373	1249	659	391	1589	1202	897	484	1318	1215	1461	1809	748	Grand Canyon, Ariz.
1505	1159	2123	1146	714	912	499	1677	1782	1146	1195	634	325	750	1116	183	Helena, Mont.
1196	1274	367	951	2410	2009	1595	813	205	2009	907	2479	2190	2615	1656	1665	Houston, Texas
563	488	892	205	1983	1709	1177	253	815	1943	856	1957	1648	2073	910	1148	Kansas City, Mo.
2214	2210	1938	1718	1026	480	736	1925	1380	404	890	1217	1415	1360	2154	1093	Los Angeles, Calif.
631	886	406	683	2558	2228	1696	307	732	2182	1043	2627	2260	2685	1385	1708	Memphis, Tenn.
2257	2228	1497	1905	3262	2321	1882	925	2629	1710	3331	3032	3457	2610	2524		Mexico City, Mexico
346	346	1340	367	1873	1818	1286	579	1303	2050	1342	1793	1484	1909	499	1092	Milwaukee, Wis.
346		1340	367	1087	1097	2668	2389	1857	713	572	2342	1165	2784	2443	1923	Minneapolis, Minn.
1340	1340		1087	1775	779	982	458	980	1748	966	1780	1471	1896	705	963	New Orleans, La.
367	367	1087		1775	1514	982	458	1286	1800	389	334	1820	918	705	918	Omaha, Neb.
2219	1873	2668	1775		532	779	2236	2362	712	1800	191	389	334	1820	918	Portland, Ore.
2010	1818	2389	1514	532		1962	1928	234	1104	970	1050	1113	1966	770		Reno, Nev.
1478	1286	1857	982	858	532		1430	1396	766	875	927	824	1070	1438	357	Salt Lake City, Utah
383	579	713	458	2236	1962	1430		949	2196	1109	2311	2427	1078	1401	1466	St. Louis, Mo.
1332	1303	572	980	2362	1928	1396	949		1784	1207	1829	1520	1945	1671	1012	San Antonio, Texas
2139	2050	2342	1748	1780	234	766	2196	1784		903	1829	1101	1046	1740	817	San Francisco, Calif.
1419	1342	1165	966	1800	1104	875	1109	1207	903		1829	1520	1945	1671	1012	Santa Fe, N. M.
2139	1793	2784	1780	191	927	927	2311	1829	309	309		143	1740	817		Seattle, Wash.
1830	1484	2443	1471	389	1050	824	2002	2328	1101	1520	309		425	1431	508	Spokane, Wash.
2255	1909	2868	1896	334	1113	1070	2427	1945	1046	1945	143	425		1747	933	Vancouver, B. C.
845	499	1802	705	1820	1966	1438	1078	1671	1740	1431	1740	1431	1747		1061	Winnipeg, Man.
1416	1092	1923	963	918	770	357	1401	1466	1004	1012	817	508	933	1061		Yellowstone Nat'l Pk.

* Source American Automobile Association

RURAL ROAD MILEAGE*

State	Surfaced mileage of primary rural state highways	Nonsurfaced mileage of primary rural state highways	Total mileage of rural roads in the U. S.	Mileage of rural roads under state control	Mileage of rural roads under local control	Mileage of rural roads under federal control
Alabama	6,751	84	60,042	6,774	52,898	370
Arizona	3,343	527	28,706	3,800	15,754	9,152
Arkansas	8,829	430	55,535	9,314	46,221	....
California	12,317	326	97,678	12,899	74,479	10,300
Colorado	3,739	3	75,810	11,818	63,204	788
Connecticut	2,533	....	10,990	2,700	8,290	....
Delaware	1,011	....	3,756	3,756	....	....
Florida	7,859	86	38,786	7,763	29,897	1,126
Georgia	10,294	2,988	89,680	12,971	76,709	....
Idaho	4,113	721	36,017	4,966	24,835	6,216
Illinois	10,351	17	104,634	10,331	94,303	....
Indiana	9,586	2	82,712	9,546	73,166	....
Iowa	8,649	43	101,488	8,770	92,718	....
Kansas	9,109	306	129,517	9,390	120,112	15
Kentucky	10,333	65	58,268	10,069	47,402	797
Louisiana	3,799	21	38,954	13,875	25,079	....
Maine	2,790	15	20,705	9,933	10,676	96
Maryland	4,331	....	17,097	4,449	12,563	85
Massachusetts	1,827	2	17,358	1,820	15,538	....
Michigan	8,294	204	93,201	8,484	84,717	....
Minnesota	9,903	10	109,661	10,780	97,730	1,151
Mississippi	3,575	....	61,287	6,266	53,992	1,029
Missouri	7,880	....	116,089	15,909	99,410	770
Montana	5,179	434	69,949	8,615	55,348	5,986
Nebraska	8,755	171	100,613	8,848	91,506	259
Nevada	2,154	....	23,801	5,616	18,185	....
New Hampshire	1,512	....	12,522	3,605	8,813	104
New Jersey	1,324	1	18,340	1,758	16,582	....
New Mexico	7,164	2,798	61,865	9,873	48,120	3,872
New York	12,816	1,444	81,472	14,465	67,007	....
North Carolina	10,204	147	62,088	60,819	....	1,269
North Dakota	6,352	340	114,439	6,764	107,261	414
Ohio	16,061	4	85,719	16,067	69,652	....
Oklahoma	9,111	528	99,607	10,206	88,779	622
Oregon	4,426	70	54,514	7,503	33,411	13,600
Pennsylvania	12,702	196	85,130	38,795	46,255	80
Rhode Island	734	....	2,521	782	1,739	....
South Carolina	7,386	395	46,242	16,459	29,783	....
South Dakota	5,519	301	98,634	6,078	91,609	947
Tennessee	7,118	13	65,047	7,403	57,066	578
Texas	28,890	474	196,434	26,827	169,607	....
Utah	3,828	964	24,039	4,744	15,359	3,936
Vermont	1,750	....	13,403	1,820	11,561	22
Virginia	8,810	81	48,945	47,503	768	674
Washington	3,735	88	50,729	5,896	40,073	4,760
West Virginia	4,436	70	34,254	32,834	1,085	335
Wisconsin	9,936	....	85,579	9,924	75,161	494
Wyoming	4,352	90	25,760	4,334	19,321	2,105
Totals	335,470	14,459	3,009,617	553,921	2,383,744	71,952

* Source Dept. of Commerce, Bureau of Public Roads, "Highway Statistics, 1948."

AUTOMOBILE MANUFACTURERS ASSOCIATION

The Automobile Manufacturers Association, founded in 1913, is an organization through which motor vehicle manufacturers voluntarily cooperate in carrying out programs that promote efficient, safe, and economical manufacture and use of motor vehicles.

The purpose of the Association is to assist in the solution of problems affecting the industry and to promote free competition in the manufacture, distribution, sale, and servicing of the industry's products.

This purpose is implemented through the following three basic types of activity:

1. The maintenance of services that can be more efficiently or effectively rendered on a joint industry-wide basis than on a separate-company basis
2. The collection of factual information concerning the manufacture, distribution, and use of motor vehicles and the distribution of such information to interested private and public groups
3. Joint cooperative activity with other industrial, social, or governmental groups to solve problems arising from the manufacture and use of passenger and commercial vehicles

Publications of the Automobile Manufacturers Association include *Automobile Facts* (monthly); *Automobile Facts and Figures* (annual); and *Motor Truck Facts* (biennial).

The general offices of the organization are in the New Center Building, Detroit, Mich. Offices are also maintained in New York City and Washington, D.C.

THE AMERICAN AUTOMOBILE ASSOCIATION ("A.A.A.")

The American Automobile Association, founded in 1902, is the world's largest motor federation, comprising some 750 state associations, motor clubs, and branches located throughout the United States, Canada, Hawaii, and Panama. Some 3,000,000 motorists belong to the organization through membership in their local affiliated motor clubs.

The A.A.A. is a civic, non-profit organization; its affairs, policies, and activities are guided by a board of directors recruited from among its membership; they serve without compensation. Since it has no stockholders, its revenues are devoted to providing specialized services for members and for the promotion of improved motoring conditions for all motorists.

Among the Association's objectives are:

Fair and equitable taxation of the motor vehicle; dedication of motor vehicle revenues exclusively to highway purposes; elimination of discriminatory motor vehicle levies; uniformity of motor vehicle laws; Federal aid for highway construction; a 40,000-mile inter-state system of high-type highways geared to the needs of modern traffic; elimination of vexatious parking problems; roadside zoning; building greater safety into the highways; extension of driver training in the high schools of the nation; promotion of travel, both at home and abroad; and elimination of travel barriers among nations.

HORSEPOWER

One horsepower is equal to 33,000 foot-pounds per minute, or 550 foot-pounds per second.

Note that power involves both the work done and the time involved. The unit of work is the foot-pound, which is equal to lifting one pound one foot. The 33,000 foot-pounds can be performed in any way, such as lifting 33,000 pounds one foot, a thousand pounds 33 feet, or one pound 33,000 feet. For example, it might take a man several days to shovel 33,000 pounds of dirt one foot into the air in a wheelbarrow, but a steam shovel could lift 2,000 pounds 16.5 feet in one minute to produce one horsepower. Work is not only lifting a weight, but moving anything against a resistance, such as turning a grindstone. If the stone had a circumference of two feet and rotated at 3,300 revolutions per minute, the stone surface would be moving at a rate of 6,600 feet per minute. If the grinding friction was five pounds, the power required to rotate the stone would be one horsepower.

To Estimate the Horsepower of a Gasoline Engine

The results obtained by using the formula given below are not exact but are close enough for all practical purposes.

Let
x=Horsepower
a=Area of one piston in square inches
b=Number of cylinders
c=Stroke of engine in feet
d=Revolutions per minute
e=Constant 1000 for four-cycle, 900 for two-cycle
then

$$X = \frac{a \times b \times c \times d}{e}$$

A boiler requires for each nominal horsepower 30 to 35 pounds of water an hour.

ELECTRICAL POWER

The kilowatt hour is the unit of electrical power. It is equal to 1.341 horsepower. Ordinarily we speak of so many kilowatts of power, but, strictly speaking, this is incorrect. We really mean a certain amount of electrical energy flowing for one hour.

HOW TO CHOOSE A CAREER

The problems of successfully choosing a career requires the careful consideration of many factors. It is of particular importance for the beginner to consider which job fields are overcrowded, and which offer the best opportunities.

There are more than 30,000 different types of work in American industry. Job competition in many of these fields is strong. High schools, colleges, and special schools are graduating students faster than job opportunities are developing. Some fields are badly overcrowded. Others—because they do not seem glamorous or for other reasons—offer big opportunities; they have more openings than they have applicants for jobs.

In 1950 about 500,000 students graduated from the four-year course in United States colleges, setting an all-time record. As the war veterans finish their college courses or drop out, the number of college graduates will decline. The enrollment and the number of graduates will rise again as the first "war babies" reach college age. Many college graduates will have increasing difficulty in finding jobs. The following fields are crowded currently and probably will continue to be: *law, personnel work, journalism, chemistry,* and *business administration* (especially accounting). On the other hand, young people and others who are looking for expanding fields with career possibilities should keep their eyes on *television, airconditioning, plastics, new chemical products,* and other relatively new fields.

Here is a brief survey of the opportunities for careers in the leading job fields.

The Professional Fields

Engineering is a rapidly growing profession, but for the next several years the number of engineering graduates will be greater than the number of openings. Later, however, the employment situation is likely to improve.

In the *teaching field* there is an oversupply of high school teachers but a great shortage of elementary school teachers. Plans to raise grade school teachers' pay will help to attract more men and women to the elementary field. Later, in the 1950's, when the "war babies" are in high school, there will be more jobs for high school teachers. In some communities there is a shortage of high school science, vocational, and physical education instructors. Few jobs offer such good beginning pay as does school teaching, which also opens the door for well-paying careers in school administration, educational writing, and other related fields.

The *reporting field* has long been crowded. Jobs are easier to find with country papers, trade papers, and house organs than with daily newspapers or major magazines.

Competition for beginning *business administration* jobs is likely to be keen, because so many young people are specializing in accounting and other business courses.

Draftsmen and *radio operators* may expect strong competition in the future. Smaller communities offer the best opportunities for beginning radio operators. *Airplane piloting, photography,* and to a lesser degree, *architecture* are all crowded fields.

There is a growing demand for *interior decorators.* But such jobs are best in prosperous times and fall off when people have less money to spend on house furnishings and decorations. Many trained interior decorators are women who combine their careers with homemaking and raising a family.

Social work currently offers good possibilities, especially to young people willing to go to college for five or more years and with executive ability, good judgment, and keen interest in people and their problems. Social workers deal with individuals, families, or groups, to relieve and improve economic and social conditions. A beginner often starts as a case worker or group worker and may later be promoted to supervisory positions over other social workers. Unlike most fields, social work expands its activities and opportunities during "hard times."

Thousands of additional *nurses* are needed. The profession is likely to continue to need many new workers each year as the country's health services grow. Girls—and boys, too—who have a "B" average or better in high school studies should be readily accepted by a local hospital or college school of nursing. Students can often find schools which give tuition scholarships and part-time jobs which pay all or part of the expenses for the training period.

Practical nurses and *nurses' aids* are also needed to assist with the home and hospital care of patients. Thousands of replacements are needed annually in this field. Boys can find many opportunities as *orderlies* in hospitals. Most practical nurses, nurses' aids, and orderlies learn their work from on-the-job training; many of these jobs are available to high school students who wish to work after school or during summer vacations. Inquire at local hospitals. Duties include caring for the patient's comfort and personal appearance, assisting doctors and nurses, helping with the housekeeping, and assisting in the diet kitchen.

There are many openings for *doctors* and *dentists.* But medical and dental colleges want only students with good grades in high school and the number of openings for entering students in these special schools is limited. In the future there will probably be more scholarships for medical students who find it necessary to work their way through the long medical course. If many young people continue to go to college to become *pharmacists,* there may be more pharmacists in the future than there are jobs.

Other health service groups, such as *veterinarians, medical X-ray technicians, medical laboratory technicians, dental hygienists, physical* and *occupational therapists,* and *dietitians,* are likely to have good opportunities for a number of years. Women will find many openings in most of these occupations.

In the larger cities, high school graduates can find jobs as *laboratory assistants* in hospitals and in factories manufacturing drugs. This is a growing field for girls, but competition is keen. Beginners with college training are often given preference over high school graduates.

Opportunities in Office Work

About 200,000 *secretaries, stenographers,* and *typists* are needed every year to fill vacancies in business and the professions. Clerical workers are in big demand in the large cities, in Washington, D.C., and in many state capitals. Beginners who hope to become private secretaries or executives should have a good business and general education and develop good work habits. Otherwise they may end up with a routine job and a small pay check.

One out of every four stenographers is a male. A boy who looks forward to a career in business administration might be wise to take secretarial training in high school and at business school during summer vacations. Then, when he finishes his college course in business, he will find it much easier to get a job as an assistant to an important executive. Part-time and vacation jobs in secretarial work are also helpful preparation.

A good beginning stenographer should be able to type at least 40 to 60 words a minute accurately and take shorthand at 80 to 100 words a minute. Good appearance, pleasant personality, ability to follow instructions and to work well with others are important qualities in this field. Stenographers may be promoted to *private secretaries, office managers,* or *supervisors.* Some become *public stenographers, court reporters,* or *legal* or *medical stenographers.*

English is a key vocational subject to be mastered by anyone specializing in clerical or sales work. Secretaries need exact knowledge of spelling and grammar, and the ability to recognize the meaning of words. Sales people need to be able to speak clear, correct English as well as to write correctly.

Selling and Service Opportunities

Sales work offers more opportunities for beginners than do most other fields. It is a growing field for women, who now obtain about half of all sales jobs. Stores today want salespeople who can really sell—not merely package-wrappers and change-makers. Many stores are interested in young high school graduates, especially if they have taken retail selling courses and related subjects.

A good appearance, pleasing personality, poise, patience, tact, good health, and ability to handle customers are necessary qualities for sales clerks. Clerks may advance to *credit clerk, department head, buyer, advertising manager, section supervisor,* or similar positions, young people can find after-school and summer jobs in sales work at local stores.

Opportunities are also good for beginning *service station attendants,* especially for young men living in large cities.

Between 60,000 and 70,000 new *telephone operators* are needed every year because so many operators quit to get married or to take other jobs. Eventually fewer operators will be needed as more of the telephone firms use automatic dial systems.

Fewer *beauty operators* are likely to be needed in the future as more women use home beauty aids.

The "Blue-Shirt" Field

About four of every ten workers in this country today have "blue-shirt" jobs. They work in the factories, in the building trades, and as transportation workers. They are skilled or semi-skilled workers who wear work clothes and are not afraid to get their fingers dirty as they operate machines and work with tools. Many of them are far happier than they would be at some desk or other "white-collar" job. The blue-shirt worker's take-home pay is good—often better than the white-collar worker's.

Opportunities for jobs in the *building trades* continue to be good. Most of the building trades—*carpentry, bricklaying, electrical work,* and others —have apprenticeship programs which train new workers in an earn-while-you-learn program which often lasts four years. These apprenticeship programs are organized by construction firms and labor organizations working together, frequently under the supervision and guidance of Government agencies. The demand for additional *carpenters, bricklayers, plumbers,* and *sheetmetal workers* is greater than the need for new *painters* and *paperhangers.* The painting and paperhanging fields are overcrowded; competition for work is strong.

Skilled and semi-skilled *factory workers* make automobiles, refrigerators, and other goods. As long as the country remains prosperous and people have money to buy goods, there will be plenty of factory jobs. Many of these consist in operating machines. Young people find beginning factory jobs as *assemblers* (who fit and fasten parts together by hand, machine, or tool), and as *floor boys and girls,* who carry supplies and materials to machine operators, sort and pack goods, and clean the floors and machines. Many of these jobs lead to advancement for boys; less often for girls. Young people can also find factory jobs as *packers,* especially during the rush season. Firms engaged in interstate business cannot employ young people under 18 years of age.

Farm jobs are declining in number, but agriculture still offers bright futures to young poeple who are willing to work hard and who—either because of experience or of special school training—are willing to approach farming as a business proposition which requires as much exact knowledge as any other business. Farming is becoming more scientific and more highly mechanized. Success in it depends on the skill of the worker, the suitability of his crop to reach a market which wants it, and the quality of his land. City youths who would like summer employment on the farm should inquire at the local office of the State Employment Service.

Where to Obtain Vocational Information

Government agencies, both state and Federal, publish up-to-date reports giving vocational information in various fields. These reports, often in pamphlet or booklet form, are available to the public at cost.

Outstanding in this work are the "Occupational Outlook" Series published by the Bureau of Labor Statistics of the United States Department of Labor. The "Occupational Outlook Handbook," which is revised frequently, may be purchased from the Superintendent of Documents, United States Government Printing Office, Washington 25, D.C.

"Occupations in the Federal Civil Service" lists opportunities in the various occupations and tells how these civil service jobs are filled. Another pamphlet is "Opportunities for Women in the Federal Civil Service." Free copies can be obtained from the United States Civil Service Commission, Washington, D.C.

"Women's Jobs—Advance and Growth" is the Women's Bureau pamphlet on the place of women in about 400 occupations. It is available from the United States Government Printing Office.

HOW TO LOOK FOR A JOB

During the great depression of the 1930's, when competition for the few jobs available was so keen, job-hunting became something of a science. In job clinics, career conferences, and round-table discussions on job-hunting techniques, authorities in employment work established specific formulas for planning, organizing, and carrying through a job hunt. As a result, the old haphazard methods have practically ceased to exist. Today, most job hunters—at least those who have benefited from vocational counseling services in school or college—know that employers expect to find evidence that applicants have prepared themselves sufficiently to know what they are offering and to be reasonably sure that they are offering it in the right place. Such preparation is an essential preliminary to the actual looking.

Preparation

The job seeker should take and resolutely hold the mental attitude that he is not so much asking for a job as he is offering for sale a commodity that, presumably, has a market value. After the psychological preparation come the concrete steps in preparation.

The prospective job hunter will need to determine (1) the nature of the service he proposes to offer; (2) the market value of this service, *i.e.*, what employers are generally paying for such service; (3) the qualifications he possesses in the way of (a) general education and specialized training; (b) work experiences; (c) special aptitudes or talents (whether he is qualified, for instance, to work in the theater or the movies, radio or television, writing, or some other field of artistic expression); (4) which business, profession, or organization may need the service he has to offer.

Looking for a Job

After preparation the next step is to locate a likely "prospect." The *"Help-Wanted" columns* of the local newspapers are an obvious source; less obvious but equally important are the advertisements in trade publications. Certain employers (notably those employing workers with technical training and skills) who do not ordinarily advertise in the newspapers often advertise in their trade publications.

Another obvious source is the *employment agency.* A recent graduate of a college or a business or technical school will, of course, make full use of whatever *placement facilities* it has to offer. *State employment* offices, and such social welfare organizations as the local "Y" should also be utilized.

Friends and acquaintances can often help. They sometimes know of an opening, or will be on the lookout; or they may give letters of introduction to persons who might be in a position to help with advice, information, or further introductions.

Sometimes a strategically placed *advertisement* pays out, but as a rule, only if the job seeker is experienced in a specialized field, for example, if he is an advertising copywriter or an executive, or an engineer, a chemist, or other technical expert. Advertisements, usually, are best placed in a trade, professional, or technical publication.

If efforts in these directions fail to produce an opening, it may be advisable to engage in some *independent prospecting.* A list of organizations which have a fairly constant need for the type of service to be offered should be made, and a letter of application sent to each, with a carefully prepared summary of the writer's education, training, and experience.[1]

This letter and summary deserve the utmost effort; they will be the basis for an estimate of the applicant and his qualifications for the work.

The letter should reflect some quality of the writer—a measure of originality and individuality that will cause it to stand out from the general run. Trick devices, however, of the "smart Alec" type should never be used. The letter should be brief, and mention only matters which bear directly on the writer's qualifications for the job in question. Each copy should be individually typed, on suitable stationery, and correct in every detail of spacing, placing, and typing. The English, punctuation, and spelling should be flawless. The summary—or resumé, as it is usually called—should be typed on a separate sheet. It should give in skeleton

---

[1]See also section on Letters of Application (page 481).

form the facts, with dates, of the applicant's general education; specialized training, work experience, if any, and other pertinent assets, such as extra-curricular activities, foreign travel, and knowledge of foreign languages.

Many "career" books give advice on job hunting, with sample letters of application and sample resumés. These examples are well worth studying; but the fact remains that a letter of application and resumé will prove effective only in so far as they truly represent the writer, and show sound thinking on his individual problem.

The Interview

One day, as a result of the quest, will come an appointment for an interview.

There is no gainsaying that this is a crucial occasion. In no longer than it takes for the job seeker to walk the distance between the door and the chair by the interviewer's desk he can win or lose a job. His dress, posture, manner of carrying himself, his walk, the expression on his face—all these things will tell the interviewer a great deal that will enter into his decision.

It goes without saying, therefore, that whatever time, thought, and effort have been given to preparation for the interview will have been well spent.

The task before the applicant is no less than that of convincing the shrewd, experienced person behind the desk not only that the applicant has what it takes to make a success of the job in question, but that he is an individual the interviewer will be proud to have in his organization. He knows that skills are not too difficult to find, but that outstanding quality is a rare commodity.

Individual quality, therefore, is what the job hunter should seek to register the moment he enters the interviewer's office. Appearance and bearing are the important criteria. It is essential to be neatly and conservatively dressed; quiet, reserved, and dignified in manner, and yet, as far as the natural nervousness inevitable to the occasion permits, at ease.

The interviewer should be permitted to take the lead and set the tone of the interview; but if the applicant is encouraged to talk he should not be afraid to speak up. He should remain physically quiet, without fidgeting, swinging his feet, drumming with his fingers, or fussing with his hair or clothing. He should not smoke unless invited to do so. He should answer questions fully and pleasantly. The interviewer should be permitted to introduce such matters as salary, paydays, hours of work, vacations, and holidays. The applicant should confine himself to presenting his qualifications for the work and his interest in securing it.

He should watch carefully for indications that the interviewer is ready to *terminate* the interview. Many an eager job seeker lingers on and on, hoping to add one more point in his favor, and as a result talks himself out of a job. When the interviewer says, "We'll let you know," or "You'll be hearing from us," it is the cue for departure. To thank the interviewer for his courtesy in granting the interview, and to express the hope of being considered for the position are enough.

And if the job seeker never hears from the interviewer he should not be discouraged. There will always be other interviews coming up, and some day there will be one that results in a job.

PERSONNEL SELECTION

The employees of a business are a vital factor in its efficient operation. Hiring the right person for a job involves not only finding a worker who can perform certain duties, but finding someone who will fit in well with the organization and who will enhance the local reputation of the business. A store clerk, for example, can either build up a faithful following or drive customers away to a competitor.

A small businessman must usually hire local workers, and often finds himself in direct competition with big business firms who scout local talent for the most promising workers. The small businessman, however, can reduce this handicap in several ways. He can (1) meet the wages offered by larger concerns; (2) offer experience in a wider variety of related jobs; and (3) stress the opportunity for more rapid advancement and greater responsibility.

Where to Find Workers

1. *Employment Agencies.* Federal, state, and privately operated employment agencies maintain lists of qualified workers in every field, and will recommend workers at no cost to the employer. Some private agencies specialize in certain types of work and can readily recommend good workers in their fields.

2. *Advertising.* Newspaper want ads can be a quick way to find workers interested in a certain type of job. Such ads should be carefully prepared to make sure that they specify exactly the qualifications desired. Careful wording will avoid interviews with unqualified persons who might answer a vaguely worded ad. The "Help Wanted" sections in local newspapers offer numerous examples of such advertising.

3. *Nearby Schools.* Most high schools, technical schools, and colleges maintain placement services for graduates. These services are always a good source of young workers anxious to learn a particular type of work, or to obtain experience in certain fields.

4. *Local Contacts.* In a small town, business associates, business clubs, and other organizations often know who is seeking a job and who is qualified for certain work.

What to Look For in an Employee

The employer should be a good judge of personalities and be able to assess the qualifications of the person he is considering for a job. Necessary personal qualifications, of course, vary with different types of work, but certain traits, such as cooperativeness, eagerness to work, and neatness, are desirable in all fields.

An interview affords the best means for the employer to get acquainted with an applicant and to study him carefully. The employer should try to put the applicant at ease during the interview, and should speak in a friendly manner. The gruff or stern approach often defeats the purpose of finding a good worker and frequently results in making the applicant nervous and ill at ease.

During the interview the employer should inquire into the past experience or training of the applicant in relation to the particular type of job open, and into his general educational background. The exact duties of the job should be thoroughly explained, and the employer should question the applicant on his ability to perform the work.

Employment application forms can also be used to good advantage. Often an applicant who may not be qualified for the present opening, is able to fill other jobs that might be open in the future. With the applications on file, the employer always has a list of possible workers on hand. Such form should provide adequate space for the following information: (1) name, address, and telephone number of applicant; (2) age, marital status, and social security number; (3) record of schools attended, the length of attendance, and the student's major subjects; (4) previous jobs held, type of work done, length of employment, and salary received; and (5) the names of at least three local residents, other than relatives, who can give character references. Space should also be provided for any additional remarks the applicant might wish to make, such as why he desires a particular job, or why he feels qualified for it.

If time permits, the following procedure is recommended for hiring a worker: (1) Have the worker fill out the company application form; (2) make a mutually convenient appointment for an interview; (3) study the application form and refer to it during the interview; (4) allow time for the consideration of the relative merits of various applicants; (5) notify the chosen applicant, and send notes to the rejected applicants to the effect that the position has been filled and that their interest has been appreciated.

ORGANIZATION OF A SMALL BUSINESS

The economy of the United States, from the standpoint of the size and number of business concerns, is largely an economy of small businesses. Of the nearly 4,000,000 business establishments in the country, more than 90 per cent are usually classified as small business.[1]

---

[1]According to the United States Department of Commerce, "small business" includes the following: manufacturing plants with 100 employees or less; wholesale establishments with less than $500,000 annual net sales volume; retail stores, service establishments, hotels, places of amusement, and construction establishments with annual net sales or receipts of less than $100,000.

Small business is found in almost all fields of business endeavor. It is concentrated in the retail and service fields, but it also plays an important part in maintaining a sound and prosperous economy through construction, manufacturing, wholesaling, and mining.

The establishment of a successful small business, whether from scratch or through the purchase of a going business, is not an easy undertaking. Hard work and long hours are to be expected, and competition from both small and large concerns may be intensive. Problems constantly arise demanding immediate decisions—decisions that in the long run will determine success or failure.

Inexperience, incompetence, lack of capital, fraud, and unwise credit practices are reported as the basic causes of *business failures*. A recent study estimated that during the second half of 1949 inefficient management due to inexperience or incompetence was the underlying cause of most failures.[1]

Selecting the Right Business

The fact that almost all studies of business failures report inexperience and incompetence as primary causes of failure indicates that one basic rule a prospective businessman should observe in selecting a business is to select a field with which he is familiar. Thus, for many persons there is no problem about what business they should go into. It is the one in which they have been employed, the one they know.

The selection of a business, however, is more complicated for individuals with but little, if any, experience, and for persons who have experience in fields with a limited and restricted economic life. In such instances, the individual should determine the business he thinks he would like most, and then, from Governmental and non Governmental sources, obtain all available information concerning the business. If the evaluation indicates that there appears to be a future for that type of business, the next step is to determine the qualifications required for its operation and the matching of such qualifications against the individual's background, ability, and experience. If the person is well qualified in all respects except experience, it is usually advisable for him to obtain employment in the field until sufficient experience and knowledge have been acquired.

Establishing a New Business

The prospective businessman, after selecting the kind of business to operate, is ready to consider the problems connected with the establishment of a new business. The primary problems are (1) capital requirements and sources of capital, (2) form of business organization, and (3) location of the business.

---

[1]"Why Do Businesses Fail?" *Dun's Review,* March, 1950.

Capital Requirement

The amount of capital required in establishing a business varies so widely, depending on the kind of business, type of establishment, location, and many other factors, that it is impossible to set an average minimum that would meet the needs of all small businesses. It is not only necessary to have cash or credit to obtain the things needed to start a business, but also to have a reserve of cash or credit to carry the business until it becomes self-supporting. For some businesses this may take only a few months; for others 3 years or more. It is most important not to underestimate the capital requirements, for to do so may result in business failure.

Sources of Capital[1]

Initial Capital. The risks of starting a small business are so great that the owner must be willing to risk his own savings in the venture. Traditionally, the initial capital for establishing a business is furnished by the owner; occasionally it is supplemented by relatives or friends.

Short-Term Credit. Subsequently, besides the plowing back of earnings, short-term credit is usually required, to take care of current operating bills until payment has been received from sales. Sources of short-term credit are (1) bank loans—usually from 2 to 6 months; (2) trade credit from suppliers—30 to 90 days; and (3) loans from commercial credit firms or banks against inventory, accounts receivable and other collateral —6 to 12 months.

Term Loans. The small businessman seeking to expand or modernize his business requires credit with maturities of 1 year to 5 years or longer. Small businesses, on the whole, must rely on commercial banks for term loans; flotations of securities by small establishments have been costly and not too successful.

Forms of Business Organization

The form of organization to be employed depends upon the planned size of the business, amount of capital to be invested, tax consideration, and other factors. The majority of small businesses are started by a single individual and operated as sole proprietorships; some are organized as partnerships, and a few as corporations.

The Individual Proprietorship[2]. A business owned and operated by one person is known as an individual or sole proprietorship. In addition to being the most common form, it is the simplest and least expensive to establish. While there are no special legal organizational requirements, for certain types of ventures *licenses* are needed. Sole proprietorship per-

---

[1]See also the section on Credit (page 280).
[2]See also sections on Corporations and Partnerships (pages 97 and 99).

mits the greatest freedom of action to the owner, who usually manages the business, receives all profits, and bears all losses. However, creditors have a legal claim not only on the investment in the business but also on the personal assets of the owner.

The Partnership. A partnership is an association of two or more persons by mutual agreement to operate a business for profit. It usually brings together greater financial resources than the individual proprietorship and enables the business to offer a more comprehensive and efficient service. Outstanding characteristics are (1) unlimited liability of each partner; (2) termination by death or withdrawal of partner or by acceptance of a new partner; and (3) the fact that the acts of one partner, within the scope of the business, are binding upon the other partners.

The Corporation. The corporation is an artificial entity separate and apart from its stockholders, officers, and directors; it may sue or be sued without in any way affecting the individuals; and it may make contracts and take part in business transactions as though it were an individual. The corporate form of organization is more expensive to establish and requires more records than the other two types of organizations; on the other hand, it offers the advantage of limited liability. Stockholders in a corporation are liable only to the extent of their actual investment in the corporation.

Location

In many instances the small businessman selects his home town, where he has friends, relatives, and business contacts, as his business location. While personal feelings deserve serious consideration, the most important factor should be the ability of the location to support the business profitably.

Selecting the City or Town. In evaluating a town or city the emphasis should be on population, employment, income, and competitive trends; what has happened in the past and the present situation are important as bases for estimating future trends.

Normally, a growing town is preferable to one that has reached the peak of development. The composition of the population and its social and economic characteristics are other factors to be considered.

The probable degree of competition should also be evaluated, together with the size of the trading area and average rental charges.

Selecting a Trading Area and Site. If the town selected is small, there is usually only one trading area or shopping center. The retail or service business will naturally be located there if a site is available. If the town selected has various trading areas, such as central shopping districts, outlying centers, principal thoroughfares and neighborhood streets, they should all be evaluated from the standpoint of the type of business. Factors to be considered include the buying habits of potential customers; where they live and how they shop; transportation employed, and degree of competition.

Since the end of World War II the "selection" of the actual site has usually amounted to taking whatever is available. If a choice of site does exist, however, a careful evaluation of the possibilities should be made.

In selecting a location for a small manufacturing plant, special consideration should be given to the availability of an adequate labor supply, to raw material factors, and to cheap and adequate transportation facilities. If a supply of skilled workers is important, a location near an industrial city may be indicated; if unskilled workers are chiefly needed, rural communities may also be considered.

Buying a Going Business

The possibility of buying a going business should also be considered. The classified sections of all major newspapers and of many trade papers give detailed listings of businesses offered for sale.

The same problems of *capital, form of organization,* and *location* encountered in establishing a new business must be considered in the purchase of a going business. The advantages and disadvantages should be carefully weighed. Sometimes owners of small establishments, for personal reasons, are forced to sell their businesses at bargain prices. By purchasing a going business it may be possible to obtain a well-equipped plant in a good location, or a well-furnished store with adequate stock. Less working capital may be needed, since income will be forthcoming from the start, and smaller outlays will be required for new equipment, fixtures, and stock.

The advantages can be determined, however, only by a careful study of all phases of the business. The owner may be trying to unload an unprofitable business—unprofitable because of mismanagement, or poor location, or for other reasons. The equipment, fixtures, and stock on hand may have been poorly selected for the requirements of the business.

An analysis of the financial statements and business records of the concern, together with a review of the income tax returns, will help not only to determine whether to purchase the business, but also to establish a fair price.

Advice should be sought from local banks, suppliers, and other sources familiar with the type of business. Such advice may help to prevent the investment of time, effort, and money in a business that is doomed to failure from the start.

Operating a Small Business

The small businessman must employ sound business methods if he is to prosper. He must also constantly seek fresh information about his business in particular, and about business conditions in general.

Merchandising Problems

Buying. Sound buying policies are essential. Sound buying results in having on hand the goods the customers want at the prices they are willing to pay. It is based on a careful analysis of the problems of *what, when, where,* and *how much* to buy. Buying policies should never be controlled solely by a desire for quantity discounts or special prices, or by attempts to anticipate a rising price trend. It is important not to over-buy, for serious financial trouble may result.

Pricing. A sound and effective pricing policy is also essential. It should cover all the operating expenses of a business and also return to the owner a fair and reasonable profit. Adequate accounting records, containing current information on all operations of the business, are the basis of a sound pricing policy.

The general price level the business expects to maintain should be determined at the time of reviewing and evaluating all the factors bearing on the establishment of the business. Competitors' prices should be observed; the general price level should be kept in line with competing stores selling similar goods. The prices of individual items must conform to the general price policy of the business. In determining the principles of individual items it is essential that the mark-up[1] needed to cover both operating expenses and a fair net profit be accurately determined. Most public libraries have numerous publications covering the basic principles of determining prices—how to determine costs, mark-up, selling prices, and profit margins.

After the individual prices are computed, they should again be compared with competitors' prices. If the average price is much below that of competitors a review should be made, to insure that no operating expenses were overlooked; if the average price greatly exceeds that of competitors, a study of sources of supply, rent, and salaries is indicated.

Selling and Advertising

In many small businesses, selling is primarily a matter of *personal salesmanship,* with the owner and one or two salesmen doing the selling. In such instances the sales program should especially consider the personalities of the people selling, and their knowledge of the needs and desires of customers. The sales program should also consider the number of potential customers who cannot be reached through personal salesmanship alone. *Advertising* should be employed to inform potential customers concerning the goods carried and the services offered by the business. Advertising[2] draws customers into the place of business; effective personal salesmanship consummates the sales.

Many forms of advertising are available for small business concerns—display signs, newspapers, magazines, direct mail, shopping news, handbills, outdoor billboards, classified section of the telephone directory, radio, television, and newsletters. In selecting the media to be employed consideration should be given to the size of the trading area served by the business, the type of business, and customers' buying habits. A neighbor-

---

[1]See also the section on Mark-Up (page 262).
[2]See also sections on Advertising and Salesmanship (pages 419 and 427).

hood store may find handbills and direct mail, together with a hanging display sign, most effective. If the trading area covers a large part of the city, local newspapers, "spot" radio announcements, television, and outdoor billboards may be most productive.

Record Keeping

Small businesses should keep a record of all business assets, current and fixed, and of claims against the business, *i.e.*, liabilities. All expenses of the business should be recorded; daily sales records should be totaled, to permit recording of income. If the business offers credit, a record must be kept of the amount owed by customers. The common terms for these records are General Ledger, Journal, Cash Book, Sales Book, and Accounts Receivable Ledger.[1]

These records will permit the owners to prepare a balance sheet showing the financial condition of the business, and a profit-and-loss statement showing whether the business is operating at a profit or a loss.

Government Regulations and Restrictions

Small businesses are subject to numerous laws and regulations. It is advisable to obtain legal advice on those that may affect a particular business. The following are a few of the regulations and restrictions affecting small business firms.

Licensing. Nearly all small businesses are subject to some form of governmental licensing control, the degree of regulation depending upon the type and location of the establishment. Certain businesses, such as restaurants, hotels, barbershops, and beauty shops, must usually meet with detailed licensing requirements. Others, such as dry good stores, suffer relatively few controls.

State Wage and Labor Restrictions. Many states impose legal restrictions on the employment of women and minors. Some states have laws limiting the working hours of men. Occasionally, there are restrictions covering minimum wages paid in retail and other establishments. Almost all states have workmen's compensation laws.

Taxes

The following are some of the principal types of taxes[2] the small businessman must consider in planning and operating a business.

Income Taxes. The Federal Income Tax Laws apply somewhat differently to corporations than they do to partnerships and individual proprietorships. For corporations there is one tax on the net income before it is distributed to stockholders, and another tax on this income when it has been received by stockholders as dividends. For a partnership or an individual proprietorship there is no income tax levied on the business as such, but earnings are taxed at individual income tax rates, whether distributed or not, and usually at a somewhat higher rate.

Employers must comply with the *withholding tax* law, *i.e.*, withhold a portion of the wages of each employee as an advance payment on his personal income tax.

Social Security Taxes. Under the Federal Social Security Act, the small businessman is required to deduct taxes from employee wages for old age and survivors insurance and for unemployment compensation.

---

[1] See also section on Keeping Accounts (page 271).
[2] See also section on Taxes (page 93).

Other Federal Taxes. Manufacturers and retailers excise taxes, license fees, and occupational taxes are other principal Federal taxes. The Collector of Internal Revenue has complete information concerning all Federal taxes.

The principal *state* taxes are property, license, sales, and use taxes, unemployment compensation, and income taxes.

The most important *local* taxes are property, license, sales, and income.

The state tax commissions and county and city officials have complete information concerning state and local taxes.

Keeping Up-to-Date

The small businessman, if he is to operate at a profit and maintain his competitive position in his community and industry or trade, must keep informed of new techniques of production, merchandising, and management in his particular field, and of trends and developments affecting business conditions in general. The successful owner is always endeavoring to improve his merchandising methods and continually checking his buying, pricing, and selling policies to insure that they are giving the utmost in customer satisfaction.

The Small Business Division of the United States Department of Commerce, through its "Establishing and Operating" series and "Small Business Aids," makes available information as to latest business methods, techniques, and operating procedures. The "Establishing and Operating" series covers specific business fields and topics such as business records, location factors, operating techniques, and merchandising methods, and gives related information. The "Small Business Aids" series consists of concise statements of specific small-business problems and proved solutions. Information on how to sell to the Federal Government will be given by the nearest Department of Commerce Field Office. A Government procurement manual containing complete and authoritative information on Government purchasing of all Federal procuring agencies, what Government agency buys what item, where the purchases are made, the regulations of the various procuring agencies, and how to get on bidding lists is available for reference at the Commerce Dept. Field Offices, and at many chambers of commerce and offices of manufacturers' groups.

Information on finance and tax problems, also, can be obtained from the Small Business Division. Typical of its publications are "Financing a New Small Business" and "The Small Businessman and Sources of Loans." The relationship of laws and regulations to competitive and trade practices is discussed in a number of other publications. All above-mentioned publications may be obtained free or at nominal cost from the Superintendent of Documents, Washington 25, D.C., or from any of the Commerce Dept. Field Offices.

BUSINESS MACHINES

It is important for the businessman to consider the various ways in which he may gain increased efficiency through the use of modern, time-saving business machines. Many routine jobs formerly done by hand are now quickly and easily accomplished by machines, at a considerable saving in time, money, and manpower. Certain machines, for example, make it possible to process all facts related to a business, giving its management a complete, accurate, and timely picture of company operations.

On the other hand, the purchase of elaborate equipment might be a definite liability for some small businesses. The businessman should, therefore, carefully balance the expense of such equipment against the need for it before buying. In the use of accounting machines, for example, such points should be considered as the size of the payroll, number of salesmen in the field, volume of sales, number of products, size of inventories, frequency of sales, seasonal nature of products, and other related factors.

Types of Business Machines

A description of some of the main types of business machines now available, the jobs they perform, and their relative values is given below. Such machines as typewriters, adding machines, and cash registers are not included; their use is well known in all types of business.

Accounting Machines. Accounting machines are designed to add, subtract, select data for printing, secure combinations of totals, sort, classify, and perform other similar operations. The basic record is a customer or account card into which the operator punches information in the form of small holes. These cards are record units which can be used and re-used in connection with other machines for the preparations of many different reports. Various models of accounting machines are available, or can be built for specified jobs. They are of value mainly to the business that requires a fast, economical means of preparing records and reports for efficient management control.

Addressing Machines. Modern addressing machines range from simple stencil devices to complex machines equipped with numerous automatic attachments, such as daters, numerators, and special selectors that pick out certain types of addresses by means of a code. In most of the simple machines, the address plates are fed automatically, either manually or electrically, into the machine, which in turn presses them against the post cards or envelopes. They are of value to a business that maintains a mailing list to which sales letters, accounts, bills, and similar material are frequently mailed.

Bookkeeping Machines. Computing machines for the accounting office are available in a number of models, many of which are equipped with a standard typewriter keyboard. Figures are entered into the machine by means of counters, similar to those of an adding machine. The operator can insert an old balance, post new transactions, and automatically obtain a new balance. The machine can also compute debit and credit balances, and accumulate and automatically print proof totals.

Calculating Machines. The calculator is similar to an adding machine, but does not print. A trained operator can make such calculations as figuring percentages, analyzing statistical reports, and other mathematical problems quickly and efficiently. Calculating machines are aids to bookkeeping and accounting; the buyer should consider them in relation to the particular accounting problems of his business.

Communication Equipment. Various specialized forms of loud-speaker and interoffice telephone equipment are available. The need for these depends in large part on the size and general layout of the office or business.

Dictating Machines. Recording or transcribing machines take dictation that can later be "played back" by a stenographer. In most of these machines the voice is recorded on either wire or tape that can be re-used after the dictated message has been "wiped off." Dictating machines are of value when the volume of correspondence is high, or when time formerly spent by the stenographer in taking dictation can be used to better advantage. The machine is also valuable to the businessman who does not employ a full-time stenographer. Letters can be dictated at any time and be transcribed later by a typist.

Duplicating Machines. Various types of duplicating machines are used for making multiple printed copies. The *mimeograph,* one of the oldest and the most commonly used, employs an inked stencil, fastened to a cylinder which revolves over blank sheets of paper. The paper can be fed into the machine either automatically or by hand. Another similar process makes use of a special gelatin-coated cylinder that retains an impression of the master copy. The *multilith* and *multigraph* processes are more specialized forms of duplicating machines; they are used for making a large number of copies in a short time. The duplicating machine is of particular value in a business that frequently requires multiple copies of reports, sales letters, brochures, and similar printed matter.

Mailing Machines. Several kinds of mailing machines perform such operations as gluing, sealing, and stamping envelopes. The importance of these to a small business is in proportion to the amount of mail sent each day, and the time that would ordinarily be spent if these operations were done by hand.

Miscellaneous Business Machines. Many other machines have been developed that can perform almost any type of job to be done in the business office. Among them are recording door-locks, time stamps, attendance-time recorders, indicating clocks, billing machines, check or bill endorsers, folding machines, coin changers and counters, automatic files, electric typewriters, and microfilm readers.

As a business grows in size and volume of work, machines can be employed to greater advantage; but to repeat, the businessman should consider the various factors before investing. Many large business-machine companies employ special representatives who will make a thorough survey of a firm's requirements and give advice on the type of machines needed. Other such companies maintain equipment that can be rented. Before investing it would be wise to consult a reputable concern.

PLANNING AND FURNISHING AN OFFICE

As the nucleus of business management, the well-planned office is a primary factor in the efficient functioning of any enterprise. Although the final design or floor plan of an office will have to conform to different requirements for each type of business, a number of general factors should always be considered.

The size of a business and the number of employees are the controlling factors. While one room is often sufficient for the operation of a small business, in large enterprises numerous departments, subdivisions, private offices, and special rooms are required. In all offices, however, the primary considerations are the same. The design and layout should provide for *the efficient flow of work throughout the office* and *the maximum comfort of the worker.*

Office Planning

Careful study should be given to the requirements of an office before any design is executed. The actual arrangement of rooms will depend on such important factors as (1) the number of employees; (2) the number of separate departments required; (3) the number of executive or private offices required; and (4) the number of special rooms and facilities required. A business employing 20 workers, for example, will not be able to function smoothly if they are all assigned to one room. On the other hand, the flow of work through the office would be seriously handicapped if the 20 workers were divided among four or five rooms. It is best to divide workers into groups according to the type of work they perform, and to provide space in accordance with their needs.

Generally, the individual worker requires as much as 120 sq. ft. of office space (including corridors, filing space, etc.). Private offices require as much as 250 sq. ft. of space, over twice the footage needed for a worker. Thus, in a business employing 50 workers and five executives, at least 7,250 sq. ft. are needed, of which 1,250 sq. ft. are used for private offices. The designer should also make allowances for expansion of the business, and not limit the space to that required by the present number of employees. In office planning it is best to avoid the following: (1) assigning too much space to private offices; (2) providing large working areas to departments requiring little space; (3) using too many partitions within the separate offices; and (4) providing storage space and special rooms in excess of actual needs.

Details of Office Arrangement

After the number and sizes of separate offices have been determined, the arrangement of offices in relation to each other should be planned. General rules, such as those listed below, should be considered in order to provide the most efficient flow of work:

1. Departments, such as the messenger and stenographic divisions, which are directly connected with the operation of other offices and departments should be easily accessible

2. Departments with related activities, such as the credit and accounting departments, should be placed adjacent to each other

3. Executive offices should be placed for maximum supervision of the entire office, but in such a way as to avoid interruptions to office workers by clients and visitors

4. Reception rooms should be placed where they are least likely to cause interruptions to the workers

5. Storage space for supplies should be easily accessible to all departments

6. Interoffice communications systems should be provided in large offices, and the telephone switchboard should be installed either in or near the reception room

Working Conditions

In addition to planning for the efficient flow of work through the offices, the designer should provide the best working conditions for employees. Some of the important factors to be considered are listed below:

1. *Lighting.* A diffused, evenly distributed light should be maintained without direct or reflected glare. Direct daylight is preferred, but when this is not available, semidirect artificial lighting is considered best. In general, 25 to 35 foot-candles of light are required for close work such as drafting, and 12 to 20 foot-candles for general desk work.[1]

---

[1] A foot-candle meter measures the intensity of illumination in a room, including both direct daylight and artificial light. Readings should be taken from each desk to assure the proper lighting conditions. Between 1.7 and 2.1 watts per square foot of lighted surface amount to 10 foot-candles.

Provisions for artificial lighting should be made in all offices, and adequate shades, such as venetian blinds, should be provided to control light in rooms using outside light. Wall colors should be considered for reflecting properties as well as for restful qualities

2. *Heating and Air Conditioning.* Proper working temperatures should be maintained in all offices; 68° F. is generally considered best. Heating and air-conditioning units should be placed to serve all parts of the office

3. *Ventilation.* Fresh air should be continuously circulated. Foul air should be removed and direct drafts should be eliminated; fans and air-blowing equipment should not blow directly on workers

4. *Noise Reduction.* Noise is a primary factor in fatigue; it should be eliminated or muffled. Ceilings, walls, floors, corridors, ventilating ducts, and doors should be sound-proofed whenever possible. Noisy business machines should be isolated and kept well oiled

5. *Rest and Recreation.* Drinking fountains and rest rooms adequate to the number of employees should be provided. In large businesses, centrally located lounges and recreation rooms should be available. Conveniently placed coat rooms and space for personal possessions should be arranged for each department

Methods of Office Planning

Several possible layouts should be planned carefully on paper, and compared. In general, the following procedure is recommended:

1. Prepare a detailed survey of the organization's needs, both present and future, including the estimated number of square feet, the number of departments, and the approximate location of departments and offices

2. Make a rough sketch of the office layout, indicating the approximate locations of fixed and movable equipment, using the scale of ¼ in. to 1 ft.

3. Study layout problems and revise the draft accordingly

4. Prepare detailed drawings and specifications

Office Furnishing and Decorating

The arrangement of furniture and equipment within the office is as important as the office design. The first step in furnishing an office is to determine the functions to be performed in the space. Generally, offices may be divided into two categories: (1) purely functional offices, used primarily for business operations in which there is little contact with the public, and (2) prestige offices, such as waiting rooms, conference rooms, reception rooms, interviewing rooms, and offices of executives and professional men.

Furnishing and Decorating the Functional Office. Efficiency of operation is the prime consideration in a functional office. Pleasant, comfortable working conditions should be provided, and the workers should be supplied with needed equipment. Chairs, tables, desks, filing cabinets, bookcases, and business machines usually constitute the essential equipment. The arrangement of these must conform to the floor space available; certain rules such as those listed below should be followed for the best utilization of office space:

1. The arrangement of office furniture should be neat and orderly

2. Main aisles through the office should be 45 in. to 60 in. in width

3. Aisles between desks should be at least 36 in. wide

4. Individual desks should be placed to permit the flow of work from one desk to another in accordance with the office routine

5. Each desk should be adjacent to an aisle, and not more than two desks should be placed end to end

6. Desks should not face windows. If possible, outside light should come from the left side of the worker

7. Desks should be arranged so that workers do not face the department supervisor or the department entrance

8. Filing cabinets should be placed against the wall if possible, and should not cut off light and ventilation

9. Aisles next to filing cabinets should be at least 36 in. wide when the file drawers are open

10. Partitions, if used, should be movable

11. Work tables and chairs should be placed near filing cabinets and bookshelves

12. Wastebaskets should be provided for all desks

13. Business machines should be accessible to workers to use them

14. Workers who frequently communicate with other departments should be placed near the office exit

15. Telephone and electrical outlets should be installed after the arrangement of desks and equipment has been determined

Selecting Furniture and Equipment. The decoration of a functional office is not as elaborate as that of a prestige office, but a number of factors should be given careful consideration.

Colors for the office walls, ceiling, and floor should be chosen for their reflecting properties and for their restful qualities. In general, light shades or pastel colors are recommended for the walls and ceiling, and darker colors for the floor. The table below gives the percentage of light reflected by various colors.

Color	Reflection	Color	Reflection
White	82%	Medium gray	46%
Gray white	76%	Dark orange	37%
Light green	70%	Medium red	20%
Pink	60%	Cadet blue	15%
Yellow	51%	Dark green	10%

Floor-covering materials should be selected for their ability to reduce noise and fatigue as well as for their appearance, durability, and cost. Some of the most popular flooring materials are tile, cork, linoleum, and rubber. As a rule, the color of floors should be dark, to prevent an upward glare of light.

Chairs should help to minimize fatigue and prevent physical strain through adjustments to the individual user. Adjustable revolving chairs or posture chairs are considered best. Upholstery of foam rubber or similar material is often recommended; it is preferable to pads or cushions.

Desks should be selected for the particular kinds of work to be performed. Numerous types are available, including work tables, interview desks, conference desks, and typewriter desks. The average, most widely used desk has a standard-size top 60 in. × 34 in. In many offices the trend is toward small, compactly fitted desks, built close to the floor. A number of models are available with adjustable height control.

Office furniture is usually made of wood, steel, or aluminum. In wood, walnut, birch, and other hardwoods are considered the best. Light or bleached finishes are not generally recommended for the functional office. Steel desks in light gray or olive with matching or harmonizing linoleum tops are widely used. Others are available in imitation mahogany or walnut finishes. Steel cabinets are recommended for filing and storage, and adjustable metal shelves are preferrd to built-in wooden shelves.

Furnishing and Decorating the Prestige Office. The prestige office is that of an executive or a professional man, or an office used largely for customer contacts. In furnishing an office of this type, the chief purpose is to create a setting that best exemplifies the type of business, and to establish an atmosphere suitable to that business. A doctor's waiting room, for example, should be comfortable and restful, decorated in pleasant cheerful colors. A reception room in a large organization, on the other hand, should be decorated in a more formal fashion appropriate to the type of business.

Furnishings for the prestige office vary with the requirements of the office and the amount of money to be invested. This type of office is generally decorated with wall-to-wall carpeting, window drapes, venetian blinds, and indirect or recessed lighting fixtures, or floor and table lamps. Furniture styles are a matter of individual taste. Period pieces of mahogany and walnut are frequently used, but contemporary designs in light and bleached finishes are also very popular.

Color schemes play an important part in the decoration of a prestige office. In general, restful colors should be used in waiting rooms and reception rooms, with some warmer colors employed to avoid monotony and drabness. The restful, neutral colors are frequently preferred for walls, ceiling, and carpets, with highlights of warmer shades "spotted" about the room in window drapes, pictures, upholstery designs, and lamp shades.

Methods of Furniture Arrangement. In large offices, particularly in prestige offices, the services of professional decorators are frequently utilized; but many businessmen design and arrange their offices with excellent results. To the amateur the following time-saving procedure is recommended:

1. Make a scale drawing of the office space, indicating doors, windows, fixed projections, and equipment
2. Mark the direction of door and window openings and indicate the space required by these with a circular line
3. Prepare a check list of the number and pieces of movable furniture to be used, and cut out patterns of these, drawn to the same scale as the office plan
4. Place the paper cutouts in various positions against the office plan, and consider the best possible arrangement.

HOW TO MAKE MONEY AT HOME

Making money at home, as opposed to regular, full-time, salaried employment, is of special interest to those thousands of persons who at times require additional earnings, either as a means of supplementing family income or of gaining those welcome extra dollars that provide luxuries not attainable through the present family budget. Frequently, too, an emergency arises which compels the earning of a *living*, rather, than a *supplementary* income, at home. Whether the purpose be "luxury" dollars, pin money, a serious program for a day-to-day living income, or a saving plan for security against a "rainy day," there are many types of home earning projects that may be employed.

The list of persons who for lack of time or opportunity may not be in position to seek regular employment may include housewives who must earn at home or not at all, students who must earn as they learn, shut-ins, handicapped persons, and elderly or retired men or women. Others who are fully employed may seek additional income through a profitable hobby or craft work, home workshop projects, or other skills or services which may be promoted in spare time at home.

Making money at home should be interesting as well as profitable—the kind of thing the worker does best because he thoroughly enjoys doing it and is fitted for it by temperament, training, or natural aptitude.

Any home money-making project the worker may decide upon as suited to his abilities and requirements should first be analyzed carefully from every possible angle before it is undertaken, or any investment made—by reading everything available on the subject, by observing the experiences of others, by studying the pitfalls as well as the advantages, and by carefully considering its long-time as well as its present earning possibilities.

Factors in Selecting a Project

Other factors that have a bearing on the type of work selected are:

Location. Does the worker live in city, town, or country? Are there accessible stores, shops, or consumer population to afford a market for his products or services? If he likes to grow things, or raise small livestock, or care for pets, for example, are the necessary land, housing, or other facilities for successful work obtainable?

Time. How much time can the worker devote to his project? He should choose an earning plan that will fit in with the time available.

Freedom of Action. Is the worker equipped to make contact with buyers of his products or services outside his home, or is it essential that they come to him? Many profitable projects are open to those who work wholly within their homes; others require outside selling, deliveries, or transportation facilities.

Future Plans and Requirements. The worker may seek only spare-time profits or he may be dependent on the money he makes at home for the entire support of himself and his family. If he plans a full-time operation he should select the type of project that is flexible; that has possibilities of expansion and growth; that can be developed, through skill and application, into an important business enterprise. Many of America's important retail and manufacturing establishments had their humble beginning in someone's kitchen, sewing room, garden, or basement workshop.

Suggestions for Home Money-Making Projects

The range of home activities for profit is so wide and so varied that it is impossible to compile an exhaustive list of suggestions. The following listings, however, represent types of projects that are being used successfully and profitably. Many of them can be launched with little or no capital investment, and most of them can be operated by either men or women, or by both working together.

Books and folios on many of these projects are available at public libraries. Others may be obtained free or at small cost from the Superintendent of Documents, Washington, D.C., through colleges and universities, national service-magazines, and from manufacturers and distributors of materials and supplies required in some of the projects.

Small Livestock and Other Breeding Projects

Syrian Hamsters. Widely used as laboratory animals and popular as pets. Rapid breeders; ready market for breeding stock. Small investment to start; $3.50 to $7.50 per pair for non-pedigreed animals; $10 per pair, maximum, for fine pedigreed stock. Limited space is required. Hamsters thrive contentedly in pens not over 1' × 2' in size. If the pens are stacked head-high, with a little air space between them, a colony of a dozen or more pairs may be cared for in a space of not more than 6 square feet. Due to the popularity of the project in recent years, and the many now engaged in it, prices are dropping gradually.

Cavies (Guinea Pigs). Biggest demand by laboratories and for breeding stock. Hutches for 20 pigs are approximately 20″ × 42″ × 18″ high; can be stacked or built in tiers for space economy. One male with five females should produce 120 pigs per year with a minimum market value of $1.00 per pig.

Rabbits. For meat, fur, wool, hides, and breeding stock. Many varieties available. Meat demand has increased rapidly in recent years. Initial cost for starting trio, two does and a buck, will be in the neighborhood of $100 for registered, pedigreed stock; considerably less for commercial animals. Ready outlet for furs and skins through established fur dealers; for meat through butcher shops and direct to hotels, restaurants, and clubs. Breeding stock is salable through classified advertising in small stock magazines and newspapers.

Chinchillas. Rare fur-bearing animals, sold mainly at this time for breeding stock. Expensive to start—about $1200 per pair. Small space required, relatively easy to raise. Each pair will raise two litters (usually two babies per litter) per year, valued at $600 per animal. The feeding cost per animal is approximately $2.75 per year. Profit possibilities overbalance the investment risk.

Earthworms. Cost little to start. Fantastically rapid increase. Require small space and little care. Big market for soil culture, breeding stock, bait outlets. Basement space is ample for propagation boxes of 500 or more breeder worms, each box is about 14" × 17" × 6" deep; boxes may be stacked. A 4' × 8' outdoor culture bed will support a population of about 50,000 earthworms. Selected breeding stock costs about $10 per thousand. Only food required is garbage, kitchen waste, lawn clippings, animal manures, or other organic waste. Crop is "harvested" every 21 days. Newly hatched stock develops to reproductive stage in 60 to 90 days. Little care required; a low-cost, high-profit money-making project.

Battery Broilers. Choice broilers from baby chicks in seven to eight weeks; bring fancy prices. Batteries cost less than $50 each; occupy 4' × 6' space. Cost of chicks, feeding, and care about 50 per cent of retail value of broilers.

Plant Culture

Mushrooms. Require basement, cave, cellar, or any building where temperature, ventilation and humidity can be controlled. Central states and northward. Ready outlet at good prices to hotels, restaurants, clubs, grocery stores, and consumers.

Horseradish. Roots can be sold, or ground and bottled product. Propagates itself and spreads indefinitely. A $\frac{1}{10}$-acre plot should yield, annually, up to $200 worth of bottled product, at retail. Wild or volunteer horseradish also a good source of profit.

Savory Herbs. A profitable home-garden project. Utilize space along garden fences; no waste. See *Farmer's Bulletin No. 1977,* United States Department of Agriculture.

Christmas Trees. A five-year project, but will produce steady return after five years, through successive year-by-year plantings. One acre will grow from 2,500 to 8,000 trees. Seedlings obtainable at low cost, in many states, through state forest service. Rough, steep, or otherwise unprofitable land may be used.

Roadside Vegetable Market. Profitable outlet for fruits and vegetables, as well as eggs, poultry, canned fruits, juices, jellies, preserves, and other farm, garden, and orchard products.

Gladiolus Bulbs. Two salable crops—flowers and bulbs. One of the most profitable crops, easy to grow, thrive in most soils, increase rapidly in volume.

House Plants. A flexible project, which one may start in as small a way as he chooses and enlarge as fast as he can propagate and pot new plants from his own cuttings, bulbs, and seeds. Government bulletins are available.

Service Projects

Typing and Associated Services. A competent typist will discover a healthy demand for "take-home" typing assignments such as addressing envelopes, typing speeches, sermons and story manuscripts, overflow typing from letter shops, etc. Such a service may be expanded to include mimeographing, multigraphing, varityping, and typing for planograph reproduction. For some of these additional equipment and added invest-ment are required. Such expansion, however, develops into a full-fledged lettershop service.

Telephone Service. Involves the use of the home telephone to supple-ment the phone services of physicians, lawyers, realtors, and others who must be reached, or have messages relayed, when away from their of-fices, or outside regular office hours. Home telephone services may also be employed for sales solicitation for dairies, laundries, fuel dealers, insur-ance companies, and similar types of businesses.

Shopping Service. Skillful shoppers find a ready demand for their buy-ing services among those who are too busy, or otherwise unable, to shop personally; particularly in demand on anniversary or gift occasions. The shopper, too, as her clientele grows, may keep a record of birthdays, anniversaries, and similar dates of which each client should be reminded in advance.

Catering. A good cook with ability to plan or supervise special dinners and luncheons, including menus, shopping, food preparations, serving, and party decorations, will find her services in good demand.

Children's Parties. A special kind of party service in which the worker acts as hostess, prepares or obtains costumes and place cards, plans and supervises games, recreation, and entertainment.

Baby Sitting. The care of children in their own homes, when parents must be away, has become "big business," with an ever-increasing de-mand for competent sitters. Workers of all ages, but mainly teen-agers, have found it profitable spare-time work. Others who have managerial ability and understand baby-sitting problems have found it profitable to organize baby-sitting agencies—training, supplying and supervising sit-ters through a central club or agency.

Survey Work. Many concerns, such as market research organizations, "pollsters," manufacturers, advertising agencies, radio stations, publish-ers, and political groups, employ local people to make local surveys (by personal contact or telephone) which become units in cross-sectional national polls of opinion or product-use information. The work is well paid, and pleasant for those who like to meet and converse with people.

Mailing List Service. Certain advertisers, mail order houses, and list companies will buy names, obtained locally, of brides, new mothers, births, deaths, anniversaries, new home owners, and others not obtain-able through established list channels. Such names are available through newspaper columns and other local sources.

Press Agency. Press releases to local, sectional, or national publications —with reference to newsworthy new manufactured products, or to promi-nent persons, interesting places, and current events—are worth money to manufacturers, individuals, clubs, and civic organizations. They should be well written and accompanied, when possible, by photographs. Ar-rangements should be made to obtain checking copies or tear sheets if and when such release material appears in print.

Invalid Care. For those who have roomy homes the care of aged persons and semi-invalids is a well-paid service and a steady source of income. Training in practical nursing is an asset but not essential.

"Bachelor Service." A mending and repair service for men who live alone—bachelors, widowers, college men, and traveling men away from home—is a welcome and remunerative money-making project.

Care of Pets. For those who have the facilities and the understanding of animals to take good care of pets while owners are away, there is a ready demand for such a service.

Small Business Projects

Magazine Subscription Agency. One of the most widely practiced of all home money making plans and one that can be built into a highly profitable full-time business. As a clientele is established and "repeat business" develops it becomes increasingly remunerative. Personal solicitation is best but many shut-ins have done well through the use of the mails and the telephone. Closely allied, and easily combined with it, is the increasingly popular book-club agency.

Photography. For the skilled amateur photographer there are many opportunities for making money with his camera, most lucrative of which is doubtless the photographing of children and pets in their homes. Ability to process his own negatives, prints, and enlargements is a marked advantage.

Furniture Refinishing. There are countless prospects, in most communities, for the repairing and refinishing of old or shabby furniture. The worker who can perform that service skillfully, in his home workshop or in the homes of his customers, will doubtless find all the work he can do. Original patterns for decoration and design will command better-than-average prices, and the pattern stencils themselves (such as Dutch, Mexican, Early American) may be sold as a "pattern service" to those who like to do their own decorating.

Home Gift Shop. People will go a long way to patronize a shop that carries distinctive souvenirs, hand-crafted items, hand-needlework, loom-work, and like merchandise. Such a shop may be utilized as an outlet for the owner's own craft work, or for the products of other home workers, sold on a commission basis.

Home Cooking. Many a substantial manufacturing business has grown from a humble start in someone's kitchen. The range of possibilities is limited only by the home worker's imagination—cakes, pies, cookies, special recipes, canned fruits, jams, jellies and preserves, candies, potato chips, and countless other home-made products for which there is a ready demand, through stores and shops or direct to consumers. It is the kind of home money-making enterprise that does its own advertising, via customer-to-customer recommendation.

Needlework. No one who sews well need ever lack a source of income. The possibilities are boundless—children's garments, women's wear, fancy work, sachets, knitting and crocheting, embroidering, making lovely things to wear out of low-cost cotton bags. Or the worker may specialize in certain highly skilled operations that few home-needleworkers can do well, such as matched-buttonmaking, buttonholing, belt- and pocket-making—all in demand by department stores, dress shops, tailor shops, professional dressmakers, and home seamstresses.

Key Shop. The making of duplicate keys requires no special skill. It is done by a machine, which requires only a modest investment. The blanks are inexpensive; once one is set up for business the prices received for duplicate keys are largely profit. Such a business, plus some classified advertising in local papers, is a lucrative home enterprise.

Key Checks and Dog Tags. A business that might well be combined with key making. Stamping outfit, lettering dies, alphabets, gauge, and hammer cost about $35. The blanks cost 5 cents each and the tags usually retail at 50 cents each; an excellent return on investment and labor.

Silk Screen Printing. An excellent home project in smaller cities and towns which have no large silk-screen printing establishments. It is easy to learn, materials and supplies are easily obtainable, and there is a steady demand from stores, restaurants, shops, schools, and churches for short runs of posters, counter cards, window displays, sports-event announcements, pennants, souvenirs, and emblems that can best be done by silk-screen methods.

Hand-Loom Weaving. A fascinating home money-making project for men or women, offering a ready market for such hand-loomed products as tapestries, afghans, table covers, scarves, luncheon sets, handbags, baby blankets, and materials for suits, dresses, coats, and draperies. Portable looms are available for as little as $20; floor-type for about $100 and up.

Tiny Tot Nursery. A day nursery where mothers can leave their children in good care while they work, shop, or attend the theater or social functions. Most parents prefer a well-regulated nursery to the baby-sitter plan, and are willing to pay well for its advantages.

"Heirloom" Rugs. The revival of interest in hooked and braided rugs makes them an excellent home money-making project; in which practically no initial investment is required. Beautiful pattern stencils are available; but the worker can command better prices if he can create original patterns of special or local interest.

Photo-coloring. A project that requires training and skill but which can be mastered by anyone of average ability, regardless of artistic aptitude. Portrait studios, commercial photographers, display firms, and stores require the services of color artists. It is a "take-home" project.

Textile Painting. No art or technical training is required—just a little practice plus a natural "feel" for color and design. The worker obtains the relatively low-cost, undecorated products—such as ties, scarves, belts, aprons, blouses, lamp shades, or any others of thousands of such items—and after decorating them skillfully, resells them as expensive hand-crafted items. The demand for such products, as gift or personal-use purchases, is practically universal.

Selling. There are countless opportunities open to those who like to sell —house-to-house, office-to-office, or combined personal, telephone, and mail approach. Popular among them are the sale of greeting cards, hosiery, lingerie, toiletries, kitchen ware, food products, brushes, book matches, advertising specialties, calendars, cleaning and polishing products, electrical appliances, and specialties of all kinds.

On many repeat-type products the salesperson may build up, over a period of time, a valuable regular clientele that will greatly simplify his sales effort and give him a steady, profitable part-time or full-time business. As regular customers are established, more and more orders may be taken by telephone; and as the salesperson and his products become known in a community, new customers and new sales volume will come his way through the recommendation of satisfied customers.

Opportunities for Students

Many of the forgoing projects are suitable for high school or college students who want to earn as they learn, such things, for example, as baby sitting, small livestock projects (where conditions permit), typing or telephone services, magazine subscriptions, amateur photography, silk-screen printing, selling, etc.

Other part-time services for which students are in popular demand are window washing, cleaning, lawn mowing, car washing and waxing, store deliveries, newspaper deliveries, Saturday and evening clerking, and restaurant or drugstore jobs.

Similar activities on a full-time basis are available to students in summer vacations. For older students there are full-time jobs in garages, stores, factories, newspaper offices, and printing plants. Many summer activities of an unusual nature, dependent upon local conditions and a student's special training or aptitude, will also present themselves.

Home Workshop Projects

The variety of home workshop products that may be made for profit is too extensive for detailed enumeration.

Woodworkers make hundreds of salable items such as lawn furniture, garden markers, doghouses, birdhouses, rustic furniture, miniature doll furniture, wall plaques, plane, boat, and railroad models, wood toys and puzzles, animal cutouts, wood carvings—all painted or decorated according to the worker's personal taste and skill.

Other home shopworkers specialize in such crafts as plastic molding, leather craft, metal craft, pottery craft, gourd craft, and metalizing baby shoes.

Women workers also have many well-paid craft services from which to choose, such as making and repairing dolls; shell craft and felt craft; and making artificial flowers, "button gardens," and candles.

Men and women alike have found interest and profit in such projects as gem-cutting, basket-weaving, fly-tying, fashioning driftwood souvenirs, and making oriental "Ming" trees.

How and Where to Sell Products or Services

Quite as important to the homeworker as his creative ability and skill, if he would turn them into profit, is his facility in marketing his products or services.

In general, there are three main ways to sell products made at home: (1) through local department stores, gift shops, general stores, and other retail outlets that will take such products on consignment and sell them on commission (or sometimes by outright purchase at wholesale prices); (2) direct to the consumer through personal selling, telephone solicitation, or local newspaper advertising; and (3) by national-publication or direct-mail advertising to mail-order buyers.

Regardless of the method of selling, the home worker should learn to figure his costs accurately, in order to establish resale prices that will return a satisfactory profit for the time and effort expended. He must figure the costs of raw materials, interest on investment, transportation, telephone, advertising, postage, general sales expense, and incidentals. Then, after allowing himself a fair remuneration for time and skill in making the things he sells, he should add a fair percentage of operating profit.

Finally, if the worker is setting up the type of business that requires a license he should first check with state or municipal authorities and obtain the necessary clearance for his operation. License fees, if a license is required, are usually nominal for small business enterprises.

COMMERCIAL ARITHMETIC

Roman Numbers

In writing numbers according to the Roman system the following seven letters are used:

I	V	X	L	C	D	M
1	5	10	50	100	500	1000

There are a few principles which should be kept in mind in reading and writing Roman numbers.

Repeating a letter repeats its value. Thus, X=10; XX=20.

The value of a smaller letter written after a larger one is added to the larger value. Thus, X=10; XV=15.

The value of a smaller letter written before a larger one is subtracted from the larger one. Thus, X=10; IX=9.

A horizontal bar placed above a letter increases its value a thousand times. Thus, CX=110; $\overline{\text{CX}}$=110,000.

Fractions cannot be written in the Roman system. In fact, the value of the Roman system today is chiefly decorative, since it is used mainly on clock faces (where IIII is used instead of IV), cornerstones, fine title pages in books, etc.

Arabic Numbers

The Arabic system uses ten figures and a decimal point, as follows

0, 1, 2, 3, 4, 5, 6, 7, 8, 9, and .

With these any number can be written.

How To Read Numbers

Trillions	Hundred-billions	Ten-billions	Billions	Hundred-millions	Ten-millions	Millions	Hundred-thousands	Ten-thousands	Thousands	Hundreds	Tens	Units
6,	3	7	4,	9	8	5,	2	3	1,	4	0	6

The number is read, "Six trillions, three hundred and seventy-four billions, nine hundred and eighty-five millions, two hundred and thirty-one thousands, four hundred and six."

In this country and France a billion is a thousand millions (1,000,000,000).
In England and Germany a billion is a million millions (1,000,000,000,000).

Addition

There are 45 combinations possible with our primary numbers, that is, the numbers from 1 to 10. The first step toward quick and accurate addition is to memorize them perfectly.

```
1   1   1   1   1   1   1   1   1
1   2   3   4   5   6   7   8   9
-   -   -   -   -   -   -   -   --
2   3   4   5   6   7   8   9  10
    2   2   2   2   2   2   2   2
    2   3   4   5   6   7   8   9
    -   -   -   -   -   -   -   --
    4   5   6   7   8   9  10  11
        3   3   3   3   3   3   3
        3   4   5   6   7   8   9
        -   -   -   -   -   -   --
        6   7   8   9  10  11  12
            4   4   4   4   4   4
            4   5   6   7   8   9
            -   -   -   -   -   --
            8   9  10  11  12  13
                5   5   5   5   5
                5   6   7   8   9
                -   -   -   -   --
               10  11  12  13  14
                    6   6   6   6
                    6   7   8   9
                    -   -   -   --
                   12  13  14  15
                        7   7   7
                        7   8   9
                        -   -   --
                       14  15  16
                            8   8
                            8   9
                            -   --
                           16  17
                                9
                                9
                                --
                               18
```

Column Addition. In adding a column of figures, do not say 5 plus 6 is 11 plus 0, plus 3 is 14, etc., but simply state the result of each addition, as 11—14—23—25. It is preferable to put down the sum of each column instead of carrying from one column to another, since it makes the correction of errors easier. In checking, begin at the left column. Your answers should be first written on a piece of scrap paper and only the total result placed at the foot of the column.

```
         8972
         9869
         4523
         6750
         8976
         7865
        ------
        46955
           25    42
           33    46
           46    33
           42    25
        ------  ------
        46955   46955
```

Horizontal Addition. Numbers written horizontally, as in invoices, need not be rewritten in vertical columns before they are added, but it is important to be sure that the units added together are of the same order. For example:

$$654+345+13+22+1704=2738$$

Bankers' or Civil Service Addition. In adding each column the number to be carried is added into the next sum. Like the above method, of which this is a variation, this can be interrupted, and yet the one who is doing the adding can take it up at the point where he left off without having to go back to the beginning.

```
2679.50
 188.75
   2.38
5463.44
 234.25
-------
     22
     23
     28
     26
     15
      8
-------
8568.32
```

Subtraction

Subtraction by Addition.

```
5 4 3 8 2 1   minuend
2 9 6 5 7   subtrahend
-----------
5 1 4 1 6 4   ans.
```

Instead of subtracting, add to the subtrahend the number needed to equal the corresponding number in the minuend. In the example above, 4 plus 7 equal 11. Carry 1 and 6 plus 6 equal 12, and so on through the rest of the figures. This is a good way to check a subtraction.

Subtraction and Addition Together. If a column consists of certain numbers to be added and others to be subtracted, you may find it easier to add all the negative numbers in one column and all the positive numbers in another column and then subtract to find the difference between the two.

```
 5 7 8 2
—4 5 6
 4 4 1 4
—7 2 3 1
   1 5
-------
 2 5 2 4
```

Division

All even numbers are divisible by 2.

A number is divisible by 3 if the sum of its digits is divisible by 3. For example, 3,882. 3+8+8+2=21. Therefore 3,882 is divisible by 3.

A number is divisible by 4 if it ends in two ciphers or in two figures which are divisible by 4. For example, 8,724 is divisible by 4 but 9,862 is not, though 6+2=8 is divisible by 4.

A number ending in 0 or 5 is divisible by 5.

An even number is divisible by 6 if the sum of its digits is divisible by 3. For example, 5,424. 5+4+2+4=15. Therefore, 5,424 is divisible by 6.

7, 11, or 13 will divide 1,001 or any of its multiples, as 2,002, 6,006, 12,012, etc.

A number is divisible by 8 if it ends in three ciphers or in three digits forming a number divisible by 8, as 154,000 or 543,816.

A number is divisible by 9 if the sum of its digits is divisible by 9. For example, 2,592. 2+5+9+2=18. Therefore, 2,592 is divisible by 9.

A number ending in 0 is divisible by 10.

A number ending in 00, 50, or 75 is divisible by 25.

A number ending in 000 is divisible by 125.

A factor of a given number is a number by which the given number is exactly divisible. For example, 4 is a factor of 16, 3 of 27, etc. The factor of a number is also a factor of all multiples of that number. Thus, 3 is a factor of 9. It is, therefore, a factor also of 18, 27, 36, 45, etc.

Multiplication

To multiply by 10, 100, etc., add as many ciphers to the multiplicand as there are in the multiplier.

The multiplicand is the number to be multiplied. The multiplier is, of course, the number by which it is to be multiplied.

To multiply by 5, 50, 500, etc., add as many ciphers to the multiplicand as there are figures in the multiplier and divide the result by 2.

To multiply by 25, 250, etc., multiply by 100, 1,000, etc., and divide the result by 4.

To multiply by any number ending in 9, multiply by the next higher number and then subtract the multiplicand.

Example. Multiply 26×49: 26×50=1,300—26=1,274.

To multiply any number of two figures by 11, write the sum of the two figures between them.

Example. Multiply 54×11. 5+4=9. Hence 594 is the answer.

If the sum of the two numbers is 10 or over add the 1 to the left-hand figure. Thus, multiply 88×11. 8+8=16. Hence, 968 is the answer.

To square any number of 9's. Beginning at the left, write 9 as many times less 1 as there are 9's in the given number, an 8, as many ciphers as 9's and 1.

Example. The square of 99=9,801, of 999=998,001

To multiply by 1¼, add 0 and divide by 8.

To multiply by 1⅔, add 0 and divide by 6.

To multiply by 2½, add 0 and divide by 4.

To multiply by 3⅓, add 0 and divide by 3.

To multiply by 5, add 0 and divide by 2.

To multiply by 6¼, add 00 and divide by 16.
To multiply by 8⅓, add 00 and divide by 12.
To multiply by 12½, add 00 and divide by 8.
To multiply by 16⅔, add 00 and divide by 6.
To multiply by 25, add 00 and divide by 4.
To multiply by 33⅓, add 00 and divide by 3.
To multiply by 50, add 00 and divide by 2.
To multiply by 66⅔, add 000 and divide by 15.
To multiply by 83⅓, add 000 and divide by 12.
To multiply by 125, add 000 and divide by 8.
To multiply by 166⅔, add 000 and divide by 6.
To multiply by 250, add 000 and divide by 4.
To multiply by 333⅓, add 000 and divide by 3.
To multiply by 7½, add 0 and subtract ¼ of that result.
To multiply by 11¼, add 0 and then add ⅛ of that result.
To multiply by 13⅓, add 0 and then add ⅓ of that result.
To multiply by 75, add 00, divide by 4, and multiply the result by 3.

Handy Multiplication and Division Tables

Most people find it convenient to know the multiplication tables by heart through 12×12. The pyramid shown on page 242 gives the tables in handy form through 25×25. The number in heavy type at the left is the multiplicand, the number just below the line is the multiplier, and the number just below the multiplier is the result. For instance, 2×2=4; 3×2=6; 3×3=9; and so on through 25×25=625. Every multiplication table is also, of course, a division table, if it is read backward. To find how many times the number in heavy type at the left will go into a given number, find the number on the lower line and read the number just above it. Thus, to find how many times 24 is contained in 408, find the heavy-type 24, run along the line until you reach 408, then read the number just above it, 17.

Here is another table, much like the one on page 242, except that the arrangement is slightly different. The one to use is the one you find easier to read.

1	2	3	4	5	6	7	8	9	10
2	4	6	8	10	12	14	16	18	20
3	6	9	12	15	18	21	24	27	30
4	8	12	16	20	24	28	32	36	40
5	10	15	20	25	30	35	40	45	50
6	12	18	24	30	36	42	48	54	60
7	14	21	28	35	42	49	56	63	70
8	16	24	32	40	48	56	64	72	80
9	18	27	36	45	54	63	72	81	90
10	20	30	40	50	60	70	80	90	100
11	22	33	44	55	66	77	88	99	110
12	24	36	48	60	72	84	96	108	120
13	26	39	52	65	78	91	104	117	130
14	28	42	56	70	84	98	112	126	140
15	30	45	60	75	90	105	120	135	150
16	32	48	64	80	96	112	128	144	160
17	34	51	68	85	102	119	136	153	170
18	36	54	72	90	108	126	144	162	180
19	38	57	76	95	114	133	152	171	190
20	40	60	80	100	120	140	160	180	200
21	42	63	84	105	126	147	168	189	210
22	44	66	88	110	132	154	176	198	220
23	46	69	92	115	138	161	184	207	230
24	48	72	96	120	144	168	192	216	240
25	50	75	100	125	150	175	200	225	250
26	52	78	104	130	156	182	208	234	260

1	2	3	4	5	6	7	8	9	10
27	54	81	108	135	162	189	216	243	270
28	56	84	112	140	168	196	224	252	280
29	58	87	116	145	174	203	232	261	290
30	60	90	120	150	180	210	240	270	300
31	62	93	124	155	186	217	248	279	310
32	64	96	128	160	192	224	256	288	320
33	66	99	132	165	198	231	264	297	330
34	68	102	136	170	204	238	272	306	340
35	70	105	140	175	210	245	280	315	350
36	72	108	144	180	216	252	288	324	360
37	74	111	148	185	222	259	296	333	370
38	76	114	152	190	228	266	304	342	380
39	78	117	156	195	234	273	312	351	390
40	80	120	160	200	240	280	320	360	400
41	82	123	164	205	246	287	328	369	410
42	84	126	168	210	252	294	336	378	420
43	86	129	172	215	258	301	344	387	430
44	88	132	176	220	264	308	352	396	440
45	90	135	180	225	270	315	360	405	450
46	92	138	184	230	276	322	368	414	460
47	94	141	188	235	282	329	376	423	470
48	96	144	192	240	288	336	384	432	480
49	98	147	196	245	294	343	392	441	490
50	100	150	200	250	300	350	400	450	500

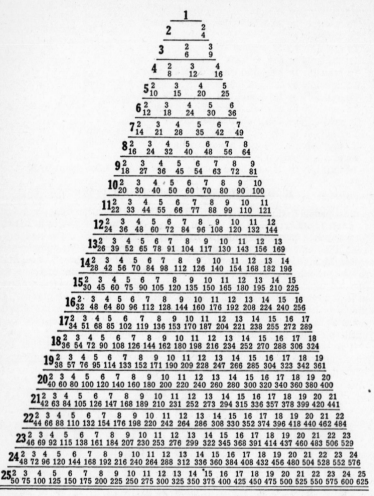

Handy Multiplication and Division Table

The Check of Nines

Addition. Add the figures in each number horizontally and divide each result by 9. Add all the remainders and divide by 9. Then add horizontally the figures in the answer, divide by 9, and compare the remainder here with the remainder from the sum of the remainders. For example:

		Remainders	
2 6 8 1	2+6+8+1=17	8	(Since 9 goes
4 7 5 2	9		into 17 only
8 3 3 9	4+7+5+2=18	0	once with 8
3 6 2 6	9		left over)
1 9 3 9 8	8+3+3+9=23	5	
	9		
	3+6+2+6=17	8	
	9	21=3	
		9	
	1+9+3+9+8=30=3		
	9		

Subtraction. Think of the minuend (see page 239) as the sum of the subtrahend and the remainder, and proceed as in addition.

Multiplication. Find the remainders in the multiplicand and the multiplier. Multiply these remainders and then find the remainder of the product. This should be the same as the remainder of the product of the two numbers. For example:

7 6 4	7+6+4=17	8
3 5	9	
2 6 7 4 0	3+5=8	8
	9	64=1
		9
	2+6+7+4+0=19=1	
	9	

Division. Think of the dividend as the product of the quotient and the divisor, and proceed as in multiplication.

Fractions

A fraction is a part of a unit.

There are two ways of writing fractions: ½ is a **common fraction**; .5 is a **decimal fraction.** In the common fraction any number may be the denominator; in the decimal fraction the denominator is 10 or some multiple of 10.

The decimal may be written .5, .6, .7, or 0.5, 0.6, 0.7, etc. The latter is safer since it shows that no whole number has been accidentally omitted before the decimal. This form is used by everyone who makes a great number of mathematical calculations.

A *proper fraction* is one which has a numerator smaller than its denominator, *e.g.*, $\frac{2}{3}$. An improper fraction is one with a numerator larger than the denominator, *e.g.*, $\frac{7}{4}$. A *mixed number* is a whole number and a fraction, *e.g.*, $14\frac{2}{5}$.

A fraction is said to be reduced to its lowest terms when the numerator and the denominator cannot both be evenly divided by any whole number except 1. $\frac{72}{80}$ reduced to its lowest terms$=\frac{9}{10}$. The practical value of this is that $\frac{9}{10}$ is much easier to work with than $\frac{72}{80}$.

Decimal fractions cannot usually be reduced to lower terms. As decimals, .5 and .025 cannot be reduced further; both, however, can be changed to common fractions and then reduced: $\frac{5}{10}=\frac{1}{2}$ and $\frac{25}{1000}=\frac{1}{40}$.

An improper fraction may be reduced to a mixed number by dividing the numerator by the denominator. Thus, $\frac{95}{50}=1\frac{9}{10}$.

A mixed number may be reduced to an improper fraction by multiplying together the whole number and the denominator of the fraction and adding the numerator. Thus, $3\frac{5}{8}=\frac{29}{8}$. (In each unit there are $\frac{8}{8}$. Therefore, in three units there are $3\times8=24+$the $\frac{5}{8}$ we already have$=\frac{29}{8}$.)

A common fraction may be changed to a decimal by adding ciphers to the numerator and dividing by the denominator. Thus $\frac{1}{2}=1.00\div2=.50$. If the division is not even it should be carried out two places and the fraction retained, or, for all practical purposes, four places and the fraction thrown away. Thus, $\frac{2}{3}=.66\frac{2}{3}$ or .6666.

The denominator of a decimal is always 1, with as many ciphers after it as there are places in the decimal. Thus, $.5=\frac{5}{10}$; $.00005=\frac{5}{100000}$.

A *complex decimal, i.e.*, a decimal with a fraction, like $66\frac{2}{3}$, is changed into a common fraction in the same way as a simple decimal. It is simplest to forget the whole number and reduce the fraction as you would any ordinary fraction. Thus, $66\frac{2}{3}=66.6666$.

Mensuration

Mensuration is the process of measuring—length, area of surfaces, volume of solids—from data of lines and angles.

A *surface* is a figure which has only two dimensions, length and breadth.

A *quadrilateral* is a plane surface with four sides and four angles.

Quadrilateral

A quadrilateral with its opposite sides parallel is called a *parallelogram.*

Parallelograms

A parallelogram whose angles are right angles is a *rectangle.*

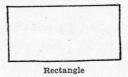

Rectangle

A rectangle with four equal sides is a *square.*

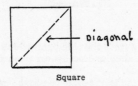

Square

A straight line drawn between opposite vertices of a quadrilateral is a *diagonal.*

The area of any parallelogram may be found by multiplying the base by the altitude.

Solid figures have three dimensions—length, breadth, and thickness.

A *prism* is a solid whose ends are congruent parallel plane figures and whose sides are parallelograms.

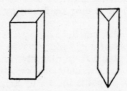

Prisms, Square and Triangular

A *cylinder* is a surface formed by one side of a rectangle rotated around the parallel side as an axis.

Cylinder

A *triangle* is a figure with three sides and three angles.

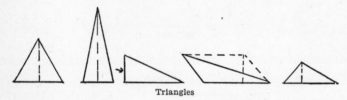

Triangles

The base of a plane figure is the side upon which it is supposed to stand. The altitude is a perpendicular line drawn from the base to the highest point on the opposite side.

The area of any triangle is one-half the base multiplied by the altitude.

The volume of a prism or of a cylinder may be found by multiplying the area of the base by the altitude. The result is expressed in *cubic* units—cu. in., cu. ft., etc., which may be reduced to bushels or any other measure of capacity.

Doubling the diameter of a pipe increases its capacity four times.

A *circle* is a plane figure enclosed by a curved line which is at all points the same distance from the center. A straight line drawn from the center of a circle to the circumference is the *radius*. The radius is one-half the length of the diameter. The circumference of a circle is found by multiplying the diameter by 3.1416. If measurements need not be exact, 3⅐ may be used instead. The diameter may, of course, be found by dividing the circumference by 3.1416; or it may be found by multiplying the circumference by .31831.

To find the area of a circle, multiply the square of the diameter by .7854.

To find the cubic contents of a cylinder or pipe, multiply the area by the height or depth. Thus, a pipe 1 ft. in diameter and 1 ft. in length contains .7854 cu. ft. To find how many gallons are contained in a pipe or cylinder, divide the cubic contents in cubic inches by 231, which is the number of cubic inches in a United States gallon.

CIRCUMFERENCES AND AREAS OF CIRCLES

Diameter	Circumference	Area	Diameter	Circumference	Area	Diameter	Circumference	Area	Diameter	Circumference	Area
1/32	.09817	.0008	17/32	1.66897	.2217	1- 1/16	3.33794	.8866	2- 1/16	6.47953	3.3410
1/16	.19635	.0031	9/16	1.76715	.2485	1- 1/8	3.53429	.9940	2- 1/8	6.67588	3.5466
3/32	.29452	.0069	19/32	1.86532	.2769	1- 3/16	3.73064	1.1075	2- 3/16	6.87223	3.7583
1/8	.39270	.0123	5/8	1.96350	.3068	1- 1/4	3.92699	1.2272	2- 1/4	7.06858	3.9761
5/32	.49087	.0192	21/32	2.06167	.3382	1- 5/16	4.12334	1.3530	2- 5/16	7.26493	4.2000
3/16	.58905	.0276	11/16	2.15984	.3712	1- 3/8	4.31970	1.4849	2- 3/8	7.46128	4.4301
7/32	.68722	.0376	23/32	2.25802	.4057	1- 7/16	4.51604	1.6230	2- 7/16	7.65763	4.6664
1/4	.78540	.0491	3/4	2.35619	.4418	1- 1/2	4.71239	1.7671	2- 1/2	7.85398	4.9087
9/32	.88357	.0621	25/32	2.45437	.4794	1- 9/16	4.90874	1.9175	2- 9/16	8.05033	5.1572
5/16	.98175	.0767	13/16	2.55254	.5185	1- 5/8	5.10509	2.0739	2- 5/8	8.24668	5.4119
11/32	1.07992	.0928	27/32	2.65072	.5591	1-11/16	5.30144	2.2365	2-11/16	8.44303	5.6727
3/8	1.17810	.1105	7/8	2.74889	.6013	1- 3/4	5.49779	2.4053	2- 3/4	8.63938	5.9396
13/32	1.27627	.1296	29/32	2.84707	.6450	1-13/16	5.69414	2.5802	2-13/16	8.83573	6.2126
7/16	1.37444	.1503	15/16	2.94524	.6903	1- 7/8	5.89049	2.7612	2- 7/8	9.03208	6.4918
15/32	1.47262	.1726	31/32	3.04342	.7371	1-15/16	6.08684	2.9483	2-15/16	9.22843	6.7771
1/2	1.57080	.1964	1	3.14159	.7854	2	6.28319	3.1416	3	9.42478	7.0686

A *square* is a parallelogram having four equal sides and four right angles. A square is equal in area to a circle when the side of the square equals 0.88623 multiplied by the diameter of the circle, or when the diameter of the circle equals 1.12838 multiplied by the side of the square.

The surface of a ball may be found by multiplying the square of the diameter by 3.1416. The cubic inches in a ball may be found by multiplying the cube of the diameter by .5236.

The distance around any plane figure is the *perimeter*.

The extent of surface inside a plane figure is the *area*. It is expressed in square units—sq. inches, sq. yards, sq. rods, etc.

Example.—Find the number of acres in a plot 36 rd. by 48 rd. How much fence would be needed to enclose it?

$$36 \text{ rd.} \times 48 \text{ rd.} = 1,728 \text{ sq. rd.}$$
$$1,728 \text{ sq. rd.} \div 160 \text{ (No. sq. rd. in one acre)} = 10\% \text{ acres.}$$

To find the amount of fence needed we simply find the perimeter.

$$2 \times (36 + 48) = 168 \text{ rds.}$$

Squares and Cubes

The *square* of a number is the result obtained when the number is multiplied by itself. Thus, $2 \times 2 = 4$. Four is the square; two is the square root.

The *cube* of a number is the result obtained when the number is multiplied by itself three times. Thus, $2 \times 2 \times 2 = 8$. Eight is the cube, two is the cube root.

The *root* of a number is one of the equal factors of that number. Thus, 4 is a root of 16; 3 is a root of 243.

This sign, $(\sqrt{\ \ })$, called the *radical sign,* denotes that the root of a number is to be found.

$\sqrt{196}$ indicates that the square root of 196 is to be found.

$\sqrt[3]{216}$ indicates that the cube root of 216 is to be found.

The number of times a number is to be multiplied by itself is indicated by a small number written above it to the right, thus, 10^5, 25^3, 40^{15}. This small number is called the *exponent*.

SQUARES, SQUARE ROOTS, CUBES, AND CUBE ROOTS OF NOS. 1 TO 100

No.	Sq.	Cube	Square Root	Cube Root	No.	Sq.	Cube	Square Root	Cube Root	No.	Sq.	Cube	Square Root	Cube Root
0.1	0.01	0.001	0.316	0.464	23	529	12167	4.795	2.843	63	3969	250047	7.937	3.979
.15	0.022	0.003	0.387	0.531	24	576	13824	4.899	2.884	64	4096	262144	8.000	4.000
.2	0.04	0.008	0.447	0.585	25	625	15625	5.000	2.924	65	4225	274625	8.062	4.020
.25	0.062	0.015	0.500	0.630	26	676	17576	5.099	2.962	66	4356	287496	8.124	4.041
.3	0.09	0.027	0.548	0.669	27	729	19683	5.196	3.000	67	4489	300763	8.185	4.061
.35	0.122	0.042	0.592	0.705	28	784	21952	5.291	3.036	68	4624	314432	8.246	4.081
.4	0.16	0.064	0.633	0.737	29	841	24389	5.385	3.072	69	4761	328509	8.306	4.101
.45	0.202	0.091	0.671	0.766	30	900	27000	5.477	3.107	70	4900	343000	8.366	4.121
.5	0.25	0.125	0.707	0.794	31	961	29791	5.567	3.141	71	5041	357911	8.426	4.140
.55	0.302	0.166	0.742	0.819	32	1024	32768	5.656	3.174	72	5184	373248	8.485	4.160
.6	0.36	0.216	0.775	0.843	33	1089	35937	5.744	3.207	73	5320	389017	8.544	4.179
.65	0.422	0.274	0.806	0.866	34	1156	39304	5.831	3.239	74	5476	405224	8.602	4.198
.7	0.49	0.343	0.837	0.888	35	1225	42875	5.916	3.271	75	5625	421875	8.660	4.217
.75	0.562	0.421	0.866	0.909	36	1296	46656	6.000	3.301	76	5776	438976	8.717	4.235
.8	0.64	0.512	0.894	0.928	37	1369	50653	6.082	3.332	77	5929	456533	8.775	4.254
.85	0.722	0.614	0.922	0.947	38	1444	54872	6.164	3.362	78	6084	474552	8.831	4.272
.9	0.81	0.729	0.949	0.965	39	1521	59319	6.245	3.391	79	6241	493039	8.888	4.290
.95	0.902	0.857	0.975	0.983	40	1600	64000	6.324	3.420	80	6400	512000	8.944	4.308
1	1.000	1.000	1.000	1.000	41	1681	68921	6.403	3.448	81	6561	531441	9.000	4.326
2	4	8	1.414	1.259	42	1764	74088	6.480	3.476	82	6724	551368	9.055	4.344
3	9	27	1.732	1.442	43	1849	79507	6.557	3.503	83	6889	571787	9.110	4.362
4	16	64	2.000	1.587	44	1936	85184	6.633	3.530	84	7056	592704	9.165	4.379
5	25	125	2.236	1.710	45	2025	91125	6.708	3.556	85	7225	614125	9.219	4.396
6	36	216	2.449	1.817	46	2116	97336	6.782	3.583	86	7396	636056	9.273	4.414
7	49	343	2.645	1.913	47	2209	103823	6.855	3.608	87	7569	658503	9.327	4.431
8	64	512	2.828	2.000	48	2304	110592	6.928	3.634	88	7744	681472	9.380	4.448
9	81	729	3.000	2.080	49	2401	117649	7.000	3.659	89	7921	704969	9.434	4.464
10	100	1000	3.162	2.154	50	2500	125000	7.071	3.684	90	8100	729000	9.486	4.481
11	121	1331	3.316	2.224	51	2601	132651	7.141	3.708	91	8281	753571	9.539	4.497
12	144	1728	3.464	2.289	52	2704	140608	7.211	3.732	92	8464	778688	9.591	4.514
13	169	2197	3.605	2.351	53	2809	148877	7.280	3.756	93	8649	804357	9.643	4.530
14	196	2744	3.741	2.410	54	2916	157464	7.348	3.779	94	8836	830584	9.695	4.546
15	225	3375	3.873	2.466	55	3025	166375	7.416	3.803	95	9025	857375	9.746	4.562
16	256	4096	4.000	2.519	56	3136	175616	7.483	3.825	96	9216	884736	9.798	4.578
17	289	4913	4.123	2.571	57	3249	185193	7.549	3.848	97	9409	912673	9.848	4.594
18	324	5832	4.242	2.620	58	3364	195112	7.615	3.870	98	9604	941192	9.899	4.610
19	361	6859	4.358	2.668	59	3481	205379	7.681	3.893	99	9801	970299	9.949	4.626
20	400	8000	4.472	2.714	60	3600	216000	7.746	3.914	100	10000	1000000	10.000	4.641

The Slide Rule

For making rapid calculations which involve multiplication, division, ratios, square roots, cube roots, squares, cubes, etc., the slide rule offers a quick and easy method. The ten-inch rule is the standard size in general use. Directions come with the rule, which can be operated after a little practice by anyone familiar with decimal fractions. Results obtained from the slide rule are not as accurate as results obtained by hand, but they are good for most practical purposes. Answers obtained with the ten-inch rule are correct to three and sometimes four figures. The rule is invaluable to engineers, mechanics, architects, etc. Estimators and accountants can make quick calculations sufficiently accurate to check all major errors. The rule furnishes an easy way to check reports and is, in fact, indispensable to anyone who makes use of any branch of applied mathematics involving the processes mentioned above. The slide rule will not add or subtract.

Multipliers for Key-operated Machines

In making calculations with key-operated machines the following multipliers are to be used:

In converting

square inches to square feet	multiply by 0.00695
square feet to square yards	" by 0.1111
cubic inches to cubic feet	" by 0.00053
cubic feet to cubic yards	" by 0.03704
cubic feet to gallons	" by 7.48224
cubic feet to feet board measure	" by 12.0
cubic inches to gallons	" by 0.00433
cubic inches to feet board measure	" by 0.00695
cubic inches to pounds steel	" by 0.284
cubic inches to pounds iron	" by 0.261
cubic inches to pounds copper	" by 0.319

Lumber: Width in inches × breadth in inches × length in feet × 0.08333 = feet board measure.

Steel: Width in inches × breadth in inches × length in feet × 3.40 = pounds.

Interest

Interest is money paid for the use of money. Throughout the United States and her territories, and, indeed, in most civilized countries, the amount of interest that can be charged is regulated by law.

If more interest than the law allows is required by the money lender it is called usurious interest. Professional money lenders, however, have many ways of evading the usury laws. In some instances they charge a bonus for the loan but the bonus does not appear in the official record. In others, they demand that a certain amount of the loan remain on deposit, which means that the borrower actually gets a much smaller sum than the one upon which he is paying interest.

INTEREST LAWS IN THE UNITED STATES AND SOME OF HER TERRITORIES AND POSSESSIONS (1950)

State	Interest Rate		State	Interest Rate		State	Interest Rate		State	Interest Rate	
	Legal Rate	Contract Rate		Legal Rate	Contract Rate		Legal Rate	Contract Rate		Legal Rate	Contract Rate
	Per Ct.	Per Ct.		Per Ct.	Per Ct.		Per Ct.	Per Ct.		Per Ct.	Per Ct.
Ala...	6	8	Ill....	5	7	Mont..	6	10	P. Rico		
Alaska.	6	8	Ind ...	6	8	Neb...	6	9	R. I...	6	
Ariz...	6	8	Iowa ..	5	7	Nev...	7	12	S. C...	6	7
Ark...	6	10	Kan...	6	10	N. H...	6	Any rate	S. D...	6	8
Cal...	7	10	Ky....	6	6	N. J...	6	6	Tenn..	6	6
Col...	6	Any rate	La....	5	8	N. M...	6	12	Tex...	6	10
Conn..	6	12	Maine..	6	Any rate	N. Y...	6	6	Utah..	6	12
Del...	6	6	Md....	6	6	N. C...	6	6	Vt....	6	6
D of C.	6	8	Mass..	6	Any rate	N. D...	4	7	Va....	6	6
Fla...	6	10	Mich..	5	7	Ohio..	6	8	Wash..	6	12
Ga....	7	8	Minn..	6	8	Okla...	6	10	W. Va.	6	6
Hawaii.	8	12	Miss..	6	8	Ore...	6	10	Wis...	6	10
Idaho..	6	8	Mo....	6	8	Pa....	6	6	Wyo...	7	10

By contract rate is meant the maximum rate, except for pawnbrokers' loans.

Interest Tables

Tables showing Simple Interest[1]

Showing the amount of interest $1.00 from one day to 120 days at various rates. To use the table, find the interest on $1.00 for the specified number of days, then multiply it by the number of dollars to be borrowed. For example, to find the interest on $200 for 60 days, at 6 per cent, find the interest on $1.00 at 6 per cent, for 60 days. The table shows that this is .009863. Multiply by 200 and you have $1.97, which is the amount of interest that will be charged.

---

[1]By courteous permission of the Lefax Corporation, Philadelphia.

Days	2%	2½%	3%	3¼%	3½%	3¾%	4%	4¼%	4½%	Days
1	.000055	.000068	.000082	.000089	.000096	.000103	.000110	.000116	.000123	1
2	.000110	.000137	.000164	.000178	.000192	.000205	.000219	.000233	.000247	2
3	.000164	.000205	.000247	.000267	.000288	.000308	.000329	.000349	.000370	3
4	.000219	.000274	.000329	.000356	.000384	.000411	.000438	.000466	.000493	4
5	.000274	.000342	.000411	.000445	.000479	.000514	.000548	.000582	.000616	5
6	.000329	.000411	.000493	.000534	.000575	.000616	.000658	.000699	.000740	6
7	.000384	.000479	.000575	.000623	.000671	.000719	.000767	.000815	.000863	7
8	.000438	.000548	.000658	.000712	.000767	.000822	.000877	.000932	.000986	8
9	.000493	.000616	.000740	.000801	.000863	.000925	.000986	.001048	.001110	9
10	.000548	.000685	.000822	.000890	.000959	.001027	.001096	.001164	.001233	10
11	.000603	.000753	.000904	.000979	.001055	.001130	.001205	.001281	.001356	11
12	.000658	.000822	.000986	.001068	.001151	.001233	.001315	.001397	.001479	12
13	.000712	.000890	.001068	.001158	.001247	.001336	.001425	.001514	.001603	13
14	.000767	.000959	.001151	.001247	.001342	.001438	.001534	.001630	.001726	14
15	.000822	.001028	.001233	.001336	.001438	.001541	.001644	.001747	.001849	15
16	.000877	.001096	.001315	.001425	.001534	.001644	.001753	.001863	.001973	16
17	.000932	.001164	.001397	.001514	.001630	.001747	.001863	.001979	.002096	17
18	.000986	.001233	.001479	.001603	.001726	.001849	.001973	.002096	.002219	18
19	.001041	.001301	.001562	.001692	.001822	.001952	.002082	.002212	.002342	19
20	.001096	.001370	.001644	.001781	.001918	.002055	.002192	.002329	.002466	20
21	.001151	.001438	.001726	.001870	.002014	.002158	.002301	.002445	.002589	21
22	.001205	.001507	.001808	.001959	.002110	.002260	.002411	.002562	.002712	22
23	.001260	.001575	.001890	.002048	.002205	.002363	.002521	.002678	.002836	23
24	.001315	.001644	.001973	.002137	.002301	.002466	.002630	.002795	.002959	24
25	.001370	.001712	.002055	.002226	.002397	.002568	.002740	.002911	.003082	25
26	.001425	.001781	.002137	.002315	.002493	.002671	.002849	.003027	.003205	26
27	.001479	.001849	.002219	.002404	.002589	.002774	.002959	.003144	.003329	27
28	.001534	.001918	.002301	.002493	.002685	.002877	.003068	.003260	.003452	28
29	.001589	.001986	.002384	.002582	.002781	.002979	.003178	.003377	.003575	29
30	.001644	.002055	.002466	.002671	.002877	.003082	.003288	.003493	.003699	30
31	.001699	.002133	.002548	.002760	.002973	.003185	.003397	.003610	.003822	31
32	.001753	.002192	.002630	.002849	.003068	.003288	.003507	.003726	.003945	32
33	.001808	.002260	.002712	.002938	.003164	.003390	.003616	.003842	.004068	33
34	.001863	.002329	.002795	.003027	.003260	.003493	.003726	.003959	.004192	34
35	.001918	.002397	.002877	.003116	.003356	.003596	.003836	.004075	.004315	35
36	.001973	.002466	.002959	.003205	.003452	.003699	.003945	.004192	.004438	36
37	.002027	.002534	.003041	.003295	.003548	.003801	.004055	.004308	.004562	37
38	.002082	.002603	.003123	.003384	.003644	.003904	.004164	.004425	.004685	38
39	.002137	.002671	.003205	.003473	.003740	.004007	.004274	.004541	.004808	39
40	.002192	.002740	.003288	.003562	.003836	.004110	.004384	.004658	.004932	40
41	.002247	.002808	.003370	.003651	.003932	.004212	.004493	.004774	.005055	41
42	.002301	.002877	.003452	.003740	.004027	.004315	.004603	.004890	.005178	42
43	.002356	.002945	.003534	.003829	.004123	.004418	.004712	.005007	.005301	43
44	.002411	.003014	.003616	.003918	.004219	.004521	.004822	.005123	.005425	44
45	.002466	.003082	.003699	.004007	.004315	.004623	.004932	.005240	.005548	45
46	.002521	.003151	.003781	.004096	.004411	.004726	.005041	.005356	.005671	46
47	.002575	.003219	.003863	.004185	.004507	.004829	.005150	.005473	.005795	47
48	.002630	.003288	.003945	.004274	.004603	.004932	.005260	.005589	.005918	48
49	.002685	.003356	.004027	.004363	.004699	.005034	.005370	.005705	.006041	49
50	.002740	.003425	.004110	.004452	.004795	.005137	.005479	.005822	.006164	50
51	.002795	.003493	.004192	.004541	.004890	.005240	.005589	.005938	.006288	51
52	.002849	.003562	.004274	.004630	.004986	.005342	.005699	.006055	.006411	52
53	.002904	.003630	.004356	.004719	.005082	.005445	.005808	.006171	.006534	53
54	.002959	.003699	.004438	.004808	.005178	.005548	.005918	.006288	.006658	54
55	.003014	.003767	.004521	.004897	.005274	.005651	.006027	.006404	.006781	55
56	.003068	.003836	.004603	.004986	.005370	.005753	.006137	.006521	.006904	56
57	.003123	.003904	.004685	.005075	.005466	.005856	.006247	.006637	.007027	57
58	.003178	.003973	.004767	.005164	.005562	.005959	.006356	.006753	.007151	58
59	.003233	.004041	.004849	.005253	.005658	.006062	.006466	.006870	.007274	59
60	.003288	.004110	.004932	.005342	.005753	.006164	.006575	.006986	.007397	60

Days	2%	2½%	3%	3¼%	3½%	3¾%	4%	4¼%	4½%	Days
61	.003342	.004178	.005014	.005432	.005849	.006267	.006685	.007103	.007521	61
62	.003397	.004247	.005096	.005521	.005945	.006370	.006795	.007219	.007644	62
63	.003452	.004315	.005178	.005610	.006041	.006473	.006904	.007336	.007767	63
64	.003507	.004384	.005260	.005699	.006137	.006575	.007014	.007452	.007890	64
65	.003562	.004452	.005342	.005788	.006233	.006678	.007123	.007568	.008014	65
66	.003616	.004521	.005425	.005877	.006329	.006781	.007233	.007685	.008137	66
67	.003671	.004589	.005507	.005966	.006425	.006884	.007342	.007801	.008260	67
68	.003726	.004658	.005589	.006055	.006521	.006986	.007452	.007918	.008384	68
69	.003781	.004726	.005671	.006144	.006616	.007089	.007562	.008034	.008507	69
70	.003836	.004795	.005753	.006233	.006712	.007192	.007671	.008151	.008630	70
71	.003890	.004863	.005836	.006322	.006808	.007295	.007781	.008267	.008753	71
72	.003945	.004932	.005918	.006411	.006904	.007397	.007890	.008384	.008877	72
73	.004000	.005000	.006000	.006500	.007000	.007500	.007999	.008500	.009000	73
74	.004055	.005068	.006082	.006589	.007096	.007603	.008110	.008616	.009123	74
75	.004109	.005137	.006164	.006678	.007192	.007705	.008219	.008733	.009247	75
76	.004164	.005205	.006247	.006767	.007288	.007808	.008229	.008849	.009370	76
77	.004219	.005274	.006329	.006856	.007384	.007911	.008438	.008966	.009493	77
78	.004274	.005342	.006411	.006945	.007479	.008014	.008548	.009082	.009616	78
79	.004329	.005411	.006493	.007034	.007575	.008116	.008658	.009199	.009740	79
80	.004384	.005479	.006575	.007123	.007671	.008219	.008767	.009315	.009863	80
81	.004438	.005548	.006658	.007212	.007767	.008322	.008877	.009432	.009986	81
82	.004493	.005616	.006740	.007301	.007863	.008425	.008986	.009548	.010110	82
83	.004548	.005685	.006822	.007390	.007959	.008527	.009096	.009664	.010233	83
84	.004603	.005753	.006904	.007479	.008055	.008630	.009205	.009781	.010356	84
85	.004658	.005822	.006986	.007568	.008151	.008733	.009315	.009897	.010497	85
86	.004712	.005890	.007068	.007658	.008247	.008836	.009425	.010014	.010603	86
87	.004767	.005959	.007151	.007747	.008342	.008938	.009534	.010130	.010726	87
88	.004822	.006027	.007233	.007836	.008438	.009041	.009644	.010247	.010849	88
89	.004877	.006096	.007315	.007925	.008534	.009144	.009753	.010363	.010973	89
90	.004932	.006164	.007397	.008014	.008630	.009247	.009863	.010479	.011096	90
91	.004987	.006232	.007479	.008103	.008726	.009350	.009972	.010595	.011219	91
92	.005041	.006301	.007561	.008192	.008822	.009452	.010082	.010712	.011343	92
93	.005096	.006369	.007644	.008281	.008918	.009555	.010191	.010828	.011466	93
94	.005151	.006438	.007726	.008370	.009014	.009658	.010300	.010945	.011589	94
95	.005205	.006506	.007808	.008459	.009109	.009761	.010409	.011061	.011712	95
96	.005260	.006575	.007890	.008548	.009205	.009863	.010519	.011178	.011836	96
97	.005314	.006643	.007972	.008637	.009301	.009966	.010628	.011294	.011959	97
98	.005369	.006712	.008055	.008726	.009397	.010069	.010737	.011411	.012082	98
99	.005424	.006780	.008137	.008815	.009493	.010172	.010846	.011527	.012206	99
100	.005478	.006849	.008219	.008904	.009589	.010274	.010956	.011643	.012329	100
101	.005533	.006917	.008301	.008993	.009685	.010377	.011065	.011760	.012452	101
102	.005588	.006986	.008383	.009091	.009781	.010480	.011174	.011876	.012575	102
103	.005642	.007054	.008465	.009180	.009877	.010583	.011283	.011993	.012699	103
104	.005697	.007123	.008548	.009269	.009972	.010685	.011393	.012109	.012822	104
105	.005751	.007191	.008630	.009358	.010068	.010788	.011502	.012226	.012945	105
106	.005806	.007260	.008712	.009447	.010164	.010891	.011611	.012342	.013069	106
107	.005861	.007328	.008794	.009536	.010260	.010994	.011720	.012458	.013192	107
108	.005915	.007397	.008876	.009625	.010356	.011096	.011830	.012575	.013315	108
109	.005970	.007465	.008959	.009714	.010452	.011199	.011939	.012691	.013439	109
110	.006025	.007534	.009041	.009803	.010548	.011302	.012048	.012808	.013562	110
111	.006079	.007602	.009123	.009892	.010644	.011405	.012157	.012924	.013685	111
112	.006134	.007671	.009205	.009981	.010740	.011507	.012267	.013041	.013808	112
113	.006188	.007739	.009287	.010070	.010835	.011610	.012376	.013157	.013932	113
114	.006243	.007808	.009370	.010159	.010931	.011713	.012485	.013274	.014055	114
115	.006298	.007876	.009452	.010248	.011027	.011816	.012595	.013390	.014178	115
116	.006352	.007945	.009534	.010337	.011123	.011918	.012704	.013506	.014302	116
117	.006407	.008013	.009616	.010426	.011219	.012021	.012813	.013623	.014425	117
118	.006462	.008082	.009698	.010515	.011315	.012124	.012922	.013739	.014548	118
119	.006516	.008150	.009781	.010604	.011411	.012226	.013032	.013856	.014671	119
120	.006571	.008219	.009863	.010693	.011507	.012329	.013141	.013972	.014795	120

Days	4¾%	5%	5¼%	5½%	5¾%	6%	6½%	7%	8%	Days
1	.000130	.000137	.000144	.000151	.000158	.000164	.000178	.000192	.000219	1
2	.000260	.000274	.000288	.000301	.000315	.000329	.000356	.000384	.000438	2
3	.000390	.000411	.000432	.000452	.000473	.000493	.000534	.000575	.000658	3
4	.000521	.000548	.000575	.000603	.000630	.000658	.000712	.000767	.000877	4
5	.000651	.000685	.000719	.000753	.000788	.000822	.000890	.000959	.001096	5
6	.000781	.000822	.000863	.000904	.000945	.000986	.001068	.001151	.001315	6
7	.000911	.000959	.001007	.001055	.001103	.001151	.001247	.001342	.001534	7
8	.001041	.001096	.001151	.001205	.001260	.001315	.001425	.001534	.001753	8
9	.001171	.001233	.001295	.001356	.001418	.001479	.001603	.001726	.001973	9
10	.001301	.001370	.001438	.001507	.001575	.001644	.001781	.001918	.002192	10
11	.001432	.001507	.001582	.001658	.001733	.001808	.001959	.002110	.002411	11
12	.001562	.001644	.001726	.001808	.001890	.001973	.002137	.002301	.002630	12
13	.001692	.001781	.001870	.001959	.002048	.002137	.002315	.002493	.002849	13
14	.001822	.001918	.002014	.002110	.002205	.002301	.002493	.002685	.003068	14
15	.001952	.002055	.002158	.002260	.002363	.002466	.002671	.002877	.003288	15
16	.002082	.002192	.002301	.002411	.002521	.002630	.002849	.003068	.003507	16
17	.002212	.002329	.002445	.002562	.002678	.002795	.003027	.003260	.003726	17
18	.002342	.002466	.002589	.002712	.002836	.002959	.003205	.003452	.003945	18
19	.002473	.002603	.002733	.002863	.002993	.003123	.003384	.003644	.004164	19
20	.002603	.002740	.002877	.003014	.003151	.003288	.003562	.003836	.004384	20
21	.002733	.002877	.003021	.003164	.003308	.003452	.003740	.004027	.004603	21
22	.002863	.003014	.003164	.003315	.003466	.003616	.003918	.004219	.004822	22
23	.002993	.003151	.003308	.003466	.003623	.003781	.004096	.004411	.005041	23
24	.003123	.003288	.003452	.003616	.003781	.003945	.004274	.004603	.005260	24
25	.003253	.003425	.003596	.003767	.003938	.004110	.004452	.004795	.005479	25
26	.003384	.003562	.003740	.003918	.004096	.004274	.004630	.004986	.005699	26
27	.003514	.003699	.003884	.004068	.004253	.004438	.004808	.005178	.005918	27
28	.003644	.003836	.004027	.004219	.004411	.004603	.004986	.005370	.006137	28
29	.003774	.003973	.004171	.004370	.004568	.004767	.005164	.005562	.006356	29
30	.003904	.004110	.004315	.004521	.004726	.004932	.005342	.005753	.006575	30
31	.004034	.004247	.004459	.004671	.004884	.005096	.005521	.005945	.006795	31
32	.004164	.004384	.004603	.004822	.005041	.005260	.005699	.006137	.007014	32
33	.004295	.004521	.004747	.004973	.005199	.005425	.005877	.006329	.007233	33
34	.004425	.004658	.004890	.005123	.005356	.005589	.006055	.006521	.007452	34
35	.004555	.004795	.005034	.005274	.005514	.005753	.006233	.006712	.007671	35
36	.004685	.004932	.005178	.005425	.005671	.005918	.006411	.006904	.007890	36
37	.004815	.005068	.005322	.005575	.005829	.006082	.006589	.007096	.008110	37
38	.004945	.005205	.005466	.005726	.005986	.006247	.006767	.007288	.008329	38
39	.005075	.005342	.005610	.005877	.006144	.006411	.006945	.007479	.008548	39
40	.005205	.005479	.005753	.006027	.006301	.006575	.007123	.007671	.008767	40
41	.005336	.005616	.005897	.006178	.006459	.006740	.007301	.007863	.008986	41
42	.005466	.005753	.006041	.006329	.006616	.006904	.007479	.008055	.009205	42
43	.005596	.005890	.006185	.006479	.006774	.007068	.007658	.008247	.009425	43
44	.005726	.006027	.006329	.006630	.006932	.007233	.007836	.008438	.009644	44
45	.005856	.006164	.006473	.006781	.007089	.007397	.008014	.008630	.009863	45
46	.005986	.006301	.006616	.006932	.007247	.007562	.008192	.008822	.010082	46
47	.006116	.006438	.006760	.007082	.007404	.007726	.008370	.009014	.010301	47
48	.006247	.006575	.006904	.007233	.007562	.007890	.008548	.009205	.010521	48
49	.006377	.006712	.007048	.007384	.007719	.008055	.008726	.009397	.010740	49
50	.006507	.006849	.007192	.007534	.007877	.008219	.008904	.009589	.010959	50
51	.006637	.006986	.007336	.007685	.008034	.008384	.009082	.009781	.01178	51
52	.006767	.007123	.007479	.007836	.008192	.008548	.009260	.009973	.011397	52
53	.006897	.007260	.007623	.007986	.008349	.008712	.009438	.010164	.011616	53
54	.007027	.007397	.007767	.008137	.008507	.008877	.009616	.010356	.011836	54
55	.007158	.007534	.007911	.008288	.008664	.009041	.009795	.010548	.012055	55
56	.007288	.007671	.008055	.008438	.008822	.009205	.009973	.010740	.012274	56
57	.007418	.007808	.008199	.008589	.008979	.009370	.010151	.010932	.012493	57
58	.007548	.007945	.008342	.008740	.009137	.009534	.010329	.011123	.012712	58
59	.007678	.008082	.008486	.008890	.009295	.009699	.010507	.011315	.012932	59
60	.007808	.008219	.008630	.009041	.009452	.009863	.010685	.011507	.013151	60

Days	4¾%	5%	5¼%	5½%	5¾%	6%	6½%	7%	8%	Days
61	.007938	.008356	.008774	.009192	.009610	.010027	.010863	.011699	.013370	61
62	.008068	.008493	.008918	.009342	.009767	.010192	.011041	.011890	.013589	62
63	.008199	.008630	.009062	.009493	.009925	.010356	.011219	.012082	.013808	63
64	.008329	.008767	.009205	.009644	.010082	.010521	.011397	.012274	.014027	64
65	.008459	.008904	.009349	.009795	.010240	.010685	.011575	.012466	.014247	65
66	.008589	.009041	.009493	.009945	.010397	.010849	.011753	.012658	.014466	66
67	.008719	.009178	.009637	.010096	.010555	.011014	.011932	.012849	.014685	67
68	.008849	.009315	.009781	.010247	.010712	.011178	.012110	.013041	.014904	68
69	.008979	.009452	.009925	.010397	.010870	.011342	.012288	.013233	.015123	69
70	.009110	.009589	.010068	.010548	.011027	.011507	.012466	.013425	.015342	70
71	.009240	.009726	.010212	.010699	.011185	.011671	.012644	.013616	.015562	71
72	.009370	.009863	.010356	.010849	.011342	.011836	.012822	.013808	.015781	72
73	.009500	.010000	.010500	.011000	.011500	.012000	.013000	.014000	.016000	73
74	.009630	.010137	.010644	.011151	.011658	.012164	.013178	.014192	.016219	74
75	.009760	.010274	.010788	.011301	.011815	.012329	.013356	.014384	.016438	75
76	.009890	.010411	.010932	.011452	.011973	.012493	.013534	.014575	.016658	76
77	.010021	.010548	.011075	.011603	.012130	.012658	.013712	.014767	.016877	77
78	.010151	.010685	.011219	.011753	.012288	.012822	.013890	.014959	.017096	78
79	.010281	.010822	.011363	.011904	.012445	.012986	.014068	.015151	.017315	79
80	.010411	.010959	.011507	.012055	.012603	.013151	.014247	.015342	.017534	80
81	.010541	.011096	.011651	.012205	.012760	.013315	.014425	.015534	.017753	81
82	.010671	.011233	.011795	.012356	.012918	.013479	.014603	.015726	.017973	82
83	.010801	.011370	.011938	.012507	.013075	.013644	.014781	.015918	.018192	83
84	.010931	.011507	.012082	.012658	.013233	.013808	.014959	.016110	.018411	84
85	.011062	.011644	.012226	.012808	.013390	.013973	.015137	.016301	.018630	85
86	.011192	.011781	.012370	.012959	.013548	.014137	.015315	.016493	.018849	86
87	.011322	.011918	.012514	.013110	.013705	.014301	.015493	.016685	.019068	87
88	.011452	.012055	.012658	.013260	.013863	.014466	.015671	.016877	.019288	88
89	.011582	.012192	.012801	.013411	.014021	.014630	.015849	.017068	.019507	89
90	.011712	.012329	.012945	.013562	.014178	.014795	.016027	.017260	.019726	90
91	.011842	.012466	.013089	.013713	.014336	.014960	.016205	.017452	.019945	91
92	.011972	.012603	.013233	.013863	.014493	.015124	.016383	.017644	.020163	92
93	.012102	.012740	.013377	.014014	.014651	.015288	.016561	.017835	.020382	93
94	.012233	.012877	.013520	.014165	.014808	.015453	.016739	.018027	.020600	94
95	.012363	.013014	.013664	.014315	.014966	.015617	.016917	.018219	.020819	95
96	.012493	.013151	.013808	.014466	.015123	.015781	.017095	.018411	.021037	96
97	.012623	.013288	.013952	.014617	.015281	.015946	.017273	.018602	.021256	97
98	.012753	.013425	.014096	.014767	.015438	.016110	.017451	.018794	.021474	98
99	.012883	.013562	.014240	.014918	.015596	.016274	.017629	.018986	.021693	99
100	.013013	.013699	.014383	.015069	.015753	.016439	.017807	.019178	.021911	100
101	.013144	.013836	.014527	.015219	.015911	.016603	.017985	.019370	.022130	101
102	.013274	.013973	.014671	.015370	.016068	.016768	.018163	.019561	.022348	102
103	.013404	.014110	.014815	.015521	.016226	.016932	.018341	.019753	.022567	103
104	.013534	.014247	.014959	.015672	.016383	.017096	.018519	.019945	.022785	104
105	.013664	.014384	.015103	.015822	.016541	.017261	.018697	.020137	.023004	105
106	.013794	.014521	.015246	.015973	.016698	.017425	.018875	.020328	.023222	106
107	.013924	.014658	.015390	.016124	.016856	.017589	.019053	.020520	.023441	107
108	.014055	.014795	.015534	.016274	.017014	.017654	.019231	.020712	.023659	108
109	.014185	.014932	.015678	.016425	.017171	.017818	.019409	.020904	.023878	109
110	.014315	.015069	.015822	.016576	.017329	.017983	.019587	.021096	.024096	110
111	.014445	.015206	.015966	.016726	.017486	.018147	.019765	.021287	.024315	111
112	.014575	.015343	.016109	.016877	.017644	.018313	.019943	.021479	.024533	112
113	.014705	.015480	.016253	.017028	.017801	.018478	.020121	.021671	.024752	113
114	.014835	.015617	.016397	.017178	.017959	.018642	.020299	.021863	.024970	114
115	.014966	.015754	.016541	.017329	.018116	.018806	.020478	.022055	.025189	115
116	.015096	.015891	.016685	.017480	.018274	.018971	.020656	.022246	.025408	116
117	.015226	.016028	.016829	.017630	.018431	.019135	.020834	.022438	.025626	117
118	.015356	.016165	.016973	.017781	.018589	.019300	.021012	.022630	.025845	118
119	.015486	.016302	.017116	.017932	.018746	.019464	.021190	.022822	.026063	119
120	.015616	.016439	.017260	.018082	.018904	.019628	.021368	.023013	.026282	120

To Calculate Interest

Multiply the principal by the number of days, and

For	4	per cent,	divide	by	90	For	8	per cent,	divide by	45
"	5	"	"	"	72	"	9	"	" "	40
"	6	"	"	"	60	"	10	"	" "	36
"	7	"	"	"	52	"	12	"	" "	30

Example.—Find the interest on $600 for two months and two days at 4 per cent.

$$600 \times 62 = 37,200 \div 90 = \$4.13$$

To find the interest at 6 per cent for 60 days, simply move the decimal point two places to the left. For example, the interest on $500 for 60 days is $5.00. When the time is more or less than 60 days it is easy to find the rate for 60 days and then add or subtract, as the case may be.

For	120 days,	multiply by 2	For	30 days,	divide by	2
"	90 "	add ½ of itself	"	15 "	" "	4
"	75 "	" ¼ of itself	"	3 "	" "	20

Example.—Find the interest on $840 for 75 days.

Interest	for	60	days =	$8.40
Interest	for	15	days =	2.10
Interest	for	75	days =	10.50

The interest on any sum of money for any length of time may be calculated through the formulas below in which

P = Principal		R = Rate	
I = Interest		T = Time	

In order to find the interest when the principal, rate, and time are given

$$I = P \times R \times T$$

Example.—Find the interest on $2,000 for three years at 6 per cent.

$$I = 2,000 \times .06 \times 3 = \$360$$

In order to find the principal when interest, rate, and time are given

$$P = \frac{I}{R \times T}$$

Example.—Find the principal when the interest is $360, the rate 6 per cent, the time three years.

$$P = \frac{360.00}{.06 \times 3} = \$2,000$$

In order to find the rate when interest, principal, and time are given

$$R = \frac{I}{P \times T}$$

Example.—Find the rate of interest on $2,000 for three years when interest amounts to $360.

$$R = \frac{360}{2,000 \times 3} = .06 \ (\frac{6}{100} = 6 \text{ per cent})$$

In order to find the time when the interest, rate, and principal are given

$$T = \frac{I}{P \times R}$$

Example.—Find the time when the principal is $2,000, the interest $360, and the rate is 6 per cent.

$$T = \frac{360}{2,000 \times .06} = 3 \text{ years}$$

Compound Interest

If interest is withdrawn as soon as it falls due on a deposit, it is called simple interest. But if it is allowed to remain, interest and principal are added together (compounded) at regular intervals, which may be a year, six months, or any other time agreed upon. On a deposit of $100 at 6 per cent annually payable twice a year, simple interest would be $3.00 each payment while the same amount at compound interest would bring in the first four payments $3.00; $3.09; $3.18; and $3.28 respectively. At simple interest at 5 per cent a sum of money doubles itself in 20 years; at compound interest it doubles itself in 14⅕ years. Compound interest is usually paid on savings bank deposits. Life insurance premiums are figured out on the basis of compound interest and returns from bonds are reckoned by compound interest.

Time in Which Money Doubles at Interest

Rate	Simple Int.	Comp. Int. (Compounded yearly)	Rate	Simple Int.	Comp. Int. (Compounded yearly)
2	50 years.	35 years.	5	20 years.	14 yrs. 75 da.
2½	40 years.	28 yrs. 26 da.	6	16 yrs. 8 mo.	11 yrs. 327 da.
3	33 yrs. 4 mo.	23 yrs. 164 da.	7	14 yrs. 104 da.	10 yrs. 89 da.
3½	28 yrs. 208 da.	20 yrs. 54 da.	8	12½ years.	9 yrs. 2 days.
4	25 years.	17 yrs. 246 da.	9	11 yrs. 40 da.	8 yrs. 16 days.
4½	22 yrs. 81 da.	15 yrs. 273 da.	10	10 years.	7 yrs. 100 da.

Table of Daily Savings at Compound Interest

(Interest at 2 Percent Compounded Annually)

Saved per Day	Saved per Year	Saved in Ten Years	Saved in Fifty Years
$ .02¾	$ 10	$ 109	$ 846
.05¼	20	219	1,692
.11	40	438	3,383
.27½	100	1,095	8,458
.55	200	2,190	16,916
1.10	400	4,380	33,832
1.37	500	5,475	42,290

Table Showing Amount of $1.00 at Compound Interest in any Number of Years from One to Twenty-five

Subtract $1.00 from the amount in this table to find the interest.

Yr.	2 per cent	2½ per cent	8 per cent	3½ per cent	4 per cent	4½ per cent
1	1.0200 0000	1.0250 0000	1.0300 0000	1.0350 0000	1.0400 0000	1.0450 0000
2	1.0404 0000	1.0506 2500	1.0609 0000	1.0712 2500	1.0816 0000	1.0920 2500
3	1.0612 0800	1.0768 9062	1.0927 2700	1.1087 1787	1.1248 6400	1.1411 6612
4	1.0824 3216	1.1038 1239	1.1255 0881	1.1475 2300	1.1698 5856	1.1925 1860
5	1.1040 8080	1.1314 0821	1.1592 7407	1.1876 8631	1.2166 5290	1.2461 8194
6	1.1261 6242	1.1596 9342	1.1940 5230	1.2292 5533	1.2653 1902	1.3022 6012
7	1.1486 8567	1.1886 8575	1.2298 7387	1.2722 7926	1.3159 3178	1.3608 6183
8	1.1716 5938	1.2184 0290	1.2667 7008	1.3168 0904	1.3685 6905	1.4221 0061
9	1.1950 9257	1.2488 6297	1.3047 7318	1.3628 9735	1.4233 1181	1.4860 9514
10	1.2189 9442	1.2800 8454	1.3439 1638	1.4105 9876	1.4802 4428	1.5529 6942
11	1.2433 7431	1.3120 8666	1.3842 3387	1.4599 6972	1.5394 5406	1.6228 5305
12	1.2682 4179	1.3448 8882	1.4257 6089	1.5110 6866	1.6010 3222	1.6958 8143
13	1.2936 0663	1.3785 1104	1.4685 3371	1.5639 5606	1.6650 7351	1.7721 9610
14	1.3194 7876	1.4129 7382	1.5125 8972	1.6186 9452	1.7316 7645	1.8519 4492
15	1.3458 6834	1.4482 9817	1.5579 6742	1.6753 4883	1.8009 4351	1.9352 8244
16	1.3727 8570	1.4845 0562	1.6047 0644	1.7339 8604	1.8729 8125	2.0223 7015
17	1.4002 4142	1.5216 1826	1.6528 4763	1.7946 7555	1.9479 0050	2.1133 7681
18	1.4282 4625	1.5596 5872	1.7024 3306	1.8574 8920	2.0258 1652	2.2084 7877
19	1.4568 1117	1.5986 5019	1.7535 0605	1.9225 0132	2.1068 4918	2.3078 6031
20	1.4859 4740	1.6386 1644	1.8061 1123	1.9897 8886	2.1911 2314	2.4117 1402
21	1.5156 6634	1.6795 8185	1.8602 9457	2.0594 3147	2.2787 6807	2.5202 4116
22	1.5459 7967	1.7215 7140	1.9161 0341	2.1315 1158	2.3699 1879	2.6336 5201
23	1.5768 9926	1.7646 1068	1.9735 8651	2.2061 1448	2.4647 1555	2.7521 6635
24	1.6084 3725	1.8087 2595	2.0327 9411	2.2833 2849	2.5633 0417	2.8760 1383
25	1.6406 0599	1.8539 4410	2.0937 7793	2.3632 4498	2.6658 3633	3.0054 3446

Yr.	5 per cent	6 per cent	7 per cent	8 per cent	9 per cent	10 per cent
1	1.0500 000	1.0600 000	1.0700 000	1.0800 000	1.0900 000	1.1000 000
2	1.1025 000	1.1236 000	1.1449 000	1.1664 000	1.1881 000	1.2100 000
3	1.1576 250	1.1910 160	1.2250 430	1.2597 120	1.2950 290	1.3310 000
4	1.2155 063	1.2624 770	1.3107 960	1.3604 890	1.4115 816	1.4641 000
5	1.2762 816	1.3382 256	1.4025 517	1.4693 281	1.5386 240	1.6105 100
6	1.3400 956	1.4185 191	1.5007 304	1.5868 743	1.6771 001	1.7715 610
7	1.4071 004	1.5036 303	1.6057 815	1.7138 243	1.8280 391	1.9487 171
8	1.4774 554	1.5938 481	1.7181 862	1.8509 302	1.9925 626	2.1435 888
9	1.5513 282	1.6894 790	1.8384 592	1.9990 046	2.1718 933	2.3579 477
10	1.6288 946	1.7908 477	1.9671 514	2.1589 250	2.3673 637	2.5937 425
11	1.7103 394	1.8982 986	2.1048 520	2.3316 390	2.5804 264	2.8531 167
12	1.7958 563	2.0121 965	2.2521 916	2.5181 701	2.8126 648	3.1384 284
13	1.8856 491	2.1329 283	2.4098 450	2.7196 237	3.0658 046	3.4522 712
14	1.9799 316	2.2609 040	2.5785 342	2.9371 936	3.3417 270	3.7974 983
15	2.0789 282	2.3965 582	2.7590 315	3.1721 691	3.6424 825	4.1772 482
16	2.1828 746	2.5403 517	2.9521 638	3.4259 426	3.9703 059	4.5949 730
17	2.2920 183	2.6927 728	3.1588 152	3.7000 181	4.3276 334	5.0544 703
18	2.4066 192	2.8543 392	3.3799 323	3.9960 195	4.7171 204	5.5599 173
19	2.5269 502	3.0255 995	3.6165 275	4.3157 011	5.1416 613	6.1159 090
20	2.6532 977	3.2071 355	3.8696 845	4.6609 571	5.6044 108	6.7275 000
21	2.7859 626	3.3995 636	4.1405 624	5.0338 337	6.1088 077	7.4002 499
22	2.9252 607	3.6035 374	4.4304 017	5.4365 404	6.6586 004	8.1402 749
23	3.0715 238	3.8197 497	4.7405 299	5.8714 637	7.2578 745	8.9543 024
24	3.2250 999	4.0489 346	5.0723 670	6.3411 807	7.9110 832	9.8497 327
25	3.3863 549	4.2918 707	5.4274 326	6.8484 752	8.6230 807	10.8347 059

TABLE SHOWING AMOUNT OF $1.00 DEPOSITED ANNUALLY AT
COMPOUND INTEREST FOR ANY NUMBER OF YEARS
FROM ONE TO TWENTY-FIVE

Periods	2 per cent	3 per cent	4 per cent
1	1.02	1.03	1.04
2	2.0604	2.0909	2.1216
3	3.121608	3.183627	3.246464
4	4.204040	4.309136	4.416323
5	5.308121	5.468410	5.632975
6	6.434283	6.662462	6.898294
7	7.582969	7.892336	8.214226
8	8.754628	9.159106	9.582795
9	9.949721	10.463879	11.006107
10	11.168715	11.807796	12.486351
11	12.412090	13.192030	14.025805
12	13.680332	14.617790	15.626838
13	14.973938	16.086324	17.291911
14	16.293417	17.598914	19.023588
15	17.639285	19.156881	20.824531
16	19.012071	20.761588	22.697512
17	20.412312	22.414435	24.645413
18	21.840559	24.116868	26.671229
19	23.297370	25.870374	28.778079
20	24.783317	27.676486	30.969202
21	26.298984	29.536780	33.247970
22	27.844963	31.452884	35.617889
23	29.421862	33.426470	38.082604
24	31.030300	35.459264	40.645908
25	32.670906	37.553042	43.311745

Discounts

Chain Discounts

A *chain discount* (called also a compound discount) is a series of discounts, like 25 per cent and 10 per cent, or 25 per cent, 10 per cent, and 5 per cent. It is quite different from the sum of the discounts. Only the first, or primary discount is from the list price. The second, or secondary, discount is taken from what is left after the first discount has been taken. The third discount is taken from what is left after the second has been taken, and so on.

The tables on pages 259 and 260 give the net amounts of $1.00 after the chain discounts most commonly used in commercial transactions have been deducted.

To illustrate its use: Find the net amount of a bill of $345 discounted at 25–10–10–5 per cent. Look first in the horizontal column at the top for the primary discount of 25 per cent. Follow this column down until you are opposite the 10–10–5 in the column at the extreme left under the heading, Secondary Discount. You see then that the net amount of $1.00 after 25–10–10–5 per cent has been taken off is .57713. Multiply this by $345 and you have $199.11, which is the net amount of the bill.

TABLE OF CHAIN DISCOUNTS*

Secondary Discount	Primary Discount														
	5	7-1/2	10	12-1/2	15	16-2/3	20	22-1/2	25	27-1/2	30	32-1/2	33-1/3	35	37-1/2
2	.931	.9065	.882	.8575	.833	.81667	.784	.7595	.735	.7105	.686	.6615	.65333	.637	.6125
2-1/2	.92625	.90188	.8775	.85313	.82875	.8125	.78	.75563	.73125	.70688	.6825	.65813	.65	.63375	.60938
5	.9025	.87875	.855	.83125	.8075	.79167	.76	.73625	.7125	.68875	.665	.64125	.63333	.6175	.59375
5 2-1/2	.87994	.85678	.83363	.81047	.78731	.77188	.741	.71784	.69469	.67153	.64838	.62522	.6175	.60206	.57891
5 5	.85738	.83481	.81225	.78969	.76713	.75208	.722	.69944	.67688	.65431	.63175	.60919	.60167	.58663	.56406
5 5 2-1/2	.83594	.81394	.79194	.76995	.74795	.73328	.70395	.68195	.65995	.63795	.61596	.59396	.58663	.57196	.54996
7-1/2	.87875	.85563	.8325	.80938	.78625	.77083	.74	.71688	.69375	.67063	.6475	.62438	.61667	.60125	.57813
7-1/2 2-1/2	.85678	.83423	.81169	.78914	.76659	.75156	.7215	.69895	.67641	.65386	.63131	.60877	.60125	.58622	.56367
7-1/2 5	.83481	.81284	.79088	.76891	.74694	.73229	.703	.68103	.65906	.63709	.61513	.59316	.58583	.57119	.54922
10	.855	.8325	.81	.7875	.765	.75	.72	.6975	.675	.6525	.63	.6075	.6	.585	.5625
10 2-1/2	.83363	.81169	.78975	.76781	.74588	.73125	.702	.68006	.65813	.63619	.61425	.59231	.585	.57038	.54844
10 5	.81225	.79088	.7695	.74813	.72675	.7125	.684	.66263	.64125	.61988	.5985	.57713	.57	.55575	.53438
10 5 2-1/2	.79194	.77110	.75026	.72942	.70858	.69469	.6669	.64606	.62522	.60438	.58354	.56277	.55575	.54186	.52102
10 10	.7695	.74925	.729	.70875	.6885	.675	.648	.62775	.6075	.58725	.567	.54675	.54	.5265	.50625
10 10 2-1/2	.75026	.73052	.71078	.69103	.67129	.65813	.6318	.61206	.59231	.57257	.55283	.53308	.5265	.51334	.49359
12-1/2	.83125	.80938	.7875	.76563	.74375	.72917	.7	.67813	.65625	.63438	.6125	.59063	.58333	.56875	.54688
12-1/2 2-1/2	.81047	.78914	.76781	.74648	.72516	.71094	.6825	.66117	.63984	.61852	.59719	.57586	.56875	.55453	.5332
12-1/2 5	.78969	.76891	.74813	.72734	.70656	.69271	.665	.64422	.62344	.60266	.58188	.56109	.55417	.54031	.51953
12-1/2 7-1/2	.76891	.74867	.72844	.7082	.68797	.67448	.6475	.62727	.60703	.5868	.56656	.54633	.53958	.52609	.50586
12-1/2 10	.74813	.72844	.70875	.68906	.66938	.65625	.63	.61031	.59063	.57094	.55125	.53156	.525	.51188	.49219
12-1/2 10 2-1/2	.72942	.71023	.69103	.67184	.65264	.63984	.61425	.59505	.57586	.55666	.53747	.51827	.51188	.49908	.47988
12-1/2 10 5	.71072	.69202	.67331	.65461	.63591	.62344	.5985	.5798	.56109	.54239	.52369	.50498	.49875	.48628	.46758
12-1/2 10 5 2-1/2	.69295	.67472	.65648	.63824	.62001	.60785	.58354	.5653	.54707	.52883	.5106	.49236	.48628	.47412	.45589
12-1/2 10 10	.67331	.65559	.63788	.62016	.60244	.59063	.567	.54928	.53156	.51384	.49613	.47841	.4725	.46069	.44297
15 2-1/2	.78731	.76659	.74588	.72516	.70444	.69063	.663	.64228	.62156	.60084	.58013	.55941	.5525	.53869	.51797
20	.76	.74	.72	.7	.68	.66667	.64	.62	.6	.58	.56	.54	.53333	.52	.5

*By courteous permission of the Lefax Corporation, Philadelphia.

Secondary Discount	40	42½	45	47½	50	52½	55	57½	60	62½	65	66⅔	70	72½	75	77½	80	85	87½	90
																	Primary Discount			
2	58800	56350	53900	51450	49000	46550	44100	41650	39200	36750	34300	32667	29400	26950	24500	22050	19600	14700	12250	09800
2½	585	56063	53625	51188	4875	46313	43875	41438	39	36563	34125	325	2925	26813	24375	21938	195	14625	12188	0975
5	57	54625	5225	49875	475	45125	4275	40375	38	35625	3325	31667	285	26125	2375	21375	19	1425	11875	095
5 2½	55575	53259	50944	48628	46313	43997	41681	39366	3705	34734	32419	30875	27788	25472	23156	20841	18525	13894	11578	09263
5 5	5415	51894	49638	47381	45125	42869	40613	38356	361	33844	31588	30083	27075	24819	22563	20306	1805	13538	11281	09025
5 5 2½	52796	50596	48397	46197	43997	41797	39597	37397	35198	32998	30798	29331	26398	24198	21998	19799	17599	13199	10999	08799
7½	555	53188	50875	48563	4625	43938	41625	39313	37	34688	32375	30833	2775	25438	23125	20813	185	13875	11563	0925
7½ 2½	54113	51858	49603	47348	45094	42839	40584	38330	36075	33820	31566	30063	27056	24802	22547	20292	18038	13528	11273	09019
7½ 5	52725	50528	48331	46134	43938	41741	39544	37347	3515	32953	30756	29292	26363	24166	21969	19772	17575	13181	10984	08788
10	54	5175	495	4725	45	4275	405	3825	36	3375	315	3	27	2475	225	2025	18	135	1125	09
10 2½	5265	50456	48263	46069	43875	41681	39488	37294	351	32906	30713	2925	26325	24131	21938	19744	1755	13163	10969	08775
10 5	513	49163	47025	44888	4275	40613	38475	36338	342	32063	29925	285	2565	23513	21375	19238	171	12825	10688	0855
10 5 2½	50018	47933	45849	43765	41681	39597	37513	35429	33345	31261	29177	27788	25009	22925	20841	18757	16673	12504	10420	08336
10 7½	4995	47869	45788	43706	41625	39544	37463	35381	333	31219	29138	2775	24975	22894	20813	18731	1665	12488	10406	08325
10 7½ 5	47453	45475	43498	41521	39544	37567	35589	33612	31635	29658	27681	26363	23726	21749	19772	17795	15818	11863	09886	07909
10 10	486	46575	4455	42525	405	38475	3645	34425	324	30375	2835	27	243	22275	2025	18225	162	1215	10125	081
10 10 2½	47385	45411	43436	41462	39488	37513	35539	33564	3159	29616	27641	26325	23693	21718	19744	17769	15795	11846	09872	07898
10 10 5	4617	44246	42323	40399	38475	36551	34628	32704	3078	28856	26933	2565	23085	21161	19238	17314	1539	11543	09619	07695
10 10 5 2½	45016	43140	41264	39389	37513	35638	33762	31886	30011	28135	26259	25009	22508	20632	18757	16881	15005	11254	09378	07503
10 10 10	4374	41918	40095	38273	3645	34628	32805	30983	2916	27338	25515	243	2187	20048	18225	16403	1458	10935	09113	0729
12½	525	50313	48125	45938	4375	41563	39375	37188	35	32813	30625	29167	2625	24063	21875	19688	175	13125	10938	0875
12½ 2½	51188	49055	46922	44789	42656	40523	38391	36258	34125	31992	29859	28438	25594	23461	21328	19195	17063	12797	10664	08531
12½ 5	49875	47844	45719	43641	41563	39484	37406	35328	3325	31172	29094	27708	24938	22859	20781	18703	16625	12469	10391	08313
12½ 7½	48563	46539	44516	42492	40469	38445	36422	34398	32375	30352	28328	26979	24281	22258	20234	18211	16188	12141	10117	08094
12½ 10	4725	45281	43313	41344	39375	37406	35438	33469	315	29531	27563	2625	23625	21656	19688	17719	1575	11813	09844	07875
12½ 10 5	44888	43017	41147	39277	37406	35536	33666	31795	29925	28055	26184	24938	22444	20573	18703	16833	14963	11222	09352	07481
12½ 10 5 2½	43765	41942	40118	38295	36471	34648	32824	31001	29177	27353	25530	24314	21883	20059	18236	16412	14588	10941	09118	07294
12½ 10 7½	43706	41885	40064	38243	36422	34601	32780	30959	29138	27316	25495	24281	21853	20032	18211	16390	14569	10927	09105	07284
12½ 10 10	42525	40753	38981	37209	35438	33666	31894	30122	2835	26578	24806	23625	21263	19491	17719	15947	14175	10631	08859	07068
15	51	48875	4675	44625	425	40375	3825	36125	34	31875	2975	28333	255	23375	2125	19125	17	1275	10625	085
15 2½	49725	47653	45581	43510	41438	39366	37294	35222	3315	31078	29006	27625	24863	22791	20719	18647	16575	12431	10359	08288
20	48	46	44	42	4	38	36	34	32	3	28	26667	24	22	2	18	16	12	1	08

Cash Discounts

A *cash discount* is a premium allowed by the seller of goods to the buyer on condition that the invoice is paid within a specified time. When cash discounts are higher than the rate of interest on the money would be for the same length of time, it is wise to borrow money from the bank, if necessary, and take advantage of the discount. The table below shows the ordinary discount rates and their equivalent interest rates figured on an annual basis:

```
½ % 10 days—net 30 days =  9% per annum
 1 % 10   "      " 30   "   = 18%  "     "
1½ % 10   "      " 30   "   = 27%  "     "
 2 % 30   "      "  4 mos. =  8%  "     "
 2 % 10   "      " 60 days = 14%  "     "
 2 % 30   "      " 60   "   = 24%  "     "
 2 % 10   "      " 30   "   = 36%  "     "
 2 % 40   "      " 60   "   = 36%  "     "
 2 % 70   "      " 90   "   = 36%  "     "
 2 % 10, 30X days—net 60 days = 36% per annum
 2 % 10, 60X  "     " 90   "   = 36%  "     "
 3 % 10 days—net  4 mos. = 10% per annum
 3 % 30   "      " 60 days = 36%  "     "
 3 % 10   "      " 30   "   = 54%  "     "
 4 % 10   "      "  4 mos. = 13%  "     "
 4 % 10   "      " 60 days = 29%  "     "
 5 % 10   "      "  4 mos. = 16%  "     "
 5 % 10   "      " 60 days = 36%  "     "
 5 % 10   "      " 30   "   = 90%  "     "
 6 % 10   "      "  4 mos. = 20%  "     "
 6 % 10   "      " 60 days = 43%  "     "
 7 % 10   "      "  4 mos. = 23%  "     "
 8 % 10   "      "  4   "   = 26%  "     "
```

MARKING GOODS

Most retail houses have a secret way of marking goods so that at a glance they can see both the cost price and the selling price. The usual way is to select a word or phrase containing ten different letters, like pink flower, regulation, etc., thus:

p i n k   f l o w e r
1 2 3 4   5 6 7 8 9 0

Sometimes an outside letter like x or z is used where a figure is repeated. Suppose the cost of an article is $2.50 and the selling price $2.75; the mark on the goods would be, if the scheme above is used,

ifr $2.75

If the cost were 44 cents and the selling price 60 cents the mark would be

kz $.60

Mark-Up

Mark-up[1] is that component which is added to a basic cost in order to arrive at a selling price.

A proper selling price should include a reasonable profit.

Profit is essential to successful business administration.

The importance of this subject is therefore obvious, and it is with this idea in mind that the table below is continuously placed before the business public.

MARK-UP TABLE

Total Deductions from Selling Price	Mark-up Percentage on Cost	Total Deductions from Selling Price	Mark-up Percentage on Cost	Total Deductions from Selling Price	Mark-up Percentage on Cost
1%	1.0101%	18%	21.9512%	35%	53.8461%
2%	2.0408%	19%	23.4568%	36%	56.25 %
3%	3.0928%	20%	25. %	37%	58.7301%
4%	4.1667%	21%	26.5823%	38%	61.2903%
5%	5.2632%	22%	28.2051%	39%	63.9344%
6%	6.383 %	23%	29.8701%	40%	66.6667%
7%	7.5269%	24%	31.5789%	41%	69.4915%
8%	8.6957%	25%	33.3333%	42%	72.4138%
9%	9.8901%	26%	35.1351%	43%	75.4386%
10%	11.1111%	27%	36.9863%	44%	78.5714%
11%	12.3595%	28%	38.8889%	45%	81.8181%
12%	13.6364%	29%	40.8451%	46%	85.1851%
13%	14.9425%	30%	42.8571%	47%	88.6791%
14%	16.2791%	31%	44.9275%	48%	92.3076%
15%	17.647 %	32%	47.0588%	49%	96.0784%
16%	19.0476%	33%	49.2537%	50%	100. %
17%	20.4819%	34%	51.5151%		

Explanation of Mark-Up Table

The column headed "Total Deductions from Selling Price," refers to the various allowances to be made on the selling price, viz.: discount, commission, overhead, and profit desired.

For example, if the discount to be allowed is
  2% of the selling price,
  5% of the selling price is allowed to a salesman for commission,
  15% of the selling price is the estimated overhead, and
  8% of the selling price is the desired profit, then

30% is the "Total Deductions from Selling Price" (including profit).

"Total Deductions from Selling Price" of 30% is equivalent to a "Mark-Up Percentage on Cost" of 42.8571% or approximately 43% as shown on "Mark-Up Table." Therefore an article costing $10 will have added to it $4.30 (43%). If sold at $14.30, all of the deductions, including profit of 8%, will have been considered.

---

[1]This information is reprinted by permission of Maurice Goldberg & Company, C.P.A., New York and Los Angeles.

Proof:

Cost of Article		$10.00
Mark-up (43%)		4.30
		$14.30

Deductions:

2% Discount	.29	
5% Commission	.72	
15% Overhead	2.15	
8% Profit	1.14	
Total Deductions (including profit)		4.30
Cost of Article		$10.00

The deductions may be changed to accord with conditions, resulting in a fluctuation of the mark-up percentage. For instance, if the selling price is to take into consideration

5% Discount
5% Overhead
5% Profit

a total of 15%, the mark-up percentage will be 17.647% or, $1.76, which amount added to the cost of $10 results in a selling price of $11.76.

MAKING CHANGE

Add enough pennies to the cost of the article to make even money, then add the larger coins.

The cost of the article is 31 cents, and the customer gives a 50-cent piece in payment. Begin with the number 31. Add four pennies to make 35. Add five to make 40 and ten to make 50.

READY RECKONER TABLES

Showing how to find the price of any number of units, such as pounds, bushels, etc., at from two cents to $3.00 per unit. The first column gives the number of units; the columns to the right of the heavy line give the prices per unit. If the number required is not in the column add together two or more numbers until it is reached. For instance, to find the price of 145 bushels, add the price of 100 bu., 40 bu. and 5 bu.

Nos.	2 ct.	3 ct.	4 ct.	5 ct.	6 ct.	6-1/4 ct.	7 ct.	8 ct.	9 ct.	10 ct.	11 ct.
2	.4	.6	.8	.10	.12	.12-1/2	.14	.16	.18	.20	.22
3	.6	.9	.12	.15	.18	.18-3/4	.21	.24	.27	.30	.33
4	.8	.12	.16	.20	.24	.25	.28	.32	.36	.40	.44
5	.10	.15	.20	.25	.30	.31-1/4	.35	.40	.45	.50	.55
6	.12	.18	.24	.30	.36	.37-1/2	.42	.48	.54	.60	.66
7	.14	.21	.28	.35	.42	.43-3/4	.49	.56	.63	.70	.77
8	.16	.24	.32	.40	.48	.50	.56	.64	.72	.80	.88
9	.18	.27	.36	.45	.54	.56-1/4	.63	.72	.81	.90	.99
10	.20	.30	.40	.50	.60	.62-1/2	.70	.80	.90	1.00	1.10
11	.22	.33	.44	.55	.66	.68-3/4	.77	.88	.99	1.10	1.21
12	.24	.36	.48	.60	.72	.75	.84	.96	1.08	1.20	1.32
13	.26	.39	.52	.65	.78	.81-1/4	.91	1.04	1.17	1.30	1.43
14	.28	.42	.56	.70	.84	.87-1/2	.98	1.12	1.26	1.40	1.54
15	.30	.45	.60	.75	.90	.93-3/4	1.05	1.20	1.35	1.50	1.65
16	.32	.48	.64	.80	.96	1.00	1.12	1.28	1.44	1.60	1.76
17	.34	.51	.68	.85	1.02	1.06-1/4	1.19	1.36	1.53	1.70	1.87
18	.36	.54	.72	.90	1.08	1.12-1/2	1.26	1.44	1.62	1.80	1.98
19	.38	.57	.76	.95	1.14	1.18-3/4	1.33	1.52	1.71	1.90	2.09
20	.40	.60	.80	1.00	1.20	1.25	1.40	1.60	1.80	2.00	2.20
25	.50	.75	1.00	1.25	1.50	1.56-1/4	1.75	2.00	2.25	2.50	2.75
30	.60	.90	1.20	1.50	1.80	1.87-1/2	2.10	2.40	2.70	3.00	3.30
40	.80	1.20	1.60	2.00	2.40	2.50	2.80	3.20	3.60	4.00	4.40
50	1.00	1.50	2.00	2.50	3.00	3.12-1/2	3.50	4.00	4.50	5.00	5.50
60	1.20	1.80	2.40	3.00	3.60	3.75	4.20	4.80	5.40	6.00	6.60
70	1.40	2.10	2.80	3.50	4.20	4.37-1/2	4.90	5.60	6.30	7.00	7.70
80	1.60	2.40	3.20	4.00	4.80	5.00	5.60	6.40	7.20	8.00	8.80
90	1.80	2.70	3.60	4.50	5.40	5.62-1/2	6.30	7.20	8.10	9.00	9.90
100	2.00	3.00	4.00	5.00	6.00	6.25	7.00	8.00	9.00	10.00	11.00

Nos.	12 ct.	12-1/2 ct.	13 ct.	14 ct.	15 ct.	16 ct.	18 ct.	18-3/4 ct.	19 ct.	20 ct.	21 ct.
2	.24	.25	.26	.28	.30	.32	.36	.37-1/2	.38	.40	.42
3	.36	.37-1/2	.39	.42	.45	.48	.54	.56-1/4	.57	.60	.63
4	.48	.50	.52	.56	.60	.64	.72	.75	.76	.80	.84
5	.60	.62-1/2	.65	.70	.75	.80	.90	.93-3/4	.95	1.00	1.05
6	.72	.75	.78	.84	.90	.96	1.08	1.12-1/2	1.14	1.20	1.26
7	.84	.87-1/2	.91	.98	1.05	1.12	1.26	1.31-1/4	1.33	1.40	1.47
8	.96	1.00	1.04	1.12	1.20	1.28	1.44	1.50	1.52	1.60	1.68
9	1.08	1.12-1/2	1.17	1.26	1.35	1.44	1.62	1.68-3/4	1.71	1.80	1.89
10	1.20	1.25	1.30	1.40	1.50	1.60	1.80	1.87-1/2	1.90	2.00	2.10
11	1.32	1.37-1/2	1.43	1.54	1.65	1.76	1.98	2.06-1/4	2.09	2.20	2.31
12	1.44	1.50	1.56	1.68	1.80	1.92	2.16	2.25	2.28	2.40	2.52
13	1.56	1.62-1/2	1.69	1.82	1.95	2.08	2.34	2.43-3/4	2.47	2.60	2.73
14	1.68	1.75	1.82	1.96	2.10	2.24	2.52	2.62-1/2	2.66	2.80	2.94
15	1.80	1.87-1/2	1.95	2.10	2.25	2.40	2.70	2.81-1/4	2.85	3.00	3.15
16	1.92	2.00	2.08	2.24	2.40	2.56	2.88	3.00	3.04	3.20	3.36
17	2.04	2.12-1/2	2.21	2.38	2.55	2.72	3.06	3.18-3/4	3.23	3.40	3.57
18	2.16	2.25	2.34	2.52	2.70	2.88	3.24	3.37-1/2	3.42	3.60	3.78
19	2.28	2.37-1/2	2.47	2.66	2.85	3.04	3.42	3.56-1/4	3.61	3.80	3.99
20	2.40	2.50	2.60	2.80	3.00	3.20	3.60	3.75	3.80	4.00	4.20
25	3.00	3.12-1/2	3.25	3.50	3.75	4.00	4.50	4.68-3/4	4.75	5.00	5.25
30	3.60	3.75	3.90	4.20	4.50	4.80	5.40	5.62-1/2	5.70	6.00	6.30
40	4.80	5.00	5.20	5.60	6.00	6.40	7.20	7.50	7.60	8.00	8.40
50	6.00	6.25	6.50	7.00	7.50	8.00	9.00	9.37-1/2	9.50	10.00	10.50
60	7.20	7.50	7.80	8.40	9.00	9.60	10.80	11.25	11.40	12.00	12.60
70	8.40	8.75	9.10	9.80	10.50	11.20	12.60	13.12-1/2	13.30	14.00	14.70
80	9.60	10.00	10.40	11.20	12.00	12.80	14.40	15.00	15.20	16.00	16.80
90	10.80	11.25	11.70	12.60	13.50	14.40	16.20	16.87-1/2	17.10	18.00	18.90
100	12.00	12.50	13.00	14.00	15.00	16.00	18.00	18.75	19.00	20.00	21.00

Showing how to find the price of any number of units, such as pounds, yards, bushels, etc., at from two cents to $3.00 per unit. The first column gives the number of units; the columns to the right of the heavy line give the prices per unit. If the number required is not in the column, add together two or more numbers until it is reached. For instance, to find the price of 145 bu., add the price of 100 bu., 40 bu., and 5 bu.

Nos.	22 ct.	23 ct.	24 ct.	25 ct.	26 ct.	27 ct.	28 ct.	29 ct.	30 ct.	31 ct.	31-1/4 ct.
2	.44	.46	.48	.50	.52	.54	.56	.58	.60	.62	.62-1/2
3	.66	.69	.72	.75	.78	.81	.84	.87	.90	.93	.93-3/4
4	.88	.92	.96	1.00	1.04	1.08	1.12	1.16	1.20	1.24	1.25
5	1.10	1.15	1.20	1.25	1.30	1.35	1.40	1.45	1.50	1.55	1.56-1/4
6	1.32	1.38	1.44	1.50	1.56	1.62	1.68	1.74	1.80	1.86	1.87-1/2
7	1.54	1.61	1.68	1.75	1.82	1.89	1.96	2.03	2.10	2.17	2.18-3/4
8	1.76	1.84	1.92	2.00	2.08	2.16	2.24	2.32	2.40	2.48	2.50
9	1.98	2.07	2.16	2.25	2.34	2.43	2.52	2.61	2.70	2.79	2.81-1/4
10	2.20	2.30	2.40	2.50	2.60	2.70	2.80	2.90	3.00	3.10	3.12-1/2
11	2.42	2.53	2.64	2.75	2.86	2.97	3.08	3.19	3.30	3.41	3.43-3/4
12	2.64	2.76	2.88	3.00	3.12	3.24	3.36	3.48	3.60	3.72	3.75
13	2.86	2.99	3.12	3.25	3.38	3.51	3.64	3.77	3.90	4.03	4.06-1/4
14	3.08	3.22	3.36	3.50	3.64	3.78	3.92	4.06	4.20	4.34	4.37-1/2
15	3.30	3.45	3.60	3.75	3.90	4.05	4.20	4.35	4.50	4.65	4.68-3/4
16	3.52	3.68	3.84	4.00	4.16	4.32	4.48	4.64	4.80	4.96	5.00
17	3.74	3.91	4.08	4.25	4.42	4.59	4.76	4.93	5.10	5.27	5.31-1/4
18	3.96	4.14	4.32	4.50	4.68	4.86	5.04	5.22	5.40	5.58	5.62-1/2
19	4.18	4.37	4.56	4.75	4.94	5.13	5.32	5.51	5.70	5.89	5.93-3/4
20	4.40	4.60	4.80	5.00	5.20	5.40	5.60	5.80	6.00	6.20	6.25
25	5.50	5.75	6.00	6.25	6.50	6.75	7.00	7.25	7.50	7.75	7.81-1/4
30	6.60	6.90	7.20	7.50	7.80	8.10	8.40	8.70	9.00	9.30	9.37-1/2
40	8.80	9.20	9.60	10.00	10.40	10.80	11.20	11.60	12.00	12.40	12.50
50	11.00	11.50	12.00	12.50	13.00	13.50	14.00	14.50	15.00	15.50	15.62-1/2
60	13.20	13.80	14.40	15.00	15.60	16.20	16.80	17.40	18.00	18.60	18.75
70	15.40	16.10	16.80	17.50	18.20	18.90	19.60	20.30	21.00	21.70	21.87-1/2
80	17.60	18.40	19.20	20.00	20.80	21.60	22.40	23.20	24.00	24.80	25.00
90	19.80	20.70	21.60	22.50	23.40	24.30	25.20	26.10	27.00	27.90	28.12-1/2
100	22.00	23.00	24.00	25.00	26.00	27.00	28.00	29.00	30.00	31.00	31.25

Nos.	32 ct.	33 ct.	33-1/3 ct.	34 ct.	35 ct.	36 ct.	37 ct.	37-1/2 ct.	38 ct.	39 ct.	40 ct.
2	.64	.66	.66-2/3	.68	.70	.72	.74	.75	.76	.78	.80
3	.96	.99	1.00	1.02	1.05	1.08	1.11	1.12-1/2	1.14	1.17	1.20
4	1.28	1.32	1.33-1/3	1.36	1.40	1.44	1.48	1.50	1.52	1.56	1.60
5	1.60	1.65	1.66-2/3	1.70	1.75	1.80	1.85	1.87-1/2	1.90	1.95	2.00
6	1.92	1.98	2.00	2.04	2.10	2.16	2.22	2.25	2.28	2.34	2.40
7	2.24	2.31	2.33-1/3	2.38	2.45	2.52	2.59	2.62-1/2	2.66	2.73	2.80
8	2.56	2.64	2.66-2/3	2.72	2.80	2.88	2.96	3.00	3.04	3.12	3.20
9	2.88	2.97	3.00	3.06	3.15	3.24	3.33	3.37-1/2	3.42	3.51	3.60
10	3.20	3.30	3.33-1/3	3.40	3.50	3.60	3.70	3.75	3.80	3.90	4.00
11	3.52	3.63	3.66-2/3	3.74	3.85	3.96	4.07	4.12-1/2	4.18	4.29	4.40
12	3.84	3.96	4.00	4.08	4.20	4.32	4.44	4.50	4.56	4.68	4.80
13	4.16	4.29	4.33-1/3	4.42	4.55	4.68	4.81	4.87-1/2	4.94	5.07	5.20
14	4.48	4.62	4.66-2/3	4.76	4.90	5.04	5.18	5.25	5.32	5.46	5.60
15	4.80	4.95	5.00	5.10	5.25	5.40	5.55	5.62-1/2	5.70	5.85	6.00
16	5.12	5.28	5.33-1/3	5.44	5.60	5.76	5.92	6.00	6.08	6.24	6.40
17	5.44	5.61	5.66-2/3	5.78	5.95	6.12	6.29	6.37-1/2	6.46	6.63	6.80
18	5.76	5.94	6.00	6.12	6.30	6.48	6.66	6.75	6.84	7.02	7.20
19	6.08	6.27	6.33-1/3	6.46	6.65	6.84	7.03	7.12-1/2	7.22	7.41	7.60
20	6.40	6.60	6.66-2/3	6.80	7.00	7.20	7.40	7.50	7.60	7.80	8.00
25	8.00	8.25	8.33-1/3	8.50	8.75	9.00	9.25	9.37-1/2	9.50	9.75	10.00
30	9.60	9.90	10.00	10.20	10.50	10.80	11.10	11.25	11.40	11.70	12.00
40	12.80	13.20	13.33-1/3	13.60	14.00	14.40	14.80	15.00	15.20	15.60	16.00
50	16.00	16.50	16.66-2/3	17.00	17.50	18.00	18.50	18.75	19.00	19.50	20.00
60	19.20	19.80	20.00	20.40	21.00	21.60	22.20	22.50	22.80	23.40	24.00
70	22.40	23.10	23.33-1/3	23.80	24.50	25.20	25.90	26.25	26.60	27.30	28.00
80	25.60	26.40	26.66-2/3	27.20	28.00	28.80	29.60	30.00	30.40	31.20	32.00
90	28.80	29.70	30.00	30.60	31.50	32.40	33.30	33.75	34.20	35.10	36.00
100	32.00	33.00	33.33-1/3	34.00	35.00	36.00	37.00	37.50	38.00	39.00	40.00

Showing how to find the price of any number of units, such as pounds, yards, bushels, etc., at from two cents to $3.00 per unit. The first column gives the number of units; the columns to the right of the heavy line give the prices per unit. If the number required is not in the column, add together two or more numbers until it is reached. For instance, to find the price of 145 bu., add the price of 100 bu., 40 bu., and 5 bu.

Nos.	41 ct.	42 ct.	43 ct.	44 ct.	45 ct.	46 ct.	47 ct.	48 ct.	49 ct.	50 ct.	51 ct.
2	.82	.84	.86	.88	.90	.92	.94	.96	.98	1.00	1.02
3	1.23	1.26	1.29	1.32	1.35	1.38	1.41	1.44	1.47	1.50	1.53
4	1.64	1.68	1.72	1.76	1.80	1.84	1.88	1.92	1.96	2.00	2.04
5	2.05	2.10	2.15	2.20	2.25	2.30	2.35	2.40	2.45	2.50	2.55
6	2.46	2.52	2.58	2.64	2.70	2.76	2.82	2.88	2.94	3.00	3.06
7	2.87	2.94	3.01	3.08	3.15	3.22	3.29	3.36	3.43	3.50	3.57
8	3.28	3.36	3.44	3.52	3.60	3.68	3.76	3.84	3.92	4.00	4.08
9	3.69	3.78	3.87	3.96	4.05	4.14	4.23	4.32	4.41	4.50	4.59
10	4.10	4.20	4.30	4.40	4.50	4.60	4.70	4.80	4.90	5.00	5.10
11	4.51	4.62	4.73	4.84	4.95	5.06	5.17	5.28	5.39	5.50	5.61
12	4.92	5.04	5.16	5.28	5.40	5.52	5.64	5.76	5.88	6.00	6.12
13	5.33	5.46	5.59	5.72	5.85	5.98	6.11	6.24	6.37	6.50	6.63
14	5.74	5.88	6.02	6.16	6.30	6.44	6.58	6.72	6.86	7.00	7.14
15	6.15	6.30	6.45	6.60	6.75	6.90	7.05	7.20	7.35	7.50	7.65
16	6.56	6.72	6.88	7.04	7.20	7.36	7.52	7.68	7.84	8.00	8.16
17	6.97	7.14	7.31	7.48	7.65	7.82	7.99	8.16	8.33	8.50	8.67
18	7.38	7.56	7.74	7.92	8.10	8.28	8.46	8.64	8.82	9.00	9.18
19	7.79	7.98	8.17	8.36	8.55	8.74	8.93	9.12	9.31	9.50	9.69
20	8.20	8.40	8.60	8.80	9.00	9.20	9.40	9.60	9.80	10.00	10.20
25	10.25	10.50	10.75	11.00	11.25	11.50	11.75	12.00	12.25	12.50	12.75
30	12.30	12.60	12.90	13.20	13.50	13.80	14.10	14.40	14.70	15.00	15.30
40	16.40	16.80	17.20	17.60	18.00	18.40	18.80	19.20	19.60	20.00	20.40
50	20.50	21.00	21.50	22.00	22.50	23.00	23.50	24.00	24.50	25.00	25.50
60	24.60	25.20	25.80	26.40	27.00	27.60	28.20	28.80	29.40	30.00	30.60
70	28.70	29.40	30.10	30.80	31.50	32.20	32.90	33.60	34.30	35.00	35.70
80	32.80	33.60	34.40	35.20	36.00	36.80	37.60	38.40	39.20	40.00	40.80
90	36.90	37.80	38.70	39.60	40.50	41.40	42.30	43.20	44.10	45.00	45.90
100	41.00	42.00	43.00	44.00	45.00	46.00	47.00	48.00	49.00	50.00	51.00

Nos.	52 ct.	53 ct.	54 ct.	55 ct.	56 ct.	57 ct.	58 ct.	59 ct.	60 ct.	61 ct.	62 ct.
2	1.04	1.06	1.08	1.10	1.12	1.14	1.16	1.18	1.20	1.22	1.24
3	1.56	1.59	1.62	1.65	1.68	1.71	1.74	1.77	1.80	1.83	1.86
4	2.08	2.12	2.16	2.20	2.24	2.28	2.32	2.36	2.40	2.44	2.48
5	2.60	2.65	2.70	2.75	2.80	2.85	2.90	2.95	3.00	3.05	3.10
6	3.12	3.18	3.24	3.30	3.36	3.42	3.48	3.54	3.60	3.66	3.72
7	3.64	3.71	3.78	3.85	3.92	3.99	4.06	4.13	4.20	4.27	4.34
8	4.16	4.24	4.32	4.40	4.48	4.56	4.64	4.72	4.80	4.88	4.96
9	4.68	4.77	4.86	4.95	5.04	5.13	5.22	5.31	5.40	5.49	5.58
10	5.20	5.30	5.40	5.50	5.60	5.70	5.80	5.90	6.00	6.10	6.20
11	5.72	5.83	5.94	6.05	6.16	6.27	6.38	6.49	6.60	6.71	6.82
12	6.24	6.36	6.48	6.60	6.72	6.84	6.96	7.08	7.20	7.32	7.44
13	6.76	6.89	7.02	7.15	7.28	7.41	7.54	7.67	7.80	7.93	8.06
14	7.28	7.42	7.56	7.70	7.84	7.98	8.12	8.26	8.40	8.54	8.68
15	7.80	7.95	8.10	8.25	8.40	8.55	8.70	8.85	9.00	9.15	9.30
16	8.32	8.48	8.64	8.80	8.96	9.12	9.28	9.44	9.60	9.76	9.92
17	8.84	9.01	9.18	9.35	9.52	9.69	9.86	10.03	10.20	10.37	10.54
18	9.36	9.54	9.72	9.90	10.08	10.26	10.44	10.62	10.80	10.98	11.16
19	9.88	10.07	10.26	10.45	10.64	10.83	11.02	11.21	11.40	11.59	11.78
20	10.40	10.60	10.80	11.00	11.20	11.40	11.60	11.80	12.00	12.20	12.40
25	13.00	13.25	13.50	13.75	14.00	14.25	14.50	14.75	15.00	15.25	15.50
30	15.60	15.90	16.20	16.50	16.80	17.10	17.40	17.70	18.00	18.30	18.60
40	20.80	21.20	21.60	22.00	22.40	22.80	23.20	23.60	24.00	24.40	24.80
50	26.00	26.50	27.00	27.50	28.00	28.50	29.00	29.50	30.00	30.50	31.00
60	31.20	31.80	32.40	33.00	33.60	34.20	34.80	35.40	36.00	36.60	37.20
70	36.40	37.10	37.80	38.50	39.20	39.90	40.60	41.30	42.00	42.70	43.40
80	41.60	42.40	43.20	44.00	44.80	45.60	46.40	47.20	48.00	48.80	49.60
90	46.80	47.70	48.60	49.50	50.40	51.30	52.20	53.10	54.00	54.90	55.80
100	52.00	53.00	54.00	55.00	56.00	57.00	58.00	59.00	60.00	61.00	62.00

Showing how to find the price of any number of units, such as pounds, yards, bushels, etc., at from two cents to $3.00 per unit. The first column gives the number of units; the columns to the right of the heavy line give the prices per unit. If the number required is not in the column, add together two or more numbers until it is reached. For instance, to find the price of 145 bu., add the price of 100 bu., 40 bu., and 5 bu.

Nos.	62-1/2 ct.	63 ct.	64 ct.	65 ct.	66 ct.	66-2/3 ct.	67 ct.	68 ct.	69 ct.	70 ct.	71 ct.
2	1.25	1.26	1.28	1.30	1.32	1.33-1/3	1.34	1.36	1.38	1.40	1.42
3	1.87-1/2	1.89	1.92	1.95	1.98	2.00	2.01	2.04	2.07	2.10	2.13
4	2.50	2.52	2.56	2.60	2.64	2.66-2/3	2.68	2.72	2.76	2.80	2.84
5	3.12-1/2	3.15	3.20	3.25	3.30	3.33-1/3	3.35	3.40	3.45	3.50	3.55
6	3.75	3.78	3.84	3.90	3.96	4.00	4.02	4.08	4.14	4.20	4.26
7	4.37-1/2	4.41	4.48	4.55	4.62	4.66-2/3	4.69	4.76	4.83	4.90	4.97
8	5.00	5.04	5.12	5.20	5.28	5.33-1/3	5.36	5.44	5.52	5.60	5.68
9	5.62-1/2	5.67	5.76	5.85	5.94	6.00	6.03	6.12	6.21	6.30	6.39
10	6.25	6.30	6.40	6.50	6.60	6.66-2/3	6.70	6.80	6.90	7.00	7.10
11	6.87-1/2	6.93	7.04	7.15	7.26	7.33-1/3	7.37	7.48	7.59	7.70	7.81
12	7.50	7.56	7.68	7.80	7.92	8.00	8.04	8.16	8.28	8.40	8.52
13	8.12-1/2	8.19	8.32	8.45	8.58	8.66-2/3	8.71	8.84	8.97	9.10	9.23
14	8.75	8.82	8.96	9.10	9.24	9.33-1/3	9.38	9.52	9.66	9.80	9.94
15	9.37-1/2	9.45	9.60	9.75	9.90	10.00	10.05	10.20	10.35	10.50	10.65
16	10.00	10.08	10.24	10.40	10.56	10.66-2/3	10.72	10.88	11.04	11.20	11.36
17	10.62-1/2	10.71	10.88	11.05	11.22	11.33-1/3	11.39	11.56	11.73	11.90	12.07
18	11.25	11.34	11.52	11.70	11.88	12.00	12.06	12.24	12.42	12.60	12.78
19	11.87-1/2	11.97	12.16	12.35	12.54	12.66-2/3	12.73	12.92	13.11	13.30	13.49
20	12.50	12.60	12.80	13.00	13.20	13.33-1/3	13.40	13.60	13.80	14.00	14.20
25	15.62-1/2	15.75	16.00	16.25	16.50	16.66-2/3	16.75	17.00	17.25	17.50	17.75
30	18.75	18.90	19.20	19.50	19.80	20.00	20.10	20.40	20.70	21.00	21.30
40	25.00	25.20	25.60	26.00	26.40	26.66-2/3	26.80	27.20	27.60	28.00	28.40
50	31.25	31.50	32.00	32.50	33.00	33.33-1/3	33.50	34.00	34.50	35.00	35.50
60	37.50	37.80	38.40	39.00	39.60	40.00	40.20	40.80	41.40	42.00	42.60
70	43.75	44.10	44.80	45.50	46.20	46.66-2/3	46.90	47.60	48.30	49.00	49.70
80	50.00	50.40	51.20	52.00	52.80	53.33-1/3	53.60	54.40	55.20	56.00	56.80
90	56.25	56.70	57.60	58.50	59.40	60.00	60.30	61.20	62.10	63.00	63.90
100	62.50	63.00	64.00	65.00	66.00	66.66-2/3	67.00	68.00	69.00	70.00	71.00

Nos.	72 ct.	73 ct.	74 ct.	75 ct.	76 ct.	77 ct.	78 ct.	79 ct.	80 ct.	81 ct.	82 ct.
2	1.44	1.46	1.48	1.50	1.52	1.54	1.56	1.58	1.60	1.62	1.64
3	2.16	2.19	2.22	2.25	2.28	2.31	2.34	2.37	2.40	2.43	2.46
4	2.88	2.92	2.96	3.00	3.04	3.08	3.12	3.16	3.20	3.24	3.28
5	3.60	3.65	3.70	3.75	3.80	3.85	3.90	3.95	4.00	4.05	4.10
6	4.32	4.38	4.44	4.50	4.56	4.62	4.68	4.74	4.80	4.86	4.92
7	5.04	5.11	5.18	5.25	5.32	5.39	5.46	5.53	5.60	5.67	5.74
8	5.76	5.84	5.92	6.00	6.08	6.16	6.24	6.32	6.40	6.48	6.56
9	6.48	6.57	6.66	6.75	6.84	6.93	7.02	7.11	7.20	7.29	7.38
10	7.20	7.30	7.40	7.50	7.60	7.70	7.80	7.90	8.00	8.10	8.20
11	7.92	8.03	8.14	8.25	8.36	8.47	8.58	8.69	8.80	8.91	9.02
12	8.64	8.76	8.88	9.00	9.12	9.24	9.36	9.48	9.60	9.72	9.84
13	9.36	9.49	9.62	9.75	9.88	10.01	10.14	10.27	10.40	10.53	10.66
14	10.08	10.22	10.36	10.50	10.64	10.78	10.92	11.06	11.20	11.34	11.48
15	10.80	10.95	11.10	11.25	11.40	11.55	11.70	11.85	12.00	12.15	12.30
16	11.52	11.68	11.84	12.00	12.16	12.32	12.48	12.64	12.80	12.96	13.12
17	12.24	12.41	12.58	12.75	12.92	13.09	13.26	13.43	13.60	13.77	13.94
18	12.96	13.14	13.32	13.50	13.68	13.86	14.04	14.22	14.40	14.58	14.76
19	13.68	13.87	14.06	14.25	14.44	14.63	14.82	15.01	15.20	15.39	15.58
20	14.40	14.60	14.80	15.00	15.20	15.40	15.60	15.80	16.00	16.20	16.40
25	18.00	18.25	18.50	18.75	19.00	19.25	19.50	19.75	20.00	20.25	20.50
30	21.60	21.90	22.20	22.50	22.80	23.10	23.40	23.70	24.00	24.30	24.60
40	28.80	29.20	29.60	30.00	30.40	30.80	31.20	31.60	32.00	32.40	32.80
50	36.00	36.50	37.00	37.50	38.00	38.50	39.00	39.50	40.00	40.50	41.00
60	43.20	43.80	44.40	45.00	45.60	46.20	46.80	47.40	48.00	48.60	49.20
70	50.40	51.10	51.80	52.50	53.20	53.90	54.60	55.30	56.00	56.70	57.40
80	57.60	58.40	59.20	60.00	60.80	61.60	62.40	63.20	64.00	64.80	65.60
90	64.80	65.70	66.60	67.50	68.40	69.30	70.20	71.10	72.00	72.90	73.80
100	72.00	73.00	74.00	75.00	76.00	77.00	78.00	79.00	80.00	81.00	82.00

Showing how to find the price of any number of units, such as pounds, yards, bushels, etc., at from two cents to $3.00 per unit. The first column gives the number of units; the columns to the right of the heavy line give the prices per unit. If the number required is not in the column, add together two or more numbers until it is reached. For instance, to find the price of 145 bu., add the price of 100 bu., 40 bu., and 5 bu.

Nos.	83 ct.	84 ct.	85 ct.	86 ct.	87 ct.	87-1/2 ct.	88 ct.	89 ct.	90 ct.	91 ct.	92 ct.
2	1.66	1.68	1.70	1.72	1.74	1.75	1.76	1.78	1.80	1.82	1.84
3	2.49	2.52	2.55	2.58	2.61	2.62-1/2	2.64	2.67	2.70	2.73	2.76
4	3.32	3.36	3.40	3.44	3.48	3.50	3.52	3.56	3.60	3.64	3.68
5	4.15	4.20	4.25	4.30	4.35	4.37-1/2	4.40	4.45	4.50	4.55	4.60
6	4.98	5.04	5.10	5.16	5.22	5.25	5.28	5.34	5.40	5.46	5.52
7	5.81	5.88	5.95	6.02	6.09	6.12-1/2	6.16	6.23	6.30	6.37	6.44
8	6.64	6.72	6.80	6.88	6.96	7.00	7.04	7.12	7.20	7.28	7.36
9	7.47	7.56	7.65	7.74	7.83	7.87-1/2	7.92	8.01	8.10	8.19	8.28
10	8.30	8.40	8.50	8.60	8.70	8.75	8.80	8.90	9.00	9.10	9.20
11	9.13	9.24	9.35	9.46	9.57	9.62-1/2	9.68	9.79	9.90	10.01	10.12
12	9.96	10.08	10.20	10.32	10.44	10.50	10.56	10.68	10.80	10.92	11.04
13	10.79	10.92	11.05	11.18	11.31	11.37-1/2	11.44	11.57	11.70	11.83	11.96
14	11.62	11.76	11.90	12.04	12.18	12.25	12.32	12.46	12.60	12.74	12.88
15	12.45	12.60	12.75	12.90	13.05	13.12-1/2	13.20	13.35	13.50	13.65	13.80
16	13.28	13.44	13.60	13.76	13.92	14.00	14.08	14.24	14.40	14.56	14.72
17	14.11	14.28	14.45	14.62	14.79	14.87-1/2	14.96	15.13	15.30	15.47	15.64
18	14.94	15.12	15.30	15.48	15.66	15.75	15.84	16.02	16.20	16.38	16.56
19	15.77	15.96	16.15	16.34	16.53	16.62-1/2	16.72	16.91	17.10	17.29	17.48
20	16.60	16.80	17.00	17.20	17.40	17.50	17.60	17.80	18.00	18.20	18.40
25	20.75	21.00	21.25	21.50	21.75	21.87-1/2	22.00	22.25	22.50	22.75	23.00
30	24.90	25.20	25.50	25.80	26.10	26.25	26.40	26.70	27.00	27.30	27.60
40	33.20	33.60	34.00	34.40	34.80	35.00	35.20	35.60	36.00	36.40	36.80
50	41.50	42.00	42.50	43.00	43.50	43.75	44.00	44.50	45.00	45.50	46.00
60	49.80	50.40	51.00	51.60	52.20	52.50	52.80	53.40	54.00	54.60	55.20
70	58.10	58.80	59.50	60.20	60.90	61.25	61.60	62.30	63.00	63.70	64.40
80	66.40	67.20	68.00	68.80	69.60	70.00	70.40	71.20	72.00	72.80	73.60
90	74.70	75.60	76.50	77.40	78.30	78.75	79.20	80.10	81.00	81.90	82.80
100	83.00	84.00	85.00	86.00	87.00	87.50	88.00	89.00	90.00	91.00	92.00

Nos.	93 ct.	94 ct.	95 ct.	96 ct.	97 ct.	98 ct.	99 ct.	$1.	$2.	$3.
2	1.86	1.88	1.90	1.92	1.94	1.96	1.98	2.	4.	6.
3	2.79	2.82	2.85	2.88	2.91	2.94	2.97	3.	6.	9.
4	3.72	3.76	3.80	3.84	3.88	3.92	3.96	4.	8.	12.
5	4.65	4.70	4.75	4.80	4.85	4.90	4.95	5.	10.	15.
6	5.58	5.64	5.70	5.76	5.82	5.88	5.94	6.	12.	18.
7	6.51	6.58	6.65	6.72	6.79	6.86	6.93	7.	14.	21.
8	7.44	7.52	7.60	7.68	7.76	7.84	7.92	8.	16.	24.
9	8.37	8.46	8.55	8.64	8.73	8.82	8.91	9.	18.	27.
10	9.30	9.40	9.50	9.60	9.70	9.80	9.90	10.	20.	30.
11	10.23	10.34	10.45	10.56	10.67	10.78	10.89	11.	22.	33.
12	11.16	11.28	11.40	11.52	11.64	11.76	11.88	12.	24.	36.
13	12.09	12.22	12.35	12.48	12.61	12.74	12.87	13.	26.	39.
14	13.02	13.16	13.30	13.44	13.58	13.72	13.86	14.	28.	42.
15	13.95	14.10	14.25	14.40	14.55	14.70	14.85	15.	30.	45.
16	14.88	15.04	15.20	15.36	15.52	15.68	15.84	16.	32.	48.
17	15.81	15.98	16.15	16.32	16.49	16.66	16.83	17.	34.	51.
18	16.74	16.92	17.10	17.28	17.46	17.64	17.82	18.	36.	54.
19	17.67	17.86	18.05	18.24	18.43	18.62	18.81	19.	38.	57.
20	18.60	18.80	19.00	19.20	19.40	19.60	19.80	20.	40.	60.
25	23.25	23.50	23.75	24.00	24.25	24.50	24.75	25.	50.	75.
30	27.90	28.20	28.50	28.80	29.10	29.40	29.70	30.	60.	90.
40	37.20	37.60	38.00	38.40	38.80	39.20	39.60	40.	80.	120.
50	46.50	47.00	47.50	48.00	48.50	49.00	49.50	50.	100.	150.
60	55.80	56.40	57.00	57.60	58.20	58.80	59.40	60.	120.	180.
70	65.10	65.80	66.50	67.20	67.90	68.60	69.30	70.	140.	210.
80	74.40	75.20	76.00	76.80	77.60	78.40	79.20	80.	160.	240.
90	83.70	84.60	85.50	86.40	87.30	88.20	89.10	90.	180.	270.
100	93.00	94.00	95.00	96.00	97.00	98.00	99.00	100.	200.	300.

SHOWING THE VALUE OF ARTICLES SOLD BY THE TON

.25	.60	.75	1-3/4	$2	2-1/4	2-1/2	2-3/4	Weight	$3	3-1/4	3-1/2	$4	4-1/2	$5	$6
.00	.00	.00	.01	.01	.01	.01	.01	10	.02	.02	.02	.02	.03	.03	.03
.00	.01	.01	.02	.02	.02	.03	.03	20	.03	.03	.04	.04	.05	.05	.06
.00	.01	.01	.03	.03	.03	.04	.04	30	.05	.05	.05	.06	.07	.08	.09
.01	.01	.02	.04	.04	.05	.05	.06	40	.06	.07	.07	.08	.09	.10	.12
.01	.01	.02	.04	.05	.06	.06	.07	50	.08	.08	.09	.10	.11	.13	.15
.01	.02	.02	.05	.06	.07	.08	.08	60	.09	.10	.11	.12	.14	.15	.18
.01	.02	.03	.06	.07	.08	.09	.10	70	.11	.11	.12	.14	.16	.18	.21
.01	.02	.03	.07	.08	.09	.10	.11	80	.12	.13	.14	.16	.18	.20	.24
.01	.02	.03	.08	.09	.10	.11	.12	90	.14	.15	.16	.18	.20	.23	.27
.01	.03	.04	.09	.10	.11	.13	.14	100	.15	.16	.18	.20	.23	.25	.30
.13	.25	.38	.88	1.00	1.13	1.25	1.38	1000	1.50	1.63	1.75	2.00	2.25	2.50	3.00
.14	.28	.42	.96	1.10	1.24	1.38	1.51	1100	1.65	1.79	1.93	2.20	2.48	2.75	3.30
.15	.30	.45	1.05	1.20	1.35	1.50	1.65	1200	1.80	1.95	2.10	2.40	2.70	3.00	3.60
.16	.33	.49	1.14	1.30	1.46	1.63	1.79	1300	1.95	2.11	2.28	2.60	2.93	3.25	3.90
.18	.35	.53	1.23	1.40	1.58	1.75	1.93	1400	2.10	2.28	2.45	2.80	3.15	3.50	4.20
.19	.38	.56	1.31	1.50	1.69	1.88	2.06	1500	2.25	2.44	2.63	3.00	3.38	3.75	4.50
.20	.40	.60	1.40	1.60	1.80	2.00	2.20	1600	2.40	2.60	2.80	3.20	3.60	4.00	4.80
.21	.43	.64	1.49	1.70	1.91	2.13	2.34	1700	2.55	2.76	2.98	3.40	3.83	4.25	5.10
.23	.45	.68	1.58	1.80	2.03	2.25	2.48	1800	2.70	2.93	3.15	3.60	4.05	4.50	5.40
.24	.48	.71	1.66	1.90	2.14	2.38	2.61	1900	2.85	3.09	3.33	3.80	4.28	4.75	5.70
.26	.53	.79	1.84	2.10	2.36	2.63	2.89	2100	3.15	3.41	3.68	4.20	4.73	5.25	6.30
.28	.55	.83	1.93	2.20	2.48	2.75	3.03	2200	3.30	3.58	3.85	4.40	4.95	5.50	6.60
.29	.58	.86	2.01	2.30	2.59	2.88	3.16	2300	3.45	3.74	4.03	4.60	5.18	5.75	6.90
.30	.60	.90	2.10	2.40	2.70	3.00	3.30	2400	3.60	3.90	4.20	4.80	5.40	6.00	7.20
.31	.63	.94	2.19	2.50	2.81	3.13	3.44	2500	3.75	4.06	4.38	5.00	5.63	6.25	7.50
.33	.65	.98	2.28	2.60	2.93	3.25	3.58	2600	3.90	4.23	4.55	5.20	5.85	6.50	7.80
.34	.68	1.01	2.36	2.70	3.04	3.38	3.71	2700	4.05	4.39	4.73	5.40	6.08	6.75	8.10
.35	.70	1.05	2.45	2.80	3.15	3.50	3.85	2800	4.20	4.55	4.90	5.60	6.30	7.00	8.40
.36	.73	1.09	2.54	2.90	3.26	3.63	3.99	2900	4.35	4.71	5.08	5.80	6.53	7.25	8.70
.38	.75	1.18	2.62	3.00	3.38	3.75	4.13	3000	4.50	4.88	5.25	6.00	6.75	7.50	9.00

$7	$8	$9	$10	$11	$12	Weight	$13	$14	$15	$16	$17	$18
.04	.04	.05	.05	.06	.06	10	.07	.07	.08	.08	.09	.09
.07	.08	.09	.10	.11	.12	20	.13	.14	.15	.16	.17	.18
.11	.12	.14	.15	.17	.18	30	.20	.21	.23	.24	.26	.27
.14	.16	.18	.20	.22	.24	40	.26	.28	.30	.32	.34	.36
.18	.20	.23	.25	.28	.30	50	.33	.35	.38	.40	.43	.45
.21	.24	.27	.30	.33	.36	60	.39	.42	.45	.48	.51	.54
.25	.28	.32	.35	.39	.42	70	.46	.49	.53	.56	.60	.63
.28	.32	.36	.40	.44	.48	80	.52	.56	.60	.64	.68	.72
.32	.36	.41	.45	.50	.54	90	.59	.63	.68	.72	.77	.81
.35	.40	.45	.50	.55	.60	100	.65	.70	.75	.80	.85	.90
3.50	4.00	4.50	5.00	5.50	6.00	1000	6.50	7.00	7.50	8.00	8.50	9.00
3.85	4.40	4.95	5.50	6.05	6.60	1100	7.15	7.70	8.25	8.80	9.35	9.90
4.20	4.80	5.40	6.00	6.60	7.20	1200	7.80	8.40	9.00	9.60	10.20	10.80
4.55	5.20	5.85	6.50	7.15	7.80	1300	8.45	9.10	9.75	10.40	11.05	11.70
4.90	5.60	6.30	7.00	7.70	8.40	1400	9.10	9.80	10.50	11.20	11.90	12.60
5.25	6.00	6.75	7.50	8.25	9.00	1500	9.75	10.50	11.25	12.00	12.75	13.50
5.60	6.40	7.20	8.00	8.80	9.60	1600	10.40	11.20	12.00	12.80	13.60	14.40
5.95	6.80	7.65	8.50	9.35	10.20	1700	11.05	11.90	12.75	13.60	14.45	15.30
6.30	7.20	8.10	9.00	9.90	10.80	1800	11.70	12.60	13.50	14.40	15.30	16.20
6.65	7.60	8.55	9.50	10.45	11.40	1900	12.35	13.30	14.25	15.20	16.15	17.10
7.35	8.40	9.45	10.50	11.55	12.60	2100	13.65	14.70	15.75	16.80	17.85	18.90
7.70	8.80	9.90	11.00	12.10	13.20	2200	14.30	15.40	16.50	17.60	18.70	19.80
8.05	9.20	10.35	11.50	12.65	13.80	2300	14.95	16.10	17.25	18.40	19.55	20.70
8.40	9.60	10.80	12.00	13.20	14.40	2400	15.60	16.80	18.00	19.20	20.40	21.60
8.75	10.00	11.25	12.50	13.75	15.00	2500	16.25	17.50	18.75	20.00	21.25	22.50
9.10	10.40	11.70	13.00	14.30	15.60	2600	16.90	18.20	19.50	20.80	22.10	23.40
9.45	10.80	12.15	13.50	14.85	16.20	2700	17.55	18.90	20.25	21.60	22.95	24.30
9.80	11.20	12.60	14.00	15.40	16.80	2800	18.20	19.60	21.00	22.40	23.80	25.20
10.15	11.60	13.05	14.50	15.95	17.40	2900	18.85	20.30	21.75	23.20	24.65	26.10
10.50	12.00	13.50	15.00	16.50	18.00	3000	19.50	21.00	22.50	24.00	25.50	27.00

SHOWING THE VALUE OF LIVESTOCK

The middle column gives the number of pounds and the top of each column the price per hundred weight.[1]

.05	.10	2.50	2.75	3.00	3.25	Weight	3.50	3.75	4.00	4.25	4.50
.00	.00	.08	.08	.09	.10	3	.11	.11	.12	.13	.14
.00	.01	.13	.14	.15	.16	5	.18	.19	.20	.21	.23
.01	.01	.25	.28	.30	.33	10	.35	.38	.40	.43	.45
.01	.02	.38	.41	.45	.49	15	.53	.56	.60	.64	.68
.01	.02	.50	.55	.60	.65	20	.70	.75	.80	.85	.90
.01	.03	.63	.69	.75	.81	25	.88	.94	1.00	1.06	1.13
.02	.03	.75	.83	.90	.98	30	1.05	1.13	1.20	1.28	1.35
.02	.04	.88	.96	1.05	1.14	35	1.23	1.31	1.40	1.49	1.58
.02	.04	1.00	1.10	1.20	1.30	40	1.40	1.50	1.60	1.70	1.80
.02	.05	1.13	1.24	1.35	1.46	45	1.58	1.69	1.80	1.91	2.03
.03	.05	1.25	1.38	1.50	1.63	50	1.75	1.88	2.00	2.13	2.25
.03	.06	1.38	1.51	1.65	1.79	55	1.93	2.06	2.20	2.34	2.48
.03	.06	1.50	1.65	1.80	1.95	60	2.10	2.25	2.40	2.55	2.70
.03	.07	1.63	1.79	1.95	2.11	65	2.28	2.44	2.60	2.76	2.93
.04	.07	1.75	1.93	2.10	2.28	70	2.45	2.63	2.80	2.98	3.15
.04	.08	1.88	2.06	2.25	2.44	75	2.63	2.81	3.00	3.19	3.38
.04	.08	2.00	2.20	2.40	2.60	80	2.80	3.00	3.20	3.40	3.60
.04	.09	2.13	2.34	2.55	2.76	85	2.98	3.19	3.40	3.61	3.83
.05	.09	2.25	2.48	2.70	2.93	90	3.15	3.38	3.60	3.83	4.05
.05	.10	2.38	2.61	2.85	3.09	95	3.33	3.56	3.80	4.04	4.28
.05	.10	2.50	2.75	3.00	3.25	100	3.50	3.75	4.00	4.25	4.50
.10	.20	5.00	5.50	6.00	6.50	200	7.00	7.50	8.00	8.50	9.00
.15	.30	7.50	8.25	9.00	9.75	300	10.50	11.25	12.00	12.75	13.50
.20	.40	10.00	11.00	12.00	13.00	400	14.00	15.00	16.00	17.00	18.00
.25	.50	12.50	13.75	15.00	16.25	500	17.50	18.75	20.00	21.25	22.50
.30	.60	15.00	16.50	18.00	19.50	600	21.00	22.50	24.00	25.50	27.00
.35	.70	17.50	19.25	21.00	22.75	700	24.50	26.25	28.00	29.75	31.50
.40	.80	20.00	22.00	24.00	26.00	800	28.00	30.00	32.00	34.00	36.00
.45	.90	22.50	24.75	27.00	29.25	900	31.50	33.75	36.00	38.25	40.50
.50	1.00	25.00	27.50	30.00	32.50	1000	35.00	37.50	40.00	42.50	45.00
.55	1.10	27.50	30.25	33.00	35.75	1100	38.50	41.25	44.00	46.75	49.50
.60	1.20	30.00	33.00	36.00	39.00	1200	42.00	45.00	48.00	51.00	56.00
.65	1.30	32.50	35.75	39.00	42.25	1300	45.50	48.75	52.00	55.25	58.50
.70	1.40	35.00	38.50	42.00	45.50	1400	49.00	52.50	56.00	59.50	63.00
.75	1.50	37.50	41.25	45.00	48.75	1500	52.50	56.25	60.00	63.75	67.50
.80	1.60	40.00	44.00	48.00	52.00	1600	56.00	60.00	64.00	68.00	72.00
.85	1.70	42.50	46.75	51.00	55.25	1700	59.50	63.75	68.00	72.25	76.50
.90	1.80	45.00	49.50	54.00	58.50	1800	63.00	67.50	72.00	76.50	81.00
.95	1.90	47.50	52.25	57.00	61.75	1900	66.50	71.25	76.00	80.75	85.50
1.00	2.00	50.00	55.00	60.00	65.00	2000	70.00	75.00	80.00	85.00	90.00
1.05	2.10	52.50	57.75	63.00	68.25	2100	73.50	78.75	84.00	89.25	94.50
1.10	2.20	55.00	60.50	66.00	71.50	2200	77.00	82.50	88.00	93.50	99.00
1.15	2.30	57.50	63.25	69.00	74.75	2300	80.50	86.25	92.00	97.75	103.50
1.20	2.40	60.00	66.00	72.00	78.00	2400	84.00	90.00	96.00	102.00	108.00
1.25	2.50	62.50	68.75	75.00	81.25	2500	87.50	93.75	100.00	106.25	112.50
1.30	2.60	65.00	71.50	78.00	84.50	2600	91.00	97.50	104.00	110.50	117.00
1.35	2.70	67.50	74.25	81.00	87.75	2700	94.50	101.25	108.00	114.75	121.50
1.40	2.80	70.00	77.00	84.00	91.00	2800	98.00	105.00	112.00	119.00	126.00
1.45	2.90	72.50	79.75	87.00	94.25	2900	101.50	108.75	116.00	123.25	130.50
1.50	3.00	75.00	82.50	90.00	97.50	3000	105.00	112.50	120.00	127.50	135.00
1.55	3.10	77.50	85.25	93.00	100.75	3100	108.50	116.25	124.00	131.75	139.50
1.60	3.20	80.00	88.00	96.00	104.00	3200	112.00	120.00	128.00	136.00	144.00
1.65	3.30	82.50	90.75	99.00	107.25	3300	115.50	123.75	132.00	140.25	148.50
1.70	3.40	85.00	93.50	102.00	110.50	3400	119.00	127.50	136.00	144.50	153.00
1.75	3.50	87.50	96.25	105.00	113.75	3500	122.50	131.25	140.00	148.75	157.50
1.80	3.60	90.00	99.00	108.00	117.00	3600	126.00	135.00	144.00	153.00	162.00
1.85	3.70	92.50	101.75	111.00	120.25	3700	129.50	138.75	148.00	157.25	166.50
1.90	3.80	95.00	104.50	114.00	123.50	3800	133.00	142.50	152.00	161.50	171.00
1.95	3.90	97.50	107.25	117.00	126.75	3900	136.50	146.25	156.00	165.75	175.50
2.00	4.00	100.00	110.00	120.00	130.00	4000	140.00	150.00	160.00	170.00	180.00
2.05	4.10	102.50	112.75	123.00	133.25	4100	143.50	153.75	164.00	174.25	184.50
2.10	4.20	105.00	115.50	126.00	136.50	4200	147.00	157.50	168.00	178.50	189.00
2.15	4.30	107.50	118.25	129.00	139.75	4300	150.50	161.25	172.00	182.75	193.50
2.20	4.40	110.00	121.00	132.00	143.00	4400	154.00	165.00	176.00	187.00	198.00
2.25	4.50	112.50	123.75	135.00	146.25	4500	157.50	168.75	180.00	191.25	202.50

[1] 100 pounds, usually abbreviated "cwt."

KEEPING ACCOUNTS

"Unsuccessful merchants," as someone has said, "are not so much unprincipled as they are incompetent." Nothing is so discouraging to incompetency as good bookkeeping; nothing makes it flourish more than sloppy bookkeeping.

Properly kept books should show at any given moment a complete and accurate picture of the way a business is going. They hold a record of what has happened and an indication of what may happen. They give a basis for sound operations and workable budgets, and, most important of all, they show weak spots which, once located, may be strengthened.

There are two systems of bookkeeping, single-entry and double-entry.

Single-Entry Bookkeeping

Single-entry bookkeeping systems are of very little value to modern business, because they are complicated, and consequently are very difficult to interpret. In order to make them comprehensive, as many books or sections of books should be carried as there are principal accounts connected with the business.

All transactions involving those accounts are recorded therein, and their effect added or deducted from the balance in that particular book or account. Single-entry records do not provide complete accounting data and it, therefore, requires special knowledge to interpret the results of the operations of a business using such records.

Double-Entry Bookkeeping

By installing a simple set of double-entry books, it is easily possible to get accurate results at a small expense. The double-entry system will accommodate itself to the means of even the smallest business, and the system can be enlarged to fit the largest and most complicated of enterprises. Primarily, double entry consists of nothing more than recording at one time the effect of any transaction on two accounts. An analysis of all business transactions would readily show that two accounts are always affected. For example—when money is paid out, the amount of cash on hand is reduced, and either an existing liability is reduced or some expense is incurred. A business in paying its rent reduces the amount of money it has by the amount it pays, and this is so recorded. The other side of this entry is recorded as a charge or debit against the rent account.

Similarly cash is received by the business in payment to it for merchandise which is sold. This is recorded as an increase of the cash (a debit), and on the other side it is credited to sales, or to payment for goods sold on open account.

Regardless of its size, a business should maintain the following books. Larger businesses may keep others in amplification of those mentioned, which are nothing more or less than an expansion of the principle involved in the simple set following: General Ledger, Cash Book, Sales Book, Purchase Book, Journal, and Accounts Receivable Ledger.

The *general ledger* should be started by a summary of the assets and liabilities of the business at its beginning or at the time that the bookkeeping system started.

An inventory should be taken of the financial position of the business with regard to the various assets and liabilities that it has at the time the system is started. If it is a new business, it will start with cash or its equivalent, and have very few accounts at the outset, but if it is an already established business, it will undoubtedly have quite a few more accounts, such as cash (bank accounts), accounts receivable, merchandise or raw material inventory, etc., among its assets, and accounts payable, notes payable, etc. among its liabilities.

The status of net worth, whether it be the sole proprietorship, partnership, or corporation should also be taken into account at this time. The balance of this account represents the business's capital investment, and should be the balance or difference between the total of its assets and the total of its liabilities.

Great care should be exercised in the original determination of the amount to be set up in these accounts, as this will avoid the necessity of subsequent corrections or changes. When finally determined, these figures are recorded in the journal and from that journal are posted as the original entries in the general ledger accounts.

The accounts outlined above having been started, they are increased or decreased at periodic intervals by the postings from the cash book, the sales book, the journal, and the accounts receivable ledger resulting from business transactions.

The *cash book* can best be kept by separating cash receipts and cash disbursements. If it is desired to keep one book, it may be most practical to have cash receipts recorded on each left-hand page, and cash disbursements on each right-hand page, or if there be a great difference between the number of entries, there being many more receipts than disbursements, or vice versa, much better results are obtained by dividing the book into two sections, one being for receipts and the other for disbursements. This book should be a columnar book, and for the majority of businesses, even the smallest, one should provide seven or more columns on each side of the book, including space for date, explanation, and a small checking column. The first thing which should appear to the extreme left of the page is the date column; the next, an explanation, in other words, space for the name of the person who sent or brought in the money; next, the net cash column, in which the exact amount of money received is recorded. There should also be a column for cash discounts which may be allowed to the customer for payment of invoices before a set date, as is common in most businesses.

In addition there should be first a column headed Accounts Receivable, in which the offsetting entry is made of the amount to be credited to the customers' individual accounts. The individual accounts for customers' charge will be carried in the accounts receivable ledger mentioned below and are posted from this column of the cash receipt book. Other columns

should be headed *Cash Sales, Notes Payable* (if money is regularly borrowed for the use of the business), and still other columns can be carried in this book if there be other sources of income or cash receipts. The idea in having this book is to show the increase in cash or, in the case of discounts, the recording of expenses experienced by allowing this discount, and also the credit columns that show from what source the money is received.

For the sake of flexibility, this book should contain a miscellaneous or general ledger column which should be a double column in which are recorded individual or miscellaneous items which are not frequent enough in their nature to require the setting up of a separate column for their classification. It will be found very practical to maintain this miscellaneous column so that any unusual items of receipt can be recorded uniformly through the same book that is used for all cash receipts.

The purpose of the double column is that the first affords space for the writing in of the name of the account to which this individual item is to be posted.

In posting this column to the general ledger accounts, the items are posted separately rather than in total, and the total is used only in proving or balancing the book at the end of the auditing period.

If a separate book is used for cash disbursements, it is usually very similar to the cash receipt book except that the totals obtained are posted in reverse of cash receipts as the very nature of the transaction is exactly opposite in effect. The same date and explanation columns are used, similarly, a column for net cash and the discount column to include items of cash discount deducted by the firm in settlement of its liabilities.

These two columns relate to accounts to be credited, and the rest of the columns relate to accounts which are debited and include accounts payable, salaries, wages, and other items of expense which are of sufficiently frequent occurrence to warrant the use of a column for their accumulation.

This book, like the cash receipt book, should also contain a general ledger column for miscellaneous entries which do not occur frequently enough to warrant the use of a column for them alone.

It might be said here and now that the best procedure both in keeping books and as a practical measure for the protection of cash is to avoid the payment of cash wherever possible, and certainly in all items in excess of $10. For this purpose, the business can keep a round fund sufficient to meet its actual cash requirements of, say, $20, $50, or $100, which is maintained as nearly as possible intact at all times, and replenished by check when more money is needed.

The entries of the check to replenish the fund are used to record the nature of the expenses for which the actual money was expended. In other words, this is the way it is done. A check is drawn for, say, $20, and this check is charged to petty cash account through the cash disbursement book and remains unaltered so long as the fund is neither increased nor decreased. Individual payments are made from time to time from this fund, and in receipt individual petty cash vouchers are made out. On a voucher of this kind is shown the person receiving the cash, the name of the expense account affected, such as postage, expressage, car fare, etc., and approval of the person authorized to make these payments.

When these slips amount to so large a sum that they leave too small an amount of cash, the slips are taken out, summarized, and analyzed, the check is drawn, and distributed in the cash disbursement book according to the analysis of the slips which it covers. The check is then cashed, and the money put back in the cash drawer, bringing the fund back to its original amount of $20 in actual cash. This system is strongly recommended to enable the deposit of all receipts, a very vital thing in the checking of money handled by a business.

The *sales book* should be a simple columnar book and should generally contain the following information, classified by columns: date column; invoice number, an explanation column, in which is entered the name of the purchaser to whom the sale is made; accounts receivable column in which are entered the total sales and from which are posted the individual items to the customer's account as carried in the accounts receivable ledger mentioned hereunder. The offsetting entry is analyzed and entered in the sales columns, one or more according to the nature of the sale and the number of subdivisions carried to record sales income.

The *purchase book* should also be a simple columnar book containing columns to receive the following information for all purchases and expenses for which bills are received: date column, an explanation column in which is entered the name of the vendor and vendor's invoice number; accounts payable column in which is entered the total amount of each invoice, and from which are posted the individual items to the customer's account as carried in the accounts payable ledger described below; a column should be provided for purchases in which are recorded all invoices for goods to be resold. Three columns should be provided for miscellaneous, bearing sub-titles as follows: two columns for nature of expense and one column for amount. The miscellaneous columns will receive offsetting entries for all items entered in the purchase book other than invoices for merchandise to be resold.

The *journal* is used for entries similar to the opening entry. In other words, to record transactions which do not involve cash, or sales, or purchases for which separate books are kept. The chief reason for keeping this book is that it is the medium through which the bookkeeper or accountant makes entries at closing or profit-and-loss determination periods. It should be but infrequently used, as its excessive use is an indication of the lack of proper books of original entry. It should also be borne in mind by persons not acquainted with accounting and bookkeeping principles that this book is unsafe in the hands of persons other than expert bookkeepers or accountants, and its use is, therefore, discouraged.

The *accounts receivable ledger* contains the individual accounts of customers to whom sales are made on credit, and each account on the left-hand side shows all items charged or debited to it, posted from the sales book (accounts receivable column), and on the right-hand side items of cash received in payment of such charges as posted from the cash receipts book (accounts receivable column).

The *accounts payable ledger* contains the individual amounts of all creditors from whom goods or services have been acquired on credit, and each amount on the left-hand or debit side shows payments made to these creditors (as posted from the cash book). The right-hand or credit side of the account will contain all items for which invoices have been received; the information for the credits is received from the accounts payable column of the purchase book. When this ledger is kept up-to-date, examination will reveal how much is owed to each of the creditors and if these amounts are listed and added will reveal the sum of the amounts owed or accounts payable as reflected in the financial statement.

For the purpose of this article, these and other amplifications of a double-entry system need not be explained, because where their use is required, the business is such that an expert accountant should be consulted for the preparation of its bookkeeping system.

On the other hand, it should be borne in mind that there are still many concerns doing a comparatively large business in which, although many records are kept, these records are not related to one another, and are not bound together to give a complete picture of the business as a whole at any time. In such cases, even the few books enumerated above, accurately kept, would be a great improvement over a large number of inaccurate and loosely related and uncontrolled books.

The biggest feature of double-entry bookkeeping and its greatest recommendation are the simple methods used that insure minimization of human error.

FINANCIAL STATEMENTS

Financial statements are prepared to show the financial condition and history of an enterprise. Compiled as of a given date, a statement covers transactions over a specified period and condition as of such date. It is presented in conformity with generally accepted accounting principles and consists of two primary forms: the *Balance Sheet,* or statement of assets, liabilities, and net worth; and the *Statement of Profit and Loss,* or income and expense statement. Supplementary information usually accompanies the two basic statements and serves to analyze and to explain certain items, such as surplus statements, loan schedules, plant and property schedules, and many others.

While financial statements are prepared periodically for single proprietorships or individuals, partnerships, and corporations, they are used also by estates, trusts, municipalities, funds, charitable and similar organizations.

Form of Statement

Standardization of form of financial statements has resulted from regulations issued by the Securities and Exchange Commission and the

Federal Housing Authority, and from recommendations of the American Institute of Accountants, various credit organizations, and others. Although no single form would cover every exigency, the form shown below is commonly used, with minor variations, by most business organizations.[1]

Balance Sheet

XYZ COMPANY
Balance Sheet
As of December 31, 19...

ASSETS

Current Assets:
Cash	$—.—		
Accounts Receivable	—.—		
Notes Receivable	—.—		
Inventories	—.—		
Other Current Assets	—.—		
Total Current Assets		$—.—	
Investments:		—.—	

Fixed Assets:
Property, Plant, and Equipment	—.—		
Less: Reserve for Depreciation	—.—	—.—	

Intangible Assets:
Goodwill, Patents, Copyright, etc.	—.—

Deferred Charges or Prepaid Expenses:
Prepaid Rent, Insurance, Taxes, etc.	—.—
Other Assets:	—.—

TOTAL ASSETS $—.—

LIABILITIES AND CAPITAL (Net Worth)

LIABILITIES

Current Liabilities:
Notes Payable	$—.—	
Accounts Payable	—.—	
Accrued Expenses (Unpaid Expenses)	—.—	
Other Current Liabilities	—.—	
Total Current Liabilities		$—.—
Fixed Liabilities (Funded Debt)		—.—

TOTAL LIABILITIES $—.—

CAPITAL (Net Worth)

Capital (for individuals and partnerships) $—.—

Capital Stock (for corporations) $—.—

Surplus:
Capital or Paid-In	$—.—	
Earned	—.—	—.—
Total Capital (Net Worth)		—.—

TOTAL LIABILITIES AND CAPITAL $—.—

(Footnotes pertaining to contingent liabilities, dividends in arrears, etc., may follow.)

[1]Substantially as recommended by the American Institute of Accountants.

Statement of Profit and Loss

XYZ COMPANY
Statement of Profit and Loss
For The Period From January 1, 19... to December 31, 19...

INCOME

Gross Sales	$—.—	
Less: Returns and Allowances	—.—	
Net Sales		$—.—
COST OF SALES		
Inventory—Beginning of Period	—.—	
Add: Purchases (incl. freight in)	—.—	
Total	—.—	
Less: Inventory—End of Period	—.—	
Cost of Sales		—.—
Gross Profit on Sales		—.—
Selling Expenses	—.—	
General and Administrative Expenses	—.—	—.—
Operating Profit		—.—
(Net Profit before other Income and Charges)		
Add: Other Income		—.—
TOTAL		—.—
Less: Other Charges		—.—
Net Profit (or Loss) for Period		$—.—

Purpose of Statement

The two major parts of a statement serve different functions. The Balance Sheet reflects the financial condition of the enterprise as of a given date, and the Statement of Profit and Loss shows the results of the business operations for the period indicated. While the Balance Sheet shows asset values, liability, and the net worth of a business, the Statement of Profit and Loss shows income and expenditures, and as a result, expresses the gain or loss of the business operations during the period.

Preparation of Statemen

Financial statements are prepared at certain intervals after the business transactions for the period have been recorded. One of the main purposes of bookkeeping is to prepare information from which statements are prepared. The statements represent the third and final step in the accounting phase.[1] The first step is the chronological recording of transactions in various "journals," such as cash receipts, cash disbursements, purchases, and sales. These journals are totaled and analyzed. The second step is classifiying the results of the journals into "ledger" accounts. Summarization is in turn made of these ledger accounts, and this

[1] See also section on Accounting (page 271).

summarization or "Trial Balance" of the ledger accounts is the starting point for the preparation of financial statements.

It is commonly agreed upon that three general elements comprise the preparation of a statement. *The recorded fact* as indicated above is the first. *The application of accounting convention* is the second element. Here variation may occur with such items as the valuation of fixed assets, the amount of an expenditure to be classified as an asset or an expense item, etc. Investments by corporations in other corporations, for example, may be carried at cost or at the current value of the investment. Work on factory buildings may be looked on as improvements to be capitalized or considered merely as repairs to be written off. Inventories may be valued at cost, or cost or market value whichever is lower. Naturally, it is essential that accounting conventions are clearly understood by anyone who attempts to analyze a financial statement. *The application of personal judgment* to the preparation of a statement is the third element. Principles of judgment have considerable bearing, for instance, on the estimated life of an asset, which in turn serves as a basis for determining its periodic depreciation or for similar appraisals.

Use and Analysis of Statement

Broadly speaking, financial statements are classified as (1) to be used *internally, i.e.,* used within the organization, and (2) to be used externally, when presented to banks, credit agencies, investors, and suppliers of materials, etc.

From a proper statement, management is able to determine the progress and efficiency of the operations of the business. From the Balance Sheet the soundness of the business can be ascertained. Comparison of the current assets (or assets that can be readily converted to cash) with the current liabilities, or with obligations that have to be met in the near future, will show the liquidity of the business, or the ability of the enterprise to dispose of its obligations easily.

In this connection, the term "working capital" is used. Working capital represents the excess or current assets over current liabilities. It shows management the current assets remaining after all immediate obligations shall have been met. A healthy condition here is usually represented by twice the amount of current assets as of current liabilities.

The "current ratio" expresses these facts in the form of a proportion. For example, current assets of $40,000 compared with $20,000 of current liabilities would represent a current ratio of 2:1.

Management may also determine the relative position of individual assets by the use of percentages. For example, the percentage of inventory to the total assets will give part of the answer to an overstocked or understocked position. Tracing this percentage for several periods will show the level of inventory fluctuation. Percentages of fixed assets, such as machinery, furniture, and other total assets, will show what portion of the total assets is tied up or unavailable for meeting current obligations.

The Statement of Profit and Loss shows whether the enterprise is operating profitably. Costs and expenses deducted from income, with the exclusion of funds reserved for taxes and other specific purposes, indicate the amount of profit available for dividend disbursements to stockholders.

Comparisons should be made of each item included in the Statement of Profit and Loss with the net sales in the form of percentages. Such comparisons indicate the percentage of the sale or income dollar that is consumed by each of the costs and expenses incurred to "run" the business. Here, comparison of percentage figures covering several years shows the trend of costs and expenses. Graphically, the rise in individual expenses will point out to management where economies are necessary.

The needs of manufacturing organizations for financial information are answered by a very specialized branch of bookkeeping and accounting known as Cost Accounting. This may vary from simple statistical records to highly intricate account systems. Frequently, Standard (manufacturing) Costs are predetermined and the Profit and Loss statement then will show standard costs and the variations therefrom. The analysis of the differences between the actual costs and the predetermined Standard Costs gives management the opportunity to spot excessive cost situations, and thus undertake steps for their cure. The further analysis of such figures into manufacturing departments helps to pin-point these cost differences.

External Use and Analysis

Banks, credit organizations, suppliers of material and investors are concerned with both the Balance Sheet and the Statement of Profit and Loss. From the information thus received they determine their relationship with the enterprise concerned.

Banks and credit organizations naturally regard stability and a business' ability to meet its obligations promptly as two fundamental factors. These may be indicated by a good current ratio maintained over a length of time, by the presence of readily marketable inventories, and by generally profitable operations. Inventory turnover (or the cost of sales divided by the average inventory) shows how readily inventory is sold during a period. The number of turnovers of inventory varies with the type of product. Another important factor in determining a possible credit is the amount of net worth of a business and/or already existing loans compared with the amount sought. Such facts, in addition to the history of an organization and prompt payment of its obligations, form the basis for extension of credit.

Organizations selling materials on credit request financial statements of their prospective customers in order to determine their ability to pay for the merchandise. The methods used to determine this are very much the same as in the case of the banks or credit organizations which grant loans.

However, the viewpoint here may be shorter in range, materials being sold normally on comparatively short credit terms. Therefore, the ratio of "Quick Assets" to current liabilities and not of current assets to current liabilities is often used. These Quick Assets are represented by such items as cash, readily marketable securities, accounts receivable (if very liquid), and, sometimes, inventory. The comparison of the Quick Assets to current liabilities is known as the "Acid Test."

The investor's viewpoint differs from the creditor's viewpoint in that the investor considers the return he will obtain on his investment, or the profit the organization will make in which he will share. Actually, the purpose of the investment will govern the phase of the statements to be considered most important. If high returns are desired, the Statement of Profit and Loss is examined to determine the extent of profits. Inventory turnovers, percentages for the period, and trend percentages are obtained for costs and expenses. If stability in investment is desired then examination of the Balance Sheet is stressed.

As an aside it may be noted here that labor unions recently received the right to inspect the financial statements of enterprises in order to determine the wages and salaries firms should be requested to pay.

As may be seen from the foregoing, the preparation of financial statements, which deal mainly with cold financial facts, may be greatly affected by the personal position, background, and education of the individual preparing these statements. The need, by credit and lending institutions and investors, for unbiased, "outside" preparation and interpretation of financial statements of companies in which they are interested has contributed to the growth of the profession of Public Accounting. States have set up criteria of education, experience, and character; only those who fulfill these requirements may become Certified Public Accountants. The certification by a Certified Public Accountant that financial statements which he has prepared "present fairly the position of the company and the results of its operations" is an indication that such statements have been prepared by a person properly trained to compile such information.

CREDIT

Credit is the "tick" in American business, because it increases sales, promotes good will, and helps to insure maximum net earnings. In addition, credit sales are larger on the average, credit customers buy more, credit develops confidence, credit attracts better trade, credit irons out business peaks, credit reduces complaints, credit sales are more economical than C.O.D. sales, and credit is a convenience to the customer.

The following classes of credit are in use by American business:

1. *Mercantile credit,* which is the potential capacity of a borrower to obtain parts and/or end items to be used in production or for wholesale distribution in return for a "confidence" promise to pay in the future;

2. *Retail credit,* which is the power of an individual to purchase completed items for consumption, in return for a promise to pay in the future—for example, a suit of clothes sold by a clothier to a customer. There are two types of retail credit, *consumer* and *installment* credit. Consumer, or individual, credit is credit granted to consumers for consumption; installment credit is another type of consumer credit, in which credit is granted to consumers for consumption, with predetermined installments made monthly or weekly;

3. *Bank credit,* which is usually short-term credit in which the bank extends credit to a businessman for temporary working capital to meet seasonal needs. This type of credit is usually accomplished with the use of promissory notes given to the bank;

4. *Investment credit,* which is long-term credit, money borrowed by industry for expansion, for acquiring fixed assets, and for permanent working capital. The credit instruments generally used are bonds, mortgages, and promissory notes;

5. *Agricultural credit,* which is long-term credit. Farmers obtain credit primarily from Federal Reserve Banks, but must apply for loans to their own local banks, to meet their needs for working capital and fixed capital.

The two main credit factors in American business, *mercantile credit* and *retail credit,* are discussed below.

Mercantile Credit

Mercantile credit affects the production and distribution of an enterprise. It is very important for the credit man to have at hand sources of credit information representing general business and financial reporting agencies, *viz.:* Dun & Bradstreet, Inc., Babson's Business Report Service, the *Wall Street Journal,* the *Journal of Commerce,* Moody Investors Service, and many others; also trade association journals published monthly, *viz.: Credit and Financial Management,* published by the National Association of Credit Men, *Credit World,* published by National Retail Credit Association, and trade journals applicable to the special industry.

Necessary sources of information pertaining to the reduction of credit risks are (1) a personal interview, (2) inspection of the debtor's business, and (3) the company's own records. The creditor should insist that the latest financial statements be submitted. Some salient questions are:

1. Is the information reliable?
2. Is there any significant evidence that sources of supply are shifted frequently?
3. Is the purchasing policy sound in respect to sources of supply and balance of accounts?
4. Is the company's position with regard to indebtedness satisfactory?
5. Are there in effect standard terms of sale?
6. Are the paying practices satisfactory?
7. What does the information in the comment column suggest—a "good" or a "bad" risk?

In determining credit limits for old and new accounts, two possible bases must be given consideration—probable purchase requirements of customers and customers' power to pay debts.

Retail Credit

The extension of credit by a retailer to his customers will increase sales but at the same time it will affect his working capital.

There are three types of retail or consumer credit: the charge account, the installment account, of which there are several variations, and personal loans.

The charge account grantor may obtain credit information from approximately 1,500 credit bureaus who are members of the Associated Credit Bureaus of America, located throughout the United States and Canada. The bureaus furnish various types of credit reports. The trade clearance and the special report bureaus are frequently used because the former provides information pertaining to the present paying habits of the applicant and the latter provides information pertaining to the identity, residence, place of business, and banking and trade status of the applicant.

The installment account grantor is primarily interested in the long-term commitments of the applicant and his paying record. Much of this information is available from the regular credit bureaus, except in some cities where there are independent bureaus specializing in the paying habits of installment buyers.

The personal loan grantor is most interested in the present and past loan-paying habits of the applicant. Lending agencies usually have their own interchange in the cities in which they operate.

The general practice of the installment creditor and the personal creditor is to conduct their personal investigations of the business and bank connections of the applicant by telephone or by letter.

While there are many special factors affecting the desirability of the credit risk, the approval is usually based on (1) ability to pay, (2) intention to pay, (3) past performance.

Additional analysis and appraisal of risks require careful study of a number of factors, *viz.*, the habits of the people, the good and bad neighborhoods, the occupational outlook, and the interpretation of credit experience.

Credit decisions based upon the factors mentioned above tend to build good will for the business.

GRAPHS

A *graph* is a diagram showing relationships. It is drawn on graph paper (which can be obtained from any stationery store or from any house that sells school supplies) and consists of a series of dots connected by a curve. The information in a graph might just as well be presented in a table, except that the graph shows at a glance what the information means, while it may take several minutes to puzzle out what the table means.

Let us see how it works. Suppose a magazine secures its only revenue from advertising and that, as with nearly all magazines, its advertising falls off during the summer. The advertising falls off, but the overhead expenses remain the same. The publisher has the information in the following table:

Month	No. of pages of advertising	Month	No. of pages of advertising
January	50	July	26
February	52	August	25
March	54	September	38
April	50	October	48
May	45	November	52
June	32	December	52

To make a picture of this he takes a piece of graph paper which is ruled off, as indicated in the accompanying diagram, horizontally and vertically into uniform squares, which in turn are divided into smaller squares. He selects 12 of the heavy vertical lines and lets each one represent a month. Then he lets the heavy horizontal lines represent the number of pages, and, for convenience, lets each heavy line represent a unit of five pages.

GRAPH 283

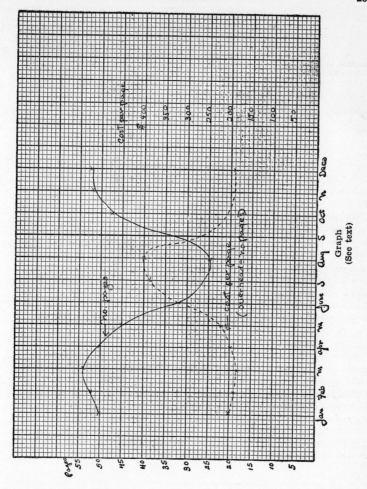

Graph
(See text)

In January the number of pages was 50. So he puts a point on the graph paper on the January vertical line where it crosses the horizontal 50-page line. In February he puts a point at 52 (about halfway between 50 and 55), and so on to the end of the year. Then he draws a smooth line through all these points. This is the——curve in the diagram above. The slump in his business (which looks alarming but which is what nearly all magazines and many other businesses have to face) is clearly evident.

Now suppose the publisher also desires to see how his overhead compares every month with his income. He finds the cost of getting a page of advertising by dividing the overhead by the number of pages. His fixed overhead charges per month are $10,000. In tabular form the information he desires is this:

Month	Cost per page to secure ($10,000÷50)
January	200
February	193
March	185
April	200
May	225
June	312
July	385
August	400
September	264
October	210
November	193
December	193

He can plot this curve on the same piece of paper. The heavy horizontal lines now represent the cost per page, each line standing for $50. In January the cost per page was $200. He makes a mark on the January vertical line where it crosses the $200 horizontal line. In February the cost per page was $193. He makes a mark on the February line slightly below the $200 mark, and so on through the table. On the diagram the curve appears in the line.......

If information of this kind is kept in "pictures" it makes it possible to compare at a glance the result of one year's work with another.

THE METRIC SYSTEM

The metric system was invented toward the close of the 18th century, and made obligatory throughout France in 1837. It is much simpler than any other system of measurement and is now used internationally by scientists, and as the national system by most countries, the chief exceptions being the British Empire, the United States, and Russia. The United States, however, has a decimal monetary system.

Units of the Metric System

The fundamental units of the metric system are the *meter,* which is the unit of length, and the *kilogram,* which is the unit of mass.

The *liter,* a measure of capacity, is defined as the volume of a kilogram of water at the temperature of its maximum density (4° centigrade), and under standard atmospheric pressure (760 millimeters). All other units are the decimal subdivisions or multiples of these.

The meter, the kilogram, and the liter are closely related. For all practical purposes, 1 cubic decimeter equals 1 liter and 1 liter of water weighs 1 kilogram. Thus, the quantity 5,432.768 meters can be immediately read as 5 kilometers, 4 hectometers, 3 decameters, 2 meters, 7 decimeters, 6 centimeters, and 8 millimeters. If the quantity is not a length, but a weight, the only change necessary is the substitution of the word "grams" for the word "meters."

The metric tables are formed by combining the word "meter," "gram," and "liter" with the six following prefixes:

Prefixes	Meaning		Units
milli-	= one-thousandth	.001	
centi-	= one-hundredth	.01	"meter" for length
deci-	= one-tenth	.1	"gram" for weight
Unit	= one	1.	or mass
deka-	= ten	10	
hecto-	= one hundred	100	"liter" for capacity
kilo-	= one thousand	1000	"are" for land area

The *joule* is a unit of both mechanical and electrical energy. It is equivalent to the work done or the heat generated in keeping up for one second a current of one ampere against a resistance of one ohm, or in raising the potential of one coulomb by one volt. Equal to 10,000,000 ergs or .73756 foot-pound.

The *calorie* is one of two recognized units of heat, of which the greater calorie is the amount of heat necessary to raise one kilogram of water 1° C., the lesser or small calorie being the amount of heat necessary to raise one gram of water 1° C.

The United States Bureau of Standards advocates use of "kilocalorie" and "calorie," respectively, for the greater and lesser calorie.

Foot-pound, horsepower, and cheval or cheval vapeur, as generally defined, vary from place to place by ½ per cent because of variations in the intensity of gravity. The relations given below are for the international standard gravity, which gives an acceleration of 980.665 centimeters per second per second.

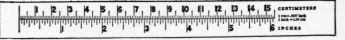

A Comparison of Centimeters and Inches

Metric Abbreviations

k	= kilo	h	= hecto	dk	= deca
m	= milli	d	= deci	c	= centi
g	= gram	m	= meter	c. c.	= cubic centimeter
hl	= hectoleter	kg	= kilogram	l	= liter
t	= ton metric	a	= are	s	= stere

Metric Conversions

Millimeters × .03937	= inches
Millimeters ÷ 25.4	= inches
Centimeters × .3937	= inches
Centimeters ÷ 2.54	= inches
Meters × 39.37	= inches
Meters × 3.28	= feet
Meters × 1.094	= yards
Kilometers × .6214	= miles
Kilometers ÷ 1.6093	= miles
Kilometers × 3.280.8	= feet
Square millimeters × .00155	= square inches
Square millimeters ÷ 645	= square inches
Square centimeters × .155	= square inches
Square centimeters ÷ 6.45	= square inches
Square meters × 10.764	= square feet
Square kilometers × 247.1	= acres
Square kilometers × .3861	= square miles
Hectares × 2.471	= acres
Hectares × .003861	= square miles
Cubic centimeters ÷ 16.387	= cubic inches
Cubic centimeters ÷ 3.70	= fluid drams
Cubic centimeters ÷ 29.57	= fluid ounces
Cubic meters × 35.314	= cubic feet
Cubic meters × 1.307	= cubic yards
Cubic meters × 264.2	= gallons (231 cubic inches)
Litres × 61.025	= cubic inches
Litres × 33.81	= fluid ounces
Litres × .2642	= gallons (231 cubic inches)
Litres ÷ 3.785	= gallons (231 cubic inches)
Litres ÷ 28.317	= cubic feet
Hectoliters × 3.53	= cubic feet
Hectoliters × 2.84	= bushels (2,150.42 cubic inches)
Hectoliters × .131	= cubic yards
Hectoliters ÷ 26.42	= gallons (231 cubic inches)
Grams × 15.432	= grains
Grams (water) ÷ 29.57	= fluid ounces
Grams ÷ 28.35	= ounces avoirdupois
Grams per cubic centimeter ÷ 27.7	= pounds per cubic inch
Joule × .7373	= foot-pounds
Kilograms × 2.2046	= pounds
Kilograms × 35.27	= ounces avoirdupois
Kilograms ÷ 908.68	= short tons (2,000 pounds)
Kilograms per square centimeter × 14.223	= pounds per square inch
Kilogram meters × 7.233	= foot-pounds
Kilograms per meter × .671	= pounds per foot
Kilograms per cubic meter × .062	= pounds per cubic foot
Kilograms per cheval × 2.235	= pounds per horsepower
Kilowatts × 1.34	= horsepower (33,000 foot-pounds per minute)
Watts ÷ 746	= horsepower
Watts × .00134	= horsepower
Watts × 44.24	= foot-pounds per minute
Calories × 3.968	= B. T. U. (British Thermal Unit)
Cheval vapeur × 0.986	= horsepower
Centigrade × 1.8 + 32	= degrees Fahrenheit

Acceleration due to gravity, international standard, 980.665 centimeters per second² or 980.665 centimeters per second per second.

Measures of Length

The meter is the unit. It is equal to 39.37 inches, or 3⅜ feet.

```
1 kilometer = 1,000 meters
1 hectometer = 100 meters
1 dekameter = 10 meters
1 decimeter = 0.1 meter
1 centimeter = 0.01 meter
1 millimeter = 0.001 meter = 0.1 centimeter
1 micron = 0.000001 meter = 0.001 millimeter
1 millimicron = 0.000000001 meter = 0.001 micron
1 foot = ⅓ yard = 30.48 centimeters
1 inch = 1/36 yard = 1/12 foot = 2.54 centimeters
1 link = 0.22 yard = 7.92 inches
1 rod = 5½ yards = 16½ feet
1 chain = 22 yards = 100 links = 66 feet = 4 rods
1 furlong = 220 yards = 40 rods = 10 chains
1 statute mile = 1,760 yards = 5,280 feet = 320 rods = 1,609.35 meters
1 hand = 4 inches
1 point = 1/12 inch
1 fathom = 6 feet
1 span = 9 inches = ⅛ fathom
1 U.S. nautical mile ⎞ = 6,080.20 feet
1 sea mile            ⎬ = 1.151553 statute miles
1 geographical mile  ⎠ = 1,853.248 meters
```

Measures of Area

The square meter is the unit, that is, a square which is one meter long on each side.

```
1 square kilometer = 1,000,000 square meters
1 hectare or square hectometer = 10,000 square meters
1 are or square dekameter = 100 square meters
1 centare = 1 square meter
1 square decimeter = 0.01 square meter
1 square centimeter = 0.0001 square meter
1 square millimeter = 0.000001 square meter = 0.01 square centimeter
1 square foot = ⅑ square yard
1 square inch = 1/1296 square yard = 1/144 square foot
1 square link = 0.0484 square yard = 62.7264 square inches
1 square rod = 30.25 square yards = 272.25 square feet = 625 square links
1 square chain = 484 square yards = 16 square rods = 10,000 square links
1 acre = 4,840 square yards = 160 square rods = 10 square chains = .4047 hectare =
     40.47 are
1 square mile = 3,097,600 square yards = 640 acres = 259 hectares
```

Measures of Volume

The cubic meter is the unit, that is, a cube each edge of which is one meter long.

```
1 cubic kilometer = 1,000,000,000 cubic meters
1 cubic hectometer = 1,000,000 cubic meters
1 cubic dekameter = 1,000 cubic meters
1 stere = 1 cubic meter
1 cubic decimeter = 0.001 cubic meter
1 cubic centimeter = 0.000001 cubic meter = 0.001 cubic decimeter
1 cubic millimeter = 0.000000001 cubic meter = 0.001 cubic centimeter
1 cubic foot = 1/27 cubic yard
1 cubic inch = 1/46656 cubic yard = 1/1728 cubic foot
1 board foot = 144 cubic inches = 1/12 cubic foot
1 cord = 128 cubic feet
```

Measures of Capacity

The liter is the unit. The liter is 1.000027 cubic decimeters, or 61.025 cubic inches, which is equal to .264178 gallons, or 2.11342 liquid pints.

```
1 hectoliter = 100 liters
1 dekaliter = 10 liters
1 deciliter = 0.1 liter
1 centiliter = 0.01 liter
1 liquid quart = ¼ gallon = 57.57 cubic inches
1 liquid pint = ⅛ gallon = ½ liquid quart = 28.785 cubic inches
1 gill = ¹⁄₃₂ gallon = ¼ liquid pint = 7.19625 cubic inches
1 fluid ounce = ¹⁄₁₂₈ gallon = ¹⁄₁₆ liquid pint
1 fluid dram = ⅛ fluid ounce = ¹⁄₁₂₈ liquid pint
1 minim = ¹⁄₆₀ fluid dram = ¹⁄₄₈₀ fluid ounce
1 firkin = 9 gallons
1 peck = ¼ bushel = 537.605 cubic inches
1 dry quart = ¹⁄₃₂ bushel = ⅛ peck = 67.200625 cubic inches
1 dry pint = ¹⁄₆₄ bushel = ½ dry quart = 33.6003125 cubic inches
1 barrel (for fruits, vegetables, and other dry commodities) 7,056 cubic inches = 105 dry
   quarts
```
Note.—

A (U.S.) gallon is a unit of capacity equivalent to the volume of 231 cubic inches
A (U.S.) bushel is a unit of capacity equivalent to the volume of 2,150.42 cubic inches

Measures of Mass

The kilogram is the unit. A kilogram is the equivalent of 2.2046 pounds avoirdupois.

```
1 metric ton = 1,000 kilograms
1 hectogram = 100 grams = 0.1 kilogram
1 dekagram = 10 grams = 0.01 kilogram
1 decigram = 0.1 gram
1 centigram = 0.01 gram
1 milligram = 0.001 gram
1 avoirdupois ounce = ¹⁄₁₆ avoirdupois pound
1 avoirdupois dram = ¹⁄₂₅₆ avoirdupois pound = ¹⁄₁₆ avoirdupois ounce
1 grain = ¹⁄₇₀₀₀ avoirdupois pound = ¹⁰⁄₄₃₇₅ avoirdupois ounce = ¹⁄₆₇₆₀ troy pound
1 apothecaries' pound = 1 troy pound = ⁵⁷⁶⁰⁄₇₀₀₀ avoirdupois pound
1 apothecaries' or troy ounce = ¹⁄₁₂ troy pound = ⁴⁸⁰⁄₇₀₀₀ avoirdupois pound = 480 grains
1 apothecaries' dram = ¹⁄₉₆ apothecaries' pound = ⅛ apothecaries' ounce = 60 grains
1 pennyweight = ¹⁄₂₀ troy ounce = 24 grains
1 apothecaries' scruple = ⅓ apothecaries' dram = 20 grains
1 metric carat = 200 milligrams = 0.2 gram
1 short hundredweight = 100 avoirdupois pounds (used in United States)
1 long hundredweight = 112 avoirdupois pounds (used in England)
1 short ton = 2,000 avoirdupois pounds
1 long ton = 2,240 avoirdupois pounds
```

WEIGHTS AND MEASURES TABLES

Linear Measure

12 inches	= 1 foot	8 furlongs	=	⎫
3 feet	= 1 yard	320 rods	=	⎬ 1 statute mile
5½ yards	= ⎱ 1 rod	1,760 yards	=	⎭
16½ feet	= ⎰	5,280 feet	=	
40 rods	= 1 furlong	6,080.20 feet	=	1 nautical mile = 1.1516 statute miles

Note.—A "knot" is a speed of 1 nautical mile per hour.

Some Special Linear Measures

1000 mils = 1 inch
72 points = 1 inch
4 inches = 1 hand
7.92 inches = 1 surveyor's link
9 inches = 1 span
18 inches = 1 cubit
2½ feet = 1 military pace
6 feet = 1 fathom
40 yards = 1 bolt (cloth)
10 chains = 1 furlong

Square Measure

144 square inches =	1 square foot
9 square feet =	1 square yard
30¼ square yards =	1 square rod
160 square rods = 43,560 square feet =	} 1 acre

160 acres =	1 quarter section
4 quarter sections = 640 acres =	} 1 square mile
36 square miles =	1 township

Cubic Measure

1,728 cubic inches = 1 cubic foot
27 cubic feet = 1 cubic yard
128 cubic feet = 1 cord

Note.—A "board foot," used in lumber measurements, is a volume equivalent to that of a board 1 ft. × 1 ft. × 1 in., or 144 cu. in.

Circular Measure

60 seconds =	1 minute
60 minutes =	1 degree
90 degrees =	1 quadrant

| 4 quadrants =
360 degrees = | } 1 circle |

A convenient method of finding the difference in time between two places, is to notice their distance apart, in degrees of longitude, and allow 4 minutes to each degree, based on the following calculation:

1,440 minutes = 1 day or revolution of the earth
1 revolution of the earth is
360 degrees; therefore,
1 degree = 4 minutes

Paper Measure

For small papers the old measure is still in use:
24 sheets = 1 quire
20 quires = ream (480 sheets)
For papers put up in cases, bundles, or frames the following measure is now used:
25 sheets = quire
20 quires = 1 standard ream (500 sheets)

Surveyor's Measure

7.992 inches = 1 link (Gunter's or surveyor's)
100 links = 1 chain (= 66 feet)
80 chains = 1 mile

Surveyor's Area Measure

625 square links	= 1 (square) pole or square rod
16 (square) poles	= 1 square chain (surveyor's)
10 square chains or 160 square rods	= 1 acre
640 acres	= 1 square mile
36 square miles	= 1 township

Mariner's Measure

6 feet = 1 fathom
120 fathoms = 1 cable length (U.S. Navy)
10 cable lengths = 1 nautical mile = 6,080 feet (Br.) = 6,080.20 feet (U.S.)
A statute mile is 5,280 feet

Time Measure

60 seconds = 1 minute
60 minutes = 1 hour
24 hours = 1 day
7 days   = 1 week
29 days, 12 hours, 44 minutes, 2.78 seconds (with a variation of 13 hours due to the eccentricity of the orbit) = 1 lunar month
28, 29, 30, or 31 days = 1 calendar month
30 days   = 1 month (in computing interest)
52 weeks and 1 day } 1 year
12 calendar months }
365 days, 5 hours, 48 minutes, and 46 seconds = 1 solar year
366 days   = 1 leap year

Apothecaries' Fluid Measure

60 minims   = 1 fluid dram
8 fluid drams = 1 fluid ounce
16 fluid ounces = 1 liquid pint
8 liquid pints = 1 gallon
(British measures differ from the above)

Apothecaries' Weight

20 grains   = 1 scruple
3 scruples = 1 dram
8 drams   = 1 ounce
12 ounces   = 1 pound

Avoirdupois Weight

27¹¹⁄₃₂ grains	=	1 dram	100 pounds =	1 short hundredweight
16 drams	=	1 ounce	112 pounds =	1 long hundredweight
16 ounces	= }	1 pound	2,000 pounds =	1 short ton
7,000 grains	= }		2,240 pounds =	1 long ton

Troy Weight

24 grains   = 1 pennyweight
20 pennyweights = 1 ounce
12 ounces   = 1 pound (Troy)

Carat (for precious stones) = 200 milligrams. The carat was formerly an ambiguous term having many values in various countries.
Carat (fineness of gold) = ½₄ (by weight) gold. For example, 24 carats fine = pure gold; 18 carats fine = ¹⁸⁄₂₄ pure gold.

Miscellaneous Unit Measurements

12 pieces = 1 dozen	165 pounds of potatoes = 1 barrel
12 dozen = 1 gross	140 pounds of apples = 1 barrel
12 gross = 1 great gross	11.7 pounds of molasses = 1 gallon
20 units = 1 score	200 pounds of lime = 1 barrel
196 pounds of flour = 1 barrel	200 pounds of pickled fish = 1 barrel
200 pounds of beef or pork = 1 barrel	63 pounds of butter = 1 tub

In measuring iron, lead, etc.

14   pounds = 1 stone
21½ stones = 1 pig

LEGAL WEIGHT IN POUNDS PER BUSHEL OF VARIOUS COMMODITIES

The bushel commonly used in the United States is the Winchester bushel which contains 2,150.42 cubic inches. This was in use both in this country and in England at the time of the Declaration of Independence and has since been approved by Act of Congress.

Commodities are sold either by the struck or level bushel or by the heaped bushel. There are no specifications as to how high the heaped bushel should be but custom decrees that it shall be "as high as may be without special effort or design." The heaped bushel is about 25 to 27 per cent larger that the struck bushel. It is often reckoned as 2747.71 cu. in. Grain, berries, beans, peas, and small fruits are usually measured by the struck bushel; apples, pears, potatoes, onions, etc., are measured by the heaped bushel.

There are 0.8 of a level bushel in a cubic foot of space. (This is found by dividing the number of cubic inches in a foot, 1,728, by the number of cubic inches in a bushel.)

There are 0.63 of a heaped bushel in a cubic foot of space (1,728 ÷ 2,747.71 = 0.63).

To find the number of bushels a bin will hold find the capacity of the bin in cubic inches (length × height × width) and multiply its capacity in cubic feet by 0.8 if the bushels are level; by 0.63 if they are heaped.

To find the number of bushels and odd pounds in a load of grain weighing a certain number of pounds, divide the pounds per bushel for the particular type of grain into the net weight of the grain. For example, a bushel of clover seeds legally weighs 60 pounds in most states. A load of clover seeds weighing 3,500 pounds would therefore contain 58 bushels and 20 pounds of clover seeds, or 3,500 divided by 60. If a state legal weight is not established for a particular grain, it is customary to use the following bushel measures: wheat, 60 pounds per bushel; barley, 48 pounds per bushel; oats, 32 pounds per bushel; rye and Indian corn, 56 pounds per bushel.

One of the most important points to remember in connection with measures for struck bushels is that a measure with a narrow diameter will not allow proper settling down nor proper heaping of the commodities. For this reason the Bureau of Standards[1] has adopted the following minimum diameters of cylindrical dry measures of various capacities:

	Minimum diameter in inches		Minimum diameter in inches
½ bushel	13¾	2 quarts	6⅝
1 peck	10⅞	1 quart	5⅜
½ peck	8½	1 pint	4

Dry commodities should never be bought nor sold in measures for liquids, since all liquid measures are about 14 per cent or 16 per cent smaller than the corresponding dry measures.

The British imperial bushel is about 3 per cent larger than the United States standard Winchester bushel. The imperial bushel contains 2,219.36 cubic inches.

It is because of the difficulties in measuring by volume that some states have laws requiring that commodities be sold by weight. In others only the commodities for which a standard weight has been legally established must be sold by weight. Whenever possible it is desirable to buy by weight instead of by volume.

The table below shows some of the more important commodities for which bushel weights have been established in more than four states. There is a wide discrepancy in the number of pounds required in the various states. In certain instances this is caused by the fact that commodities which have to be shelled or husked are in some states measured with the shell or husk on while in others there must be enough of the commodity for a bushel *after* the shell or husk has been taken off.

---

[1]The tables on the following pages are reprinted from Bureau of Standards material.

COMMODITIES FOR WHICH BUSHEL WEIGHTS HAVE BEEN
ESTABLISHED IN MORE THAN FOUR STATES

	Alfalfa seed	Apples			Barley	Beans						Soy	Beets
		Apples[1]	Dried	Apple seeds		Beans[1]	Castor	Green (unshelled)	Green or string	Lima	Miscellaneous varieties		
Federal Statutes	...	[2]50	...	...	48	...	...	...	...	...	...	...	...
Alabama	60	[3]50	24	40	48	[9]60	46	30	...	...	...	...	50
Arizona	...	...	...	...	...	...	...	...	...	...	...	...	...
Arkansas	...	[3]50	24	...	48	[4]60	...	...	...	...	...	...	...
California	...	...	...	...	50	...	...	...	...	...	...	...	...
Colorado	...	...	...	...	48	60	...	...	...	...	...	...	...
Connecticut	...	48	25	...	48	[9]60	...	...	24	...	...	...	[5]60
Delaware	...	...	...	...	...	...	...	...	...	...	...	...	...
District of Columbia	...	...	...	...	...	...	...	...	...	...	...	...	...
Florida	...	[3]48	24	...	48	[6]60	[6]48	...	...	...	[7]78	...	...
Georgia	...	...	24	...	47	[4]60	...	...	...	...	...	...	...
Hawaii	...	...	...	...	48	...	...	...	...	...	...	...	...
Idaho	60	[3]48	24	...	48	60	46	...	...	...	...	...	56
Illinois	60	[3]47	24	...	48	[4]60	46	...	24	...	[8]24	...	60
Indiana	...	...	...	...	...	...	...	...	...	...	...	...	...
Iowa	60	48	24	...	48	[9]60	[6]50	56	...	56	...	...	56
Kansas	60	48	24	...	48	60	46	38	...	...	...	...	56
Kentucky	...	...	24	...	47	[4]60	45	...	...	...	...	...	...
Louisiana	...	...	...	...	32	...	...	...	...	...	...	...	...
Maine	60	44	25	...	48	60	...	...	24	56	[10]47	58	[11]60
Maryland	60	[3]50	28	...	48	[9]60	[12]50	...	...	...	...	...	...
Massachusetts	...	...	...	...	...	...	...	...	...	...	...	...	...
Michigan	...	48	22	...	48	60	46	...	...	...	...	...	56
Minnesota	60	[3]50	28	...	48	60	...	...	...	56	[10]47	...	50
Mississippi	...	...	26	...	60	[4]60	46	...	...	...	...	...	...
Missouri	...	48	24	...	48	60	46	56	...	...	...	...	...
Montana	...	45	...	...	48	60	...	...	...	...	...	...	50
Nebraska	60	[3]48	24	...	48	[9]60	[6]50	56	...	56	...	...	56
Nevada	60	[3]48	24	...	48	60	46	...	...	...	...	...	56
New Hampshire	...	...	25	...	48	[4]60	...	...	24	...	...	58	60
New Jersey	...	...	...	...	...	...	...	...	...	...	...	...	...
New Mexico	60	45	24	...	48	60	46	...	...	...	...	...	56
New York	...	...	...	...	...	...	...	...	...	...	...	...	...
North Carolina	60	...	24	40	48	[9]60	46	30	...	...	...	60	50
North Dakota	60	50	28	...	48	60	...	...	...	55	[10]47	...	60
Ohio	...	48	24	...	48	60	...	...	...	...	...	...	56
Oklahoma	60	48	24	...	48	60	46	...	...	...	...	...	60
Oregon	...	...	...	...	...	...	...	...	...	...	...	...	...
Pennsylvania	60	45	25	...	48	[9]60	[6]46	...	...	...	...	...	56
Rhode Island	...	48	25	40	48	60	46	...	...	...	...	...	50
South Carolina	...	[3]50	24	40	48	[9]60	46	30	...	...	...	...	50
South Dakota	60	48	24	...	48	[9]60	[6]50	50	...	[9]56	...	...	56
Tennessee	...	[3]50	24	40	48	[9]60	46	30	...	...	...	...	50
Texas	60	[3]50	28	...	48	[4]60	46	...	24	...	[8]24	...	60
Utah	...	...	...	...	...	...	...	...	...	...	...	...	...
Vermont	60	44	25	...	48	60	...	28	24	...	...	58	60
Virginia	60	...	28	...	48	[13]60	46	...	...	...	...	[13]60	...
Washington	...	...	...	...	...	...	...	...	...	...	...	...	...
West Virginia	60	[3]48	24	40	48	[14]60	46	38	24	56	...	58	56
Wisconsin	60	44	25	...	48	60	46	...	30	56	...	...	50
Wyoming	...	[3]48	...	...	48	60	46	...	...	...	...	...	56

[1]Not defined, except as noted.   [2]Green or ripe.   [3]Green apples.   [4]White.
[5]Mangelwurzel; beets, table size, 50 pounds.   [6]Shelled.   [7]Velvet in hull.   [8]Wax.
[9]Dry or dried.   [10]Windsor (broad).   [11]Also sugar, turnip, and mangelwurzel.
[12]Called "castor beans or seed" in the law.   [13]Navy and soya.   [14]Dried, shell.

COMMODITIES FOR WHICH BUSHEL WEIGHTS HAVE BEEN ESTABLISHED IN MORE THAN FOUR STATES (*Cont.*)

	Blackberries	Bluegrass seed	Bluegrass seed (English)	Bran	Broomcorn seed	Buckwheat	Cabbage	Canary seed	Carrots	Cement	Charcoal	Cherries	Chestnuts
Federal Statutes													
Alabama	[5]48	14		20	42	50	50	60	50	80	22	156	50
Arizona													
Arkansas		14		20	48	52							
California						40							
Colorado		14				52							
Connecticut				20		48			50		[2]20		
Delaware											[2]20		
District of Columbia													
Florida				20									
Georgia		14		[3]20		52							
Hawaii													
Idaho		[4]14	22	20		50			50				
Illinois		14		20	48	52			50		20		
Indiana													
Iowa		14		20	50	48			50		20	40	
Kansas		[4]14	22		30	48			50			156	
Kentucky		14	14	20		56							
Louisiana													
Maine	40			20		48			50				
Maryland		14		20		48			50				
Massachusetts													
Michigan		14				48			50				
Minnesota		14			57	50			45				50
Mississippi		14		20		48							
Missouri		14		20		52			50				
Montana		14		20		52			50				
Nebraska		18		20	50	50			50		20	40	
Nevada		14	22	20		50			50				
New Hampshire				20		48			50				
New Jersey													
New Mexico		14		20		52			50	80	20		
New York													
North Carolina	[5]48	14		20	44	50	50	60	50	80	22	156	50
North Dakota		14		20	30	42			45				50
Ohio				45	50	50			50				
Oklahoma		14		20	48	52			50				
Oregon													
Pennsylvania		14		20	50	48	50		50	100	20	156	[6]50
Rhode Island				20		48			50		20		
South Carolina	[5]48	14		20	42	50	50	60	50	80	22	156	50
South Dakota		14				50			50				
Tennessee	[5]48	14		20	42	50	50	60	50	80	22	156	50
Texas		14		20	48	52			50	80	22		
Utah													
Vermont						48			50		20		50
Virginia		14		20		48			50				57
Washington													
West Virginia	48	14	22	20	57	48	50	60	50	100	20	156	50
Wisconsin		14		20		50			50				
Wyoming									50				

¹With stems; without stems, 64 pounds.　²Commercially dry.　³Wheat bran.　⁴Native.
⁵Undefined; dried, 28 pounds.　⁶Hulled.

		Coal					Corn, including Indian corn or maize					
	Clover seed	Coal[1]	Anthracite	Mineral	Stone	Coke	In the ear	In the ear (unhusked)	Popcorn (in ear)	Popcorn (shelled)	Shelled	Sweet
Federal Statutes											[2]56	
Alabama	[3]60				80	40	70	[4]75	70	56	56	
Arizona												
Arkansas	60						[5]70	74			56	
California											252	
Colorado	60			80			70				256	
Connecticut	60		80								256	
Delaware											256	
District of Columbia												
Florida								70			56	
Georgia	60				80		70				56	
Hawaii											256	
Idaho	·60						70				56	
Illinois	[6]60	80				40	70		70	56	56	
Indiana												
Iowa	60	80				40	[7]70	[7]75	70	56	[7]56	50
Kansas	60		[8]76		[8]76		[5]70	75	70	56	56	
Kentucky	60						[9]70	75			56	
Louisiana	60										256	
Maine	60										256	
Maryland	[10]60	76					70				56	
Massachusetts												
Michigan	60		80				70				56	
Minnesota	60						70				56	48
Mississippi	60				80		72				56	
Missouri	60			80			70				56	
Montana	60			76			70				56	
Nebraska	60	80				40	[11]70	[7]75	70	56	[7]56	50
Nevada	60						70				56	
New Hampshire	60										256	
New Jersey												
New Mexico	60			80		40	70	72	70	56	56	
New York												
North Carolina	[12]60				80	40			[13]70		56	
North Dakota	60				80		70				56	48
Ohio	60	[14]70				40	68		42		56	[15]45
Oklahoma	[10]60			80			70	72			56	
Oregon												
Pennsylvania	60		75		80	40	[5]70				56	
Rhode Island	60	80				40	70				56	
South Carolina	[19]60				80	40	[5]70	[4]74		56	56	
South Dakota	60						70		70	56	56	50
Tennessee	[19]60				80	40	[7]70	[4]74	[13]70	56	56	
Texas	[6]60		80			40	(16)		70	56	56	
Utah												
Vermont	60						[5]70	72	[18]70	56	56	
Virginia	60		80				70				56	
Washington												
West Virginia	60	80				40	[17]68				56	50
Wisconsin	[10]60						70				[2]56	
Wyoming							70				56	

[1] Not defined, except as noted.
[2] Not stated whether shelled or unshelled, but presumed from the weight shown to be shelled.
[3] Red and white and crimson; burr clover, 10 pounds; Japan clover (lespedeza), 25 pounds.
[4] Corn, green, with shucks, 100 pounds per bushel. [5] Husked.
[6] Clover seed, sweet, unhulled, 33 pounds, Illinois; 23 pounds, Texas. [7] Field corn.
[8] "Stone coal"; the term includes anthracite, cannel, bituminous, and other mined coal.
[9] Corn in the ear, in Kentucky, 70 pounds from November 1 to January 1 following, and from January 1 to November 1 following, 68 pounds; in Mississippi, in connection with public local grain warehouses, "not exceeding 80 pounds" during the months of October and November only.
[10] Also alsike (or Swedish), 60 pounds. [11] Field corn, husked.
[12] Red and white; clover burr, 8 pounds; German clover (also more commonly known as crimson clover), 60 pounds; Japan, lespedeza, 25 pounds.
[13] Not stated whether in the ear or not, but from the weight shown it is presumed to be in the ear.
[14] Cannel coal. [15] Shelled. [16] Corn in the ear in Texas, 70 pounds after December 1, and 72 pounds for new crop before December 1. Green corn (roasting ears), 50 pounds. [17] In ear, dry; in ear, green, 72 pounds. [18] Cured, in cob. [19] Red and white.

COMMODITIES FOR WHICH BUSHEL WEIGHTS HAVE BEEN ESTABLISHED IN MORE THAN FOUR STATES (Cont.)

	Corn meal (including Indian meal)			Cotton seed			Cranberries	Cucumbers	Emmer[2]	Flaxseed (linseed)	Gooseberries	Grapes
	Corn meal[1]	Bolted	Unbolted	Cotton seed[1]	Sea Island cotton seed	Upland cotton seed						
Federal Statutes	...	...	...	...	...	...	...	...	...	56	...	...
Alabama	...	48	48	32	...	...	...	48	...	56	...	360
Arizona	...	...	...	...	...	...	...	...	...	56	48	...
Arkansas	48	...	...	33-1/3	...	...	...	...	...	56	...	...
California	...	...	...	...	...	...	...	...	...	...	...	...
Colorado	50	...	...	...	...	...	...	...	...	...	...	...
Connecticut	50	...	...	...	44	30	32	48	...	55	...	...
Delaware	...	44	48	...	...	...	...	...	...	...	...	...
District of Columbia	...	...	...	...	...	...	...	...	...	...	...	...
Florida	48	...	...	32	44	...	...	...	...	...	...	...
Georgia	...	48	48	30	...	...	...	...	...	56	...	...
Hawaii	...	...	...	...	...	...	...	...	...	...	...	...
Idaho	48	...	...	...	...	...	...	...	...	56	...	...
Illinois	48	...	48	32	...	...	33	48	40	56	40	...
Indiana	48	...	...	...	...	...	...	...	...	...	...	...
Iowa	48	...	...	...	...	...	...	48	40	56	...	440
Kansas	...	...	...	...	...	...	...	48	40	56	...	548
Kentucky	50	...	...	...	...	...	...	...	...	56	...	...
Louisiana	...	...	...	...	...	...	...	...	...	...	...	...
Maine	50	...	...	...	44	30	32	...	...	56	...	...
Maryland	48	...	...	...	...	...	...	...	...	56	...	...
Massachusetts	...	...	...	...	...	...	...	...	...	...	...	...
Michigan	50	...	...	...	...	...	40	...	...	56	...	...
Minnesota	...	...	...	...	...	...	36	48	...	56	...	...
Mississippi	48	44	48	32	...	...	...	...	...	56	...	...
Missouri	50	...	...	33	...	...	...	48	...	56	...	...
Montana	50	...	...	...	...	...	...	...	...	56	...	...
Nebraska	48	...	...	...	...	...	...	48	48	...	...	440
Nevada	48	...	...	...	...	...	...	...	...	56	...	...
New Hampshire	50	...	...	...	...	...	32	...	...	56	...	...
New Jersey	...	...	...	...	...	...	...	...	...	...	...	...
New Mexico	50	...	...	32	...	...	...	48	...	56	...	...
New York	...	...	...	...	...	...	...	...	...	...	...	...
North Carolina	...	48	48	30	44	...	...	48	...	56	48	548
North Dakota	...	...	...	...	...	...	36	48	...	56	...	...
Ohio	48	...	...	...	...	...	...	...	...	56	...	48
Oklahoma	50	...	...	32	...	...	...	48	...	56	...	...
Oregon	...	...	...	...	...	...	...	...	...	...	...	...
Pennsylvania	50	...	...	...	...	...	32	48	...	56	40	48
Rhode Island	50	...	...	...	44	30	...	...	...	56	...	...
South Carolina	...	48	48	630	...	...	32	48	...	56	48	548
South Dakota	50	...	...	...	...	...	32	48	...	56	...	440
Tennessee	...	50	48	28	...	...	...	48	...	56	48	548
Texas	50	...	48	32	...	...	33	48	...	56	40	...
Utah	...	...	...	...	...	...	...	...	...	...	...	...
Vermont	50	...	...	...	...	...	32	48	40	55	...	...
Virginia	48	...	...	30	...	...	...	...	...	56	...	...
Washington	...	...	...	...	...	...	...	...	...	...	...	...
West Virginia	48	46	...	32	44	...	36	750	...	56	40	360
Wisconsin	50	...	...	...	44	30	35	750	...	56	...	...
Wyoming	...	...	...	...	...	...	...	...	45	56	...	...

[1]Not defined.   [2]See also "Spelt or speltz."   [3]With stems, 48 pounds.   [4]With stems.
[5]With stems; without stems, 60 pounds.   [6]Long staple.   [7]Green.

COMMODITIES FOR WHICH BUSHEL WEIGHTS HAVE BEEN ESTABLISHED IN MORE THAN FOUR STATES (Cont.)

	Hair			Hempseed	Herds grass	Hickory nuts	Hominy	Horseradish	Hungarian grass seed	Kafir corn	Kale	Lime		Malt	Millet	
	Plastering[1]	Plastering (unwashed)	Plastering (washed)									Lime[1]	Slaked		Millet or millet seed[1]	Japanese barnyard
Federal Statutes																
Alabama	8			44	45	50	62	50	48	56		[2]80	40		[10]50	
Arizona																
Arkansas															50	
California																
Colorado				44								80				
Connecticut					45	50		50			[3]12	70				
Delaware																
District of Columbia																
Florida															50	
Georgia	8			44								[2]80				
Hawaii																
Idaho		8	4	44					50	56		[2]80		32	50	
Illinois		8	4	44		50			50	56		80		38	50	35
Indiana																
Iowa				44		[4]50			50	56		80			50	
Kansas		8	4	44		50				56		[2]80		38	[5]50	
Kentucky	8			44					50			[2]35			50	
Louisiana																
Maine	[6]11			44	45				48		12	70			50	35
Maryland				44	45				50			80		[7]34	[8]50	
Massachusetts																
Michigan				44					50			70			50	
Minnesota		8	4	44		50			48			80			48	
Mississippi				44					50			[2]80		38	50	
Missouri				44					48					38	50	
Montana				44					50			[2]80		30	50	
Nebraska				44		[4]50				56		80			50	
Nevada				48					50	56				32	50	
New Hampshire					45							70				35
New Jersey																
New Mexico				44					50	56		[2]80			50	
New York																
North Carolina	8			44		[9]50	62	50	48	50	10	[2]80	40		50	
North Dakota		8	4	50		50			48			80			50	
Ohio				44		50	60		50	56		70		34	50	
Oklahoma				44					48	56		80		38	50	
Oregon																
Pennsylvania	8			44	45	50	60	50	50	56		80		38	50	
Rhode Island				44					50			70		38	50	
South Carolina	8			44		50	62	50	48	56	12	[2]80	40		[10]50	
South Dakota				44		[4]50			50	56		80			50	
Tennessee	8			44		50	62	50	48		30	[2]80	40		[10]50	
Texas		8	4	44		50			48	50					50	35
Utah																
Vermont					45			56	50	56				34	50	
Virginia	8			44					48			[2]80		38	50	
Washington																
West Virginia				44	45	50	60	50	50	56	15	[2]70	40	34	50	35
Wisconsin	8			44		50			48			(11)		[7]34	50	
Wyoming										56						

[1]Not defined, except as noted. [2]Unslaked. [3]Commercially dry. [4]Hulled.
[5]Hungarian. [6]Well dried and cleaned, used in masonry. [7]Barley malt.
[8]German and American. [9]Without hulls. [10]German, Missouri, and Tennessee.
[11]"Seventy pounds for a bushel of lime; 80 pounds for a bushel of unslaked lime."

	Oats	Onions			Orchard grass seed	Osage orange seed	Parsnips	Peaches		Peanuts	Pears[1]
		Onions[1]	Bottom onion sets	Top onion sets				Peaches[1]	Dried		
Federal Statutes	[2]32										
Alabama	32	[3]57	32	28	14	33	45	350	[13]33	22	[15]50
Arizona											
Arkansas	32	57			14				33		
California	32										
Colorado	32	57									
Connecticut	32	52					45	52	33		52
Delaware											
District of Columbia											
Florida	32	56						[4]54	24	22	55
Georgia	32	57							[13]33	[5]25	
Hawaii	32										
Idaho	32	57					50	48	33		
Illinois	32	57	32	30	14	33	50	48	33	[6]20	58
Indiana											
Iowa	32	52	32	28	14	32	45	48	33	22	45
Kansas	32	55					48	48	33		50
Kentucky	[7]32	57	36		14				39	[5]24	
Louisiana	32										
Maine	32	52			14		45	48	33	[6]20	58
Maryland	32	54			14			[8]40		22	
Massachusetts											
Michigan	32	54			14	33	50		28		
Minnesota	32	52	32	28	14		42	48	28	22	45
Mississippi	32	57							33	[5]24	
Missouri	32	57		28	14	36	44	48	33		48
Montana	32	57					50				45
Nebraska	32	57	32	28	14	32	50	48	33	22	45
Nevada	32	57					50	48	33		
New Hampshire	32	52					45	48	33	[6]20	58
New Jersey											
New Mexico	32	57	32	30	14		42	48	33	22	48
New York											
North Carolina	32	[3]57	32	28	14	33	50	350	25	[9]22	[15]56
North Dakota	32	52	32	28	14		42		28	22	45
Ohio	32	56		[10]28			50	48	33		
Oklahoma	32	57		28	14	36	44	48	33	22	48
Oregon											
Pennsylvania	32	50		[10]28	14		50	48	[13]33	22	50
Rhode Island	32	50					50	48	33		
South Carolina	32	[3]56	32	28	14	33	50	350	25	23	[15]36
South Dakota	32	52	32	30	14	32	48	48	33	20	45
Tennessee	32	[3]56	32	28	14	33	50	350	26	23	[15]56
Texas	32	57	32	30	14		50	50	28	[11]20	58
Utah											
Vermont	32	52					45	48		[6]20	58
Virginia	32	57			14		50		[14]32	[12]22	
Washington											
West Virginia	32	55	32	28	14	33	42	48	33	23	50
Wisconsin	32	50	[10]32				44	48	33		48
Wyoming	32	57					50	48			

[1]Not defined, except as noted.   [2]Hulled or unhulled.   [3]Matured.   [4]Green.
[5]Called ground peas in the law.   [6]Roasted; green, 22 pounds.   [7]Shelled.
[8]Peaches, peeled, 40 pounds; unpeeled, 32 pounds; not stated whether dried or not.
[9]Spanish, 30 pounds.   [10]Not stated whether top or bottom onion sets.
[11]Roasted; green, Georgia or Virginia, 22 pounds; Spanish, 24 pounds.
[12]Virginia; Spanish, 30 pounds.   [13]Unpeeled; peeled, 38 pounds.
[14]Unpeeled; peeled, 40 pounds.   [15]Matured; dried, 26 pounds.

COMMODITIES FOR WHICH BUSHEL WEIGHTS HAVE BEEN ESTABLISHED IN MORE THAN FOUR STATES (*Cont.*)

	Peas[1]	Green, un-shelled	Plums	Irish or white	Sweet	Quinces	Rape seed	Raspberries	Red top or red top seed	Rhubarb or pie-plant	Rice, rough (or unhulled)	Rutabagas	Rye	Rye meal
Federal Statutes....	60												56	
Alabama	[2]60	30	64	60	55	[3]48	50	48	14	50	[16]45	50	56	
Arizona														
Arkansas	60			60	50				14				56	
California													54	
Colorado					60								56	
Connecticut	[4]60	[13]26	48	60	54	48			14		45	[17]55	56	50
Delaware														
District of Columbia														
Florida			40	60	56	48							56	
Georgia	60			60	55						43		56	
Hawaii													50	
Idaho	[5]60			60	50								56	
Illinois	[4]60	32		60	50	48	50		14		45	50	56	50
Indiana														
Iowa	[4]60	50	48	60	50	48	50		14			60	56	
Kansas	60	30	52	[16]60	[6]50	48						50	56	
Kentucky	60			60	55								56	
Louisiana													32	
Maine	60	28		60	54	48		40	14		44	60	56	50
Maryland	[4]60			60	60		50		[7]14				56	
Massachusetts														
Michigan	60		[4]28	60	56				14				56	
Minnesota	[8]60			60	55		50		14	50		52	56	
Mississippi	60			60	54								56	
Missouri	60	56		60	56				14			50	56	
Montana	60			60									56	
Nebraska	[4]60	50	48	60	50	48	50		14			60	56	
Nevada	[5]60			60	50								56	50
New Hampshire	60	28		60	54	48							56	
New Jersey														
New Mexico	60			60	50	48	50					50	56	
New York														
North Carolina	[2]60	30	64	56	[14]56	[3]48		48	14	[9]50	44		[10]56	
North Dakota	60			60	46		50			50		52	56	
Ohio	60		50	60	50								56	
Oklahoma	60	56		60	55		50		14			50	56	
Oregon														
Pennsylvania	[4]60	28	64	60	54	48	50	48	14		45	60	56	50
Rhode Island	60		64	60	54								56	50
South Carolina	[2]60	[11]30	64	60	50	[3]48	50	48	14	[9]50	44	60	56	50
South Dakota	[4]60	56	48	60	54	48	50		14			50	56	
Tennessee	[2]60	30	64	60	50	[3]48		48	14	[9]50			56	
Texas	[4]60	32		60	50	48	50		14		45	50	56	50
Utah														
Vermont	60	28	48	60	54	48			[15]14				56	
Virginia				60	56					40			56	
Washington														
West Virginia	[2]60	[12]30	60	60	50	48	50	48	14			50	56	50
Wisconsin	60	30		60	54		50		14		45	56	56	50
Wyoming				60	50								56	

[1] Not defined, except as noted.   [2] Dry.   [3] Matured.   [4] Dried.   [5] Shelled, dried peas.
[6] Sweet potatoes, seed, sorted, 1¼ inches diameter and under 45 pounds.
[7] Red top grass seed (chaff); fancy, 32 pounds.   [8] Smooth peas.   [9] Called pieplant in the law.
[10] Seed.   [11] Not stated whether shelled or unshelled.   [12] Green, shelled, 50 pounds.
[13] Dried, in pod.   [14] Green; kiln dried, 47 pounds.   [15] In chaff; recleaned, 32 pounds.
[16] Not defined.   [17] Called rutabaga turnips in the law.

COMMODITIES FOR WHICH BUSHEL WEIGHTS HAVE BEEN ESTABLISHED IN MORE THAN FOUR STATES (*Cont.*)

	Salt													
	Salt[1]	Coarse salt	Fine salt	Sand	Shorts	Sorghum seed	Spelt or speltz[2]	Spinach	Strawberries	Timothy seed	Tomatoes	Turnips	Walnuts	Wheat
Federal Statutes						50	40		48	45	56	55		60
Alabama						50	40		48	45	56	55	50	60
Arizona														
Arkansas	50					50				60		57		60
California														60
Colorado	80									45				60
Connecticut		70	70		20			[3]12		45	56	[4]50		60
Delaware										45	56	[4]50		60
District of Columbia														
Florida	60					56						54		60
Georgia										45		55		60
Hawaii														60
Idaho	80					50				45	56	55		60
Illinois		55	50		20	50	40	12		45	56	55	50	60
Indiana														60
Iowa	80			130	20	[5]50	40			45	50	55	[6]50	60
Kansas	80		55			50	40	14		45	56	55	[7]50	60
Kentucky	50		55							45		60		60
Louisiana														60
Maine		[8]70	[9]60			50		12	40	45	56	[14]50		60
Maryland		70	56			50				45	60	60		60
Massachusetts														
Michigan	[10]56									45		58		60
Minnesota						57	40			45	50	55	50	60
Mississippi	50					42				45		55		60
Missouri	50					42				45	45	[11]42		60
Montana	50									45				60
Nebraska	80			130	20	[5]50	48			45	56	55	[6]50	60
Nevada	80					50				45	56	56		60
New Hampshire		70	50		20				12	45	56	55		60
New Jersey														
New Mexico				130		50				45	50	56		60
New York														
North Carolina	50					50		10	48	45	56	50	[6]50	60
North Dakota	80					57	40			45	50	60	50	60
Ohio						50				45	56	60	[12]50	60
Oklahoma	80					50				45	45	[11]42		60
Oregon														
Pennsylvania		85	[13]62	100	20	50	40	12	48	45	56	56	[11]50	60
Rhode Island		70	50		20					45	56	50		60
South Carolina	50					50		12	48	45	56	50		60
South Dakota		80		130		50	45			45	50	55	[6,7]50	60
Tennessee	50					50		30	48	45	56	50	50	60
Texas		55	50		20	50		12		45	56	55	50	60
Utah														
Vermont		70	56						12	45	56	60		60
Virginia	50									45	60	55		60
Washington														
West Virginia		70	50	130	20	57	40	15	48	45	56	55	50	60
Wisconsin		70	50		20			14		45	56	42		60
Wyoming							45				56	55		60

[1] Not defined, except as noted.
[2] See also "Emmer." Spring emmer has frequently been erroneously called speltz, this name being a misspelling of spelt, which is a distinct crop. The differences between spelt and emmer are pointed out in U. S. Dept. Agr. Farmers' Bulletin 466.
[3] Commercially dry. [4] Summer; rutabaga or Swedish turnips, 55 pounds.
[5] Sorghum saccharatum seed. [6] Hulled. [7] Black.
[8] Turk's Island salt or other grades of coarse salt. [9] Liverpool salt or other grades of fine salt.
[10] Michigan salt. [11] Common. [12] Domestic. [13] Ground. [14] Common English.

STANDARD BARREL MEASURE

The capacity of the standard barrel for fruits, vegetables, and other dry commodities has been fixed by Act of Congress. Except for the cranberry barrel and the lime barrel, which is graded on a weight basis, the capacities of the standard barrel and its subdivisions for the commodities mentioned above are as follows:

Size	Cubic inches	Bushels[1]	Quarts[1]
Barrel	7,056	3.281	105
¾ barrel	5,292	2.461	78¾
½ barrel	3,528	1.641	52½
⅓ barrel	2,352	1.094	35

The capacities of the standard cranberry barrel and its subdivisions are as follows:

Size	Cubic inches	Bushels[1]	Quarts[1]
Cranberry barrel	5,826	2.709	86⁴⁵⁄₆₄
¾ cranberry barrel	4,369.5	2.032	65¹⁄₆₄
½ cranberry barrel	2,913	1.355	43¹¹⁄₃₂
⅓ cranberry barrel	1,942	0.903	28²⁹⁄₃₂

MEASURING OIL, WATER, ETC.

The unit of measurement for cisterns, tanks, etc., is the gallon, which consists of 231 cubic inches. A cubic foot of space contains 1,728 cubic inches ÷ 231, which equals 7.48 gallons.

To find the number of gallons which a cistern or a tank will hold, multiply the capacity in cubic feet by 7.48.

Water

1	cubic inch	.03617	pound
12	cubic inches	.434	pound
1	cubic foot	62.5	pounds
1	cubic foot	7.48052	U. S. gallons
1.8	cubic feet	112.0	pounds
35.84	cubic feet	2,240.0	pounds
1	cylindrical inch	.02842	pound
12	cylindrical inches	.341	pound
1	cylindrical foot	49.10	pounds
1	cylindrical foot	6.0	U. S. gallons
2.281	cylindrical feet	112.0	pounds
45.62	cylindrical feet	2,240.0	pounds
1	imperial gallon	10.0	pounds
11.2	imperial gallons	112.0	pounds
224	imperial gallons	2,240.0	pounds
1	U. S. gallon	8.355	pounds
13.41	U. S. gallons	112.0	pounds
268.1	U. S. gallons	2,240.0	pounds

Note.—The center of pressure of water against the side of the containing vessel or reservoir is at two-thirds the depth from the surface. One cubic foot of salt water weighs 64.3 pounds.

[1]Struck measure.

Other Liquids (pounds per cubic foot)

Liquid	Pounds	Liquid	Pounds
Alcohol: ethyl	50.4	Oils—(cont.)	
methyl	50.5	Lard	57.4
Aniline	64.5	Lavender	54.7
Benzene	56.1	Linseed (boiled)	58.8
Bromine	199.0	Neat's foot	57.0–57.2
Carbolic acid (crude)	59.2–60.2	Olive	57.3
Carbon disul.	80.6	Palm	56.5
Chloroform	93.0	Pentane	40.6
Ether	45.9	Peppermint	56.0–57.0
Gasoline	41.0–43.0	Petroleum	54.8
Glycerin	78.6	Pine	53.0–54.0
Milk	64.2–64.6	Poppy	57.7
Naphtha (petroleum ether)	41.5	Resin	59.6
		Sperm	55.0
Oils: amber	49.9	Soya-bean	57.3
Camphor	56.8	Train or whale	57.3–57.7
Castor	60.5	Turpentine	54.2
Cocoanut	57.7	Valerian	60.2
Cottonseed	57.8	Wintergreen	74.0
Creosote	64.9–68.6	Water	62.4

Note.—Milk, at 68° Fahrenheit, weighs 8.60 pounds a gallon, provided it contains 3 per cent of butter fat; cream at the same temperature weighs 8.37 pounds a gallon, if it has in it 28 per cent of butter fat. When cream contains 40 per cent of fat it weighs 8.28 pounds a gallon.

TABLE OF SOLUBILITIES

(S—soluble in water. I—insoluble in water. P—slightly soluble in water. Ia—insoluble in water and dilute acids.)

	Aluminum	Ammonium	Antimony	Arsenious	Barium	Bismuth	Cadmium	Calcium	Cobalt	Copper	Ferrous (Fe++)	Ferric (Fe+++)	Lead	Magnesium	Manganese	Mercurous (Hg+)	Mercuric (Hg++)	Nickel	Potassium	Sodium	Silver	Zinc
Acetate	S	S	—	—	S	—	S	S	S	S	S	—	S	S	S	P	S	S	S	S	S	S
Bromide	S	S	P	S	S	P	S	S	S	S	S	S	P	S	S	I	I	S	S	S	Ia	S
Carbonate	—	S	—	—	I	I	I	I	I	S	I	—	I	I	I	S	I	—	S	S	I	I
Chlorate	S	S	—	—	S	—	S	S	S	S	S	—	S	S	S	S	S	—	S	S	S	S
Chloride	S	S	P	S	S	P	S	S	S	S	—	S	P	S	S	I	P	S	S	S	Ia	S
Chromate	—	S	—	—	I	I	—	I	I	I	I	—	I	I	—	S	P	—	S	S	I	S
Hydroxide	I	S	P	S	S	I	I	P	I	I	I	I	I	I	I	S	I	I	S	S	—	I
Iodide	S	S	P	P	P	I	S	S	S	—	I	S	I	S	S	I	I	S	S	S	Ia	S
Nitrate	S	S	—	I	S	S	S	S	S	S	S	S	S	S	S	I	S	S	S	S	S	S
Oxide	I	—	I	P	S	I	P	I	I	I	I	I	I	I	I	I	I	I	S	S	I	I
Phosphate	I	S	—	—	I	I	I	I	I	I	I	I	I	I	P	I	I	I	S	S	I	I
Sulphate	S	S	—	—	Ia	S	S	P	P	S	S	S	Ia	S	S	P	I	S	S	S	P	S
Sulphide	—	S	Ia	Ia	—	S	Ia	—	I	Ia	S	—	Ia	S	I	Ia	Ia	I	S	S	Ia	I
Sulphite	—	S	—	—	I	—	S	P	P	I	S	P	—	I	—	—	I	—	S	S	S	P

MEASURING COAL, COKE, AND CHARCOAL

The estimates in the table below are according to the Bureau of Standards at Washington, D. C. Remember that a "long" ton weighs 2,240 pounds avoirdupois while a "short" ton weighs 2,000 pounds avoirdupois. The long ton is the common measure in Great Britain, the short ton in the United States and Canada.

(Weights are approximate only)

Anthracite coal (piled loose):
1 cubic foot = 50 to 57 pounds
A short ton = 35 to 40 cubic feet
1 long ton = 39 to 45 cubic feet

Bituminous coal (piled loose):
1 cubic foot = 44 to 54 pounds
1 short ton = 37 to 45 cubic feet
1 long ton = 42 to 51 cubic feet

Coke (piled loose):
1 cubic foot = 23 to 32 pounds
1 short ton = 62 to 87 cubic feet
1 long ton = 70 to 97 cubic feet

Charcoal (of pine and oak):
1 cubic foot = 15 to 30 pounds

The average weight of the various kinds of anthracite coal in pounds per cubic foot is as follows:

Size	White ash	Red ash
Egg	57.0	53.0
Stove	56.5	52.5
Chestnut	55.5	52.0
Pea	53.5	51.0
Buckwheat	53.0	50.5

To find how much coal a bin will hold find its volume in cubic feet (length × width × height). Divide this by the number of cubic feet in a ton (for ordinary estimates 54 is used for anthracite coal, 50 for bituminous coal), and the result is the amount of coal the bin will hold.

Example: Find the number of tons of anthracite coal that a bin 24 ft. long, 4 ft. wide and 6 ft. high will hold.

$$24 \times 4 \times 6 = 576 \text{ cu. ft.}$$
$$576 \div 54 = 10\tfrac{5}{8} \text{ tons}$$

For the making of steam one ton of coal is equal to two cords of wood.

MEASURING WOOD

Wood is measured by the cord. A cord is a pile of wood 8 ft. long, 4 ft. wide, and 4 ft. high. It contains 128 cubic ft.

To find the number of cords in a given pile of wood, find the number of cubic feet in the pile (length × width × height) and divide by 128.

Example: Find the number of cords in a pile of wood 8 ft. wide, 6 ft. high, and 12 ft. long.

$$8 \times 6 \times 12 = 576 \text{ cu. ft.}$$
$$576 \text{ cu. ft.} \div 128 \text{ cu. ft.} = 4\tfrac{1}{2} \text{ cords}$$

Example: A wood shed is 16 ft. long, 12 ft. wide, and 8 ft. high. How many cords of wood can be piled in it?

$$16 \times 12 \times 8 = 1,536 \text{ cubic ft.}$$
$$1,536 \div 128 = 12 \text{ cords of wood}$$

WEIGHTS OF VARIOUS SUBSTANCES
(From the Smithsonian Physical Tables)

Solids (pounds per cubic foot)

Material	Pounds	Material	Pounds
Asbestos	125–175	Leather: dry	54
Asphalt	69–94	greased	64
Basalt	150–190	Lime: mortar	103–111
Brick	87–137	slaked	81–87
Caoutchouc	57–62	Limestone	167–171
Celluloid	87	Litharge:	
Cement, set	170–190	artificial	580–585
Chalk	118–175	natural	490–500
Chrome yellow	374	Marble	160–177
Clay	122–162	Mica	165–200
Coal, soft	75–94	Paper	44–72
Copal	65–71	Paraffin	54–57
Emery	250	Peat	52
Feldspar	159–172	Pitch	67
Flint	164	Porcelain	143–156
Fluorite	198	Quartz	165
Gamboge	75	Resin	67
Gas carbon	117	Rock salt	136
Gelatin	180	Sandstone	134–147
Glass: common	150–175	Slag, furnace	125–240
Graphite	144–170	Slate	162–205
Gum arabic	80–85	Soapstone	162–175
Gypsum	144–145	Tallow	57–60
Ivory	114–120		

Woods (pounds per cubic foot)

Wood	Pounds	Wood	Pounds
Alder	26–42	Hazel	37–49
Apple	41–52	Hickory	37–58
Ash	40–53	Holly	47
Bamboo	19–25	Iron-bark	64
Basswood	20–37	Juniper	35
Beech	43–56	Laburnum	57
Blue gum	62	Lancewood	42–62
Birch	32–48	Lignum vitae	73–83
Box	59–72	Locust	42–44
Butternut	24	Logwood	57
Cedar	30–35	Mahogany	41
Cherry	43–56	Mahogany, Spanish	53
Cork	14–16	Maple	39–47
Dogwood	47	Oak	37–56
Ebony	69–83	Pear tree	38–45
Elm	34–37	Plum tree	41–49
Fir or pine, American white	22–31	Poplar	22–31
Fir or pine, larch	31–35	Satinwood	59
Fir or pine, pitch	52–53	Sycamore	24–37
Fir or pine, red	30–44	Teak, Indian	41–55
Fir or pine, spruce	30–44	Walnut	40–43
Fir or pine, yellow	23–37	Water gum	62
Greenheart	58–65	Willow	24–37

RESISTANCE TO CRUSHING FOR VARIOUS MATERIALS

(Square inch)

Material	Resistance to crushing in pounds per square inch
Brick:	
soft-burned	3,000– 6,000
hard burned	4,500– 6,500
vitrified	8,500–25,000
Brownstone	7,300–23,600
Concrete	800– 3,800
Granite	9,700–34,000
Limestone	6,000–25,000
Marble	7,600–20,700
Sandstone	2,400–29,300
Tufa	7,700–11,600

TENSILE STRENGTH OF METALS

(*From the Smithsonian Tables*)

(Given in pounds per square inch. The values can be considered only as approximations.)

Metal	Tensile Strength in lbs. per sq. in.
Aluminum wire	30,000–40,000
Brass wire	50,000–150,000
Bronze wire, phosphor, hard-drawn	110,000–140,000
Bronze wire, silicon, hard-drawn	95,000–115,000
Bronze	60,000–75,000
Cobalt, cast	33,000
Copper wire, hard-drawn	60,000–70,000
German silver	40,000–50,000
Gold wire	20,000
Iron, cast	13,000–33,000
Iron wire, hard-drawn	80,000–120,000
Iron wire, annealed	50,000–60,000
Lead, cast, or drawn	2,600–3,300
Magnesium, hard-drawn	33,000
Monel metal, cold-drawn	80,000–100,000
Nickel, hard-drawn	155,000
Palladium	39,000
Platinum wire	50,000
Silver wire	42,000
Steel	40,000–330,000
Steel wire, maximum	460,000
Steel, specially treated nickel steel	250,000
Steel, piano wire, 0.033 in. diam.	357,000–390,000
Steel, piano wire, 0.051 in. diam.	325,000–337,000
Tantalum	130,000
Tin, cast or drawn	4,000–5,000
Tungsten, hard-drawn	590,000
Zinc, cast	7,000–13,000
Zinc, drawn	22,000–30,000

MODULUS OF RUPTURE, TRANSVERSE TESTS FOR VARIOUS WOODS

(From the Smithsonian Tables)

Material	Modulus[1] lbs. per sq. in.	Material	Modulus[1] lbs. per sq. in.
Ash, white	10,800	Maple, silver	5,800
Basswood	5,000	Maple, sugar	9,100
Beech	8,200	Oak, red	7,700
Cedar, red	5,200	Oak, white	8,300
Cedar, white	4,200	Pine, longleaf	8,700
Cypress, bald	6,800	Pine, white	5,300
Elm, white	6,900	Spruce, red	5,700
Fir, grand	6,100	Sycamore	6,500
Hemlock, Eastern	6,700	Walnut, black	9,500
Hickory, pecan	9,800	Yew, Western	10,100

[1]Recommended allowable working stress (interior construction): ⅛ tabular value.

SPECIFIC GRAVITY

The density of a substance compared with the density of the same amount of another substance is called its specific gravity. With solids and liquids the standard of comparison is water; with gases it is air. The quality of a substance, *e.g.*, milk, can often in large measure be determined by determining its specific gravity.

Table of Specific Gravities

Iridium	23.000	Diamond	3.550	Beeswax	.960
Platinum	21.500	Plate glass	2.760	Lard	.947
Gold, pure	19.258	Marble	2.720	Butter	.942
Mercury, pure	14.000	Salt	2.130	Ice	.920
Silver	10.500	Brick	2.000	Petroleum	.880
Copper	8.788	Ivory	1.870	Turpentine	.870
Brass	8.000	Sugar	1.600	Hickory, dry	.840
Steel	7.840	Honey	1.456	Alcohol	.840
Tin	7.290	Milk	1.032	White pine, dry	.400
Cast iron	7.200	Water	1.000	Cork	.240

WATER PRESSURE PER SQUARE INCH

Depth in feet	Pressure in pounds	Depth in feet	Pressure in pounds
6	2.60	90	38.98
8	3.40	100	43.31
10	4.33	110	47.64
15	6.49	120	51.98
20	8.66	130	56.31
25	10.82	140	60.64
30	12.99	150	64.97
35	15.16	160	69.31
40	17.32	170	73.64
45	19.49	180	77.97
50	21.65	190	82.30
60	25.99	200	86.63
70	30.32	215	93.14
80	34.65	230	99.63

MEASURING ICE

Ice weighs 57.5 pounds per cubic foot. There are 30 cubic inches in a pound. To get the weight of a block of ice multiply its length by its breadth by its thickness. If it is 16 in. long × 10 in. wide × 8 in. thick it will contain 1,280 cubic inches. Since there are 30 cubic inches in a pound there will be 1,280 ÷ 30 = 42⅔ pounds in the block.

CONVERSION OF CENTIGRADE AND FAHRENHEIT TEMPERATURES

Fahrenheit and centigrade temperatures may be converted by means of two simple formulas. To convert Fahrenheit to centigrade, subtract 32° from the Fahrenheit and multiply by 5⁄9. To convert centigrade to Fahrenheit, multiply the centigrade by 9⁄5 and add 32. For example, to convert 50° Fahrenheit, subtract 32, which leaves 18, and multiply by 5⁄9; the result is 10° centigrade. To convert 50° centigrade, multiply by 9⁄5, which gives a product of 90, and add 32; the result is 122° Fahrenheit.

The following is a comparison of centigrade and Fahrenheit temperatures.

C	F	C	F	C	F	C	F
−40	−40	−12	10.4	16	60.8	44	111.2
−39	−38.2	−11	12.2	17	62.6	45	113.
−38	−36.4	−10	14.	18	64.4	46	114.8
−37	−34.6	− 9	15.8	19	66.2	47	116.6
−36	−32.8	− 8	17.6	20	68.	48	118.4
−35	−31.	− 7	19.4	21	69.8	49	120.2
−34	−29.2	− 6	21.2	22	71.6	50	122.
−33	−27.4	− 5	23.	23	73.4	51	123.8
−32	−25.6	− 4	24.8	24	75.2	52	125.6
−31	−23.8	− 3	26.6	25	77.	53	127.4
−30	−22.	− 2	28.4	26	78.8	54	129.2
−29	−20.2	− 1	30.2	27	80.6	55	131.
−28	−18.4	0	32.	28	82.4	56	132.8
−27	−16.6	+ 1	33.8	29	84.2	57	134.6
−26	−14.8	2	35.6	30	86.	58	136.4
−25	−13.	3	37.4	31	87.8	59	138.2
−24	−11.2	4	39.2	32	89.6	60	140.
−23	− 9.4	5	41.	33	91.4	61	141.8
−22	− 7.6	6	42.8	34	93.2	62	143.6
−21	− 5.8	7	44.6	35	95.	63	145.4
−20	− 4.	8	46.4	36	96.8	64	147.2
−19	− 2.2	9	48.2	37	98.6	65	149.
−18	− 0.4	10	50.	38	100.4	66	150.8
−17	+ 1.4	11	51.8	39	102.2	67	152.6
−16	3.2	12	53.6	40	104.	68	154.4
−15	5.	13	55.4	41	105.8	69	156.2
−14	6.8	14	57.2	42	107.6	70	158.
−13	8.6	15	59.	43	109.4	71	159.8

72	161.6	92	197.6	112	233.6	132	269.6
73	163.4	93	199.4	113	235.4	133	271.4
74	165.2	94	201.2	114	237.2	134	273.2
75	167.	95	203.	115	239.	135	275.
76	168.8	96	204.8	116	240.8	136	276.8
77	170.6	97	206.6	117	242.6	137	278.6
78	172.4	98	208.4	118	244.4	138	280.4
79	174.2	99	210.2	119	246.2	139	282.2
80	176.	100	212.	120	248.	140	284.
81	177.8	101	213.8	121	249.8	141	285.8
82	179.6	102	215.6	122	251.6	142	287.6
83	181.4	103	217.4	123	253.4	143	289.4
84	183.2	104	219.2	124	255.2	144	291.2
85	185.	105	221.	125	257.	145	293.
86	186.8	106	222.8	126	258.8	146	294.8
87	188.6	107	224.6	127	260.6	147	296.6
88	190.4	108	226.4	128	262.4	148	298.4
89	192.2	109	228.2	129	264.2	149	300.2
90	194.	110	230.	130	266.	150	302.
91	195.8	111	231.8	131	267.	151	303.8

SOME INTERESTING TEMPERATURES

	Degrees Centigrade	Degrees Fahrenheit
Freezing point of mercury	−39	−38
Freezing cold storage	{ −18 0	0 +32
Freezing point of water	0	32
Danger of frost	+4	39
Proper temperature for household refrigerator	{ 7 13	45 55
Temperature for gymnasium, or rooms where occupants are actively engaged in physical work or exercise	13	55
Temperature for rooms where occupants are not exercising	{ 20 21	68 70
Normal temperature of the human body determined by thermometer under the tongue	37	98.6
Melting point of tallow	52.8	127
Boiling point of alcohol	75	167
Boiling point of water at normal pressure	100	212
Melting point of common soft solder	185	365
Melting point of lead	327	621
Melting point of aluminum	659	1,220

FACTS ABOUT THE EARTH

Surface area	196,950,000 sq. mi.
Radius at the equator	3,963,338 mi.
Radius at the poles	3,949,992 mi.
One degree of latitude at the equator	68.70 mi.
One degree of latitude at the pole	69.41 mi.
Mean distance to the sun	92,897,416 mi.
Mean distance to the moon	238,857 mi.
Mean density	5.52 grams per cubic centimeter

TIME

"Time is a great deal more than money. If you have time you can obtain money—usually. But though you have the wealth of a cloakroom attendant at the Carlton Hotel, you cannot buy yourself a minute more of time than I have, or the cat by the fire has."—ARNOLD BENNETT in *How to Live on Twenty-Four Hours a Day.*

Standard Time

Since March 19, 1918, standard time has been the legal time throughout the United States. Like the standard time in nearly every other country in the world, it is measured from the prime meridian at Greenwich, England. Eastern standard time is 75° west from Greenwich; Central standard time is 90° west from Greenwich; Mountain standard time is 105° west from Greenwich; Pacific standard time is 120° west from Greenwich; and Alaskan standard time is 150° west from Greenwich.

United States Eastern standard time is used from the Atlantic Ocean to a line through Toledo, O.; Norton, Va.; Johnson City, Tenn.; Ashville, N. C.; Atlanta and Macon, Ga., and Apalachicola, Fla.

United States Central standard time is used from this first line to a line through Mandan, N. D.; Pierre, S. D.; McCook, Neb.; Dodge City, Kan., and along west line of Oklahoma and Texas. Standard Mountain time is used from the second line to a line that forms the western boundary of Montana, thence follows the Salmon River westward, the western boundary of Idaho southward, the southern boundary of Idaho eastward, and thence passes southward through Ogden and Salt Lake City, Utah; Parker and Yuma, Arizona.

United States Pacific standard time is used from the third line to the Pacific Ocean.

Exact time signals, based on precise astronomical calculations, are sent out daily at 3 A.M., noon, and 3 P.M., Eastern standard time, from the United States Naval Observatory at Washington, D. C. The signals are transmitted by telegraph control lines which automatically operate the radio stations at Arlington and Annapolis. At noon the stations at Key West and at San Diego are also operated.

Daylight-Saving Time

When daylight-saving time is adopted the clock is advanced one hour. The usual time for it to begin is the last Sunday in April, and the usual time for it to end is the last Sunday in September. There are, however, many local variations. The custom is more often observed in the Eastern states than elsewhere

Differences in Time Between New York City and Other United States Cities

When it is noon, Eastern standard time, in New York City, the time in various other cities of the United States is as follows:

Atlanta, Ga.	Noon	Milwaukee, Wis.	11:00 A.M.
Baltimore, Md.	Noon	Minneapolis, Minn.	11:00 A.M.
Boston, Mass.	Noon	New Haven, Conn.	Noon
Chicago, Ill.	11:00 A.M.	New Orleans, La.	11:00 A.M.
Cleveland, Ohio	Noon	Philadelphia, Pa.	Noon
Dallas, Texas	11:00 A.M.	Pittsburgh, Pa.	Noon
Denver, Colo.	10:00 A.M.	Portland, Ore.	9:00 A.M.
Detroit, Mich.	Noon	St. Paul, Minn.	11:00 A.M.
Houston, Texas	11:00 A.M.	Salt Lake City, Utah	10:00 A.M.
Indianapolis, Ind.	11:00 A.M.	San Francisco, Calif.	9:00 A.M.
Kansas City, Mo.	11:00 A.M.	Seattle, Wash.	9:00 A.M.
Los Angeles, Calif.	9:00 A.M.	St. Louis, Mo.	11:00 A.M.
Louisville, Ky.	11:00 A.M.	Washington, D.C.	Noon

Differences in Time Between New York City and Various Foreign Cities

When it is noon, Eastern standard time, in New York City, the time in various other cities and parts of the world is as follows:

Amsterdam	5:00 P.M.	Madrid	5:00 P.M.
Berlin	6:00 P.M.	Manila	[1]1:00 A.M.
Brussels	5:00 P.M.	Melbourne	[1]3:00 A.M.
Buenos Aires	1:00 P.M.	Moscow	8:00 P.M.
Cape Town	7:00 P.M.	Paris	5:00 P.M.
Copenhagen	6:00 P.M.	Peking	[1]1:00 A.M.
Durban	7:00 P.M.	Rome	6:00 P.M.
Havre	5:00 P.M.	Stockholm	6:00 P.M.
Istanbul	7:00 P.M.	Vienna	6:00 P.M.
Johannesburg	7:00 P.M.	Yokohama	[1]2:00 A.M.
Leningrad	8:00 P.M.		
London	5:00 P.M.	[1]Denotes next day.	

Ship Time

Until recently time on shipboard was marked off by bells, as follows:

Time, A.M.		Time, A.M.		Time, A.M.	
1 Bell	12:30	1 Bell	4:30	1 Bell	8:30
2 Bells	1:00	2 Bells	5:00	2 Bells	9:00
3 "	1:30	3 "	5:30	3 "	9:30
4 "	2:00	4 "	6:00	4 "	10:00
5 "	2:30	5 "	6:30	5 "	10:30
6 "	3:00	6 "	7:00	6 "	11:00
7 "	3:30	7 "	7:30	7 "	11:30
8 "	4:00	8 "	8:00	8 "	Noon

The time P.M. was the same as the time A.M.

The day commenced at noon and was divided as follows:

Afternoon Watch, noon to 4 P.M.   First Watch, 8 P.M. to midnight
First Dog Watch, 4 P.M. to 6 P.M.   Middle Watch, midnight to 4 A.M.
Second Dog Watch, 6 P.M. to 8 P.M.   Morning Watch, 4 A.M. to 8 A.M.
                    Forenoon Watch, 8 A.M. to noon

Recently many ships have abandoned this in favor of the system followed in ordinary civil life in which the day commences at midnight and comprises the hours which elapse before the following midnight. In some instances, the hours are counted from 0 to 24, but, generally, they are divided into two series of twelve hours each in which the hours are marked A.M. or P.M., as the case may be.

The International Date Line

The international date line is an imaginary line in the Pacific Ocean at which dates change. It runs mainly along the 180th meridian of longitude but zigzags here and there so that closely associated groups of islands will have the same calendar. This is the line upon which eastbound travelers set their calendars back one day and repeat a day, and westbound travelers set it ahead one day or skip a day. The necessity for this is caused by the rotation of the earth. A traveler going in the same direction that the earth is moving, *i.e.,* one going east, travels with respect to the sun at the rate the earth is moving, plus the rate at which he is moving over the surface of the earth. A traveler moving in the opposite direction, *i.e.,* to the west, would travel with respect to the sun at the rate he is moving over the surface of the earth, minus the speed of the rotation of the earth. Without the date line there would be endless confusion all over the world.

The Watch as a Compass

If you are lost in the woods and your watch is keeping correct time you can locate the cardinal points of the compass in the following manner. Hold the watch flat in your hand like a compass with the face upward. Hold a small stick or match straight up at the edge of the watch and turn the watch until the shadow of the stick falls along the hour hand nearest to the actual hour of day. This hand will then point toward the sun. In the morning south will lie halfway between the hour hand and XII, forward. At noon south will lie along the shadow cast by the match. In the afternoon south will lie halfway between the hour hand and XII, backward. If the watch is running according to daylight-saving time, it is one hour fast by the sun, and adjustments should be made accordingly.

International
Date Line

The Thirteen-Month Year

The 13-month year was endorsed by the League of Nations in 1926. A number of business houses would welcome it because of the greater convenience.

According to the scheme there would be 13 months of 28 days, each containing four weeks, each week beginning on Sunday and ending on Saturday. Every month would be like every other month, and days would fall on identical dates. That is, the first of every month would always be on Sunday, the second on Monday, etc.

The 13-month would come between June and July and would be like all the other months.

The last day in every year would be dated December 29, and, since it is an extra day, would be called Year Day, and would not have a weekday name, such as Monday or Tuesday.

In leap years a similar day would be inserted as June 29, to be known as Leap Day, thus providing a midsummer holiday as well as the midwinter holiday which December 29 would give.

Bankers' Time Table

For periods of less than one year the following table may be found useful. From it one can tell at a glance the number of days between any day in any month and the corresponding day in any other month for any period of time not greater than one year. To find the number of days between October 25 and April 25, take October in the first column, follow the line through to April; the number is 182. From December 10 to October 10 is 304 days. To find the number of days between uneven dates, between April 9 and August 20, for instance, find the number of days between April 9 and August 9, and add to it the number of days from August 9 to August 20. From the table you see that there are 122 days between April 9 and August 9. Add to this the 11 days between August 9 and August 20 and you have 133 days.

From any day of	To the Same Day of the Next											
	Jan.	Feb.	Mar.	Apr.	May	June	July	Aug.	Sept.	Oct.	Nov.	Dec.
Jan.	365	31	59	90	120	151	181	212	243	273	304	334
Feb.	334	365	28	59	89	120	150	181	212	242	273	303
Mar.	306	337	365	31	61	92	122	153	184	214	245	275
Apr.	275	306	334	365	30	61	91	122	153	183	214	244
May	245	276	304	335	365	31	61	92	123	153	184	214
June	214	245	273	304	334	365	30	61	92	122	153	183
July	184	215	243	274	304	335	365	31	62	92	123	153
Aug.	153	184	212	243	273	304	334	365	31	61	92	122
Sept.	122	153	181	212	242	273	303	334	365	30	61	91
Oct.	92	123	151	182	212	243	273	304	335	365	31	61
Nov.	61	92	120	151	181	212	242	273	304	334	365	30
Dec.	31	62	90	121	151	182	212	243	274	304	335	365

Reckoning Time for Ordinary Interest

In ordinary interest calculations the year is reckoned as having 12 months of 30 days each, making 360 days in all. In finding time for more than a year this basis is used. For instance, find the time between June 29, 1911, and March 4, 1930.

Years	Months	Days
1929	14	34
1911	6	29
18	8	5

Since it is impossible to subtract 29 days from four days you borrow a month, which makes it 34 days but leaves you only two months in the column to the left. Six months cannot be subtracted from two and so you borrow a year, making it 14 months, but leaving you with a year less in the "Years" column.

Reckoning Time for Accurate Interest

The United States Government and certain bankers compute accurate rather than ordinary interest, that is, they count on a basis of 365 days to a year. It is much more troublesome to work out than ordinary interest. There are tables for it as well as for ordinary interest, but since they are seldom used in the general run of commercial transactions they are not included here. A simple way to find out the accurate interest is to find the ordinary interest. Ordinary interest is as much greater than accurate interest as $360/60$ is greater than $360/365$, which is $1/72$. Therefore, to find the accurate interest subtract $1/72$ of it from itself. Similarly, to find the ordinary interest, add $1/72$ of the accurate interest to itself.

SPLICING ROPE

Rope is said to be spliced when the two ends are joined together by untwisting their strands for a short distance and threading the strands of each rope under and over the strands of the other to form a joint. To avoid increasing the thickness of the rope at the joint, the loose ends of the strands are cut to varying lengths and thinned down to points. The strands of one rope are then twisted into the vacant spaces in the other rope and the tapered ends threaded.

Stages in making common forms of splice. Left, short splice joining two rope ends. Right, eye splice, for making a loop.

KNOTS

The knot most commonly used is the overhand knot (1). By making a second overhand knot over the first the square or reef knot (2) is made. The bowline (3) forms a loop that will not draw and can be undone very quickly. The clove hitch (4) is one of the best knots for fastening a line. It is very secure. The timber hitch (5) is used for hoisting or towing heavy timbers, the sheepshank (6) for shortening a rope when neither end is free.

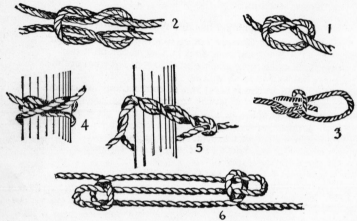

Knots in common use. 1. Overhand. 2. Square or Reef. 3. Bowline. 4. Clove hitch. 5. Timber hitch. 6. Sheepshank.

AMERICAN LABOR UNIONS

Approximately 15,000,000 workers belong to labor unions, more than three-fourths of which are affiliated with either the **American Federation of Labor** (AFL) or the **Congress of Industrial Organizations** (CIO). Besides these federations, there are many unaffiliated unions such as the Railroad Brotherhoods, the United Mine Workers, the International Association of Machinists, and numerous independents. Since 1935, there has been a great growth of unionism in mass-production industries such as steel, cement, automobiles, rubber, and aluminum.

Workers are organized into *local* unions which are subordinate to *national* or *international* unions which in turn are affiliated with the national federations. The charter of each national union gives it exclusive jurisdiction over a given trade or industry, though jurisdictional disputes are common on both an inter-federation and on an intra-federation scale. The real power within the federations is in the hands of the national unions.

Most of the craft unions are affiliated with the AFL, while most of the industrial unions are in the CIO. The objectives of both are largely the same—to further the economic interests of workers by collective bargaining and by securing favorable legislation. Within the AFL, there are state federations of labor, local trade and labor councils, and departments which are composed of unions having interests in a particular industry such as building. The CIO has state and local industrial councils which parallel AFL organizations, but it has no departments.

NATIONAL LABOR RELATIONS BOARD

In 1934, Congress established a National Labor Relations Board to operate under NRA. In 1935, the **National Labor Relations Act** was established, providing for a new Board to consist of three members, appointed by the President with the consent of the Senate. The Board had two principal functions: (1) to prevent unfair labor practices by employers (interference with the exercise by employees of the right to organize and bargain collectively, domination of unions, anti-union discrimination, and refusal to bargain collectively); (2) to certify unions as the duly chosen bargaining representatives of the workers in a designated bargaining unit. In respect to unfair labor practices, the Board could direct an employer to cease and desist from the practice complained of; it could also order the employer to take affirmative action, such as reinstatement of employees with back pay.

The Act was amended in 1947 by the **Taft-Hartley Act.** As amended, the statute bars certain unfair practices by unions, such as intimidation of employees and refusal to bargain collectively. The closed shop is outlawed, as are jurisdictional strikes and secondary boycotts. Unions are also required to file specified data with the Board and union officers operating under the Act are compelled to sign non-Communist affidavits. The membership of the Board has been increased to five, and its judicial functions have been separated from its prosecuting functions by delegating to the Board's General Counsel final authority to act for the Board in respect to the issuance of complaints in unfair labor practice cases.

FAIR LABOR STANDARDS ACT

This law, also known as the Wage and Hour Act, has been described as providing a ceiling for hours, a floor for wages, and a break for children.[1] It applies to those employees who are engaged in interstate commerce or in producing goods for interstate commerce or in a process or occupation directly essential to such production. Thus, a typical employee covered by the Act is one who is employed in a factory or wholesale establishment engaged in receiving or shipping goods in interstate commerce.

Exemptions from the Act include: bona fide executive, administrative, professional, or local retailing personnel;[2] outside salesmen;[2] employees of retail or service establishments; agricultural workers; certain employees engaged in activities of irrigation systems; certain employees of seafood and fishing industries; employees of certain forestry and logging operations; employees of weekly, semiweekly, or daily newspapers having a circulation of less than 4,000; employees of street, suburban, or interurban electric railways, and of local trolley or motorbus carriers; switchboard operators of public telephone exchanges with not more than 750 stations; seamen; employees of taxicab companies; employees engaged in the delivery of newspapers; and employees engaged in the first processing of agricultural products within the area of production.[2]

Those employees whose hours are subject to regulation by the Interstate Commerce Commission and those employed in the first processing of dairy products, cotton, cottonseed, and sugar are exempted from the hours but not from the wages provisions. Partial exemption from the hours provision is also extended to those in seasonal industries and those operating under guaranteed employment contracts. In such instances, overtime need not be paid unless the seasonal work extends over more than 14 weeks a year, or the workday exceeds 12 hours or the workweek exceeds 56 hours.

Wage and Hour Coverage

The Fair Labor Standards Act, as amended in 1950, contains provisions for minimum wage and overtime, but does not deal blanket-fashion with

---

[1] For Child Labor Provisions see page 460.

[2] Exemptions thus designated are governed by special regulations issued by the Administrator of the Act. All other exemptions are self-executing in accordance with provisions of the Act.

industries as a whole. Coverage under the Act depends upon the nature of the employment of the particular employee. The employer is required to meet the minimum wage and overtime requirements of the Act for each of his employees who is engaged in commerce or in the production of goods for commerce. "Commerce" is defined by the Act to mean "trade, commerce, transportation, transmission, or communication among the several states or between any state and any place outside thereof."

Coverage under the minimum wage and overtime provisions of the Act is not limited to employees working on an hourly wage. Provisions of the Act apply whatever the method of payment—hourly, weekly, by piece-work, monthly, or on any other basis. The general minimum-wage requirement of the Act is that each covered and nonexempt employee must be paid at the rate of not less than 75 cents an hour.

Compensation for overtime—work after 40 hours in a workweek—is due when the employee customarily receives his pay. Such overtime payments must be at the rate of not less than one and one-half times the "regular rate" at which the employee is actually employed and paid, except as otherwise specially provided.

The Act provides for exceptions for the 75-cents-an-hour minimum rate for certain learners, apprentices, messengers, and handicapped workers. However, none of those excepted can be employed at a subminimum rate except under special certificate issued in accordance with regulations promulgated by the Administrator.

Because of the widespread dissatisfaction over portal cases, Congress, in 1947, enacted the Portal-to-Portal Act which provided that time spent in travel or in other activities which were preliminary or postliminary to the employee's principal activities was not to be counted as working time unless compensable by contract, custom, or usage.

Administration. The Fair Labor Standards Act provides for an Administration of the Wage and Hour Division in the Department of Labor. The Administrator is authorized to supervise the payment of unpaid minimum wages or overtime compensation; and upon receipt of a written request from an employee claiming unpaid minimum wages or overtime compensation, the Administrator is authorized to bring court action to recover the amount of the claim.[1] The Federal Government may prosecute willful violation of the Fair Labor Standards Act. Upon conviction, the employer may be fined up to $10,000 and, in the case of a second conviction, imprisoned for up to six months.

WORKMEN'S COMPENSATION

Workmen's compensation is a form of social insurance that provides monetary compensation for injuries arising in the course of employment. In recent years, this compensation has been extended to cover some, but not all, occupational diseases.

---

[1] In accordance with the Act, the employee has the right to sue his employer independently and recover up to double the amount of back wages due.

In the United States, all states, the Territories of Alaska, Hawaii, Puerto Rico, the Virgin Islands, and the Federal Government have enacted workmen's compensation laws. The Bureau of Employees' Compensation of the United States Department of Labor administers the Act of Sept. 7, 1916, which provides workmen's compensation benefits for civil employees of the United States who suffer injuries in the line of duty. Certain large groups of workers, such as railroad employees and seamen, are not covered by compensation laws, largely because the workers feel that employers' liability laws give them greater protection. Also not covered by compensation laws in general are farm laborers, domestic servants, and employees of nonprofit institutions.

Workmen's compensation laws in the United States are characterized by the following provisions:

1. *Waiting time before compensation becomes payable.* A waiting time has been prescribed in all states except Oregon, and ranges from less than one week to ten days.

2. *Temporary disability.* Compensation for temporary disability ranges from 80 per cent to 50 per cent of the worker's wage. Thirty-seven states have set a maximum time limit during which payments are allowed, ranging from 156 to 1,000 weeks.

3. *Permanent total disability.* Twenty-two states and the Federal Government provide a fraction of the worker's former wage each week. Other states limit compensation to between 260 and 1,000 weeks; total maximum compensation, where limited, ranges from $3,000 to $15,750.

4. *Permanent partial disability.* Special payments for permanent partial disability are made, scaled according to the member or faculty lost. Payment for extra disability (*e.g.*, the loss of a second eye) out of special funds is provided by 41 states, Alaska, Puerto Rico, District of Columbia, Hawaii, and the Federal Longshoremen's Act.

5. *Medical care.* Medical care and surgical appliances which may be necessary for injured workers are provided for in compensation laws, although practice in this matter varies considerably from state to state.

6. *Death.* In the case of death, 47 states pay funeral expenses in addition to compensation. In most of the states the widow receives 40 per cent or more of the weekly wages until death or remarriage, plus an allowance for each child under a certain age.

7. *Rehabilitation.* Provision for rehabilitation was first made by Massachusetts (1918) through surgery, re-education, and other means, and was copied in the next year by nine other states. In 1920 Congress agreed to match with equal sums all amounts appropriated by the states for rehabilitation. At present, all states are cooperating in this program.

8. *Occupational diseases.* Diseases which result from certain occupations are fully covered under the laws of 24 states, and certain specific diseases are covered under the laws of 17 states.

Most states have established official agencies for the technical administration of workmen's compensation laws. The administrative officials of these state agencies and those of the Canadian provinces are organized into the International Association of Industrial Accident Boards and Commissions.

SOCIAL SECURITY ACT

The Social Security Act is a national law, passed by Congress and approved by the President on August 14, 1935. The purpose of the Act and its subsequent amendments is to prevent and relieve the misfortunes that come when earnings are cut off by lack of work, old age, blindness, or death; and when children are left with no one to support them or when they lack necessary care. Five of the aid programs covered by the Act provide for direct cash payments to qualified individuals.

The Social Security Administration,[1] part of the Federal Security Agency, administers the Act, and is responsible for Federal old-age and survivors insurance and for public assistance for the aged, the blind, and dependent children in families that have lost their breadwinner. Since August 20, 1949, the Department of Labor has been responsible for the unemployment insurance program. Three maternal and child-welfare programs are also provided under the Act—maternal and child-health services, services for crippled children, and child-welfare services.

Old-Age and Survivors Insurance

The old-age and survivors insurance program protects wage-earners in industrial and commercial employment and their families when either old age or death ends their earnings. In addition, the amendment of 1950 provides coverage (effective Jan. 1, 1951) for the following groups: (1) *self-employed persons* whose annual net income through self-employment is at least $400, excluding farmers, physicians, lawyers, and certain other specified professional groups; (2) *agricultural workers* who are regularly employed to the extent that they work five months or more for the same employer and earn at least $50 in each quarter; (3) *domestic workers,* not employed in farm homes, who work for a single employer for at least 24 days in a calendar quarter with cash wages of at least $50 for the quarter; (4) *employees of non-profit organizations* where two-thirds of the employees are in favor of the program and the employer is willing to pay his share; (5) *employees of state and local governments* in cases where special agreements have been made between the state and Federal governments (excluding public employees already covered under a retirement system); and (6) *specially covered employees* such as full-time life insurance salesmen, agent drivers, or commission drivers (who distribute most products except milk), and full-time traveling and city salesmen except retail salesmen and industrial home workers.

The old-age and survivors insurance program is wholly Federal in operation and is administered by the *Bureau of Old-Age and Survivors Insurance* of the S.S.A. Monthly benefits directly related to the employee's past wages are provided for wage earners who meet certain qualifications when they stop work at or after the age of 65, to their wives at the same age, or to a wife regardless of age with a child of 18 or younger in her care. In the event of an insured worker's death, payments are made to his widow when 65 or over or while she has a child of 18 or younger in her care, to the children, or to dependent parents when they are 65 or over, if they were receiving 50% or more of their support from the wage

---

[1]Hereafter referred to as the S.S.A.

earner. In addition, the 1950 amendment provided for lump-sum benefits, payable to survivors of insured deceased wage earners in every death case; husband insurance benefits, payable to dependent husbands (65 or over) of women wage earners; and widowers (65 or over) with the same qualifications. Under the 1950 amendment, a beneficiary may not earn more than $50 a month in covered employment without losing his benefits. After the age of 75 benefits are payable regardless of the amount of earnings.

To qualify for benefits under the old-age and survivors insurance program, a worker must have been employed and earned wages for a certain length of time. The Act provides that any calendar quarter in which a worker has earned $50 or more is to be considered a "quarter of coverage." The number of quarters required varies for each individual in accordance with the age of the worker. To be fully insured a worker must have six quarters of coverage in every case and also either one quarter of coverage for each two calendar quarters after January 1, 1951; or one quarter of coverage for each two calendar quarters after he became 21 years old; or a total of 40 quarters of coverage.

The employer and employee each pay the same amount toward the benefits at a fixed percentage of the worker's earnings. The rates listed below give the percentages to be paid through 1969 after which the employer and employee will each pay 3¼% of the employee's wage.[1]

1950—1953—1½%	1960—1964—2½%
1954—1959—2%	1965—1969—3%

This money goes into an *Old-Age and Survivors Insurance Fund* from which the benefits are paid. The 1950 amendment also provided for a flat wage credit of $160 per month made for each month spent in the armed services by World War II veterans. Credit, however, is not provided if the period of service is credited toward any other Federal retirement benefit.

Public Assistance

Aid to the needy aged, the blind, dependent children, and the permanently and totally disabled is based upon Federal-state cooperation. *The Bureau of Public Assistance* of the S.S.A. administers the provisions of the act relating to these types of public assistance. Services under the program include direct cash benefits, medical care, and provisions for the mother, caretaker, or guardian of the dependent child.

Maternal and Child Welfare[2]

The Social Security Act provides three programs for children and mothers which are administered through Federal grants to states to

---

[1] The self-employed pay 1½ times these rates.
[2] See section on Aid to Dependent Children (p. 461)

assist in the development of maternal and child-health services, services for crippled children, and child-welfare services. These are administered by the *Children's Bureau* of the S.S.A. Maternity clinics, child-health conferences, health services for children of school age, immunization services, dental and mental health services, and nutrition education programs are encouraged. State crippled children's agencies provide service programs that include skilled medical, surgical, nursing, medical-social, and physical therapy care. Child-welfare services, under state and local programs, provide the assistance of social workers to parents, administrators of children's services, and others in meeting the problems of dependent, neglected, and delinquent children, and of children in danger of becoming delinquent.

Employment Security

A joint Federal-state program provides a two-fold service—job insurance and job placement. Each state has its own unemployment insurance law under which jobless workers receive weekly out-of-work benefits.

When a man loses his job, he is required to file his claim at the local employment office. If no job is found for him, his benefit payments begin at the end of a waiting period, which is usually one week or more, depending upon the state law. The amount of benefits received by the worker and the length of time for which he may receive such benefits also depend upon the state law.

Public employment offices register unemployed workers, whether or not they are insured under the state law, and try to find work for them free of charge. The *Bureau of Employment* of the Department of Labor administers the Federal part of the program.

FARMING IN THE UNITED STATES

The agriculture of any area depends primarily on climate, soil, topography, and markets. Perhaps the two most important climatic features which determine the type of farming in a given area are the length of the frost-free season and the rainfall. The southern part of the United States has 200 days or more between frosts, which is sufficient time for the growth of cotton. The northern fringe of the country, as well as much of the Rocky Mountain area, has less than 140 days of frost-free season, which is insufficient for the growth of corn.

The eastern half of the country has more than 20 in. of rainfall per year. Most of the western half has less than 20 in., although the northern Pacific coast has a very high rainfall. Twenty inches is about the minimum rainfall required to produce crops without irrigation or special procedures to conserve moisture.

The areas with a heavy concentration of farming are those which have a favorable combination of climate, soil, topography, and markets. Most of such areas are in the eastern half of the country. The exceptions to this are the irrigated valleys of the Pacific coastal states. The largest concentration of farming is in the corn belt—a strip of land about 250 miles wide and 800 miles long extending from western Ohio to eastern Nebraska.

Another area with concentrated agriculture is the northern Atlantic seaboard. This area has excellent markets and in many parts is also favored with respect to climate, soil, and topography. The central valley of California has excellent soil and topography and excellent climate for fruit growing, but irrigation must be practiced.

Because of the widely varying conditions in different parts of the country, farmers grow many different crops. The most important crop is corn; it occupies about one-fourth of the crop area. Hay and wheat each occupy about one-fifth. A large proportion of the total crop area is devoted to crops which are used for livestock feed. These crops include corn, hay, oats, and sorghums. Together they account for about three-fifths of the total crop area.

Table 1 indicates the sources of farm income in the United States. A little more than half of the total is from three animals—cows, sows, and hens. Vegetables account for a higher proportion of the farm income than either wheat or cotton.

TABLE 1

UNITED STATES GROSS FARM INCOME

(Average of 1946 and 1947)

Gross income is cash income from sales, plus
value of products used for human consumption on the farm.

Item	Gross income in millions of dollars	Per cent of total
Crops		
Wheat	$2129	7
Rye, rice, buckwheat	188	1
Feed crops	1989	7
Cotton and cotton seed	1852	6
Soybeans, flaxseed, peanuts	846	3
Tobacco	992	3
Fruits and nuts	1668	5
Vegetables[1]	2594	8
Sugar and sirup crops	228	1
Forest products	375	1
Greenhouse and nursery products	381	1
Other crops	189	1
Total crops	$13,431	44
Livestock and livestock products		
Dairy products	$4648	15
Cattle and calves	4396	14
Hogs	4042	13
Eggs	1901	6
Chickens	1062	4
Turkeys	258	1
Sheep, lambs, and wool	498	2
Other	153	1
Total livestock	$16,958	56
Total crops and livestock	$30,389	100

[1]Includes truck crops, farm gardens, dry field peas, dry edible beans, potatoes, sweet potatoes.
Source of data: "Agricultural Statistics" 1948, pp. 591–593.

Types of Farms

The general tendency in all business in the United States is toward increased specialization. Such specialization permits a division of labor, with each person becoming skilled at one job. However, the high degree of specialization common in manufacturing is not usually possible in farming because of the seasonal nature of the work, and the fact that most individual farms do not specialize in any one product, but produce several different kinds. Still, the long-time tendency is toward some degree of specialization.

Dairy farms are located largely in the Northeast and the states bordering the Great Lakes. Most of the hog farms are in the corn belt. Beef-cattle and sheep ranches utilize most of the land in the Rocky Mountain states.

Fruit and vegetable farms are located chiefly in the states bordering the Atlantic and Pacific Oceans and the Great Lakes.

The present type of farming in each region is the result of years of experimentation. A newcomer should not try a "new" type of farming until he is certain that his new idea is not merely one that farmers in the area tried out years ago and discarded when they found it did not pay.

Sizes of Farms

The average farm size for the entire United States in terms of acres was 195 in 1945; it varied from 56 acres per farm in Massachusetts to 2,533 acres per farm in Wyoming. These figures do not necessarily indicate that the farms in Wyoming are large businesses. It takes a very large area to support a family where the topography is rough and the rainfall is low. The average acreage per farm in the northern states was 180, in the southern states 131, and in the western states 639.

The 1945 census classified the farms of the United States according to economic classes. The study was based primarily on the total value of the farm products sold or used in farm households in 1944. With this classification as a basis, the farms have been divided into three groups, which may be called small, medium, and large (table 2). The *small farms* produced less than $1,200 worth of products per farm. On many of these farms there were other than farm sources of income. The small farms accounted for 42 per cent of all the farms, but produced only 7 per cent of the value of farm products. Half of them were located in the southern states.

TABLE 2

SMALL, MEDIUM, AND LARGE FARMS[1]
(United States, 1944)

Size of farm business	Value of farm products per farm in 1944	Number of farms (millions)	Per cent of all U. S. farms	Total value of products (millions)	Per cent of total value of products
Small	Less than $1,200	2.5	42	$ 1,368	7
Medium	$1,200 to $19,999	3.3	56	12,866	71
Large	$20,000 or more	0.1	2	4,004	22
	Totals	5.9	100	$18,238	100

[1]Basic data from the United States Census.

The *medium-sized farms,* which accounted for 56 per cent of all farms in the country, produced almost three-fourths of the total value of farm products; the *large farms,* which constituted only 2 per cent of the farms, produced almost one-fourth of the value. A little more than half of these large farms were located in the western states.

By most business standards all the small and medium-sized farms are "small business"; even some of the large farms would be so considered. A manufacturing enterprise producing not over $20,000 worth of goods in a year is small business. Some of the large farms were owned by corporations, but most of them were operated by individual farm families.

Kinds of Farm Organization

There are many kinds of farm organization; and it is important to understand the differences between them and the place in the economy of each kind. Farms may first be divided into (1) family farms and (2) large-scale farms. On family farms most of the work is done by the farmer and his family. Most of the farms in the United States are family farms. In 1945 only 47 per cent of all farms had any hired help; and the farms which had hired labor averaged only 182 days of such help.

Family Farms.—Family farms may be divided into four groups: subsistence, residential, commercial, and part-time.

Subsistence Farms. Subsistence farms are those which emphasize production for home use, with only small amounts produced for sale. The family job is farming; there is little or no nonfarm income. Subsistence farms may have a high standard of living with respect to food, but since there is little cash there can be no plumbing, radios, automobiles, refrigerators, or other modern conveniences. In pioneer days all farms were subsistence farms. Today, significant numbers of such farms exist in the southern Appalachian and the Ozark Mountains.

Residential Farms. On a residential farm, farm production is slight, and very little is sold; the family depends largely on nonfarm income. Some owners of residential farms are unskilled laborers, some skilled laborers, and some highly successful professional men.

Family-Commercial Farms. Most of the agricultural production of the United States is from family farms which are operated as businesses; they include the medium-sized farms discussed previously and many of the large farms. Family-commercial farms emphasize production for sale. The only items produced for home use are those which can be produced efficiently. Most of the products are sold, and all or most of the family income is from farming. Some labor may be hired, depending on the amount of family help available. The operator works with both his hands and his head.

Part-Time Farms. A part-time farm is a combination of a residential farm and a commercial farm. The owner of such a farm is a man with two jobs, one of which is farming. It is important to distinguish between part-time and residential farming. A residential farmer is a city worker who has decided to live in the country and do a little farming when he feels like it. A part-time farmer makes farming a business; he will often find that his farming interferes with vacation trips or family picnics.

Large-Scale Farms.—Large-scale farms are those with a number of workers under one manager. The manager's time is taken up almost completely with management. There are relatively few such farms in the United States, although most business other than agriculture is organized on a large-scale basis. A comparison of the advantages of large-scale and individual operation as applied to *any business* should help to explain why there are not more large-scale farms.

Advantages of Large-Scale Operation	Advantages of Individual Operation
Volume of business in buying and selling	Greater interest in the business by the owner-manager
Division of labor—each man can be a specialist in his job	Greater interest in the business by laborers
Long life—business is not liquidated when manager dies or retires	Flexible labor supply—in emergencies workers put in longer hours and members of the family help out
Standardized production—large quantities, all made the same	Possibility of making quick decisions—no board of directors to consider

The main problems of large-scale farms are those of labor. In fruit and vegetable farming, one man can supervise a great many workers; there are, therefore, a considerable number of large-scale fruit and vegetable farms. In most types of farming, however, the workers are scattered all over the land; hence, the supervision of a large number of uninterested workers involves prohibitive expense.

The main trend in American agriculture has been to continue the family farm, in order to get the advantages of individual operation listed above, *but to cooperate with other farmers on jobs for which large-scale operation is particularly advantageous.* For example, farmers often cooperate to hire a technical expert, known as the county agent.

Factors in Success of a Family-Commercial Farm

Prices. In discussing the factors that affect profits prices must always be put at the top of the list, even though the individual farmer does not have much control over them. As an example of the importance of prices, farm business records for 28 dairy farmers in Montgomery County, New York, in 1944 showed an average labor income of $2,087[1]. In 1933 the average labor income of the same 28 farmers, operating on the same farms with the same kind of farming, was $-569. These figures might suggest that prices alone determine farm income. However, a study of the 28 individual farms showed that in 1944 one farmer had a labor income of $6,311, while another had a labor income of $-272. In 1933 one farmer had a labor income of $199, while another had a labor income of $-2,597.

The difference between the average labor incomes of the 28 farmers in 1944 and in 1932 was $2,656. The difference between the most successful and the least successful farmer in 1944 was $6,583. This fact indicates that there are factors other than prices which affect farm profits.

Success in farming actually depends on many factors, a fact which makes it difficult to determine which are the most important. A casual observer of a farm business often attributes success or failure to the wrong cause.

For example, success may be attributed to the method of feeding the

---

[1] A farmer's labor income is what he gets for his year's work after paying all business expenses and interest on all the capital invested; but in addition to his labor income he has the use of a house, and farm products for family use.

hens, when, as a matter of fact, the hens are not paying, but the cows are keeping both the farmer and the hens. The farmer may attribute a good bean crop to the date of planting, when it is really due to good soil. A neighbor may think a farmer's failure to prosper is the result of poor fertilization practices, when it is really the result of doctors' and hospital bills.

The actual reasons for success or failure stand out more clearly after a study of the records of many farm businesses. The discussion which follows purposes to summarize the findings from thousands of farm records for many different years.

Size of Business. Farm records over the years indicate that farms large enough to keep two to four men profitably employed are more successful than those which furnish work for less than two men. The table below, which shows the usual relationship between size and profits, could be duplicated many times for other years, other types of farming, and other regions.

TABLE 3

RELATION OF SIZE OF BUSINESS TO LABOR INCOME[1]
(100 Dairy Farms, Oneida County, New York, 1942–43)

Size of farm business	Number of farms	Man equivalent	Number of cows	Pounds of milk produced per cow	Labor income
One-man farms	18	1.2	10	7,500	$ 473
One-and-a-half-man farms	35	1.6	15	7,246	932
Two-man farms	27	2.0	23	6,874	1,483
Three-man farms	20	2.8	34	7,710	1,968

[1]Data from Cornell University Mimeographed Report A. E. 465.

Farm-management records show the advantages of large businesses to be primarily economy in the use of labor, equipment, and capital. With a very small business, a considerable proportion of the time is spent in getting ready for a job and in finishing it. For instance, in doing chores, it takes as long to get into the haymow to throw down hay for 3 cows as it does for 30. It does not take ten times as long to get 50 cows from pasture as it does to get 5. It does not take five times as long to clean up the milking machine for 50 cows as it does for 10. With a one-man business a farmer spends most of his time in "getting ready" and "finishing up."

Another reason for economy of labor on a two- to four-man farm is that it is difficult for a man to do many farm operations alone. Thus, a farm which actually has too little business to keep two men profitably employed often has a second man because it is impossible to do some of the work without him.

Greater efficiency in the use of equipment is another advantage of the larger businesses. It takes almost as much equipment to run a 100-acre dairy farm as it does to run a 200-acre farm. Very little farm equipment, even on a large farm, is used to full capacity. As more equipment is invented it becomes increasingly important to have a large business. For example, not many years ago potatoes were planted by hand, the bugs knocked off into a can of kerosene, and the potatoes dug with a potato hook. Use of equipment under such operations was as efficient with a 1-acre potato patch as with a 50-acre field. Today, with expensive machines used for planting, spraying, and digging, it is important to have enough business to keep the machine efficiently employed.

Rates of Production of Crops and Animals. Over the years, farm management records have indicated that, within the limits of the actual practice of farmers, the higher the yield of crops or the production of animals, the higher the labor income of the farmer. With yields much below the neighbors' average, a farmer usually makes less than a hired man's wages.

A few farms are successful in spite of low yields, for the yield, though very important, is only one factor affecting farm profits. The importance of good yields is sometimes stressed to the disparagement of that of size, and the advice is offered, "Farm fewer acres and do it better." This is mixing good advice with bad. It is not necessary to reduce the size of the farm below that adapted to modern machinery in order to get better crop yields or production per animal.

Many factors must be considered to obtain good rates of production. One of the most important is to secure good land and good animal breeds. The choice of a farm is a very important milestone in a farmer's life; so is the choice of animals. A farmer should be a good judge of both.

The farmer's problem is to adjust his crop yields and the production per animal to the conditions with which he works. It is a mistake to suggest that every farmer should get 10,000 lb. of milk per cow, or 190 eggs per hen, or 400 bu. of potatoes per acre. These fixed goals are too high for some and too low for others. The most profitable adjustment of yields depends on many factors. These include the price of land, the quality of the animals, the cost of labor, the price of fertilizer, and the price of product. It is not desirable that every farmer should attempt to get the maximum possible crop yields or production per animal. Extremely high yields are expensive. There is plenty of evidence that good yields are profitable, while extremely high yields are usually obtained at a high cost.

Selection and Combination of Enterprises. In deciding on the best combination of enterprises for any one farm there are also many factors to be considered. The most important of these are:

1. Relative profits of different enterprises. Because of differences in climate, soil, topography, and markets certain areas have definite advantages in the production of some products, while other areas lend themselves to other products. It is to the advantage of each area to concentrate as much as possible on the production of items most profitable in the area

2. Labor distribution. It is desirable to choose a group of enterprises which require labor throughout the year, in preference to a selection which causes seasonal peaks in labor requirements

3. Relative amounts of tillable and untillable land. Where considerable untillable land is available, the enterprises chosen should provide a use for this land, such as grazing livestock

4. Use of by-products
5. Maintenance of productivity
6. Rotation
7. Risk
8. Distribution of income throughout the year
9. Use of buildings and machinery
10. Capital available
11. Type of farming done by neighbors
12. Personal preference

One of the common errors in advising farmers in the selection of enterprises is overemphasizing some one of the above factors at the expense of the others. For example, much has been said concerning the risk involved in one-crop farming; yet most one-crop areas have chosen to operate in this manner because they have found it pays best. In most one-crop areas, such as the potato region of northern Maine, there is a great difference between the profits to be derived from the most profitable enterprise and the next most profitable. On the other hand, wherever there is a situation in which two or three enterprises are about equally profitable, a diversified agriculture is almost certain to result.

Sometimes personal preference is thought of as the most important factor to be considered in selecting enterprises. A would-be farmer with a strong personal preference should be careful to select a farm which is adapted to that kind of farming. It is unfortunate when a strong preference as to kind of farming and an equally strong preference for a particular farm are antagonistic.

Some persons get their personal preferences and the relative profits of different enterprises mixed up. Farmers and others will discuss the questions of whether beef will pay in New York, or apples in Iowa, or hogs in Massachusetts. Unless an individual is promoting beef, apples, or hogs, this is no way to look at the matter. The real problem is whether *on this farm* beef will pay better than the enterprises with which it competes. It is not a question of whether apples will pay in Iowa, but of whether they will pay as well as corn. Will hogs in Massachusetts pay as well as poultry?

Labor Efficiency. Labor is the most expensive item in the cost of farm operation, whether the farmer hires help or not. The farmer's own time is valuable, because he usually has the alternative of taking another job at good wages.

Labor is used most efficiently on a moderately large farm with good yields of crops and production per animal, and with enterprises so combined that the labor requirements are spread out through the year.

The use of well-tested labor-saving machines is always important. Some farmers buy so much machinery that they lose money, but there are probably many more who have too little equipment.

Changes in the layout of the farm or the arrangement of the buildings offer possibilities of increased efficiency on many farms. Farmers often get into the careless habit of doing chores in an inconveniently arranged barn.

Planning the work ahead will help on many farms, though a farmer's plans are always subject to change without notice from the weather man. It is important to keep a list of jobs which need doing, in order that when the weather changes, the farmer can know immediately which is the most pressing job in the changed situation. Doing work on time is one way to save labor and do a better job. This is particularly true of weed control. If weeds are killed when they are small, it will take less time than if the job is postponed.

Efficiency in the Use of Farm Equipment. Few, if any, farm businesses are large enough to justify ownership of all the modern equipment. Dairy farms are an example. Some are too small to justify a milking machine. Some which are large enough to afford a milking machine have too little business to warrant owning a hay baler. Some which are large enough to have both of these machines are not yet large enough to own a bulldozer. Certainly there are very few farms large enough to need a well-drilling outfit. It would take quite a business to keep a well-drilling outfit busy.

If a farm business is not large enough to make efficient use of a particular piece of machinery the farmer has about six possible courses to follow. These are to:

1. Buy the machine but use it inefficiently
2. Do without the machine, but attempt to compete with the man who has a business large enough to use it. In principle, this means using a sickle and flail against a combine
3. Buy the machine, and make full use of it by doing custom work for others in addition to doing his own work
4. Go in with the neighbors on cooperative ownership of the machine
5. Hire someone who owns the machine to do the job
6. Enlarge his farm business to the point where it justifies ownership of the machine

The first two choices listed above are not good. Each of the last four choices has its value, and it is not uncommon for one farmer to practice all of them at once—for different machines. For example, one farmer does the following:

He owns a hay baler, and does some custom work for others
He owns a silo-filling outfit in cooperation with a neighbor
He hires another neighbor to "combine" his grain
He puts four farms together into one unit in order to justify ownership of most of the modern equipment which he needs to use

It is good business for most farmers to practice all four of these plans. If the farm is not large enough to afford a milking machine, the only choice is to enlarge the business. Neither custom-operation nor share-ownership with the neighbors will work with this machine. On the other hand, if a man needs to have a well drilled his best course is to hire a well-driller.

Getting Started on a Family-Commercial Farm

Personal Qualifications. Some persons who may succeed in specialized jobs in a city are not qualified for farming, because farming calls for versatility. A good farmer is a combination of businessman, mechanic, naturalist, and laborer.

On a modern farm, most of the products are sold, and most of the necessities for the family are purchased. The farm is a business, and sound business principles must be applied if it is to succeed.

Mechanical ability has always been important in farming, but the great increase in the use of complicated machines in recent years has made this ability much more important than formerly. Occasionally, a farmer can depend on hired men for this mechanical ability, but usually he must not only be the mechanic but must also instruct the men and be on guard against their carelessness.

The farmer's job is growing plants and animals. He must know the scientific principles of crop and animal production, and he must also know the practical application of these principles to his own farm. An important requirement for success in farming is a keen interest in growing things. With all our scientific production, we have not outgrown the old adage, "The eye of the master fatteneth his cattle."

Good health and good physical strength are important for both the farmer and his wife. While modern machinery has reduced the amount of heavy physical labor on the farm and in the home, there are still many jobs which require a strong back. Running a farm is no job for either the physically or the mentally handicapped.

Education and Experience. In preparing for farming one should consider both education and experience. One alone is not enough, nor can either substitute for the other.

The importance of education is underemphasized by persons without it, and is likely to be overemphasized by persons who have it. Farm management records indicate that the farmers with higher education, on the average, run larger businesses, do a better job of farming, and make more money than those with less. Some college graduates have made spectacular failures, and some men who can hardly read and write have been very successful farmers. However, records indicate that these are exceptions rather than the rule.

Education, then, is not a guarantee of success in farming. It cannot overcome the handicaps of lack of ability, inexperience, or poor soil. For any individual farmer, education improves the chances of achieving financial success. Farming deals with living things. There are many difficult and intricate problems. Farming is becoming more of a science and less of an art. The more this becomes true, the greater will be the importance of education. Willingness to accept new ideas is becoming increasingly important in farming; a successful farmer must not be the last to lay the old aside. Farm management records indicate that persons with the most formal education find it easiest to adopt new ideas.

Farm experience is very important for success in a farm business. The knowledge necessary for success in any business is largely gained by practical experience, and farming is no exception. People who have never tried to run a farm often fail to realize the importance of actual experience.

Getting Control of Capital. A big problem in starting farming is capital. To finance an average farm at present, including stock and tools, requires about $25,000, and if one wishes to be a better-than-average farmer it takes more than this amount. To acquire the use of this capital is naturally a considerable problem. Farmers have done this by a number of different methods. Some of these are:

1. Working at some job other than farming to save money
2. Working on the home farm, gradually working into the business, and eventually buying all or part of the farm
3. Using the "hired-man-tenant" method of saving money, and getting established in farming
4. Inheriting or being given a farm

In using the "hired-man-tenant" route to farm ownership, a young man works as a hired man until he has obtained some experience, saved a little money, and established a good reputation in the community. Next he may have an opportunity to rent a farm, with the landlord furnishing most of the capital. He will then gradually accumulate some livestock and equipment. After he has accumulated enough livestock and equipment to run a farm, he may have an opportunity to buy a farm, borrowing all or most of the purchase price.

This method of acquiring control of the capital to farm may appear slow and difficult, but experience has shown that young men who start out this way become farm owners as early as or earlier than those who start by any other route. Those who have started by taking another job to save money have commonly been disappointed in the amount of their savings at the end of years in the other job. The young man who starts by the hired-man-tenant route is more likely to save money, since he is under more pressure to do so.

Most young men who start farming need to borrow money. An important question is where to borrow it. For financing a farm mortgage the most common single source of credit is private individuals. It is important to keep this in mind because this type of credit receives little publicity. We hear much about credit from banks and Government agencies, but these are not the main sources of farm mortgage credit.

A common method of financing the purchase of a farm is to get a *first mortgage* from the Federal Land Bank, a local bank, or a life insurance company, and a *second mortgage* from a local individual. Often the second mortgage is held by the person who sells the farm.

In this method of financing, the confidence of the local individual is of the utmost importance. Individuals commonly make loans on the basis of their confidence in the person to whom they are lending money. A young man who has established a good reputation in his local community will usually have no difficulty in borrowing all the money he ought to have. Men who have difficulty in borrowing money are those who have not established a good reputation. See also section on the Department of Agriculture (page 345) for Federal lending agencies.

Choosing a Farm

A check list of points to consider when buying a farm is given below. Of all the points in the check list, *climate* is one of the most likely to be overlooked. Any person on any day of any year can see the topography of a farm. A well-trained person can see the soil any day when it is not frozen. With respect to climate, however, a person might be wrong, even after several years' observations or after "asking the neighbors." Anyone can see the weather, but climate is weather over a period of years. It is easy to be misled by a period of unusually favorable weather. The only way to choose a climate with any degree of certainty is to look at the records of the United States Weather Bureau, Department of Commerce, Washington, D. C.; and even the Weather Bureau records do not give all the information needed. There are many local variations in climate not shown by the records.

Of all the various features of soils, *drainage* is the most likely to be limiting in the United States. While some well-drained soils are so infertile as to be practically worthless, most of them are good soils; poorly drained soils, of course, are generally difficult to farm profitably.

Good buildings can usually be bought cheaper than they can be built. For this reason a farm with good buildings in good repair is likely to be a better "buy" than a similar farm with buildings which are inadequate or run down. The difference in price of two such farms is seldom enough to cover the cost of reconditioning the poor buildings.

What to Consider Before Buying a Farm

Acreage
Crops
Pasture
Woods
Farmstead, roads, waste, etc.
Total

Location
Kind of road
Amount of travel on road
General condition of roads important to this farm
Accessibility in all seasons
Distance to school
Quality of school
Churches, community organizations
Quality of farms in neighborhood
Distance to electric-light line
Type of neighbors
Residential opportunities

Markets for Important Products

Climate
Annual rainfall
Growing season rainfall
Average days between killing frosts
Frequency of drought, hail, flood, etc.

Timber
Species
Condition

Houses
Present use
General condition and appearance
Foundation
Roof
General arrangement
Number of rooms
Lights
Running water
Bathroom
Furnace
Hardwood floors
Other features

Soils
Names of types of soil
Acreage of each type
Texture
Lime
Drainage
Natural productivity
Present productivity
Stones
Weeds

Topography

Elevation at the buildings
Effect of topography on ease of cultivation
Effect of topography on air drainage
Effect of topography on erosion
Effect of topography on hauling in and out of barn

Layout

Size and shape of fields
Convenience to farmstead
Obstructions in fields
Condition and adequacy of fences

Building Layout

Location with respect to highway
Location with respect to each other
Site of farmstead

Water Supply

House
Barn
Pasture
Spray
Irrigation

Orchard

Acres
Age
Varieties of fruit
Condition

Barns

Present use
Dimensions
General condition and appearance
Foundation
Roof
General arrangement
Adequacy
Lights
Running water
Drinking cups
Concrete floor
Modern stanchions

Amount of Taxes

Productive Capacity

Acreage and expected yield of the different crops
Number of each kind of stock that can be carried

Where to Go For Advice on Farm Problems

The best persons to give advice on how to get started in farming or on living in a given rural community are the successful farmers in that community. There are farmers in every community who are both qualified and willing to give advice and suggestions about farms for sale or rent, about opportunities for jobs as hired men on successful farms, and about opportunities for residential farming for persons who may wish to live in the country and work in town.

The County Agricultural Agent

Each agricultural county has a county agricultural agent, who is employed jointly by the Extension Service of the State Agricultural College, the United States Department of Agriculture, and the farmers of the county. This agent is a trained agricultural specialist who is familiar with farm and rural conditions in his county. His job is to assist farm people with their problems of production, management, and marketing. He cannot make real estate appraisals and does not operate a real estate or employment office. He is, however, in a position to give much helpful advice to persons interested in farming or living in the country, and to refer them to farmers and others who can give them specific information about opportunities to buy or rent farms and rural homes, and opportunities for jobs as hired men on successful farms. Persons interested in learning about these opportunities are urged to consult the local county agricultural agent, his office is usually at the county seat.

The State Agricultural Colleges

In each state there is an agricultural college, supported by public funds, which has available a wealth of information concerning the scientific and technical aspects of the farming of the state. Bulletins are available for free distribution to residents of the state. The United States Department of Agriculture in Washington, D. C., provides the names and addresses of all agricultural colleges in this country on request.

Seedtime and Harvest

The dates for planting and harvest of some of the more important crops are given below. These dates show when the job normally begins in each area; most of the work is done after the dates given here.

Crop	Job	State	Date
Winter wheat	Planting	Kansas	September 10
Winter wheat	Planting	Michigan	September 1
Winter wheat	Harvest	Kansas	June 20
Winter wheat	Harvest	Michigan	July 10
Spring wheat	Planting	North Dakota	April 10
Spring wheat	Harvest	North Dakota	August 10
Winter oats	Planting	Georgia	October 1
Winter oats	Harvest	Georgia	May 20
Spring oats	Planting	Iowa	April 1
Spring oats	Harvest	Iowa	July 10
Corn	Planting	Georgia	March 10
Corn	Planting	Iowa	May 1
Corn	Harvest for silage	Iowa	September 10
Corn	Harvest for grain	Georgia	September 20
Corn	Harvest for grain	Iowa	October 20
Alfalfa	Harvest first cutting	Missouri	May 25
Alfalfa	Harvest first cutting	New York	June 15
Cotton	Planting	Georgia	April 1
Cotton	Picking	Georgia	August 20
Tobacco	Transplanting	Kentucky	May 15
Tobacco	Harvest	Kentucky	August 25
Potatoes	Planting	Georgia	February 10
Potatoes	Planting	New Jersey	March 20
Potatoes	Planting	Maine	May 10
Potatoes	Harvest	Georgia	May 10
Potatoes	Harvest	New Jersey	July 1
Potatoes	Harvest	Maine	September 1
Dry beans	Planting	New York	May 20
Dry beans	Harvest	New York	September 1
Elberta peaches	Harvest	Georgia	July 10
Elberta peaches	Harvest	New Jersey	September 1
Delicious apples	Harvest	Virginia	September 15
Strawberries	Picking	Louisiana	February 1
Strawberries	Picking	Arkansas	May 1
Strawberries	Picking	New Jersey	June 1
Cantaloupes	Harvest	California	May 1
Cantaloupes	Harvest	Maryland	July 15
Asparagus	Harvest	California	March 1
Asparagus	Harvest	New Jersey	May 1

DATES OF KILLING FROSTS, WITH LENGTH OF GROWING SEASON, IN VARIOUS PARTS OF THE UNITED STATES

(Figures based on United States Weather Bureau information)

Station	Averages for 28 to 40 years			Station	Averages for 28 to 40 years		
	Spring — Average date of last killing frost	Fall — Average date of first killing frost	Length of growing season between average dates of killing frosts (Days)		Spring — Average date of last killing frost	Fall — Average date of first killing frost	Length of growing season between average dates of killing frosts (Days)
Birmingham, Ala.	Mar. 16	Nov. 11	240	Savannah, Ga.	Feb. 28	Nov. 28	273
Mobile, Ala.	Feb. 17	Dec. 12	298	Thomasville, Ga.	Mar. 6	Nov. 20	259
Montgomery, Ala.	Mar. 3	Nov. 19	261	Boise, Idaho	Apr. 23	Oct. 17	177
Flagstaff, Ariz.	June 3	Sept. 29	118	Lewiston, Idaho	Apr. 5	Oct. 26	204
Phoenix, Ariz.	Feb. 5	Dec. 6	304	Pocatello, Idaho	Apr. 28	Oct. 6	161
Tucson, Ariz.	Mar. 19	Nov. 19	245	Cairo, Ill.	Mar. 29	Nov. 1	217
Yuma, Ariz.	Jan. 12	Dec. 26	348	Chicago, Ill.	Apr. 13	Oct. 26	196
Fort Smith, Ark.	Mar. 21	Nov. 10	234	Peoria, Ill.	Apr. 15	Oct. 20	188
Little Rock, Ark.	Mar. 17	Nov. 13	241	Springfield, Ill.	Apr. 11	Oct. 22	194
Eureka, Calif.	Jan. 26	Dec. 20	328	Evansville, Ind.	Apr. 2	Oct. 30	211
Fresno, Calif.	Feb. 9	Dec. 1	295	Fort Wayne, Ind.	Apr. 23	Oct. 16	176
Independence, Calif.	Apr. 11	Oct. 28	200	Indianapolis, Ind.	Apr. 15	Oct. 24	192
Los Angeles, Calif.	Jan. 3	Dec. 28	359	Charles City, Iowa	Apr. 27	Oct. 6	162
Red Bluff, Calif.	Mar. 6	Dec. 5	274	Des Moines, Iowa	Apr. 19	Oct. 11	175
Sacramento, Calif.	Feb. 6	Dec. 10	307	Dubuque, Iowa	Apr. 19	Oct. 18	182
San Bernardino, Calif.	Mar. 15	Nov. 23	253	Keokuk, Iowa	Apr. 15	Oct. 19	187
San Diego, Calif.	None	None	365	Concordia, Kan.	Apr. 12	Oct. 20	191
San Francisco, Calif.	Jan. 7	Dec. 29	356	Dodge City, Kan.	Apr. 15	Oct. 25	193
Denver, Colo.	Apr. 26	Oct. 14	171	Iola, Kan.	Apr. 7	Oct. 20	196
Grand Junction, Colo.	Apr. 16	Oct. 24	191	Wichita, Kan.	Apr. 10	Oct. 27	200
Pueblo, Colo.	Apr. 23	Oct. 14	174	Bowling Green, Ky.	Apr. 14	Oct. 22	191
Hartford, Conn.	Apr. 19	Oct. 18	182	Lexington, Ky.	Apr. 16	Oct. 22	189
Milford, Del.	Apr. 19	Oct. 25	189	New Orleans, La.	Feb. 20	Dec. 9	292
Apalachicola, Fla.	Feb. 11	Dec. 13	305	Shreveport, La.	Mar. 8	Nov. 15	252
Avon Park, Fla.	Jan. 12	Dec. 25	347	Greenville, Me.	May 25	Sept. 20	118
Jacksonville, Fla.	Feb. 15	Dec. 11	299	Portland, Me.	Apr. 27	Oct. 17	173
Miami, Fla.	Infrequently			Grantsville, Md.	May 20	Sept. 29	132
Tampa, Fla.	Jan. 13	Dec. 27	348	Boston, Mass.	Apr. 13	Oct. 29	199
Atlanta, Ga.	Mar. 23	Nov. 9	231	Alpena, Mich.	May 10	Oct. 7	150
Augusta, Ga.	Mar. 16	Nov. 13	242	Detroit, Mich.	Apr. 24	Oct. 18	177
Macon, Ga.	Mar. 16	Nov. 11	240	Grand Haven, Mich.	May 1	Oct. 19	171

Station	Last frost	First frost	Days
Grand Rapids, Mich.	May 1	Oct. 17	169
Ludington, Mich.	May 10	Oct. 18	161
Marquette, Mich.	May 9	Oct. 14	158
Duluth, Minn.	May 10	Oct. 5	148
Minneapolis, Minn.	Apr. 25	Oct. 13	171
Moorhead, Minn.	May 8	Oct. 1	146
Meridian, Miss.	Mar. 17	Nov. 11	239
Vicksburg, Miss.	Mar. 8	Nov. 15	252
Columbia, Mo.	Apr. 13	Oct. 19	189
St. Joseph, Mo.	Apr. 12	Oct. 15	186
St. Louis, Mo.	Apr. 2	Oct. 29	210
Springfield, Mo.	Apr. 8	Oct. 28	203
Havre, Mont.	May 11	Sept. 22	134
Helena, Mont.	May 2	Oct. 1	153
Kalispell, Mont.	May 5	Oct. 5	149
Miles City, Mont.	Apr. 30	Oct. 6	158
North Platte, Nebr.	Apr. 29	Oct. 20	160
Omaha, Nebr.	Apr. 14	Oct. 3	189
Valentine, Nebr.	May 4	Oct. 10	152
Reno, Nev.	May 8	Oct. 14	155
Winnemucca, Nev.	May 11	Sept. 29	141
Concord, N.H.	May 3	Oct. 7	153
Atlantic City, N.J.	Apr. 6	Nov. 7	215
Trenton, N.J.	Apr. 13	Oct. 27	197
Roswell, N. Mex.	Apr. 7	Oct. 31	207
Santa Fe, N. Mex.	Apr. 24	Oct. 19	178
Albany, N.Y.	Apr. 23	Oct. 14	174
Buffalo, N.Y.	Apr. 26	Oct. 23	180
Canton, N.Y.	May 3	Sept. 30	150
Setauket, N.Y.	Apr. 11	Nov. 8	211
Syracuse, N.Y.	Apr. 23	Oct. 22	182
Asheville, N.C.	Apr. 11	Oct. 22	194
Charlotte, N.C.	Mar. 18	Nov. 11	238
Raleigh, N.C.	Mar. 23	Nov. 9	231
Wilmington, N.C.	Mar. 10	Nov. 17	246
Bismarck, N. Dak.	May 16	Sept. 27	140
Devils Lake, N. Dak.	May 15	Sept. 23	131
Williston, N. Dak.	May 15	Sept. 25	133
Cincinnati, Ohio	Apr. 12	Oct. 25	196
Cleveland, Ohio	Apr. 16	Nov. 5	203
Columbus, Ohio	Apr. 19	Oct. 23	187
Dayton, Ohio	Apr. 19	Oct. 25	189
Toledo, Ohio	Apr. 20	Oct. 22	185
Oklahoma City, Okla.	Mar. 28	Nov. 7	224
Baker, Ore.	May 12	Oct. 3	144
Portland, Ore.	Mar. 6	Nov. 24	263
Roseburg, Ore.	Mar. 30	Nov. 19	234
Erie, Pa.	Apr. 20	Oct. 31	194
Harrisburg, Pa.	Apr. 9	Oct. 30	204
Pittsburgh, Pa.	Apr. 20	Oct. 20	183
Scranton, Pa.	Apr. 22	Oct. 15	176
Charleston, S.C.	Feb. 23	Dec. 5	285
Columbia, S.C.	Mar. 15	Nov. 18	248
Greenville, S.C.	Mar. 27	Nov. 10	228
Huron, S. Dak.	May 4	Oct. 2	151
Pierre, S. Dak.	Apr. 30	Oct. 8	161
Rapid City, S. Dak.	May 1	Oct. 4	156
Yankton, S. Dak.	May 1	Oct. 9	161
Chattanooga, Tenn.	Mar. 21	Nov. 11	235
Knoxville, Tenn.	Mar. 30	Nov. 2	217
Memphis, Tenn.	Mar. 17	Nov. 10	238
Nashville, Tenn.	Mar. 30	Oct. 30	214
Abilene, Texas	Mar. 25	Nov. 12	232
Amarillo, Texas	Apr. 11	Nov. 2	205
Brownsville, Texas	Jan. 30	Dec. 26	330
Corpus Christi, Texas	Jan. 26	Dec. 27	335
Del Rio, Texas	Feb. 22	Nov. 29	280
El Paso, Texas	Mar. 21	Nov. 14	238
Fort Worth, Texas	Mar. 11	Nov. 17	251
Galveston, Texas	Jan. 21	Dec. 28	341
Palestine, Texas	Mar. 7	Nov. 23	261
San Antonio, Texas	Feb. 24	Dec. 3	282
Taylor, Texas	Mar. 6	Nov. 26	265
Modena, Utah	May 17	Oct. 2	138
Salt Lake City, Utah	Apr. 13	Oct. 22	192
Lynchburg, Va.	Apr. 4	Oct. 25	204
Norfolk, Va.	Mar. 19	Nov. 16	242
Richmond, Va.	Mar. 29	Nov. 2	218
Wytheville, Va.	Apr. 17	Oct. 16	182
Northfield, Vt.	May 21	Sept. 25	127
Seattle, Wash.	Mar. 14	Nov. 24	255
Spokane, Wash.	Apr. 12	Oct. 13	184
Walla Walla, Wash.	Mar. 31	Nov. 5	219
Elkins, W. Va.	May 4	Oct. 12	161
Parkersburg, W. Va.	Apr. 18	Oct. 19	184
Green Bay, Wis.	May 5	Oct. 9	157
La Crosse, Wis.	Apr. 29	Oct. 9	163
Madison, Wis.	Apr. 29	Oct. 17	171
Milwaukee, Wis.	Apr. 22	Oct. 23	184
Cheyenne, Wyo.	May 14	Oct. 2	141
Lander, Wyo.	May 18	Sept. 20	125
Yellowstone Park, Wyo.	May 23	Sept. 16	116

NORMAL TEMPERATURE BY MONTHS AT SELECTED POINTS IN THE UNITED STATES
(Figures in degrees Fahrenheit, based on U. S. Weather Bureau records)

Station (AP = Airport)	January	February	March	April	May	June	July	August	September	October	November	December	Annual mean
Birmingham, Ala.	45.1	48.0	55.4	63.3	71.1	77.9	80.2	79.2	74.8	64.8	53.9	46.4	63.3
Mobile, Ala.	51.5	54.7	59.7	66.3	74.4	80.3	81.4	81.0	78.1	69.3	58.6	52.2	67.3
Phoenix, Ariz.	51.2	55.1	60.7	67.0	75.0	84.5	89.8	88.5	82.7	70.6	59.7	52.0	69.7
Little Rock, Ark. AP	41.4	44.9	53.0	62.1	70.3	77.4	80.9	79.8	74.1	63.6	52.1	44.2	62.0
Eureka, Calif.	46.9	47.2	48.3	49.9	52.0	54.3	55.5	56.0	55.9	53.6	51.1	48.2	51.6
Fresno, Calif. AP	45.5	50.3	54.4	60.2	67.2	75.7	81.3	79.5	72.0	62.3	52.4	45.1	62.2
Los Angeles, Calif.	54.6	55.5	57.5	59.4	62.2	64.4	70.2	71.1	69.0	65.3	60.9	56.6	62.4
Sacramento, Calif.	45.8	50.1	54.3	58.1	63.3	69.4	73.2	72.9	69.3	62.9	53.6	46.2	59.9
San Diego, Calif. AP	54.0	55.5	57.0	59.0	61.3	65.0	68.5	69.6	68.2	64.1	59.3	55.5	61.4
San Francisco, Calif.	49.9	52.2	54.2	55.0	56.9	58.5	59.1	59.1	60.9	60.5	59.3	55.3	56.1
Pueblo, Colo. AP	28.3	32.1	40.8	49.4	58.9	68.6	74.2	72.7	64.6	51.2	38.3	30.1	50.8
Hartford, Conn. AP	25.5	27.2	35.0	46.7	57.5	67.1	72.5	68.9	61.7	51.2	39.5	29.8	48.5
Dover, Del.	35.1	35.5	43.2	53.1	63.7	72.5	76.6	74.7	68.8	57.5	46.4	37.0	55.4
Jacksonville, Fla.	55.4	58.0	62.6	68.7	75.0	79.9	81.8	81.7	78.3	71.1	62.2	56.3	69.3
Miami, Fla.	67.9	68.0	70.3	73.9	77.2	80.0	82.1	82.1	80.9	78.0	72.4	69.1	75.1
Atlanta, Ga.	42.6	45.3	52.0	61.0	69.9	76.0	78.1	77.0	72.4	63.0	52.1	44.7	61.2
Thomasville, Ga.	51.0	54.8	60.2	66.7	73.3	79.5	81.8	81.0	76.8	68.2	58.5	52.5	67.1
Boise, Idaho AP	27.9	33.6	41.4	49.1	56.1	64.5	72.5	71.0	61.2	50.1	39.7	30.4	49.8
Chicago, Ill. AP	22.3	25.0	34.5	46.9	56.8	68.1	74.4	71.6	64.9	52.5	39.8	26.9	49.5
Peoria, Ill. AP	22.1	25.0	36.0	49.9	60.7	71.9	77.6	75.0	67.7	53.5	39.8	28.1	50.5
Evansville, Ind. AP	31.6	34.9	44.4	54.9	63.3	75.2	79.1	77.3	69.5	57.0	44.4	34.8	54.8
Indianapolis, Ind.	28.4	34.1	40.0	52.1	62.9	71.9	75.7	74.0	66.9	55.7	42.3	32.2	52.9
Des Moines, Iowa	20.1	23.7	35.9	50.0	61.8	71.1	76.7	74.7	65.8	54.4	39.5	26.5	50.4
Dubuque, Iowa	19.1	22.3	34.0	48.7	60.3	69.4	74.8	72.1	64.1	52.5	38.1	25.0	48.6
Concordia, Kan.	27.9	30.8	42.0	53.4	63.3	73.6	79.5	77.9	69.2	56.9	42.7	31.0	54.0
Dodge City, Kan. AP	31.1	33.9	43.5	53.7	64.3	73.3	79.1	77.8	69.6	57.1	43.6	33.0	54.9
Lexington, Ky. AP	32.9	35.4	43.7	54.3	64.3	72.2	75.9	74.5	68.5	57.4	43.8	35.8	55.0
New Orleans, La.	54.2	57.3	62.8	68.8	74.5	80.6	82.4	82.2	79.2	71.0	61.6	55.6	69.3
Shreveport, La. AP	46.0	49.9	57.3	64.8	72.6	80.4	83.2	81.7	75.9	65.6	55.0	48.1	65.0
Greenville, Me.	12.8	13.5	24.5	37.1	45.7	59.2	65.1	62.3	55.2	44.5	30.6	18.8	39.4
Baltimore, Md.	33.8	34.8	42.3	53.6	64.7	72.7	77.2	75.5	68.5	58.2	46.3	37.2	55.4
Boston, Mass. AP	27.9	28.8	35.6	46.4	57.1	66.5	71.7	69.9	63.2	53.6	42.0	32.5	49.6
Escanaba, Mich.	15.4	15.4	24.2	37.9	49.6	60.7	66.0	64.3	57.1	46.0	33.1	22.4	41.0
Grand Rapids, Mich.	24.5	23.7	33.4	47.0	58.0	67.8	72.3	69.7	62.7	51.2	38.4	28.5	48.1
Duluth, Minn.	7.9	11.4	23.7	37.0	47.4	57.2	63.9	62.6	55.1	44.1	30.0	15.9	38.0
St. Paul, Minn. AP	12.6	15.8	29.1	45.6	57.9	67.1	72.1	69.4	61.3	48.6	32.5	19.0	44.2
Jackson, Miss. AP	48.6	50.8	58.5	65.2	72.5	79.6	81.6	81.3	77.0	65.9	55.8	49.1	65.5
St. Louis, Mo.	31.1	34.8	44.1	56.1	67.0	75.0	78.8	77.5	70.5	58.8	45.4	34.9	56.2
Springfield, Mo. AP	32.3	34.0	45.2	56.0	63.4	72.5	76.8	75.7	68.9	58.2	45.7	36.2	55.7
Havre, Mont.	12.9	13.6	27.1	43.7	53.4	62.0	68.3	65.4	56.4	44.5	31.2	20.4	41.6
Kalispell, Mont.	20.4	23.3	32.9	43.6	51.4	57.7	64.0	63.5	53.5	43.5	32.4	24.9	42.5

NORMAL TEMPERATURE BY MONTHS AT SELECTED POINTS IN THE UNITED STATES (Cont.)

(Figures in degrees Fahrenheit, based on U. S. Weather Bureau records)

Station (AP = Airport)	January	February	March	April	May	June	July	August	September	October	November	December	Annual mean
North Platte, Nebr.	22.9	26.6	36.6	48.6	58.7	67.5	72.9	70.8	62.1	49.7	36.6	26.7	48.3
Omaha, Nebr. AP	20.9	24.3	36.1	51.0	62.4	70.7	75.2	73.2	65.7	53.4	38.3	26.4	49.8
Winnemucca, Nev.	28.6	33.5	40.0	46.7	53.9	62.8	70.6	69.3	59.2	48.3	38.4	30.0	48.4
Concord, N. H. AP	19.0	20.3	29.1	41.6	52.9	61.7	67.4	65.5	58.0	47.8	35.4	24.0	43.6
Trenton, N. J.	30.5	30.7	39.1	49.8	61.1	69.5	74.5	73.0	66.9	55.6	44.4	34.4	52.5
Albuquerque, N. Mex.	34.1	34.7	46.1	54.8	63.8	72.6	77.0	75.9	67.6	56.7	43.2	37.0	55.7
Buffalo, N. Y. AP	23.9	24.7	31.3	43.8	55.9	64.9	68.6	68.4	61.6	51.1	38.5	28.8	46.8
Canton, N. Y.	16.6	15.8	27.8	41.9	54.2	62.1	68.4	66.5	58.8	47.5	35.0	21.8	43.2
Charlotte, N. C.	41.2	43.9	50.4	59.8	68.9	75.5	78.8	77.1	71.5	61.7	50.6	43.0	60.2
Bismarck, N. Dak.	8.0	11.6	25.2	43.1	54.5	64.2	70.5	68.2	58.1	45.2	28.5	15.7	41.1
Devils Lake, N. Dak.	1.8	5.3	19.8	38.8	52.6	61.2	67.2	64.8	55.9	42.4	24.5	9.5	37.0
Cincinnati, Ohio	30.3	32.8	40.9	52.4	63.1	71.2	75.1	73.6	67.1	57.0	44.6	36.4	55.2
Cleveland, Ohio	26.5	27.4	34.0	45.4	57.9	67.1	71.4	70.0	63.9	53.6	40.9	31.2	49.2
Oklahoma City, Okla.	36.4	39.6	50.0	59.8	67.7	76.0	80.6	79.7	72.8	61.5	48.8	39.3	59.4
Portland, Ore.	39.4	42.1	46.9	51.8	56.9	62.4	66.7	66.7	61.7	54.2	46.8	41.2	53.1
Roseburg, Ore.	41.2	43.4	47.1	51.0	56.0	62.5	67.4	68.0	62.9	53.9	45.9	41.8	53.1
Pittsburg, Pa.	30.7	32.3	39.6	51.2	62.4	70.7	74.6	72.9	66.4	55.7	43.2	34.2	52.8
Scranton, Pa.	26.6	27.3	35.7	48.1	59.4	67.8	71.7	69.8	62.9	51.9	40.5	30.7	49.4
Providence, R. I.	27.2	29.0	35.7	46.6	58.5	68.3	73.4	71.0	63.2	52.2	40.4	31.6	49.7
Charleston, S. C.	49.9	52.4	57.4	64.5	72.7	78.9	81.4	81.0	76.6	67.8	58.1	51.7	66.0
Huron, S. Dak. AP	11.3	14.3	28.9	45.1	56.4	66.2	71.8	69.4	61.3	47.7	31.5	18.7	43.6
Rapid City, S. Dak.	20.0	21.9	31.5	44.1	54.0	64.2	71.0	69.5	60.2	47.6	34.6	25.1	45.3
Knoxville, Tenn. AP	38.6	40.8	47.5	57.3	66.7	73.8	76.7	75.4	69.4	58.5	46.5	39.1	57.4
Nashville, Tenn. AP	38.6	41.6	49.2	59.0	68.2	75.6	79.1	77.8	71.8	61.0	49.0	41.0	59.3
Amarillo, Texas AP	33.1	36.1	45.3	53.8	62.1	71.4	75.9	74.6	67.8	55.8	43.8	35.5	54.6
Brownsville, Texas AP	59.8	62.6	68.2	73.7	78.6	82.4	83.6	83.9	80.6	74.9	67.2	61.2	73.1
El Paso, Texas AP	43.6	48.6	54.9	62.3	70.0	78.0	83.4	78.0	72.3	62.0	51.1	43.7	62.0
Fort Worth, Texas AP	44.4	47.3	56.7	64.1	72.2	79.9	85.2	82.7	75.9	65.7	54.5	46.5	64.5
Galveston, Texas	53.8	56.3	62.4	68.7	74.8	80.7	83.8	83.5	80.1	72.7	63.3	56.4	69.5
San Antonio, Texas AP	52.3	55.4	62.8	69.1	75.1	81.0	84.8	83.5	79.0	70.5	60.3	53.7	68.9
Modena, Utah	26.7	31.0	38.2	46.0	53.5	63.3	70.7	69.2	60.0	48.0	36.4	28.1	47.6
Salt Lake City, Utah	29.2	33.8	41.7	49.6	57.4	67.4	77.0	74.5	64.4	52.5	41.1	31.9	51.6
Lynchburg, Va. AP	35.3	38.0	45.4	55.6	65.9	73.1	76.1	74.3	67.9	57.2	45.2	37.3	56.5
Norfolk, Va.	40.6	42.7	48.2	56.8	66.2	74.4	78.7	77.4	71.6	62.5	51.4	43.1	59.5
Burlington, Vt. AP	18.8	19.4	29.1	43.3	56.6	65.7	70.3	67.9	60.3	49.2	36.3	24.4	45.1
Seattle, Wash.	40.8	42.8	46.4	51.1	56.6	61.4	65.5	65.1	60.3	53.7	46.8	42.6	52.8
Spokane, Wash. AP	27.4	31.3	39.7	48.4	55.5	69.0	69.0	68.1	59.2	48.3	38.5	30.5	48.2
Parkersburg, W. Va.	32.5	34.2	42.8	53.4	63.8	71.4	75.4	73.9	67.3	56.1	43.8	35.2	54.2
Madison, Wis.	16.7	19.1	30.6	45.4	57.6	67.2	72.1	69.8	62.4	50.3	35.2	22.8	45.8
Rock Springs, Wyo.	19.5	23.7	32.0	42.2	52.0	60.1	68.6	66.4	56.7	45.8	31.0	23.9	43.4
Sheridan, Wyo. AP	19.3	22.6	31.4	43.3	52.0	61.5	68.4	66.5	56.3	44.6	32.7	22.8	43.4

NORMAL PRECIPITATION BY MONTHS AT SELECTED POINTS IN THE UNITED STATES
(Figures in inches, based on U. S. Weather Bureau records)

Station (AP = Airport)	January	February	March	April	May	June	July	August	September	October	November	December	Annual total
Birmingham, Ala.	5.52	5.23	5.70	4.81	3.95	4.46	5.17	4.26	3.38	2.42	3.31	5.14	53.35
Mobile, Ala.	4.85	5.52	5.98	4.63	4.32	5.43	6.89	6.92	5.00	3.60	3.64	5.02	61.80
Phoenix, Ariz.	.80	.79	.68	.40	.12	.07	1.07	.95	.75	.47	.70	1.00	7.80
Little Rock, Ark. AP	4.73	3.84	4.62	5.19	4.78	3.76	3.50	3.75	3.17	2.71	4.19	4.14	48.38
Eureka, Calif.	7.11	6.67	5.23	3.33	1.80	.72	.11	.18	1.01	2.33	5.18	6.28	39.95
Fresno, Calif. AP	1.73	1.47	1.58	.95	.44	.08	.01	.01	.21	.57	.93	1.45	9.43
Los Angeles, Calif.	3.10	3.14	2.78	1.04	.45	.08	.01	.02	.17	.68	1.20	2.63	15.30
Sacramento, Calif.	3.72	3.09	2.57	1.51	.77	.15	.00	.02	.38	.92	1.88	3.03	18.02
San Diego, Calif. AP	2.06	2.09	1.72	.77	.35	.05	.03	.04	.08	.54	.76	1.87	10.36
San Francisco, Calif.	4.54	3.93	3.14	1.61	.80	.18	.02	.01	.45	1.12	2.35	3.95	22.10
Pueblo, Colo. AP	.31	.47	.59	1.31	1.60	1.36	1.94	1.82	.75	.66	.36	.50	11.67
Hartford, Conn. AP	3.94	3.99	3.90	3.36	3.60	3.08	4.37	4.29	3.49	3.52	3.55	3.97	45.06
Dover, Del.	3.46	3.25	4.09	3.63	3.58	3.65	4.72	4.86	3.73	2.89	3.09	3.27	44.22
Jacksonville, Fla.	2.80	3.09	2.91	2.38	4.02	5.33	6.71	5.81	7.35	4.46	1.98	3.02	49.86
Miami, Fla.	2.27	2.11	2.63	3.41	7.15	7.17	5.60	5.88	8.65	7.74	3.26	1.98	57.85
Atlanta, Ga.	4.95	4.79	5.30	3.61	3.47	3.74	4.65	4.45	2.99	2.59	3.03	4.70	48.27
Thomasville, Ga.	4.10	4.61	4.09	3.34	3.63	5.45	6.70	5.75	4.88	2.96	2.68	4.31	52.50
Boise, Idaho AP	1.73	1.48	1.35	1.18	1.43	.92	.24	.19	.53	1.24	1.28	1.57	13.14
Chicago, Ill.	1.90	2.15	2.56	2.54	4.06	3.48	3.43	3.02	3.20	2.56	2.51	2.07	31.86
Peoria, Ill. AP	1.78	2.07	2.73	3.38	4.04	3.77	3.58	3.12	4.03	2.29	2.37	1.77	34.95
Evansville, Ind. AP	3.74	3.34	4.19	3.90	3.86	4.04	3.42	3.36	3.31	2.82	3.74	3.54	43.26
Indianapolis, Ind.	2.95	2.83	3.93	3.62	3.89	3.62	3.34	3.31	3.40	2.78	3.55	2.98	40.20
Des Moines, Iowa	1.05	1.16	1.78	2.56	4.08	4.41	3.33	3.80	3.91	2.25	1.58	1.12	31.03
Dubuque, Iowa	1.30	1.43	2.03	2.16	3.90	4.16	3.34	3.66	3.92	2.43	1.85	1.27	31.85
Concordia, Kan.	.49	.89	1.11	2.16	3.84	4.15	3.10	3.21	2.66	1.88	1.09	.66	25.24
Dodge City, Kan. AP	.37	.78	.94	2.00	2.85	3.19	2.67	2.40	2.08	1.35	.93	.57	20.13
Lexington, Ky. AP	4.18	3.62	4.32	3.50	3.81	4.05	3.65	3.45	3.07	2.59	3.34	3.77	43.35
New Orleans, La.	4.34	4.38	4.72	5.24	4.60	5.88	6.37	5.80	5.03	3.30	3.14	4.79	57.59
Shreveport, La. AP	3.93	3.40	4.11	4.63	4.23	3.50	3.56	2.70	2.80	2.69	3.65	4.29	43.49
Greenville, Me.	2.88	2.72	2.96	2.92	3.22	3.72	4.26	4.37	3.75	3.56	3.08	3.13	39.57
Baltimore, Md.	3.50	3.49	3.71	3.34	3.54	3.88	4.64	4.37	3.37	2.89	2.56	3.37	42.66
Boston, Mass. AP	3.61	3.37	3.57	3.34	3.18	2.89	3.49	3.62	3.14	3.15	3.33	3.45	40.14
Escanaba, Mich.	1.49	1.55	1.89	2.23	2.93	3.22	3.33	3.19	3.32	2.63	2.13	1.75	29.66
Grand Rapids, Mich.	2.35	2.31	2.48	2.77	3.44	3.48	2.92	2.61	3.53	2.81	2.77	2.57	34.04
Duluth, Minn.	.97	1.09	1.54	2.06	3.25	3.91	3.76	3.18	3.31	2.31	1.45	1.15	27.98
St. Paul, Minn. AP	.92	.95	1.43	2.35	3.27	4.14	3.57	3.01	3.07	2.20	1.30	1.06	27.27
Jackson, Miss. AP	4.94	4.85	5.48	5.33	4.67	4.13	4.54	3.88	2.91	2.59	3.41	5.46	52.19
St. Louis, Mo.	2.34	2.63	3.38	3.81	4.34	3.82	2.98	2.99	3.46	2.72	2.83	2.21	37.51
Springfield, Mo.	2.34	2.43	3.39	3.86	5.19	4.68	4.21	4.09	3.52	3.05	2.79	2.31	41.86
Havre, Mont.	.73	.50	.51	.99	2.04	2.86	1.87	1.22	1.29	.67	.61	.61	13.90
Kalispell, Mont.	1.57	1.14	.95	.80	1.46	2.06	1.10	.87	1.24	1.06	1.35	1.45	15.05

NORMAL PRECIPITATION BY MONTHS AT SELECTED POINTS IN THE UNITED STATES (Cont.)

(Figures in inches, based on U. S. Weather Bureau records)

Station (AP = Airport)	January	February	March	April	May	June	July	August	September	October	November	December	Annual total
North Platte, Nebr.	.39	.55	.86	2.06	2.78	3.22	2.74	2.39	1.35	1.07	.47	.53	18.41
Omaha, Nebr. AP	.70	.92	1.37	2.51	3.77	4.56	3.54	3.05	3.21	2.17	1.07	.93	27.80
Winnemucca, Nev.	1.03	.94	.96	.84	.88	.72	.21	.20	.41	.62	.68	1.08	8.57
Concord, N. H. AP	3.00	2.89	3.03	2.78	3.01	3.19	3.56	3.54	3.45	2.85	3.08	3.13	37.51
Trenton, N. J.	3.31	3.41	3.40	2.94	3.08	3.09	3.94	4.75	3.40	2.78	2.73	3.35	40.18
Albuquerque, N. Mex.	.46	.32	.47	.81	1.25	.94	1.22	1.62	1.58	.83	.52	.61	10.63
Buffalo, N. Y. AP	3.30	2.95	2.57	2.56	3.10	2.82	3.03	3.08	2.92	3.29	3.02	3.36	36.00
Canton, N. Y.	2.50	2.27	2.50	2.18	3.00	3.29	3.50	3.65	2.35	3.03	3.16	2.69	35.12
Charlotte, N. C.	4.00	4.30	4.17	3.31	3.63	4.22	5.10	5.07	2.99	2.95	2.57	3.86	46.17
Bismarck, N. Dak.	.38	.39	.87	1.19	2.23	3.29	2.28	1.63	1.44	.91	.48	.48	15.51
Devils Lake, N. Dak.	.47	.51	.78	1.52	2.03	3.56	2.57	2.48	1.63	1.25	.72	.54	18.06
Cincinnati, Ohio	3.48	3.07	3.89	3.12	3.70	3.66	3.31	3.41	2.65	2.51	2.85	2.98	38.63
Cleveland, Ohio AP	2.51	2.51	2.71	2.44	3.12	3.12	3.35	2.77	3.33	2.78	2.64	2.44	33.82
Oklahoma City, Okla.	1.19	1.14	1.98	3.29	4.88	3.67	3.45	2.89	3.05	2.86	1.87	1.50	33.18
Portland, Ore.	6.60	5.52	3.91	2.87	2.19	1.52	.61	.64	1.98	3.12	6.10	6.72	41.78
Roseburg, Ore.	5.31	4.49	3.28	2.27	1.93	1.09	.32	.34	1.27	2.61	4.66	5.34	32.91
Pittsburg, Pa.	3.05	2.62	3.03	2.92	3.21	3.81	4.05	3.23	2.58	2.52	2.29	2.86	36.17
Scranton, Pa.	3.03	3.04	3.20	2.77	3.27	3.67	4.03	3.69	3.17	3.03	2.77	3.02	38.69
Providence, R. I.	3.70	3.78	3.49	3.21	2.96	3.15	3.17	3.45	3.25	2.75	3.21	3.47	39.59
Charleston, S. C.	3.02	3.08	3.02	2.53	3.00	4.59	6.89	6.53	4.53	3.27	2.14	2.72	45.32
Huron, S. Dak. AP	.56	.56	.91	2.24	2.98	3.79	3.16	2.46	1.57	1.28	.59	.57	20.67
Rapid City, S. Dak. AP	.45	.50	.97	1.43	2.94	3.04	2.08	1.70	1.20	.94	.49	.44	16.18
Memphis, Tenn.	4.81	4.36	5.26	4.78	4.19	3.55	3.18	3.36	2.80	2.68	4.24	4.51	47.72
Nashville, Tenn.	4.76	4.13	5.11	4.13	3.87	4.00	3.88	3.71	3.42	2.49	3.50	4.20	47.20
Amarillo, Texas AP	.51	.73	.71	1.83	2.79	2.84	2.84	3.08	2.30	1.66	.92	.80	21.01
Brownsville, Texas AP	1.81	1.49	1.57	1.73	2.58	3.17	2.27	2.86	5.82	3.60	2.28	1.87	31.05
El Paso, Texas AP	.46	.42	.36	.26	.33	.58	1.99	1.70	1.25	.80	.50	.52	9.17
Fort Worth, Texas AP	2.05	1.83	2.32	4.02	4.65	3.35	2.61	2.62	2.49	2.81	2.58	1.87	33.20
Galveston, Texas	3.41	2.93	2.63	3.06	3.42	4.37	3.71	4.28	5.57	4.36	3.33	3.75	44.87
San Antonio, Texas AP	1.46	1.75	1.84	3.19	3.20	2.46	2.17	2.42	3.05	2.23	1.90	1.61	27.28
Modena, Utah	.85	.98	1.03	.89	.76	.32	1.08	1.29	.78	.74	.59	.83	10.14
Salt Lake City, Utah	1.31	1.57	1.98	2.05	1.92	.80	.51	.85	.98	1.44	1.35	1.43	16.19
Lynchburg, Va. AP	3.10	3.26	3.54	2.95	3.63	3.79	4.21	3.78	3.31	3.15	2.33	3.26	40.64
Norfolk, Va. AP	1.76	3.33	3.77	3.23	3.81	4.22	5.75	5.22	3.23	3.04	2.16	3.34	44.20
Burlington, Vt. AP	1.76	1.57	2.04	2.15	2.85	3.38	3.50	3.48	3.23	2.97	2.66	1.88	31.61
Seattle, Wash.	4.94	3.89	3.05	2.38	1.87	1.33	.63	.70	1.77	2.84	5.03	5.60	34.03
Spokane, Wash. AP	2.16	1.81	1.20	1.13	1.42	.69	.69	.62	.90	1.17	2.09	2.19	16.07
Parkersburg, W. Va.	3.58	3.23	3.49	3.19	3.38	4.00	4.29	3.51	2.76	2.48	2.57	3.03	39.51
Madison, Wis.	1.38	1.56	2.07	2.77	3.85	3.76	3.88	3.21	3.72	2.43	1.78	1.63	32.04
Rock Springs, Wyo.	.40	.72	.66	1.24	1.02	.78	.72	.80	.63	1.04	.54	.35	8.90
Sheridan, Wyo. AP	.85	.72	1.16	1.92	2.65	2.04	1.22	.91	1.27	1.07	.63	.64	15.08

Breeds of Dairy Cows

There are 5 major breeds of dairy cattle kept in the United States. The fat and the total solids content of the milk of each breed is given below. The average production of fat per cow per year is about the same for all 5 breeds, assuming equal care and quality of animals. For example, in comparing Holsteins and Jerseys, the total amount of milk produced by one cow will be higher for Holsteins, in about the same proportion as the fat content of the milk is lower. There are good and poor cows in each breed. The choice of breed depends primarily on the premium which the market pays for milk with a high fat content. If the premium is small, Holsteins are kept. If it is large, Jerseys or Guernseys are kept.

Milk Yield of Dairy Cows in the United States

Breed	Fat content of milk (per cent)	Other solids in milk (per cent)	Total solids in milk (per cent)
Jersey	5.4	9.5	14.9
Guernsey	4.9	9.6	14.5
Brown Swiss	4.1	9.3	13.4
Ayrshire	4.0	9.0	13.0
Holstein	3.5	8.8	12.3

Dimensions in Modern Dairy Barns

Width. 34 ft. on the inside
Stable Height. 7 ft. 9 in. to 8 ft. 3 in. from platform
Cross Alleys. 4 ft. wide. There should be alleys at each end of cow stanchions, and also in the middle if the row is long
Width of Cow Stalls. Eight-tenths of platform length. Most barns have stalls too narrow. For large cows they should be 4 ft. or wider. Variable widths from 3 ft. 6 in. to 4 ft. 6 in. are desirable

Following are desirable dimensions for various items in a modern dairy barn. Small variations from these dimensions are not a serious handicap.

Feed alley	4 ft.	
Manger	2 ft.	
Curb		6 in.
Platform	5 ft.	2 in.
Gutter	1 ft.	4 in.
Drive	8 ft.	
Gutter	1 ft.	4 in.
Platform	5 ft.	2 in.
Curb		6 in.
Manger	2 ft.	
Feed alley	4 ft.	
Total	34 ft.	

Poultry Houses

Leghorns. Allow 3 sq. ft. of floor space per hen
Heavy breeds. Allow 4 sq. ft. of floor space per hen

Estimating Barbed Wire for Fences

The following table shows the estimated number of pounds of barbed wire required to fence the space or distances mentioned, with 1, 2, or 3 lines of wire, based upon each pound of wire measuring 1 rod (16½ feet).

	1 Line	2 Lines	3 Lines
1 square acre	50⅔ lb.	101⅓ lb.	152 lb.
1 side of a square acre	12⅔ lb.	25⅓ lb.	38 lb.
1 square half acre	36 lb.	72 lb.	108 lb.
1 square mile	1280 lb.	2560 lb.	3840 lb.
1 side of a square mile	320 lb.	640 lb.	960 lb.
1 rod in length	1 lb.	2 lb.	3 lb.
100 rods in length	100 lb.	200 lb.	300 lb.
100 feet in length	6¼₆ lb.	12¼ lb.	18¾₆ lb.

APPROXIMATE CAPACITY OF CYLINDRICAL SILOS
(for Corn Silage)

Depth of silage after settling 2 days	Diameter of the silo in feet					
	10	12	14	16	18	20
(feet)	(tons)	(tons)	(tons)	(tons)	(tons)	(tons)
5	4	6	9	11	14	17
10	10	15	20	26	33	41
15	18	25	34	45	57	70
20	26	38	51	67	85	105
25	36	52	70	92	116	143
30	47	67	91	119	151	187
35	58	84	114	149	188	232
40	70	101	138	180	229	280
45	82	118	160	213	271	334
50	94	137	186	248	319	389
55		155	212	283	365	444
60			240	319	415	500

A ton of timothy hay in a well settled mow occupies approximately 450 cu. ft. A ton of clover hay in a well settled mow occupies approximately 550 cu. ft.

THE DEPARTMENT OF AGRICULTURE

On May 15, 1862, President Abraham Lincoln signed the bill establishing what is now the United States Department of Agriculture as a separate agency, with bureau status and headed by a commissioner. On February 9, 1889, the Department was raised to cabinet rank.

The primary functions of the Department are to compile and distribute useful information concerning agriculture, and to conduct research and educational programs. In addition, the Department directs the conservation, marketing, and regulation of farm products, including crops and livestock, for the purpose of protecting both the farmer and the consumer.

Toward this end the Department maintains a number of specialized agencies. The functions of the most important of these are listed below.

The *Agricultural Research Administration* comprises the Office of the Administrator, the Office of Experiment Stations, and the Bureaus of Agricultural and Industrial Chemistry, Animal Industry, Dairy Industry, Entomology and Plant Quarantine, Human Nutrition and Home Economics, and the Bureau of Plant Industry, Soil, and Agricultural Engineering. The Administrator of the Agricultural Research Administration has the following duties: (1) to administer the research and regulatory activities of the Administration; (2) to coordinate the Department's entire research program, with the exception of economic research; (3) to cooperate with the directors of state agricultural experiment stations in the development of an integrated agricultural research program for the nation; (4) to administer the program of research grants to the state experiment stations under various Federal Acts; (5) to administer the Research and Marketing Act of 1946.

The *Office of Experiment Stations* represents the Department in the administration of the Acts of Congress under which funds are provided for agricultural research by state agricultural experiment stations in the 48 states, Alaska, Hawaii, and Puerto Rico.

The *Bureau of Agricultural and Industrial Chemistry* operates the four Regional Research Laboratories, and a number of other field stations. It is primarily concerned with the development of new and wider industrial uses for agricultural products and by-products.

The *Bureau of Animal Industry* conducts scientific investigations of the cause, prevention, treatment, control, and eradication of diseases and parasites of domestic animals. It is also concerned with the breeding, feeding, and management of domestic animals, including poultry, and with the methods of improving the quality and usefulness of their products.

The *Bureau of Dairy Industry* conducts scientific research on the breeding, nutritive requirements, and management of dairy cattle. It also conducts research on the physiology of reproduction and milk secretion, the manufacture of milk products and by-products, and the efficient operation of dairy manufacturing plants.

The *Bureau of Entomology and Plant Quarantine* conducts research programs to develop methods to control, eradicate, or prevent spread of injurious insects and to utilize insects which are beneficial. It also conducts cooperative programs to control or eradicate important insect pests and plant diseases, and is responsible for the enforcement of quarantines to prevent the introduction and spread of insect pests and plant diseases into the country.

The *Bureau of Human Nutrition and Home Economics* conducts research on goods and services for everyday living, and furnishes families with facts to increase their social and physical well-being.

The *Bureau of Plant Industry, Soils, and Agricultural Engineering* conducts research on problems concerning crops, soil, machinery, storage, transportation, and housing. Among the problems studied are those of weather, disease, weeds, fertilization, mechanical operations of insect control, and other environmental factors affecting the growing and storage of farm products. An important activity is the introduction and testing of promising seeds and plants from foreign countries for possible domestic use.

The *Commodity Exchange Authority* administers the Commodity Exchange Act. Its functions are primarily to prevent price manipulation and to prevent dissemination of false and misleading crop and market information affecting prices.

The *Extension Service* is the cooperative educational agency under which the Department of Agriculture and the state agricultural colleges carry on educational programs on agriculture and homemaking among people in rural areas. It encourages membership in the 4-H clubs and emphasizes health nutrition and sanitary standards as important considerations in efficient agricultural production. The Service also fosters group study and discussion of broad agricultural problems and policies.

The *Farm Credit Administration,* through organizations operating under its supervision, provides a complete cooperative credit service for farmers and their cooperative marketing, purchasing, and business service associations.

The *Farmers Home Administration* provides small farmers with credit to improve farming operations or to become owners, and supplements its loans with individual guidance in sound farm and home management.

The *Forest Service* is responsible for promoting the conservation and wise use of the nation's forest lands, which comprise one-third of the total land area of the United States.

The *Commodity Credit Corporation* makes loans to producers to finance the carrying and orderly marketing of agricultural commodities.

The *Production and Marketing Administration* administers the Department's production and marketing programs, including agricultural conservation, production goals, acreage allotments, marketing quotas, price support, storage facilities, surplus disposal, and other programs.

The *Rural Electrification Administration* finances the construction of electric power facilities in the unserved rural areas, and administers the extension and improvement of rural telephone services. Cooperatives are the principal borrowers, but the Administration also lends to public power districts and commercial power companies.

The *Soil Conservation Service* is responsible for the development and prosecution of a national program to bring about physical adjustments in land use that will further human welfare, conserve natural resources, establish a permanent and balanced agriculture, and reduce the hazards of floods and siltation.

Staff and Service Agencies

The *Bureau of Agricultural Economics* is the central statistical and economic research agency of the Department. It gathers, evaluates, and reports on data on a broad range of economic subjects which pertain to agriculture.

The *Office of Budget and Finance* is responsible for the financial affairs of the Department, including the acquisition and distribution of funds.

The *Office of Foreign Agricultural Relations* primarily acquires and disseminates information on the foreign demand for and competition with United States agricultural products. It also coordinates the technical assistance in agriculture that is extended by the United States to foreign governments.

The *Office of Information* plans, coordinates, and directs the informational activities of the Department.

Other staff agencies include the *Office of Personnel,* the *Office of Plant and Operations,* and the *Office of the Solicitor.*

PLANNING A HOME GARDEN

Home gardening can be an important source of flowers and fresh vegetables for the family, as well as an excellent form of outdoor exercise and recreation. From a financial standpoint, a well-planned and well-managed garden can consistently yield crops that more than repay the relatively low cost of seeds, tools, fertilizer, and other necessary materials. It is important, however, that the garden be carefully planned.

Choosing a Proper Site

The following rules are generally accepted in choosing a garden site:

1. The plot should receive at least six hours of direct sunshine each day, and should be protected from the wind
2. The ground should be level and well drained, although some sloping plots can be utilized, provided that the rows of plants can be terraced to avoid erosion
3. The garden should be located near a convenient water supply
4. The soil should be rich enough to show a good crop of weeds or grass; marshy ground, soil consisting of gravel and subsoil fill, and soil contaminated by chemical wastes should not be utilized
5. The plot should be located in an area not likely to receive excessive storm drainage or stream overflow

The site of a flower garden should receive special attention. A study should be made of the landscape around the home, and a site should be chosen that will fit in with this and make the most attractive addition to the scene. The gardener should consider how the garden will appear from all sides, and try to visualize it in bloom. It is an excellent plan to plot the garden on paper.

Making a Good Plot

Once a good location has been chosen, the garden plot should be planned and a seed bed prepared according to the following directions:

1. Remove all rubbish, stones, weeds, and grass
2. If the soil is excessively sandy or clayey, add manure or compost, which should be spread evenly over the soil before spading
3. Spade or plow the soil to a depth of 8 to 10 in. until the soil is dry and level, and all clods have been worked down
4. Rake the surface of the soil until the ground is smooth enough to permit making shallow trenches for the seeds

Berry and Herb Gardens

Strawberries and similar perennial herbs can be grown successfully by the home gardener. Plots and seed beds should be prepared in the same manner as for vegetable gardens. Any soil in which potatoes grow well is suitable for this type of plant. Good surface drainage is essential; and care should be taken not to set the plants too close together.

Planting

Only a small quantity of seeds is required for planting the average garden; and in the long run the best brands are the cheapest. The types of vegetables to be planted depend mainly on the time of year and weather conditions. The following table lists some of the most common vegetables, grouped according to the approximate times they can be planted, and their relative requirements for cool and warm weather.[1]

APPROXIMATE PLANTING TIME FOR VEGETABLES

Cold-hardy plants for early spring planting		Cold-tender or heat-hardy plants for late spring or early summer planting			Hardy plants for late summer or fall planting except in the North (plant 6 to 8 weeks before first fall freeze)
Very hardy (plant 4 to 6 weeks before frost-free date)	Hardy (plant 2 to 4 weeks before frost-free date)	Not cold-hardy (plant on frost-free date)	Requiring hot weather (plant 1 week or more after frost-free date)	Medium heat tolerant (good for summer planting)	
Broccoli Cabbage Lettuce Onions Peas Potatoes Spinach Turnips	Beets Carrots Chard Mustard Parsnips Radishes	Beans, snap Cucumbers Okra New Zealand spinach Soybeans Squash Sweet corn Tomatoes	Beans, lima Eggplant Peppers Sweet potatoes	Beans, all Chard Soybeans New Zealand spinach Squash Sweet corn	Beets Collards Kale Lettuce Mustard Spinach Turnips

The principal planting errors of most inexperienced gardeners are (1) sowing seeds too deep; (2) sowing too many seeds; (3) sowing seeds too close together; and (4) failing to properly thin out excess plants. In vegetable gardens, care should also be taken to plant perennial plants, such as asparagus and rhubarb, at one side of the plot where they can be handled conveniently without interfering with the annual spading and plowing of other parts of the garden. The following table gives a ready guide to the proper spacing of plants and seeds in the vegetable garden when grown intensively for hand culture.[1]

[1]From the United States Department of Agriculture publication, *Growing Vegetables in Town and City.*

SPACING OF VEGETABLE PLANTS OR SEEDS

Crop	Distance between— Rows	Distance between— Plants or hills in rows	Depth to cover seeds or roots	Seeds or plants required for— 1 ft. of row or per hill	Seeds or plants required for— 100 ft. of row	Seeds or plants required for— 1 acre
	In.	In.	In.	No.		Lb.
Asparagus[1]	30	18	8		70 plants	3
Beans, lima (bush)	28	4	1½	4	¾ pound	100
Beans, lima (pole)[2]	36	24	1½	[2]4	½ pound	60
Beans, snap (bush)	28	3	1½	5	¾ pound	100
Beans, snap (pole)[2]	36	24	1½	[2]4	¼ pound	40
Beets	16	3	¾	6	1 ounce	12
Broccoli, sprouting[3]	30	18	½	3	1 packet	¼
Brussels sprouts[3]	30	18	½	3	1 packet	¼
Cabbage[1]	30	18			70 plants	¼
Cabbage, Chinese[3]	24	10	½	4	1 packet	¼
Carrots	16	1½	½	20	¼ ounce	4
Cauliflower[1]	30	18			70 plants	¼
Celery and celeriac[1]	24	6		2	200 plants	¼
Chard	24	6	¾	4	1 ounce	12
Chervil	16	2	½	15	¼ ounce	4
Chives	16	2	½	15		
Chicory, witloof	20	4	½	10	1 packet	2
Collards[3]	30	18	½	3	1 packet	¼
Corn salad	16	10	½	5	1 packet	2
Corn, sweet	36	12	1½	2	¼ pound	15
Cress, upland	16	3	¼	20	1 packet	2
Cucumbers[2]	72	72	1	[2]12	½ ounce	2
Dandelion	16	8	¼	10	1 packet	2
Eggplant[1]	36	30			40 plants	¼
Endive	20	10	½	10	1 packet	2
Florence fennel	20	4	½	20	¼ ounce	3
Garlic[1]	16	3	1½	4	1 pound	325
Horseradish[1]	30	18	2		70 roots	
Kale[3]	24	10	½	4	1 packet	4
Kohlrabi	16	4	½	10	¼ ounce	4
Leeks	16	3	½	20	¼ ounce	4
Lettuce, head[1]	16	12			100 plants	¼
Lettuce, leaf	16	6	½	10	1 packet	2
Mustard	16	6	½	10	1 packet	2
Okra	36	18	1	3	1 ounce	8
Onions, seed	16	3	½	20	¼ ounce	4
Onions[1]	16	3		4	{ 1 qt. sets / 400 plants }	600 / 3
Parsley	16	4	¼	20	¼ ounce	2
Parsnips	16	3	½	15	½ ounce	3
Peas, garden (dwarf)	18	1	1½	12	1 pound	120
Peas, garden (tall)	24	1	1½	12	1 pound	120
Peas, black-eye	28	3	1½	5	½ pound	60
Peppers[1]	30	18			70 plants	¼
Potatoes	30	12	4	1	7 pounds	1,200
Radishes, spring	12	1	½	15	1 ounce	12
Radishes, summer or winter	20	3	½	10	½ ounce	6
Rhubarb[1]	42	42	4		30 roots	
Rutabagas	20	4	½	20	¼ ounce	2
Salsify	20	2	½	15	1 ounce	12
Shallots[1]	16	2			600 plants	
Sorrel	20	6	½	10	¼ ounce	2
Soybeans	24–36	3	1½	5	½–1 pound	45–90
Spinach	12	4	½	12	½ ounce	10
Spinach, New Zealand	30	12	1	3	1 ounce	4
Squash, bush[2]	48	48	1	10	½ ounce	3
Squash, trailing[2]	96	48	1	10	½ ounce	2
Sweet potatoes[1]	36	12			100 plants	
Tomatoes,[1] not staked	48	48			26 plants	⅛
Tomatoes,[1] staked	36	24			51 plants	¼
Turnips	16	3	½	20	¼ ounce	2

[1]Plants or sets. [2]Hills of about 4 plants each.

[3]Four or 5 seeds planted in 1 spot where plants are to stand; later thinned to 1 plant.

Special attention should be given to the *arrangement of plants in the flower garden*. If the garden is against a hedge or wall, the taller flowers should be planted in the rear, then the intermediate sizes, then the low plants, at the front. Color schemes should be considered when planting, in order that the garden in bloom may present an artistic blend of colors. Seeds should be planted about 2 to 4 in. apart in rows or in circles, if that arrangement is preferred. Flower seeds should not be planted too deep, and should be sprinkled lightly after planting. The following table gives the principal characteristics of some popular annual flowers.[1]

PRINCIPAL CHARACTERISTICS OF SOME ANNUAL FLOWERS

Common name	Height of plant in feet	Color	Preference for sun or shade	Hardiness to cold
Aster, China	2	purple, rose, and white	sun	half hardy
California poppy	1	yellow, orange	sun	very hardy
Cape marigold	1	yellow, orange	sun	hardy
Chrysanthemum, summer	2	yellow, white	sun	tender
Cornflower	2½	blue, rose, and white	sun or shade	very hardy
Dahlia	3	red, yellow, and white	sun	tender
Forget-me-not	1	blue	partial shade	hardy
Four-o'clock	1½	crimson, yellow, and white	sun	tender
Larkspur	2½	blue, pink, and white	sun	very hardy
Marigold, Aztec	2	yellow, orange	sun	hardy
Marigold, dwarf	1	golden yellow	sun	tender
Mignonette	1½	greenish	sun	half hardy
Nasturtium, dwarf	1	scarlet, orange, and yellow	sun	tender
Pansy	1	purple, yellow, and blue	sun or shade	hardy
Petunia	1	rose, purple, and white	sun	tender
Phlox, Drummond	1	red, lilac, buff, and white	sun	hardy
Pink	1	scarlet, pink, and white	sun	hardy
Poppy	2	scarlet, pink, and white	sun	very hardy
Rose everlasting	1½	pink and white	sun	half hardy
Snapdragon	2	scarlet, yellow, and white	sun	very hardy
Sorghum	4	green	sun	tender
Strawflower	2½	lemon yellow	sun	hardy
Sunflower	4	yellow	sun	hardy
Zinnia	2½	rose, scarlet, yellow, and orange	sun	hardy

Transplanting

Many types of flowers and vegetables can be grown more successfully if they are first planted in a protected place, to prevent damage by unfavor-

[1]From the United States Department of Agriculture bulletin, *Growing Annual Flowering Plants.*

able weather conditions. They are transplanted to the open garden later, when they have developed a sturdy root growth. This procedure is simple for some types of flowers that can be planted indoors in boxes. Other flowers and vegetables, however, require special hotbeds and cold frames; for the small gardener it is advisable to buy these plants from nurseries rather than to try to grow them from seed.

Making a Rock Garden

A rock garden is easy to build and can be an attractive addition to the home landscape. The following make excellent sites: (1) natural banks of rocks; (2) slopes or banks of earth; (3) natural rises in the ground, or excavated piles of earth; and (4) depressions in the ground, or old excavations. The rock garden should be in the open sunlight, away from trees but protected from the wind.

The preparation of the plot depends largely on the site chosen. If a natural bank of rocks has been selected, it is only necessary to make paths between the rocks for plants, and fill in with pockets of good soil. If rocks are to be brought to the site the directions below should be followed:

1. Select weather-beaten stones or rocks in various sizes and shapes, avoiding the use of too many small rocks
2. Place stones in the soil, starting at the bottom of the mound, slope, or depression, and gradually work upward
3. Slant stones toward the ground to form pockets for soil and rain. Cover three-fourths of each stone with earth
4. Place good top soil or sand and gravel, depending on the type of plants to be used, in the pockets. Use ample soil and allow it to settle for several days before planting

Native perennial plants make the best choice for a rock garden. Low plants are best for the main part of the garden, but somewhat taller plants may be used for the borders and background. The general recommendations for planting and care of the rock garden are the same as those given for other types.

Care of the Garden

After it is planted, a garden requires constant care. Some of the necessary routines are described below:

1. The garden should receive a good watering at least once a week. This is preferable to light sprinklings at frequent intervals. The best method is to apply water along the length of the furrows between the rows of plants
2. Weeds, which rob the cultivated plants of nutrients and water, should be pulled or hoed under whenever they appear
3. In nonirrigated soils with a low moisture content a mulch of straw, dry grass, leaves, or similar material should be applied over the soil to help conserve water
4. The constant danger of insects and plant diseases should be controlled. Every gardener should have a duster or sprayer for applying fungicides or insecticides[1]

---

[1]Information concerning the control of insects and diseases in the home garden can be obtained for a nominal fee from the United States Department of Agriculture.

HOME DESIGN AND CONSTRUCTION

The information on construction details given in this section refers mainly to an individual home, in order that in either building or buying a house the reader may have a general knowledge of construction and be able to discriminate between good and bad quality. A large structure is only an enlargement of a home; the information given here can, therefore, be utilized for constructions of any type.

Building a house falls into two parts, namely, planning and construction. If an architect is employed the house will be made to order; if stock plans, which are available from both private and governmental sources, are used the house will be of ready-made design. Without deprecating the function of an architect, it may be stated that ready-made plans are often excellent, for both layout and construction detail. The architect may interpret and elaborate on the client's ideas, but the greater the divergence from simple and standard construction, the greater the cost.

Architect

The function of the architect is to indicate on prepared plans his and the client's ideas on the way the house should be built. Briefly, he builds on paper and tears down with an eraser, thus saving the expense and disappointment of preventable errors. His plans show the layout of the rooms and specify the method of construction and the materials to be used. The architect also prepares *specifications* which prescribe in detail the quality of material and the workmanship.

General Contractor

The general contractor receives the architect's plans and specifications and prepares an estimate of the cost of construction.

If the estimate submitted is satisfactory to the owner, a contract is prepared. It consists of plans, specifications, and the contract document. The contract document need not be prepared by an attorney; the forms can be obtained at a stationer's or a legal-supply shop, or directly from the American Institute of Architects.

Location

The location of the house should be carefully considered for view, privacy, and exposure. It is traditional to place the service portions of the house toward the rear of the lot; but this tradition need not be followed if, for example, the street is exceptionally noisy, or if the prevailing summer winds blow from the rear.

351

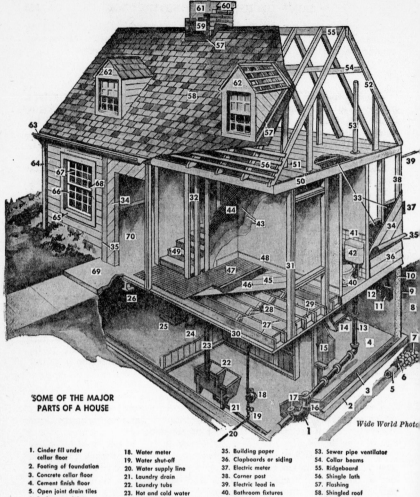

SOME OF THE MAJOR PARTS OF A HOUSE

Wide World Photo

1. Cinder fill under cellar floor
2. Footing of foundation
3. Concrete cellar floor
4. Cement finish floor
5. Open joint drain tiles
6. Burlap over joints
7. Crushed rock
8. Soil
9. Membrane waterproofing
10. Concrete foundation
11. Electric fuse box
12. Electric conduit
13. Sewer line
14. Cellar stairs
15. Cellar partition
16. Sewer trap
17. Cleanout plugs

18. Water meter
19. Water shut-off
20. Water supply line
21. Laundry drain
22. Laundry tubs
23. Hot and cold water
24. Hot water storage tank
25. Heating plant
26. Steel I-beam
27. Floor joists
28. Bridging
29. Firestops
30. Sill
31. Studs doubled
32. Single studs
33. Insulation in walls and ceiling
34. Diagonal sheathing

35. Building paper
36. Clapboards or siding
37. Electric meter
38. Corner post
39. Electric lead in
40. Bathroom fixtures
41. Bathroom tilework
42. Flush tank
43. Three coats of plaster
44. Metal lath
45. Diagonal sub-flooring
46. Building felt
47. Finish flooring
48. Baseboard
49. Staircase
50. Plate
51. Attic floor
52. Rafters

53. Sewer pipe ventilator
54. Collar beams
55. Ridgeboard
56. Shingle lath
57. Flashing
58. Shingled roof
59. Chimney
60. Chimney cap
61. Flue lining
62. Dormer windows
63. Gutter or eaves trough
64. Leader or down spout
65. Window frame
66. Window stiles
67. Muntins
68. Meeting rail
69. Doorstep
70. Entrance

352

Generally, the house should not be set in the middle of the plot, leaving several small areas of grass at the sides, front, and rear. The open area should be localized, to permit a garden or other plantation.

Foundation

The foundation walls, which support the house, should extend at least 6 in. below the frostline and above ground, so that they will not heave and crack during freezes and thaws.

Vertical cracks in concrete foundations usually indicate a settling of the structure; they should not occur. Hairline cracks are not important; they are caused by volume changes in the concrete. If, however, the concrete is uneven, has holes in it, and broken corners, probably too little cement was used or the concrete was placed carelessly in the forms.

Brick or masonry foundation walls should be smooth, true to lines and surface, and fairly uniform. To test them pick at the mortar with a knife blade. If the mortar crumbles easily, too much sand was used, or a poor quality of cementing material. It is a good idea to drive a nail into a vertical joint to see whether the mortar has been skimped. Corners of the building and window and door openings should be vertical and even. Wooden jambs and trim around doors and windows should fit snugly against the masonry. Joints between wood and masonry should be carefully filled with mortar. The sills of all windows, particularly the cellar windows, should drain outward. Areaways under windows should have a drainage outlet for rain water and snow.

Check the wall thickness through a cellar window. The minimum for concrete is 8 in., for brick or concrete blocks 12 in. Examine the joint between the top of the wall and the sill to make sure that there are no air spaces.

Walls

The side walls of the upper structure may be covered with wood siding, shingles, brick, stucco, or stone, or may be built entirely of brick, stone, concrete, or a combination of such materials. When used properly they are all good.

A *wood-framed house* is one in which the vertical supporting members are wood studs at least 2 × 4 in. in size and usually spaced 16 in. on centers. On the outside of these studs are nailed boards or sheathing, laid diagonally for maximum rigidity and strength in the walls. The exterior surface is applied in the form of wood siding, shingles, stucco, a layer of brick (veneer), or an enclosure of stone. Some houses are *framed with steel*. Light steel sections, bolted together as a skeleton frame, permitting variation in design, take the place of the wood frame; the companion materials used in the walls are changed very little.

If *wood siding* has been used, examine the condition of paint on the siding; particularly notice whether the paint film is dense and opaque, and whether the wood is showing through. If it is, repainting should be done immediately. Repainting is also indicated for painted surfaces which are dull and chalky. Run your hand over some of the boards to see that the painted surface is fairly free from blisters or scales; if these are present, they should be sanded down before repainting is done. It is a good rule to paint wood houses every three to five years.

The siding should be laid evenly, with overlapped and tight butt joints. At the house corners, the siding may be mitered or fitted snugly against vertical corner boards.

The woods most in use today are red cypress, western red cedar, redwood, southern yellow pine, Douglas fir, West Coast hemlock, Ponderosa pine, spruce, yellow poplar, and several others. If you are lucky enough to own a century-old New England landmark, the wood is probably white pine. By scraping off some of the paint you can determine the type of wood— if you are an expert.

Shingle-covered walls may be stained for the sake of appearance or treated with some kind of creosote oil for greater durability. Shingles should be fastened with noncorroding nails, *i.e.*, zinc, copper, zinc-coated, or cement-coated. The shingles should be at least ⅜ of an inch thick at the bottom. For side walls, shingles 24 in. long should be exposed not more than 11 in. to the weather; 18-in. shingles not more than 8½ in.; and 16-in. shingles not more than 7½ in. Smaller exposures require more shingles but make a thicker wall covering.

If side walls are *stuccoed,* look for signs of cracking or of mortar spalling off. Outside stucco is usually a mixture of portland cement and sand, applied to a metal base, which should be furred out ¼ of an inch or so from the sheathing so that the stucco can be forced through the mesh and form a tight bond. Heavy, waterproof building paper is applied over the sheathing, either separately or as an integral part of the mesh. One requirement for a permanent stucco finish is that no water shall seep behind it. Flashing strips (noncorrosive metal) over tops of windows and at other horizontal projections covering the edges of stucco work will prevent seepage. Window sills should have a groove or drip underneath, so that water will drip clear of the wall and not run down over the face. Incidentally, the stucco should start from a water table several inches above the finished grade to prevent staining and disintegration of the mortar on account of ground moisture or splashing rain. No matter what the material, look it all over carefully for defects or careless workmanship.

If the house has a *brick exterior,* the walls may be of solid brick or of brick veneer (a layer 4 in. thick) to serve as an outside finish to a frame wall. Varied effects can be obtained with either common brick or face brick, which is more decorative—and more costly.

Exposed brickwork should be built of hard, well-burned brick which is durable; but the mortar joints between the bricks must be laid carefully. Joints should be *filled,* not merely closed up at the outer edge of the brick. If the joints are pointed (finished) so that a ledge is left at the edge of every brick, opportunity is afforded for water to collect and seep through the walls of the building.

Headers are bricks laid lengthwise into the wall. In a solid brick wall, 13 in. thick, the headers are commonly concealed. In an all-brick wall, header courses should occur at least once to every 6 regular "stretcher" courses or the equivalent of 2 header bricks to every square foot of wall. Brick veneer should be well tied to the framework by metal bonds, well-spiked to the framework; this feature should be concealed. Copper ties are preferred for durability.

A white deposit appearing on the surface of brickwork is called efflorescence; it is usually due to moisture penetrating the interior of the masonry, dissolving the soluble salts in the materials and carrying them to the surface, where they are deposited by evaporation. It can be removed by washing or a good driving rain. Efflorescence seen on older houses or recurring on newer houses is a sign of defective construction, such as faulty roof drainage or open joints in masonry or around windows and doors, with resultant leakage.

Gutter and Flashing

Provision should be made for carrying rain water and melting snow from the roof of the house to the ground without damage to the house or its foundation. Rustproof gutters, without any sag, should be placed at all eaves; down-spouts, preferably of copper, zinc, or aluminum, should extend to the ground, where they should be cemented into an upright cast-iron or glazed-clay pipe protruding above the ground, and thence should drain into the sewer. If the down-spouts are not connected to a drainage system, they should be provided at the bottom with a curved elbow and discharge onto a flat stone or slab. There should be strainers over the inlets from the gutters to the down-spouts, to keep leaves, etc., from clogging up the pipe. The strips and fittings which hold the down-spouts in place should also be of non-rusting metal. Iron painted to resemble copper or bronze can be detected with a magnet; zinc, copper, or other non-ferrous metals will not be attracted.

Above each window, in frame construction, there is a joint between the outside trim and the wall. This should be "flashed" or protected by a sheet of copper or other noncorrosive metal. Window frames in masonry walls should be well-caulked to stop up all air spaces between the frame and the wall. Unfortunately, this is not common practice.

Chimneys from the Outside

The chimney should be plumb and erected on a substantial masonry foundation, constructed to prevent cracking or settling. If it is an exterior chimney the vertical joints between the chimney and the side walls, in frame construction, should be tight, to shut out the elements.

The chimney should be high enough to be above air currents which may interfere by blowing directly down the flues. Winds, at times, swoop up one slope of a peak roof and then swirl downward into a low chimney on the other side. A chimney at the peak will draw well, and so will a high chimney on the slope, provided, of course, that the fireplace and flues are correctly designed. There is no certainty possible, but try to judge whether the top of your chimney is safely above a draft down-zone. It should be 3 ft. above a flat roof, at least 2 ft. above the ridge of a sloping roof, and preferably capped; but capping should not decrease the required flue area.

Blinds

Blinds or shutters are now used mostly for appearance rather than utility. In colonial types of homes they suit the decor, but in other types they are incongruous. They provide security, however, during your absence and add protection in severe climates.

Screens

Copper screens last longest. The frames should be fitted tightly and firmly together. If they are of the sliding type, see that the tongues which slide in the grooves are unbroken and straight and that each screen is numbered for the opening in which it belongs. It is a good idea to screen the bottom of doors, and to have such screening reinforced, to prevent scuffing.

Structural Features

The framework is the backbone of the house. Scrutinize the *inside basement walls* even more carefully than you did the outside. They should be free from unduly large bulges. Be sure that the masonry where it supports the floor beams and girders has not been crushed. Look for indications of leaks; the best time to look for these is after a rainy spell. *Joints* around windows should be tight, to prevent entrance of air or moisture.

The *basement floor* should be dry; look for water stains along the angles between floor and walls. If drainage has been taken care of outside, so that the water is carried away from the foundation walls, you will be fairly safe on this score. If it has not, the builder may have obtained a watertight cellar by mopping hot pitch on the outside of the wall, or by using, below ground, a rich cement mortar. You can determine this by digging down a little on the outside of the wall. Since it is difficult and expensive to waterproof a building satisfactorily from the inside, this should be a careful inspection on your part. All holes where pipes come through the foundation wall should be cemented. Tap all around the floor to be sure there are no bubbles in the finish or hollow spaces beneath to cause the floor to crack. A floor drain is an advantage. It permits washing down the floors and provides for an overflow from the tubs, but it is no indication of watertightness. Some cities prohibit floor drains. If present, they should never be connected directly with the sewer, for the water which seals the trip in the drainpipe is likely to dry up and admit sewer gas. In some localities, danger from sewers backing up may necessitate a back-water valve in the drainpipe. Some builders slope the cellar floor toward a drain so that water runs off quickly.

The concrete floor should have a hard, smooth, troweled, uncracked surface. Check *cellar-entrance steps,* which should be sound and sturdy, and without projections which can be easily broken. See whether there is danger of rain or snow accumulating on these steps or at the bottom of the area. If so, there should be an area drain. The *basement door* should be large enough to permit carrying in furniture or parts of a new boiler.

Floor Beams

The floor beams or joists support the load on the first floor, and in turn are supported at one end by the basement wall and at the other end by a steel or wood girder, or by the opposite wall. In the average house the floor beams are of *wood,* although *steel beams* and also *reinforced concrete beams* have been recently introduced in residential construction. Wood joists should be evenly spaced about every 16 in. and be "bridged" about every 8 ft. of their length with snugly-fitted cross braces securely nailed with 2 nails at the top of one joist and the bottom of the next. The bridging stiffens the joists and helps to distribute the heavy loads.

Examine the joists for sagging and warping and for cracks, especially vertical cracks. Look carefully at any joists which have been cut to permit piping. Small holes along the middle of a beam for piping or electric wiring can have a weakening effect. The presence of knots is not a serious defect, unless there are a great many toward the center of the span or near the edges.

The *size of the joists* will depend on several factors: distance between the supports, the assumed load, and the kind and grade of lumber used.

Between the floor joists you should see the rough or *subfloor* of nominal 1-in. boards, not over 8 in. wide (shrinkage in wider boards may distort the finished floor), preferably laid diagonally to the joists. Diagonal flooring stiffens the house in a horizontal plane against heavy winds. It should extend to the outside edge of the vertical studs, in frame construction, and be fitted tightly against the inside of masonry walls. The subfloor should never be omitted in the first floor of a house. It makes the floors stronger and stiffer and helps to prevent squeaking, is an excellent insulator, and serves as a working platform during the building of the house. Look through the cracks in adjacent boards and make sure that a heavy-coated or *waterproof building paper* has been laid on the subfloor. A waterproof paper will not only cut off drafts and dust from the cellar but will also prevent any dampness from below getting into and warping the finished floor.

Numerous knots are permissible in the subfloor, provided the knots are sound. A No. 2 common grade of lumber is suitable for this purpose. Do not condemn the house if you observe *blue-stained lumber;* the stain is a harmless fungus which does not affect the strength of a beam or floor. You can test the soundness and hardness of the wood by sticking a penknife into it. However, blue-stained lumber would be objectionable in paneling or woodwork that is to have a natural, unpainted finish.

Floor beams resting directly on basement walls should have at least 3 in. of support. Make sure there is *ventilation* around the ends of all wood beams resting on masonry. If the ends of the joists are sealed into the wall, they cannot dry out and may even absorb moisture from the wall. In such event decay is to be expected. When wood beams frame into a masonry wall, the ends should be beveled with a "fire cut," so that in case of a fire burning through one or two joists before it can be controlled, the joists can fall down without destroying the wall. With masonry walls, every fourth joist should be anchored to the wall with wrought-iron pin anchors.

In most frame houses the floor beams rest on wood sills laid around the top of the basement wall and set in a full mortar bed. This still provides a level, even support for the vertical framing pieces called studs, and the mortar insures a weatherproof and verminproof joint between the bottom of the sill and the masonry. See that the wood sill is *bolted to the masonry* every 8 ft. along the wall. During hurricanes many homes are blown off their foundations simply because these anchor bolts have been omitted.

Stick the point of your knife into the sill at various spots to see whether the wood is sound. Occasionally, the sills absorb an excessive amount of moisture; in such cases they are likely to decay. This danger can be avoided by the use of sills chemically treated with either creosote or salts, or by the use of heartwood.

Termites

Termites are prevalent in certain sections of the country, more particularly in the South. They will not attack wood that has been given proper chemical treatment. Termites live mostly in the ground, are blind, and avoid light. They build slender shelter tubes up the walls of a house, from the ground to the sills and joists, to obtain moisture. Destruction of these tubes will kill all termites. In a termite-infested district, look for signs of these tubes and for the white pellets deposited by termites; insist upon termite shields. These are metal sheets placed on top of the foundation walls and bent down at a 45-degree angle for 2 in. or so on each side of the wall. It is also a wise precaution to have the lumber for sills, joists, and studs treated chemically. All-heart California redwood also offers considerable resistance to termites. Creosoted material, because of its odor, is seldom used above the foundations.

Floor Beams of Steel or Concrete

, Examine all joists that have had holes punched in them for piping. Holes less than 3 in. in diameter, if on the center line, have little weakening effect. Similar holes near flanges, however, may be dangerous.

Unless the ceiling is plastered, the concrete slab will be visible between the beams at all points. The concrete should be smooth and fit snugly against the beams at all points. Good concrete work is of vital importance in such floor systems.

Inside the Walls

You may be able to see, near the basement ceiling and in the attic, the rough boarding or sheathing which, in the wood-framed house, is nailed to the outside of the studs. In certain sections of the country insulating boards are employed as sheathing. Since these boards vary in quality, thickness, efficiency, and strength, the product of each manufacturer should be given separate consideration. Lumber sheathing should be nailed diagonally unless the house is stuccoed, in which case horizontal sheathing has been found the better; diagonal bracing, however, must be used at all corners of the house to provide against high-wind pressures. Heavy building paper should always be used between the sheathing and the outside wall covering; it will prove invaluable in shutting out the wind, even though it is negligible as an insulator.

Fire Stops

Spaces between studs or openings for pipes should be blocked off or "fire stopped" at all floor levels, but especially at the first floor. Even a 1-in. board helps somewhat (one reason for extending the subflooring to the outside face of the studs), but incombustible filling is better. It should completely occupy the hollow space between floor joists and studs to a height of 3 in. above the floor level. Loose material should be held in place with a rust-resistant wire mesh or wood strips at least 2 in. thick. Without fire stops these spaces may act as veritable flues in case of fire. Unblocked spaces permit warm air in the cellar to pass up to the top of the house and escape, thus increasing the fuel bill. They also permit the passage of rats and mice from the basement to the upper part of the house. The house built by speculators seldom has fire stops; but if you are building your own house insist upon them. It is good and cheap insurance.

It is also a wise precaution to have the entire basement ceiling, or at least the area over the heating plant, protected with metal lath and plaster or some fire-resistant material. There should be at least 15 in. overhead clearance. This also applies to wood framing at the sides of the furnace or boiler.

Test the various basement windows to be sure that they are securely hinged and that the hardware works, and see that the windows are not broken or warped to permit air leaks. The coal chute opening should preferably have a heavy metal frame to withstand hard service.

Basement partitions should also be carefully examined, to see that they are fastened at both top and bottom and are not mere makeshifts.

Chimneys

If your house has a potential fire hazard, the chances are that it lies in the details of the chimney construction. Make sure there is a good fire-clay flue lining ¾ of an inch thick inside the brickwork or masonry and extending from below the flue opening to 2 in. above the cap. Under certain circumstances the flue lining may be omitted, but then the chimney walls must be 8 in. thick, if of brick, with a special firebrick lining; or 6 in. thick, if of reinforced concrete. But insist upon a flue lining for the ordinary chimney.

Have no wood within 2 in. of any chimney wall, and no wood within 4 in. of the back wall of the fireplace. The violation of this rule causes countless fires. MAKE SURE THAT:

1. Chimneys shall not rest upon or be carried by wooden floors, beams, or brackets, or be hung from wooden rafters;

2. Chimneys shall be built upon concrete or masonry foundations properly proportioned to carry the width imposed without danger of settlement or cracking;

3. All spaces between chimneys and wooden joists or beams shall be filled with loose cinders, loose mortar refuse, gypsum block, or other porous incombustible material to form a fire stop;

4. The incombustible material shall be supported by strips of sheet metal or metal lath set into the brickwork and nailed to the wooden beams, forming a buckled, flexible joint between, or by similar strips of metal nailed to the woodwork with the inner edge close to the chimney;

5. No wooden studding, furring, lathing or plugging shall be placed against any chimney or in the joints thereof. Wooden construction shall either be set away from the chimney or the plastering shall be directly on the masonry, or on metal lathing, or on incombustible furring material. Wood furring strips, placed around chimneys to support base or other trim, shall be insulated from the masonry by asbestos paper at least ⅛ in. thick, and metal wall plugs or approved incombustible nail-holding devices attached to the wall surface shall be used for nailing;

6. All fireplaces and chimney breasts shall have trimmer arches or other approved fire-resistive construction supporting hearths. The arches and hearths shall be at least 20 in. wide, measured from the face of the chimney breast. The arches shall be of brick, stone, or hollow tile, not less than 4 in. thick. A flat stone or a reinforced concrete slab may be used to carry the hearth instead of an arch, if it be properly supported and a suitable fill be provided between it and the hearth. The length of trimmer arches and hearths shall be not less than 24 in. longer than the fireplace opening. Hearths shall be of brick, stone, tile, or concrete, as may be specified.

Flooring

Entirely satisfactory finished flooring may be had in various materials, although wood is the one most commonly used. The most beautiful wood flooring is probably a clear grade of quarter-sawed (*i.e.*, sawed at right angles to the annual rings of the tree) hardwood, such as white oak, although plain-sawed material is also attractive and durable. Strips are carefully matched for color and grain in the best floors. Since a price difference of about 30 per cent exists between first- and second-grade oak, it is often wise to use the lower grade in bedrooms and upper-story rooms, where it is not objectionable to have a few defects in the wood.

Quarter-sawed (also called edge-grain or vertical-grain) southern pine and Douglas fir are two good choices for floor woods. Edge-grain western larch and West Coast hemlock are other good woods.

Be sure that the wood floors, and also the interior finish or woodwork, are installed after the plaster has dried out. Although flooring is carefully dried in a kiln by the modern manufacturer, if it is laid in a damp house it will absorb moisture. This will cause expansion and, probably, warping.

When the house is heated, the wood dries out, the flooring shrinks, and cracks appear; the result is squeaky floors. Wide flooring strips, though attractive and used in colonial-type houses, will expand or contract more than narrow strips. The remedy here is to delay the finished flooring until plaster is thoroughly dried out—at least two to three weeks after the last coat is applied.

As you walk over a floor, notice whether it squeaks, or seems to deflect or spring under your weight. If the floor joists are adequate and a subfloor has been included, neither of these things should happen. You can tell whether the floors are level by stretching a string across them.

Tile Work

The best indication of good workmanship in floors, walls (particularly bathrooms), wainscots, or mantels is a clean-looking over-all job.

Tile floors should be smooth, without raised tiles or depressed areas. Joints should be regular and uniform throughout. If white tile has been used, the floors should appear white all over; numerous discolored tiles indicate soft, inferior material. The pattern should be carried out accurately. Fittings around fixtures should be done neatly. There should be no visible opening between the tile floor and the threshold.

Tile work on walls, for instance, in baths or kitchens, should be smooth, have neat, uniform joints, and be free from chipped or broken tiles. The top, or cap, course of the tile wall or wainscot should be level and neatly returned into the plaster surface above. Slight stains in the center of wall tile are due to the wetting of tile for proper setting. They disappear after a short time as the work dries. In colored tile, a variation in shade is typical.

Trim and Millwork

This is the woodwork around doors and windows, paneling, moldings, staircases, and similar features. It may be painted or stained, or finished in a natural grain. Do not be misled by imitation graining. Most woods are more attractive in their natural grain than when finished to imitate a more expensive wood. Different woods lend themselves to different treatments. Your own judgment and taste should be your guide, but bear in mind the relation of trim and woodwork to flooring and the room as a whole. Narrow trim is popular today because it is neater-looking and more economical. Hardwood trim, such as birch, red gum, or oak, is attractive when given a natural, varnished, lacquered, waxed, or oil finish. So are the softer pines in the knotty grades that are selected especially for paneling. Other softwoods are generally painted to suit the room decorations. Be sure there are no open joints, hammer marks, warped pieces, or signs of nailing.

Woodwork manufacturers kiln-dry their various products to prevent shrinkage after installation. Unless this dry millwork is protected from dampness, before as well as after it is installed in the house, it will absorb moisture and lose the benefits of this drying. Millwork should be painted on the back with a good paint primer before it is installed. Although this is an inexpensive method of protection, it is not common practice. Many of the more careful builders actually measure the humidity in the newly plastered house and, by means of the heating plant, in cold or continued wet weather dry out the house properly before the kiln-dried woodwork is installed. After that it remains for the home owner to avoid excessive dryness (with further shrinkage) during the long winter heating season. Usually this means water pans on radiators, or humidifiers, and a relative humidity of from 40 to 60 per cent. Natural dampness, even during a rainy period in midsummer, is seldom detrimental to woodwork. It is the excessive drying out in overheated rooms, through several weeks or months, that causes glued joints to open.

Over the door, where the side casings meet the horizontal "header" the trim is often mitered, that is, fitted at an angle. If this joint is tight, as all joints should be, it is an indication of careful workmanship. If the joint has opened at the bottom, however, the wood has shrunk after installation; if the joint has opened at the top, it has taken on too much moisture and expanded—it was probably installed before the wet plaster had dried out. Many doors have the trim applied with square-cut butt joints, without molding, which are more economical and less likely to open.

The baseboard should fit snugly against the floor and the wall at all points. Make sure that walls have been plastered back of the baseboard. Cracks between the baseboard and the floor are favorite retreats for waterbugs and other insects. Why baseboards? To cover the joint between wall and floor, to protect walls from furniture and vacuum cleaners, and to add to the appearance of solidity. A chair rail—a molding which encircles a room at a height of about 3 ft.—is sometimes added to protect the wall from the backs of chairs.

Some builders avoid a crack between the floor and the base molding by nailing the shoe mold to the subfloor, stopping the finished floor at the inner face of the base mold. Then, even if the baseboard shrinks, it will not pull the shoe mold away from the floor, nor will any shrinkage of the finished floor pull the molding away from the baseboard.

Wainscoting and paneling seem somewhat mysterious to most of us, particularly with reference to the methods of making plywood panels out of veneer, or thin sheets of wood. For the better class of plywood, 5-ply construction is usually preferred. This is the result of skillful laying together and gluing under high pressure of 5 thin sheets of wood. The wood in the outer layers is carefully selected for appearance and for ease of finishing. Simpler and cheaper plywood, designated 3-ply, is made with 3 sheets.

The core for workmanlike plywood must be chosen for strength, stability, and minimum variation under atmospheric conditions. The face wood is selected for appearance and durability. The idea that veneer covers an inferior base does not apply to well-manufactured plywood. Color and grain of wood should be matched in the different panels, if the wood is finished in natural grain.

Doors

Doors should swing freely and close tightly without sticking. They should be high enough to admit large pieces of furniture, as well as tall people. If there is a threshold under the front-entrance door, there should be no opening for the admittance of cold, snow, and bugs. Be sure that the back and side doors remain in position. Interior doors should be hung so that they clear the rugs and should not interfere with other doors and electric-light wall brackets. They should latch readily and stay latched.

Outside doors, which are subject to rain and cold on one side and warm, dry air on the other, should be at least 1¾ in. thick at the edges, and the panels considerably thinner. Inside doors are usually only 1⅜ in. thick. Doors may be of either solid wood or plywood, of either hardwood or softwood. The solid door has stiles and rails (the thicker vertical and horizontal framework) of one piece; the veneered or plywood doors have veneer applied over a built-up core. In hardwood designs for certain styles of architecture, specially-planned or flush plywood doors are occasionally required, but generally such doors are too heavy and costly.

Door panels are set in grooves in the stiles and rails; enough clearance is allowed for expansion of the panels under abnormal conditions. However, the panels should fit snugly in the grooves not to rattle.

No wood patches or wedges should be present; they indicate a second-grade door. Large panels are nearly always built up of 3 or 5 plys of veneer, glued together. Small panels may be solid. Various methods are used to join the different parts of a door. Examine the joints for neatness and workmanship. Glazed doors should be set in putty; and in a veneered exterior door it is good practice to have a beveled strip along the lower edge of the opening before it is glazed, in order that water running down the glass shall not get in between the veneer and the core.

Windows

The exposed portions of the frame and sash should preferably be of hardwood, from such species as red cypress, genuine white pine, and redwood, although less durable woods may often be used.

In most cases window sash will be the common double-hung type. The choice, however, between double-hung sash and casements is largely a matter of the most appropriate window for the house. With casements, a full window opening for ventilation can be utilized. The advantage of double-hung windows lies in the ease with which ventilation can be had on bad days. Also, such windows are easily screened and fairly weather-tight. Since, however, there is always a certain amount of play between windows and frames, it is economical to have them weather-stripped. This also applies to doors, more particularly to casements. Interlocking metal weather strips should be placed around the edges. Weather stripping should not interfere with the opening of doors or windows.

The meeting rails, where the upper and lower sash are locked together, may have a joint that is straight, beveled, or stepped. The latter two bring the sash together when the window is locked and give the most weather-tight joints. The underside of the lower sash should be thoroughly puttied and painted, to exclude moisture. When looking at windows, also test shades and be sure there are no cracked panes of glass.

In casement windows, notice whether they are hung to swing inward. These windows are extremely hard to make watertight, so look for signs of leaks. Outswinging casements require a special type of inside screens. Wood casements are preferably 1¾ in. thick, as are exterior doors.

Examine wood sash for signs of decay and steel sash for signs of rust. Notice whether there is a draft around windows and look for crevices in window framing. Also examine the glass, to see whether it is flawless or wavy and distorted.

Partitions

The house is divided into rooms by walls or partitions. A well-built wall has double studs at the sides of door openings, and across the top a double header, with the pieces set on edge for maximum stiffness. If the studs rest on floor joists, any shrinkage in the joists will cause a corresponding settling in the partition, and probably a plaster crack at the ceiling.

Lath

These general types of lath are in use: *wood lath, metal lath,* and *plaster lath,* also *insulation boards* which are used as lath substitute.

In partition walls and in side walls of wood-framed houses the lath is nailed to the vertical with 2 × 4 in. studs, spaced 16 in. on centers. Plaster is then applied over the lath in 2 or 3 coats. In masonry walls furring or nailing are usually nailed to the wall, and the lath then nailed to these strips and plastered. Since it is not possible to see the lath, except perhaps in attic or basement, it should be judged from the general appearance and solidity of the plaster applied as a covering.

Plaster

Miscellaneous, random plaster cracks probably mean poor plaster or lath, or inferior workmanship. In a new house an outline of the lath should never show through the plaster; if there is such an outline it means thin, skimped plaster.

Examine the walls to see whether they are smooth, without valleys and hills. The joints between trim and plaster should be tight. Tap on the walls to see whether they are of plaster or composition wallboard. Such wallboards are used to replace both lath and plaster when costs are being held down.

If plaster is exposed on walls or ceilings, see whether there are any chalky, light-colored spots; these spots indicate "dry-outs" where the water in the plaster evaporated before the plaster was set. These places will always be soft and subject to cracking. If *damp* spots have occurred, these can be cured by supplying heat and ventilation immediately, unless the dampness has come from a leaky roof or wall.

If the plaster has a sandy appearance and the sand can be brushed off by rubbing your hand over it, the plaster is oversanded, weak, and easily destroyed.

Painted Walls and Wallpaper

Interior flat finishes using the oil type of paint present a pleasing matte appearance. If the paint finish shows streaks and hair cracks, it indicates that the priming coats were not properly designed and that a refinishing coat should be applied.

Your personal taste in wallpaper, as well as its condition, should be your standard.

Closets

There is more "to" a closet than just the size. The walls should be completely plastered, as unfinished openings may admit vermin. Some builders raise the closet floors to a level with the threshold so that they can be easily cleaned.

Kitchens

Beech, birch, or maple flooring or linoleum make excellent floors for the kitchen.

The sink should be about 35 in. above the floor and be fitted tightly against the wall at the back. Examine the enameled surface of the sink; if it is rough and the iron is beginning to show through it will be difficult to keep clean.

Avoid a range that has too many corners to clean and too much metal to shine. An insulated oven is an advantage.

Staircase

See that the staircase is easy to walk up and down and is not squeaky. The railings should be secure. Balusters should be firmly mortised into holes in the steps. Steps should not bend under your weight, and there should be sufficient clearance overhead so that a tall person can descend with safety.

Bathroom

The tile floor should be of unglazed, ceramic mosaic, glazed floor tile, faience, or plastic tile. The edges should be cut evenly and the pieces fitted snugly against the base. If the walls appear to be tiles, tap them, so that you may know whether they are real or imitation tile. The latter does not condemn the house, but you should know what you are buying. Wall tile should be installed wherever water may be splashed. Examine plumbing fixtures, which should be modern. Many changes in design and use have occurred in the past 20 years. Be sure the fixtures, such as bathtub and medicine cabinet, are of adequate size for your family.

Roof Anchorage

Rafters should be notched over and spiked to the side wall plate over the studs. With masonry walls this plate should be fastened to the walls by means of anchor bolts embedded securely in the masonry. Proper anchorage is extremely important, but it is often overlooked in a house.

In examining side walls see whether the outside sheathing has been carried up to the roof boarding. Note also whether *fire stops* have been inserted between the studs, to shut off drafts and prevent the rapid spread of fire.

Over the rafters is laid the *roof sheathing,* which should be of a good grade of lumber. Look at the undersurface for stains or signs of leakage. Shingle roofs are better laid of solid sheathing than of shingle lath. Although the latter permits ventilation for the shingles, it lessens roof insulation, and has less fire resistance.

Roofs

Roofs are usually of wood shingles, slate, tile, metal, or asbestos shingles.

Inspect as much of the roof surface as possible. For any shingle roof the slope should be at least 1:2; that is, the roof should rise 6 in. in every foot, measured horizontally. For tile or slate a slightly steeper pitch should be used. For sheet metal, a nearly flat roof is permissible, if it has enough slope to take care of drainage.

Be sure that *flashing* or rustproof material is used around chimneys, at vent pipes, around skylights, and at the channels for water formed at the intersection of roof surfaces. This flashing should extend far enough to prevent water from backing up over the top of the flashing.

Ascertain for how long a period the roof is guaranteed.

Garage

Find out whether the garage has adequate fire protection.

The same careful inspection should be given to the garage as to the rest of the house. The garage should be adequately lighted and heated. There should be a supply of water and a floor drain. Examine the doors to see whether they work adequately. Be sure that both garage and driveway are large enough for your car.

Hardware

Finished hardware comprises such articles as door handles, locks, bolts, hinges, window lifts and pulleys, and shutter fasteners. They may be of cast iron, wrought iron, wrought steel, cast or wrought brass, or bronze. Plated hardware of good quality may be satisfactory; but on doorknobs and surrounding plates and escutcheons, the plating may wear off.

All hardware in bathrooms should be of bronze or brass with nickel or chromium finish, to insure that they are rustproof. The best criterion for hardware is that it be reliable for its purposes.

Plumbing

A detailed explanation of plumbing and heating systems would be too technical for the purposes herein set forth. If the house itself is satisfactory the purchaser should retain a competent engineer or contractor to check over carefully the plumbing and heating installations.

A good plumbing system is never obtrusive. It supplies water whenever desired and takes care of all household drainage in a sanitary and efficient manner.

The water-supply system consists simply of a cold-water pipe from the source of supply, with a connection to each of the plumbing fixtures requiring water. To provide hot water, one branch of pipe is usually run in coils through a heating apparatus, frequently a special gas heater. For storage purposes there is usually a hot-water tank; the hot water, being lighter than the cold, rises, and the cold water falls, thus maintaining by gravity a constant circulation.

A hot-water supply must have not only proper-sized piping but also a satisfactory hot-water heater. The hot-water storage tank should have a capacity, for even a small family, of 30 gal.; for a larger family a capacity of at least 7 gal. per person is needed.

Water may be heated in many ways and with different fuels. Today, many gas companies furnish expert advice on all phases of hot-water heating.

Drainage and Sanitation

The drainage or waste system carries off various kinds of household waste. It also protects against gas entering the house from the sewer, and provides air pipes or vents necessary for the successful operation of the system.

Observe the general character of the plumbing as to both materials and workmanship. See whether flanges are installed to cover any holes where piping comes through the floor. Look for signs of corrosion, particularly at joints.

Cesspools and Septic Tanks

If the house is in a rural district it has its own sewage-disposal system. The cesspool cannot be too strongly condemned.

A septic tank, underground and watertight, is the safest and most satisfactory method of sewage disposal. A septic tank can be tested for watertightness by filling it with water in the afternoon and noting the water level the next afternoon. A drop of more than half an inch during 24 hours indicates a leaky tank.

Heating

Your house may be heated by coal, oil, or gas, through the medium of steam, hot water, or warm air. Any of these methods will be adequate if the design and installation are correct. Only an expert can determine this for you.

In any heating unit you should check the workmanship, especially around connections. Look for any obviously defective material. If everything seems to be in good condition, and the boiler or furnace is of reputable make, you can call in the expert.

The entire question of the heating system to be selected depends on the initial cost and the upkeep in relation to the comfort and satisfaction to be derived. Be sure that the heating system is operated correctly; if the manufacturers' directions are not followed, trouble will result even in a perfect system.

Electric Wiring

The connecting link between the feed wires and the electric lights and appliances in your house is the electric wiring. Most of it is concealed, but some parts may be visible, such as those in the cellar or the attic. In many communities electric wiring is inspected by a municipal or a fire insurance inspector, who issues certificates of inspection. Such certificates are the best possible evidence that the requirements of good workmanship and the necessary technical requirements have been met; these certificates should be checked on.

These certificates, of course, do not indicate the number or the location of circuits and outlets; the purchaser must decide for himself whether they are adequate. The purchaser should also examine switches and lighting fixtures.

As with heating and plumbing, an expert should be called in to examine electric wiring, and cables, conduits, fuses, and circuits.

LUMBER

Kinds of Lumber

Lumber is divided into three kinds: (1) *Yard lumber,* meaning lumber that is less than 6 in. thick; (2) *Structural timbers,* meaning lumber that is 6 in. or more in both thickness and width; and (3) *Factory or shop lumber* meaning lumber that will be cut up and used in manufacturing.

Yard lumber less than 2 in. thick and less than 8 in. wide is called *strips.* Yard lumber less than 2 in. thick but 8 in. or more wide is called *boards.* All yard lumber except strips, boards, and timbers is called *dimension lumber.* Dimension lumber is therefore 2 in. but less than 7 in. thick, and any width. When it is 2 in. and less than 4 in. thick and 8 or more in. wide it is called *planks.* When it is 2 in. but less than 6 in. thick and less than 8 in. wide it is called *scantlings.* When it is 4 in. but less than 6 in. thick and 8 in. or more wide it is called *heavy joists.*

Framing lumber is a common lumber called technically dimension and heavy joist lumber. It is 2 in. or more in thickness and 4 to 12 in. wide.

From it the frameworks of buildings are made. The most important sub-divisions of the framework are, the *posts,* or *stanchions,* which form the main interior support for the building; the *sills,* which form the lowest part of the structure, resting as they do on the foundation walls, and furnish a nailing base for the studs and joists; the *girders,* or *sleepers,* which form the main horizontal supports for the floors and partitions; the *joists,* which are the horizontal timbers directly supporting the floor or ceiling; the *studs,* which are uprights to which sheathing boards or laths are nailed; the *plates,* which are the horizontal timbers which support the trusses or rafters of a roof; the *ribbons,* which are narrow strips framed into the studs to support the floor or ceiling joists; the *collar ties,* which are boards to keep the roof from sagging or spreading; the *rafters,* which are the sloping timbers which support the roof; and the *lookouts,* which are bracketlike pieces which support the overhanging part of a roof.

Lumber as it comes from the saw is called *rough. Surfaced lumber* has been planed. *Worked lumber* has been matched (dressed so as to make a close tongue-and-groove joint at the edges or ends when laid together) shiplapped (dressed so as to make a close rabbeted or lapped joint) or patterned (made into a pattern or mold).

Smoothly finished lumber with very few defects, suitable for natural finishes or paint, is called select lumber. Lumber which contains defects but is still good for structural purposes is called common lumber. Each of these divisions has many subdivisions. The United States Bureau of Standards under the auspices of the United States Chamber of Commerce and the National Association of Lumber Manufacturers have worked out a table of blemishes and defects indicating the kinds and quantities that will be allowed in the various grades of wood.

Grading of Lumber

Grading of wood, however, cannot in the nature of things be an exact science. Dimensions can, of course, be measured exactly but one man's summing up of the quality of a plank may not be the same as another's. Five per cent is the variation allowed for differences in judgment.

It is possible today to buy grade-marked lumber. More than 7,000,000-000 ft. of grade-marked pine and fir are produced annually by American mills. The National Lumber Manufacturers' Association guarantees the integrity of such wood and if the customer is dissatisfied he can call for a reinspection of the lumber. The Association will send an inspector and will allow only the five per cent margin for human fallibility which has been mentioned in the preceding paragraph. Grade marking is simply a guarantee which protects the customer.

Lumber is graded from the better side, and if lumber is surfaced on one side only it is graded from that side.

It is also possible to buy short lengths instead of the customary long lengths. Farmers, for example, and small builders can save from 15 per cent to 25 per cent by using short lengths.

TABLE OF BOARD FEET

Size in inches	Length in Feet							
	10	12	14	16	18	20	22	24
1x2	1-2/3	2	2-1/3	2-2/3	3	3-1/3	3-2/3	4
1x3	2-1/2	3	3-1/2	4	4-1/2	5	5-1/2	6
1x4	3-1/3	4	4-2/3	5-1/3	6	6-2/3	7-1/3	8
1x5	4-1/6	5	5-5/6	6-2/3	7-1/2	8-1/3	9-1/6	10
1x6	5	6	7	8	9	10	11	12
1x7	5-5/6	7	8-1/6	9-1/3	10-1/2	11-2/3	12-5/6	14
1x8	6-2/3	8	9-1/3	10-2/3	12	13-1/3	14-2/3	16
1x10	8-1/3	10	11-2/3	13-1/3	15	16-2/3	18-1/3	20
1x12	10	12	14	16	18	20	22	24
1x14	11-2/3	14	16-1/3	18-2/3	21	23-1/3	25-2/3	28
1x16	13-1/3	16	18-2/3	21-1/3	24	26-2/3	29-1/3	32
1x18	15	18	21	24	27	30	33	36
1x20	16-2/3	20	23-1/3	26-2/3	30	33-1/3	36-2/3	40
1-1/4x4	4-1/6	5	5-5/6	6-2/3	7-1/2	8-1/3	9-1/6	10
1-1/4x6	6-1/4	7-1/2	8-3/4	10	11-1/4	12-1/2	13-3/4	15
1-1/4x8	8-1/3	10	11-2/3	13-1/3	15	16-2/3	18-1/3	20
1-1/4x10	10-5/12	12-1/2	14-7/12	16-2/3	18-3/4	20-5/6	22-11/12	25
1-1/4x12	12-1/2	15	17-1/2	20	22-1/2	25	27-1/2	30
1-1/2x4	5	6	7	8	9	10	11	12
1-1/2x6	7-1/2	9	10-1/2	12	13-1/2	15	16-1/2	18
1-1/2x8	10	12	14	16	18	20	22	24
1-1/2x10	12-1/2	15	17-1/2	20	22-1/2	25	27-1/2	30
1-1/2x12	15	18	21	24	27	30	33	36
2x4	6-2/3	8	9-1/3	10-2/3	12	13-1/3	14-2/3	16
2x6	10	12	14	16	18	20	22	24
2x8	13-1/3	16	18-2/3	21-1/3	24	26-2/3	29-1/3	32
2x10	16-2/3	20	23-1/3	26-2/3	30	33-1/3	36-2/3	40
2x12	20	24	28	32	36	40	44	48
2x14	23-1/3	28	32-2/3	37-1/3	42	46-2/3	51-1/3	56
2x16	26-2/3	32	37-1/3	42-2/3	48	53-1/3	58-2/3	64
2-1/2x12	25	30	35	40	45	50	55	60
2-1/2x14	29-1/6	35	40-5/6	46-2/3	52-1/2	58-1/3	64-1/6	70
2-1/2x16	33-1/3	40	46-2/3	53-1/3	60	66-2/3	73-1/3	80
3x6	15	18	21	24	27	30	33	36
3x8	20	24	28	32	36	40	44	48
3x10	25	30	35	40	45	50	55	60
3x12	30	36	42	48	54	60	66	72
3x14	35	42	49	56	63	70	77	84
3x16	40	48	56	64	72	80	88	96
4x4	13-1/3	16	18-2/3	21-1/3	24	26-2/3	29-1/3	32
4x6	20	24	28	32	36	40	44	48
4x8	26-2/3	32	37-1/3	42-2/3	48	53-1/3	58-2/3	64
4x10	33-1/3	40	46-2/3	53-1/3	60	66-2/3	73-1/3	80
4x12	40	48	56	64	72	80	88	96
4x14	46-2/3	56	65-1/3	74-2/3	84	93-1/3	102-2/3	112
6x6	30	36	42	48	54	60	66	72
6x8	40	48	56	64	72	80	88	96
6x10	50	60	70	80	90	100	110	120
6x12	60	72	84	96	108	120	132	144
6x14	70	84	98	112	126	140	154	168
6x16	80	96	112	128	144	160	176	192
8x8	53-1/3	64	74-2/3	85-1/3	96	106-2/3	117-1/3	128
8x10	66-2/3	80	93-1/3	106-2/3	120	133-1/3	146-2/3	160
8x12	80	96	112	128	144	160	176	192
8x14	93-1/3	112	130-2/3	149-1/3	168	186-2/3	203-1/2	224
10x10	83-1/3	100	116-2/3	133-1/3	150	166-2/3	183-1/3	200
10x12	100	120	140	160	180	200	220	240
10x14	116-2/3	140	163-1/3	186-2/3	210	233-1/3	256-2/3	280
10x16	133-1/3	160	186-2/3	213-1/3	240	266-2/3	293-1/3	320
12x12	120	144	168	192	216	240	264	288
12x14	140	168	196	224	251	280	308	336
12x16	160	192	224	256	288	320	352	384
14x14	163-1/3	196	228-2/3	261-1/3	294	326-2/3	359-1/3	392
14x16	186-2/3	224	261-1/3	298-2/3	336	373-1/3	410-2/3	448

Board Measurement

Lumber is measured in board feet. A board foot is a square foot of board one inch or less than one inch, thick. If no thickness is mentioned it is understood to be one inch. Each of the following diagrams represents a board foot of lumber.

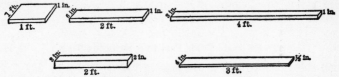

Various forms of a board foot of lumber

To find the number of board feet in a piece of lumber multiply the length in feet by the width in inches and the thickness in inches and divide by 12. Lumberyard practice, however, is as follows:

To find the board feet in a piece of timber one inch thick and

           4 in. wide, take ⅓ of the length
           6 in. wide, take ½ of the length
           8 in. wide, take ⅔ of the length
           9 in. wide, take ¾ of the length
         10 in. wide, take ⅚ of the length
         12 in. wide, take the length
         14 in. wide, add ⅙ to the length
         15 in. wide, add ¼ to the length

If the lumber is

        2 in. by 4 in. $(2 \times 4 = 8)$, take ⅔ of the length
        2 in. by 8 in. $(2 \times 8 = 16)$, take ⅓ of the length, etc.

To ascertain the board measure contents of a number of pieces of lumber of the same width and thickness and of various lengths, multiply the number of pieces of each length by their respective lengths and treat as one piece. For example, to find the number of feet in ten pieces of lumber 2 in. × 4 in. thick and 10 ft. long and ten pieces of the same width and thickness 12 ft. long and ten pieces of same width and thickness 16 ft. long, multiply the different lengths separately $(10 \times 10 = 100;$ $10 \times 12 = 120;$ $10 \times 16 = 160)$, add the results $(100 + 120 + 160 = 380)$. Since it is all 2 in. by 4 in., take two-thirds of the length. This will give 253 ft., which is the total board measure of the pieces of lumber in question.

Doubling any one dimension of a piece of lumber doubles its volume; doubling two dimensions makes the volume four times as much; doubling all three dimensions makes the volume eight times as much. Thus, a piece of lumber 1 in. thick × 2 in. wide, 12 ft. long contains 2 bd. ft. A piece of lumber 1 in. thick × 4 in. wide, 12 ft. long contains 4 bd. ft. A piece of lumber 1 in. thick × 4 in. wide, 24 ft. long contains 8 bd. ft. A piece of lumber 2 in. thick × 4 in. wide, 24 ft. long contains 16 bd. ft.

In practically all transactions in the United States lumber is stocked and sold at so much per thousand board feet.

Moldings, screening strips, splines, etc., are bought and sold by the linear foot. The unit is usually 100 linear feet.

To Estimate Cubic Feet in a Log

If the diameter of the log is the same all the way along, measure it in inches and then square it (*i.e.*, multiply it by itself). Multiply the result by .7854 and then multiply by the length of the log in feet. Divide by 144 and the result will be the number of cubic feet in the log. If the log is tapering, find the diameter at each end and divide by two to get the average diameter. Then proceed as above.

To Estimate Cubic Feet in a Standing Tree

Find the circumference of the tree in inches. Divide by 3.1416. This gives the diameter. From this point proceed as in estimating the cubic feet in any other log (see preceding paragraph).

TABLE SHOWING CUBICAL CONTENTS OF ROUND TIMBER

Length in feet	Diameter in inches															
	6	7	8	9	10	11	12	13	14	15	16	17	18	19	20	21
8	1.57	2.14	2.79	3.53	4	5	6	7	8	10	11	12	14	16	17	19
9	1.76	2.40	3.14	3.97	5	6	7	8	9	11	12	14	16	18	20	22
10	1.96	2.67	3.49	4.42	5	7	8	9	10	12	14	16	18	20	22	24
11	2.16	2.94	3.84	4.86	6	7	8	10	12	13	15	17	19	22	24	26
12	2.35	3.20	4.19	5.30	6	8	9	11	13	15	17	19	21	24	26	29
13	2.55	3.47	4.54	5.74	7	9	10	12	14	16	18	20	23	26	28	31
14	2.75	3.74	4.89	6.19	7	9	11	13	15	17	19	22	25	28	31	34
15	2.94	4.05	5.24	6.63	8	10	12	14	16	18	21	23	26	30	33	36
16	3.14	4.27	5.58	7.07	9	11	12	14	17	20	22	25	28	32	35	38
17	3.33	4.54	5.93	7.51	9	11	13	16	18	21	24	27	30	33	37	41
18	3.53	4.81	6.28	7.95	10	12	14	16	19	22	25	28	32	35	39	43
19	3.73	5.07	6.63	8.39	10	13	15	17	21	23	27	30	33	37	41	45
20	3.92	5.34	6.98	8.84	11	13	16	18	21	25	28	31	35	39	44	48

TABLE SHOWING CUBICAL CONTENTS OF ROUND TIMBER (*Cont.*)

Length in feet	Diameter in inches																
	22	23	24	25	26	27	28	29	30	31	32	33	34	35	36	37	38
8	21	23	25	27	29	32	34	37	39	42	45	48	50	53	57	60	62
9	24	26	28	31	33	36	38	41	44	47	50	53	57	60	64	67	70
10	26	29	31	34	37	40	43	46	49	52	56	59	63	67	71	75	79
11	29	32	35	37	41	43	47	50	53	57	61	65	69	73	77	82	86
12	32	34	38	41	44	47	51	55	58	62	67	71	76	80	85	90	94
13	34	37	41	44	48	51	56	60	63	68	72	77	82	87	92	97	102
14	37	40	44	48	52	55	60	64	68	73	78	83	88	94	99	105	110
15	40	43	47	51	55	59	64	69	73	78	84	89	95	100	106	112	118
16	42	46	50	55	59	63	68	73	78	83	89	95	101	107	113	119	126
17	45	49	53	58	63	68	73	78	83	89	95	101	107	114	121	127	135
18	48	52	57	61	66	72	77	82	88	94	100	106	114	120	128	134	142
19	50	55	60	65	70	75	81	87	93	99	106	112	120	127	135	142	151
20	53	58	63	68	74	79	85	91	98	105	112	118	126	134	142	149	159

Standard Dressed Sizes of Lumber

The standard yard board is $^{25}/_{32}$ in. thick; the standard industrial board is $^{26}/_{32}$ in. thick.

The standard yard dimension of 2-in. Stock not more than 12 in. wide shall have in finished sizes a thickness of 1⅝ in., whether it is surfaced on one side or both sides. The standard industrial dimension shall be 1¾ in. thick.

The finished widths of a finish surfaced on one or two edges shall be ⅜ in. off on standard lumber 3 in. wide; ½ in. off on standard lumber 4 to 7 in. wide; ¾ in. off on standard lumber 8 to 12 in. wide. The finished widths of boards and dimension, surfaced on one or two edges, shall be ⅜ in. off on lumber of standard widths less than 8 in., and ½ in. off on lumber of standard widths of 8 to 12 in.

The abbreviations S1S, S2S, S1E, S2E, mean surfaced (or dressed or planed) one side, surfaced two sides, surfaced one edge, and surfaced two edges respectively. S4S means surfaced on all four sides.

TABLES SHOWING THICKNESSES AND WIDTHS OF FINISHED LUMBER, S1S OR S2S AND OR S1E OR S2E

FINISH, COMMON BOARDS AND STRIPS, AND DIMENSION
(The thicknesses apply to all widths and the widths to all thicknesses)

Product	Size, board measure		Dressed dimensions at standard commercially dry shipping weight and moisture content		
	Thickness	Width	Standard thickness, yard	Standard thickness, industrial	Standard width
	Inches	Inches	Inches	Inches	Inches
Finish..............	...	3	5/16	...	2-5/8
	...	4	7/16	...	*3-1/2
	...	5	9/16	...	*4-1/2
	...	6	11/16	...	*5-1/2
	1	7	25/32	26/32	*6-1/2
	1-1/4	8	1-1/16	...	*7-1/4
	1-1/2	9	1-5/16	...	*8-1/4
	1-3/4	10	1-7/16	...	*9-1/4
	2	11	1-5/8	1-6/8	*10-1/4
	2-1/2	12	2-1/8	...	*11-1/4
	3	...	2-5/8	...	...
Common boards and strips	1	3	25/32	26/32	2-5/8
	1-1/4	4	1-1/16	...	3-5/8
	1-1/2	5	1-5/16	...	4-5/8
	...	6	...	...	5-5/8
	...	7	...	...	6-5/8
	...	8	...	...	7-1/2
	...	9	...	...	8-1/2
	...	10	...	...	9-1/2
	...	11	...	...	10-1/2
	...	12	...	...	11-1/2
Dimension	2	2	1-5/8	1-6/8	1-5/8
	2-1/2	4	2-1/8	...	3-5/8
	3	6	2-5/8	...	5-5/8
	4	8	3-5/8	...	7-1/2
	Over 4	10	Off 3/8	...	9-1/2
	...	12	...	...	11-1/2

*Based on kiln-dried lumber. Other figures were obtained by measuring the wood at standard commercially dry shipping weight, with moisture content allowed for each species.

SIDING, FLOORING, CEILING, PARTITION, SHIPLAP, AND DRESSED AND MATCHED
(The thicknesses apply to all widths and the widths to all thicknesses except as modified by the last footnote below)

Product	Size, board measure		Dressed dimensions at standard commercially dry shipping weight and moisture content	
	Thickness	Width	Standard thickness	Standard face width
Bevel siding	. . .	4	*7/16 by 3/16	3-1/2
	. . .	5	10/16 by 3/16	4-1/2
	. . .	6	. . .	5-1/2
Rustic and drop siding (shiplapped)	. . .	4	9/16	3-1/8
	. . .	5	3/4	4-1/8
	. . .	6	. . .	5-1/16
	. . .	8	. . .	6-7/8
Rustic and drop siding (dressed and matched)	. . .	4	9/16	3-1/4
	. . .	5	3/4	4-1/4
	. . .	6	. . .	5-3/16
	. . .	8	. . .	7
Flooring	. . .	2	5/16	1-1/2
	. . . .	3	7/16	2-3/8
	. . .	4	9/16	3-1/4
	1	5	25/32	4-1/4
	1-1/4	6	1-1/16	5-3/16
	1-1/2	. . .	1-5/16	. . .
Ceiling	. . .	3	5/16	2-3/8
	. . .	4	7/16	3-1/4
	. . .	5	9/16	4-1/4
	. . .	6	11/16	5-3/16
Partition	. . .	3	3/4	2-3/8
	. . .	4	. . .	3-1/4
	. . .	5	. . .	4-1/4
	. . .	6	. . .	5-3/16
Shiplap	1	4	25/32	3-1/8
	. . .	6	. . .	5-1/8
	. . .	8	. . .	7-1/8
	. . .	10	. . .	9-1/8
	. . .	12	. . .	11-1/8
Dressed and matched	1	4	25/32	3-1/4
	1-1/4	6	1-1/16	5-1/4
	1-1/2	8	1-5/16	7-1/4
	. . .	10	. . .	9-1/4
	. . .	12	. . .	11-1/4

*Minimum, 7/16.

In tongued and grooved Flooring and in tongued and grooved and shiplapped Ceiling 5/16″, 7/16″, and 9/16″ thick, board measure, the tongue or lap shall be 3/16″ wide, with the over-all widths 3/16 inch wider than the face widths shown above.

In all other patterned material, 11/16″, 3/4″, 1″, 1¼″, and 1½″ thick, board measure, the tongue shall be ¼″ wide in tongued-and-grooved lumber, and the lap 3/8″ wide in shiplapped lumber, with the over-all widths ¼″ and 3/8″ wider, respectively, than the face widths shown above.

The standard dimensions of rough lumber, commercially dry, shall be enough larger than the standard dimensions of finished lumber of the corresponding size to allow the surfacing of one or both sides and one or both edges to standard finishes.

FACTORY FLOORING, HEAVY ROOFING, DECKING, AND SHEET PILING

(The thicknesses apply to all widths and the widths to all thicknesses)

Size, Board Measure		Dressed dimensions at standard commercially dry shipping weight and moisture content			
					Standard Face Width Grooved[1] for Splines
Thick-ness	Width	Standard Thickness	D&M	Ship-lapped[1]	
Inches	Inches	Inches	Inches	Inches	Inches
2	4	1⅝	3⅛	3	3½
2½	6	2⅛	5⅛	5	5½
3	8	2⅝	7⅛	7	7½
4	10	3⅝	9⅛	9	9½
...	12	...	11⅛	11	11½

[1]In patterned material 2 in. thick and thicker, the tongue shall be ⅜ in. wide in tongue-and-grooved lumber and the lap ½ in. wide in shiplapped lumber, with the over-all widths ⅜ in. and ½ in. wider, respectively, than the face widths shown above.

Odd Lengths

With the following exceptions which are permissible in grades of building lumber, odd lengths of yard lumber and structural timbers are not considered in American Lumber Standards:

2 by 4 in., 6 and 8 in.—9 and 11 ft. long

2 by 8 in. and 10 in.—13 ft. long

2 by 10 in.—15 ft. long

8 by 8 in., 10 by 10 in., 10 by 12 in., 12 by 12 in., 14 by 14 in., 16 by 16 in., 18 by 18.—11 and 13 ft. long

6 by 16 in., 6 by 18 in., 8 by 16 in., 8 by 18 in.—15 and 17 ft. long

Structural Material

Structural material has three basic grades: dense select, select, and common. All grades shall be sound except where decay is specifically allowed.

According to its uses it is separated into the divisions indicated by the following tables:

Joist and Plank

Joists, Rafters, Scaffold Plank, Factory flooring, etc.

Nominal thicknesses: 2 to 4 in.

Nominal widths: 4 in. and wider

Standard thicknesses, S1S or S2S: ⅜ in. off

Extra standard thickness, 2 in., S1S or S2S: ¼ in. off

Standard widths, 4 to 7 in., S1E or S2E: ⅜ in. off; ⅜ in. and wider: S1E or S2E: ½ in. off

Standard lengths, multiples of 2 ft.

Beams and Stringers
Beams, Girders, Stringers, etc.

Nominal thicknesses: 5 in. and thicker
Nominal widths: 8 in. and wider
Standard lengths: Multiples of 2 ft.
S1S, S1E, S2S, or S4S: ½ in. off each way

Posts and Timbers
Posts, Caps, Sills, Timbers, etc.

Nominal sizes: 6 by 6 in. and larger
Standard lengths: Multiples of 2 ft.
S1S, S1E, S2S, or S4S: ½ in. off each way.

Softwood Factory and Shop Lumber

Softwood factory planks are graded from the poorer side, although both sides are taken into consideration.

The standard dressed thicknesses of such lumber are shown in the table below. All other thicknesses are special. The standard lengths are 6 ft. and over in multiples of 1 ft.

Size, board measure in inches	Finished thicknesses, S1S or S2S, at commercially dry shipping weight and moisture content	
	Standard	*Extra standard*
	Inches	*Inches*
1	$2\frac{5}{32}$	$2\frac{6}{32}$
1¼	$1\frac{5}{32}$	—
1½	$1\frac{13}{32}$	—
2	$1\frac{26}{32}$	—
2¼	$2\frac{1}{8}$	—
2½	$2\frac{3}{8}$	—
3	$2\frac{5}{8}$	—
4	$3\frac{5}{8}$	—

Note.—It is to be understood that any association which publishes and administers rules for factory lumber under the American Lumber Standards, will not be required to furnish 1-in. factory lumber in both the standard and extra-standard thicknesses.

There are two grades of cuttings in factory plank. No. 1 cuttings are free from defects on both sides. No. 2 cuttings shall admit any of the following defects:

Light blue stain on one side, not larger in extent than one-half the area of one side.
Medium brown kiln or heart stain covering half the surface on one face, or a greater area of lighter stain, or a proportionate amount on two sides.
A small, sound and tight knot which does not exceed ⅝ in. in diameter.
A small pitch pocket not over ⅛ in. wide nor over 1 in. long in Western pine and California pine.
One or more small season checks whose combined length does not exceed 8 in.
Light pitch or small pitch streaks that do not form a pronounced defect.
Slightly torn grain on one side.

Sizes of Cuttings

Stiles shall be 5 and 6 in. wide by 6 ft. 8 in. to 7 ft. 6 in. long. They may be either No. 1 or No. 2 in quality.

Bottom rails shall be 9 and 10 in. wide by 2 ft. 4 in. to 3 ft. long. They may be either No. 1 or No. 2 in quality.

Muntins shall be 5 and 6 in. wide by 3 ft. 6 in. to 4 ft. long. They may be either No. 1 or No. 2 in quality.

Top rails shall be 5 and 6 in. wide by 2 ft. 4 in. to 3 ft. long. They must be of No. 1 cutting quality, but shall be considered as No. 2 cuttings.

Sash cuttings shall be 2½ and 3½ in. in width by 28 in. and over in length.

Laths[1]

Wood laths may be of pine, spruce, Douglas fir, hemlock, or other soft woods. Many laths are made of metal, gypsum, or special composite materials. A good standard size is 1½ in. wide, ⅜ in. thick, and 4 ft. long. Dealers often estimate laths at the rate of two to each square foot. This gives plenty of margin for waste. A more accurate measurement is shown on the table below:

Wood Laths

Size of lath in.	Laths per square yard	Pounds of nails per 1,000
1 in. × 2⅔ ft.	26.0	9
1 × 2⅔	26.0	7
1 × 4	19.5	14
1 × 4	19.5	10
1⅛ × 4	19.0	14
1⅛ × 4	19.0	10
1½ × 4	14.5	14
1½ × 4	14.5	10
1⅝ × 4	14.4	14
1⅝ × 4	14.4	10

Clapboards

Clapboards are four feet long and are sold by the thousand. Laid four inches to the weather, one clapboard will cover 1⅓ square feet. Generally clapboards are laid over sheathing paper.

In estimating the number of clapboards needed, openings are, as a rule, disregarded unless they amount to 4 sq. ft. or more.

Roofing

The pitch or slant of a roof is determined by the angle of its rise. To determine it, divide the height at the highest point by the distance (measured horizontally) required to reach this height. Thus, if the height of the ridgepole is equal to ¼ of the distance from the edge of the roof to the center, the pitch of the roof is stated as being ¼ pitch. This

[1]See also section on Plastering, pages 408 and 409.

rule is for simple roofs only, and does not consider roofs containing two slopes before reaching their highest point. The diagram below shows how carpenters determine some of the more common pitches.

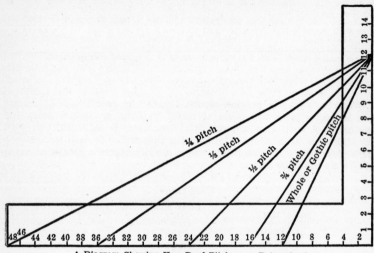

A Diagram Showing How Roof Pitches are Determined

The area of a roof may be found by getting the area on the level of the plates on which the rafters rest. Then, for the different pitches adding the following percentages:

One-fourth pitch, add to area on square	12 per cent
One-third pitch, add to area on square	20 per cent
One-half pitch, add to area on square	42 per cent
Three-eighths pitch, add to area on square	25 per cent
Five-eighths pitch, add to area on square	60 per cent
Three-fourths pitch, add to area on square	80 per cent

Cornice projections must be added to the above dimensions.

The length of the *rafters* for the various pitches can be found as follows:

Pitch	Rafter Length W ×	L ×	Pitch	Rafter Length W ×	L ×
¼	0.56	1.12	½	0.71	1.42
⅓	0.60	1.20	⅝	0.80	1.60
⅜	0.63	1.25	¾	0.90	1.80

W = Width of building over plates,
or, if rafters extend into
cornice, over cornice.
L = ½ of W.

The rise in inches per foot for the various pitches is as follows:

¼	6
⅓	8
⅜	9
½	12
⅝	15
¾	18

Roofing is generally estimated in units of 100 sq. ft. The materials most frequently employed are shingles, slate, tin, tarred paper, gypsum, etc. Many city building ordinances demand the use of fireproof material.

Shingles are sold by the thousand or by the bundle. The standard bundle contains 250 shingles and bundles are not divided. Ordinary shingles are 16 in. long and have an average width of 4 in. They are laid with 4 in., 4½ in., 5 in., or 5½ in. exposed to the weather. The amount exposed depends upon the pitch of the roof; the steeper the pitch, the greater the amount of shingle exposed. The following table shows the usual estimate per 100 sq. ft:

Length (in Inches) of Shingle Exposed to the Weather	Number of Shingles per 100 Sq. Ft.	Pounds of Nails Required
4	1000	4
4½	900	3.9
5	800	3.5
5½	700	3.3

There are a great many other sizes of shingles. Manufacturers will be glad to furnish information as to the number needed with various exposures. Manufacturers of slate and other special roofings will also be glad to furnish specifications.

In estimating shingles openings are disregarded, as a rule, unless they amount to 4 sq. ft. or more in which case they are subtracted.

Red Cedar Shingles[1]

Preparation of Shingles.—If shingles are not to be stained, wet thoroughly with water before applying. If stain is to be used, dip, when thoroughly dry, two-thirds of their length in stain and dry in a loose pile. Do not soak shingles in stain. To secure very uniform color, give brush coat after laying, as a second coat. Do not use cheap stains, especially those mixed with kerosene or benzene.

Shingle Nails.—Do not use an ungalvanized nail. A hot-dipped, zinc-coated, cut iron nail or a hot-dipped, zinc-coated, copper-bearing steel wire nail is preferable, as such nails are covered with a 6 per cent to 10 per cent coating of pure zinc and in themselves are remarkably resistant to rust.

---

[1] By courtesy of the Red Cedar Shingle Bureau, Chicago, Ill.

Insist on carpenters using either of these nails, as they will double the life of your shingle roof. Pure copper or pure zinc nails are excellent, but expensive. For shingles measuring 5 butts to 2 in. or thinner, use 3d nails. For thicker shingles use 3½d or 4d nails.

Metal Work.—Use old style I. C. C. hand-dipped and heavily coated tin in flashing around chimneys. For ridge roll and valleys use either copper or at least 20-gauge heavily galvanized iron, or 14-in. best quality old-style tin, heavily coated.

Laying Shingles.—Starting at eaves, lay first course, two-ply, allowing 1¼ in. projection over crown mould and 1 in. projection at gables; 16-in. shingles that measure 5 butts to 2 in. or thicker should be laid 4½ in. or 5 in. to the weather; 18-in. shingles should be laid 5½ in. to the weather; 24-in. shingles should be laid 7½ in. to the weather. All shingles should be spaced at least ⅛ in. apart.

Break all joints 1⅛ in. (side lap), seeing that no break comes directly over another on any three consecutive courses. This covers all nails and is extremely essential for a serviceable roof.

Use a straight edge to insure straight courses. Nail 16-in. shingles 6 in. or 6½ in. from butt; 18-in. shingles 7 in. from butt, and 24-in. shingles 9 in. from butt. Nail ⅝ in. to ¾ in. from sides, with only two nails in each shingle. Do not drive nail heads into shingles.

Flooring

To estimate the amount of regular tongue-and-groove flooring, needed 2¼ face, add one-third of the total number of square feet in the room. For example, if a room is 10 ft. wide by 12 ft. long, it contains 120 sq. ft. To get the amount of flooring needed, add one-third, which is 40. You will, therefore, need 160 sq. ft. to cover the entire room.

For wider flooring add about one-fourth to the total number of square feet in the room.

On underflooring add one-fourth. Different widths change this figure a little but it is practically right for any underflooring.

In laying diagonal underflooring, add one-fourth for squared-edged flooring, one-third for matched flooring.

The final flooring should be laid as late as possible in building operations to avoid damage.

Quantity of Flooring and Nails Needed to Cover 100 Square Feet

Hardwood Floors

Thick-ness	Face		Board Feet	Nails. (pounds)
⅝	1½	....	145	1.2
1³⁄₁₆	2¼	....	134	3.3

Pine Floors

Thickness	Face		Board Feet	Nails (pounds)
$1\frac{3}{16}$	$2\frac{1}{4}$	....	134	4.3
$1\frac{5}{16}$	$3\frac{1}{4}$	....	128	3.4
$1\frac{3}{16}$	$5\frac{1}{4}$	....	120	2.2
$1\frac{1}{16}$	$2\frac{1}{4}$	....	168	6.8
$1\frac{1}{16}$	$3\frac{1}{4}$	....	160	5.3
$1\frac{1}{16}$	$5\frac{1}{4}$	....	150	3.5
$1\frac{5}{16}$	$2\frac{1}{4}$	....	200	10.0
$1\frac{5}{16}$	$3\frac{1}{4}$	....	180	7.7
$1\frac{5}{16}$	$5\frac{1}{4}$	....	180	4.9
$1\frac{5}{8}$	$5\frac{1}{8}$	....	246	8.9
$2\frac{5}{8}$	$5\frac{1}{8}$	....	369	18.4

Subfloors

Thickness of Subfloors		Stock Sizes	Board Feet	Nails (pounds)
1″		1×6	120	3.0
		1×8	114	2.3
		1×10	113	2.7
		1×12	112	4.5
2″		2×6	240	...
		2×8	228	...
3″		3×6	360	...
		3×8	342	...

Plywood

Plywood is the name given to boards made up of plies or thin veneers of wood cemented or glued together with the grain of each layer placed at right angles to the layer on either side of it. It has numerous advantages in comparison with solid timber, including lightness combined with strength, and great width without a joint, as much as 2½ yd. in width being possible. Plywood is much less likely to warp or split than solid wood. It is used in making furniture, paneling walls, making boxes, chair seats, etc.

Preserving Lumber

Lumber can be preserved by treating it with coal-tar creosote or zinc chloride. The pressure treatment should be used but this demands fairly elaborate equipment, and where facilities are not available spraying, brushing, or dipping must be resorted to.

One gallon of creosote oil will give two coats to every 100 sq. ft. of lumber unless there are defects which make the surface absorb a larger amount than this. This creosote oil makes an excellent paint for farm buildings, fences, etc., since in addition to giving them an attractive brown color it greatly increases their resistance to decay.

For the treatment of lumber a 2 per cent to a 5 per cent solution of zinc chloride is used. The lumber is steeped in this solution, one day for each inch of thickness and an extra day for luck at the end.

NAILS

Approximate number to a pound of various kinds and sizes

Common Nails and Brads

Size	Length and Gauge	Approx. Number to Pound
2d	1 inch No. 15	876
3d	1¼ inch No. 14	568
4d	1½ inch No. 12½	316
5d	1¾ inch No. 12½	271
6d	2 inch No. 11½	181
7d	2¼ inch No. 11½	161
8d	2½ inch No. 10¼	106
9d	2¾ inch No. 10¼	96
10d	3 inch No. 9	69
12d	3¼ inch No. 9	63
16d	3½ inch No. 8	49
20d	4 inch No. 6	31
30d	4½ inch No. 5	24
40d	5 inch No. 4	18
50d	5½ inch No. 3	14
60d	6 inch No. 2	11

Shingle Nails

Size	Length and Gauge	Approx. Number to Pound
3d	1¼ inch No. 13	429
3½d	1⅜ inch No. 12	345
4d	1½ inch No. 12	274
5d	1¾ inch No. 12	235
6d	2 inch No. 12	204

Fence Staples

Made of No. 9 wire

Length	Number to Pound	Length	Number to Pound
¾	132	1¼	87
⅞	120	1½	72
1	108	1¾	65
1⅛	96	2	58

JOINTS

Lapped Joint

A lapped joint is one formed when one beam overlaps another.

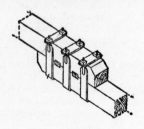

Fished Joint

A fished joint is formed when two beams meet end to end. The cover plates are called fish plates.

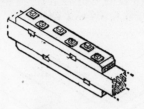

Scarfed Joint

A scarfed joint is made by cutting away two pieces of wood to make them fit into each other. Scarfed joints are secured by bolting, nailing, riveting, etc. Wedges are often used to tighten up the joint.

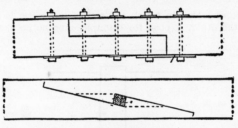

Keyed Joint

Keys are pieces of hard wood which are used either to join two pieces of wood together or to keep them from sliding over each other.

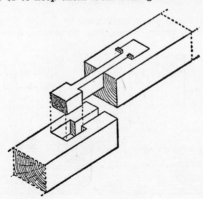

Halved Joint

In making a halved joint the two pieces of timber are cut to half the depth and secured with bolts, nails, screws, or wooden pegs. This is one of the simplest and most useful of joints.

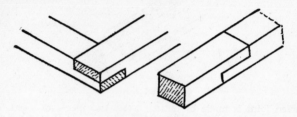

Housed Joint

A housed joint is one in which the end of one piece is let down into the body of the other. A post, for example, may be housed in a bottom cross rail, etc.

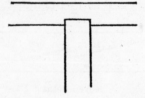

Mortise and Tenon Joint

A mortise and tenon joint is formed by fitting a projection from a piece of wood, *i.e.*, a tenon, into a hole in another piece of wood called a mortise.

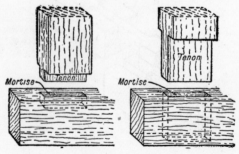

Dovetail joints are forms of mortise and tenon joints, so called because the tenon flares like a dove's tail.

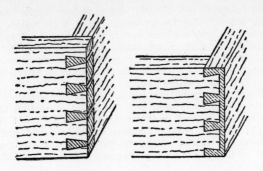

Miter Joint

A miter joint is formed by the junction of two similar blocks or moldings, the meeting ends of which are equally beveled. The illustrations will make this clearer:

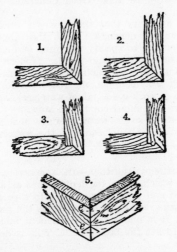

Miter. 1. Common form. **2.** Miter where wooden members are of different widths. **3.** Greek miter. **4.** Tongued miter. **5.** Keyed miter, *i.e.*, wooden keys glued and driven into the saw cuts at an angle.

CONCRETE

Concrete is a compound of sand and gravel or crushed stone bound together by cement, the whole being mixed with water. *Reinforced concrete* is like ordinary concrete except that metal is embedded in it to make it capable of taking tensile loads. *Prestressed concrete* is concrete which is subjected to an initial precompression by any of several means to such an extent that the member itself will not be forced into tension regardless of the forces acting upon it.

Various types of cement are manufactured for use in construction work, the most commonly used being portland cement. Before the invention of portland cement in 1824 the adhesive agent was lime mortar of one kind or another. Portland cement comes in barrels and bags. One barrel of portland cement weighs 376 lb. net and is the equivalent of four bags of 94 lb. each. This material should not be allowed to rest on the ground.

All cement work uses the same materials but proportions vary. The proportions are expressed thus: 1:2:4, which means 1 part of the cement to 2 parts of sand and 4 parts of gravel. The materials are always listed in the same order.

How to Make Good Concrete[1]

Until the recent discovery that the strength, durability, and water-tightness of concrete are dependent upon the proportion of water to cement it was customary to specify mixtures as one part cement to a certain number of parts of sand and pebbles. Modern practice is to state the amount of mixing water for each sack of cement, varying according to the class of work. For example, the recommended mixture for sidewalks and that class of work is 4¼ gal. of water per sack of cement, when sand and pebbles are in a moist condition. Moisture in the aggregates is free to act on the cement, so less water is added in this case than if these were absolutely dry. Had these been dry, the correct amount of water would be 5½ gal. for each one-sack batch.

Cement Binds Particles Together.—In a concrete mix, cement and water form a paste which, upon hardening, acts as a binder cementing the particles of sand and pebbles together into a permanent mass. The use of too much mixing water thins or dilutes the paste, weakening its cementing qualities. It is important that cement and water be used in proper proportions to get the best results. This is dependent upon the work.

The accompanying tables give recommended quantities of water for different classes of work and also suggest proportions of cement to sand

---

[1]By permission of the Portland Cement Association.

and pebbles to use in trial batches. The trial batch for sidewalks is 1 part cement to 2 parts sand and 3 parts pebbles (1:2:3 mix). It may be necessary to change the amounts of sand and pebbles as will be described to obtain a smooth, plastic, workable mix. Under no conditions vary the amount of water from the quantity shown.

RECOMMENDED MIXTURES FOR SEVERAL CLASSES OF CONSTRUCTION

Intended primarily for use on small jobs

Kind of Work	Gallons of Water to Add to Each One Sack Batch			Trial Mixture For First Batch			Maximum aggregate size
	Dry sand and pebbles	Moist sand and pebbles	Wet sand and pebbles	Cement	Sand	Pebbles	
				Sacks	Cu. ft.	Cu. ft.	In.
Foundation walls which need not be watertight, mass concrete for footings, retaining walls, garden walls, etc.	7-1/2	6	5	1	3	5	2
Watertight basement walls and pits, walls above grounds, dams, lawn rollers, hand tamper, shoe scrape, hotbeds, cold frames, storage and cyclone cellar walls, etc.	6-1/2	5	4-1/4	1	2-1/2	3-1/2	1-1/2
Water storage tanks, well curbs and platforms, cisterns, septic tanks, watertight floors, sidewalks, stepping stone and flagstone walks, driveways, porch floors, basement floors, garden and lawn pools, steps, corner posts, gate posts, piers, columns, chimney caps, concrete for tree surgery, etc.	5-1/2	4-1/4	3-3/4	1	2	3	1
Fence posts, clothes-line posts, grape-arbor posts, mailbox posts, etc., flower boxes and pots, benches, bird baths, sundials, pedestals and other garden furniture, work of very thin sections.	4-1/2	3-3/4	3-1/2	1	2	2	3/4

The trial proportion (1:2:3) suggested for sidewalks may result in a mixture that is too stiff, too wet, or which lacks smoothness and workability. This is remedied by changing slightly the proportions of sand and pebbles, *not the water*. If the mix is too wet, add sand and pebbles slowly until the right degree of wetness is obtained. If the mix is too stiff cut down the amounts of sand and pebbles in the next batch. In this way the best proportions for any job may be determined.

How to Obtain Workable Mixture.—A workable mixture is one of such wetness and plasticity that it can be placed in the forms readily, and that with spading and tamping will result in a dense concrete. There should be enough cement-sand mortar to give good smooth surfaces free from rough spots, and to bind pieces of coarse aggregate into the mass so they will not separate out in handling. In other words the cement-sand mortar should completely fill the spaces between the pebbles and insure a smooth plastic mix. Mixtures lacking sufficient mortar will be hard to work and difficult to finish. Too much sand increases porosity and cuts down the amount of concrete obtainable from a sack of cement.

A workable mix for one type of work may be too stiff for another. Concrete that is to be deposited in thin sections like fence posts must be more plastic than for more massive construction such as walls. A good rule to follow is to proportion the sand and pebbles to obtain the greatest volume of concrete of correct plasticity for the work to be done.

Aggregates.—Sand and pebbles or crushed rock are usually spoken of as "aggregate." Sand is called "fine aggregate" and pebbles or crushed stone "coarse aggregate." Fine aggregates such as rock screenings include all particles from very fine (exclusive of dust) up to those which will pass through a screen having meshes ¼ in. sq. Coarse aggregate includes all pebbles or broken stone ranging from ¼ in. up to 1½ or 2 in. In thin walls of slabs the largest pieces of aggregate should never exceed one-third the thickness of the thinnest section. Maximum sizes of aggregate for different classes of work are shown in the table.

Sand should be clean and hard, free from fine dust, loam and clay, and vegetable matter. These foreign materials prevent bond between the cement and sand thereby reducing the strength of the concrete. Concrete made with dirty sand hardens very slowly and often will not harden sufficiently to be used for its intended purpose.

Sand should be well graded, the particles should be not all fine nor all coarse, but should vary in size from fine up to that which will just pass through a ¼-in. mesh screen. If the sand is well graded the finer particles help to fill the spaces between the larger ones.

Pebbles or crushed stone should be tough, fairly hard, and free from foreign matter. Stone containing considerable soft, flat, or elongated particles should not be used.

Bank-Run Gravel.—Bank-run gravel is the natural mixture of sand and pebbles taken from a gravel bank. In this material fine and coarse aggregates are seldom present in proper proportions, usually containing too much sand. Money can be saved by screening out the sand and recombining in proportions according to the class of work.

Water.—Water used in mixing concrete should be clean, free from oil, alkali, and acid. In general, water that is fit to drink is good for concrete.

Measuring Materials.—All materials, including water, should be accurately measured. A pail marked on the inside at different heights to indicate quarts and gallons will be found handy for measuring water. A pail may also be used for measuring cement, sand, and pebbles. In mixing one-

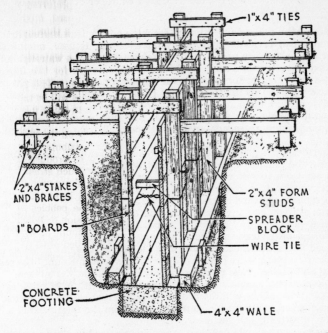

1"x 4" TIES

2"x 4" FORM STUDS

SPREADER BLOCK

WIRE TIE

2"x 4" STAKES AND BRACES

1" BOARDS

CONCRETE FOOTING

4"x 4" WALE

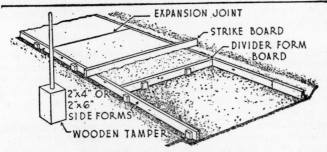

EXPANSION JOINT

STRIKE BOARD

DIVIDER FORM BOARD

2"x 4" OR 2"x 6" SIDE FORMS

WOODEN TAMPER

TOP: Forms for a concrete foundation
BELOW: Sidewalk construction
By the Portland Cement Association

sack batches it is not necessary to measure cement, as one sack holds exactly 1 cu. ft. Sand and pebbles are then most conveniently measured in bottomless boxes made to hold 1 cu. ft., 2 cu. ft., or other volumes desired.

Mixing the Concrete.—Although machine mixing is preferred, first-class concrete can be mixed by hand. Whichever way is used, mixing should continue until every pebble is completely coated with a thoroughly mixed mortar of cement and sand.

If a tight floor is not available for mixing concrete a watertight mixing platform should be made. It should be large enough for two men using shovels to work upon at one time. A good size is 7 × 12 ft. This platform is preferably made of matched lumber so that the joints will be tight. Strips are nailed along three sides to prevent materials from being pushed off in mixing.

The measured quantity of sand is spread out evenly on the platform and on this the required amount of cement is evenly distributed. The cement and sand are turned with square pointed shovels to produce a mass of uniform color, free from streaks of brown and gray. Such streaks indicate that cement and sand are not thoroughly mixed. The required amount of coarse aggregate is then measured and spread in a layer on top of the cement-sand mixture. Mixing is continued until the pebbles have been uniformly distributed throughout the mass. A depression or hollow is then formed in the middle of the pile and the correct amount of water added while the materials are turned. This mixing is continued until the cement, sand, and pebbles have been thoroughly and uniformly combined.

The concrete should be placed in the forms within 30 minutes after mixing. It should be well tamped or spaded as it goes into the forms. This operation forces the coarse aggregate back from the face, making a dense concrete with smooth surfaces.

Extreme care should be taken to avoid excessive handling or working of concrete once it is placed in the form. Such "puddling" causes water in the mix to rise to the surface, thus resulting in a weakened material.

Curing.—Do not permit the newly placed concrete to dry out. Protect it from the sun or drying winds for a week or ten days, otherwise the water necessary for proper hardening will evaporate, resulting in loss of strength. Floors, walks, and similar surfaces can be protected by covering with earth or straw kept moist by occasional sprinkling as soon as the concrete has hardened sufficiently so that it will not be injured.

Walls and other sections which cannot be conveniently covered by this method can be protected by hanging moist canvas or burlap over them and wetting down the work frequently for ten days or so after placing. In cold weather work should be protected but need not be kept moist.

Reinforcement.—Reinforcement is the term used to describe the steel rods or mesh that are placed in the concrete to increase its strength where subjected to forces tending to bend or pull it apart. Care should be taken to place the reinforcement in correct position and in the part of the concrete mass where it will be most effective.

HOW TO FIGURE QUANTITIES

Quantities of Cement, Fine Aggregate and Coarse Aggregate Required for One Cubic Yard of Compact Mortar or Concrete

Mixtures			Quantities of Materials				
			Cement in sacks	Fine aggregate		Coarse aggregate	
Cement	F. A. (Sand)	C. A. (Gravel or stone)		Cu. Ft.	Cu. Yd.	Cu. Ft.	Cu. Yd.
1	1.5	....	15.5	23.2	0.86	.....	.....
1	2.0	....	12.8	25.6	0.95	.....	.....
1	2.5	....	11.0	27.5	1.02	.....	.....
1	3.0	....	9.6	28.8	1.07	.....	.....
1	1.5	3	7.6	11.4	0.42	22.8	0.85
1	2.0	2	8.3	16.6	0.61	16.6	0.61
1	2.0	3	7.0	14.0	0.52	21.0	0.78
1	2.0	4	6.0	12.0	0.44	24.0	0.89
1	2.5	3.5	5.9	14.7	0.54	20.6	0.76
1	2.5	4	5.6	14.0	0:52	22.4	0.83
1	2.5	5	5.0	12.5	0,46	25.0	0.92
1	3.0	5	4.6	13.8	0.51	23.0	0.85

1 sack cement = 1 cu. ft.; 4 sacks = 1 bbl. Based on tables in "Concrete, Plain and Reinforced," by Taylor and Thompson.
C. = Cement in sacks
F.A. = Fine aggregate (sand) in cu. ft.
C.A. = Coarse aggregate (pebbles or broken stone) in cu. ft.
(Quantities may vary 10 per cent either way depending upon character of aggregate used. No allowance made in table for waste.)

Materials Required for 100 sq. ft. of Surface for Varying Thicknesses of Concrete or Mortar

Pro-portion	1:1-1/2			1:2			1:2-1/2			1:3		
Thickness in inches	C.	F.A.	C.A.	C.	F.A.	C.A.	C.	F.A.	C.A.	C.	F.A.	C.A.
3/8	1.8	2.7		1.5	3.0		1.3	3.2		1.1	3.4	
1/2	2.4	3.6		2.0	4.0		1.7	4.3		1.5	4.4	
3/4	3.6	5.4		3.0	6.0		2.5	6.3		2.2	6.8	
1	4.8	7.2		4.0	7.9		3.4	8.4		3.0	8.9	
1-1/4	6.0	9.0		4.9	9.9		4.2	10.5		3.7	11.1	
1-1/2	7.2	10.8		5.9	11.9		5.1	12.7		4.4	13.3	
1-3/4	8.4	12.6		6.9	13.9		5.9	14.7		5.2	15.7	
2	9.6	14.4		7.9	15.8		6.8	16.9		5.9	17.7	

	1:2:2			1:2:3			1:2-1/2:3-1/2			1:3:5		
3	7.7	15.4	15.4	6.5	13.0	19.3	5.5	13.6	19.1	4.3	12.8	21.3
4	10.2	20.4	20.4	8.6	17.2	25.8	7.3	18.1	25.4	5.7	17.0	28.4
5	12.8	25.6	25.6	10.8	21.6	32.2	9.1	22.6	31.8	7.1	21.3	35.5
6	15.4	30.7	30.7	12.9	25.8	38.6	10.9	27.2	38.2	8.5	25.6	42.6
8	20.6	41.0	41.0	17.2	34.4	21.6	14.6	36.4	51.0	11.4	34.1	57.0
10	25.6	51.2	51.2	21.5	43.2	64.4	18.2	45.3	63.5	14.2	42.5	71.0
12	30.7	61.4	61.4	25.8	51.6	77.2	21.8	54.5	76.3	17.0	51.1	85.1

Condensed Specifications for Sidewalks[1]

One-Course Sidewalks

Cement. Shall meet the requirements of the Standard Specifications of the American Society for Testing Materials (Serial Designation C150–49).

Fine Aggregate. Shall consist of natural sand or screenings from hard, tough, crushed rock, gravel, or slag. Must be clean and well graded. All fine aggregate shall pass a ¼-in. screen and 95 per cent shall be retained on a 100-mesh screen.

Coarse Aggregate. May be pebbles, broken stone, or blast-furnace slag. Must be clean, hard, durable, and uncoated. All coarse aggregate shall pass a 1-in. screen and 95 per cent shall be retained on a ¼-in. screen.

Water. Shall be clean enough to drink.

Joint Filler. Shall be premolded strips of bitumen-filled fiber or mineral aggregate, ½-in. thick, as wide as the thickness of the sidewalk, and at least 2 ft. long.

Forms. Shall be of lumber 2 in. thick or of steel of equal strength. Flexible strips may be used on curves. They shall be rigidly held to line and grade by stakes or braces.

Division Plates. Shall be of ⅛-in. steel as wide as the depth of the slab and as long as the width of the walk.

Subgrade. Shall be well drained and compacted to a firm surface with a uniform bearing power.

Drains. Where necessary, 4-in. concrete tile drains shall be laid to protect the walk from damage by frost action.

Sub-base. On poorly drained soil, where drains are impracticable, a 5-in. sub-base of cinders, gravel, or other porous material shall be constructed. It shall be thoroughly tamped and drained into the street gutter.

Thickness and Proportions. The walk shall never be less than 5 in. thick. Concrete shall be mixed in the approximate proportions of 1 part cement, 2 parts fine aggregate, and 3 parts of coarse aggregate with a maximum of 6¼ gal. of water per sack of cement, including the moisture in the aggregates.

Concrete. Shall be mixed until each particle of fine aggregate is coated with cement and each particle of coarse aggregate is coated with mortar, and not less than one minute.

Placing and Finishing. Concrete shall be placed immediately after mixing. It shall be tamped and struck off with a template and shall be floated with a wood float until the surface has a true contour. Care shall be taken to not bring to the surface an excess of water and fine sand by overfinishing.

Jointing. The walk shall be cut into separate rectangular slabs not greater than 6 ft. on any one side. The surface edges of each slab shall be rounded to a ¼-in. radius. Markings shall be exactly at cuts between slabs.

Expansion Joints. Shall extend from the surface to the subgrade and shall be at right angles to the sidewalk surface, and completely filled with compressible material. A ½-in. expansion joint shall be made across the walk at approximately 50-ft. intervals. At all places where the walk intersects a curb line or another walk, 1-in. expansion joints shall be made.

Curing. Finished concrete shall be kept wet for seven days.

Two-Course Sidewalks[2]

(Same as specifications for one-course sidewalks, except the following paragraphs which should be substituted for those of corresponding headings in One-Course Sidewalk Specifications.)

Thickness and Proportions. Two-course walks shall never be less than 5 in. thick. They shall consist of a base 4¼ in. thick, composed of concrete in the approximate proportions of 1 part cement, 2½ parts fine aggregate, 4 parts coarse aggregate, and a maximum of 6¼ gal. of water per sack of cement; and a top coat ¾ in. thick, composed of mortar in the proportions of 1 part cement and 2 parts fine aggregate.

Placing and Finishing. The base shall be thoroughly compacted by tamping and shall

---

[1] By the Portland Cement Association.
[2] One-course walks are recommended.

be struck off with a template which shall leave it ¾-in. below the finished surface. The top coat shall be placed within 45 minutes after the base course is laid. It shall be struck off and finished with a wood float until the surface has a true contour.

Forms and Curing

A great deal of concrete must be set in *forms*. It is economy to buy new wood for forms, since nail holes, etc., in old wood must be closed up to prevent imperfections in the concrete. White pine and spruce, being light and strong, are excellent for forms. One-inch slabs are used for small jobs; for beam sides, etc., 2-in. slabs are used. The wood must be dressed on one side and the edges; it is better to have it dressed all around. Forms should be simply made so that they can be used again. Most of them are put together with cleats. Forms should be thoroughly cleaned and oiled before the concrete is placed, to keep the concrete from sticking to the wood and to keep the wood from warping under the influence of the water from the concrete. Forms are also made of metal. At the present time, several commercial makes of prefabricated forms (wood, metal, and combinations of wood and metal) are available.

Newly placed concrete should be protected until it has thoroughly hardened. The water in the mixture begins a slow chemical action, and if the mixture is exposed to the sun this water, so necessary for the proper hardening of the concrete, will evaporate. The concrete, especially if the surface is large, should, therefore, be protected by moist sand, canvas, etc., which should be placed as soon as the mixture has hardened sufficiently to prevent surface injury. In cold weather the materials should be heated to begin with and the finished work should be protected from frost.

Bonding, in the event that there are more courses than one, can be done with a heavy wire brush if the forms are removed as soon as the concrete can bear its own weight. Otherwise a sharp instrument must be used.

Forms should never be removed until the concrete has hardened enough to resist whatever pressure may immediately be brought to bear upon it. Records should be kept of the dates of pouring and removing forms. The following table, taken from the Engineering Regulations of the Building Code of the District of Columbia, shows the length of time which the work should remain undisturbed:[1]

	No. of Days	
	April 1 to Nov. 1	Nov. 1 to April 1
For slabs less than 3-ft. span	3	6
For slabs more than 3 ft. and less than 8 ft.	7	10
For slabs more than 8 ft. and less than 15 ft.	12	15
For slabs more than 15 ft. and all 15 beams	15	21
For columns and walls	3	12

Concrete expands and contracts with heat and cold at practically the same rate at which steel expands and contracts, thus making it possible to

[1]Table applies to the District of Columbia only. Generally, the length of time depends upon climatic and weather conditions.

combine the two materials. Concrete is a poor conductor of heat; steel is an excellent one. Steel at high temperatures softens; this is why a casing of concrete is placed around nearly all structural steel.

Reinforced concrete is one of the most adaptable of all building materials. Concrete has great resistance to compression; steel has great tensile strength. This, combined with the equal rate of expansion and contraction of the two materials, the plasticity of the mixture, and its great lasting qualities make this a building material almost without equal.

PORTLAND CEMENT STUCCO CONDENSED SPECIFICATIONS[1]

GENERAL

Preparation of Surface

All hangers, fasteners, trim, or other fixed supports or projections of any kind shall be in place previous to the application of stucco. In masonry backing the surface shall be cleaned thoroughly before stucco is applied and shall be sufficiently rough to provide a good mechanical bond for the first coat.

Flashing

Flashing shall be in place previous to the application of stucco in the following locations: at the top and along sides of all openings wherever projecting trim occurs; across the wall and under coping, cornices, or brick sills with mortar joints, flashing to project beyond upper edge of stucco; under built-in gutters and around roof openings; at the intersection of walls and roofs; and at all other points where flashing would prevent water from getting behind the stucco.

Water Protection

All horizontal exposed surfaces, which are of stucco, such as copings, cornices, belt courses, shall be given sufficient fall to prevent water from accumulating on such surfaces. In general, the construction shall protect the surface against excessive concentrated water flow, all horizontal projections being provided with overhanging drips and watertight joints. Stucco wall surfaces shall be stopped 6 in. above grade line.

MATERIALS

Cement

Portland cement shall conform to the current standard specifications of the American Society for Testing Materials.

---

[1] By courtesy of the Portland Cement Association.

Fine Aggregate

Fine aggregate shall consist of clean sand, screenings from crushed stone or pebbles, graded from fine to coarse, passing when dry a No. 4 screen, with not more than 20 per cent through a No. 50 screen, free from dust or other deleterious materials.

Water

Water shall be clean, free from oil, acid, strong alkali, or vegetable matter.

Coloring Materials

Only permanent mineral oxides that are fully guaranteed by the manufacturer to be unaffected by lime, cement, or weathering shall be used in coloring.

Hydrated Lime

Hydrated lime shall meet the requirements of the standard specifications of the American Society for Testing Materials and when used shall not exceed one-fifth the volume of the cement.

Reinforcement

The principle to be followed is to create a continuous metal-mesh reinforcement over the entire surface to be stuccoed, and to have this of a character similar to the reinforcing system of reinforced concrete. To meet such a requirement demands that the reinforcement have large enough openings to allow the mortar to fill the space back of the mesh reinforcement completely.

Metal lath if used as a reinforcement (without back-plastering) should have as large mesh openings as possible, be furred out ¼ in. from sheathing, and weigh not less than 3.4 lb. per sq. yd. Special care must be used to encase the lath completely by pushing the mortar through so that the mortar is "keyed" over the lath. Unless this is done the purpose of having the lath act strictly as a reinforcement is defeated.

CONSTRUCTION

Proportions

Mortar for all coats shall be mixed in the proportions of 1 part by volume of portland cement to not less than 3 nor more than 5 parts by volume of damp, loose, aggregate. Hydrated lime may be added up to 25 per cent by volume of the portland cement. The final coat should be similarly mixed, except that the color of the cement should be selected and any desired coloring matter added.

Mixing

Ingredients shall be thoroughly mixed before water is added. It is positively essential that a definite system be used which will produce uniform mixes for all coats. The quantity of water shall be determined by trial and thereafter used in the proper proportions. The use of a machine mixer is advocated for uniformity of mixing if the work is of sufficient size to warrant its use. Ordinarily a mortar box will suffice.

Framing

Spacing of studs shall not exceed 16 in. Studding shall run from foundation to rafters without intervening horizontal members, tied together below 2nd-floor joists with 1×4-in. boards let into the inner faces of the studs. In open construction without sheathing the spacing of studs shall not exceed 12 in. The corners of all walls shall be braced diagonally to secure the necessary rigidity of the structure. Bridging of studding with 2×4-in. braces shall occur at least once in each story height.

Sheathing

Sheathing boards shall not be less than 6 in., nor more than 8 in. wide, dressed to a uniform thickness, laid horizontally, and fastened securely to each stud. Over the sheathing shall be laid, horizontally, beginning at the bottom, any standard asphalt-saturated roofing felt weighing 15 lb. per square, the bottom layer lapping the baseboard and each strip lapping the strip below and all flashing at least 2 in.

Application of Reinforcement

Reinforcement shall be placed horizontally and fastened with approved furring devices not more than 8 in. apart over the surface. Vertical laps shall occur at supports. The sheets shall be returned around corners at least 6 in. for sheathed construction and 16 in. for open construction. Corner beads shall not be used.

Furring

All reinforcement shall be furred out from the studs, sheathing, or base ¼ in. by any device which will not reduce the effective section of the scratch coat.

Half-Timbering

Embedded trim or half-timbering shall be securely nailed directly upon sheathing or studs, and shall have the inside corners of vertical members grooved into which the mortar of the first coat shall be forced, forming a watertight joint. All joints on horizontal members shall be flashed.

Masonry Walls

Concrete, concrete block, brick, hollow tile and similar walls shall be rigid and constructed upon solid footings, all units being set in portland cement mortar. The surface on which stucco is to be applied shall be clean, free from all dust, dirt or loose particles, preferably rough and of coarse texture. Wood lintels over wall openings shall not be used. Monolithic concrete walls shall be roughened by hacking, wire brushing, or other effective means. Concrete block, tile, or brick units shall have the joints cut back even with the surface. Clay tile shall be hard burned with dovetail or heavy, ragged scoring. Clay brick walls shall be composed of rough, hard burned clay brick, and if painted or waterproofed shall be covered with reinforcing fabric before overcoating with stucco.

Wetting the Surface

Immediately preceding the application of the stucco, the surface of the wall shall be evenly wetted but not saturated. Water shall not be rapidly absorbed from the plaster, nor remain standing on the surface.

Retempering

Retempering by the addition of water shall not be permitted.

Consistency

Only sufficient water to produce a workable consistency shall be used.

Application of Stucco Coats on Frame Construction

The application shall be carried on continuously in one general direction without allowing the stucco to dry at the edges. If it is impossible to work the full width of the wall at one time the joining shall be at some natural division of the surface, such as a window or door. The scratch coat shall be shoved thoroughly through the metal reinforcement, forming a solid mass against the sheathing paper, thus completely encasing the metal. This coat shall be ⅜ in. thick, fully covering the face of the reinforcement, and shall have its surface heavily cross-scratched to provide a strong mechanical key or bond. Allow this coat to become thoroughly dry. It shall be wetted down but not saturated before applying the second coat. The second, or browning, coat shall be at least ⅜ in. thick over the face of the first coat; it shall be rodded straight and true in every direction, or left untrue, giving a wavy effect, as the desired finish would suggest. If the finish is to be a float-type finish, the second coat shall be brought to a good even surface with wood floats. This coat shall be wet down for at least three days and allowed to become thoroughly dry before the finishing coat is applied. The finish coat shall be applied not less than one week after the application of the second coat and shall vary in thickness from ⅛ in. to ¾ in., depending upon the texture of the finish coat.

Scratch Coat on Masonry Walls

Mortar shall be troweled on to a thickness of approximately ⅜ in., heavily cross-scratched, and allowed to become thoroughly dry before the browning coat is applied. (From this point on use specification covering "Application of Stucco Coats on Frame Construction.")

Freezing

Methods shall be employed to keep the stucco above 50° F. during application and for 48 hours thereafter.

Curing

Each coat shall be protected from drying rapidly from effects of intense sunlight or wind until it has sufficiently hardened to permit sprinkling. Each coat shall be kept moist by sprinkling for at least two days following its application.

Back-Plastered Construction

In back-plastered construction, the metal lath shall be furred out from the face of the studs by an approved furring device and the mortar of the first, or scratch, coat applied with sufficient force to push it through the openings of the metal lath forming keys behind. The back-plastering coat shall not be applied until the scratch coat has hardened sufficiently to prevent injuring the keys of the scratch coat. The back-plastered coat shall not be less than ½ in. thick back of reinforcement, composed of the same proportions and materials as the scratch coat, and shall be applied from side to side of the hollow space between studs. The application of the browning and finish coats on back-plastered construction is identical with other methods as previously given.

Open Construction

In open construction the studs shall have parallel strands on No. 18 W & M gauge or heavier soft-annealed wire stretched tightly across their faces at 6-in. intervals to serve as a backing for the standard 15-lb. asphalt-saturated roofing felt. Metal reinforcement shall be applied over the entire surface held in place by approved furring devices, lapping at least 2 in. on all horizontal laps and at least 6 in. on all vertical laps. All metal reinforcement shall be returned around corners at least 16 in. Corner beads will not be permitted.

Finish Coat

The finish coat should be any color selected. Color can be varied by the admixture of cement coloring material, and can also be varied by the choice of light, medium, or very dark cement.

PREPARED PORTLAND CEMENT STUCCO

Although to the average plasterer the preparation, proportioning, mixing, and application of portland cement stucco is a simple operation, it is possible to obtain a more uniform quality of stucco by using prepared portland cement stucco. This may be obtained from retail stores, completely mixed, in properly proportioned packages, ready for the addition of water. This prepared stucco gives the advantage of factory-measured and -proportioned materials, machine mixing, and grinding of the coloring pigment with the cement and selected materials.

Application of Stucco Coats

Portland cement stucco shall be applied in three coats. The first base (or scratch) coat, ⅜ in. thick, shall be cross-scratched and allowed to damp-cure from a fine water spray for not less than 48 hours after setting. The second base (or brown) coat, ⅜ in. thick, shall be applied over a dampened and cured first coat, rodded level, broomed to a rough surface, and damp-cured for at least 48 hours. The third (finish) coat shall be applied over the dampened and cured second coat, to a thickness of ⅛ in. to ¼ in., steel-troweled to a smooth even surface, and when set shall be damp-cured for not less than 72 hours.

Back-Plastered Construction

In back-plastering, care should be taken that complete embedment of the reinforcement is accomplished without injury to the first plaster coat already in place.

Hair or Fiber

Hair or fiber should be used only in the first coat of mortar in back-plastered metal lath construction, or for the underside of horizontal surfaces.

Finishing

The architect should bring to his client's attention the possibilities in portland cement stucco colors and textures. In the choice of these, samples may be submitted by competent stucco contractors and in every case a definite sample of texture and color should be furnished by the architect for the basis of bids.

The application of the finish is a distinct craft and the plastering contractor should endeavor to use only experienced workmen to obtain good results. Many variations of color and texture are possible.

Materials Required for 100 Square Feet of Surface for Various Thicknesses of Stucco

Thickness	Proportions			
	1:3		1:3-1/2	
	Cement (sacks)	Sand (cubic feet)	Cement (sacks)	Sand (cubic feet)
1/8 inch	.36	1.10	.33	1.15
1/4 inch	.73	2.20	.65	2.29
3/8 inch	1.10	3.30	.98	3.44
1/2 inch	1.47	4.40	1.31	4.59
3/4 inch	2.22	6.60	1.91	6.87
1 inch	2.94	8.80	2.62	9.18
1-1/4 inches	3.68	11.00	3.28	11.45

These quantities may vary 10 per cent in either direction due to the character of the sand and its moisture content. No allowance is made for waste.
If hydrated lime is used (20 per cent by volume of cement) decrease these quantities 12 per cent.

Overcoating Old Houses with Stucco

"Overcoating" is the term generally applied to the method of using portland cement stucco as a covering for the exterior surfaces of old houses. The structural framework of such houses invariably possesses useful life, usually being built of staunch, seasoned timber. The problem which this rejuvenation process solves is how to preserve and utilize the value of this worth-while structure, while eliminating the dilapidated appearance. The preparation of the surface of the old wall to receive the stucco overcoat requires but a minimum of treatment.

In adding an inch or more of stucco to this surface it is of course necessary that all the original projections or trim, such as window and door frames, be extended or built out proportionately to this depth. The majority of houses which are overcoated are of frame construction, with siding boards. After the extension of the trim a layer of a substantial, waterproof building paper should be applied directly on the siding, which should be renailed if found loose. The sheet of reinforcement is attached over this paper, being furred out ¼ in. so that it will be in the approximate center of the stucco slab and to insure its positive and complete embedment in the mortar.

When the old surface is of masonry it should be sufficiently rough to give the first coat of mortar a good mechanical bond. If the wall is painted or otherwise glazed, reinforcement should be fastened over it and standard procedure followed.

The advantages of overcoating an old house with portland cement stucco may be summarized as follows: Increased property value is assured by better appearance; upkeep in painting and repairing has been cut; the house has been insulated against temperature changes, resulting in a saving in the cost of heating; and the fire safety of the structure has been increased.

BRICKWORK

The standard dimensions for building brick, established by the United States Bureau of Standards, are as follows:

8   in. in length
3-¾ "   " width
2-¼ "   " height

Though these dimensions are still considered standard, the dimensions in all building products are currently being coordinated on multiples of 4 inches when placed in the finished wall. Under this system of dimensional standardization, brick instead of being 8 in. in length would be 7½ in. where made for ½-in. mortar joint, and 7⅝ in. where made for ⅜-in. mortar joint, thus giving an over-all length of brick and joint of 8 in., or two (2) 4-in. modules. Similar dimensional differences are made in width and height.

SOLID BRICK WALLS IN RUNNING BOND

Sq. Ft. Wall Area	4" WALL No. of brick	8" WALL No. of brick	12" WALL No. of brick
1	6.16	12.32	18.48
10	62	124	185
20	124	247	370
30	185	370	555
40	247	493	740
50	308	616	924
60	370	740	1,109
70	432	863	1,294
80	493	986	1,479
90	555	1,109	1,664
100	616	1,232	1,848
200	1,232	2,464	3,696
300	1,848	3,696	5,544
400	2,464	4,928	7,392
500	3,080	6,160	9,240
600	3,696	7,392	11,088
700	4,312	8,624	12,936
800	4,928	9,856	14,784
900	5,544	11,088	16,632
1000	6,160	12,320	18,480

Mortar

One barrel of lime, 1 cu. yd. of sand, and 4 bags of cement will lay about 1,200 standard-size bricks with the standard ⅜-in. joint. If the joint is thicker more mortar will be needed; if thinner less will be needed. Lump lime is better if properly slaked, but hydrated lime can also be used. For the above mixture six 50-lb. bags of hydrated lime will be needed. Bricks should be dipped in a soft-soap solution to keep mortar drippings from adhering to them.

In ordinary work one man should be able to lay about 800 bricks a day, but there are many factors which cause a variation in this figure. Odd sizes, corners, projections, etc. make a difference in time. And it takes longer to lay press bricks (the kind used in fireplaces) than to lay ordinary bricks.

Modern bricklayers in action.

Bonding

Bricks are laid in a number of different patterns, and the beauty and soundness of the work depend upon these patterns or "bonds," as they are called by bricklayers. Bricks laid without bonding would present an appearance like this:

A wall laid in this fashion would depend upon the strength of the mortar while in a bonded wall each brick helps to resist downward pressure.

Bricks laid so that the shorter face shows are called *headers;* bricks laid the long way are called *stretchers*.

Other popular methods of bonding are these:

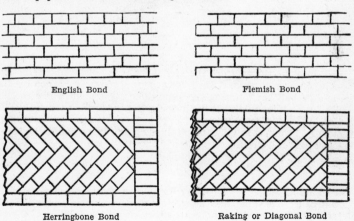

English Bond Flemish Bond

Herringbone Bond Raking or Diagonal Bond

For thick walls a bonding like the one below gives great strength:

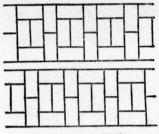

Bond for Thick Walls

In nearly all cities brickwork is regulated by laws which prescribe the use of good, well-burnt bricks and a firm mortar or cement. Damp courses are prescribed to keep down moisture which might arise through the bricks which, being porous, might form good conductors.

When the wall has progressed 4 or 5 ft. a scaffold should be built to carry on the upper part of it. Since the safety of the workman depends upon this scaffold and since it can be used again and again, it is simple economy to build a good one.

To Make a Rounded Arch of Brick or Stone

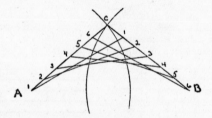

First, measure the width of the arch. This is the distance covered by a straight line drawn from A to B. Then describe from each point a half circle, each half circle having the same radius. The point where the half circles intersect is equidistant from A and B. Next divide the two lines AC and AB into equal parts (the number of equal parts does not particularly matter) and connect as indicated in the diagram. The curve at the base is an exact part of a circle.

Scaffolding

Any kind of temporary structure for seating spectators at a parade or show is called a scaffold, but the scaffold most commonly met with is the elevated platform used by workers, *e.g.*, bricklayers, in building.

Such a scaffolding is made of poles placed horizontally, vertically, and obliquely and fastened securely together. The main part of the structure is formed by the vertical poles, or standards, and the horizontal poles, which may be either ledgers or putlogs. The oblique poles, or braces, are for the purpose of strengthening the structure. The putlogs are short timbers placed at right angles to the ledgers, or long horizontal timbers.

In bricklayers' scaffolds the putlogs are allowed to rest one end against the brickwork; but in masons' scaffolds the whole structure must be independent of the wall in order to avoid disfiguring it.

In setting up a bricklayers' scaffold the first step is to place the standards singly or in pairs, 6 ft. to 8 ft. apart in a straight line with one another parallel with the walls of the building and 4 ft. to 6 ft. in front of it. They should be sunk 2 ft. or more into the ground.

When the standards are placed the ledgers are lashed to them at a distance of from 5 ft. to 6 ft. from the ground. Three-strand Manila cords may be used for the lashing, tied generally with the "builders' knot" or clove hitch (see page 314). Wire ropes are sometimes substituted, and there are patented systems of fastening which do away with the ordinary lashing. After the ledgers are lashed the putlogs are placed about 5 ft. apart. One end of the putlog rests on the ledger, the other on the wall where it is given a bearing of some 6 in. The platform is laid across the putlogs, the planks falling the long way, parallel with the building. No plank should project more than 6 in. beyond the putlog. A guard rail is erected about 3 ft. 6 in. from the platform.

Rising standards are lashed to those embedded in the ground. A putlog which touches a standard may form the base for the next rising standard. When double uprights are used they are paired in uneven lengths and the shorter timber, or puncheon, forms the base for the standard which is lashed to the longer timber.

Scaffolding poles are made generally of pine or spruce. They are 30 ft. to 50 ft. long and between 6 in. and 9 in. in diameter. Putlogs are about 6 ft. long and 4 in. square except at the end which enters the wall. Here they are cut down to about the size of a brick end, $2\frac{1}{2}$ in. $\times$ $3\frac{1}{2}$ in. Platform planks are between 12 ft. and 14 ft. long, about 8 in. wide, and an inch and a half to 2 in. thick. The ends are often bound with strap iron to keep them from splitting.

When a tall scaffolding is not needed a series of horses or trestles may answer the purpose. These should be 5 ft. wide and 5 ft. high and placed on six or seven 2 in. $\times$ 10 in. planks laid close together. This should be kept sufficiently far back from a green wall not to throw it out of plumb.

STONEWORK

The ordinary unit in estimating stonework is the perch, which is equal to 24.75 cu. ft. The cubic yard is also used. Percentages vary but on an average one-ninth is allowed for mortar and filling, that is, 2.75 cu. ft. to each perch.

To find out the amount of stone needed find the dimensions of the wall in feet (width × height × thickness) and divide by 22. The figure 22 is obtained by subtracting the amount allowed for mortar from the whole amount of the perch. To find the number of perches divide the number of cubic feet in the wall by the number of cubic feet in a perch (24.75).

WELDING

Welding is a method of joining two pieces of metal together by the application of heat, with or without the application of pressure and with or without the addition of filler metal in the form of welding rods or electrodes.

There are 37 different welding processes in commercial use today. Many of these processes lend themselves to high-production rates only. Others are equally suitable for low-rate production, job shop repairs, and even minor home repairs or work projects. Among the latter processes are *shielded metal-arc welding, oxyacetylene (or other fuel gas such as propane, butane, etc.) welding, and torch brazing.*

Except for the brazing processes, the difference between the welding processes is in the method of heating. In the brazing processes a lower-melting-point filler metal is used and capillary attraction is a factor in distributing the molten metal through the joint.

All commonly used metals can be welded by the use of the proper processes, proper joint preparation, proper filler metal, and proper technique. When correctly welded, the joint will be equal in service properties to the parts joined.

Knowledge and experience are necessary for good welding. Before one attempts any welding job, it is advisable to consult the American Welding Society, 29 West 39th Street, New York, N.Y., for information regarding specific applications.

SOFT SOLDERING

Soft soldering is a means of joining two pieces of metal together with another metal melted into the joint. Solders are generally made of tin, lead, or a tin-lead alloy, with or without additions of antimony, silver, arsenic, or bismuth, to impart special properties. These solders may be used in the form of wire (or string) bars, powders, or ingots. A common solder is a 50-50 mixture of tin and lead; a 60-40 solder is also used widely.

The parts to be soldered should be mechanically or chemically cleaned and a flux should always be used. The flux serves to clean the joint, prevent oxidation, and lower the surface tension of the solder, thus increasing its melting properties. Fluxes may be composed of rosin or rosin alcohol, citric acid in water, zinc chloride, ammonium chloride, and muriatic acid. Glycerine is added to some fluxes to increase wetability. Lactic acid, levulinic acid, sulfonated alcohol, and turpentine are added for different metals. Soldered joints should be thoroughly cleaned to prevent corrosive action by a flux residue.

Solder is applied with a soldering "iron" made of a short, stout copper bar pointed at the working end and fitted at the other end into an iron shank, which is in turn fitted into a wooden handle. The iron may be heated electrically or over a gas flame. Care must be taken not to allow it to become red-hot. When the proper temperature is reached the end should be filed on an ordinary file, dipped in the flux, and pressed against the solder, which spreads over and "tins" the end. The end is then applied to the joint which has been already covered with the flux.

Brazing, which employs higher-melting-point alloys and more involved methods of heating, is sometimes erroneously referred to as hard soldering, but should not be confused with the above process.

EXCAVATIONS

Estimates for excavations are usually figured in cubic yards or cubic feet. If there is any doubt as to the nature of the underlying surface the owner or architect should have borings made to determine how deep one has to go before a firm foundation can be secured and to find out whether shoring and pumping will be necessary. If the job is a large one this should in any case be done. Costs depend upon all these items and also upon whether the excavated material is to be removed from the site, or redistributed for grading. Bids can usually be obtained for removal of earth in accordance with plans, with rock excavation as an "extra" at a unit price per yard. The unit price will vary for general rock or rock for piers. Be sure to include excavation for sewer and water trenches. Great care in the beginning may save much trouble later on.

DAMS

Earth dams should never be more than 100 feet high. *Masonry dams* may be of any height; dams over 100 feet high are practically always of masonry.

The area to be covered by a dam should first be cleared of trees, top soil, and other organic matter which would soften in water. A trench should then be dug where the center of the dam is to be, deep enough to reach a solid base. The center of the trench should be filled with a core wall of concrete or puddled clay. This wall is built up with the banks, which are made of earth, the excavated material being used for this purpose. The 'nside slope should be protected from the waves by slabs of concrete or something which answers the same purpose. The core wall should be somewhat higher than the high-water mark of the reservoir. This is a safety factor.

The largest earth dam in the world is the one which impounds Gatun Lake on the Isthmus of Panama. It is more than a mile long, has a base width of nearly half a mile and contains more than 20,000,000 cubic yards of material. The water which it holds in check has an area of 171 square miles.

PLASTERING

Plaster is made of gypsum, plus an aggregate—sand or one of the lightweight aggregates, such as perlite or vermiculite. The plaster may be fibered or unfibered. Either two or three coats of plaster are necessary for a well-finished wall, depending upon the type of lathing used.

Plastering is generally estimated by the square yard. Suppose the problem is to plaster a room 10 ft. long, 8 ft. wide, and 8½ ft. high. It has two windows, 3 ft. × 6 ft., and one door, 3 ft. × 7 ft. Find the cost of plastering the walls and ceiling at 50 cents per sq. yd.

The area of the walls of a room is found by multiplying the perimeter by the height. (The perimeter is the distance around the room.) Therefore:

$$10 + 8 + 10 + 8,$$

or, as it may be more easily expressed,

```
2 × (10 + 8) = 36 ft. perimeter of room
8½ × 36 = 306 sq. ft. in the walls
8 × 10 = 80 sq. ft. in the ceiling
306 sq. ft. + 80 sq. ft. = 386 sq. ft. in both ceiling and walls
2 × 3 × 6 = 36 sq. ft. in windows
3 × 7 = 21 sq. ft. in the door
36 + 21 = 57 sq. ft. in both doors and windows
386 − 57 = 329 sq. ft., net area of walls and ceiling
329 sq. ft. ÷ 9 sq. ft. = 36½ sq. yd.
36½ × .50 = $18.25, cost of plastering the room
```

Plastering Bases and Lathing

Plastering bases are those materials or constructions which receive the base coat of plaster. These bases are usually divided into two classes, (1) lathing bases that are secured to the structure to provide a relatively smooth and level surface, (2) masonry bases. Gypsum lath is frequently used as a plastering base. It may be nailed to wood framing or furring, and may be secured to wood or metal furring with special clip attachments. Generally, it is used in sheets ⅜ in. thick × 16 in. wide × 48 in. long, although other sizes are available. The usual requirements for nailing gypsum laths call for 4 nails per lath on each stud on the sidewalls, and 5 on the ceiling. Lath nails should be of 13-gauge wire, be 1⅛ in. long, and have a ⅜-in. head. They should be driven home so that the head is just below the paper surface, without breaking the paper. Gypsum lath should be applied with the long dimension horizontal, and with vertical joints staggered. All lath ends must have bearing on wood framing, headers, or nailing blocks, and be securely nailed. Metal corner lath on inside corners helps to reinforce the joints.

Metal lath makes a strong plastering base because the steel becomes embedded in the plaster and so produces a reinforced plaster slab. The following table gives the various types and weights of metal, wire, and wire fabric laths.

TYPES AND WEIGHTS OF METAL LATH, WIRE LATH, AND WIRE FABRIC, AND SPACING, CENTER TO CENTER OF SUPPORTS[1]

Type of lath	Minimum weight of lath, lb. per sq. yd.	Maximum allowable spacing of supports, in.				
		Vertical supports			Horizontal supports	
		Wood	Metal		Wood or concrete	Metal
			Solid partitions	Others		
Flat expanded metal lath	2.5 3.4	16 16	16 16	12 16	0 16	0 13-1/2
Flat rib metal lath	2.75 3.4	16 19	16 24	16 19	16 19	12 19
3/8-in. rib metal lath[2]	3.4 4.0	24 24	... ...	24 24	24 24	19 24
Sheet metal lath	4.5	24	24	24	24	24
Wire lath	2.48	16	16	16	13-1/2	13-1/2
V-stiffened wire lath	3.3	24	24	24	19	19
Wire fabric[3]	....	16	0	16	16	16

(Reprinted from the Manual of Gypsum Lathing and Plastering)

[1]Lath may be used on any spacings, center to center, up to the maximum shown for each type and weight.
[2]Rod-stiffened or V-stiffened flat expanded metal lath of equal rigidity and weight is permissible on the same spacings as 3/8-in. rib metal lath.
[3]Minimum weight: paper-baked wire fabric, No. 16-gauge wire, 2 × 2 in.-mesh, with stiffener.

Wood lath is also an important lathing material. No. 1- or No. 2-grade wood lath of white pine, spruce, or other soft wood, free of knots, sap, and bark should be used. This lath should be spaced ¼ in. to ⅜ in. apart. The lath should be fastened to each stud with a 3d, 16-gauge wire nail. Wood lath should be soaked in water overnight before application and made wet again before the plaster is applied. Soaking is necessary to prevent the wood from absorbing water from the plaster, then swelling and causing the plaster to loosen. See also wood laths on page 377.

Plastering Methods

A three-coat application of plaster is required over metal or wood laths. It consists of a first coat, or scratch coat, of plaster which is applied directly to the plastering base, cross-raked, and allowed to set and to dry partially; a second coat, or brown coat, of plaster which is surfaced out to the proper grounds, left rough, and allowed to set and to dry partially; and a third, or finish, coat of plaster. The two-coat application of plaster is similar in every respect, except that the cross-raking of the first coat is omitted and the second coat of plaster is applied within a few minutes to the unset first coat. This two-coat method is generally accepted practice in applying plaster to masonry and gypsum lath, except in certain localities where the three-coat method predominates. The three-coat method is often preferred since it develops a harder and stronger base coat. The set and partially dried first coat has a strong suction which draws much of the excess water from the second coat. The second coat is thereby densified because the water-to-gypsum ratio is reduced, thus producing a stronger plaster.

Condensed Specification for Three-Coat Plastering

1. The first coat is made of sand and lime in a 2:1 mixture.[1] Enough clean water should be added to make the mixture hold together well. This coat should be about ¼ to ½ in. thick, depending on the type of lath used, and should be scratched or roughened to form a key for the next coat.

2. The second coat should be applied not sooner than 48 hours after the application of the first coat, and should have a thickness of about ⅜ in. It should be a 3:1 mixture of sand and lime, to which hair may be added. Strips of plaster 4 or 5 in. wide, carefully plumbed and leveled, should be laid at intervals to serve as a guide for the rest of the coat. The space between these strips should then be filled and the surface scoured with a wooden float. If the plaster shows a tendency to dry, water should be sprinkled on with a brush. This scouring should be done two or three times with an interval of 6 to 24 hours between. Small inequalities should be leveled at this time. The coat is then ready to be keyed for the next coat. This is done by going over it with a wire brush or a nail float.

3. The final, or surface, coat is made of lime putty. When putty made from Finishing Hydrated Lime is used the proportions should be 4½ parts of putty to at least 1 part of good gauging plaster. This is equivalent, approximately, to 3 lb. of dry hydrated lime to 1 lb. of dry gauging plaster. When putty made from high calcium quicklime is used the proportions should be 4 parts of lime putty to at least 1 part of good gauging plaster. The ingredients should be mixed together thoroughly and applied by first covering all of the second-coat surface. This should be followed up immediately with another coat to form an even surface. This final coat should be troweled, and brought to a true, even, smooth surface, free from checks, cracks, and other blemishes.

4. Plaster should be protected until it is thoroughly dry. In the hot summer months doors and windows should be kept closed to prevent it from drying before it has crystallized. In winter it should not be allowed to freeze, and in very wet weather artificial means of drying should be provided. Local building specifications often call for the temporary closing of a building and other measures to insure the proper drying of plaster.

Many varieties of base-coat and finish-coat plaster are manufactured; they require only the addition of water at the job site. It is important to follow the manufacturer's specifications for these carefully. Small repairs are generally made with plaster of Paris or a prepared patching plaster.

---

[1] The use of cattle or goat hair is optional. If hair is used, it should be in the proportion of 1 lb. of hair to every 2 or 3 cu. ft. of the mortar.

PAINTING

Materials

Painting could be much cheaper for the home owner and hours could be much better for the painter if painting were not practically confined to the spring and fall of the year. There is no need for this. Outside painting can be done at any time of the year when the atmosphere is dry and the thermometer 40 or more degrees Fahrenheit, and there is no danger of a sudden drop in temperature. Interior painting can be done at any time of the year and it is better not to have it in the rush seasons, but in the winter. The ideal temperature for inside work is between 60 degrees and 70 degrees Fahrenheit.

In painting as in most other fields the most economical way to begin is to *buy the best materials*. There are many manufacturers today whose names are guarantees of the soundness of their products. It is important not only to choose good paint but suitable paint. Exterior paints should be used only for exteriors; interior paints only for interiors. Chemists have for many generations been studying the qualities of paints; they know now what kinds will stand exposure and what kinds will not, what kinds will give a glossy coat and what kinds will gave a dull finish, what kinds are good for undercoats and what kinds should be used on the surface. Continued research work has led to the development of new paint products such as rubber base paints, one-coat exterior paints, mildew-resistant and fire-retardant paints, and many others which add to the quality or life of paint on a surface.

Mixing Paints

In mixing paints a clean flat wooden paddle is used. It is best to have two pails so that the paint can be poured from one to the other during the mixing process. With ready mixed paints the pigment is stirred thoroughly and the liquid added a little at a time. For the final coat these paints should not, as a rule, be thinned. If, however, they have been left uncovered (and no paint should ever be left uncovered when not in use) thinning may be necessary.

For mixing paste paints the paste should be put in a mixing keg that will hold at least twice the amount of paste needed. A very small quantity of oil should be added until the mixture becomes easily workable. If the paint is to be tinted, the tint is now added, having first been mixed with oil or turpentine. The tint should be added slowly since it takes only a little to color a white paint. The tint should be tested by brushing it on a sample surface. After the color has been thoroughly mixed in, the turpentine is added and stirred in, then the final amount of linseed oil. Last of all the drier is added.

Paint formulas vary, but for ordinary work the following estimate has been given: For each 100 pounds of white lead or paste use between 6½ and 7 gallons of linseed oil. Turpentine may be added to thin out the mixture.

Turpentine should never be added before at least a part of the oil has been added, since it makes mixing difficult.

The proportions of linseed oil and turpentine vary according to the kind of surface desired. For a full-gloss finish the proportions are about ⅕ turpentine and ⅘ linseed oil. For a semigloss, about ⅓ turpentine and ⅔ linseed oil; for a flat finish, about ¾ turpentine and ¼ linseed oil. If a dead flat effect is desired, as for enamel undercoats and certain other interior work, turpentine alone should be used. It is best in this case to mix the paint and allow it to stand overnight. The small amount of oil that is in the paste will rise to the top. All the liquid on top should be poured off and the paint mixed with fresh turpentine. Paint mixed in this way will dry entirely without gloss. If the paint is to be exposed to the sun more turpentine should be added to prevent blistering and only boiled linseed oil should be used. For unexposed work raw linseed oil may be used.

Paint should be mixed so that it is thin enough to brush out freely, but not too thin to hide the surface upon which it is to be used.

Brushes

After one has bought the best and most suitable paint the next step is to buy a good brush. Once more it is economy to buy the best. The finest paint in the world will not give good results if it is streaked with bristles and if it is spattered or spread on unevenly. The best brushes are bound in leather or metal and set in cement or vulcanized rubber. Bristles set in vulcanized rubber will not come out in any kind of paint.

The size and style of a brush is a matter for each painter to decide for himself, but the size most commonly used for outside walls is a 4-inch flat brush with bristles about 4¾ inches long. Shorter bristles wear out more quickly and make the brush less easy to handle. A wall stippling brush to eliminate brush marks should have bristles about 3½ inches long. Oval paint and varnish brushes are useful for certain kinds of work and wear out less quickly than flat brushes.

Paint brushes not in use should be kept suspended in linseed oil. The paint should first be wiped out and the oil should cover the bristles entirely and come about an inch above the ferrule. The bristles should not touch the bottom of the container or they will become bent. As a makeshift the brush may be cleaned by wiping it with rags and washing out the remainder of the paint in a container of benzene, gasoline, or kerosene.

Varnish should never be allowed to dry on a brush. If it does it may be removed with alcohol mixtures or turpentine. Varnish brushes may be kept in linseed oil or varnish but all the oil should be wiped out before the brush is used.

Shellac brushes may be kept suspended in shellac but the best treatment is to clean them with alcohol immediately after using.

Lacquer brushes should be cleaned wth lacquer thinner.

Brushes used in bronze paints should be washed clean with turpentine as soon as they have been used.

Brushes should not be cleaned near a fire or flame, and painters should not experiment with new cleaners. Ammonia, for example, added to some of the lacquer varnishes gives a poison gas which may result in an extremely sore throat or even more serious consequences.

New brushes must be broken in, and they should be broken in on a priming coat, not on a finish coat. Loose bristles should first be worked out and the brush dipped into the paint (a brush should never be dipped in more than two or three inches) and wiped several times across the mixing paddle. An old brush is more satisfactory for poking into corners and for grille work.

Surface Preparation

The surface to be painted should be properly prepared. This is usually a very simple matter. New wood should be gone over with a duster and a putty knife to remove dirt, plaster, etc. Knots and sappy places should be brushed with turpentine, solvent naphtha, or a coat of aluminum knot primer applied about 20 minutes before the application of the priming coat. Otherwise the pitch in the lumber will be drawn out by the sun and the surface will be discolored.

Moisture is at the bottom of most paint difficulties. It is not enough for the surface only to be dry; the structure must be dry through and through or the paint will blister when the sun draws the moisture to the surface. A blistered surface may be scraped clean with a putty knife and painted over. The scraped patches should be touched up with paint before the whole job is gone over.

When paint has cracked or scaled it is best to remove it with a blowtorch before applying new paint, but the blowtorch should be handled only by a professional painter because of the fire hazard.

Priming Coats

If any one coat of paint is more important than any other, it is the priming coat, which is the foundation. The application of this coat should not be delayed too long. It forms a protective coat which keeps out moisture due to fogs, rains, etc.; yet, if it is thin enough, it allows the moisture within to escape.

The formula for the priming coat must be varied to suit the kind of wood to which it is applied. Porous woods which absorb oil readily, like bass, cedar, white pine, and boxwood, require an extra amount of oil in the priming coat. Woods with an oily fiber, like cypress, yellow pine, fir, hemlock, spruce, and gum require an excess of turpentine for the priming coat. In case any one of these woods has an excess of gum it is advisable to add one pint of solvent naphtha 160 degrees, to each gallon of the priming coat. The priming coat should be allowed to dry thoroughly, the length of time necessary depending upon the weather conditions, the paint formula, and the wood; but it should not be allowed to remain so long that it is chalky or badly weathered. Otherwise the finish will appear faded.

Estimate of Coverage

It is difficult to give an estimate of the amount of paint required for a surface, for so much depends upon the surface, whether it is rough or smooth, exposed or protected, painted or unpainted, porous or hard. Under average conditions a gallon of good paint will cover 300 square feet sometimes as much even as 500 square feet. An expert hand with the brush can cover nearly 25 per cent more than an inexperienced hand. Dark paints have a greater coverage than light paints because they can be spread thinner. It takes more paint to cover a dark surface with light paint than it takes to cover a light surface with dark paint, since the paint must be spread on more thickly.

Painting Shingles

New shingles should be dipped in paint or stain a few days before they are laid. The best method is to use a barrel containing stain or paint and to dip a dozen or so shingles at a time, butt end down, to a depth of 6 or 8 inches and to stand them in a trough to catch the drippings. After the shingles are laid, a second coat should be applied with an old paint brush which will go into all the cracks and joints.

Painting Cement and Stucco

Cement and stucco surfaces should be clean and thoroughly dry. Freshly formed cement needs a treatment to neutralize the free lime present or oil paints will be damaged. This treatment consists of a neutralizing wash made of two or three pounds of zinc sulphate crystals dissolved in a gallon of water, brushed or sprayed on the surface and allowed to dry before the paint is applied. This treatment is unnecessary on stucco that has been allowed to age. Since the priming coat must bind the loose particles of cement on the surface and at the same time supply a good foundation for the succeeding coats, it is advisable to add an extra quantity of oil or varnish to the formula. Any good house paint is suitable for the finishing coats.

Painting Brick

In painting bricks an excess of oil is used in the priming coat. The application of paint to a brick wall is an excellent way to seal up the pores and prevent the penetration of moisture, which often causes dampness and decay.

Painting Interiors

In doing interior painting ventilation is desirable; an electric fan may answer the purpose quite well. All dust should be removed and the floor and the furniture which cannot be removed easily should be carefully covered with light duck, heavy muslin, or old sheets.

The plan of painting should be figured out before the brush is dipped into the pail. Floor painting should begin in the far corner of the room so that the painter will end up at the door. Wall painting should begin in the upper left-hand corner of the room.

New plaster, like new stucco, should be treated for free lime to keep the surface from "burning." The treatment is a solution of zinc sulphate crystals in the proportions of two pounds to a gallon of water. The solution is applied with a brush. Next, the wall is sandpapered and the small cracks filled with plaster of Paris or a crack filler. When the surface is entirely smooth it is ready to be sized and primed. *Old plaster* in good condition needs only to be dusted. Particles of paint must be wiped off with a wire brush. Grease may be washed off with a solution of sal soda or ammonia and water. Old calcimine, if in bad condition, should be washed off. Cracks should be filled as in the case of new plaster and the whole surface sanded smooth.

Wallboard should be smoothed before it is sized and primed. This operation involves the filling in of all joints, cracks, etc.

Wallpaper which is still tight to the walls and in good condition may be dusted and painted over, but work done under such circumstances cannot be guaranteed.

A good *sizing* for plaster or wallboard is a coat of first-class interior varnish, thinned with turpentine and colored with a little of the wall paint.

The best primer is a coat of flat wall paint which contains an excess of linseed oil. Wallboard is more porous than plaster and therefore requires a greater proportion of oil.

Wall paint is usually faster drying than exterior paint and the brushing is somewhat more difficult. If the paint is too thin it will run and if it is improperly applied it will not be smooth. The general rule is to begin in the upper left-hand corner working from left to right and from ceiling to floor in strips a foot or two wide. Narrow strips are painted so that the edge of each painted area can be smoothly joined to the one that has preceded it before it has had a chance to set. The brush should never be pressed down too hard. Small brush marks disappear as the paint dries if the paint is properly flowed on. Too much brushing should be avoided since it brings the oil to the surface and gives a gloss. Once an area has been left it will not help but injure it to go over it again with the brush.

Stippling

Stippling is done with a regular stippling brush. Paint for this coat should be quite thick and the stippling should be done while it is still wet. Usually two painters work together, the second following the first with the stippling brush.

Sponging

A novel finish is sometimes applied with a sponge, either a deep sea or a rubber sponge cut flat on one side, the flat side being used to apply the paint. The sponge is dipped into a little paint which has been poured into a shallow container and tapped on the surface. The sponge should be pressed against the wall and pulled away straight without twisting the hand. It is advisable to soak the sponge in benzene or water before beginning and every five or ten minutes while working in order to keep it fluffy and remove the accumulations of paint. A small sponge should be used for corners.

A wad of cheesecloth, crepe paper, muslin, or burlap, may be used in the same way, except that the hand is twisted in using these implements instead of being held straight as with the sponge.

Scumbling

For scumbling a wall a harmonizing or contrasting color is applied over the dry ground color and while it is still wet a wad of newspaper is placed firmly against the wall and rolled downward and over, thus allowing the ground coat to show through.

Starching

For starching a wall a handful of starch is dissolved in just enough cold water to cover it and boiling water is added until it has reached a thick jellylike consistency. It is then thinned with cold water until is has a consistency about like that of milk and brushed on with an ordinary flat wall brush. A pinch of dry color may be added. If the wall has a gloss finish it is best to wipe it down with vinegar or alcohol before the starch coat is applied.

Only new walls should be starched since the process merely serves to bring out defects in old ones.

Pasteurized buttermilk may be used instead of starching with much the same result. It is brushed on and then stippled with a wall stippling brush.

When it is wished to freshen the wall this starch or buttermilk coat is simply washed off.

A painted wall can be satisfactorily washed only when the entire wall is washed. Washing small patches leaves rings.

Washing Walls

A good solution for washing a wall is prepared by shaving a small cake of pure white soap or soap flakes into a quart of water. Dissolve about two ounces of glue in another quart of water and mix the two liquids together. A little flour may added to make a thicker solution or a little sal soda or washing powder to make a stronger solution. The whole mixture is applied with a soft sponge, working from the bottom up and the wall is then wiped down with a chamois skin. If the wall is badly soiled the solution should be allowed to stand for two or three minutes to loosen the dirt and then washed off with a clean sponge and a pail of clean water.

Walls coated with a thin film of grease may be treated with the same solution, only an extra amount of sal soda or ammonia should be added.

Another recommended mixture for cleaning a wall is made by dissolving one ounce of soap flakes in sixteen ounces of water and adding about three ounces of turpentine. The mixture is kept agitated and applied with a brush or a sponge.

Varnishing

Both the varnish and the room in which it is used should be warm. In very cold weather the varnish should be placed near a radiator or in a pail of warm water (never before an open fire) for an hour or two before using.

Painting Radiators

Bronze and aluminum paints should not be used on radiators since they reduce the emission of heat as much as 20 per cent. A white or light-colored wall paint protects the metal and retards the heat practically none at all. When it is desired to reduce the heat given out by pipes, as in a furnace room or basement, the pipes should be painted with a bronze or aluminum paint, but when it is desired to increase the heat a light or white paint should be used.

PAPER HANGING

Paper is sold by the roll. Most American papers are 18 inches wide. A single roll is 24 feet long; a double roll is 48 feet long. If the paper has to be matched it is best to use a double roll to reduce the waste to a minimum.

In order to estimate the amount of paper that will be needed, find the distance around the room and subtract the width of the doors and windows. Divide the result in feet, which is the net perimeter of the room, by 1½ feet (width of one strip of paper, if it is standard American paper). This gives the number of strips of paper needed. To find out the number of strips in a roll of paper divide the length of the roll by the height of the wall.

New walls are prepared by sanding the surface to make it even and by washing and sizing to make the paper stick.

For ordinary papers a stiff paste made of wheat or rye flour is generally used, with a little formalin or carbolic acid added to prevent decomposition and attacks from insects. For heavy embossed or leather papers a glue paste is used and thin tacks are driven in lightly so that they can be taken out when the paper is dry.

In hanging figured paper great care should be taken to keep the pattern perfect. In covering projecting or recessed corners the paper should be cut so that only half an inch or so turns the corner. The paper hanger should work away from a window rather than towards it, so that the overlapping edges do not face the light. This makes them much less conspicuous.

For medium-weight paper something more than a pint of paste will be needed for each roll. Light papers will need less and heavy papers will need more.

SIZING

Size is any one of a number of gelatinous materials used to give glaze to a surface. Ordinary painter's size is glue with too much water in it to allow it to harden, usually five quarts of water to one pound of glue. To prepare the sizing, add one pound of glue to two quarts of boiling water. Stir until the glue is thoroughly mixed, and then add three quarts of water.

WHITEWASHING

Whitewash is made of slaked lime mixed with water to a thin paste. It should be applied with a brush and the surface to which it is applied should be rough. It is excellent for use on fences, barns, brickwork, etc.

Government specifications for a whitewash which is almost as good as paint are as follows:

Slake half a bushel of lime with boiling water, keeping it covered during the process. Strain it and then add a peck of salt dissolved in warm water, three pounds of rice which has been boiled to a thin paste, half a pound of Spanish whiting, and a pound of clean blue which has been dissolved in warm water. Mix thoroughly and let stand for three days. Then heat and apply with a brush while still very hot.

ADVERTISING

Advertising is the printed, written, spoken, or pictured presentation of a product, service, or idea, sponsored by the advertiser for the purpose of influencing sales, use, or action. This is done today in various ways—through announcements in newspapers and magazines, by radio and television, through mail, billboards, car-cards, spectacular electric signs, or any other medium which will carry the advertiser's selling message to the public.

Large-scale distribution, typical of present-day business, depends upon advertising for its success; and almost every type of business realizes the importance of advertising in mass selling. Advertising is the selling tool employed to interest potential customers in a product or service. In some instances advertising is expected not only to attract attention and gain interest but also to stimulate desire and get action. This is true with lower-priced and convenience goods. With higher-priced shopping goods and with technical products, advertising is used primarily to attract attention and to interest prospects, with the completion of the sale left to regular salesmen.

Much confusion has arisen in discussions concerning the relative merits of advertising. Consumer groups, in particular, often condemn advertising as an unnecessary and wasteful charge added to the purchase price. They contend that it stimulates desires for many unnecessary products and services; furthermore, that it tends to standardize consumer goods, and also makes it difficult for the small nonadvertising competitor to remain in business. The proponents of advertising take the opposite point of view. They claim that advertising lowers prices to consumers because large-scale distribution made possible by this tool results in large-scale, lower-cost production. They claim that if advertising were eliminated the overall cost of marketing would go up substantially and that prices would necessarily be much higher.

Both these points of view are extreme; examples can be given to uphold both sides. Practically, advertising is an important tool in distribution. As such it may be efficient or inefficient, good or bad, depending upon the way it is employed. When used properly it is an unusually effective implement for distributing large quantities of mass-produced goods at the lowest possible cost. When used improperly it may maintain artificially high prices or persuade people to purchase items for which they have little need. An intelligent view of advertising sees it as an important adjunct to personal selling which promotes sound products and services at the lowest possible cost.

An analysis of advertising indicates that it is especially effective in the following ways:

1. It introduces new products and services to the market by familiarizing potential consumers with the uses of the offerings.

2. It helps to obtain desirable wholesaler and retail dealers for the offerings by making it easier for them to sell.

3. It paves the way for the salesman by acquainting prospects with his company and the nature of its products.

4. It informs potential customers of new developments and new applications of existing products.

5. It makes it possible under certain conditions to complete the selling task even in the absence of salesmen.

Effective advertising must be based on a sound product. Misrepresentation may sell goods, but it also builds ill will. Since the advertiser who misrepresents his product harms not only the public but the whole industry as well, organized efforts have been made to prevent objectionable advertising. One of these was the model statute against fraud in advertising drafted in 1911 by the magazine *Printers' Ink*. This statute has since been enacted by 42 states, in either the original or a modified form, and covers 93 per cent of the population of the United States.

Further Government control over advertising was achieved by the Federal Trade Commission Act (1914), as amended by the Wheeler-Lea and other Acts. These gave the Federal Trade Commission, among others, the power to prosecute for unfair methods of competition and unfair or deceptive acts and practices, including false advertising. This legislation, in combination with the Food, Drug, and Cosmetic Acts of 1906 and 1940, which prohibit the sale of any food, drug, or cosmetic that is adulterated or misbranded, protect the consumer from injurious products. Another protection for the consumer against fraudulent advertising is the National Better Business Bureau, with offices throughout the United States and Canada. A protection to the advertiser against misrepresentation by publications is the Audit Bureau of Circulations; its function is to find out the net paid circulation of newspapers and magazines. Practically all magazines and newspapers which accept advertising voluntarily submit audited accounts to the A.B.C.

Most firms turn over the entire problem of advertising to advertising agencies. This practice generally costs the advertiser nothing because the agency receives a commission from the medium in which the advertisement appears. The medium returns to the agency 15 per cent of the cost of space or time sold to the advertiser. With this return the agency can offer its clients many services in addition to preparing advertisements, and still make a profit.

Agencies are usually equipped to handle every phase of the program. They may help with research. They prepare the advertisements and select the media in which the ads are to be run. They may also assist in other phases of marketing and even in product-development.

Market Research

It is easy to lose money in advertising; the best prevention lies in marketing research, which provides a careful study of (1) the product and (2) the market. Expert research staffs eliminate "blind" advertising. Such a staff will (1) find out how the product compares with others in the same field and suggest improvements, if any are needed, (2) study the market and determine the potential buyers of the product, and (3) make a study of advertising media, to determine which will bring in the greatest returns.

Many considerations enter into this work. The market for the product may consist of men, or women, or both: different groups require different appeals. The woman of wealth, for instance, will not be induced to buy through the kind of advertising that will interest the less wealthy woman; and different parts of the country require different types of approach.

Preparing the Advertisement

It is not necessary to have a detailed knowledge of the highly technical skills involved in preparing an advertisement in order to plan advertising. However, an understanding of the components of an advertisement, of their functions and preparation, and of how they are combined into usable form is essential.

The customary parts of an advertisement are (1) heading or headline, (2) illustration, (3) copy, and (4) company or product identification. These may be arranged in many ways. Headlines may appear anywhere in the advertisement. Copy may vary from a few words to a detailed description of the offering. The illustration may be very simple, it may be a reproduction of a fine painting or there may be no illustration at all. In any case, the four basic ingredients noted above *must* be considered in preparing an advertisement. The first step is to visualize the idea. Headlines and copy must then be considered, and a decision made on the illustration and the type. Finally, these must be assembled in finished form for reproduction. Now we shall briefly examine these steps.

Visualization and Layout. The first rule in preparing an advertisement is to capture attention. If the ad does not "stop" the prospect, it cannot make sales. Attention should be arrested by either an effective layout, a telling headline, or, preferably, by both. That is why the first step in preparing an advertisement is to visualize its appearance.

First, a rough sketch or layout is prepared in which headline, illustration, copy, company identification, and any other features are drawn to scale. This is the equivalent of a blueprint; it indicates in what manner the various components are to appear.

The layout should have two important characteristics—(1) it should be interesting to look at, (2) it should convey a feeling of movement and action.

The layout, like any other work of art, should observe the principles of design. It should be balanced properly. A lopsided advertisement will interfere unpleasantly with the desired effect. The materials that go into the layout should be harmonious in shape, color, and tone. They should be knit together logically and should stress ideas according to their relative importance. Emphasis is secured through contrast; the contrast may be in color, type, size, or many other features.

Another characteristic which advertising people strive for is distinctiveness. This feature may be achieved by emphasis or exaggeration, by unusual use of white space, by action pictures, by striking type- or border-treatment, or even by sheer simplicity.

The size of the space to be used is an important factor. It will depend upon the type of advertisement and the purposes behind it. There are many natural advantages in the use of large space, but often this is unnecessary and wasteful. A major error by a novice in advertising with comparatively little money to spend is using it all on one or two large ads. Usually he will be disappointed with the relatively weak results. The same amount spent on a series of smaller advertisements would be far more effective.

Headlines and Copy. Headlines and copy are developed after the advertisement is laid out. The headline is used to capture attention and to arouse interest. It should appeal to the reader's self-interest. A good headline holds out a specific promise to do something that people want done. It should be exciting, and as clear and concise as possible. It may be informative, or may create a desire for further information, or may have news value. The headline carries the heaviest burden of attracting desirable readers. No other part of the copy is worked over more thoroughly by experienced advertising men.

A headline is often used as a caption for a picture; but it should do more than simply describe the picture. Good headlines often combine a number of functions. They are particularly effective in appealing to the desired type of reader.

The most common weakness of many headlines is that they are neither specific nor vivid. They utter dull platitudes, and fail to challenge the reader's curiosity. The headline should express a worth-while idea in the fewest possible words. Some ideas require more words than others; but the headline should be kept short.

Sometimes a secondary or subordinate headline, called a subcaption, helps to round out the idea in the headline. It may clarify the headline, introduce the product, or present the idea in a different light. The headline and subheadline are usually considered together; they provide the cue to the copy which follows.

The Copy

The text or reading matter in the advertisement is called advertising copy. (In radio or television programs the "commercials" are the copy.) In most advertisements, the major burden of delivering the message falls upon the copy. It is the function of copy, supported by illustrations, to express the message in such a way that it will leave both a favorable and a lasting impression.

It is absolutely essential that the copy be adapted to the prospects who are to be influenced and to the media in which it is to appear, as well as to the product. Copy aimed at factory purchasing agents is written very differently from that expected to influence housewives. Copy published in trade papers is quite unlike that printed in the tabloids. Unless these considerations are kept in mind the advertisement will not arouse interest in the desired reader.

The first job of copywriters is to get at the facts. Good copy involves preliminary research, study, and analysis. Every product or service has unsuspected or unexploited angles. Market- and product-research uncovers many concrete facts which the copywriter may use imaginatively and convincingly. Often a good source of copy information is a competitor's advertising.

The copywriter must know the basic principles of good writing. He must be able to write clearly and convincingly and to convey the exact shade of meaning the advertisement requires. Artificiality and superficial cleverness will not hold the reader; common sense and sincerity are far more convincing. Trickery in copy more often distracts from the real message than it attracts attention to the advertisement. It should never be forgotten that the function of advertising is to sell, not merely to entertain.

In preparing copy, it is important that the proper types of advertising appeals be used. These are the buying motives, or the "reasons why" prospects should purchase the product. The appeals will vary with the type of product and the type of prospects to whom the advertising is directed. The best results are obtained when the appeals of the seller meet the wants of the buyer. Therefore, a thorough knowledge of how and why people buy a product is necessary for the preparation of successful advertising.

Certain rules have been found effective in enhancing the selling power of copy. These follow:

1. Dramatize the facts
2. Present the facts from the consumer's point of view
3. Be specific—give details
4. Localize your testimonial material whenever possible
5. Use "performance evidence" when you can
6. Use statements that ring true
7. If a reduced price is a fact, give a good reason for it

Copy is often classified on the basis of action desired from the reader or listener as (1) institutional, or good-will and (2) selling, or immediate-action. The first is intended to build up friendship for and confidence in the company, its policies and products. Selling copy, on the other hand, looks for quick response in the form of purchases or inquiries.

Another classification of copy is by the style employed or the method of approach. These are (1) news or editorial, (2) "reason why," (3) explanatory, (4) humorous, (5) testimonial, (6) conversational, (7) "teaser," (8) human-interest, (9) institutional, (10) "trick," and others. Obviously, these groups are not at all mutually exclusive. The important thing to remember is to employ the type of motivation and mode of expression consonant with the product or service being advertised.

The Use of Illustrations

The primary functions of illustrations are to attract the reader's attention and to convey part of the message. It is not necessary (nor possible) to have illustrations in all types of advertisements, but whenever it is possible they should be used because of their strong psychological effect. The illustration simplifies the problem of presenting a mental image of the product. This is necessary if the reader is to remember the product or service long enough to buy it.

Certain types of pictures attract more attention than others. Pictures of children and animals are particularly effective. A large, simple picture gets more attention than several small pictures. In the last analysis the pictures utilized will depend upon the advertisement under consideration.

Study has demonstrated that the product pictured in the advertisement gets more attention if it is shown in use, especially when it is accomplishing something for the user. For example, a hat or shirt that is being worn, making a man look neat and successful, is superior to a picture of a single hat or shirt. Seeing the product in use stimulates desire in the reader.

Illustrations are used to emphasize the truthfulness of claims. Photographs are particularly convincing. Most people believe what they see. Illustrations are also used to show, even to dramatize, details of a product. Drawings or "close-up" photographs can show all special features.

The illustration should invariably be integrated with the rest of the advertisement. The picture should be closely related to the product or service advertised. If the illustration is used solely because of its attention-getting power, it may distract the reader from the copy, and much of the total impression-value be lost.

There are five major types of illustrative material used in advertising. These are (1) photographs, (2) original drawings, (3) original paintings, (4) charts, and (5) technical drawings. Of these the most commonly used is the *photograph*. *Original paintings* by outstanding artists are so expensive that they are beyond the reach of the average small advertiser. They are effective, but must be used in relation to the product or service being advertised. *Original drawings,* on the other hand, are heavily employed, especially in newspaper advertising. "Line" and "wash" drawings are very effective, and seldom approach good paintings in cost. However, unless the art work is done by competent artists, the advertisement will suffer.

Charts are unusually effective in presenting facts or reasons for buying; they make it easy to grasp the essential points. *Technical drawings* are often employed in trade papers and in direct advertising to explain the workings of complicated products.

Choice of Type

The selection of type is a technical matter which must relate to the over-all theme and purpose of the advertisement. Here the type expert must decide. The problem requires an artistic sense in addition to "visual psychology." Type should be chosen for its ability to express the exact shade of feeling intended. Hand lettering adds further distinction.

Italics or bold-face type may be used for emphasis, also for contrast. Borders are sometimes used to enhance the effect of unity or to support enclosed material, but their use is decreasing. Type (and borders, if used) should be suited to the subject and the audience, and should take into consideration the kind of paper, the amount and purpose of the copy, and the kind of illustration.

Advertising Production

The final stage in preparing the advertisement for production is the *assembly of the elements*. The various components and the layout are sent to the printer. He sets up the advertisement in accordance with the layout, following all instructions meticulously. When he has finished, proofs are made and sent to the advertiser. These are carefully examined for possible needed corrections, and returned to the printer. He makes the necessary adjustments and returns final proofs to the advertiser. When these are approved the advertisement is ready to be run.

Media Selection

Approximately $5,000,000,000 is spent for advertising annually. This sum is apportioned among the various advertising media, which include newspapers, radio and television, direct mail, magazines, business and trade papers, and a number of others.

An important problem faced by the advertiser, naturally, is the selection of media to reach the largest number of potential customers per dollar spent. Such a choice can be made intelligently only after careful study of each medium, to learn the type of coverage each can offer. Any larger advertising agency has a media expert whose primary duty is to suggest the best media in the best combinations for the advertiser. A brief examination of the leading media follows.

Newspapers have always been considered very effective for local advertising and in the last few years their value in nation-wide advertising has been recognized. Today they dominate the scene; they absorb approximately 35 per cent of all advertising expenditures. Newspapers offer heavy coverage at comparatively low cost, in localized areas. They can be utilized on short notice; this fact makes them particularly effective for most types of retailing. They are strong "traffic builders" and are depended upon heavily by retailers.

Radio and television is the second largest medium, accounting for close to 15 per cent of advertising budgets. National advertisers use this medium primarily to build up good will, but local programs have proved effective also in selling merchandise or services. However, analysis of "listenership" and the effect of such programs on buying habits discovers substantial discrepancies in the reports submitted by different research firms which evaluate radio and television programs.

Undoubtedly the greatest interest today lies in the potential growth of television. The effects of this new medium can hardly be overestimated; it is already affecting radio advertising expenditures. Rapid development of television programming, plus greatly increased sales of television receivers, is stimulating sponsor interest all over the country. However, television advertising technique is still in its infancy and the cost of good programs is extremely high. Technical advances should soon lower costs and increase the effectiveness of television advertising.

Direct mail has grown very rapidly since the end of World War II. Over 12 per cent of advertising funds are spent on this medium. It is very effective in achieving selective contacts with potential buyers; experts claim it to be another form of personal selling. Retailers, especially department stores and home-furnishings firms use it very successfully. Direct mail is a somewhat expensive medium, but there is comparatively little waste.

This medium is also unusually adaptable to the needs and requirements of different advertisers. It may be employed for large campaigns or small ones and in various forms and shapes; it may be used nationally or locally. For these reasons it is depended upon heavily by small businessmen with relatively little money to spend. They can achieve a high local coverage by printing inexpensive circulars, handbills, leaflets, announcements, etc., and distributing them quickly, either by mail or in person.

Magazines account for another 11 per cent of all advertising expenditures. They are particularly effective in developing national recognition for a firm and its products. Circulation of the larger magazines run into many millions; and they claim that each copy is read by many people. However, the cost of such advertising (as high as $25,000 per page) precludes its use by smaller firms.

Outdoor advertising, a comparatively small medium, is growing in importance. Expeditures for it are about 5 per cent of the total. Outdoor advertising has been held back somewhat because it has been esthetically abused, but correction of this misuse has eliminated much of the feeling against it. The importance of this medium lies in its ability to increase the local intensity of a marketing campaign. Coverage can be adapted to meet the requirements of any situation. The medium is flexible enough to be used either by the storekeeper who wants only one sign posted or by the large concern selling nationally, which supplements its advertising in other media with the outdoor form. The ads may range from small placards to very large signs electrically lighted to attract evening passers-by.

The remainder of the advertising budget is spent largely for promotional material, such as point-of-sale displays, samples, premiums, contests, and consumer education. These are employed to tie in with both advertising and personal selling. Their use has been growing rapidly in recent years and may be expected to grow further. These are very flexible devices; they may be used to initiate, maintain, or bolster a sagging campaign.

From a practical standpoint, the advertiser wants returns; but there are other aims, such as higher standards of art and higher forms of public service. The trend since 1900 has been "Truth in Advertising," a motto that should govern advertising in future years because it is a guarantee that business will reach "the possible attainment of that ideal state in which the fact that an article is advertised through any medium will be alone a guarantee of its worth."

SALESMANSHIP

Salesmanship is the skill or art of presenting goods, services, or ideas in a way to make people want goods and services or accept ideas; it is the art of satisfying the needs of people. It has also been defined as the art of helping people to buy intelligently. Selling is a twofold process. The first step is to uncover the needs or latent desires of people; the second, to persuade them that it is to their advantage to fill those needs by purchasing a firm's product or services.

Selling concepts have changed very much in the last 25 years. However, present-day sales principles are not too well understood by most people. In spite of the service which salesmanship has rendered to our economic system many people still consider selling a necessary evil rather than a creative skill. So much criticism is voiced about the heavy costs of distribution that many persons think of salesmanship as a wasteful and questionable pursuit. Even salesmen often share this point of view. For these reasons, this occupation has had difficulty in achieving professional status.

It is true that many years ago salesmen did engage in questionable practices. The old concept of selling demanded that the salesman get the order by fair means or foul. Current thinking is very different. Today's salesman is definitely expected to help the customer buy. The salesman must so win over the customer that he will regard the salesman as a friend and buy from him again and again. This type of selling requires the thorough training of the salesman, in order that he may fully understand the needs of his "prospects" and may give them valuable assistance. The modern, trained salesman does not consider his job finished when the item has been sold and delivery made. He will follow up the purchase by seeing that his customer knows how to use the product properly. If the sale is to a dealer the salesman will help him promote and sell the item. Such a salesman is truly a merchandise counselor whose visits are looked forward to by his customers.

Formerly it was the practice to hire salesmen rather haphazardly and, if they failed, to let them go. Seldom did the executive in charge consider the possibility that his methods were responsible for the failure of his men. Today, however, the duties of the selling job are analyzed very carefully; men are selected to meet the requirements of specific positions, and are carefully trained and supervised. Then, if the salesman falls down, the executive in charge bears the brunt of criticism. This approach developed because more and more businessmen came to the conclusion that poor salesmen were a serious liability to their firms.

For the remainder of this article we will examine modern salesmanship methods primarily from the point of view of the wholesale salesman, because wholesale selling necessarily includes most of the techniques employed in retail and specialty selling. A little thought will convince the reader that no dealer will buy a product for resale unless he is first convinced that the product is a good "buy." Therefore, the wholesale salesman must face the dual problem of (1) "selling" the dealer as a potential user of the product, and (2) of selling to him as a businessman who must see a profit in the resale of the item.

Requirements for Salesmanship

A good salesman should have an *agreeable personality* as well as thorough training and should like to meet people. Firms expect their salesmen to be loyal, honest, dependable, and courteous. Men with these characteristics plus a thorough training should be very effective in their jobs.

Before the novice undergoes regular sales training, it is important that personality deficiencies be ironed out. Irritating characteristics must be eliminated. Speech defects must be cleared up and the vocabulary enlarged to include a firm grasp of the terms needed for the types of selling involved. The appearance and dress of novices must pass muster; here again constructive suggestions are of great benefit. Besides having a pleasant attitude and the ability to get along with people, in some types of selling the salesman must be able to write a good sales letter.[1] This is a more difficult ability to develop.

The properly equipped salesman must be *fully trained* in every phase of the sales presentation. He must be thoroughly grounded in a knowledge of his industry, his firm, and the product it manufactures or the service it sells. He must be trained in the psychology of selling as well as in effective presentation. His training should include the techniques of finding prospects, getting interviews, and in then giving complete, convincing demonstrations which will result in sales. He should also be able to describe clearly any additional promotional services that the firm expects him to render. With such training, plus the usual selling equipment, the new salesman should be ready to do a satisfactory job. These factors in sales training will now be discussed in detail.

Factors in Sales Training

Familiarity with his industry as a whole is a prime requisite for a salesman if he is to meet competition successfully. His customers will expect him to be familiar with competing firms and their products, typical practices in the industry, and its business methods. He should know what trends are significant and should be able to pass on this information to his customers.

Thorough knowledge of his own firm and its business organization is even more important; it is customary to give new men this detailed information. They should be told of its historical development, and of its current activities and objectives. They should be introduced to all executives with whom they may expect to come in contact, and to the work of those departments which will have a direct bearing on their sales. These depart-

---

[1]For information regarding Sales Letters, see page 490.

ments include packing, shipping, scheduling, record-keeping, and especially credit-granting.

In this connection it should be noted that a major area of conflict usually exists between salesmen and credit men. Salesmen naturally tend to sell every prospect that they can; but sometimes customers are weak credit risks. Credit men, on the other hand, have to see that losses are held to a minimum, and often refuse to approve sales on credit to such customers. The natural reaction of salesmen working on a commission basis is to feel that they are being injured by persons who fail to understand the complexities of selling. Conflict is bound to develop between credit men and salesmen unless the work of each is carefully explained to the other. Introducing salesmen to credit men tends to eliminate this friction, for once individuals get to know each other socially it is much easier to lessen conflicts.

A knowledge of the firm includes many other areas. Distribution policies should be explained to the salesman; he should be taught how and why the marketing channels utilized by the firm have been selected. Contracts in use, price schedules, terms of sales, advertising campaigns, and any other features of the marketing program should be outlined in detail. A salesman should also be familiar with the transportation and delivery methods of his firm. This information should include the time required for production and shipment, the cost of transportation, and the problems of damage in transit; and it should cover the difficult subject of returns and allowances.

The salesman should also know the firm's method of production, the manufacturing processes, the raw materials entering into the product, the workmanship, patent rights, etc., and be thoroughly grounded in the physical characteristics of the product. These include sizes, shapes, styles, colors, packaging, and any other aspects which might be of value in selling. All too often a salesman fails to stress desirable features built into the product by the firm's engineering department; these features possess valuable sales appeal. This neglect is discovered so often that many firms make strong efforts to keep salesmen abreast of new features. They are often required to go through a modified factory-training course, or at least to demonstrate the uses of the new devices in special-training meetings. All such information is taught in terms of interest to distributors, dealers, and users.

Salesmen often fail because of an inadequate knowledge of their offering. Obviously, unless the salesman thoroughly understands the uses and values of his products or services he cannot do an effective job of selling; *thorough knowledge* of the offering is a prerequisite for sound sales demonstration. Such knowledge enables the salesman to guide and control the sales interview, and to meet objections effectively. Most important, it enables him to suit the offerings to the specific needs of his prospects.

Psychology of Salesmanship

A knowledge of selling psychology is absolutely essential to salesmen. Training in psychology of salesmanship deals primarily with the motives of human behavior. All people want goods and services. However, their reasons for wanting various items differ, and in many instances the desire for the product must be deliberately aroused. The art of salesmanship consists largely in showing prospective buyers how certain goods may satisfy their wants.

There are many lists of desires (needs or wants) and motivations common to all people; the following is typical:

1. Food and drink—all people eat and drink
2. Comfort—pleasant and relaxed surroundings
3. Affection—doing things for loved ones
4. Pride—the desire to excel
5. Need for amusement and entertainment (including vacations)
6. Imitativeness—we wish to keep up with our neighbors
7. Sense of ownership—borrowing or renting is not sufficient for many people
8. Fear or caution—we take care of ourselves and others
9. Desire for gain or profit—we buy bargains
10. Wish to construct—people like to make things with their own hands

By utilizing such information the salesmen can adapt his approach to specific types of prospects. While most wants are common to all people, it is very important that the salesman fit his offering to the specific needs of each prospect by playing up the most effective type of motivation. The sales presentation should fulfill the special desires of the prospect. In this connection it should be noted that most things are sold on the basis of *ideas* rather than on the basis of physical properties alone. Care should be taken to distinguish between emotional and rational buyers. Most consumers are considered to be in the former category because of their tendency to "buy with the heart" rather than with the head. Industrial and business buyers, on the other hand, are noted for their scientific approach to purchasing and can be convinced more easily with facts and figures than with frills and fancies.

Psychological training should include information regarding the personality and character traits of prospects. This should be helpful in overcoming sales resistance. The salesman should develop the faculty of keen observation and sensitivity to the reactions of prospects. He must be flexible—he must not only know his prospect but also be able to adjust to him quickly.

Sales Presentations

After the salesman has received training in psychological fundamentals he may be taught how to make a sales presentation. It is agreed that instruction in the preparation of a selling talk is essential for most men. However, there is considerable disagreement as to how much of the selling talk should be memorized. For many products sales managers insist that sales presentations be memorized and given without change. These are known as "canned" presentations. Most sales executives, however, prefer more or less standardized extemporaneous presentations. This does not mean that the salesman may say anything he pleases. He has been trained in selling techniques and is expected to memorize detailed outlines of necessary selling information; but he is given leeway in his use of language and method of presentation.

The decision on whether to use memorized or extemporaneous presentations usually depends upon the type of offering and the salesman; also upon the type of prospect and the number of times he will be called upon. The memorized presentation is effective in selling comparatively simple or inexpensive items, especially when the prospect is not a technical buyer, and will be called upon only once, or at long intervals. When this is the situation comparatively poor salesmen may be employed, and trained in a technique which will give the highest ratio of sales per dollar of expense. The extemporaneous presentation is effective in selling products and services which require a number of visits and which are purchased only after careful consideration. Usually a higher type of salesman is required, one who can adjust rapidly to changing situations. In most sales situations the extemporaneous rather than the memorized talk is preferable.

The selling talk should be carefully planned and prepared. It crystallizes all that the salesman knows about the offering in terms of the prospect's needs. It should be developed around the basic buying motives. When properly presented it has a number of major advantages over the unprepared approach. It covers all the ground, leaving no gaps. It insures logical order. It not only saves time for the salesman and the prospect; it is especially valuable for the novice. When he might fail if left to his own devices, with such preparation he can sell effectively from the beginning. The prepared talk stimulates the salesman's confidence in his ability to conduct the sales interview and helps him to present his case more convincingly. Most sales managers believe that a salesman with a pleasant personality who has taken the trouble to thoroughly digest the standard sales presentation is well on his way to success.

Techniques of Selling

Now our salesman is ready to begin selling. The first problem is to find potential customers; this is known as prospecting. Sometimes it is simple, sometimes quite complicated. While the firm will usually give the salesman as much assistance as it can, in most cases he is dependent upon his own ingenuity.

Prospects may be culled from various directories, such as the telephone book, membership lists of trade associations and clubs, city directories, and various other compiled listings. For many types of selling, however, these are less effective than some of the well-known prospecting systems. These include:

1. Endless-chain system
2. Center-of-influence technique
3. Personal observation technique
4. Direct-mail sales
5. "Cold turkey" canvassing

The *endless-chain* system is predicated upon the simple idea that you can use each customer or prospect as a "lead" to other prospects. Some time during the sales presentation, usually at or near the end, the salesman asks the prospect to suggest any other persons who might be interested in the offering. The *center-of-influence technique* is based upon the idea that if a key person in a community or group can be convinced of the merit of the offering, he will suggest a number of other prospects. The name of the influential person may be very effective in getting the next interview. *Personal observation technique* is one of the simpler prospecting techniques. Simply by being alert the salesman can spot prospects for many types of products, even items as diversified as automobiles and home furnishings. *Direct-mail* leads usually result from advertising campaigns in which readers request further information. *"Cold turkey" canvassing* is the simplest of all prospecting methods. Without any preliminary contact the salesman works from door to door or office to office, hoping to stimulate interest in his proposition. Most salesmen object to this type of selling, but experience has proved that it brings results if the salesman perseveres.

Before a salesman makes contact with the prospect he should find out as much as he can about him. This is known as the *pre-approach*. Every bit of pertinent information the salesman can unearth may be helpful during the presentation. It is desirable to learn the best time for interviewing the prospect. His needs and interests are also very important to know. With this information the salesman can best adapt his offering to the prospect's requirements. Pre-approach analysis is helpful because it conserves time that might otherwise be wasted on poor leads. It also helps to give the salesman enthusiasm and confidence.

Information about prospects is often available at the salesman's home office; old records and reference material may be of great value. Study should also comprise an analysis of the territory. Additional sources of information are Government reports, marketing surveys, trade-association compilations, surveys by salesmen, leads from correspondence, and salesmen carrying related lines. Initiative and imagination are necessary for successful pre-approach work.

Although it is important for salesmen to be able to size up prospects rather quickly, there is danger in this practice. While a good salesman wastes little time on weak potential customers and, consequently, maintains a high record of sales, there is the possibility of over-reaching himself by belittling or avoiding a prospect because the initial impression does not promise a sale. Every salesman can cite instances in which unassuming prospects and questionable leads resulted in surprisingly easy sales. The study of prospects prior to making contact with them helps greatly in developing sound sales strategy. Salesmen often mistakenly cut down on this phase of the work because it seems to be a waste of time; but they actually make the ultimate sales presentation more difficult.

Contact with the Prospect

The salesman is now ready to make contact with the prospect. His first problem is to obtain the interview. This difficulty has been exaggerated unduly. In most cases the salesman need only present his card, or request to see the prospective buyer to be given the opportunity. What transpires once he makes the contact is a different problem.

If, however, the interview is not readily granted other methods must be tried. A simple device employed by many firms is to send out advance announcements. Cards or letters timed to precede the call of the salesman are mailed to prospects in order to break the ice. These may be quite effective. Often sending in the salesman's card with a message on it which should appeal to the buyer will result in an interview. Sometimes an appeal to good fellowship, self-interest, or curiosity will induce the prospect to see the salesman. Psychologically, the salesman should expect to get the interview.

Various other devices and maneuvers are employed to make contact with the prospect. Some firms offer free services—for example, polishing furniture or checking up on an oil burner or radio free of charge. Once contact is made the salesman may work into his presentation. A number of cooking-utensil firms hold parties in the home of prospects, supplying the food besides doing the necessary work. All they ask is an opportunity to show the guests how efficiently their utensils perform. A sales practice frequently considered questionable has developed in many parts of the country. Salesmen will claim that they are making a survey, but once they are in the home or office will launch into the sales demonstration. The best technique for getting interviews, as we outlined in the discussion on prospecting, is that which is developed from preceding contacts.

A crucial stage in selling is the *initial phase of the sales interview*. The salesman must secure favorable attention quickly or he may find it impracticable to continue. If the prospect is not immediately interested or favorably impressed he may dismiss the salesman at once. For this reason he must be very careful in his approach. First, the salesman's appearance and attitude should of themselves insure a friendly reception. Second, great care should be given to the opening statements, which should refer to the prospect's problems and focus his full attention upon the salesman and his offering. Different devices are used to accomplish this end. The salesman may show the customer samples, models, manuals, or pictures which the latter may like to examine; the salesman may also refer to mutual friends, or give concrete facts which will interest the prospect.

During the initial stage of the interview, in addition to winning favorable attention, the salesman must check the information he acquired concerning the prospect prior to the interview. Once he is sure of his facts the salesman can go on to create interest. Certain cautions are in order. The salesman should proceed slowly in utilizing his information and in presenting his samples or models. He should wait for responses in order to gauge attention. He should see that the prospect is comfortable, to make sure that he will listen to the proposition in detail.

Many salesmen follow a standard procedure in *building up interest*. They begin with selling points that bear directly on the prospect's problems, hoping to capture his attention, then quickly tie in the prospect's problems with the selling points of the offering. They next emphasize the way in which the offering will supply his needs or solve his problems. In presenting these points salesmen are on the alert for the dominant buying motive. Usually certain points or features stimulate a prospect more than others; and these selling points, when stressed, become the key to the sale.

All buyers have inhibitions which must be overcome. Either they have been buying from sources which they consider satisfactory, or they do not wish to try something new. These are major hurdles in any sales presentation. Buyers do not like to be high-pressured; a shrewd salesman lets the prospect feel that he is making the decision. In this respect suggestions are more effective than high pressure. The basic problem is to arouse the feeling of need and to show how the offering solves the need. The salesman must adjust the speed of his presentation to the mind of the prospect. Genuine enthusiasm is contagious.

Even if the prospect indicates a desire to own the product the sale may be far from over. Conflicts with older desires in the mind of the buyer may tend to postpone decision. At this stage it is necessary to solidify desire into conviction. This may be done by the use of tests, guarantees, facts, and statistics, and testimonials from satisfied users.

With certain products it is possible to prove to the prospect by tests that they will meet his needs. For example, if it is stated that a ladder will support a certain number of pounds, weights can be placed on the object to prove it. With fabrics, in which tensile strength is an important asset, a simple, small hand device can make the test on the spot. It is easy to prove that a ball-point pen will make carbon copies by having the prospect write on manifold paper forms.

Guarantees may be used to clinch sales, especially of technical merchandise and equipment. Any doubts regarding quality must be resolved. If the salesman's firm guarantees the product, the prospect is more likely to buy. Sometimes, unfortunately, salesmen make statements which are not backed up by the contract. Such improper practices result in much ill will.

Facts and statistics are effective in selling to technical buyers. Proof of this nature will often convince them when descriptions of the product seem to get nowhere.

Testimonials are useful in selling consumer goods. The average person tends to believe what he reads or hears, especially if it is said by someone of importance or someone he knows. If a satisfactory trial has been made by some well-known person the implication is that it will also be satisfactory to the prospect. That is why many salesmen find the name of a local purchaser effective in selling to others.

At this stage of the sales demonstration it is suggested that the salesmen use positive expressions, avoiding neutral or negative statements. The prospect likes to hear what the offering will do for him, not, as a rule, what it will not do. In this connection, many sales managers caution their men against mentioning competitors' products unless forced to do so by the prospect.

"Objections" Techniques

At any stage of the sales presentation the prospect is likely to raise objections. These may be simple and unimportant or they may be serious. Some salesmen are irritated by objections, but that is the wrong attitude. Objections are guideposts to the prospect's reactions, and a good salesman is on the alert for them and makes the most of them. He listens carefully before answering. Perhaps he repeats the question, so that both he and the prospect understand it exactly. Then he answers it, for he knows full well that unless he meets it adequately the sale will not be made.

A number of techniques are used to answer objections. First there is the "reverse English" or "boomerang" technique. Sometimes the question raised by the prospect can be turned into a strong selling point. For example, the prospect may object to a light-colored automobile. The salesman then points out that a light-colored car is safer than a dark-colored one because the former can be seen more easily at night.

A second technique is to "reverse positions." If the prospect's objections as to quality are unfounded the salesman may suggest that the prospect tell exactly what is wrong with the item; and he will have difficulty finding specific warranted complaints. The salesman will then examine each feature with the prospect, at the same time making the necessary selling points.

In some cases the salesman agrees that the objection of the prospect is well founded; the salesman then stresses a superior feature which compensates for the lack. For example, if, in the sale of a ball-point pen, the prospect objects that such pens eliminate individuality in handwriting the salesman agrees, but points out that only a ball-point pen can make carbon copies or write on all types of surfaces under a wide variety of conditions.

Once in a while a salesman will answer an objection with a direct denial; but the utmost caution should be used in employing this type of answer. Under most circumstances it will alienate the prospect and preclude any possibility of a sale. In certain cases, however, it is necessary to deny a statement made by the prospect. This is especially true when the reputation or business practices of the salesman's firm are impugned unfairly.

Never magnify an objection. A poor salesman may build up a simple objection into so complex a discussion that a sale is impossible. Avoid arguments in handling objections; no one wins, and the atmosphere is not conducive to a sale. Many salesmen anticipate possible objections and forestall them by working both the objection and the answer into the regular prepared presentation.

Getting the order is the acid test in selling; some salesmen seem able to do everything but complete the sale—they cannot bring themselves to ask for the order. Various techniques may be used for the closing. There is no reason why this should not be done at the right time. In this respect it should be noted that it is not always necessary to go through the complete presentation before trying to close. A "trial close" is tried by a good salesman at different points along the way. Quite often the sale can be completed in short order especially when the prospect asks for a certain type of item. Sometimes, a lengthy presentation will do more harm than good. Some firms employ an "up-the-sleeve offer," in which an additional item or a discount is offered by way of inducement. When the product is in short supply the "standing-room-only" technique is usually effective. The prospect is advised that unless he buys immediately, he may not be able to buy at all. The simplest type of closing is that in which there is *implied consent*. As the salesman finishes the presentation, having eliminated any objections, he takes out his order book and begins to write up the order. Naturally, unless the prospect stops him, it is taken for granted that the sale is being consummated.

The modern salesman is expected to do more than merely take an order. He must cooperate with other departments within the marketing division, especially with advertising and sales promotion. He is expected to assist the dealer in every way possible—by showing him how the product can be sold, pointing out different selling methods, instructing the dealer's salespeople, and assisting in setting up point-of-sale displays.

The salesman may be expected to perform service work on the product both before and after the sale, and to assist in credit and collection duties. Usually he will be asked to submit reports and records of his activities. He will also be expected to attend sales meetings, conventions, exhibits, and demonstrations which may help him to improve his techniques or at which he can meet prospects.

From the foregoing it is evident that the modern salesman's work is far from simple; yet a man who acquires the necessary training and maintains a pleasant and cooperative attitude is usually successful.

The Successful Salesman[1]

The successful salesman:

1. Does not argue; he sells
2. Does not contradict his prospect nor tell him he is wrong
3. Does not deliver a speech; he illustrates his conversation
4. Does not forget that figures and a pencil are the best evidence
5. Never puts questions that may call for a "no"
6. Never gets excited
7. Never speaks against his competitors; he slowly but surely proves the advantage of his own product
8. Speaks of the advantages of his offering and does not discuss prices
9. Never smokes when calling on a prospect, unless he is invited to do so
10. Wears nothing so original or eccentric that it will attract his prospect's attention
11. Never speaks uncertainly, but always with the authority of a man who knows
12. Never raises his voice (especially at the closing) but always speaks clearly enough to be understood
13. Does not let the conversation deviate from his aim: an order
14. Does not tolerate any doubt concerning the qualities of his product; he is sure of his representations
15. Does not jabber; he lets his prospect talk. One can be a very fine lawyer but a very poor salesman
16. Does not use high-pressure methods
17. Does not allow circumstances to get the best of him; he dominates them
18. Does not fear competition—that may lead him to success
19. Never fails to keep his word; he is never late
20. Never stops working and increasing his sales
21. Does not forget the value of frequent, opportune visits. The law of averages is inexorable. Repeated visits bring him his reward: orders and friends
22. Does not forget that his customer and friends will help him

[1]Adapted from *Think* Magazine, June 1936

23. Never neglects his customers; he knows what that means
24. Never wastes his time; he works his territory methodically and consistently
25. Never is satisfied with one order when he can have more
26. Does not stay home on rainy days; his prospects are likely to be in then, and there will not be many visitors
27. Does not rest on Saturday afternoon; he can meet prospects then whom he cannot see on other days
28. Never lacks self-confidence, confidence in his product, his company, and his leaders
29. Does not acknowledge "bad times" nor depressions; he transforms difficult times into productive periods, adapting himself to the job and the circumstances
30. Does not scatter his faculties; he concentrates his thoughts and efforts
31. Never turns down cooperation
32. Never admits failure while on duty

TALKING

One of the most common human activities is talking. Even as infants we begin to express our desires and convey our thoughts by word of mouth. We want other people to understand what is on our minds, and we transmit these ideas by speech.

Talking is also one of our most revealing habits. It gives a strong insight into the speaker's personality. Over 2,000 years ago, Demosthenes said that "as a vessel is known by the sound whether it is cracked or not, so men are proved by their speeches whether they be wise or foolish." This statement is every whit as true today. When a person begins to speak our impressions of him tend to change for better or worse. His speech, coupled with his appearance, makes a lasting impression. For this reason, if for no other, the way in which a person talks should be given serious attention.

Communication with others is most commonly carried out by word of mouth. This is quite as true in business as in other walks of life. Business executives must be skilled in communicating with others, for failure to develop this ability results in misunderstandings. Effective speech is an incalculable aid toward attaining social or business success.

Effective speakers are made, not born. Speech may be improved in many ways. It is necessary to build a good vocabulary because words are the tools of speech. Grammatical errors must be eliminated consciously until correct speech becomes natural. Enunciation and pronunciation must also be cultivated to make sure that listeners can easily grasp what is being said.

Various techniques may be employed to correct speech deficiencies. Speaking in front of a mirror, for instance is very helpful. It will quickly reveal mannerisms which are distracting or unattractive. The speaker can observe his facial expressions and improve upon them. Another technique is the use of a voice recorder. A record of the voice should be made and listened to critically. While the first reaction to the playback will probably be shock, after one overcomes this initial reaction, he can readily distinguish and correct speaking defects.

Think before you speak. Do not talk just to make conversation. If you are in doubt about what to say, listen. One of the basic principles of salesmanship is that most people enjoy talking much more than listening. A customer will sometimes talk himself into a sale when the best unaided efforts of the salesman might fail.

An intelligent speaker adjusts his way of talking to his listeners. Do not talk "over the heads" of people, nor as if you were superior to them. Either attitude is irritating. Use language and expressions which befit the situation. Be pleasant and natural. Everyone dislikes artificiality, but respects sincerity. If you talk in an interesting, engaging manner, people are bound to like you and look forward to seeing and hearing you again.

SLANDER AND LIBEL

Slander and libel are different forms of defamation; *slander* is defamation by spoken word, whereas *libel* is defamation by writing, print, picture, effigy, sign, or otherwise than by speech. Some courts have held that the reading of a defamatory letter or a broadcast over the radio from a script is libel and not slander.

No defamation can constitute the basis of an action to recover damages unless it is "published." In the law of defamation "publication" has a special meaning. It is the communication of the defamatory matter to another person. A libel is not published if it is read *only* by the person defamed; and a slander is not published if it is heard *only* by the person defamed. However, no person defamed can recover damages when he, himself, communicates or by his conduct is responsible for the communication of, the defamatory matter, or if he authorizes its publication. To illustrate, when a person who receives a defamatory letter exhibits it to another, the publication is not actionable.

There are *two classes of defamation;* one is defamatory per se, the other is not. A defamation is slander per se or libel per se if the words on their face, without other proof, are recognized as injurious; but if the words on their face are not injurious, but become so only as a result of the surrounding circumstances, the defamation is not per se. In the former case damage is presumed to follow from the language used, whereas in the latter case damage must be alleged and proved.

Generally, words are libelous per se, *i.e.,* no special damage need be alleged and proved, if they expose or even tend to expose a person to public hatred, shame, disgrace, or contempt.

Some words may constitute libel per se but not slander per se. The distinction has an ancient origin. It rests on the fact that a libel is a more permanent form of defamation than a slander and can, therefore, be more readily circulated with greater possibility of causing damage to the person defamed.

Words are slanderous per se if they impute the commission of a crime or the possession of a loathsome or contagious disease, or if they prejudice a person in his profession, trade, or business.

When the words are libelous per se or slanderous per se the person defamed is entitled to recover damages without regard to the motive with which the publication was made. Such motive is unimportant. If malice is proved the person defamed can recover *exemplary damages,* that is damages greater than the actual loss, and imposed for punishment.

In all actions of slander or libel, whether per se or not, the words must be *false.* Falsity is presumed; it need not be proved. Truth must be established by the person who published the defamation.

Under some circumstances a person who is sued for defamation may plead *privilege.* The privilege grants immunity for what is otherwise defamatory, whether per se or not. Privilege may be *absolute* or *qualified.* It rests on public policy. Generally, a privileged communication is one made in good faith by some person to another when both have an interest in the subject matter of the communication. For example, defamatory statements, even if malicious, made in a judicial proceeding which are material and relevant to the issues there involved are absolutely privileged.

Derogatory statements by an employer concerning a former employee constitute a qualifiedly privileged communication if made in answer to inquiries by a prospective employer.

Newspapers have no special privilege in the absence of statute. Fair and impartial reports by newspapers of judicial, legislative, or executive proceedings are privileged. Comment or criticism that is fair and reasonable gives immunity to newspapers. Public welfare requires that newspapers shall have the right of making such criticism and comment. However, actual malice defeats the defense of fair comment and criticism.

All persons who either cause or participate in the publication of defamations are liable. A newspaper owner is liable for a libel printed in his newspaper, even though it was made without his knowledge or consent; the author is also liable.

ORGANIZATION OF CLUBS AND PARLIAMENTARY LAW

Clubs

A club is a group of people organized for a purpose—generally social, business, political, or educational, but not for profit.

One or more persons usually start to organize a club after informal discussions. They invite some other interested persons to come to the first meeting. When they convene, one person generally "takes the chair" and, after gaining the attention of the people present, explains the purposes for which they have met. This person may retain the chairmanship during the meeting, or he may suggest that another be chosen as a temporary chairman. Someone will then rise and say, "I move that Mr.—— retain the chairmanship for this meeting," and someone else will say, "I second the motion." The chairman then announces to the group, "You have heard the motion: That Mr.—— retain the chairmanship for this meeting. Are there any other nominations?" If there are none, he calls for a vote by saying, "All those in favor, say 'aye,' all those against say 'no.' " He then counts the votes, and says, "The ayes have it, and Mr.—— retains the chair during this meeting."

The chairman appoints a temporary secretary, or one is elected from those present. Both temporary officers serve until their successors are elected in accordance with rules the club will later adopt. A committee should be selected by the chairman to draft a constitution and bylaws. The meeting is then adjourned.

At the next meeting a copy of the proposed constitution and bylaws is given to the chairman, who reads it and moves "for the adoption of the constitution and bylaws as read." When this motion is seconded, he reads the constitution, section by section, permitting time for discussion and amendments, if any are proposed, before putting each section to a vote. When the constitution has been adopted, the bylaws are taken up in the same manner. Since the future activities of the club will be governed by these rules, and conditions may change, flexibility is desirable. It is advisable to provide that the constitution and bylaws may be amended.

Constitution of ——— Club[1]

ARTICLE I: NAME

The name of the club shall be ———.

ARTICLE II: PURPOSE

The purpose of this club is ———.

---

[1]This is a basic constitution; the actual text of a specific constitution depends on the purpose of the group, and other special circumstances.

ARTICLE III: MEMBERSHIP

Membership in this club shall be granted to those over ———— years, and ————
(state prerequisites).

ARTICLE IV: OFFICERS

The officers of the club shall be a president, a vice president, a secretary, and a
treasurer.

ARTICLE V: MEETINGS AND QUORUM

Section 1. Regular meeting shall be held (fix time and place).
Section 2. The annual meeting shall be held (fix time and place).
Section 3. Special meetings may be called by the president; or, on request of ————
members, the president shall call such meeting.
Section 4. ———— members of the club in good standing, shall constitute a quorum
for transacting business.

ARTICLE VI: AMENDMENT

This constitution may be amended at any meeting of the club by a two-thirds vote,
a quorum being present.

Bylaws

ARTICLE I: DUTIES OF THE OFFICERS

Section 1. It shall be the duty of the president to preside at all meetings of the club
and perform all duties pertaining to his office.
Section 2. In the absence or disability of the president, the vice president shall perform the duties of the president.
Section 3. The secretary shall keep and record the minutes of club proceedings. He
shall send notice of meetings, notify officers of election, and perform such other duties
as his office may require.
Section 4. The treasurer shall receive and keep the club's funds in ———— bank,
and pay out the same only on order of the president. He shall make an annual report
of receipts and disbursements.

ARTICLE II: ELECTION OF OFFICERS

Section 1. All officers shall be elected by ballot at the annual meeting and shall
assume office at the close of that meeting.
Section 2. No member shall be eligible to office who has not been a member of the
club for one year.
Section 3. No member shall hold the same office more than ———— years in succession, and filling an unexpired term shall be considered as a term in office.
Section 4. Should an officer resign before new elections are held, the president shall
appoint some member in good standing to temporarily assume the office, and direct
the secretary to send notice of a special meeting at the next regular meeting, when the
vacancy can be filled.

ARTICLE III: MEMBERSHIP

Section 1. Candidates must be proposed by a member and must be seconded by another member, and the vote shall be held at the meeting following that at which membership was proposed. ———— negative votes shall exclude a candidate, and the same
name may not be proposed more than once during a club year.
Section 2. The secretary shall notify the treasurer of the election of new members,
whereupon he shall notify the elected members, with instruction to send dues to the
treasurer. Failure to pay such dues within ———— days shall forfeit membership.
Section 3. Resignation from membership shall be in writing. Members in arrears
for one year shall be dropped.

ARTICLE IV: DUES

Section 1. The annual dues shall be $——, payable at the first regular meeting after the annual meeting.

Section 2. When an election to membership takes place within ———— months of the expiration of the fiscal year, the dues shall be credited to the following year.

ARTICLE V: COMMITTEES

Section 1. At the regular meeting next previous to the annual meeting, the president shall appoint the following committees to report at the annual meeting: a nominating committee to present a list of candidates for election to office for the following year; an auditing committee to report on the correctness of the treasurer's accounts.

Section 2. The president shall appoint such special committees as he considers necessary at any time, or, on the majority vote of the members present at any meeting, he shall appoint committees as they direct.

ARTICLE VI: AMENDMENTS

These bylaws may be amended at any meeting by a two-thirds vote, a quorum being present.

ARTICLE VII: PARLIAMENTARY AUTHORITY

Cushings' *Manual of Parliamentary Practice* shall be the parliamentary authority on all matters not covered by the constitution and bylaws of the club.

ARTICLE VIII: SUSPENSION OF BYLAWS

These bylaws may be suspended in case of emergency by unanimous vote of all those present at a meeting at which a quorum is present.

Order of Business

1. Call to order by the presiding officer
2. Reading of minutes of previous meeting by the secretary, corrections, if any, vote of acceptance
3. Treasurer's report (as necessity requires at annual meeting)
4. Committee reports
5. Unfinished business
6. New business
7. Program of the day
8. Good and welfare
9. Adjournment

When the constitution and bylaws have been adopted, the permanent officers are elected. The candidates for office may be chosen by a nominating committee, who present their slate, or the presiding officer may call for nominations from the floor. Nominations from the floor do not have to be seconded.

Nominating and voting must be held in the manner set forth in the bylaws. When such officers have been elected, the newly elected president takes the chair; the temporary secretary retains his office until the end of the meeting, when he turns over his records and the minutes of all meetings to his successor.

The club is then fully organized to function. It can decide to apply for a state charter by incorporating as a nonprofit organization, so that the individual members shall not be personally liable for any debts the club may contract. The laws of the states vary; an attorney should be consulted concerning proper incorporation.

Motions

Matters of interest to the organization which require approval by the membership are brought before the club by motion. A member who desires to make a motion rises and addresses the presiding officer by title, as "Mr. Chairman" or "Madam Chairman." This officer grants recognition by calling the member's name. If two members rise, the officer should recognize the one whose voice he first heard. Not until one is recognized may the motion be made. The proper way to make a motion is to introduce the substance of the motion by saying, "I move that ——," or "I move to ——."

The motion may not be discussed or voted upon before approval is obtained by another member. Approval is accomplished by that member saying, "I second the motion," but only after recognition has been granted to him by the presiding officer.

The member who made the motion has the privilege of withdrawing it at any time before it is put to a vote. The motion to withdraw need not be seconded, unless objection is made, in which event a motion to withdraw must be made, seconded, and carried by majority vote of the members present.

If the motion is not thus withdrawn the presiding officer restates the motion and discussion ensues. If there is no discussion the matter is put to a vote. While the motion is pending no other unrelated business may be introduced. However, certain other motions may be made with reference to the main motion. These are:

1. *Motion to amend.* The member who introduced the motion may accept a proposed amendment after it has been regularly made and seconded. If he refuses to accept it, the members first vote upon the amendment, and in the event it is carried, the motion, as amended, is then brought to vote.

The proposed amendment must relate to the subject matter of the main motion, otherwise it may not be entertained. An amended motion may be further amended only once. There can be no amendment of an amendment to an amendment.

2. *Motion to refer to a committee.* At times it may be advisable to obtain the benefit of the view of a committee before putting a motion to a vote, in which event it may be referred to such committee by motion regularly made, seconded, and carried.

3. *Motion to postpone or lay on the table.* When it is deemed advisable to defer putting the motion to a vote, it can be postponed by motion regularly made, seconded, and carried to a certain future time, in which case it can only be considered at that time; or it can be laid on the table, in which case it may be considered at any time.

4. *Motion to close debate or to call the previous question.* After some discussion and in order to force a vote, a motion is made to call for the previous question; if such motion is carried, the main motion must be voted upon.

Voting

The action of the membership is reflected by vote. There are several methods of voting:

1. *By the voice* (viva voce) or by show of hands. The presiding officer calls for a vote by requesting those in favor to say "aye," and after they have responded he requests those opposed to say "no." He judges the responses by ear and announces the result. Sometimes the voting is by show of hands.

2. *By rising.* If there is any doubt as to who won by the previous method of voting, the presiding officer requests those in favor of the motion to rise and remain standing until counted. When the count is reported, these members are seated and those opposed rise. They are counted, and after they sit down the vote is announced.

3. *By unanimous consent.* In routine and minor matters when it is obvious that there is no difference of opinion, the presiding officer, after stating the motion may say, "There being no objection, the motion to ———— will stand approved as read."

4. *By roll call.* When the motion is put to a vote each member's name is called and he or she answers "yes" or "no" and the votes are recorded. When the entire roll has been called, the "yes" and "no" votes are totaled, and the result announced.

5. *By ballot.* The voting methods previously discussed reveal how the members voted. At times members may not wish to disclose how they voted; if ballots are used the voting is secret.

A member may change his vote at any time before the result is announced, except when the ballot method is used, for then there is no way of identifying the voter.

Quorum

A quorum is the number of members fixed by the bylaws as the number that must be present to transact business which will bind the entire membership.

Committees

Committees are small groups of members with special duties. The officer authorized by the bylaws appoints members to the committees. Such designees must accept or decline promptly. If a member accepts he can resign only by notifying such officer. The committees function under the authority of a chairman appointed by the president or by the entire board of officers.

There are *standing* and *special* committees. A standing committee is one which continues, while a special committee ceases to exist when it completes the work for which it was formed. Each committee has its own secretary who records the work of the group and prepares reports which are signed by the chairman. When the chairman renders the report to the membership he does not say, "I wish to report," but "Your committee wishes to report."

Amendments

Amendments to the constitution and bylaws should be submitted in writing. They should be voted upon by the greatest number of members possible after appropriate deliberation. Therefore, a copy of the proposed amendment should be mailed to each member with a notice stating the date of the meeting when voting thereon will take place.

Adjournment

An adjournment for a short period during the meeting is a recess; a continuation of the meeting to another time is an adjournment.

A motion to adjourn must be seconded; it may not be debated or amended, and after it has been voted, it cannot be reconsidered.

Unfinished Business

Business left unfinished at a meeting must be disposed of as old business at the next succeeding meeting before any new business may be called for discussion.

The Minutes

The operations of the club are recorded in permanent form in a minute book. The minutes are kept and signed by the secretary. After a meeting is called to order it is customary for the presiding officer to request the secretary to read the minutes of the previous meeting, and if the minutes as read require amendment by deleting or adding thereto a proper motion to such effect is made and seconded. If no amendment is made, the minutes are approved as read by appropriate motion to that effect. These minutes need not be detailed, but should recite the names of the officers who were present and absent, and contain a summary of committee reports and a record of all motions and their disposition, together with a brief statement of other matters that were discussed at the meeting.

Resolutions

A resolution is a formal expression of opinion by the club as a body. It is generally adopted after motion by a majority vote of those present at the meeting. It is in writing and dated; a copy is made part of the minutes of the meeting at which it was adopted and the original is transmitted to the person or body affected by its subject matter. The nature and purpose of the resolution will determine to what extent it is publicized.

Resolution against Toll Roads

Whereas: The free use of the public highway is a fundamental principle of government.

Whereas: Motor vehicle owners of the United States through special taxes are today largely meeting the costs of the construction of these highways, *and*

Whereas: So-called express highways are simply a step in the further improvement of our public highway system which will be found necessary in those localities where traffic is heavy and congestion great,

Be It Resolved: That the National Automobile Chamber of Commerce opposes any effort to place control of any part of the public highways in the hands of private promoters, and

Be It Further Resolved: That the National Automobile Chamber of Commerce emphatically supports the principle that **the public highways shall be kept forever free to the general public.**

(*Voted by directors of National Automobile Chamber of Commerce, February 1, 1928.*)

If it is decided to incorporate the club, the following form of resolution might be used. Most banks, however, have their own form of resolution for such a purpose.

Resolution Authorizing Club to Open a Bank Account

Resolved: That the treasurer of ————— be and he is hereby authorized to open an account in the ————— bank at its branch located at —————, City of —————, in the name of such club, and that said bank be, and hereby is, authorized to honor checks drawn against funds deposited in the said bank by this club, when they are signed by the treasurer and the president.

Program

The program of a club will, of course, be dictated by its aims and purposes. The specific purpose for which the club is organized constitutes its over-all program.

Most clubs have a special committee, known as the program committee, whose function is to arrange the program of activities to be held under the auspices of the club at stated intervals during the club year. The committee might decide to sponsor a series of lectures or debates, or a musical program, or a series of concerts. If the organization does not have members with special talents to present such programs, the committee generally looks outside the group. If they decide on a lecture series, for instance, they can consult with an organization to obtain speakers or lecturers. There are many such organizations. The American Red Cross, local and Federal district attorneys' offices, local police and Federal narcotics agents, the National Federation of Business and Professional Women's Clubs, and many others will be glad to send speakers, usually free of charge, to speak on their special topics to interested groups. Debates may often be arranged through a local debating society.

In the event that a subject of importance to the club arises with which the members are not particularly well acquainted, it may be advisable to organize a special committee which would first conduct an investigation for the purpose of ascertaining all relevant facts and then report to the membership. Proper resolutions could be adopted on the basis of their findings. The committee might then be directed to meet with governmental agencies, or other authorities, to urge that they act in a way to alleviate or help solve the particular problem. Civic and business groups would probably be most interested in this type of program activity. Other groups might find other types of programs more suitable.

MARRIAGE

Legally, marriage is a relationship founded on contract. It is also a status to which the state is a party and, therefore, the legislative bodies of *each state* have jurisdiction to prescribe the qualifications of the parties; to declare how marriages are to be solemnized and who may perform the marriage ceremony; to define the rights, duties and obligations of the parties; to determine the effect of the marriage on property rights; and to enumerate the causes for its annulment or permanent or limited dissolution. Congress has similar power in the District of Columbia and in the territories of the United States.

The general laws of the state as to marriage apply to the residents or citizens of the state, and to those who are subject to its jurisdiction; and each state has the right to determine the marital status of its citizens under its laws. The general rule is that the validity of a marriage is determined by the law of the place where it was contracted. If valid there it will be valid in all states, unless both parties left the state of their domicile to evade its law. Such departure would have rendered the marriage invalid if the statute expressly provides that such a marriage is invalid: if the statute does not so expressly provide, then the general rule applies. This general rule, however, has no application if such marriage is contrary to the public policy of the state which the parties left—in cases, for instance, of polygamy, incest, or miscegenation.

Statutes in the various states require the procurement of a *marriage license* from an authorized person designated by statute. Many states require a physical examination and a blood test to show that the parties do not have venereal disease. The *solemnization* of a marriage is necessary, except in those states which recognize common law marriages.

A *common law marriage* is a marriage without formal solemnization. It is based upon an actual and mutual agreement between parties having legal capacity to marry, consummated by their living together as husband and wife openly and publicly; and it must contemplate a permanent union. In states where such marriages are recognized, they are as fully valid as ceremonial marriages, and the parties may not voluntarily change their status. Where parties contract a valid common law marriage, it will be considered valid after removal by the parties to another state where such marriages are not recognized. If such a marriage is recognized by a state, a subsequent statute declaring such marriages invalid shall not affect any previous common law marriage. Such statutes are constitutional if they have no retroactive effect.

In order to contract a valid marriage each party must have *legal and mental capacity* at the date of the marriage. Although it is difficult to define the necessary degree of such mental capacity, the general test is whether the person understands the duties and responsibilities which are involved in such relationship. No particular form or degree of insanity invalidates a marriage. At common law, and in some states, the marriage of a person who lacks sufficient mental capacity, and, therefore, cannot give free consent, is absolutely void, and such marriage will be declared invalid in any legal proceeding whenever the question arises, whether during the lifetime of the parties or after the death of either or both of them. However, in some states, the statutes provide that such a marriage is only voidable, so that the marriage is valid until set aside in a proceeding for that purpose during the lifetime of the parties. Either the insane or the sane person, when the latter did not know of the other's insanity, can bring the proceeding.

Physical capacity is also necessary. The marriage of one physically incapable of sexual intercourse is not void but voidable; it is valid until set aside in a legal proceeding by the person who does not suffer from the disability. Such person may, however, ratify the marriage. The impotency must be permanent and incurable. Barrenness or sterility or mere sexual weakness or frigidity will not render a person incompetent to marry.

Generally, an infant is not permitted to marry until he or she has attained the *age of legal consent* (see table below). Some statutes fixing the marriage age expressly or by clear inference provide that a marriage of a person below such age shall be absolutely void. In the absence of such express or implied declaration, such marriages are voidable. In some states, one who marries before reaching the age of consent may avoid the marriage before reaching such age, but in most states he or she may do so only on reaching the age of consent. Once such person attains the age of consent and elects to affirm the marriage, he or she may not thereafter disaffirm. Continued cohabitation will give rise to a presumption of an election to affirm. Where only one of the parties is under the age of consent at the time of the marriage, the other may not avoid the marriage on such ground.

Persons of different races or color may *intermarry,* unless such intermarriage is prohibited by statute. Many states absolutely prohibit marriages between white and Negroes; between whites and mulattoes; between whites and Indians; between whites and Mongolians; and between whites and Japanese. Such a prohibited intermarriage is void, and either party may disregard it; its invalidity may be shown at any time, either before or after the death of one party or both parties. Such statutes have no retroactive effect; marriages contracted before the enactment of such statutes remain valid.

A person who has already contracted a valid marriage is incapacitated from contracting another marriage while the former remains in existence. All states prohibit *bigamous marriages.*

Imprisonment does not disqualify a person from marrying. In those states that declare a person imprisoned under a death or a life sentence to be civilly dead, the spouse of such person may remarry, even though no decree dissolved the earlier marriage.

Consent is the basis of marriage; it must be mutual, free, and voluntary. Where the consent is induced by *duress or fraud* which goes to the essence of the relationship the marriage is voidable. Not every fraud affords ground for dissolution. Fraudulent representation of willingness to have children, fraudulent promise to have a religious ceremony, deceptive concealment of serious physical defects which will endanger the health of the other party or of the children of the marriage, or deceptive concealment of mental disease will furnish a basis for dissolution. Cohabitation with full knowledge of the fraud, not merely living together under the same roof, prevents the invalidation of such marriage. Ratification may also be established in other ways. Oral or written forgiveness will suffice, provided it was given after full knowledge of the fraud. However, fraudulent representations as to character, wealth, or social position do not constitute fraud that will invalidate the marriage.

Marriage is an executed contract and is distinguished from the *engagement to marry*. Contracts to promote marriage through *marriage brokers* are against public policy; a contract to pay a fee or commission to another to negotiate a marriage is void and unenforceable.

When a valid contract to marry has been made and is subsequently repudiated and disavowed, or there is a failure to go through with the marriage, there is a breach which gives rise to a cause of action for breach of promise. However, many states have outlawed such actions.

MARRIAGEABLE AGES AND SOME OTHER REQUIREMENTS FOR MARRIAGE IN THE UNITED STATES[1],[9]

Alabama.—Age of consent: male 17; female 14. Personal or written consent of parents is required, with $200 bond when male is under 21 or female is under 18, unless such minor has been previously married.

Arizona.—Males under 18 and females under 16 may not marry. Consent of parents is required when male is under 21 or female is under 18.

Arkansas.—Age of consent: male 18, female 16. Written consent of parents or guardian is required when male is under 21 or female is under 18.[2]

California.—No age under which persons may not lawfully marry, but verified written consent of parent or guardian is required and must be filed with licensing clerk when male is under 21 or female is under 18; approval by court order is required when male is under 18 or female is under 16.

Colorado.—No age under which person may not lawfully marry but consent of parent or guardian is required when male is under 21 or female is under 18; court order is also required if either party is under 16.

Connecticut.—No minimum statutory age is fixed; written consent of guardian signed in presence of a witness and acknowledged before a notary must be filed with registrar; if either party is a minor a similar consent is required of the parent or guardian; court order is also required if either party is under 16.[3]

Delaware.—Age of consent: male 18, female 16. Written consent of parents or guardian, signed in presence of 2 witnesses, is required when male is under 21 or female is under 18.[4]

District of Columbia.—Age of consent: male 18, female 16. Oral or written consent of parent or guardian attested by witnesses is required when male is under 21 or female is under 18, unless such minor has been previously married.[5]

Florida.—No license will be granted to male under 18, nor to female under 16, with or without consent, unless they acknowledge under oath that they are parents or expectant parents of a child, in which case granting of license is discretionary with the judge. If either party is under 21, written, acknowledged consent of parents is required, unless both parents are dead or infant has been previously married.

Georgia.—Age of consent: male 17, female 14. If female is under 18 the consent of parents is required. If both parties are under 21, a notice must be posted, unless parent or guardian of infant female personally consents.[6]

Idaho.—License will not be issued to a person under 15, except to a female upon order of court after hearing; no license will be issued to a person under 18 unless written, acknowledged consent of his or her father, mother, or guardian is obtained.

Illinois.—Age of consent: male 18, female 16. Personal appearance and affidavit of consent of parents are required when male is under 21 or female is under 18.

Indiana.—Age of consent: male 18, female 16. Consent of parent is required when male is under 21 or female is under 18 unless she has lived in the county where license is sought for 1 month before making application, and has no parent living within the state.

Iowa.—Age of consent: male 16, female 14. Consent of parents is required when male is under 21 or female is under 18.

Kansas.—Age of consent: male 14, female 12. Consent of parent is required when male is under 21 or female is under 18, evidenced by written certificate if not given personally; approval of judge is also required when male is under 18 or female is under 16.[2]

Kentucky.—Age of consent: male 16, female 14. When either party is under 21 and has not been previously married, written consent of father is required, or if father is dead or absent from state, consent of mother is required, attested by 2 subscribing witnesses and proved by oath of the witnesses.

Louisiana.—Age of consent: male 18, female 16, unless evidence of extraordinary circumstances is presented to judge. Minors must have parents' consent, or, if both be dead, the consent of their tutor.

Maine.—Age of consent: male 14, female 12. Consent of parents is required when male is under 21 or female is under 18; if either is under 16 consent of judge is required.[3]

Maryland.—Age of consent: male 18, female 16. Parents may not permit marriage unless a physician certifies that female is pregnant. Consent of parents is required when male is under 21 or female is under 18; and they must swear or affirm that the person to be married is of age at which marriage is lawful.[7]

Massachusetts.—Age of consent: male 14, female 12; but if male is under 18 or female is under 16 the court may permit marriage if parents within the state consent; if neither is living consent of legal guardian is required; if parent is living but residing out of the state notice must be given to such parent.[3]

Michigan.—Age of consent: male 18, female 18. Consent of one parent is required when female is under 18.[3]

Minnesota.—Age of consent: male 18, female 16; or male 16, female 15 if parents consent and judge approves. Consent of parents is required when male is under 21 or female is under 18.[3]

Mississippi.—No minimum legal age of consent; but consent of parents is required when male is under 21 or female is under 18.[3]

Missouri.—No license can be granted to person under 15 except on court order. Written, sworn consent of either parent is required when male is under 21 or female is under 18.[2]

Montana.—Age of consent: male 18, female 16. Consent of either parent is required when either party is a minor.

Nebraska.—Age of consent: male 18, female 16. Written consent in affidavit form of either parent is required when either party is a minor.

Nevada.—Age of consent: male 18, female 16. Parent's consent is required when male is under 21 or female is under 18. Consent must be either personal or in writing, attested by two witnesses, one of whom must appear personally and swear that he either saw the parent sign the consent or acknowledge that it was signed.

New Hampshire.—Age of consent: male 20, female 18. Judge may grant permission if special circumstances warrant when male is not less than 14 or female is not less than 13.[3]

New Jersey.—At common law age of consent of female is 12; no other statutory age of consent. Consent of parent is required when male is under 21 or female is under 18, but approval by judge is required when male is under 18 or female is under 16. In special circumstances (if female is pregnant) no consent of parent or court is required.[8]

New Mexico.—Age of consent: male 18, female 16. Written consent of parents is required when male is under 21 or female is under 18. In special circumstances the court may authorize marriage.

New York.—Age of consent: male 16, female 14. Written consent of parents is required when male is under 21 or female is under 18; but written approval by judge is required where female is under 16.

North Carolina.—Age of consent: male 16, female 16. Written consent of either parent by both parties is required when either party is under 18.

North Dakota.—Age of consent: male 18, female 15. Consent of parents of male is required when he is under 21, or of parents of female when she is under 18. Consent must be given before judge personally or by certificate attested by 2 witnesses, one of whom must personally appear and testify to the signatures on the written consent.

Ohio.—Age of consent: male 18, female 16. Consent of parents is required when either party is under 21. Consent may be given personally or in writing.[3]

Oklahoma.—Age of consent: male 18, female 15. Court may authorize marriage of persons under such age if the female is pregnant or has an illegitimate child; written, acknowledged consent of parents is required when male is under 21 or female is under 18.

Oregon.—Age of consent: male 18, female 15. Consent of parent is required when male is under 21 or female is under 18, unless no parent lives in the state and female has lived in the county for 6 months.[3]

Pennsylvania.—Age of consent: male 16, female 16; but marriage may be authorized by court if persons are under such age. Consent of parents is required by minor; it may be given personally, or in writing attested by 2 witnesses and properly acknowledged.

Rhode Island.—Age of consent: male 14, female 12. Written consent of parent is required when the male has attained the age of 18 and the female has attained the age of 16; consent of court is required when the male is under the age of 18 or the female is under the age of 16.

South Carolina.—Age of consent: male 14, female 12 (common law). Written consent of parent is required when either party is under 18.

South Dakota.—Age of consent: male 18, female 15. Consent of parent is required when either is a minor.

Tennessee.—Age of consent: male 16, female 16. Judge may authorize marriage regardless of age for good cause.[3]

Texas.—Age of consent: male 16, female 14. Consent of parents is required when male is under 21 or female is under 18.

Utah.—Age of consent: male 16, female 14. Consent of either parent is required if male is under 21 or female is under 18.

Vermont.—Age of consent: male 16, female 14. Written consent of parent is required when male is under 21 or female is under 18; but approval of court is also required when male is under 18 or female is under 16.

Virginia.—Age of consent: male 18, female 16. If a physician certifies that female is pregnant and parent consents, license may be issued. Infants, unless previously married, must have personal or written, acknowledged consent of father, if living, or else of mother; if both be dead, court may authorize license.

Washington.—Age of consent: male 14, female 12 (common law). Consent of parent is required when male is under 21 or female is under 18; no consent may be given when female is under 15.[2]

West Virginia.—Age of consent: male 18, female 16. Consent of parents is required when either is under 21.

Wisconsin.—Age of consent: male 18, female 15. Consent of parent is required when male is under 21 or female is under 18.[3]

Wyoming.—Age of consent: male 18, female 16. Consent of parents is required when either party is a minor.

Alaska.—Age of consent: male 21, female 18. No other consent by parent or guardian is required.

Hawaii.—Age of consent: male 18, female 16. Consent of parent is required when either party is under 20.

Puerto Rico.—No statutory age of consent; but parents' consent is required when either is under 21.

Virgin Islands.—Age of consent: male 16, female 14. Personal, or attested, written consent of father, or if dead, mother, or if both are dead, guardian, is required when the male is under 21 or when the female is under 18 and has not been previously married.

---

[1]Wassermann or other standard laboratory blood tests are required for marriage for both applicants in all but the following states: Arizona, Arkansas, Dist. of Columbia, Georgia, Maryland, Minnesota, Mississippi, Nevada, New Mexico, South Carolina, and Washington. In Alabama, Louisiana, and Texas, a physician's venereal certificate is necessary for the male, which is void in 10 to 15 days, depending on the state. In Oklahoma, no venereal test is required, but if either person is infected, a certificate should be obtained from a physician; failure to do so carries a penalty and imprisonment.

[2]Applicants must wait three days to obtain license to marry.

[3]Applicants must wait five days to obtain license to marry.

[4]Nonresident applicants must wait 96 hours to obtain license to marry. When one party is a resident, they must wait 24 hours. No wait necessary after obtaining license.

[5]Applicants must wait three clear days for license to marry (not counting either day of application or day of issuance).

[6]No waiting period for license if both applicants are 21; if under 21, they must wait five days.

[7]Applicants must wait 48 hours to obtain license to marry.

[8]Applicants must wait 48 hours to obtain license, which should be obtained 24 hours prior to the ceremony. License valid for 30 days.

[9]It is not necessary to wait for any length of time after license is obtained except in New Jersey, where a 24-hour wait is required; in New York, where a 24-hour wait is required except when one of the parties is a member of the armed forces of the Allied Nations or a member of the United States Merchant Marine (in which case there is no delay, but three days must elapse from time of examination and blood test); in Rhode Island, where a five-day wait is required if the woman is a nonresident; and in Vermont, where a five-day wait is required.

RIGHTS AND DUTIES OF HUSBAND AND WIFE

Modern legislation has altered the old common law rule that regarded husband and wife as one legal unit with the husband having all the rights. The trend is to give equality, although this has not yet been fully accomplished.

Because the husband is head of the family, his name becomes the family name, not by law but by custom. He has the right to determine the place of residence, and the wife must follow him when he changes the residence. This right is not unlimited. He must act reasonably and have proper regard for her comfort, health, safety, and general welfare. He must provide an independent home in which his wife is mistress. He may not compel her to live in a home with members of his family where she is subjected to unwarranted interference in the control and management of the household. Her refusal without proper cause to move to a new domicile selected by him may constitute abandonment or desertion. However, his misconduct may give her the right to establish a different and separate domicile. The circumstances which will give her this right vary in the different states, and her rights depend upon statute.

The husband is under a duty to protect his wife, and has no right to inflict punishment on her.

Both spouses are under a duty to cohabit. Cohabitation includes not only the right to sexual intercourse, but also the right to each other's society, companionship, and affection.

Both parties have the right to complete religious freedom and worship in accordance with their respective beliefs.

Support; Property Rights; Earnings

The husband has the duty to adequately support and maintain his wife in accordance with his ability, regardless of her own financial means, or of her independent ability to support herself. This duty is a continuing one while the relationship exists, although by statute a husband may be absolved from such responsibility if the wife commits certain statutory matrimonial offenses such as abandonment of him without cause, or adultery.

No like duty rests on the wife. In some states, however, by statute the husband and wife may contract for mutual support, and under some statutes the wife may be chargeable with the support of her husband, if he is destitute and she has financial means.

At common law a wife's earnings belonged to her husband, unless he agreed or consented that she should retain them. In most states this rule has been modified so that in certain cases the wife may retain her earnings without his consent. It is, however, the duty of the wife to render household services to her husband, for which she is not entitled to be paid by him.

Notwithstanding the statutory right to dower and inheritance that a wife may have in some states, at common law the husband's property that he acquired before or after marriage belonged to him and the wife acquired no interest whatever thereto.

Household goods belong to the husband unless the couple has agreed to the contrary. In some states the wife may not remove any household goods without her husband's consent, even if she leaves him because of his misconduct. He may sell his personal property without her consent and may also do the same with his real estate, except in states where the wife has dower rights. In such states her written consent must first be obtained.

At common law the husband acquired the right to his wife's property. In some states, as a result of constitutional or statutory provision, married women retain their rights to the property which they owned before marriage.

In Arizona, California, Idaho, Louisiana, New Mexico, Nevada, Texas, and Washington there are community property laws which in essence provide that all property acquired during marriage by the husband or wife, or both, belongs beneficially to both during the continuance of the marriage relationship.

Liabilities of Husband

The husband is liable for *necessaries* supplied and furnished to the wife. Food, clothing, and medical expenses are necessaries. He is also liable in some states for her *debts* contracted before marriage. However, in some states his liability for such debts is limited to the value of the property received by him from her; in others, statutes expressly release him from all liability for such debts.

Under modern statutes married women are solely liable for *torts* they may commit or have committed. At common law neither may sue the other for torts; but by statute, in some states, such actions may be maintained.

Wills and Inheritance

In most states a married woman may make wills. In some states she may disinherit her husband, in others she may not. In many states the husband cannot completely disinherit his wife, nor may he during his lifetime fraudulently transfer his property in a way that will deprive her of her dower rights or of any other statutory right she may have in his property.

Citizenship Rights

Formerly, in the absence of statute, an alien woman who married a citizen of the United States acquired citizenship automatically. This is no longer the law. It is now provided by Federal statute that "any alien who, after September 21, 1922, and prior to May 24, 1934, has married a citizen of the United States, or any alien who married prior to May 24, 1934, a spouse who was naturalized during such period, and during the existence of the marital relation may, if eligible to naturalization, be naturalized" upon compliance with certain requirements of the naturalization laws but need not file a declaration of intention and must have resided continuously in the United States for at least one year. "Any alien who on or after May 24, 1934 has married or shall hereafter marry a citizen of the United States, or any alien whose husband or wife was naturalized on or after May 24, 1934 and during the existence of the marital relationship or shall hereafter be so naturalized may, if eligible for naturalization, be naturalized" upon compliance with certain requirements of the naturalization laws, but need not file a declaration of intention and must have resided continuously in the United States at least three years. "The naturalization of any woman on or after May 24, 1934, by any naturalization court, upon proof of marriage to a citizen or the naturalization of her husband and proof of but one year's residence in the United States is validated only so far as relates to the period of residence required to be proved by such person under the naturalization laws. The naturalization of any male person on or after May 24, 1934, by any naturalization court, upon proof of marriage to a citizen of the United States after Sept. 21, 1922, and prior to May 24, 1934, or of the naturalization during such period of his wife, and upon proof of three years' residence in the United States is validated only so far as relates to the period of residence required to be proved by such person under the naturalization laws."

DIVORCE AND SEPARATION

A *divorce* is a dissolution of a marriage for a cause arising after the marriage was entered into. An *annulment* of a marriage is for a pre-existing cause. A *separation* does not dissolve nor annul the marriage; it only separates the parties, either permanently or temporarily, for a cause arising after the marriage.

Since the state has an interest in every marriage, the parties have no right to dissolve it by themselves. Therefore, an *agreement for a divorce* is invalid on grounds of public policy.

A divorce or annulment can be obtained only through legal proceeding. A separation may be obtained by legal proceeding, or, if the parties are living apart they may enter into a separation agreement. However, an agreement to separate in the future made while the parties are living together is void. In no event may the agreement completely absolve the husband from his obligation to properly support his wife and children in accordance with his financial ability.

There is *no national law of divorce* or separation in the United States. Each state by statute has prescribed the grounds for divorce and separation as well as the residential requirements and forms of procedure.

The right of the guilty party to *remarry* during the lifetime of the former spouse is regulated by statute. In the absence of statute restricting or prohibiting remarriage, the guilty party may remarry. In many states, the statute prescribes a minimum time which must elapse before the guilty party may remarry. A statute which either completely prohibits remarriage of the guilty party or fixes a minimum length of waiting time has no extraterritorial effect. To illustrate: A husband is divorced in a state which prohibits remarriage before the expiration of a three-year period and leaves the state before the time is up, and remarries in another state. Then, if the marriage in that state is valid according to the laws of that state, the marriage is legal, although it is in contravention of the laws of the state where the divorce was obtained.

Although in most civil actions a judgment by default may be obtained against the defendant, in matrimonial actions of divorce, annulment, and separation the plaintiff must establish his or her case before the court even though the defendant fails to contest the action.

A woman who obtains a judgment of divorce may resume her *maiden name* if she chooses. The court will usually award custody of minor children to the wife, whether she is plaintiff or defendant, unless she is found not fit, and it may grant right of visitation to the party who is not awarded custody. In most states, when a wife is granted a judgment of divorce the court will direct the husband to pay her *alimony*, which is an allowance for support and maintenance; generally, the court will not award a wife alimony if the husband obtains such a judgment. In many states, however, the court has discretionary power to award the wife alimony even when it was the husband who obtained the divorce judgment. Such power will be exercised only if circumstances warrant. In all states the court will require the husband to pay for the support and maintenance of minor children, no matter who obtains the judgment of divorce.

The amount of alimony for the wife and/or minor children which the court may require the husband to pay rests on the court's discretion; it will depend on the circumstances of each case. The amount may be increased or decreased on application to the court if changed circumstances warrant.

After divorce the minor children continue to *bear the father's name*. However, under some circumstances, on notice to the father and for good cause shown, the court may permit the name of such minors to be changed, even over the father's objection. This relief is rarely granted. If the mother remarries after obtaining a judgment of divorce and the father fails to pay support for the minors as directed, or otherwise fails to act as a dutiful father, the court may permit the minors to assume the name of the wife's second husband, particularly when children have been born from the second marriage.

The judgment of divorce may be set aside for good cause upon timely application to the court and notice to whichever party obtained the judgment. Fraud or imposition on the court is always a proper ground for obtaining such relief. If the court did not acquire jurisdiction because the plaintiff was not a bona fide resident of the state, or if such plaintiff was a bona fide resident but the defendant was not properly served as required by statute, the judgment will be set aside, even in the absence of fraud. The right to have such judgment vacated may be lost through failure to make timely application to the court, or as a result of affirmative misconduct which would make it inequitable to grant such relief. If parties who have been divorced or separated become reconciled, they may apply to the court to set aside the judgment of divorce or separation. This right, however, is statutory and the procedure is governed by the applicable statute, which must be followed.

In most states a valid judgment of divorce does not become effective until after a statutory period of time, generally fixed in the judgment, has elapsed.

The United States Constitution, Article IV, Section 1, requires each state to give full faith and credit to the judicial proceedings of every other state. This is known as the Full Faith and Credit Clause. In obedience to it, a valid judgment of divorce or separation is valid in every other state, even though the ground for which such judgment was granted is not recognized in such other state.

However, since each state is sovereign, with power to determine whether the state in which such judgment was obtained had proper jurisdiction, another state may refuse to recognize such judgment if it determines that the plaintiff was not in fact a bona fide resident of the state in which it was granted. To illustrate: If a husband, married and matrimonially domiciled in New York, went to Florida or any other state and resided there for whatever period of time the law of that state required before commencing a divorce action there, then served the summons and complaint on the wife in New York, where she had continued to reside, the judgment of divorce in that state would not be recognized in New York. The wife, however, would have to prove that the husband's residence in the granting state was not bona fide. Determination of such questions by a New York court will depend upon the facts in each case. Temporary sojourn or mere duration of time will not suffice to confer jurisdiction on the granting state. It is the intent to acquire a *permanent* domicile that controls. However, even if the granting state did not have jurisdiction because the plaintiff had not in fact become a bona fide resident of that state, the judgment would be entitled to recognition if the defendant either filed an appearance in that action or otherwise participated as a litigant.

In a recent decision of the United States Supreme Court, the facts were as follows: The wife sued her husband in New York for separation in 1943: after trial she was granted a judgment of separation and he was directed to pay alimony. In January 1944 he went to Nevada, where he started an action for divorce in 1945. The wife did not appear in that action and the husband obtained a final judgment of divorce which did not require him to pay alimony.

The husband paid alimony as directed by the New York judgment of separation until he obtained his judgment in Nevada, when he stopped making payments. The wife then sued the husband in New York to recover the arrears.

The question to be decided was whether the judgment of separation survived the Nevada judgment for divorce. The majority of the New York court concluded that the Nevada judgment was valid in so far as it affected the marital status of the parties, but that it was invalid with respect to alimony. New York did not have to give full faith and credit to that part of the Nevada judgment because of the interest of the state of New York in abandoned domiciliaries of the state. An abandoned spouse might be left destitute, and so become a public charge.

GROUNDS FOR DIVORCE IN THE UNITED STATES

State	Residence requirements for divorce	Divorces are granted because of								
		Adultery	Desertion	Cruelty	Nonsupport	Impotency	Alcoholism	Insanity	Separation	Felony conviction
Alabama	1 yr.	x	x	x	x	x	x	x		x
Arizona	1 yr.	x	x	x	x	x	x		x	x
Arkansas	90 days	x	x	x		x	x			x
California	1 yr.	x	x	x	x		x			x
Colorado	1 yr.	x	x	x	x	x	x	x		x
Connecticut*	3 yr.	x	x	x	x		x	x		
Delaware	2 yr.	x	x	x		x	x			
Dist. of Columbia	2 yr.	x	x						x	x
Florida	90 days	x	x	x	x	x	x			
Georgia*	1 yr.	x	x	x		x	x			x
Idaho	6 wk.	x	x	x	x		x	x		x
Illinois	1 yr.	x	x	x		x	x			x
Indiana	1 yr.	x	x	x	x	x	x	x		x
Iowa	1 yr.	x	x	x			x			x
Kansas*	1 yr.	x	x	x	x	x	x			x
Kentucky*	1 yr.	x	x	x			x		x	x
Louisiana	1 yr.	x	x	x	x		x		x	x
Maine	1 yr.	x	x	x	x	x	x			
Maryland	1 yr.	x	x				x			
Massachusetts	5 yr.	x	x	x	x	x	x			x
Michigan	1 yr.	x	x	x	x	x	x			x
Minnesota	1 yr.	x	x	x			x	x	x	x
Mississippi	1 yr.	x	x	x			x	x		x
Missouri	1 yr.	x	x	x	x	x	x			x
Montana	1 yr.	x	x	x			x			x
Nebraska	2 yr.	x	x	x	x	x	x			x
Nevada	6 wk.	x	x	x	x	x	x	x	x	x
New Hampshire	†	x	x	x	x	x	x			
New Jersey	2 yr.	x	x	x						
New Mexico	1 yr.	x	x	x	x	x	x	x		x
New York	§	x								
North Carolina	6 mo.	x				x				
North Dakota	1 yr.	x	x	x	x		x	x		x
Ohio*	1 yr.	x	x	x	x	x	x	x		
Oklahoma	1 yr.	x	x	x	x	x	x			x
Oregon*	1 yr.	x	x	x		x	x	x		x
Pennsylvania	1 yr.	x	x	x		x				x
Rhode Island	2 yr.	x	x	x	x	x	x			x
South Carolina	1 yr.	x	x	x			x			
South Dakota	1 yr.	x	x	x	x		x	x		x
Tennessee	2 yr.	x	x	x		x	x			x
Texas	1 yr.	x	x	x			x			x
Utah	3 mo.	x	x	x	x	x	x	x	x	x
Vermont	1 yr.	x	x	x	x			x	x	
Virginia	1 yr.	x	x			x		x		x
Washington*	1 yr.	x	x	x	x	x	x	x	x	
West Virginia	2 yr.	x	x	x			x			x
Wisconsin	2 yr.	x	x		x	x	x		x	x
Wyoming*	60 days	x	x	x	x	x	x	x		x
Territories of the United States										
Alaska	2 yr.	x	x	x	x	x	x	x		x
Hawaii	2 yr.	x	x	x	x		x	x		
Puerto Rico	1 yr.	x	x	x			x		x	x
Virgin Islands	6 wk.	x	x	x		x	x	x		x

*Fraud is also recognized as a ground for divorce.
†Jurisdiction of the court is limited to cases where there is jurisdiction over the parties.
§Adultery only is a ground for divorce, but residence in the state is not necessary.

CHILDREN

The father of a family has the primary obligation to support his minor children; and upon his death the mother is bound to support them. If she is unable to, she may apply for financial assistance to her state or local government. Most states provide by statute for such financial aid, with fixed amounts for various cases.

The mother of a *child born out of wedlock* may institute paternity proceedings, and, if paternity is established, the father can be judicially compelled to pay a fixed amount for the support of such child; or the father may voluntarily assume to pay support. If he does not do so, or if paternity is not established by judicial proceeding, the mother is bound to support the child.

If any parent neglects to furnish necessaries to an infant,[1] a *stranger* who supplies such necessaries may compel payment from the parent by legal action. The parent's obligation to pay will be implied.

The obligation to support infant children or to pay for necessaries rests upon the parent only while such infant is a member of the parent's household. If the child voluntarily leaves the parent's house to make his own way in the world, no such duty rests upon the parent.

This duty rests only upon the *natural parents*. A stepfather is not legally bound to pay for the support of his stepchildren, except where statute imposes such obligation.

A child is not legally bound to *support his parent* unless such obligation is imposed by statute, as it is in most states.

Adoption procedures are regulated by statute and must be strictly observed. Extra-legal adoptions, frequently referred to as "baby black markets," have resulted in criminal prosecutions and convictions. There are many agencies which may be consulted for help in effecting a proper and legal adoption. It would be wise to consult a Government agency first, to obtain the names of such bona fide organizations.

The natural parents are relieved from their legal obligation to support a child who is legally adopted by others; the obligation is assumed by the adopting parents. In many states an adopted child may inherit from his adoptive parents.

The *earnings of a minor child* generally belong to the father, but infants who receive gifts, or acquire property by will, retain them; the parent has no right to such property.

Children born out of wedlock may be *legitimized* in several ways. Public acknowledgment by the father is sufficient in some states; in others legal adoption is necessary. In some states legitimacy may be established through legal proceedings. Marriage of the parents is generally sufficient. In many states, by statute, birth certificates need not contain the state-

---

[1]An infant, as prescribed by law, is a child who has not attained the age of majority. The age of majority varies in the several states. At common law, the infant reaches majority at age 21, except where a different age is prescribed by statute.

ment that an infant is illegitimate, and need not contain the marital status of the mother. The name of the putative father of a child born out of wedlock may not be entered without his consent.

In most states *guardianship proceedings* are regulated by statute. In some states infants over a certain age may choose their guardians, subject to the court's approval. The relationship between the guardian and his ward is personal and sacred. Trust and a confidential relationship occurs between the ward and his guardian, who owes the ward the highest degree of fidelity. He may not act to the ward's adverse interest.

A minor child who is deprived of proper parental care is a *ward of the state*. Courts have jurisdiction, independent of statute, over minors. Where statute exists, however, this jurisdicion may be regulated by statutory, as well as by relevant constitutional, provisions.

In divorce actions, the court has broad discretionary power to award custody of an infant to either party. The primary consideration in determining to whom custody is awarded is the best interest and welfare of the child. The child's preference will be considered, if he or she is of sufficient age and intelligence; however, the child does not control the decision. The custodial provisions are not unalterable. If subsequent events prove that the child's best interests and welfare require a change, the court, on due application, and after taking testimony, will make proper and adequate custodial provision, even to the extent of giving custody to grandparents or other members of the family.

CHILD LABOR

Employment of children is regulated in the United States by child labor laws of the individual states and, to a certain degree, by the **Federal Fair Labor Standards Act.**

As to state regulation of child labor, every state has a child labor law. These laws usually apply to the employment of minors up to 16 or 18 years of age. In general, they fix the minimum age at which a child may go to work, regulate the maximum daily and weekly hours that he may work, prohibit night work, require work permits or employment certificates as a condition for his employment, and prohibit work in hazardous occupations.

Although in most states a minimum age of 14 is set for employment, 22 states have now adopted laws which set 16 as the minimum age for employment during school hours or in factories at any time. Many states also prohibit employment of minors below 18 years of age in specified hazardous occupations, such as in mines or in work with explosives, or in operating dangerous machines. In a majority of the states, the work of children between 14 and 16 is limited to 8 hours a day and 48 a week, and nearly all prohibit night work for children under 16. Over one-third of the states, however, have limited the maximum weekly hours for children under 16 to 40 or 44, while nine states have established a 40- or 44-hour week also for minors of 16 and 17. Work permits are required for minors under 16 in practically all the states, with about one-half the states requiring such certificates up to 18.

A proposed amendment to the Constitution that would give Congress power to regulate child labor throughout the country in intrastate industries also was submitted to the states by Congress in 1934. It has not yet been adopted by 36 states, as is required to make it part of the Constitution.

AID TO DEPENDENT CHILDREN

Forty-seven states have programs for aid to dependent children which meet the requirements of the Social Security Act, thus entitling them to receive Federal grants for this purpose. Eligibility requirements and the amount to be paid are determined by the state. Under the original Act the Federal government participated only in the budget needs of the dependent child, but under the 1950 amendment, this was expanded to include the needs of the mother, caretaker, or guardian as well. The Federal government contributes its share of payments made by a state within the limits of $27 a month for the first dependent child and $18 a month for each additional dependent child in the family. The Federal government's share is three-fourths of the first $12 of the average monthly payment per child plus one-half of the remainder of expenditures within the maximum.

WILLS

A will expresses a person's desire concerning the guardianship of his children, the administration of his estate, and the distribution of his property after his death. It is called a testamentary instrument.

A *codicil* is also a testamentary instrument which modifies a prior will in some particular, as by revoking a prior disposition of some or all of the property, or by enlarging or reducing a legacy, by making an entirely new legacy, or by changing the guardian, the trustee of any trust, or the executors.

A male person making a will is called a *testator,* a female a *testatrix.*

The person charged by the testator or testatrix with the responsibility of carrying out the terms of a will is called an *executor,* if male, and an *executrix,* if female.

A will can be made by any competent person of sound mind. No special mental capacity is required. A person is competent if he has the capacity to understand the nature and extent of his property, to know the relationship of those who would naturally be the object of his bounty, and to know and understand what he is doing.

Generally, statutes in the various states provide that persons over 18 may make wills relating to personal property and those over 21 wills relating to real property.

Wills must be executed in the form and manner prescribed by statute. In most states a will must be in writing, and subscribed at the physical end of the document, and attested in the presence of witnesses; if it is not subscribed in the presence of such witnesses, the testator must acknowledge the will. The witnesses must sign their names in the presence of the testator.

Oral wills, called *nuncupative wills,* are valid as to personal property only if made by a soldier while in actual military service, or by a mariner while at sea.

The number of witnesses required is fixed by statute—either two or three. They need not know the terms of the will. Their signatures merely attest to the fact that the testator was then of sound mind. In some states a witness cannot be a legatee.

A will may be printed, typed, or handwritten. No special language need be used. Statutory formalities must be strictly complied with and the testator's wishes must be clearly stated. A lawyer should be consulted before a will is made; he should prepare it and attend to its proper execution. Thousands of wills have been declared invalid because they were not prepared by lawyers. Lay persons cannot be expected to know the necessary statutory provisions.

Wills and codicils may be executed on any day, including Sundays and legal holidays.

Upon the death of the testator the will must be *probated, i.e.,* proved in a special court, in some states called a surrogate's court, in others a probate court. When proof is submitted that the will was executed with all legal requirements, a decree is made admitting the will to probate. The person designated as executor, after duly qualifying to act, marshalls the assets of the estate and, after first paying all debts and administration expenses (including Federal and state inheritance taxes) distributes the estate in accordance with the terms of the will. In some cases the inheritance tax is not payable from estate assets, but from individual legacies. After attending to all this, the executor files his account, which must be judicially approved.

The will should dispose of all property of the testator. When a will does not make specific disposition of particular property it is advisable to have a *residuary clause* to provide for disposition of such property. If there is no such clause the residue of the estate will be disposed of as if the person had died without a will.

A person may make any disposition of his property he wishes, except that in some states he may not completely disinherit his wife and children.

If a testator does not wish to give outright his wife or children complete control of money or property, but wishes to regulate the use of such property, a *trust* should be set up. It is best to have a corporate trustee, because if an individual is designated his death would unnecessarily delay the administration of the estate. Moreover, banks have special competence in such matters. A trustee must also file his account and have it judicially settled.

Will[1]

I, JOHN DOE, of (city) ————, (state) ———— being of sound and disposing mind and memory, do hereby make, publish and declare this to be my Last Will and Testament, and hereby revoke all Wills and Codicils by me at any time heretofore made.

First: I direct all my just debts, funeral and testamentary expenses be paid by the executrix hereinafter named as soon as conveniently may be after my decease.

Second: I give, devise and bequeath unto my son, JAMES DOE, Ten Thousand Dollars ($10,000).

Third: All the rest, residue and remainder of my estate, both real and personal, of whatsoever kind and nature, and wheresoever the same may be situate, of which I shall be seized or possessed, or to which I may in any way be entitled at the time of my death, I give, devise and bequeath unto my beloved wife, MARY DOE, to be hers absolutely.

In the event that my said wife shall predecease me, or that we shall die in the same accident, then in either of such events, I hereby give, devise and bequeath my entire residuary estate to my friend, RICHARD ROE, of the city of ————, state of ————.

In the event that my said wife shall predecease me, or that we shall die by the same accident, and in the event also that RICHARD ROE shall not survive me, then I give, devise and bequeath my entire residuary estate as aforesaid to my brother, CHARLES DOE, of the city of ————, state of ————.

Fourth: I hereby nominate and appoint my wife, MARY DOE, to be executrix of this, my Will, and I direct that she be permitted to qualify as such without the giving of a bond or other security, in any jurisdiction. In the event that my wife, MARY DOE, shall fail to qualify, or cease to act as such executrix, then I nominate and appoint the GUARANTY TRUST COMPANY OF NEW YORK, or its successors, to be executor of this my Will, it also to be permitted to act without bond or other security. I authorize said GUARANTY TRUST COMPANY or its successors, to sell and convey, at public or private sale, all or any of my real estate, on such terms, prices, considerations and conditions as it shall deem to be for the best interests of my estate.

In witness whereof, I have hereunto subscribed my name and affixed my seal this ———— day of ————, 19—.

Witnesses:

John Doe (seal)

    John Jones
    Henry Smith
    Charles Green

The foregoing instrument was subscribed by the above named testator, JOHN DOE, at the city of ————, county of ————, state of ———— on this ———— day of ————, in the year one thousand nine hundred and ———— in our presence, and was at the same time and place published and declared by him to us to be his Last Will and Testament, and thereupon we, at his request, and in his presence, and in the presence of each other, did subscribe our names thereto as attesting witnesses, this attestation clause having first been read aloud to us in the presence of said testator.

Names	*Residences*
John Jones	No. ————, ———— Street, (city), (state)
Henry Smith	No. ————, ———— Street, (city), (state)
Charles Green	No. ————, ———— Street, (city), (state)

[1]This is only a suggested form. The reader is advised to secure a form, valid in his state, from a lawyer or legal stationer for use on a specific occasion.

Codicil[1]

I, JOHN DOE, of the city of ————, county of ————, state of ————, having made my Last Will and Testament bearing date the ———— day of ————, in the year one thousand nine hundred and ————, do now make and publish this Codicil thereto which is to be taken as an addition to and a part of my Last Will and Testament.

First: I revoke the legacy of Ten Thousand Dollars ($10,000) to my son, JAMES DOE, and give him in lieu thereof 100 shares of common stock in the X, Y, Z Corporation, now in my safe deposit vault in the Guaranty Trust Company in New York.

Second: I hereby give, devise, and bequeath Ten Thousand Dollars ($10,000) to the American Red Cross, Inc.
And I hereby ratify and confirm my Last Will and Testament in every respect save so far as any part of the same is inconsistent with this Codicil.

In witness whereof at the end of this Codicil to my Last Will and Testament I have subscribed my name and affixed my seal this ———— day of ————, one thousand nine hundred and ————.

John Doe (seal)

Subscribed by the above mentioned testator in the presence of each of us and at the same time declared by him to be a codicil to his Last Will and Testament, and thereupon we, at his request, and in his presence, and in the presence of each other, signed our names as subscribing witnesses.

Witnesses:
John L. Jones No. ————, ———— Street, (city), (state)
Charles Green No. ————, ———— Street, (city), (state)

[1]This is only a suggested form. The reader is advised to secure a form, valid in his state, from a lawyer or legal stationer for use on a specific occasion.

PUBLIC SCHOOLS

Public education in the United States is big business, and one that is growing rapidly. In 1950 the total amount spent on the public schools was almost $5,000,000,000. This huge sum paid the salaries of approximately 1,000,000 teachers, principals, and school administrators and the salaries of tens of thousands of other school employees: clerks, custodians, nurses, cafeteria workers, school-bus drivers, maintenance workers, and many others. It also built thousands of new schoolrooms and paid for great quantities of school equipment and supplies. For local retail merchants, for the building trades, and for the manufacturers and distributors of school equipment and supplies, ranging from lead pencils to 50-passenger buses, the schools and their employees are important customers.

Attendance

Currently attending the nation's public schools are about 25,600,000 children and youth—20,000,000 in the elementary schools and 5,600,000 in the secondary schools. The United States Office of Education predicts that by 1960, because of the wartime rise in the national birth rate, the total will rise to 32,000,000, with 24,800,000 in the elementary grades and 7,200,000 in the high schools. If this prediction is correct, it will require even greater expenditures on school construction, school equipment, and staff salaries, merely to maintain the kinds of schools we now have.

Operation and Control

Each state is legally responsible for the education of the children within its borders. The public schools are operated and controlled, therefore, according to *state* law—and not according to any over-all national regulations on the one hand, nor to the decisions of local communities on the other. Because education is a state function, the school system of each state is the product of the laws of that state.

In practice most of the states delegate much of their authority to local school districts. These districts are of many sizes and types, ranging from small communities with a single one-teacher school to the largest cities and counties. Sometimes school districts cut across county and city boundaries, to take in part or all of two or more units of local government. Altogether there are nearly 100,000 local school districts, maintaining some 185,000 schools.

The governing body for the local school system is a board of education of three or more members. Boards with five or seven members are common; they are usually the recommended type for districts other than the very smallest and the very largest. Authority is given to the local school board to determine school expenditures in the district, employ the school staff, and generally oversee the local schools. Although its powers and duties are subject to state law, this board has much to do with the scope and quality of education in its district. The administrative officer who carries out the policies and directives of the board is usually known as the superintendent of schools, a professionally trained leader for the supervisors, principals, teachers, and other school employees who work under his direction.

Requirements for Teachers

Except in rare instances teachers are not employed under civil service but can enter their profession only after obtaining a teaching certificate, or license. In nearly all cases this certificate is now issued by state departments of education, after the applicant has completed certain required professional preparation. Requirements vary greatly from state to state, also within a state, for different kinds of work. In 1948 half the states would issue certificates only to citizens of the United States. About one-fourth of them required an oath of allegiance. Twenty-eight states required a certificate of good health. Over three-fourths of the states had set a minimum age—for the most part 18 years. In nearly half the states a certificate valid in the elementary schools required a minimum of two years of college preparation—in a few states of one year. In 19 states, however, the minimum preparation for an elementary license was four years. For certificates valid in junior and senior high schools, most of the states required at least four years of special preparation, and a few states a minimum of five years. Responsibility for selecting persons with suitable personality traits and sound characters is usually laid on the training institutions.

Teachers are usually employed under written contracts, often with standard contract forms issued by the state departments of education. As a rule, initial contracts are valid for one year. After a specified probationary period of about two years, the contracts in many states become continuous, and can be breached only for good cause sustained in public hearings or in the courts. Where such contracts are authorized teachers are said to have "tenure." The form and duration of contracts, as with teaching certificates or licenses, are determined by state law, and vary widely from state to state.

Education a State Function

Because education is a state function rather than a Federal responsibility, practices, as one would expect, vary from one state to another. The sizes and types of school districts vary. The amount of state aid may range from almost none to more than four-fifths of the total school expenditures. Requirements are far from uniform for the certificates or licenses of teachers and other professional employees. Different textbooks and teaching materials are recommended; different age limits are set for compulsory school attendance; different standards for schoolhouse construction are approved. Yet in spite of these and other differences, the general pattern of schooling is strikingly similar in the various states. All the schools tend to adopt the practices that proved their worth in the communities which first tried them out. Parents who move from one state to another insist on schools that are generally comparable to those they left. In general, all children who are physically and mentally able to do so are required to attend an approved school, either public or private, from the ages of about six to sixteen years.

Special Features of the System

The public school system of the United States is both new and unique. It is a product of the past century; and the secondary portion, the American high school, is chiefly the product of the past 50 years. The system is unique in its teaching emphasis and in its scope. More than any other system of education, ours concerns itself with the pupil's total personal development; our schools try to adjust their work to the interests and needs of the individual. Also, in the United States the door of educational opportunity is open to more children, and for a longer time, than in almost any other land. Elementary schools for all are found in many countries, but the opportunity to attend high school is seldom given to so large a proportion of a nation's youth as in the United States.

The standard portion of the school program consists of 12 grades. For administrative purposes this is often divided into an eight-grade elementary school and a four-year high school. In thousands of districts, however, there are three divisions: a six-grade elementary school, a three-year junior high school, and a three-year senior high school. There are several other grade groupings, all variations of these basic patterns. An impressive start has also been made toward extending the school system downward, to include the kindergarten and sometimes the nursery school. Also, the movement to establish two-year community colleges as part of the public school system is well under way.

Current emphases in public education include, among others: (1) increased attention to the so-called "three R's"; (2) an improved program of citizenship education; (3) school camps and other work-experience opportunities, especially for older students; (4) safety education and driver training; (5) instruction in family living; (6) increased attention to cultural and spiritual values; (7) cultivation of world good will and international understanding; (8) consumer education and thrift; (9) a community-centered curriculum; (10) greater use of audio-visual materials and devices in education; and (11) education for the conservation and wise use of natural resources.

ADULT EDUCATION

Throughout the United States today a new concept of formal education has taken hold. In the elementary schools and high schools and in colleges and universities, millions of adults are enrolled for the pursuit of knowledge, while countless other persons study at home through correspondence courses.

Adult education in its narrowest sense has meant until recently a preoccupation with arts and crafts—people tinkering with tools, learning to paint, or to fix leaky faucets: taking courses in dilettante fashion to help while away the evening hours. In addition, for many years civic groups and women's clubs have been presenting comprehensive lecture programs and forums for the discussion of the current political situation or the popular literary vogue. Such activities have been valuable and continue to help adults to spend their middle and late years usefully by pursuing hobbies.

Since the beginning of this century, education as a social institution has developed dramatically. In 1890, only 7 per cent of the eligible population attended high schools, whereas in 1950 approximately 75 per cent attend. A college education, in consequence, has become part of the social experience of millions of the population. Although such education meets diverse needs, such as general education, preprofessional training, training for a business career, etc., many adults today are increasingly dissatisfied with their lack of understanding of current issues and with their personal and social conditions. Such people are turning to adult education schools and services for help in their dilemma.

Elementary schools are providing literacy training, citizenship programs, and remedial arithmetic through special adult schools, during afternoons and evenings. Such schools are for those who were deprived of such formal education in their early years, as well as for the foreign-born who need help in orientation. Many high schools have adopted methods suitable to adults who wish to acquire a secondary school education. Courses are often given on an accelerated plan; a year's work in any subject may be covered in one term. The subject matter is treated on an adult level by teachers especially interested in adult problems. A major drawback, however, at this educational level is the lack of teaching materials with which to stimulate adult thinking.

Colleges and universities, through their extension divisions and adult education schools, have developed extensive programs for adults, regardless of their previous educational background. The Universities of California and Wisconsin are typical of state universities, in that they give courses for adults on campus and at extension centers throughout their respective states; hold institutes to discuss special training and vocational problems, and offer opportunities for study through correspondence.

Some private universities, for instance, the University of Chicago and New York University, have developed extensive programs of evening study designed to meet the needs of adults in an urban milieu. Most conventional degree-granting colleges make it their primary role to train and educate young people for life by teaching them certain techniques and methods of inquiry; whereas schools for adults aim to help those beyond the normal school age to advance professionally, and to develop educationally and socially.

Not all adult education goes on in educational institutions. Extensive programs are offered by community groups: the Y.M.C.A., certain labor organizations, agricultural extension services, etc. Correspondence study is also a major means of adult education. In New York State alone, of the 2,000,000 adults enrolled in formal and informal activities, approximately 500,000 attend schools and colleges; the remaining 1,500,000 engage in less formal educational activities.

Among the noteworthy phenomena in adult education today are the "Great Books" classes offered in all parts of the country under the auspices of such organizations as the Great Books Foundation of Chicago. At such classes, held generally at public libraries, adults, in Socratic fashion, discuss with lay leaders the timeless values of the great books. The major purpose of such study is to stimulate thought.

An illustration of the great popularity of correspondence study is the United States Armed Forces Institute, which at its inception in December 1941, at Madison, Wisconsin, offered 64 courses on the secondary and junior-college levels, to approximately 2,500 students. Today it is a huge educational institution, giving, as of May 1950, 321 correspondence courses and approximately 6,000 courses by contract with 48 cooperating colleges and universities through their extension divisions. On April 1, 1950, there were approximately 111,000 students actively enrolled in USAFI courses, with an additional 7,500 students enrolled through USAFI for courses with contracting schools. USAFI also offers work for men in the armed forces overseas. Approximately 48 per cent of USAFI enrollments are in academic courses at the high school level, 23 per cent at the college level, and 29 per cent on the vocational-technical level. The International Correspondence School is an example of a proprietary institution which has exerted great influence on the technical training of hundreds of thousands of skilled mechanics throughout the country by means of its comprehensive courses.

If the current interest in adult education is maintained (and the likelihood is that it will be accelerated) every community will be offering adult education services for all purposes to approximately 70,000,000 people within the next ten years. Because of the steadily increasing longevity of the population of the United States, and because of the shortened work week, now approximately 37½ hours, many adults are finding such adult educational activity a happy occupation for their free time.

INVITATIONS

Noteworthy events in the course of business are often celebrated by formal receptions, luncheons, banquets, etc. In such cases the invitations should be in keeping with the occasion, that is, they, too, should be formal. The examples shown below indicate the general style which should be followed.

> The Public Service Commission
> of the
> Commonwealth of Pennsylvania
>
> requests the pleasure of
>
> Mr. _____
>
> company at the formal opening
>
> of the new offices of
>
> The Commission
>
> on Thursday, the fifth of September
>
> at two o'clock in the afternoon
>
> in the North Office Building
>
> Harrisburg, Pennsylvania

Reproduced by courtesy of the Bailey, Banks & Biddle Company of Philadelphia, Pa.

First National Bank of Philadelphia
requests the pleasure of your company at a
Luncheon to be served at the Banking House
Tuesday, January the twelfth, 19
between twelve o'clock noon and one o'clock P. M.

Livingston E. Jones
President

R. s. v. p.

The Retail Lumbermen's Association of Philadelphia

requests the pleasure of your company

at its Twenty-fifth Anniversary

on Wednesday, the thirtieth of April

at half after six o'clock

in the Rose Garden of the Bellevue-Stratford

R.s.v.p.
Charles P. Maule
2500 South Street

VISITING CARDS

A man's social cards should always have "Mr." in front of the name, and the name should always be written out in full. The address (either the home or, if the man is a bachelor, the club address) may be added, but there should be nothing else.

The rule for business cards is somewhat different. The title is usually omitted, its place being taken by an announcement of the company represented in the lower left-hand corner. Examples of good practice in business cards are shown below.

Charles M. Kinsolving

Rhoades & Company
Members of the New York Stock Exchange

27 William Street
New York City

HARVEY WILSON

REPRESENTING
THE BABCOCK & WILCOX TUBE CO.
PACKARD BUILDING
PHILADELPHIA, PA.

Reproduced by courtesy of the Bailey, Banks & Biddle Company of Philadelphia, Pa.

W. WALTER WILSON

PRESIDENT
FIRST MILTON NATIONAL BANK   MILTON, PA.

NATIONAL FOLDING BOX COMPANY

CHAMPE S. ANDREWS
DIRECTOR OF SALES   MAIN OFFICE AND FACTORY
NEW HAVEN, CONNECTICUT

MR. FRANK BRADLEY HARDER

Reproduced by courtesy of the Bailey, Banks & Biddle Company of Philadelphia, Pa.

Dr. Harvey Shoemaker

1727 Spruce Street
Philadelphia

LETTERS

Many types of business letters can be written effectively after only a little direction and practice. We exempt from this classification those letters that people have to be compelled to read, such as circulars and advertisements, which have special laws and are often written by experts; and we exempt letters of application, adjustment letters, and a few others; but the ordinary letter of the kind that a person in business has to write every day of his working life is a fairly simple matter. There are only a few rules. One of them is: *Know what you want to say,* and another is: *Let your reader learn it as soon as you possibly can.*

Beginning a Letter

The first sentence of a letter usually indicates whether or not the writer has a clear idea of what he is driving at. In order to let his correspondent know at once the writer may place a line by itself at the right between the heading and the body of the letter reading: "Subject: Your order of December 16"; or if the letter, though addressed to a firm, should go to a specific person or department: "Attention of Mr. Brownell," or "Mail Order Department."

The openings given below are good examples of brief, but clear and definite ways to begin a letter:

You will recollect that in our estimate for lead pipes we allowed . . .

I have received your letter of March 14.

If I seem insistent in the matter of an appointment for October 2, I am sorry but . . .

As I have not received an answer to my letter of December 9, I think perhaps it did not reach you so I am enclosing a copy.

Will you please refer to my letter of February 4. In addition to the reasons given there . . .

Your letter of June 30 was very helpful.

The proposition which you set forth in your letter of May 11 is very interesting. Before I give you a final decision, however, I should like to ask . . .

After receiving your letter of March 19, regarding the sale of the lot on the north corner of Hulton and Franklin Streets, I went into the matter of the title very fully with Messrs. Mann and Graham . . .

It is evident from your letter of November 13 that mine of November 9 is not clear to you.

About the burglary insurance on the laboratory, I agree with you that . . .

This letter is about a number of things:

1. . . .
2. . . .
3. . . .
4. . . .

This is to confirm our telephone conversation of this morning . . .

So much has been written about phrases to be avoided in the beginning of a letter that it ought not to be necessary to say anything about them here. "Yours of the 31st ult. to hand and contents noted" does exactly what we have just said the beginning of a letter should do, but there are two grave objections to it. One is that it is old-fashioned, like "Your esteemed favor"; the other is that it is not personal and, therefore, lacks individuality.

Ending a Letter

The middle of an ordinary routine letter should present no special difficulties if the writer exercises the usual care, but the ending he may find awkward. It is hard to take leave gracefully. The main thing to avoid is trailing dimly off into space. Always end with a complete sentence. Do not write:

> Hoping to hear from you soon,
> Sincerely yours,

but:

> May we hear from you soon?
> Sincerely yours,

If the letter is a long one there should be a summary of its main points at the end. Above all, the ending, like the beginning, should be clear-cut and definite. Such endings are the following:

Let me thank you for your splendid cooperation in this matter.

Will you give me all this information as soon as you get it?

Let us get together one day next week—I suggest Thursday at my Fifth Avenue office at two o'clock—and talk the whole matter over.

I hope you can see me on Wednesday.

I hope the delay has caused you no inconvenience.

I am sure that with your cooperation we shall be able to handle this sale in a way that will be profitable to all of us.

May I hear from you about this?

If you are willing to do this, I think we can demonstrate to your satisfaction that it will be a profitable plan for you.

I await further word from you.

Thank you for all the trouble you have taken in the matter.

Will you please let me know just what the situation is?

I trust your judgment and leave the matter entirely in your hands.

If you will send a duplicate sheet, I think we can straighten out the whole matter.

If we can be of any further use in the matter, kindly let us know.

Please send us the above information at the earliest possible moment so that we may avoid delay in delivering the material.

Form of Letters

There are very few standard rules that can be given for the arrangement of the letter on the page.

The margins should be regular with a little more space at the bottom than at the sides. Either the block style (see page 479) or the indented style (see page 480) is good. If the letter is short it should be placed a little above the center of the page with generous side margins. Ordinarily the side margins should be from an inch to an inch and a half wide with indentations of an additional inch. If the letter is more than one page long the margin at the bottom should be almost one and a half times those at the sides.

For the sake of clearness it is a good general rule to give each idea a separate paragraph; but simple ideas of kindred sorts may be considered and treated as one idea and grouped in a single paragraph. Too many paragraphs make a letter scrappy in appearance and give equal stress to important and unimportant ideas.

Use a double space between paragraphs, a single space between lines. This sets off the paragraph effectively and keeps the expression of a single idea compact within a small area. Incidentally, it does away with most two-sheet letters, and so saves stationery and prevents the loss of part of the communication.

Emphasis may be obtained by underlining, by typing in capitals or red letters, or through other similar devices which are good as long as they are used sparingly. Do not try to gain emphasis through startling variations from the conventional form. A good letter does not attract too much attention to itself. Arrange your matter naturally. If you have to state facts and make comments, begin with the facts. If your letter contains a résumé of events or transactions, the chronological arrangement is the natural one.

The only safe rule in business correspondence is: *One letter, one subject,* for it is probable that the different topics of your letter may require the attention of different persons or departments in the organization you are addressing. Also the filing system may demand that your letter on two subjects be filed in two different places at the same time.

Very few business letters need to be more than one page long though, of course, there is no definite rule. How long should a man's legs be? Long enough to reach the ground. How long should a business letter be? Long enough to accomplish its purpose.

No letter is complete until it has given all the necessary information. This may take half a page or it may take 20 pages.

It is not in good taste to use more than one printed letterhead. Every sheet after the first should be of plain paper of the same quality and size as the first.

Never send a letter that is blurred, blotted, or disfigured with erasures.

If you have forgotten something, do not add it in a postscript. That is saved for especially important items. Rewrite the letter. In the long run it will be economy.

Fold your letter so that it will be easy to open. Do not bring the edges exactly together.

The envelope is the last part of the letter to receive your attention but it is the first to attract that of your correspondent. Insufficient postage, irregular punctuation, awkward spacing, the omission of "Mr.," violently colored paper or ink prejudice your correspondent against your letter even before he opens it.

There are certain parts to every letter, whether it be long or short, that are as essential as eyes and legs and arms to a human being. They are:

1. *Heading.* In a great many business houses the heading is printed on the stationery; but whether printed, typed, or written by hand, the heading consists of the name and address of the firm and the date. Of course if an individual is writing, it consists simply of his address and the date. The day of the month and the complete number of the year (not just '51) should be given.

2. *Address.* This consists of the name and address of the person to whom the letter is written and should be the same both outside and inside the letter. It is the approved custom today to use as little punctuation as possible. Very seldom nowadays does one see a comma at the end of each line. The address should be clear. If house numbers immediately precede street numbers, the shortest number should be written out in full. Not 117 7 Street, but 117 Seventh Street. The state abbreviation approved by the Post Office Department (see page 511) should be used. The name of the state should never be omitted. There are a dozen Bostons, a dozen and a half Brooklyns, and two dozen Washingtons in the United States. "City" is not sufficient, even if the sender lives in New York, Chicago, or Boston. The name of the city should be written out in full, and the postal zone number should be designated, if it is known.

The title of respect should never be omitted before the name of the addressee, and, if possible, it should be the right one. Many men with thoroughly illegible handwritings have been offended when their scrawls have been misread and replies have come addressed to "Miss" instead of "Mr." So and So. Other titles in good use besides the ordinary "Mr.," "Mrs.," and "Miss" are Reverend, Doctor, Professor, Honorable (abbreviated to Rev., Dr., Prof., Hon.), but no name should be preceded by more than one title. If the name is followed by "Esq.," use no tiltle before it; *e.g.*:

John B. Reynolds, Esq.

In the United States a woman should not be addressed by her husband's title. The wife of a physician is not Mrs. Dr. Hubbard, but simply Mrs. Hubbard.

If you are writing to a person in a special position or department, the letter will be delivered more promptly if a line is added designating the position or department. For instance:

Mr. Frank D. Whitney
Head of the Collection Department
Mallory, Barret, and Co.
119 Peachtree Street
Atlanta 3, Ga.

3. *Salutation.* This varies with the type of letter. "Dear Sir:", "Dear Mr. Roe:", and "Gentlemen:" are all good for most purposes. In addressing women the corresponding forms are "Dear Madam:", "Dear Miss Roe:", and "Ladies:". For special types of salutation see page 499. In business communications the salutation is usually followed by a colon.

4. *Body of the letter.*

5. *Complimentary close.* In business the following forms are commonly used:

Yours sincerely,
Sincerely yours,
Very truly yours,
Yours truly,
Faithfully yours,

Such a closing as "Yours respectfully" should not be used unless the letter is addressed to someone in a position that commands respect, like a Senator or a governor. "Yours gratefully," "Yours respectfully," or "Yours cordially," should not be used unless there is a genuine reason for it. "Earnestly yours," "Cooperatively yours," and the like are sometimes recommended, but it is better for a beginner to stick to "Yours sincerely." You cannot possibly go wrong.

If you are asking for a favor do not send thanks in advance. To do so takes the favor for granted and destroys the receiver's pleasure in conferring it.

6. *Signature.* The signature to a letter, like all business signatures, should be legible. It should be written with black or blue ink, not with pencil nor with a rubber stamp. Business women often put "Mrs." or "Miss" in parentheses before their names in order to avoid embarrassment. When a letter is signed for a business firm the name of the firm is typewritten first, then the handwritten signature is placed just below it. No title like "Mr." or "Dr." should be used in the signature. If the person who wrote the letter cannot be on hand to sign it and the letter needs to go out at once he may delegate this task to his stenographer, who writes his name in full with her initials beneath it.

Some examples of correct signatures are the following:

NATIONAL BANKING COMPANY

Russell H. Walker

Cashier

Charles G. Hopkins

a.w.p.

If the letter has been dictated to a stenographer there should be some means of identifying it. This is usually done by placing the initials of the dictator followed by a colon and the initials of the stenographer on the left-hand side of the page about two or three lines below the signature:

RC:EM

If there are enclosures with the letter this fact should be indicated on the letter. This makes it possible for the one who receives the letter to know whether he has everything he is supposed to have. Enclosures are usually indicated by writing the word "Enclosure" just below the identification initials:

RC:EM
Enclosures 2

                 The name of the firm
                      Address

                                              Date
Salutation:

The body of the letter comes in these lines.
In this letter it is printed block style.
The heading is not at the "head" but at the
bottom of the page. This position is suitable
in letters that may be classified as either
personal or official.

In most instances the name of the firm and the
address are already printed on the stationery.
The date line is, of course, always filled in
with the typewriter.

The complimentary close always begins in the
middle of the page whether the letter is typed
in indented or block style.

                    Complimentary close,

                    Handwritten signature

                    Typewritten name of signer

Name of Addressee
Street and No.
City, Zone No., State

Identification
Initials

                      The name of the firm
                       Kind of business
                          Address

                                                    Date

Name of Addressee
Street and No.
City, Zone No., State

Salutation:

        The body of the letter comes in these
lines. It may be printed with indentations as
in this letter or in the block style as in the
letter on page 479.

        The date might have been put below the
address of the firm at the top of the page. It
should be put wherever it looks best.

                        Complimentary close,

                        Name of company

                        Handwritten signature

                        Title

Identification
Initials

Letters of Application

Many factors besides the letter itself enter into the result that a letter of application may produce. General business conditions and particular business conditions in the firm applied to are sometimes such that the finest possible letter will not even arouse an expression of interest; but an outstandingly good letter may live through a period of depression and bring a response long after it was written. Business houses do, occasionally, at least, consult their application files; a letter in one of them is, in a sense, a permanent record of your qualifications.

Letters of application should never be written on social stationery. Plain white paper of standard business size (8½×11 in.) with the standard-sized envelope (6½×3½ in.) is best. Freak envelopes are occasionally used, sometimes with good effect, but on the whole tricks like this are not well received in business.

In large firms where no one is known to you by name, address the personnel manager. He usually has charge of hiring and firing.

Do not enclose a stamped, self-addressed envelope with a letter of application. There are, however, three enclosures which may be of real service:

1. Samples of your work, if its nature permits
2. Letters of recommendation
3. A photograph of yourself

The letter should be typewritten unless it is in answer to an advertisement which especially requests that it be in handwriting.

The letter of application must shoot for a definite mark. The person who writes that he will take almost anything at whatever salary he can get advertises that he is not much good. To ask for a job at the bottom in order to learn the business from the ground up is a different matter, and an excellent way for a young person to get a foothold in business.

The letter must be concrete. A pretty lot of words, however gracefully and neatly strung together, will not do if the essential information is lacking. The human tendency to run off the track and talk about something irrelevant is one reason why so many big houses have standard application blanks with just room enough after each question for a short answer, often a single word, or a check mark.

The letter should be short. Its main object is to secure an interview for the applicant (very few jobs are given without this) ; it should, therefore, awaken the reader's interest in the writer. This can be done in a few paragraphs. It might almost be laid down as an ironclad rule that a letter of application should never be more than a page long.

What is the essential information which a letter of application should contain? Let us look at an application card. There will be variations, but the one given below is a fair sample of what the prospective employee will be asked to fill out:

Name in full

(The name should be printed, not written, and the last name should be written first, followed by a comma, then by the first name)

Address   Street   Town

Telephone number

Date of birth   Married or single

Position applied for

Salary

Last employer   Address

How long employed

Were you ever employed here before   Dept.

Remarks

Photographs are sometimes asked for; but this does not mean that a handsome cabinet-sized picture should be sent. A small, unmounted picture (about 3 in. square) is sufficient.

If you have special equipment, you should make a point of mentioning it. If you are filling out a blank and there is no other place for it, include it under "Remarks."

If you can refer to someone known to the firm to which you are applying, do so. The kind of letter of recommendation that you can carry around with you is practically worthless, but if you can indicate that you would be very happy to have your prospective employer talk confidentially with your former employer or with whoever is recommending you, that will help. Letters from former school teachers, relatives, and old friends of the family carry little weight. In any case the letter of recommendation should, like the letter of application, be specific. If the position applied for is in a bank the officials will want to know whether the applicant is honest. In such a case the letters of recommendation should be from men of proved integrity. If the position is in an advertising office, the letter should be from an advertising man, if possible. If the position is in engineering, the letter should be from someone familiar with your work in this field.

Original letters of recommendation should never be sent. They should be copied on the typewriter with COPY in capital letters at the top. In brackets just before the signature should be the word (Signed).

In applying for an executive position you should emphasize the way you can handle men; for salesmanship, personality is the important factor; with stenographic work, it is speed, accuracy, and dependability. All items should point in the same direction.

An application blank may ask for the reason you are applying. Some reasons should never be given, no matter how true they are. One is that you need the job. That is not of interest to your employer. What he wants to know is how well you can do the job. Another is that you are out of work. If you are asked why you left your former employer, do not take the opportunity to deliver yourself of your opinion of him, particularly if the opinion is unfavorable. Simply say that you felt that you would find better opportunity for advancement elsewhere or that you were getting into a rut and wished to develop yourself along some other line, or something else of this sort. Employers value highly the virtue of loyalty, and, having nothing else to go on, judge what your attitude toward them might be by what your attitude toward your former employer is.

The question of salary, unless specifically asked in the application blank, might better be saved for the interview. It is easier to come to terms face to face. Sometimes a letter is so high-flown that the prospective employer, while interested, feels that he cannot afford such a man. Sometimes a man who would be glad to get a position at $50 a week describes himself so grandiloquently (and it may be added, so inaccurately) that those to whom he is applying think they have a $50,000-a-year man to deal with. Honesty is the best policy, here as elsewhere.

A word might be said about applying for a job which you think ought to exist but does not. Most of us hold jobs that someone else has made for us; but the most fortunate and brilliant people in business create jobs for themselves. It is hard to apply for a job that is not there, and the letters applying for it demand very special attention. The first letter should indicate that the applicant has something to talk over which he believes will interest the firm. He should ask to see a specific person, if not by name, at least by job, such as the publicity director or the supervisor of machinery. An interview should follow this letter; during the course of it the applicant may be asked to set forth his ideas in writing. Even if he has convinced the supervisor, he must remember that the supervisor also has people to convince, for instance, vice presidents and directors and super-supervisors. This letter should be a model of brevity and conciseness.

It is sometimes easier to act indirectly in applying for a job, that is, to act through an agency. Sometimes the agency writes the letter to be sent out; sometimes the applicant writes it. The following is a good example of the kind of letter an agency might send:

PELHAM NASH AND CO.
Agents for High Grade Positions
101 Belton Street
New York 16, N.Y.

Please use Ref. 2981-B

James Howard Cook
Editor of *Radio Gazette*
333 Tenth Avenue
New York 24, N.Y.

Dear Sir:

We know a well-educated young man who is interested in finding a permanent position as publicity director, house-organ editor, or in sales-promotion work with a corporation associated with the radio industry or a closely allied field. He has asked us to address you in his behalf.

This man has had nine years of editorial experience with radio publications and is capable of assuming complete management of a publicity department or house organ for a manufacturer or advertising agency. He has a broad knowledge of present conditions in the radio industry, he is thoroughly familiar with radio from the technical viewpoint, and he has a wide acquaintance in this field. In his various positions and in free-lance publicity work he has also become well known as a writer of feature articles on radio and other subjects. This work has included both technical and popular articles for magazines and newspapers.

In addition to all this, our client has a valuable knowledge of all phases of editorial work. He has had actual experience in editing copy, planning and directing art work, laying out pages, ordering engravings, selecting proper type faces, making up at stones and with dummy, contracting with authors, making surveys, and preparing statistics. These qualifications together with his complete understanding of radio problems should render his services invaluable in the position suggested.

It will be a privilege to send you further information regarding him. This will involve no obligation on your part. His record cannot fail to convince you of his ability.

May we send the details?

> Very truly yours,
>
> PELHAM NASH AND CO.
>
> *Pelham Nash*
> President

N:T

Letters of Recommendation

All letters of recommendation should be carefully dated, and the information as to when and where the person writing the letter knew the person about whom the letter is written should be very definite. You can never tell what a person's career may be after he leaves you.

The "To-Whom-It-May-Concern" letter does not, except under unusual circumstances, carry a great deal of weight, nor do the letters which a person carries around with him. The letters of real value are usually those addressed by one person to another in behalf of a third and those sent confidentially through the mails. The first letter below is an example of the first type.

Dear Mr. Blanton:

This letter is in behalf of a young man, Robert Howell, who has just completed a cruise around the world as chief radio operator on the *President Lincoln,* and is now ready to settle down.

Your new short-wave station at Milbrook is very attractive to him, and he would like a position with you if you have an opening. He worked with me at 2GY for a year and a half before he sailed and I found him an excellent operator. I would take him back, only, as you know, 2GY is temporarily suspended. He has a letter from the captain of the *President Lincoln,* a copy of which I am enclosing.

If you are interested will you let me know when it will be convenient for you to see him?

> Sincerely yours,

The captain's letter follows. It is a "To-Whom-It-May-Concern" letter, but the circumstances give it much more value than this type of letter generally has. Young Mr. Howell wants a new job, and his new employer will be sure to wish to consult his former employer. But by the time Howell has the job the captain of the ship will be far out at sea; hence, what he said before he left must be taken at face value.

To Whom It May Concern:

This is to certify that Robert Howell was chief operator on the *President Lincoln* on her around-the-world voyage which began on July 2, 19—. I found him at all times quick and reliable. In my opinion he is a good operator, and I think any station which secures his services will be fortunate. He left me entirely of his own accord.

Sincerely yours,

The letter given below is an example of the kind which is sent by mail. Such letters should be treated as entirely confidential and the writer of one should speak honestly. It is not wise, however, to make bald derogatory statements. You do not know what the person may be like now. Simply say, "My experience was . . ." or "My feeling is . . ." or something else of the sort.

Dear Mr. Smith:

Richard Allen, whose letter you sent me, worked for us during our first year in business. Before that time he had been a salesman for our friend, John Roe. What success he had with Roe I do not know. With us however, he was not a great success but I always liked him personally. After he left us he got the idea of a specialty shop dealing in fine metalwork. I never went into the idea with him fully and so can pass no opinion as to whether it is sound or not. What he has in mind now I have not the least idea. I am sorry not to be more helpful.

Sincerely yours,

Letters of Introduction

It is a fortunate man who at one period of his career or another has not been asked for a letter of introduction which he would rather not write. When one has been so asked it may be necessary to send a separate sealed letter by mail to the person to whom the introduction is addressed, but this should be done only in extreme cases. Letters that you would rather not write should be kept formal and noncommittal; of course, if you can help it, they should not be written at all. No letter of introduction nor any other letter which is to be delivered by hand should be sealed. The letter of introduction should bear on the outside, "Introducing Mr. John Jones," or a similar legend. This enables the one to whom the letter is addressed to speak to his caller at once by name and thus prevents embarrassment. The full name of the one who is being introduced should also be incorporated in the body of the letter, so that if the envelope is thrown away the one to whom the letter is given can refer to the letter.

Mr. Jones may present the letter in person, or, if he prefers, may enclose it with a note of his own to the addressee asking when it will be convenient for him to call. The tone of a letter of introduction depends upon the degree of intimacy the writer has with the person to whom he is writing. The two examples that follow illustrate both an informal and a formal letter of introduction.

Dear Jim:

This is to introduce an old friend of mine, John Jones. You've heard me talk about him before now. I'm sorry to have to introduce him by letter because it's one of those things I'd especially like to do in person. John is going to cover the Lawrence Co. territory for the Balkson people from now on and will be in your neighborhood about once a month. I think he can be of use to you and you to him. Anyway, I think you will enjoy knowing each other.

Sincerely yours,
Richard

Dear Mr. Allen:

I am sending you this letter by a young man, John H. Jones, who has been with us four years. He has worked out a selling plan for Babson pumps which seems practical to me. I wonder how it will strike you. He can explain it for himself better than I can explain it for him, and whether you approve it or not I think you will find it interesting.

Sincerely yours,
Richard Smith

Do not ask a man, except in a sealed letter, to see another man as a favor to you, unless the letter is a favor to him; do not write it, except, as was indicated above, when you can find no way out of doing so. There should be a reason behind every letter of introduction (and behind every other letter, especially in business), and the reason should be given in the body of the letter itself.

Letters of introduction should be acknowledged by the person to whom they are addressed. A brief note assuring the writer of the letter that it was a pleasure to receive it is all that is necessary:

Dear Mr. Grant:

It was a great pleasure to meet Mr. Simmons, who came to the office yesterday with your letter. I look forward to seeing him again.

Sincerely yours,

Letters of Congratulation

Friendliness in business is as heart-warming a quality as it is in other departments of life. It is a gracious thing to let a person who has had a piece of good fortune know that you are rejoicing with him.

Dear Mr. Moffitt:

It made me very happy to read in the *News* this morning that you have been made manager of the Springfield office. It is work which I know from experience you are admirably fitted to do, and I am not the only one of your friends here in your old home who will rejoice to see you back where you belong.

Most cordially yours,

Order Letters

In writing an order letter, be sure that you give an exact description of what you want. State size, quantity, color, price (approximate, if exact price is unknown), and, if you are ordering from a catalog, the catalog number. Most mail order houses provide special blanks for their customers. These should be used when they are available.

If you are ordering several different items arrange them in table form, making a separate paragraph of each.

State how payment is to be made. It is no longer considered good form to say "Enclosed please find check," but simply, "You will find check enclosed," the reason being that in the first instance the recipient is not doing you a favor by finding the check, and there is no sense in asking him as if he were. "Please charge this to my account" is entirely correct.

State how delivery is to be made unless it is perfectly obvious, as in the case of a department store with a regular system for delivering everything.

Be sure that your address and your name are on the order.

All these rules may seem like instructions for a child in the first grade, but every one of them is violated hundreds of times a day by presumably intelligent men and women.

143 HAMPTON BOULEVARD
SILVER SPRINGS, NEW YORK

October 14, 19—

National Screw Co.
543 West 86th Street
Chicago 18, Ill.

Gentlemen:

Please send me by express the following screws as listed in your revised price list of January 4, 19—:

Iron wood screws

2 gross	¼ in., No. 4 @ .24	$ .48
2 gross	½ in., No. 7 @ .32	.64
2 gross	⅞ in., No. 14 @ .70	1.40
10 gross	1¾ in., No. 16 @ 1.20	12.00

Brass wood screws

4 gross	½ in., No. 4 @ .40	1.60
8 gross	¾ in., No. 9 @ .90	7.20
2 gross	2 in., No. 10 @ 2.05	4.10
		$27.42

I am enclosing a check for $27.42.

Sincerely yours,

B:N

Letters of Confirmation

For the sake of record it is advisable to put into writing the substance of a conversation, especially if the conversation was in the nature of a contract. Such a letter is the following:

I am very glad to put into writing the agreement which we have made with you by which we are to have the benefit of your help and experience in scouting for new accounts, advising us on current problems, and helping us in other ways as occasion may arise.

It is understood that we are to pay you $1,200 a year, beginning November 1, payments of $100 monthly to be made by check.

Mr. French and I are looking forward to a very happy and profitable relationship. I know that it will be pleasant for us and I hope it will be for you.

Often the letters may be shorter, such as:

This is to confirm our telephone conversation of this morning, at which time it was agreed that you would send us immediately by parcel post ten gross of pencils, No. 2, Blenkinsop.

Reminders

A good many reminder letters are the "Why-in-hell-don't-you. . . ." kind. There is no excuse for them. One like the following gets better attention and leaves a better feeling behind:

Please consider this just a reminder that your company has not as yet returned the receipts for the numerous dies we sent you about two weeks ago.

Will you please give this matter attention so that our records can be properly closed?

Stop-Gap Letters

If, for any reason, a letter cannot be answered at once it should be acknowledged and the reason given for the delay. This delay often occurs when information is asked for that will take some time to assemble, or when the person to whom the letter is addressed is away from the office.

1. This is just to acknowledge the pictures which you sent to Miss Bancroft. She has been suddenly called away from the office for a few days. You will hear from her as soon as she returns.

2. It may take us several weeks to assemble all the information for which you ask in your letter of November 1, since the greater part of it must come from our office in Springfield. As soon as we get it, however, I will send it on to you. Please be patient with us.

Form Letters

In a business in which the same situation occurs many times and each time demands exactly the same treatment, and a treatment has been found that is agreeable and satisfactory, it is unnecessary to try to vary it. For example, in a publishing house where 15 to 30 unsolicited book manuscripts come in every day, all that is necessary is a polite notice to each author that his manuscript has been received and will be given most careful attention. Such notices may be sent out as letters; often they are on printed cards. Later, when the manuscript has been read, the situation varies. The author may have given instructions for the return of the manuscript and have enclosed stamps or coin for the purpose, or the publisher may wish to make suggestions for revision, in which case a personal letter must be written. Many times there are form paragraphs which may be used, with slight variations, in many letters—if the situation warrants it. But form letters must be used with discretion; and if a form letter is sent in answer to another letter, it must really answer the questions asked.

Letters of Resignation

Most resignations are given orally, but some firms prefer or even demand them in writing. The conventional form is to express regret at leaving, to give some reason for it, to express pleasure (if any) at the associations which the connection has afforded, and to suggest a time at which the resignation shall become effective. The following letter was written by a young man resigning a position in the suburbs for one in the city:

I am sorry to have to tell you that I am obliged to sever my connection with Bennett, Inc.; but there are personal reasons why it is advisable for me to have a position in town rather than in West Gardens.

If possible, I should like to leave at the end of the week. Will you let me know whether this will be convenient?

Letters of Complaint

The first rule of letters of complaint is: *Be sure you are right;* the second is: *Then go ahead;* and the third is: *Watch your step,* which means *Be courteous.*

The following letter brought immediate response. The fact that the receipt was enclosed so that the company which sold the chairs did not have to ask for more information may have had something to do with it.

On April 29 I bought from you two desk chairs. The enclosed receipt will give you a record of the transaction. The salesman said that one was in stock and that the other would be in a day or so and that both would be delivered before the end of the week. Ten days have passed and I have heard nothing.

Will you please look into the matter at once and see whether you can find out what the difficulty is?

Letters of Adjustment

Letters of adjustment need not be in answer to letters of complaint. The following, for instance, is about a mistake in deductions. Notice that the letter contains no hint that there was any intent to defraud on the part of the one paying the bill. It is simply a statement of facts with a polite request that proper adjustment be made.

In regard to your remittance of $1,564.98 received January 18, we note that you deducted a 2 per cent discount before you deducted the 15 per cent agency commission. In other words, from our charge of $1,602.69, you are entitled to $32.15 discount, not $37.71, as you have it. There is a difference of $5.56 in our favor.

In order that we may keep our records in check we ask that you kindly remit this difference at your earliest possible convenience.

In letters of adjustment words with unpleasant associations like "failure," "complaint," "trouble," "neglect," and "refuse" should be avoided. "Your complaint of April 1" might just as well be simply "Your letter of April 1." "Your failure to send a check" might just as well be "By some oversight the check which you mentioned in your letter was not enclosed."

Do not use the words "You say" in this manner: "You say that the shipment was four crates short." This seems to imply that you believe that the person to whom you are writing is not telling the truth. "The customer is always right" is one of those slogans that can be practiced only up to a certain point. It makes an excellent beginning policy; but there are unfair customers, and the business concern which deals with them (and this means all business concerns with many contacts) must be firm. Politeness can be overdone. Rubbing it on too thick is in itself a form of discourtesy. Fair dealing is the cornerstone.

Many times letters of adjustment can be avoided by writing a letter of the kind shown below. This was written in connection with a certain kind of plumbing that was to be installed in an office building. In this instance the extra cost did reach a fairly important total, but it was a contingency for which the house that had ordered it was prepared, and there was no angry interchange of letters when the bill was presented.

We are making the changes for which you asked in your letter of November 10. If the extra cost involved does not assume an important total you will hear no more from us about it. If, on the other hand, it assumes such proportions, we are quite sure that you will give us consideration and help meet the extra expense.

Sales Letters

Every letter is at least glanced at by the person who receives it. If it is a sales letter, that may be all that is ever done to it, for sales letters as a class are not welcomed. More time and money and more expert attention are lavished upon them than upon any others, and yet more of them go into the waste basket.

Form is important in all letters but more so in sales letters than in others, for it is the form that determines whether it will get a second glance. A sales letter is not, strictly speaking, an advertisement. An advertisement is impersonal, while a sales letter, even though it be mimeographed, is directed to you because the one who sent it has some connection with your name which makes him believe that you will be interested in his product. The good salesman knows who his customers are; he does not write his letters "blind."

A point which may be worth adding is that the easier names are to get, the less likely they are to be of value as prospects for sales letters. The very fact that they are easy to get probably means that they are already on many lists and receiving letters from all of them.

Sales letters are often planned in campaigns, the number of letters running as high as ten or twelve. In such cases the article to be sold is an expensive one. Less costly articles will stand only one letter; it must, therefore, be a good one.

There is only one way to find out how good a sales letter is—to try it. The usual practice is to try it first on a small group of people before sending it to a large one. Where the mailing list is very long, six and seven trial letters are sometimes sent before a final one is selected.

High-pressure compulsion in sales letters is going out. Never club your prospect into insensibility. Do not try to make him believe that the advantage is all on his side. He will know, unless he is fit to be an inmate of an insane asylum, that you are not telling the truth.

Make buying a pleasure. Appeal to your prospect's pride, to his sense of comfort or economy, to his desire for efficiency, to his hope for a better social position than he now occupies.

In cases where you expect the customer to do the ordering, make it easy for him. Enclose a card with business reply postage on it. Urge him to act at once. If the prospect is a business man with a secretary he will probably dictate a note or ask her to attend to the matter; the reply card is not so essential.

Many devices are used to attract attention. The most radical of these are usually not desirable. They get attention, but it is the same kind a man would get by walking around balancing a pencil on the end of his nose.

Sometimes letters are written by hand in the hope that they will win more notice than the typewritten letter. If they are long and if the handwriting is at all difficult to read, no one will bother with them. There is a belief that farmers and women have time enough to read all the mail they get; but they will not read it unless it is lively and interesting. The salesman who thinks all he has to do to persuade them into buying something is to write a long, dull letter about it has nothing but disappointment ahead.

Everybody wants facts in a sales letter, not promises and glittering generalities. The tendency is to group the facts in a series of short paragraphs, the reason being that short paragraphs are easier to read than long ones.

If the statement is made that your article is lower in price than any other in its class, give the reason, or the assumption will be that it is also inferior in quality. If it is actually inferior in quality, you have no business marketing it.

Timeliness is of enormous value in a sales letter. Special Christmas and holiday appeals, if well done, bring good returns. Letters sent to a bride placing oneself at her service for invitations, flowers, trousseau, silver, etc., are likely to command attention. Alert companies see hundreds of opportunities that sleepier ones pass by. A sign painter, for example, on learning that a certain radio supply house was to open a shop in a new location wrote at once the following letter:

When you move to Nassau Street who will make your signs? How much will they cost? How soon can they be delivered? Will they be distinctive?

These are some of the questions that you have no doubt been asking yourself during the last week. May we offer our services? We have every modern facility for doing excellent work at a reasonable cost. The best way for you to judge is to see for yourself.

Phone Nicholson 7623 and our representative will call.

The following letter was written by the manager of an inn in the country to a prospective guest who was obliged to cancel a reservation:

I have your letter of April 30 saying that you cannot come to Glenfield on Friday, and I have accordingly canceled your reservation. I am very sorry you cannot be here. Glenfield is more than usually beautiful this spring. I hope you will be able to come later.

The letter below is a good example of the kind of letter a nurseryman might send out at the end of the season:

The following are some of the surplus stock on our hands now, which we are selling at greatly reduced prices because we do not wish to carry it over until another season. All are good healthy plants, as you can easily see for yourself if you will visit our nurseries on Martin Boulevard at the Merrick Crossing. The prices are f.o.b. nursery.

Assorted evergreens	1 to 2 feet high @	$1.00 each
Rhododendrons	1½ to 2 feet high @	2.00 each
Rhododendrons	2 to 3 feet high @	3.00 each
Cedars	4 to 5 feet high @	.50 per foot
Oriental arborvitæ	4 to 5 feet high @	5.00 each
English juniper	5 to 6 feet high @	6.00 each
American holly	2 to 3 feet high @	4.00 each
Golden arborvitæ	4 to 5 feet high @	6.00 each

Assorted flowering shrubs, extra heavy, 6 years old, 50 cents to $1.00 each
Assorted French lilacs, all colors, 2 to 4 feet high @$2.00 each

We have also a good many other varieties, which will be sold at very attractive prices. Pay us a visit and we will save you money.

It is always a good plan to try to put yourself into the place of the person to whom you hope to make the sale. If what you have to offer is a trucking service, these are some of the questions which a sensible customer will wish to have answered:

Is this trucking concern responsible in case of fire or collision in transit?
Are its men courteous and competent?
Will they be careful?
Will they arrive at the house when they say they will or must I wait for them an hour or two?
How much insurance per van load will I get?
How much will the cost of everything amount to?
Can I get a better service than this?

Other points which a trucking service used with effect were the fact that they owned outright every van they operated so that the responsibility was entirely theirs, and the further fact that their men were employed by the year rather than by the season, thus enabling the company to employ good ones.

Credit Letters

In 1947 nearly 118 billion dollars' ($118,000,000,000) worth of retail business was transacted in the United States. According to the annual Retail Credit Survey, almost one-third of this was done on credit. This means that modern business is built largely upon credit; and there are today many agencies which make a business of finding out just how good is the credit of various commercial organizations. The most famous is Dun and Bradstreet, which publishes quarterly rating books giving, as nearly as can be determined from signed statements of the firms, the financial ratings of business houses. The National Association of Credit Men and the Credit Clearing House are others; but nearly every house has ways of its own to find out the advisability of extending credit. One of these is to ask for a statement from the customer himself; another is through his own ledger accounts, which, if active, tell an up-to-date and fairly accurate story; a third is through the personal knowledge of the credit manager, who should be a man with wide knowledge of human nature and tact enough to deal with it pleasantly. Salesmen have intimate contacts with customers and are excellent sources of information with regard to the firm's local standing and its actual operating conditions. They know whether the staff is adequate and capable, and whether the general appearance and equipment are attractive and up-to-date.

A customer who is asked for a financial statement from any of these agencies should furnish it promptly. Refusal is often taken as evidence of financial weakness. The signed statement should be accurate, for it must stand in law. In most states there is legal protection for those who have been defrauded through false statements. Many houses voluntarily submit statements of their financial standing, a custom which is becoming more and more general.

Credit is extended on the basis of the character of the customer, his ability, and his capital. For the kinds of questions asked by those seeking to learn the credit capacity of a business, see pages 281 and 282. The length of time for which credit is extended varies in different kinds of business. Farmers go from crop to crop. Small dealers often prefer weekly or monthly statements with no discount, while larger ones prefer the chain discounts (trade discounts). Cash discounts always amount to more than the interest on the money would be, and a failure to take advantage of a cash discount is considered evidence of financial weakness. Every business has its own system; the customary practice is the wise one to follow.

The following credit letters are self-explanatory:

Gentlemen:

I wish to establish an account with you, beginning at once with an order for 100 pairs of black Boy Guide shoes, No. 14, C. Will you please let me know what credit information you desire so that I can send it immediately?

Sincerely yours,

Dear Mr. Bush:

It is a great pleasure to grant you the credit for which you asked in your letter of March 8. The goods are ready and will go forward at once. Our terms are three per cent, ten days; net, 30 days for the amount of your order.

We hope that this is the beginning of a long and happy relationship.

Sincerely yours,

Gentlemen:

Thank you very much for your order of June 17 for turpentine barrels amounting to $267.85. We are now preparing the barrels for shipment and are anxious to deliver them promptly. However, we cannot find on our records that we have previously furnished you with barrels, and we are, therefore, without the information which our credit department demands before we can open an account. Will you be so good as to fill out the enclosed form and return it to us at once so that we can make shipment? The information will, of course, be treated as confidential.

Again let us thank you for your order. We hope it will be the first of many.

Sincerely yours,

Gentlemen:

In answer to your letter of February 10 inquiring as to the credit standing of the Standard Cotton Co. of Eastville, may we say that we have always found them entirely satisfactory as customers? They always discount our bills promptly. The highest amount of credit they have ever asked from us was about $800.

Sincerely yours,

Gentlemen:

We are very sorry to be obliged to refuse the credit for which you asked in your letter of January 9, but the information which we have been able to obtain does not seem sufficient to warrant it. As soon as further information is available we shall be glad to go into the matter again. In the meanwhile we shall be very glad to send the goods C. O. D., if you will authorize us to do so.

Sincerely yours,

Collection Letters

Most letters have one purpose; collection letters have two purposes—to get the money and to keep the customer.

Collection letters usually run in series, though it is sometimes useless to prolong the series beyond five or six letters.

The first should be simply a formal reminder. This may be a statement of the bill with "Overdue" or "Please remit" stamped upon it. Better still, it may be a formal printed statement somewhat like "May we call your attention to this overdue account?" Or it may be a printed or multigraphed form with the dates and the amount of the debt filled in by hand in the blank spaces. "This is to call your attention to your account for March amounting to $540, a bill for which was sent you on April 1. (Signed) E. J. Howe Co."

The series to follow should be carefully planned but should not be routine. The personal element will often bring about payment when nothing else will. For this reason some of the best collection men, even in large companies, have no form collection letters. If a man does not pay his bill there must be a reason. He may be temporarily unfortunate; if this is true he should write frankly to his creditor stating the reasons. If his character is good and his reasons valid he should not have difficulty in getting an extension of time. The following letter, which was sent after a formal reminder was received attached to the bill, is an example:

Will you give me a little time on this? I have just buried my mother after a four-months illness, and I am about flat broke. I will certainly take care of it and would have done so long ago were it not for the frightful expenses I have had to carry.

Once an account is overdue the debtor must not be let alone. The older the account the harder it is to get a settlement. But there should always be time between letters for a reply. It is wise, too, in some cases, to suggest partial payment instead of waiting longer for full payment. Thus:

I have just got around to the letter that you wrote in answer to my letter to you of April 7 regarding an outstanding account of $11.30.

I suggest that you do not wait until you are in a position to remit the full amount. Send us something on account and try to have it in our hands before the close of the present month. We should then be willing to give you a reasonable length of time in which to pay any remaining balance.

Even small accounts must be treated with firmness. One item of less than five dollars is not much, but a hundred or two of them begin to make inroads on almost anybody's business.

Gentlemen:

Again we must remind you of a little account of $3.45. It is of long standing. We are not in the least worried about the size of the account, but we are disturbed over the fact that you seem to ignore our letters pertaining to it. Perhaps you have concluded not to pay it. In that event won't you kindly give us your reason? The account is apparently correct and we can see no reason why the amount should not be liquidated right now.

Please grant us the courtesy of a reply by return mail.

Very truly yours,

Gentlemen:

You know all about this little account that we have against you for $3.45. We regret to be obliged to inform you that our credit department has decided that the item is worthless and we are charging it off to profit and loss.

Perhaps in the near future you may conclude that it is to your interest to reinstate your name with us and will decide to pay this small item.

Yours very truly,

The following series of letters was used with great success in connection with a national campaign for selling a group of travel books:

1. Please accept our many thanks for your order of "Pocket Travels." Your set is being shipped today, all charges prepaid.

In accordance with our special offer, you are to examine these books thoroughly, and if you find that they are not all that you believed them to be, or wished them to be, return them to us within the examination period, and you will owe us nothing.

But if when you have completed your examination of "Pocket Travels" you feel that you will enjoy reading them (and we are sure that this will be the case) mail us $3.50, and $3 a month each month thereafter until the full amount is paid—and the complete set is yours.

The majority of our customers take the cash discount rather than be bothered with the installment payments, and you may do so if you prefer.

Yours very truly,

The following statement of the account, properly filled in, was printed on the lower margin of the above letter:

STATEMENT OF ACCOUNT:

Amount of order.............$———
Amount paid.................$———
Balance due.................$———
Installments now due.........$———

$23.27 pays in full, if remitted within ten days.

2. We are very glad that you have decided to keep the complete set of "Pocket Travels." Kindly accept our many thanks.

Undoubtedly, your interest in searching out the hidden treasures of this invaluable work has caused you to completely overlook sending us your first remittance of $3.50.

Now that your attention has been directed to your delinquency, won't you kindly let us have your check by return mail.

Thank you!

Yours very truly,

STATEMENT OF ACCOUNT:

```
Amount of order.............$————
Amount paid................$————
Balance  due...............$————
Installments now due.......$————
```

3. We are rather surprised that your first payment on your account has not been received by us.

The books were sent you, at your request, on a seven-day approval basis, with the understanding that you would return them to us within that period if they were not satisfactory. The seven days have long since expired, and we must now ask you to send us the first payment of $3.50 at once.

Your check or money order, returned to us with this letter in the enclosed envelope, will receive proper credit.

Yours very truly,

STATEMENT OF ACCOUNT:

```
Account number...............————
Amount of order.............$————
Installments now due........$————
```

P. S. When you write us about this account, or if you forward to us a remittance, be sure to attach this letter.

4. Again I must remind you that the first payment on the books you ordered has not been received.

Can it be possible you are intentionally neglecting this? I hardly think so. What I do think is that you are perhaps a little careless or a little busy, and put it off until to-morrow.

Won't you justify my faith in your integrity and honesty by attaching a check or money order to this letter for the payment now due and mail it to me in the enclosed envelope?

Yours very truly,

STATEMENT OF ACCOUNT:

```
Account Number...............————
Amount of Order.............$————
Installments Now Due........$————
```

P. S. If you write us about this account, be sure to attach this letter to yours.

5. Fifteen days ago we called your attention to the fact that your account was in arrears. Up to this date we do not find that we have received remittance to bring your account up to date.

When we offered these books to you on the intallment plan, we were confident that you would live up to the schedule of payments regularly and punctually. This fact is confirmed by your signature on the original order that we hold.

We are very anxious to bring your account up to date, and must request that you forward to us your remittance for the amount now due, promptly.

Yours very truly,

STATEMENT OF ACCOUNT:

```
Account number...............————
Amount of order.............$————
Amount paid................$————
Balance  due...............$————
Installments now due.......$————
```

P. S. If you write us about this account, be sure to attach this letter to yours.

Account No. ——————————
Amount ——————————

6. Please understand that in calling your attention to the above account, no action concerning your credit standing is contemplated at this time. It generally suffices to send this final notice to bring a settlement by return mail.

7. Any good reason for not paying this account should be reported to this office *immediately*. (THIS IS FOR YOUR OWN PROTECTION.)

We have been exceptionally lenient in your case, in hope of receiving an amicable settlement, without interruption of our cordial relations.

Regretfully, we must abandon our former policy and disclaim any liability for damage or loss resulting from the next steps we propose to take in securing the amount you owe us.

Our claim against you will be sent to our attorneys for necessary legal action unless you respond to this last notice within five days.

The outcome depends entirely upon yourself.

Yours truly,

It is useless to keep on further threatening an account. If the maker was not frightened the first two or three times he will not be frightened the next two or three. If you say you are going to place the matter in the hands of a lawyer, either do so or, if the account is too small to bother with any longer, write it off the books.

The notice below is the kind a lawyer sends when he begins his campaign. The steps that follow are the lawyer's business and hardly within the scope of this book.

The above account has been placed in my hands for immediate collection in the amount of $51.53, with interest to date.

It is imperative that I receive a check by return mail if further action and expense are to be avoided.

Inter-Office Correspondence

It is easy for a person who is not very busy to delude himself into thinking he has a great deal to do by sending numerous long memorandums to people in his own office; but in a well-regulated office where the workers trust one another, it should not be necessary to exchange many written messages.

Memorandums should be sent to save time. Even the simplest requests may be put into writing for this reason, *e.g.*, "Please let me have the profit and loss cards for July." But if the man who has the profit and loss cards sits only about two feet from you, ask him for them.

Memorandums may be sent as reminders.

Most important of all, memorandums may be sent as records of items of importance.

The length of a memorandum depends upon its subject. The confirmation of an order may require only three lines while the presentation of an idea for a new magazine or for some other entirely new or complicated project may require more than 100 pages.

All memorandums should be dated; and it is a good plan to initial them in ink for identification.

Memorandum

From: Mr. Bennett
To: Mr. Patterson

  This confirms verbal instructions to make 10,000 copies of "Green Branches."
Orders are coming in far beyond our expectations and we shall want these as quickly
as possible.
These books are to be absolutely uniform with the first edition.
Please let me know how soon they can be delivered.

(Date)

Large business houses have special memorandum forms: to individuals
whose word carries special weight or whose memorandum volume is unusually large personal blanks are supplied. For instance, the president of a
firm might send a memorandum thus:

BALCH, INCORPORATED
654 Fifth Ave.

Memorandum from
The President

  For various reasons I have an idea that June sales will be practically nil. They will
certainly approach this figure in the regular trade department where publications
have been postponed.
  Under these circumstances it becomes necessary to curtail all advertising expenses
—if not to eliminate them entirely. Will you, therefore, see that this is done?
  Discussion of further advertising, promotion, etc. that will be appearing in the
month of July will be had during the month of June.

(Date)

One should be very careful about putting a reprimand in the form of a
memorandum. It may be more difficult, but in general it is much better to
do this kind of thing by word of mouth. What is said may be forgotten and
forgiven, but what is written continues to rankle.

The same holds true of letters of dismissal. Even if such a letter is sent
(and often it goes, as a matter of routine, with the final pay check) it is
far kinder to say to the departing employee that you are sorry it is necessary that he leave and give him your best wishes for good luck elsewhere.
This seems easy, but many strong men shrink from it. The dismissed employee, however, who is so spoken to goes away with a much warmer feeling in his heart than if he had merely received a printed pink or blue slip.
Employees who leave with a grudge, especially if there is something to
warrant it, can do the firm they quit a great deal of harm.

Official Letters

Official letters are more formal than general letters. The salutation is
"Sir:" or "Sirs:" as the case may be; there are no abbreviations and all
titles of respect are written out in full. Such letters are addressed to the
editors of magazines and newspapers for publication, to men in official
positions, to committees or boards.

Officer	*Letter Address*	*Letter and Verbal Salutations* (1) *Formal and* (2) *Informal*
The President	The President of the United States	(1) Mr. President (2) My dear Mr. President
The Vice President	The Hon. John Smith, Vice President of the United States	(1) Sir (2) My dear Mr. Vice President
Ambassadors	His Excellency the Italian Ambassador (For United States Ambassadors The Hon. John Jones)	Your Excellency
Cabinet Officers	The Hon. Secretary of the Treasury	(1) Mr. Secretary (2) My dear Mr. Secretary
Senators	Senator John Smith	(1) Sir (2) My dear Senator
Congressmen	The Hon. Henry Jones	(1) Sir (2) My dear Congressman Jones
Governors	His Excellency the Governor of Delaware	(1) Your Excellency (2) Dear Governor
Supreme Court Justices	The Chief Justice of the United States: or, The Hon. John Smith, Associate Justice of the United States	(1) Mr. Justice (2) My dear Mr. Justice
Cardinal or Archbishop	His Grace the Archbishop of Philadelphia	Your Grace
Bishops (Protestant or Roman Catholic)	The Right Rev. John Smith The Right Rev., the Bishop of Delaware	(1) Right Reverend and dear sir (2) My dear Bishop Smith

Law of Letters

Be sure that everything you write will bear reading before a jury of 12 good men and true. Pay careful attention to syntax, for if the meaning is doubtful your letter will be interpreted according to the laws of grammar. Indecent, fraudulent, or seditious matter is unlawful, and letters of an abusive or libelous nature will subject the sender to punishment if he shows them to or allows them to be seen by a third person. In letters answering questions as to a man's financial or personal standing, do not assume too much responsibility. Do not flatly say that the man is not reliable, but that your experience with him will not warrant your endorsing him.

Many letters are permanent records of contracts and they should be so written that there will be no loophole for the man you are dealing with, should he happen to be dishonest. In accepting a contract follow the exact conditions imposed. If the offer is made by mail and no other method is specified, accept by mail, by return mail if possible. If there is a request for acceptance by telegraph, or telephone, or if a time limit is set, comply absolutely, or the contract is not binding. If you make the slightest change in the original terms of the contract it is not binding until it has been accepted by the other party. A contract holds good if the acceptance is made in the prescribed way, even if the acceptance is delayed or completely lost in transit. A man has the right to revoke an offer any time before it is accepted; but the acceptor has no right to revoke unless he makes provision for it in his acceptance.

Agreements made on Sundays and on legal holidays are not valid.

The law of the state where the acceptance is made governs the transaction.

It may be worth adding that a letter is the property of the person who writes it, not of the person to whom it is written, and no letter can be legally published without permission from the author. This does not apply to letters that are introduced into court as evidence.

A carbon copy of a letter is legally considered a duplicate of the original.

Want Ads

"Situation wanted" ads should be brief and definite. Here is a good sample of the kind not to write:

Man (45) wishes position at anything; has had 20 years' business experience; can furnish references. K657 *Times.*

All that anyone knows from the advertisement is that the man is 45 years old. No clue whatsoever is given as to the kind of business experience scattered over those 20 years. He offers references, but almost anyone can produce references of one kind or another. Contrast this advertisement with the one below:

Mechanic, 37, locksmith, carpenter, electrician; own tools; steady; reasonable. *Times* 15A.

The second ad tells briefly what the man can actually do and states that he owns his own tools. He might have added something about references, but no doubt has them where they can be produced.

The "Help wanted" advertisement should follow the same rules. Here is a good example:

WANTED.—Clerical worker, young man, by fire insurance company. Must be good at figures; fire insurance experience preferred. Reply in own handwriting stating experience and salary desired. *Herald* S17.

WORDS OFTEN MISPRONOUNCED

Bad grammar betrays all language; bad spelling betrays written, and bad pronunciation spoken, language. From a man's accent we can usually tell what section of the country he comes from, and how far up the ladder of education he has climbed. Correct usage varies in different localities; and if you grew up saying *tomāto*, there is no reason why you should change now to *tomäto*. Snobbishness in speech is almost as despicable as it is in character. It is nearly always the half-educated man who says *ither* and *nither* to impress other people in his community, if they all happen to say *ēēther* and *nēēther*. Many words admit of two pronunciations. Choose the one that attracts least attention to yourself. Other words have *only one correct pronunciation*. Read the following list carefully. You probably accent some of these words wrongly without realizing it.

accept—ăk-sĕpt', *not* ĕk-sĕpt'.
acclimate—ă-klī'-māt, *not* ăk'-klĭm-āt.
accurate—ăk'-ū-rāt, *not* ăk'-kĕr-ĭt.
across—à-krŏs', *not* à-krŏst'.
address—ă-drĕs', *not* ăd'-drĕs.
à la carte—ä-lä-kärt', *not* ä-lä-kärt'ĕ.
alias—ā-lĭ-ăs, *not* ā-lī'-ăs.
aviation—ā-vĭ-ā'-shŭn, *not* ăv-ĭ-ā-shŭn.
aviator—ā'-vĭ-ā-tĕr, *not* ăv'-ĭ-ā-tĕr, even though certain distinguished fliers pronounce it thus.

bona fide—bō-nà fī'-de, *not* bō-nà fīd.

chasm—kăzm, *not* kă'-zŭm.
chef—shĕf, *not* chĕf.
chic—shēēk, *not* chĭck.
chiropodist—kī-rŏp'-ō-dĭst, *not* chī-rŏp'-ō-dĭst.
column—kŏl'-ŭm, *not* kŏl'-yŭm.
contribute—kŏn-trĭb'-ut, *not* kŏn'-trĭb-ūt.
corps (*military*)—kōr; *pl.*, kōrz.

data—dā'-tà, *not* dä'-tà.
deficit—dĕf'-ĭ-sĭt, *not* dē-fĭ'-sĭt.
digest—dī'-jĕst (*n.*—, *Reader's Digest; v.*—, dĭ-jĕst').
diplomacy—dĭ-plō'-mà-sĭ, *not* dĭ-plō'-mà-sĭ.
discipline—dĭs'-ĭ-plĭn, *not* dĭ-sĭp'-lĭn.
drowned—dround, *not* droun'-dĕd.

exquisite—ĕks'-kwĭ-zĭt, *not* ĕks-kwĭz'-ĭt.
extempore—ĕks-tĕm'-pō-re, *not* ĕks-tĕm-pōr'.

fellow—fĕl'-ō, *not* fĕl'-ĕr.

government—gŭv'-ĕrn-mĕnt, *not* gŭv'-ĕr-mĕnt.

habeas corpus—hā'-bē-ăs kôr'-pŭs, *not* hăb'-ē-ăs kôr'-pŭs.
Hawaii—hä-wī'-ē.
Hawaiian—hä-wī'-yàn.
hoof—hōōf, *not* hŏŏf. See *roof*.

inquiry—ĭn-kwīr′-ĭ, *not* ĭn′-kwĭ-rĭ.
interesting—ĭn′-tēr-ĕst-ĭng, *not* ĭn-tēr-ĕst′-ĭng.
iron—ī′ûrn, *not* ī′-rŭn.

khaki—kä′-kē, *not* kăk′-ĭ.
library—lī′-brĕ-rĭ, *not* lī′-brĭ.

mediocre—mē-dē-ō′-kēr, *not* mĕd′-ĭ-ō-kēr.
mischievous—mĭs′-chĭ-vŭs, *not* mĭs-chēē′-vŭs.

natatorium—nā′-tà-tō-rĭ-ŭm, *not* năt′-à-tō-rĭ-ŭm.
New Orleans—nū ôr′-lē-ănz, *not* nū or-lēēnz′.
news—nūz, *not* nōōz.

partner—pärt′-nēr, *not* pärd′-nēr.
penalize—pē′-năl-īz, *not* pĕn′-ăl-īz.
posse—pŏs′-ē, *not* pŏs.
pro rata—prō rā′-tà, *not* prō răt′-à, *nor* prō răt′-tà.

recognize—rĕk′-ŏg-nīz, *not* rĕk′-ēr-nīz.
roof—rōōf, *not* rŏŏf.

salmon—săm′-ŭn, *not* săm′-ŭn.
sort of—sôrt ŏv, *not* sôrt′-ēr.
speedometer—spēd-ŏm′-ē-tēr.
stupid—stū′-pĭd, *not* stōō′-pĭd.
suburb—sŭb′-ûrb, *not* sŭ′-bûrb.
suite—swēt, *not* sōōt.

table d'hôte—täb′lē-dōt, *not* tä′-bl-dō-tē.
theater—thē′-à-tēr, *not* thē-ā′-tēr.

used—ūsd, *not* ūst.
ultimatum—ŭl-tĭ-mā′tŭm, *not* ŭl-tĭ-mä′-tŭm.

verbatim—vēr-bā′-tĭm, *not* vēr-băt′-ĭm, *nor* vēr-bà′-tĭm.

what—when—where, and **which** are pronounced hwŏt, hwĕn, hwâr, hwĭch, *instead of* wŏt, wĕn, wâr and wĭch.

WORDS OFTEN CONFUSED

Accept. All of us *except* John *accepted* the invitation.
Except. I *except* no one when I say he is the greatest man living.

Advice (noun). That is not good *advice.*
Advise (verb). Let me *advise* you. (This word is abused in business correspondence. Don't use it unless you are really giving advice.)

Affect, to influence or change something which already exists. Ignorant people believe that the moon *affects* crops.
Effect, to cause or produce something. The new law *effected* a political reform.

Altar. He knelt at the *altar.*
Alter. The coat was *altered* to fit.

Beside, by the side of. He sat *beside* the manager.
Besides, in addition to. *Besides* all this, we have eight more coming.

Canvas. A *canvas* tent.
Canvass. A *canvass* for votes.

Capacity, power of receiving. He has the *capacity* to learn the work.
Ability, power to do. He has the *ability* to do this work.

Capital. Albany is the *capital* of New York. There is strife between *capital* and labor.

Capitol. State house. The national *capitol* is at Washington.

Censor, one who examines. Moving pictures pass a board of *censors* before they appear before the public.

Censure, to blame. The stenographer was *censured* severely for her carelessness.

Continual, often repeated. The morning was broken into by *continual* interruptions.

Continuous, never stopping. The *continuous* noise of a dozen typewriters is distracting to one unaccustomed to it.

Credible, believable. A *credible* yarn.

Creditable, praiseworthy. A *creditable* performance.

Emigrant. The *emigrant* from Russia settled on the East Side of New York.

Immigrant. The *immigrant* to the United States found himself among people who could not speak his language.

Expect, to look forward to. I *expect* the shipment tomorrow morning.

Suspect, to distrust. The robber was *suspected* of murder.

Export. We *export* supplies to other countries.

Import. We *import* sugar from Cuba.

Few refers to number. Very *few* of the melons were defective.

Less refers to quantity. There is *less* cotton produced in the South since the advent of the boll weevil.

Finally, at last.

Finely, adverb derived from *fine*.

Find, to discover. He *found* the leak.

Locate, to place. *Locate* Tasmania on the map. The store will be *located* in New York.

Invent. Edison *invented* the phonograph.

Discover. Columbus *discovered* America.

Lay, to put down. *Lay* the book on the desk.

Lie, to recline. I shall *lie* down for a while.

Miner. Many *miners* have to spend their working hours underground.

Minor. A *minor* is one who is not yet 21.

Practicable, capable of being put into practice. That is a *practicable* scheme.

Practical, pertaining to, or governed by, actual use and experience. He has *practical* ideas about management.

Precede, to go before. The marshal will *precede* the parade.

Proceed, to go forward. The meeting will now *proceed*.

Principal, chief, leader; sum on which interest accrues.

Principle, general truth, information, or belief.

Quiet. At last the children are *quiet*.

Quite. He lay *quite* still.

Respectfully, with respect. *Respectfully* submitted.

Respectively, singly considered. When the teacher called the roll the boys answered *respectively* to their names.

Set (transitive).

Sit. (intransitive). Set the basket there and then sit down over here by me.

Stationary, not movable. The desk is *stationary*.

Stationery. Often the character of a firm is judged by the *stationery* on which its letters are written.

Therefor, for this or that or it, etc. We bought 17 cases and paid *therefor* $60.

Therefore, for that reason. We liked the idea, and *therefore* submitted it to you.

To (preposition).

Too (adverb).

Two (adjective). I gave *two* rabbits *to* my brother but they were *too* heavy for him to carry.

WORDS OFTEN MISSPELLED

Rules for spelling are so complicated and are qualified by so many exceptions that it is almost useless to bother with them. But this is one worth remembering, for it holds true in practically all cases where *ei* or *ie* are found after *l* or *c*. (Believe, lieutenant; receive, conceit.) *Leisure* is an exception.

> When the letter *c* you spy
> Place the *e* before the i
> When the letter *l* you see
> Place the *i* before the e

A good speller is a good visualizer. Often he can tell which of two spellings is correct by writing them both on a slip of paper and seeing which one "looks right." Cultivate this faculty. Try to remember how the word looks on the printed page.

If there is still doubt, consult an unabridged dictionary. You will find it profitable to memorize the following list. These words are responsible for more errors than any others.

acceptable	bankruptcy	deficit
accidentally	benefited	delinquent
accommodate	business	describe
accuracy	calendar	develop
achievement	column	disappear
across	committee	embarrassing
address	commodity	enclose
adequate	communicate	erroneous
advertisement	computation	expense
all right	consignment	feasible
apparent	correspondence	February
auditor	credentials	financial
balance	debtor	fiscal

foreclosure	notary	remittance
foreign	noticeable	replies
forty-four	occasion	salable
governor	occurring	salary
guarantee	omission	secretary
incidentally	opportunity	security
indispensable	parallel	separate
insistent	parcel	similar
intelligible	partner	since
inventory	picnicking	stenographer
label	planning	stopped
ledger	policy	subscription
liquidate	prejudice	surprise
manageable	privilege	tariff
meant	promissory	tenant
miscellaneous	publicity	truly
momentary	pursue	Tuesday
mortgage	quietly	twelfth
necessary	quite	Wednesday
negotiable	recommend	wholesale
nickel	reliability	

MISTAKES TO AVOID IN GRAMMAR

A. Don't say, *that kind of a man,* but *that kind of man.*

Accept. Don't say, *accept of. Accept* is sufficient.

Again. Don't say, *Do it over again,* or *Return back again,* but *Do it over, Return.*

Ain't. This word has had a long life and shows no sign of dying, but it has never been used by careful writers and speakers.

And. *And* connects only words, phrases, or clauses of equal rank. *Be sure and come,* therefore, should be, *Be sure to come.* It is foolish to write *and etc.,* for etc. means *and so forth.* Be careful not to use too many *ands;* they destroy clearness.

Anywheres. This is a vulgarism for *anywhere. Any place* is incorrect. So are *everywheres* and *every place.* Use *anywhere* and *everywhere.*

As. Don't say, *He as did it,* for *as* is never a pronoun. Substitute *who* or *that.*

Don't say, *Not as I know of,* but *Not that I know of.*

At. *Where am I at?* is not good English except for humorous emphasis.

Badly. *He looks bad* is correct unless you are referring to his manner of looking out of his eyes. Similarly, *The rose smells sweet* instead of *sweetly,* for the rose has no sense of smell. Always use the adverb when you are describing the verb, the adjective when you are describing the noun.

Balance. Don't say *balance* when you mean *rest* or *remainder. Balance* has reference to the difference between the credit and the debit columns of an account.

Between. Don't say, *divided between five men,* but *divided among five men. Between* refers to two.

Don't say, *between you and I,* but *between you and me,* since the pronouns form the compound object of the preposition, *between*. You would never say *between I and you and the gatepost*.

Can. Don't say, *Can I go to the ball game?* unless you are asking your physician about your physical ability. *May* is the proper verb to use to get permission.

Cooperate. Don't say, *cooperate together. Cooperate* means to work together.

Complected. Use *complexioned*.

Dangling participles. Never introduce a participle into a sentence unless you are sure there is something there for it to modify. *Walking into the room his eye lighted on a stranger* is inexcusable because it might so easily have been, *When he walked into the room he saw a stranger*. Keep special guard over *replying, hoping, answering, trusting*, etc.

Date. A thing does not date *back* to 1888; it dates *from* 1888.

Different is followed by *from*, never by *than*.

Do. This is one of the most abused words in the language.

Don't say, *He done it. Done* is the past participle and should always be preceded by some part of the verb *to have*.

He don't like it is as incorrect as *He do not like it*.

Don't tack *I don't think* on the end of what you say. Most of the time you say exactly the opposite from what you mean. *We won't get to Philadelphia this week, I don't think*, means, *I don't think we won't get to Philadelphia this week*.

Each. *Each, any, every one, any one, either, neither*, etc. require a singular verb. Not *Each are here*, but *Each is here*, because you are talking about only one person.

Foot. Don't say, *ten foot high*, but *ten feet high*. A *ten-foot pole* is correct, however.

Funny. *It's a funny thing. When one member of that family gets sick they all get sick.* Use *singular, odd*, or *strange*, and save *funny* for the places where it is really needed.

Gent. This is a vulgarism. Don't use it, and don't use the other word that is equally objectionable, *pants*.

He. It is correct to say, *"This is he"* when you acknowledge over the telephone that you are John Smith. The verb *to be* has the value of the sign of equality (=) and should always be followed by the nominative case. A pronoun is always a substitute. Be sure that you have made perfectly clear what it stands for.

Don't use pronouns unnecessarily, as in this sentence: John, *he* began the fight, but Bill, *he* was ready for it, and pretty soon the whole crowd, *they* all pitched in. This construction is allowable when it is used for emphasis, *e.g.*, Jones, the organizer and promoter of this company, *he*, I say, is the man we want.

Here. Don't say, *this here letter* or *that there book*, but simply *this letter* or *that book*.

Its, it's. Its is a possessive pronoun. *It's* is a contraction for *It is*. The child loves *its* dog. *It's* very warm today.

Let. This verb is followed by the objective case. *Let you and me do it,* not *Let you and I do it.*

Like. *Like* is a preposition, *as* is a conjunction. It is ungrammatical to say, *Do like I do.* Say either *Do as I do* or *Do like me.*

Myself. Don't say, *John and myself are here,* but *John and I are here. Myself* is used reflexively or for emphasis, as *I cut myself* or *I, myself, will do it.*

Neither ... nor, either ... or. These conjunctions are used in pairs, always *nor* with *neither* and *or* with *either.* Place them as near as possible to the terms they connect. Don't say, *We shall either go Thanksgiving Day or Christmas,* but *We shall go either Thanksgiving Day or Christmas.*

Negatives. Avoid the double negative as you would influenza. Never say, *I don't hardly know, I ain't got none, not by no means, I did not see no one,* but *I hardly know, I have none, by no means, I saw no one.*

Nights. Don't say, *I work nights,* but *I work at night* or *every night.*

Of. Don't say, *I would of, should of,* or *could of* done it. *Of* is never a verb.

Off of. *Of* is unnecessary.

Ought. Don't say *had ought. Ought* should never be preceded by a helping verb.

Overly. It is a vulgarism to say, *I am not feeling overly well.*

Pair. Don't say *a new pair of shoes,* but *a pair of new shoes.*

Party. Except in legal parlance, *party* is not correctly used to refer to one person. *Party to a contract,* but not *the party with the tortoise-shell spectacles.*

Rather. *I would rather* is better form than *I had rather.*

Say. It is crude to say, *I want a say in this matter.* Better, *I want to say something about this matter.*
Don't say, *It said,* or *They said,* for *The Tribune said,* or *The people said.*

Seldom. *Seldom ever* should be *seldom, if ever.*

Size. Don't say, *A good size order,* but *A good-sized order.*

Some. Don't say, *I like it some,* but *I like it somewhat.*
Don't say, *He is some better,* but *He is somewhat better.*

Subject. The agreement between subject and predicate is very troublesome, especially when they are separated by some other part of the sentence. *The cost of necessities are constantly increasing* should be *is constantly increasing* because you are talking about the *cost,* not the *necessities. The captain, as well as the crew, were present* should be *was present,* for it is the captain whose presence you are interested in. *We shall all go to Boston, John, you and me,* should be, *We shall all go to Boston, John, you and I. John, you,* and *I* are explanatory modifiers of *we* and should therefore be in the nominative case.

Suspicion. *Suspicion* is often improperly used for *suspect. I suspected something was wrong,* not *I suspicioned something was wrong.*

Tense. Be sure that your verb refers exactly to the time when the action took place, and don't switch awkwardly from the past to the present in the same sentence.

Them. *Them* is a pronoun and should not be used for an adjective. Don't say, *them boys,* but *those boys.*

This, that, these, those. Don't say *these kind,* because *kind* is singular and should be modified by a singular adjective. *This kind* or *these kinds, that sort* or *those sorts.*

Up. Don't tack *up* on at the end of a verb. Not, *He divided up his work,* but *He divided his work.*

Was. Never say, *You was,* but always *You were.* Don't say, *If I was you,* but *If I were you,* for you are expressing an impossibility, and the subjunctive mode is needed.

Without. Distinguish from *unless.* Don't say, *Without you go,* but *Unless you go.*

Will. Don't say, *What will I do?* but *What shall I do? Will* with the first person denotes determination on the part of the speaker. Hence, *Shall I close the door?* and *Will I do it? I will not!* are both correct.

When. Don't say, *Good English is when you speak and write well,* because *when* is used to express time. See *where.*

Where. Don't say, *Typewriting is where you use the typewriter,* because *where* is used to express place.

Who. *Who* refers to persons, *which* to things, *that* to either persons or things. Be careful to use the objective case, *whom,* when the pronoun is the object of a preposition or a verb. *To whom did you give it? Whom do you wish to see?* are correct.

PUNCTUATION

Carelessness in punctuation is likely to cause trouble. Compare, "The office boy says the boss is a fool" with "The office boy," says the boss, "is a fool." The fashion in punctuation, as in words, changes from time to time and the best way to acquire good habits of punctuation is to notice the usage of standard magazines. The following rules, however, will cover most ordinary cases:

1. The *period* is placed at the end of a declarative or an imperative sentence, and after all initials and abbreviations. It is not placed after 1st, 2nd, 3rd, 10th, etc.

2. The *comma* indicates the smallest degree of separation of thought in the sentence, but it is the most troublesome of all the marks of punctuation. It is better to use it too little than to use it too much. It is used:

    a. To separate words, phrases, or clauses in a series.
        He laid his coat, hat, umbrella, and cane on the table.
    b. To set off "Yes," "No," and words of direct address.
        Come here, John. Yes, sir.
    c. To set off explanatory modifiers.
        The last day, Friday, was very rainy.
    d. To set off words which interrupt the regular grammatical flow of the sentence.
        Let the conference close, I beg you, as soon as the speech is over.

e. To clarify the meaning of a long involved sentence, especially when there is danger of misinterpretation.

When the heat of midsummer made the boys irritable and lessened their efficiency, practical economy directed the manager to install electric fans and other devices for making them as comfortable as possible.

f. To separate the members of a short compound sentence.

Be square with your workers, but make them realize that you are square.

g. To show an omission.

Industry is the key to success; idleness, the bolt that bars the door.

Macon, Georgia, June 16, 1920.

h. To give emphasis.

He worked hard, and won success.

i. Before *not* when it introduces a contrasting phrase or clause.

Acquire the habit of questioning everything you read, not to find fault with it, but to learn the truth from it.

j. To separate a direct quotation from the rest of the sentence except when it is very long.

Then Jackson said, "Let me hear from you."

3. The *semicolon* is placed between the members of a compound sentence when either contains a comma, when a comma is insufficient, or when the conjunction is omitted.

When he hands in his report, his power ceases; he has no authority to enforce his decisions.

What I tell you is of no consequence; what I do—behold!

4. The *colon* is used to introduce. It is placed after *as follows,* after the salutation of a business letter, and before a long quotation or an enumeration of details.

It is also used in writing the time of day in figures.

Here was the proposition: Twenty men were to work for eight days—

My dear Sir:

The statement is as follows: He works from 8:45 to 5:30.

5. The *dash* is wrongly used by many people when they are in doubt as to what other mark of punctuation to use. It is properly used to indicate an abrupt break in the thought, to replace marks of parenthesis, or to emphasize some part of the sentence.

Just at that moment the door opened slowly and—but you had better finish the story for yourself.

If you decide to keep it—and you surely will—send five dollars today.

You have everything to gain—nothing to lose.

6. The *hyphen* should be used when it is absolutely necessary to divide a word at the end of a line. Always divide words according to pronunciation.

The hyphen is used with many compound words about which no rules can be given and about which even the dictionaries disagree.

7. *Marks of parenthesis* are used to enclose a word or group of words strongly subordinate to the rest of the sentence.

> The last epidemic caused 500,000 deaths (these facts can be verified) and a total economic loss of nearly four billion dollars.

8. *Brackets* are used to enclose supplementary or explanatory matter not originally found in the text.

> Then he [Neal] signed the paper.

9. *Quotation marks* are used to enclose a direct quotation.

> Stevenson said, "The difficulty is not to write but to write what you mean."

The title of a book, play, or magazine article may be enclosed in quotation marks or may have a line drawn under it. A single line drawn underneath a word, or a group of words, denotes that it is to be printed in italics.

> I was reading *The Voice of the City* when Fred asked me to go to *Twelfth Night*.

10. The *apostrophe* is used to indicate the possessive case, to indicate omitted letters, and to form the plural of letters, figures, and symbols.

> Scott's ambition was the result of his mother's teaching.
> I'll see about it.
> Dot your i's and cross your t's.

It is not used in the following pronouns: *its, hers, his, ours, theirs, yours.* Please read the above sentence again. This is a very common mistake.

11. The *exclamation point* is used to show strong or sudden feeling.

> Oh! Fine!

12. The *question mark* is placed at the end of a direct question. It is used in parentheses to indicate doubt.

> Who is there?
> It happened twice, once in 1819 (?) and again in 1901.

CAPITALIZATION

Capital letters are used to begin every sentence, every line of poetry, every direct quotation, every important word in the title of a book, and every proper noun or adjective.

The pronoun "I" and the exclamation "O" are always capitalized.

The words North, East, South, and West are capitalized when they refer to sections of the country but not when they merely indicate direction.

All titles of persons begin with capital letters.

All names of the Deity should be capitalized.

Any particularly important word may be capitalized, and if special emphasis is desired the entire word may be typed in capitals.

ABBREVIATIONS

Abbreviations should never be used in formal writing, nor in any place where they would create doubt as to the meaning.

The following abbreviations of the states and territories are officially recognized by the Post Office Department.

Ala., Alabama	N. C., North Carolina
Ariz., Arizona	N. Dak., North Dakota
Ark., Arkansas	Nebr., Nebraska
Calif. California	Nev., Nevada
Colo., Colorado	N. H., New Hampshire
Conn., Connecticut	N. J., New Jersey
C. Z., Canal Zone	N. Mex., New Mexico
D. C., District of Columbia	N. Y., New York
Del., Delaware	Okla., Oklahoma
Fla., Florida	Pa., Pennsylvania
Ga., Georgia	P. I., Philippine Islands
Ill., Illinois	P. R., Puerto Rico
Ind., Indiana	R. I., Rhode Island
Kans., Kansas	S. C., South Carolina
Ky., Kentucky	S. Dak., South Dakota
La., Louisiana	Tenn., Tennessee
Mass., Massachusetts	Tex., Texas
Md., Maryland	Va., Virginia
Mich., Michigan	Vt., Vermont
Minn., Minnesota	Wash., Washington
Miss., Mississippi	W. Va., West Virginia
Mo., Missouri	Wis., Wisconsin
Mont., Montana	Wyo., Wyoming

Miscellaneous Abbreviations and Signs

abst., Abstract
a.c., Alternating current
acc., acct., a/c, Account
A.D., Since the birth of Christ
Anno Domini, literally, In the year of our
   Lord
ad, advt. (*pl.*, ads), Advertisement
admr., Administrator
agt., Agent
A.M., Before noon, (ante meridiem)
Amer., American
amt., Amount
anon., Anonymous
A1, First class
ans., Answer
Assn., Association
asst., Assistant, assorted
av., advp., avoir., Avoirdupois
ave., Avenue

B.A., Bachelor of Arts
bal., Balance
bbl., Barrel
bdl., Bundle
b.e., B/E, Bill of exchange
bkt., Basket
b.l., B/L, Bill of lading
bldg., Building
b.p., B/P, Bills payable
b.r., B/R, Bills receivable
B.Sc., Bachelor of Science
b.s., Balance sheet
b.s., B/S, Bill of sale
bu., Bushel
bt., Bought
bx., Boxes

c. or ct., (*pl.*, cts.), Cent
C., Centigrade
ca., Circa, about
cap., Capital
c.c., Cubic centimeter
cf., Compare
chgd., Charged
c.i.f., Cost, insurance, and freight
cm., Centimeter
cml., Commercial
c.o., Carried over
c/o, Care of
c.o.d., Cash on delivery
com., Commercial, commission
C.P.A., Certified public accountant
cr., Credit, creditor, crate
cs., Cases

C.S.T., c.s.t., Central standard time
ctge., Cartage
cu., Cubic
c.w.o., Cash with order
cwt., Hundredweight

d.c., Direct current
D.D., Doctor of Divinity
D.D.S., Doctor of Dental Surgery
dept., Department
dft., Draft
disct., Discount
div., Dividend
do., Ditto, the same
doz., Dozen
Dr., Doctor; dr., Debtor, dram

E., East
e.e., Errors excepted
e.g., For example (exempli gratia)
Eng., England, English
E.S.T., e.s.t., Eastern standard time
et al., And elsewhere; and others
etc., And so forth
ex., Example; exchange; extract
exp., Export; express; expense

F., Fahrenheit
f.a.s., Free alongside ship
fcp., Foolscap
ff., Following
fig., Figure
f.o.b., Free on board
for'd., Forward
frt., fgt., Freight
Fr., French
ft., Foot, feet; fort

g., Gram
gal., Gallon
G.M.T., g.m.t., Greenwich mean time
govt., Government
gr. gro., Great gross
gro., Gross
G.T.C., Good till canceled
guar., Guarantee

HE, High explosive
hhd., Hogshead, hogsheads
h.p. or hp, Horsepower

ib., ibid., In the same place (ibidem)
id., The same
i.e., That is (id est)
i.h.p., Indicated horsepower

512

imp., Imported, important
in., Inch
inc., Incorporated
incog., Incognito
ins., Inches; inspector; insurance
int., Interest
inv., Invoice
invt., Inventory
I O U, I owe you

lat., Latitude
lb., Pound
LL.B., Bachelor of Laws
LL.D., Doctor of Laws
long., Longitude
l.t., Long ton
Ltd., Limited

M.A., Master of Arts
mdse., Merchandise
mem. or memo., Memorandum
mfd., Manufactured
mfg., Manufacturing
mfr., Manufacturer
mgr., Manager
m.o., Money order
MS., ms., MSS., mss., Manuscript, manu-
    scripts
M.Sc., Master of Science
M.S.T., m.s.t., Mountain standard time
mun., Municipal

N., North
N.B., Note carefully (nota bene)
n.l., Not permitted (non licet)
no., nos., Number, numbers
N.P., Notary public

o/a., On account of
O.K., All correct
oz., Ounce

p., Page
p. & l., Profit and loss
payt., Payment
pc., Piece
p.c., Per cent. See also per ct.
pd., Paid
per an., By the year
per ct., Per cent
p. ex., For example
Ph.D., Doctor of Philosophy
pk., Peck
pkg., Package
P.M., Afternoon (post meridiem)
P.O., Post Office
pop., Population
pp., Pages

p.p., Postpaid
pr., Pair
pref., Preferred
pres., President
P.S., Postscript
P.S.T., p.s.t., Pacific standard time

q.v., quod vide, which see
qr., Quarter
qt., Quart

Rd., rd., Road
rec'd, Received
rect., Receipt
reg., Registered
ret., Returned
R.F.D., Rural Free Delivery
R.R., Railroad
Ry., Railway

S., South
sec., sec'y, Secretary
s.d., S/D, Sight draft
sdy, Sundries
ser., Series
sh., Share
shipt., Shipment
sq., Square
S.S., Steamship
St., Street
stbt., Steamboat
stor., Storage
str., Steamer
super., Superfine
supt., Superintendent

t.b., Trial balance
temp., Temporary
t.f., Till forbidden
tr., Transpose
treas., Treasurer

v., vs., Versus; against
ves., Vessel
via, By way of
viz., Namely

W., West
W/B, Way bill
wt., Weight

yd., Yard
yr., Year

&, And
$, Dollar
%, Per cent
#, Number
@, At, at the rate of

A BUSINESS DICTIONARY

A GUIDE TO ABBREVIATIONS

Abbr. = abbreviated

A. D. = Anno Domini (Year of our Lord)

adj. = adjective

adv. = adverb

A. M., a. m. = before noon (ante meridiem)

B. C. = before Christ

Colloq. = colloquial

Eng. = England, English

etc. = et cetera (and so forth)

F. = Fahrenheit

fem. = feminine

Fr. = France, French

i. e. = id est (that is)

interj. = interjection

masc. = masculine

n. = noun

pl. = plural

P. M., p. m. = afternoon (post meridiem)

prep. = preposition

pron. = pronoun

sing. = singular

sq. = square

U. S. = United States

v. i. = verb intransitive

v. t. = verb transitive

A

A1, a registry mark denoting that a ship is in first class condition; first-rate.

a-bey-ance, a temporary holding back, as the settlement of an estate.

ab-scond, to flee in haste from one's home or duty; disappear to avoid arrest.

ab-stract (ăb′străkt), *n.* A summary comprising the principal parts of a larger work: *v. t.* **(ăb-străkt′),** to take away; steal.

ac-cept-ance, an agreement to terms; an agreement to pay a note.

ac-cept-er, the one who receives or promises to pay a bill of exchange or draft. Also, ACCEPTOR.

ac-ces-so-ry, one who aids or abets; a confederate.

ac-com-mo-da-tion, that which fills a want or desire; the loan of money as a favor.

ac-com-mo-da-tion pa-per, a note made or endorsed by one person for another as a favor, as distinguished from a note given for value received.

ac-com-plice, a companion in crime; a confederate.

ac-count, *v. t.,* to reckon; compute: *n.,* a statement or memorandum of business transactions; bill.

ac-count-a-bil-i-ty, responsibility; the state of being liable.

ac-count-a-ble, answerable for one's actions; punishable.

ac-coun-tan-cy, the art or practice of a skilled bookkeeper.

ac-coun-tant, an expert bookkeeper, especially one skilled in keeping financial records.

ac-count cur-rent, a running account showing the amount due at the present time.

ac-count sales, the statement of a broker or salesman showing the amount of sales, freight, commission, expenses, etc.

ac-cred-it, *v. t.,* to accept as true; give credit to.

ac-knowl-edg-ment, the legal admission of a truth; an avowal; a receipt; a certificate issued by the public officer before whom an acknowledgment has been made.

ac-quit, to set free; release; forgive.

ac-quit-tal, the act of setting free; the judicial verdict of "Not guilty."

ac-quit-tance, a release from debt or other liability.

ac-tion, motion; deed; achievement; feat; battle; suit at law.

ac-tion-a-ble, giving grounds for a lawsuit.

ac-tive ac-count, an account showing many deposits and withdrawals.

a-cu-men, keenness of perception; sharpness.

ad-den-dum, *n.* (*pl.* **addenda**), something added.

ad-dress, *v. t.,* to speak or write to; direct: *n.,* speech; bearing; residence.

ad-dress-ee, the person to whom anything is addressed.

ad-dress-o-graph, a machine for directing letters, etc.

ad-duce, to bring forward in proof; cite; quote.

ad-journ, *v. t.,* to postpone to another time: *v. i.,* to leave off for a future meeting.

ad-ju-di-cate, to determine in court.

ad-junct, an addition; a thing joined to another.

ad-ju-ra-tion, an oath or solemn charge.

ad-jure, to entreat earnestly; charge upon oath.

ad-just-er, one who settles claims, etc.

ad-just-ment, settlement of a legal claim or a disputed account; arrangement.

ad-min-is-ter, to manage; dispense; settle, especially the estate of one who dies without a will.

ad-min-is-tra-tor, one who manages, directs, or governs affairs, especially one who manages the estate of one who has died intestate.

ad-min-is-tra-trix, a woman appointed by law to settle the estate of a deceased person.

ad va-lo-rem, according to value; said of a tax or duty upon goods as distinct from a specific charge for a certain number or quantity.

ad-vance, an increase in price or value; payment beforehand.

ad-vo-cate, a lawyer or counselor in court; a pleader.

af-fi-da-vit, a sworn declaration in writing.

af-fil-i-ate, *v. t.,* to adopt; to receive into a club or society; *v. i.,* to be closely connected with.

af-fir-ma-tion, ratification; confirmation.

af-flu-ence, wealth.

af-flu-ent, rich.

a-genc-y, operation; the carrying on of business for another; the place where such business is carried on.

a-gent, one authorized to act for another; a substitute; one who handles the business of another.

ag-gra-va-tion, in law, anything which increases a crime or damages.

ag-gres-sion, unlawful infringement upon another's rights.

ag-i-o (ăj'ĭ-ō), *n.,* the difference in value between various kinds of money; an exchange premium; discount.

a-gra-ri-an, *adj.,* pertaining to land: *n.,* an advocate of redistribution of public lands.

a-gra-ri-an-ism, the principles of those who believe in a redistribution of public lands.

a-gree-ment, a contract; mutual understanding; concord of opinions or feelings.

à la carte, according to the bill of fare.

al-a-mode, *adv.,* in the fashion: *adj.,* fashionable. Also, A LA MODE.

al-der-man, *n.,* a city official next in rank to the mayor.

a-li-as, an assumed name.

al-i-bi, the plea of having been elsewhere when a crime was committed.

al-ien, a foreigner: *adj.,* strange; foreign; different.

al-ien-ate, to estrange; transfer.

al-i-mo-ny, an allowance made by court from her husband's estate to a divorced woman.

al-le-ga-tion, positive assertion or declaration.

al-lege, *v. t.,* to assert positively but without proof; *n.,* a plea or an excuse.

al-li-ance, a union; partnership; compact; coalition.

al-low-ance, an admission; a definite amount granted for some purpose; a deduction from the gross weight or amount of goods.

al-loy, *n.,* any metallic compound: *v. t.,* to mix or combine metals.

al-ter-a-tion, a change.

a-mal-gam, a mercurial compound; union.

a-mal-ga-mate, to mix or blend, as a race.

a-mal-ga-ma-tion, the union of mercury with another metal; a consolidation; union.

a-man-u-en-sis, (*pl.,* **amanuenses**), one who writes dictation; a secretary.

am-a-teur, a non-professional.

am-big-u-ous, capable of being understood in two or more ways.

a-merce, to punish by fine or deprivation of a right.

am-nes-ty, a general pardon for political offenders.

a-mor-tize, to clear off or liquidate, as a debt, by a sinking fund.

a-mount, *n.,* the sum total: *v. i.,* to reach; be equal to: AMOUNT GROSS, the total sum: AMOUNT NET, the total sum minus deductions for expenses, discounts, etc.

am-pere, the unit in measuring the strength of an electric current.

an-nals, a record of events as they happen, year by year.

an-nex, *v. t.,* to add; to unite a smaller thing to a greater: *n.,* a supplementary building.

an-no Do-mi-ni, in the year of our Lord: *abbr.,* A. D.

an-no-tate, to supply with notes.

an-nu-al, yearly.

an-nu-i-tant, one who is entitled to receive a certain sum of money each year.

an-nu-i-ty, a yearly allowance or income.

an-nul, to do away with.

an-swer-a-ble, liable; responsible.

an-te-date, to date before the actual time; to occur before.

an-te me-rid-i-em, before noon: *abbr.,* A. M.

an-ti-quat-ed, obsolete; old-fashioned.

a-poth-e-ca-ries' weight, the system used in weighing drugs in which a pound equals 12 ounces.

ap-pel-lant, one who appeals to a higher court.

ap-pel-late, pertaining to appeals.

ap-per-tain, to belong by right.

ap-pli-ance, an article of equipment.

ap-pli-ca-ble, suitable.

ap-pli-cant, a candidate for a position.

ap-pli-ca-tion, a request; the act of demonstrating the practical use of.

ap-plied, used.

ap-point-ment, the act of assigning or being signed to an office or trust.

ap-por-tion, to assign in right proportion; allot; divide.

ap-prais-al, valuation.

ap-praise, to estimate the value of.

ap-prais-er, one who sets a value on goods or merchandise, especially that subject to duty.

ap-pre-ci-a-ble, capable of being estimated or valued.

ap-pre-ci-a-tion, an increase in market value; a just valuation of the worth of.

ap-pre-hend, to arrest; understand; fear.

ap-pre-hen-sion, arrest; comprehension; anxiety.

ap-pren-tice, a beginner; one placed in the hands of another for instruction in a trade or craft.

ap-prise, to set a value on. Also, APPRIZE.

ap-pro-pri-a-tion, the act of setting apart funds for a particular purpose, especially by the Government.

ap-prox-i-mate, *v. t.,* to bring near: *v. i.,* to come close to: *adj.,* nearly but not quite accurate.

ap-pur-te-nance, that which belongs to something else; an accessory.

a pri-o-ri, from the former.

ar-bi-ter, a judge; an umpire.

ar-bi-trage, the buying and selling of stocks, etc., for the profit arising from the difference in price of the same commodity in different markets at the same time.

ar-bit-ra-ment, a decision by chosen judges.

ar-bi-tra-ry, not governed by law; unreasonable.

ar-bi-trate, to settle a dispute; mediate.

ar-bi-tra-tion, the settling of a dispute by mutual agreement.

ar-bi-tra-tion of ex-change, the process of comparing and adjusting the difference in money values or rates of exchange among various countries for the purpose of international business transactions.

ar-bi-tra-tor, one chosen to settle a dispute. Also, ARBITER.

arch-e-type, the original pattern or model.

ar-chi-pel-a-go, a sea full of islands; a body of islands.

ar-chive, more often in (*pl.,* **archives**), a record kept for evidence.

a-re-a, any surface inclosed within a given space.

ar-ro-gate, to assume; claim unduly.

ar-ro-ga-tion, the taking of more than belongs to one by right.

ar-son, a malicious setting fire to a building.

ar-ti-cle, an item; a single piece of goods; a distinct division of a contract or other document.

ar-ti-cle, an item; a single piece of goods; a distinct division of a contract or other document.

ar-ti-cles of part-ner-ship, a written agreement defining the powers and purposes of an association for the promotion of a joint enterprise.

ar-ti-san, a trained workman; mechanic.

as-perse, to slander.

as-per-sion, calumny; injury.

as-sas-sin, one who kills by secret assault.

as-sault, *n.,* a violent attack: *v. t.,* to attack violently.

as-say, *n.,* the act of testing; a risk: *v. t.,* to try; ascertain the purity of.

as-say-er, one who tests the purity of metals and coins.

as-sem-blage, an audience; the fitting of various parts together, as of an automobile.

as-semble, *v. t.,* to collect; gather together: *v. i.,* to meet; convene.

as-sess, to value for taxation; to set a charge upon; fix damages.

as-sessed tax-es, taxes on income, houses, etc.

as-sess-ment, an official estimate of value for taxation; a tax on property; a share of expenses.

as-sets, *n. pl.,* property which may be used in the payment of debts; all that one owns: AVAILABLE ASSETS; Assets on which there is no lien or claim, so that the owner is free to dispose of them as he wishes.

as-sign-ment, the transference of a right or title to another; the thing transferred; an allotment to some particular person or for some special use.

as-sign-or, one who transfers an interest or right; one who sets aside something for a special person or use. Also, ASSIGNER.

as-size, a court for the trial of civil or criminal cases.

as-so-ci-ate, *n.,* a confederate: *v. t.,* to join; accompany: *v. i.,* to unite.

as-so-ci-a-tion, a union; confederacy; combination of persons for the promotion of a business undertaking, usually without charter.

as-sur-ance, an agreement to pay on a contingency almost certain to occur; a pledge; confidence; insurance.

as-ter-isk, the mark (*) used in printing.

at-las, a collection of maps in a volume.

at-tach-ment, the legal seizure of property to force compliance with a judicial decision.

at-tain-der, the depriving of civil rights of those under death sentence.

at-test, to bear witness to; certify; give proof.

at-tes-ta-tion, testimony under oath; an official declaration.

at-tor-ney, a legal agent: POWER OF ATTORNEY, a written authority for one person to transact business for another.

at-tor-ney gen-er-al, the chief law officer of a state.

auc-tion, a public sale in which the article falls to the highest bidder.

auc-tion-eer, one licensed to conduct a public sale in which the property falls to the highest bidder.

au-dit, *n.,* an official examination of accounts or claims: *v. t.,* to examine or adjust, as accounts or claims: *v. i.,* to act as an examiner.

au-di-tor, one appointed to examine accounts.

aus-pices, *n. pl.,* leadership; support; patronage.

aus-pi-cious, favorable.

au-then-tic, genuine; trustworthy.

au-then-ti-cate, to establish as correct or genuine.

au-then-ti-ca-tion, in law, the verification of a document; the act of proving genuine or true.

au-thor-i-ta-tive, having due authority.

au-thor-i-ty, power or right; testimony; a person in power.

au-to-graph, one's signature in his own handwriting.

au-ton-o-mous, self-governing.

au-ton-o-my, self-government; political independence.

au-top-sy, a post-mortem examination to find out the cause of death.

aux-il-i-ary, *adj.,* aiding: *n.,* an assistant.

av-er-age, *adj.,* ordinary; midway between two extremes: *n.,* the mean value; an estimate; the general type: *v. t.,* to reduce to a mean: GENERAL AVERAGE, a proportionate contribution levied on a ship or cargo to cover loss or damage at sea: PARTICULAR AVERAGE, the compensation paid by an underwriter for damage to a part of a ship or its cargo from ordinary wear or mishaps: PETTY or PETIT AVERAGE, allowance for incidental expenses on a voyage, shared by ship and cargo.

av-o-ca-tion, a secondary occupation; a diversion.

av-oir-du-pois, a system of weights in which one pound = 16 ounces.

B

back, *n.,* the hinder part: *v. t.,* to furnish with a back; support: *adj.,* toward the rear; overdue.

back-er, a supporter.

bad debts, uncollectible accounts.

bail, *v. t.,* to liberate on security, *n.,* surety.

bail-ee, one to whom goods are committed in trust.

bail-iff, a sheriff's deputy.

bail-i-wick, a sheriff's district.

bail-ments, *n. pl.,* in law of contracts, the delivery of goods by one person to another in trust for a special purpose.

bal-ance, *n.,* a pair of scales; poise; the difference between two sums or weights: *v. t.,* to adjust; equalize; weigh.

bal-ance of trade, the difference between the money value of exports and imports.

bal-ance sheet, a statement of open accounts in tabular form to show assets and liabilities, profit and loss.

bank, *n.,* an establishment for the custody, exchange, or issuing of money; *v. t.,* to put in a bank.

bank-a-ble, receivable at a bank.

bank bill, a banker's draft.

bank book, a depositor's pass book containing a record of credits and charges.

bank cred-it, the amount which one is allowed to draw from a bank with, or without, security.

bank dis-count, a deduction equal to the interest at a given rate on the principal of a note from the time of discounting until it becomes due.

bank draft, a bill of exchange drawn by one bank on another.

bank-er, one engaged in the custody, exchange, or issuing of money.

bank note, a promissory or other note payable at a bank.

bank-rupt, *n.,* a debtor (persons or corporation) who is legally declared unable to meet his obligations in full, and whose estate is to be liquidated for the benefit of creditors: *adj.,* insolvent: *v. t.,* to impoverish.

bank-rupt-cy, failure in business; the state of being legally declared unable to pay one's debts.

bargain, *n.,* an agreement; a contract; a gainful transaction: *v. i.,* to haggle.

bar-ris-ter, a counselor at law: Eng.

bar-ter, to traffic; bargain.

batch, a quantity of something, especially of bread baked at the same time.

bear, one who sells stocks, etc., for future delivery in the hope that the market price will fall.

bear-er, one who holds a note, draft, or bill of exchange.

bench, a body of judges.

bench war-rant, a legal paper providing for the arrest of an offender given out by the judge instead of the magistrate.

ben-e-fac-tion, the act of benefiting; a gift of charity.

ben-e-fac-tor, one who confers a benefit.

ben-e-fi-ci-a-ry, one who is benefited or assisted, as by a will.

be-queath, to hand down to by heritance.

be-quest, a legacy.

berth, *n.,* a bed in a ship or railway carriage; enough room for a ship to anchor: *v. t.,* to allot an anchorage to.

be-times, early; in good season.

bi-an-nu-al, twice a year.

bi-as, *n.,* prejudice: *v. t.,* to prejudice; influence.

bib-li-og-ra-phy, a list of books relating to a special subject; the science which deals with the history and description of books.

bid, *v. t.,* to offer; to propose as a price; to command: *v. i.,* to make an offer: *n.,* a price offered at auction.

bi-en-ni-al, happening once in two years; continuing for two years.

big-a-my, the offense of having more than one husband or wife at the time.

bill, *n.,* an account for goods sold, services rendered or work done; a copy of a proposed law; a printed advertisement; negotiable paper: *v. t.,* to make a list of; to advertise by bills.

bill book, a book in which a record is kept of notes and drafts issued or received.

bill do-mes-tic, a bill of exchange or draft payable in the country in which it is drawn. Also, BILL INLAND.

bill for-eign, a bill of exchange or draft payable in a country other than the one in which it was drawn.

billhead, a printed form for bills, etc., with the business address at the top.

bil-lion, in the United States and France, one thousand millions; in England and Germany, one million millions.

bill of en-try, a memorandum of goods entered at the custom house whether for import or export.

bill of ex-change, a written order or request from one person or house (the drawer) to another (the acceptor) to pay to the person named a certain sum at a specified future time.

bill of health, a statement given to the master of a vessel, signed by the consul or other official, giving an account of the sanitary conditions and general health of the ship and crew.

bill of la-ding, a paper acknowledging receipt of goods to be shipped and promising to deliver them safely to the designated person or place.

bill of mor-tal-i-ty, an official record of the number of births and deaths in a place within a given period.

bill of sale, a formal paper given by the seller to the buyer of personal property to declare and establish the title of the latter.

bills pay-a-ble, bills of exchange, drafts, or promissory notes issued by ourselves and payable to others.

bills re-ceiv-a-ble, bills of exchange, drafts, or promissory notes, issued by others and payable to ourselves.

bi-me-tal-lic, consisting of, or relating to, the use of two metals in a system of coinage, as gold and silver.

bi-month-ly, occurring every two months.

bird's-eye, seen from above, as by a flying bird; hence, general, not detailed.

birth-rate, the increase of population in a given district within a certain period as shown by the percentage of registered births within a specified period.

birth-right, any right or privilege to which a person is entitled by birth.

bi-sect, to cut into two equal parts.

bis-sex-tile, *n.,* leap year: *adj.,* pertaining to leap year.

bi-week-ly, fortnightly, not semi-weekly, which means twice a week.

black-leg, a swindler; a gambler who cheats; a nonunion workman.

black list, a list of persons deserving punishment, or a list of those who are undesirable in business transactions: *v. t.,* to enroll as undesirable or culpable.

black-mail, *v. t.,* to secure money by threats: *n.,* extortion of money by threats.

blank, any empty space: an unfilled space in a written or printed document; a lottery ticket which does not draw a prize; a disk of metal before it is stamped; the white spot in the center of a target.

block-ade, *n.,* the shutting up of a place, as a port: *v. t.,* to surround and shut up.

block sys-tem, the system which provides for the safety of a railway line by dividing it into short sections and allowing only one train on a section at a time.

blood mon-ey, money obtained at the cost of another person's life; the reward paid for the capture or discovery of a murderer; money paid to the next of kin of a person slain by another.

blue laws, severely strict laws, especially those which interfere unduly with personal freedom.

blue rib-bon, a mark of distinction or success; the highest award in a competition.

board, *n.,* a council; a group of people selected to manage a public or private affair: *pl.,* the stage.

board foot, a measure equal to the volume of a piece of timber one foot long, one foot wide, and one inch thick.

board meas-ure, measurement in board feet.

bod-y-guard, one, or those who defend the person of another, usually some high official.

bod-y pol-i-tic, the people living under an organized government considered collectively.

bo-gus, not genuine.

bo-na fi-de, genuine.

bo-nan-za, a rich vein of ore; anything which brings wealth or fortune.

bond, *n.,* a tie; an obligation; a

formal deed issued by a government or corporation as a money security: *v. t.,* to mortgage.

bond cred-i-tor, a creditor whose debt is secured by bonds.

bond debt, a debt secured under bond.

bond-ed, held under pledge for payment of duties secured by bonds.

bond-ed goods, goods held in a bonded warehouse.

bond-ed ware-house, a warehouse under guarantee for strict observance of the revenue laws.

bond-hol-der, one who owns or holds bonds.

bonds-man, one who stands responsible for the payment of another's debt.

bo-nus, a premium; a special allowance beyond what is strictly due.

boo-dle, graft; bribe money.

book, *n.,* a volume; register; record; a list of race horses and the bets made on them: *v. t.,* to register; record.

book debts, accounts charged on the books of a business.

book-ing of-fice, a ticket office.

book-keep-er, one who keeps account; an accountant.

book-keep-ing, the keeping of a record of business transactions in systematic order: SINGLE ENTRY, the system which requires only one entry for each transaction: DOUBLE ENTRY, the system which requires two entries for every transaction, one on the debit, and one on the credit side of the ledger.

book-mak-er, a professional betting man.

boom, *n.,* a sudden advance in prices: *v. t.,* to push forward with great energy.

booth, a temporary structure at fairs, markets, polling places, etc.

bor-ough, a municipality organized into a self-governing body under a mayor and other officials.

boun-ty, generosity; a premium offered by the Government to induce men to enlist in the army or navy; a special allowance or premium given to encourage some branch of trade or manufacture.

bourse, a stock exchange for the transaction of business, especially the stock exchange of Paris.

boy-cott, *v. t.,* to combine against a person so as to hinder his trade or profession: *n.,* the act or state of combining against a person; the combination.

brand, *n.,* a burning piece of wood; any kind of trademark; a mark of infamy: *v. t.,* to mark by burning with a hot brand or by other means.

brand new, quite new.

breach, the breaking of any obligation; a quarrel.

breach of trust, violation of a legal trust or duty.

break-age, allowance made by a shipper for fracture by accident.

break-ing bulk, the opening of a bundle of merchandise while in process of transportation.

break-wa-ter, any structure to lessen the force of waves.

bri-ber-y, the act or practice of corrupting or influencing another through gifts.

brief, *adj.,* short; condensed: *n.,* abridged statement for the instruction of a lawyer; a condensed argument.

brief-less, without clients.

broad-side, a printed or oral attack upon some public person.

brochure, a pamphlet or booklet dealing with a subject of current interest.

bro-ker, one who acts as an agent for another; a buying and selling agent; a middleman who works for a commission.

bro-ker-age, the business of a broker; his commission.

buck-et shop, an office for gambling in stocks, grains, etc., in small amounts organized in such a way that it is difficult to distinguish between it and a legitimate stock broker's establishment.

budg-et, a statement of the financial need of the year to come of a nation, organization, etc.

buf-fer, any contrivance which serves to deaden the shock of two bodies striking together.

build-ing and loan as-so-ci-a-tion, an organization to aid its members in buying or improving real estate with money, loaned or subscribed by the other members.

bull, a speculator who buys in expectation of a rise in price, or to bring about a rise: opposed to *bear*.

bul-le-tin, *n.,* an official report: *v. t.,* to publish by bulletin.

bul-lion, uncoined gold or silver in bars or ingots.

bun-co, a swindling game.

bun-combe, anything done for mere show.

bunk, *Slang,* nonsense.

bu-reau, an office; a governmental department.

bu-reauc-ra-cy, a government by bureaus.

bur-sar, the treasurer of a college; a purser.

buy-er's op-tion, a purchaser's privilege of taking something within a certain period.

by-law, a private rule framed by a corporate body.

C

ca-bal, a secret combination of a few persons for carrying out a special design, usually evil.

cab-a-ret, a restaurant where the guests are entertained by music, dancing, vaudeville acts, etc.

cab-i-net, a committee of the heads of the Government departments.

ca-ble, a submarine telegraph line.

ca-ble-gram, a message sent by cable.

cal-cu-late, to compute; reckon.

cal-cu-la-tion, an estimate; computation; an opinion.

cal-cu-la-tor, one who or that which reckons.

cal-en-dar, a register of the days, weeks, and months of the year; a list.

call, *n.,* a summons; a demand for payment of money due; a request to a stockholder to pay an instalment on his subscription; a request from a government or corporation to the holders of redeemable bonds to present them for payment; a contract demanding the delivery of a certain amount of stock or goods at a stipulated price within a specified time: *v. t.,* to summon.

call loan, a loan of money subject to payment on demand.

ca-lor-ic, of or pertaining to heat.

cal-o-rie, the small calorie is the amount of heat necessary to raise one gram of water 1° centigrade. The great calorie is the amount of heat necessary to raise one kilogram of water 1° centigrade, in other words, 1,000 small calories. Also, CALORY.

ca-lum-ni-ate, to accuse falsely and maliciously.

cam-ou-flage, the art of disguising or deceiving by false appearances; any variety of concealment.

can-cel, to mark out writing by drawing lines across it; destroy; annul; revoke.

can-dle pow-er, the illuminating power of a standard candle taken as a unit to measure the power of any other light.

can-vass, *n.,* solicitation; inspection: *v. t.,* to examine; *v. i.,* to solicit.

cap-i-tal, accumulated wealth; property of a corporation or individual at a stated time; wealth or goods used in production.

cap-i-tal-ism, an economic system based on capital employed by capitalists; a system of which the operation is chiefly effected by private enterprise under competitive conditions.

cap-i-tal-ist, one possessing great wealth.

cap-i-tal-ize, to convert into money which may be used in production; apply to the purposes of business.

cap-tion, a heading; as of a chapter, or the legend accompanying a picture; a certificate of arrest.

car-at, the weight used for weighing precious stones, etc. Also, KARAT.

car-di-nal points, north, east, south, and west.

card in-dex, an index in which each item is listed on a separate card.

carte blanche, absolute freedom; a signed paper given to another to fill in as he chooses.

car-ton, a pasteboard box.

cash, ready money; coin.

cashbook, a book containing an ac-count of money received or paid out.

cash-ier, one in charge of the receiving and paying out of money in a bank or trading establishment.

cash-ier's check, a check drawn upon a bank by itself and signed by its cashier.

cash sale, a sale of goods for cash or payment within 30 days.

cast-ing vote, the deciding vote cast by a president or chairman.

cas-u-al-ty, an accident; in war, losses by death, disease, etc.

cat-a-log, *n.,* an arranged list: *v. t.,* to enter in such a list; to make a register of. Also, CATALOGUE.

cat-e-go-ry, a class.

cen-sor, an inspector; a critic.

cen-sus, any official enumeration of population.

cen-ti-grade, divided into a hundred degrees.

cen-time, a French coin equal to one hundredth part of a franc, or about one-fifth of a cent.

cer-tif-i-cate, a written testimony.

cer-tif-i-cate of de-pos-it, a statement issued by a bank that a person has on deposit a certain sum of money.

cer-ti-fi-ca-tion, the act of testifying through a written statement.

cer-ti-fied check, a check guaranteed good by the bank upon which it is drawn.

cer-ti-fy, to testify in writing.

chair-man, the presiding officer of an assembly.

cham-ber of com-merce, an association of merchants or traders for the promotion of their business interests.

chap-ter, an organized branch of some fraternity or other organization.

char-gé d'af-faires, one who transacts business for an ambassador in his absence or at a court where no ambassador is appointed.

char-la-tan, an impostor.

chart, a map, especially for the use of sailors; any tabular list of instructions or facts.

char-ter, *n.,* an official grant of certain rights, as to an association or corporation: *v. t.,* to establish by charter; to hire for one's own use.

char-tered, granted by charter; protected by charter.

char-ter par-ty, a mercantile lease for a vessel or a part thereof.

chas-sis, the frame of an automobile or airplane.

chat-tel, usually in *pl.,* movable personal property.

chauf-feur, the driver of an automobile.

check, *n.,* a restraint; hindrance; small mark used to show that an item has been attended to; an order on a bank for payment of money on demand; ticket: *v. t.,* to stop; curb; reprove; verify. See *Cheque.*

check-book, a book containing blank checks.

check-mate, *n.,* the winning move at chess; defeat: *v. t.,* to defeat utterly.

cheque, an order on a bank. Same as *check.*

chit, a memorandum; a voucher. India, China, etc.

chron-o-log-i-cal, relating to the order of time.

chro-nol-o-gy, the science of dates.

chro-nom-e-ter, an instrument for measuring time accurately.

ci-pher, *n.,* zero; the symbol, 0; naught; a person or thing of extremely small value; a secret code or the key to it: *v. i.,* to write in codes; to work with arithmetical figures.

cir-cu-lar, a printed or written letter addressed to the public or to a group of people.

cir-cu-lar note, a note issued by bankers for travelers so that they may obtain money from correspondents at various places.

cir-cum-stan-tial, pertaining to, or inferred from, the circumstances; incidental.

cir-cum-stan-ti-ate, to describe exactly or minutely.

ci-vil-ian, one engaged in civil, not military affairs.

civ-il ser-vice, the service of the Government, not military nor naval.

claim, *v. t.,* to demand; assert as true: *n.,* a title.

claim-ant, one who demands a thing as his by right.

clear-ance, a cleaning out; the passage of negotiable paper through the clearing house; settlement of claims, etc.; a customhouse certificate that a ship is free to leave.

clear-ance pa-pers, certificates issued by a customhouse stating that a vessel has complied with the law and is ready to leave.

clear-ing, the settlement of balances against each other by banks and other business agencies, carried on at a clearinghouse.

clear-ing house, the place where banks send their representatives daily to exchange drafts, bills of exchange, etc.

clerk, a salesman; an office correspondent, or keeper of records.

cli-ent, the patron of a lawyer, architect, or other expert.

cli-en-tele, a body of people who seek expert advice.

closed shop, a shop closed to non-union workers.

clo-sure, the act of closing; stopping a debate by the vote of the majority.

co-a-lesce, to unite; fuse; combine.

co-a-li-tion, a union; combination.

c. o. d., collect on delivery, a call for payment for merchandise at the time of its delivery.

code, a system of laws or rules; a system of symbols used for brevity and secrecy.

cod-i-cil, an addition; postscript to a will.

co-di-fy, to systematize.

cof-fer, a chest.

cof-fer-dam, a watertight inclosure for the protection of workmen.

cog, a notch or tooth, as on a wheel.

col-lat-er-al, additional security.

col-league, an associate, not a partner.

col-lec-tor, one authorized to collect money for another.

col-lude, to conspire secretly and with evil intent.

col-lu-sion, a secret and unlawful agreement.

col-por-tage, the system of distributing religious literature by travelers.

col-por-teur, a person employed to give away Bibles and religious tracts.

com-men-su-ra-ble, having a common measure.

com-men-su-rate, equal in measure or extent; proportionate.

com-men-ta-ry, a series of explanatory remarks.

com-merce, extended trade; intercourse.

com-mer-cial, *adj.,* pertaining to trade: COMMERCIAL PAPER, notes, draft, bills of exchange and other negotiable paper used in business transactions.

com-mis-sion, *n.,* an agent's allowance or percentage for transacting business; a document investing one with authority or rank; a duty; trust; a body of men joined to perform some duty: *v. t.,* to empower, authorize: COMMISSION BROKER, one who buys and sells for a commission.

com-mis-sion-er, an officer in charge of some branch of public service.

com-mit-ment, the act of committing; a sending to prison. Also, COMMITTAL.

com-mit-tee, persons appointed to deal with some matter.

com-mod-i-ty, an article of commerce: *pl.,* merchandise; goods.

com-mon car-ri-er, a public conveyer of persons or goods for compensation and for all persons without discrimination.

com-mon law, the unwritten law which has grown out of customs and usages.

com-mon sense, sound, practical judgment in ordinary affairs.

com-mon-weal, the general public welfare.

com-mon-wealth, the public good; the whole mass of people in a state.

com-mu-ta-tion, change; substitution of something less severe; the changing of an electric current by means of a commutator.

com-mu-ta-tion tick-et, a transportation ticket sold at a reduced rate, to be used during a certain period of time.

com-mute, *v. t.,* to exchange; substitute; lessen the severity of: *v.*

i., to buy at a reduced rate, as a railroad ticket.

com-mut-er, one who changes or exchanges; one who buys a railroad ticket at a reduced rate to be used during a limited period of time.

com-pact, an agreement; contract.

com-pa-ny, a band of associates for industrial or commercial purposes; assembly.

com-pen-di-um, an abridgement; a brief summary.

com-pen-sate, to atone; make amends for.

com-pen-sa-tion, recompense; remuneration; requital.

com-pe-tence, a sufficiency. Also, COMPETENCY.

com-pe-tent, capable; fit; qualified.

com-pet-i-tor, a rival.

com-plain-ant, a grumbler; a plaintiff or petitioner.

com-ple-ment, a full number; something which completes; the amount by which a given angle or arc falls short of 90 degrees.

com-ple-men-ta-ry, forming or pertaining to the completing part.

com-plic-i-ty, a partnership in guilt.

com-po-nent, *adj.,* constituent; composing: *n.,* a necessary portion or part.

com-pos-i-tor, one who sets type.

com-pound in-ter-est, interest on both principal and interest.

com-pro-mise, *n.,* the settlement of a dispute by certain concessions from both parties: *v. t.,* to adjust or settle by mutual agreement: *v. i.,* to make an adjustment by concessions.

comp-trol-ler, a public officer who has charge of the accounts of officials under him.

com-pute, to calculate; reckon.

con-cede, to grant; admit.

con-cern, a business.

con-ces-sion, a grant; the act of yielding.

con-ces-sion-aire, a person holding a concession or having a special privilege.

con-cur-rence, agreement; consent.

con-cur-rent, acting in conjunction.

con-fed-er-a-cy, a league; alliance.

con-fed-er-ate, *v. i.,* to unite: *adj.,* leagued: *n.,* an ally; an accomplice.

con-fer, *v. t.,* to bestow: *v. i.,* to consult together.

con-fer-ence, a meeting for consultation; a gathering; crowd.

con-fi-dence, something told in secret.

con-fi-den-tial, secret.

con-firm, to approve; ratify.

con-fir-ma-tion, additional evidence.

con-niv-ance, voluntarily winking at wrongdoing.

con-nive, to pretend not to see; to aid secretly.

con-nois-seur, a critical judge, as of any work of art.

con-sen-sus, general agreement of opinion.

con-serv-a-tism, the tendency to adhere to existing conditions and institutions and to oppose radical change.

con-ser-va-tion, preservation.

con-serv-a-tive, one opposed to radical changes.

con-sid-er-a-tion, a fee.

con-sign, to deliver formally to another.

con-sign-ee, the person to whom goods are sent for sale or superintendence.

con-sign-ment, the act of delivering formally; the thing sent.

con-sign-or, one who sends goods to another. Also, CONSIGNER.

con-sol-i-date, to make solid; combine.

con-stit-u-en-cy, the supporters of a member of Congress or other public official.

con-stit-u-ent, an adherent; a component element.

con-sti-tu-tion, fundamental laws, as of a nation or society.

con-straint, repression; compulsion.

con-struc-tive, having the power or tendency to help or uplift.

con-strue, to interpret.

con-sul, a nation's commercial agent in another country.

con-sul gen-er-al, the chief consul.

con-su-lar, pertaining to the consul.

con-su-late, the office or term of residence of a consul.

con-sum-er, one who makes ultimate use of a product.

con-text, the parts of writing which immediately precede or follow a part quoted.

con-tin-gen-cy, a possible occurrence.

con-tin-gent, adj., accidental; possible: n., a possibility; quota.

con-tra-band, adj., illegal; n., forbidden goods.

con-tract (kŏn-trăkt'), v. t., to draw together; shorten; bargain; become affected with: n., (kŏn'-trăkt), a written agreement.

con-trac-tor, one of the parties to a contract; one who undertakes to supply or construct.

con-trol-ler, an officer who oversees and verifies public accounts.

con-vene, v. i., to assemble: v. t., to cause to meet together.

con-ven-tion, an assembly; an arbitrary social custom.

con-ver-sant, familiar with.

con-vey, to carry; transmit; cede.

con-vey-ance, the act of transmitting; a vehicle; the change of property from one owner to another.

con-vey-an-cer, one who draws up deeds, etc.

con-vo-ca-tion, the act of calling together, especially formal assemblies.

con-voy (kŏn-voi'), v. t., to go with as protector: n., (kŏn'-voi), an escort, as of a ship.

coop-er-age, the business of making barrels, etc.; the charge for such work.

co-op-er-ate, to work together, or conjointly.

co-op-er-a-tion, the act of working together.

co-or-di-nate, v. t., to harmonize: adj., equal; of the same order: n., one who or that which is of the same rank.

co-or-di-na-tion, the state of being in harmony or working together.

co-part-ner, a joint partner.

cop-y, manuscript to be set in type.

cop-y-right, the exclusive right to reproduce, publish, or sell a literary or artistic work for a number of years.

cord, a measure for wood (128 cu. ft.).

co-re-spond-ent, the person charged with guilt in a divorce suit.

cor-ner, to drive into a position from which escape is impossible: CORNER THE MARKET, to buy up a controlling interest in property or stock.

cor-ner-stone, the stone at the corner of a building.

cor-o-ner, an officer who investigates the causes of sudden or violent death.

cor-po-rate, united in a body.

cor-po-ra-tion, a body of persons legally authorized to act as a single person and having distinct rights and liabilities.

corps (*pl.,* **corps**), a body of troops; any body of persons associated in a common work.

cor-re-late, *v. i.,* to be related by parallelism, etc.: *v. t.,* to connect by disclosure of mutual relationship.

cor-re-la-tion, a mutual or reciprocal relation.

cor-re-spond-ence, agreement; communication by means of letters.

cor-re-spond-ent, one with whom communication is carried on by mail; one who sends communications to another by mail.

cor-rob-o-rate, to verify.

cos-mo-pol-i-tan, *n.,* one who is at home anywhere in the world: *adj.,* free from local prejudices.

cos-mop-o-lite, a citizen of the world.

cost, *n.,* price; expense; outlay: *v. t.,* to be the price of; to cause to bear or suffer.

coun-cil, an assembly for consultation; a municipal body.

coun-cil-man, a member of the council; of a township, borough, etc.

coun-cil-or, a member of a council.

coun-sel, *n.,* advice; adviser: *v. t.,* to give advice to.

coun-se-lor, *n.,* one who gives advice, especially a lawyer.

coun-ter, *n.,* a shop table; one who or that which keeps an account: *adv.,* in opposition: prefix meaning contrary.

coun-ter-act, to oppose; neutralize.

coun-ter en-try, an entry in an opposite sense.

coun-ter-bal-ance, *v. t.,* to offset: *n.,* a force or weight equal to another.

coun-ter-feit, *v. t.,* to copy or imitate with the purpose of deceiving: *n.,* a forgery; an imitation made to deceive: *adj.,* false; spurious.

coun-ter-mand, *v. t.,* to change, contradict, or revoke an order: *n.,* a contrary order.

coun-ter-mine, *n.,* any means by which an enemy's plans are defeated: *v. i.* and *v. t.,* to dig an underground passageway in order to meet and destroy similar works of the enemy; to defeat by secret means.

coun-ter-sign, *v. t.,* to sign with an additional signature: *n.,* a password.

count-ing-house, a room where accounts are kept and bookkeeping is done.

coup, a master stroke of strategy.

cou-pon, an interest certificate, attached to bonds, etc., to be torn off when due; the detachable part of a theater ticket, etc.

cov-er-ture, a cover; the legal status of married woman.

co-work-er, a fellow worker.

craft, ability; manual art; a guild; vessels.

crafts-man, a skilled mechanic.

cre-den-tial, a testimony of one's ability. Usually in *pl.*

cred-it, *v. t.,* to believe; ascribe; to enter on the credit side of an account: *n.,* belief; honor; reputation; balance due; the amount which a person can obtain from a bank or other business house.

cred-i-tor, one to whom another owes money or goods.

cri-sis, a turning point; an emergency.

cri-te-ri-on, a standard by which something can be measured.

cross-ex-am-i-na-tion, the questioning of a witness by the opposing party.

cross-pur-pose, a contrary purpose.

cross-ques-tion, to cross-examine; question closely.

cul-de-sac, a passageway open at only one end; a blind alley.

cul-mi-nate, to reach the apex; to come to the final result.

cul-mi-na-tion, summit; climax.

cu-mu-la-tive, forming a heap or mass.

cur-ren-cy, circulation; that which is used for money.

cus-to-di-an, a keeper; guardian.

cus-to-dy, guardianship.

cus-tom-house, the place where duties are paid, and vessels are entered and cleared.

cus-tom-house brok-er, an agent who attends to the clearing of goods and vessels for another.

D

dam-ag-es, compensation paid for a specified injury, loss, or wrong.

da-ta, *n. pl.,* (*sing.,* **datum**), a collection of facts.

day-book, a book in which business accounts of the day are kept.

day la-bor-er, a workman who is paid by the day.

day let-ter, a telegram sent at special rates with the understanding that regular telegrams shall have precedence in time of sending.

days of grace, the time allowed for the payment of a note after it falls due.

dead let-ter, a letter which cannot be delivered and is sent to the dead-letter office to be opened and returned to the sender; anything which has lost its authority.

dead-lock, a complete standstill.

deal, *n.,* quantity; part; division; trade; bargain: *v. t.,* to distribute; divide: *v. i.,* to conduct business.

deal-er, one who buys and sells.

de-base, to lower.

deb-it, *n.,* a recorded account of a debt; *v. t.,* to charge with debt.

debt, that which is due from one to another; obligation.

debt-or, *n.,* one who owes something to another.

dec-ade, a period of ten years; a group of ten.

dec-i-mal, *adj.,* pertaining to, or reckoned upon, the number, ten: *n.,* a decimal fraction.

de-cree, *n.,* an edict; law; command: *v. t.,* to ordain; determine by law.

de-duct, to take away.

deed, *n.,* a written document for the transfer of land or other real property; an instrument; *v. t.,* to transfer by deed.

de-face, disfigure; blemish.

de fac-to, actually existing or done.

de-fal-cate, to embezzle.

de-fame, to slander; libel.

de-fault, neglect; failure: *v. i.,* to fail: *v. t.,* to make a failure in.

de-fault-er, an embezzler; one who fails to pay or to do.

de-fend-ant, one who is sued in a court of law.

de-fense, *n.,* a protection; excuse; bulwark; plea.

de-fer, to delay; postpone; give in to the judgment of another.

de-fi-cien-cy, a falling short.

def-i-cit, a shortage, as of money.

de-fraud, to cheat.

de-fray, to pay; bear the expenses of.

de ju-re, by right of law, distinguished from *de facto.*

de-le, *v. t.,* to erase; cancel; take out: the mark (§) indicating that a word, etc., is to be deleted.

del-e-gate, *n.,* a representative; agent: *v. t.,* to send as a representative; in trust.

del-e-ga-tion, a body of delegates; the act of authorizing an agent or a group of agents.

de-lete, to take out; erase. See *dele.*

de-lin-quent, *adj.,* failing in duty: *n.,* one who falls short in the performance of duty.

de luxe, made unusually fine, as an edition *de luxe* of an author's books.

de-mon-e-tize, to deprive of standard value, as money; to withdraw from circulation.

de-mur-rage, the delay of a vessel, railroad car, etc., after the time allowed for loading, etc.; money paid for such a delay.

de-mur-rer, one who objects, a pause or delay in law.

de-port, to banish; to carry from one country to another.

de-pose, bear witness to.

de-pos-it, *v. t.,* to put in place of security; put in a bank; intrust: *n.,* that which is laid or set down; money in the bank; DEPOSIT SLIP, a dated slip which a depositor leaves with a deposit stating the character and amount of the funds deposited.

de-pos-i-ta-ry, one to whom something is intrusted; a storehouse; guardian. Also, DEPOSITORY.

dep-o-si-tion, testimony under oath.

de-pos-i-tor, one who places in trust; one who lodges money in the bank.

de-pot, a warehouse; a railway station.

de-pre-ci-ate, *v. i.,* to fall in value:

v. t., to reduce the value of; to disparage.

de-pre-ci-a-tion, a fall in value or market price.

de-pres-sion, a period of commercial dullness.

dep-u-ta-tion, the sending of a deputy or representative; a person or a group of persons sent to represent another.

dep-u-ty, a delegate; a substitute.

de-sid-er-a-tum, anything greatly desired.

de-vise, *v. t.,* to contrive; invent; bequeath: *n.,* a will.

dev-i-see, one to whom a legacy has been left.

de-vis-er, one who invents or contrives.

de-vis-or, one who bequeaths.

dic-ta-phone, an instrument like a phonograph, used for dictating to a stenographer.

dic-tate, to express orally for another to take down in writing; to declare with authority; order.

dic-ta-tion, the act of speaking words which are to be taken down; words so spoken.

dic-tum, a positive assertion.

dil-a-to-ry, tending to cause delay; late.

di-rec-tor, *n.,* one who, or that which, guides or directs: *pl.,* a body of persons appointed to manage the affairs of a corporation or other organization.

di-rec-to-rate, *n.,* the office of a director; a body appointed to manage the affairs of an organization.

di-rec-to-ry, a guidebook; a book of names and addresses; a board of managers or directors.

dis-burse, to pay out; expend.

dis-burse-ment, money expended.

dis-charge, *v. t.,* to unload; free;

dismiss: *n.*, the act of unloading; the thing unloaded; performance, as of duty; an explosion; dismissal.

dis-count, *n.*, a deduction made for prompt payment; the deduction made on money lent; *v. t.*, to deduct for prompt payment; lend at a discount; to allow for exaggeration in.

dis-crim-i-nate, select; distinguish.

dis-crim-i-na-tion, discernment; an unfair distinction.

dis-par-i-ty, inequality; disproportion.

dis-pen-sa-ry, a place where medicines are given away.

dis-pen-sa-tion, distribution; dealing out in portions; relaxing of the laws or canons in special cases.

dis-pense, to deal out: to dispense with, to do without.

dit-to, the same thing as before.

di-ur-nal, daily; pertaining to the daytime.

div-i-dend, a share of the profits from a business, etc.; a number to be divided.

div-i-dend war-rant, a formal paper through which a shareholder obtains his dividend.

dock-age, a cutting down or off; accommodation at a dock; money paid for it.

dock-et, a summary; list; schedule: *v. t.*, to indorse.

doc-u-ment, an official paper giving evidence or proof.

doc-u-men-ta-ry, pertaining to official records and papers.

dol-drums, *n. pl.*, the calm equatorial zone; dullness.

do-main, territory governed; dominion.

do-mes-tic, pertaining to the household; native, not foreign.

dou-ble-faced, dishonest; deceitful.

dou-ble name pa-per, a note, draft, bill of exchange, or other negotiable paper which is additionally indorsed by some one approved by the bank which accepts or discounts it.

dow-ry, *n.*, the property a bride brings to her husband at the time of her marriage; gift, possession.

draw, *v. t.*, to obtain from a deposit: *v. i.*, to write a formal demand.

draw-ee, one on whom an order, bill of exchange, or draft is drawn.

draw-er, one who draws a draft, bill of exchange, etc.

droit, legal right; justice.

drudge, *v. i.*, to labor at mean or unpleasant tasks: *n.*, a slave; menial.

drudg-er-y, slavish work.

dry goods, textile fabrics, etc.

due, *adj.*, owed; owing; payable: *n.*, that which belongs or may be claimed by right; *pl.*, money payable at regular intervals for membership in a club, etc.

due bill, an informal acknowledgment of a debt in writing.

du-plex, double; twofold.

du-pli-cate, *v. t.*, to make an exact likeness of: *n.*, copy; facsimile.

dur-ance, imprisonment; custody.

du-ress, constraint; imprisonment; durance.

du-ty, tax levied by the government on certain exports, imports, or other articles.

E

ear-nest, a token; something given or done in advance as a pledge.

earn-ings, *n. pl.*, money received for services; wages.

ease-ment, in law, any of several rights, short of ownership, which one may have in the land of another, the right of passage, for instance.

e-co-nom-ic, frugal; thrifty.

e-co-nom-ics, the science that treats of the production and distribution of wealth.

e-con-o-mist, one who studies the theory of the production, etc., of wealth; one who is frugal.

e-con-o-my, thriftiness; a judicious use of wealth.

ed-it, to revise, correct or adapt for publication.

e-di-tion, the whole number of the copies of a work published at a time; a literary work in its published form.

ef-fects, personal estate.

ef-fi-cien-cy, the power of producing the desired effect.

El Do-ra-do, a fabulously rich country; any place where money may be made easily and in large quantities.

em-bar-go, a restraint imposed by law upon commerce; the act of stopping vessels or transportation by railway.

em-bez-zle, to steal that which has been intrusted to one's care.

em-bez-zle-ment, the stealing of property that has been intrusted to one's care.

e-men-da-tion, an improvement in the reading of a text.

e-mer-gen-cy, a crisis; anything which comes suddenly and unexpectedly.

em-i-grant, one who leaves his own country to settle in another.

em-i-grate, to leave one country or state to reside in another.

em-is-sa-ry, a person sent on a mission.

e-mol-u-ment, profit; compensation; salary; wages.

em-ploy-ee, one who works for another.

em-ploy-er, one who hires another to work for him.

em-ploy-ment, occupation; business.

em-po-ri-um, a trading place; a large shop.

en-dorse, to authorize; write on the back of, as a check. Also, INDORSE.

en-dow, to enrich; furnish with a fund.

en-dow-ment, property or income appropriated to any object; gifts of nature.

en-tail, *v. t.,* to fix an estate inalienably upon certain heirs: *n.,* the act of entailing; an estate left to a particular heir or heirs.

en-trée, an entrance; freedom of access; a dish served between the chief courses at the table. *Fr.*

en-tre nous, between ourselves; confidentially. *Fr.*

en-trust, *v. t.,* to place in faithful keeping; confide. Also, INTRUST.

en-try, the act of recording in a book; the thing so recorded; the act of taking possession; the giving an account of the arrival of a ship in port.

en-vel-op, to cover by wrapping, etc., hide.

en-ve-lope, that which infolds or covers, usually sealed for safe conveyance by post, etc.; a covering.

eq-ui-ty, in finance, the difference between the actual value of a property and the total of all claims against that property.

eq-ui-ty of re-demp-tion, the time allowed a mortgagor to reclaim property by paying the obligation due.

er-ra-tum, (*pl.* errata), an error in writing or printing.

er-rors and o-mis-sions ex-cept-ed, usually abbr. E. and O. E., a mark used on bills, etc., to denote that corrections will be made later on.

es-cheat, *v. t.,* to forfeit; take possession of, as of property to which there are no heirs: *v. i.,* to revert: *n.,* property which falls to the state by forfeiture or failure of heirs.

es-crow, a deed, bond, or other written agreement given over to a third person, to be given up to the grantee only when certain conditions are fulfilled.

es-prit de corps, a spirit of common devotedness, sympathy, interest, etc., existing among persons of the same profession, society, etc. *Fr.*

et-i-quette, conventional rules of society; good breeding.

e-ven-tu-al-i-ty, a possible occurrence.

e-vict, to put out or dispossess by legal process; expel or remove by force.

ev-i-dence, proof; testimony.

ex ca-the-dra, with authority.

ex-cep-tion, something omitted or excluded; objection.

ex-cess, an undue amount; overabundance; an added charge.

ex-cess prof-its tax, a tax imposed on business profits which exceed "normal" or "standard" profits. An excess profits tax was levied by the United States in both world wars and from 1933–1945.

ex-change, a trading place; a central office for the transaction of business; the settling of accounts between parties at some distance from each other.

ex-change bro-ker, one who deals in the exchange of money, especially foreign bills of exchange and money.

ex-cheq-uer, a public treasury.

ex-cise, *n.,* a tax levied upon goods within a country; a tax upon certain trades; duty: *v. t.,* to levy a tax or duty upon; cut out.

ex-clu-sive, restricted to a privileged few.

ex-e-cute, to carry out; make valid by signature or seal; put to death under sentence of the law.

ex-e-cu-ted, carried out according to law.

ex-ec-u-tive, one charged with administrative work.

ex-ec-u-tor, one appointed by a testator to carry out the terms of a will.

ex-ec-u-trix, the female form of executor.

ex-hib-it, *v. t.,* to display: *n.,* a collection of objects shown before the public; something shown in court and held to be used for further evidence.

ex-hi-bi-tion, a display; demonstration.

ex-i-gen-cy, a pressing need; an emergency.

ex li-bris, from the books of.

ex of-fi-ci-o, by right of office but without other special authority.

ex-on-er-ate, to free from blame; justify; acquit.

ex-or-bi-tant, excessive.

ex parte, one-sided, as *ex parte* evidence.

ex-pe-di-ent, advisable.

ex-pe-dite, to quicken the progress of.

ex-pend, to spend; use.

ex-pend-i-ture, the act of laying out time, money, energy, etc.

ex-pense, cost; the paying out of money.

ex-pen-sive, costly.

ex-pert, one specially qualified by study and practice; a specialist.

ex-ploi-ta-tion, the act of making use of or obtaining profit by.

ex-port, *v. t.,* to send out of a country, as merchandise, etc.: *n.,* any goods sold and sent to another country.

ex-po-sé, an undesirable or an embarrassing disclosure. *Fr.*

ex post fac-to, happening or enacted after the deed is done; retrospective.

ex-press-age, the charge for a thing sent by express.

ex-press mon-ey or-der, a money order issued at one express office and payable at another.

ex-pur-gate, to cleanse; remove offensive matter from.

ex-tem-po-re, without previous study or preparation.

ex-tem-po-rize, *v. i.,* to speak without notes on the spur of the moment; improvise; speak extempore: *v. t.,* to compose on the spur of the moment.

ex-tend, *v. t.,* to stretch out; expand; continue: *v. i.,* to reach; be prolonged.

ex-ten-sion, the allowance of additional time to a debtor by a creditor; enlargement; expansion.

ex-tort, to obtain by unjust compulsion.

ex-tor-tion, the act of obtaining by force, threats, or injustice.

ex-tor-tion-ate, unreasonable; excessive; oppressive.

ex-tor-tion-er, one who demands and obtains by unjust means.

ex-tra-dite, to deliver or surrender under an extradition treaty or special agreement.

ex-tra-di-tion, the surrender under treaty or special agreement of a fugitive from justice by one government to another.

eye wit-ness, one who saw a thing done.

F

Fa-bi-an, practicing a policy of delay such as that of Fabius who acquired the name of "Delayer" by his policy of avoiding direct engagements with Hannibal.

fab-ric, cloth woven or knit; texture, as of cloth, etc.

face val-ue, the nominal value which appears on a bond, coupon, piece of money, or other financial instrument.

fa-cil-i-tate, to make easy.

fac-sim-i-le, an exact reproduction.

fac-to-ry, a place where goods are made; a manufactory.

fac-to-tum, one who does all kinds of work.

Fah-ren-heit, the name of a thermometer having 32 degrees as the freezing and 212 degrees as the boiling point of water.

fail-ure, bankruptcy.

fake, *v. t.,* to cheat; deceive; swindle: *n.,* a scheme for swindling; a hoax; false report of news.

fak-er, a swindler; street peddler.

fa-kir, an oriental beggar or wonder-worker.

fall, *n.,* a drop; overthrow, ruin; autumn: *v. i.,* to drop; be disgraced.

false pre-tense, a willful misrepresentation of facts with the purpose of cheating aonther.

fea-si-ble, practicable.

fed-er-al, pertaining to league or treaty; pertaining to a country made up of states, as the United States and Switzerland or its government.

fed-er-al re-serve bank, a system of banks organized by the United States Government, to act as an

agent in maintaining reserves, issuing money in the form of bank notes, and lending money to other banks.

fee, *n.,* payment for services; an inherited estate; land held of a superior: *v. t.,* to pay a fee to.

feel-er, something put forth to obtain information.

fee sim-ple, an estate held in one's own right without restrictions.

fel-o-ny, a serious crime punishable by death or imprisonment.

fi-as-co, a complete or ignominious failure.

fi-at, a decree; a command; an order of court authorizing certain proceedings.

fi-du-ci-ar-y, *n.,* a trustee: *adj.,* held in trust.

fig-ure-head, a person only nominally important.

file, *n.,* an orderly arrangement of letters or papers; any device for so arranging them; a series; line; tool: *v. t.,* to arrange in order.

fi-nance, *n.,* the science of handling money, especially with regard to its investment; revenue or income of an individual, corporation, or government: *v. t.,* to manage the monetary affairs of; raise or supply money for.

fi-nan-cial, pertaining to money; pecuniary; fiscal.

fin-an-cier, one who is skilled in conducting matters of finance.

fine, *n.,* money exacted as penalty: *v. t.,* to punish by imposing a money penalty upon.

fi-nesse, stratagem.

first-hand, obtained direct from the first source.

first-rate, of the highest excellence.

fis-cal, pertaining to the public treasury; financial.

fixed charges, charges which be-

come due at stated intervals, like rent, taxes, etc.

fix-ture, any fixed appliance.

float, to start a company, scheme, etc., by furnishing money.

flot-sam, wreckage of a ship or of a ship's cargo found floating on the sea.

fluc-tu-ate, to rise and fall; waver, hesitate.

fly-leaf, a blank leaf at the beginning or end of a book.

fold-er, a circular or time table, etc.

fo-li-o, the page number in a book.

font, a complete assortment of printing types of one size.

forced sale, a sale under legal compulsion.

fore-close, to take away the right of redeeming mortgaged property.

fore-clo-sure, the act of cutting off from further chance to redeem property: said of a mortgage.

fore-gone, determined beforehand; unavoidable.

for-eign bill, a draft or bill of exchange payable in a foreign country.

fore-man, the spokesman of a jury; a chief workman; overseer; a supervisor.

fore-sight, the power of seeing beforehand; provident care.

forge, to counterfeit.

forg-er, one who counterfeits handwriting with the intent to deceive.

forg-er-y, the act of criminally imitating the handwriting of another; the act of making counterfeit coins.

for-mu-la, a prescribed rule or model; an expression of chemical composition; expression of a mathematical problem by means of symbols; a prescription.

for-mu-late, to reduce to a definite

statement; to put in terms of a prescription, rule, or recipe.

foun-da-tion, the base or lowest part of a structure; basic principles; an endowed institution.

foun-dry, a place where metals are cast.

fran-chise, liberty; freedom; right; privilege; right of suffrage.

frank, *n.,* free postage: *v. t.,* to send or carry a letter free of charge.

frank-ing priv-i-lege, the right of sending letters, packages, telegrams, etc., free of postal charges.

fra-ter-ni-ty, a brotherhood; a secret society.

free a-long-side ship, free delivery of merchandise to the side of an outgoing vessel. *Abbr. f. a. s.*

free list, a list of goods or merchandise admitted to a country free of duty; a list of those entitled to something free of charge.

free on board, free delivery of goods to the conveyance by which they are to be transported. *Abbr. f. o. b.*

free port, a port where merchandise may pass duty free.

free trade, trade or commerce free from tariffs or customs duties.

freight, *n.,* the cargo of a ship; goods loaded on a vessel, car, etc.; the charge for the transportation of goods: *v. t.,* to load with goods; to hire for carrying goods.

freight-age, charge for freight; cargo; act of freighting.

freight-er, one who charters or loads a ship or car; a vessel which carries a load but no passengers.

func-tion, *n.,* duty; office; event; action; public or official ceremony; a mathematical quantity connected with and varying with another: *v. i.,* to act.

func-tion-ar-y, *n.,* an official; one who fills an important position.

fund, *n.,* stock; capital; money set apart for some special purpose: *v. t.,* to provide a fund; to place in a fund.

fun-da-men-tal, basic; essential; pertaining to the foundation.

fund-ed, in the form of bonds bearing regular interest; invested in public securities.

fund-ed debt, a public debt which has been put in the form of bonds bearing regular interest.

funds, quick capital; available financial resources.

fu-tures, merchandise, commodities, or securities bought or sold for future delivery.

G

gage, *n.,* a standard of measure; the distance between the rails of a railway line: *v. t.,* to measure; to find out. Also, GAUGE.

gain, *n.,* advantage; winnings: *v. t.,* to obtain; earn: *v. i.,* to make progress; increase.

gain-ful, advantageous.

gar-nish-ee, *n.,* one who controls the property of another until the claims of a third party are settled: *v. t.,* to attach property by law for the payment of debt.

gauge, see *gage.*

gaug-er, an official whose business it is to ascertain the contents of casks.

gav-el, a small mallet used by a presiding officer or chairman.

gen-er-al-ize, *v. t.,* to make general in scope or meaning; to reduce to a general law or statement: *v. i.,* to draw general inferences.

gold brick, a swindle.

goods, movable property; merchandise; wares.

goods and chat-tels, movable property.

good will, the established popularity of a business house or trade.

graft, unlawful acquisition of money, especially from the Government; a bribe: *v. i.,* to practice grafting; to accept bribes.

graft-er, one who through position or business is able to accept public money without having rendered service for it.

grand ju-ry, a jury which inquires into an offense to see if there is sufficient evidence to bring an indictment, that is, to recommend it to the petty, or trial, jury.

grant, *n.,* the act of conferring; a gift; bestowal; privilege: *v. t.,* to give; confer; admit; concede; transfer; impart.

grant-ee, the person to whom property is transferred by law.

grant-or, the person who transfers property by law.

graph, a diagram showing a system of interrelations by points, often connected by lines.

gra-tu-i-ty, a free gift.

green-back, a U. S. note with a green back.

gross, twelve dozen; the entire amount.

ground plan, the plan of the ground floor of a building.

guar-an-tee, *n.,* a surety; a promise; a pledge: *v. t.,* to be responsible for; warrant; secure the performance of.

guar-an-tor, one who gives a guarantee.

guar-an-ty, a legal surety; a guarantee.

guard-i-an, one who has charge of the property or person of another, as of a minor or someone else incapable of managing his own affairs.

guild, a fraternity; an association.

H

ha-be-as cor-pus, you may have the body; a writ or order to bring a person into court.

hab-er-dash-er, a dealer in small dress wares; usually, in U. S., a dealer in men's furnishings.

hall-mark, a mark of genuineness or purity.

hand-bill, a loose printed sheet circulated for advertising purposes.

hand-book, a book for the hand; a guidebook or manual.

har-bor mas-ter, an official whose duty is to see that the regulations of the government are observed in a harbor.

head-quar-ters, the center of authority.

hear-ing, a judicial trial.

high seas, the open sea, beyond the waters owned by certain nations.

hire, *v. t.,* to engage for a stipulated reward; to rent: *n.,* a consideration paid for the use of anything; wages.

hire-ling, one who serves for pay; a mercenary person.

hol-o-caust, a total destruction, as by fire.

hon-o-ra-ri-um, a fee paid for professional services.

hon-or-a-ry, conferring or possessing something as a token of high esteem.

horse-pow-er, the power of a horse estimated at 33,000 pounds raised one foot in one minute.

hun-dred-weight, the twentieth part of a ton; 100 pounds avoirdupois.

hy-drau-lic, pertaining to fluids in motion; operated by water.

hy-poth-e-cate, to pledge, as life insurance, as a security for a debt or other obligation.

I

i-bi-dem, a Latin word meaning in the same place: *abbr., ib., ibid.*

il-le-gal, unlawful.

il-leg-i-ble, not easy to read; badly written.

il-le-git-i-mate, unlawful; unauthorized; born out of wedlock.

im-peach, to accuse.

im-peach-a-ble, liable to trial in court, or to arraignment.

im-peach-ment, the act of calling to trial; charges of maladministration brought up against high officials.

im-pe-cu-ni-ous, without money; hard up.

im-pli-cate, to involve; entangle; bring into connection with.

im-pli-ca-tion, an entanglement; a tacit inference.

im-plic-it, to be understood, though not expressed in words.

im-port (ĭm-pōrt′), *v. t.,* to bring into one's country: (ĭm′pōrt), *n.,* merchandise brought into a country from abroad.

im-port-er, a merchant who brings in goods from abroad.

im-post, a tax, especially duty levied on goods brought into a country.

im-pos-tor, one who imposes on others; one who deceives under false character or pretensions.

im-print (ĭm-prĭnt′), *v. t.,* to fix in the mind or memory: *n.* (ĭm′-prĭnt), the name of the printer or publisher of a book with the time and place of publication; an impression.

im-prob-i-ty, want of integrity or principle.

im-promp-tu, offhand; without preparation.

in-ca-pac-i-tate, to deprive of capability or natural power.

in-cen-di-a-rism, the act of maliciously burning property.

in-cen-di-a-ry, *n.,* one who maliciously sets fire; one who inflames the passions, or excites violence: *adj.,* relating to arson; tending to arouse sedition.

in-ci-den-tal, *adj.,* casual; accidental: *n. pl.,* small expenses.

in-close, to shut in or surround; fence in; encompass. Also, ENCLOSE.

in-clo-sure, a space or thing surrounded; that which surrounds; something included in the envelope with a letter.

in-clu-sive, inclosing; comprehensive.

in-cog-ni-to, *adj.,* in disguise: *adv.,* under an assumed name: *n. (fem.,* **incognita**), one who travels under an assumed name.

in-come, the yearly receipts of a business or of a person; salary; revenue: GROSS INCOME, the entire receipts from a business: NET INCOME, the part of an income which remains after expenses are paid.

in-come tax, a tax levied upon the receipts of an individual or a business.

in-com-pat-i-bil-i-ty, the state of not being able to live together in harmony.

in-com-pe-ten-cy, inability. Also, INCOMPETENCE.

in-com-pe-tent, incapable; not admissible or allowable.

in-cor-po-rate (ĭn-kôr-pō-rāt′), *v. t.,* to combine into one body or corporation; embody: *v. i.,* to unite so as to become a part of another body: (ĭn-kôr′-pō-rāt), *adj.,* united in one body; incorporated.

in-cor-po-ra-tion, a combination,

especially of persons legally authorized to carry on business under certain conditions.

in-cre-ment, increase; gain; produce; UNEARNED INCREMENT, the accumulation of interest on money without effort on the part of the owner.

in-cum-ben-cy, the state of holding any office or benefice.

in-cum-bent, *adj.,* obligatory; resting upon as a duty: *n.,* one who holds an office or benefice.

in-cur, to encounter; to become subject or liable to; contract.

in-debt-ed, being under monetary or other obligation.

in-de-fea-si-ble, that cannot be made null or void, as a title.

in-dem-ni-fi-ca-tion, reimbursement for loss or damage; reparation.

in-dem-ni-ty, security against loss, injury, or damage; repayment for loss.

in-dent-ed, held by agreement, especially as an apprentice.

in-den-ture, *n.,* a mutual legal agreement: *v. t.,* to bind by written agreement, as an apprentice.

in-dex (*pl.,* **indexes, indices**), a pointer or an indicator; a table of contents; the figure or symbol showing the power or root of a quantity, as 4^a, 4^2.

in-dict, to charge with, as crime.

in-dict-a-ble, liable to be charged with crime or misdemeanor.

in-dict-er, one who charges another with crime. Also, INDICTOR.

in-dict-ment, a formal charge against a person; a written accusation against a prisoner.

in-dig-e-nous, native.

in-di-gent, destitute.

in-dis-pen-sa-ble, necessary.

in-dorse, to write on the back of, as a check, etc.; guarantee; approve; ratify. Also, ENDORSE.

in-dor-see, the person to whom a check, etc., is made payable.

in-dorse-ment, approval.

in-dors-or, one who signs over a check; one who approves, ratifies, or recommends.

in-dus-tri-al-ism, a state of society founded upon the development of manufacturing industries.

in-dus-tri-ous, hard-working.

in-dus-try, assiduity; habitual diligence; a particular branch of manufacture or trade.

in-ef-fi-cien-cy, want of power or skill.

in-ef-fi-cient, incapable.

in-ex-pe-ri-ence, a want of personal trial and practice with life; lack of practice of any kind.

in-fant, in common law, any person under the age of twenty-one. The statute law varies in different states.

in-for-mal, unceremonious; unofficial.

in-i-ti-ate, to introduce; begin.

in-i-ti-a-tion, the act of introducing, as into a society, club, etc.; the rites by means of which one is introduced into such an organization.

in-i-ti-a-tive, the power of taking the lead; the energy which dares new enterprises.

in-junc-tion, legal restraint on certain proceedings.

in-no-va-tion, the introduction of a novelty; a change.

in-op-por-tune, unseasonable.

in-quest, a judicial or official inquiry into the causes of sudden death; the jury making the inquiry.

in re, concerning.

in-scribe, to write; to address formally; to dedicate.

in-scrip-tion, the act of printing or engraving for publication; the dedication of a book or a poem to a person; that which is written or engraved, as an inscription on a monument.

in-sol-ven-cy, the state of being unable to pay all debts.

in-sol-vent, *adj.,* unable to pay all debts; bankrupt: *n.,* one who is not able to pay all his debts.

in-spect, to examine carefully, so as to ascertain quality, errors, etc.

in-spec-tion, a careful survey; an official examination.

in-spec-tor, one who examines.

in-stall, to invest with office or rank; to set up for use.

in-stal-la-tion, the act of investing with office or rank.

in-stall-ment, a part payment; a part of anything produced at one time, as a serial in a magazine.

in-stall-ment plan, the system of paying a debt or price due in payments.

in-stan-ter, without delay.

in sta-tu quo, in the former state.

in-sti-tu-tion, an organized group for promoting a particular object.

in-stru-ment, the means by which anything is accomplished; a document containing the terms of a contract.

in-sub-or-di-nate, not submitting to authority; mutinous; riotous.

in-sub-or-di-na-tion, rebellion against authority.

in-sur-a-ble, capable of being insured against loss or damage.

in-sur-a-ble in-ter-est, a right or title to a person or property insured to sustain a contract in the event of the loss insured against.

in-sur-ance, *n.,* the act or system of insuring against loss, damage, accident, etc.; the system by which a person pays a *premium* to protect himself against a specific loss or *risk*.

in-sur-ance bro-ker, an agent who handles insurance.

in-sur-ance pol-i-cy, the written contract between the insurer and the insured.

in-sur-ance trust, a trust created by a life insurance policyholder who directs that the amount of the policy shall be paid at his death to a trustee, who shall invest and administer it for the beneficiary.

in-sure, to make sure; protect against loss, damage, accident, etc.

in-ter-course, reciprocal dealings between individuals, nations, etc.; commerce; fellowship.

in-ter-est, premium paid for the use of money.

in-ter-im, the meantime.

in to-to, in general; in the whole.

in tran-sit, on the way.

in vac-u-o, in a vacuum.

in-val-id, having no force or effect.

in-val-i-date, to destroy the force of; cancel; nullify.

in-va-lid-i-ty, a want of legal force.

in-ven-to-ry, a list of goods, as an *inventory* of a merchant's stock.

in-vest, *v. t.,* to clothe, as with office or dignity; to lay out so as to obtain interest: *v. i.,* to put money into.

in-vest-ment, the act of placing money so that it will draw interest.

in-ves-tor, one who lays out money for profit.

in-voice, a written account of merchandise sent to a person with the prices attached; a bill.

in-voice book, a book in which a record of invoices is kept.

in-volved, financially embarrassed.

ip-so fac-to, as a result of the act itself.

ip-so ju-re, by the law itself.

ir-re-deem-a-ble, not convertible: said of paper money; not redeemable.

i-tem, a separate particular; a bit of news.

i-tem-ize, to state by separate entries.

i-tin-er-a-ry, a guide book; a diary of an extended trip; the plan of a long journey.

J

jet-sam, goods thrown overboard to lighten a ship's cargo in time of danger. Also, JETTISON.

jet-ti-son, *n.,* the act of throwing goods overboard to relieve a ship: *v. t.,* to throw overboard.

jet-ty, a structure extending into the water to influence the tide, current, etc.; a wharf.

job-ber, a middleman; an agent who does odd pieces of work; one who dabbles in stocks.

job lot, an odd assortment of merchandise.

join-er, a skilled woodworker.

joint note, a promissory note signed by two or more persons each of whom is responsible for a proportionate share of its payment.

joint and sev-er-al note, a promissory note signed by several persons, each of whom is liable for the whole amount in the event the others fail to make payment.

joint stock, stock that is held in common with another or others.

joint stock com-pa-ny, a group of people organized to conduct business with capital held in common.

joint ten-an-cy, tenure of property with others in such a way that when one of the joint owners dies his share goes to the others to the exclusion of his heirs.

join-ture, property settled on a woman at the time of her marriage to be used after the death of her husband.

jour-nal, a daily paper or other periodical; a diary; a ship's logbook; an account of daily transactions and events.

jour-ney-man, a mechanic who has fully learned his trade.

judge, *n.,* an arbiter; a referee; *v. t.,* to pass sentence upon: *v. i.,* to pass sentence; estimate.

judg-ment, the decision of a court.

judg-ment note, a promissory note containing a power of attorney authorizing a judgment without process in case of nonpayment when due.

ju-di-ca-ture, a court of justice, and the extent of its jurisdiction.

junc-tion, the place where railroads, rivers, etc., meet; point of union.

ju-ror, one who serves on a jury.

ju-ry, a body of men, usually twelve, selected according to law, and sworn to examine and declare truth on the evidence in a legal case before them.

K

kar-at, a unit of weight for precious stones; a term used to express the purity of gold. Also, CARAT.

kil-o-gram, 1,000 grams or 22 lb. avoirdupois.

kil-o-li-ter, 1,000 liters or 264.18 gallons.

kil-o-me-ter, 1,000 meters or 3,280.8 feet.

kil-o-watt, a unit for measuring the

power of an electric current; 1,000 watts.

L

la-bel, *n.,* a slip of paper, etc., attached to anything stating contents, destination, ownership, etc.: *v. t.,* to mark with such a slip.

la-bor, *n.,* toil; exertion; work; pain: *v. i.,* to toil. Also, LABOUR.

lab-o-ra-to-ry, a place for scientific research.

La-bor Day, a legal holiday, usually the first Monday in September.

la-bor-er, one who does work which requires little skill.

land-ed, possessing, or consisting of land; captured and brought to shore.

land-hold-er, a holder or proprietor of land.

land-la-dy, a woman who lets houses, apartments, etc., to tenants; the mistress of an inn or hotel.

land-lord, the owner of lands or buildings which he rents to others; the master of an inn, hotel, etc.

land poor, having real estate which does not produce enough income to pay taxes on it.

lapse, *v. i.,* to pass or slip away; to fail in moral conduct or duty; to pass from one thing to another by some omission: *n.,* a slight failure in duty.

lar-ce-ny, theft.

lar-gess, a liberal gift. Also, LARGESSE.

lathe, a machine in which articles are held and rotated while being shaped and polished by means of a tool.

law, *n.,* a rule prescribed by authority or custom; statute; the legal profession; a principle deduced from practice or observation; a scientific statement of facts observed in natural phenomena; an established principle.

law-ful, legal; just.

law-less, unruly, not restrained by authority.

law-suit, an action in court for the recovery of a right or the settlement of a claim.

law-yer, one who practices law.

leak-age, allowance made for the quantity of anything that passes in or out; the quantity which leaks.

leap year, a year of 366 days; a year divisible by 4, as 1920.

lease, *n.,* the time for which property is rented; a written contract for the renting of property: *v. t.,* to let grant by lease; take possession of by contract.

lease-hold, tenure by contract for a certain time; property so held.

ledg-er, the principal account book of a mercantile or other business house.

leg-a-cy, a bequest by will; anything handed down by an ancestor.

le-gal, lawful; pertaining to law.

le-gal-i-ty, lawfulness.

le-gal-ize, to make lawful.

le-gal ten-der, currency or coin authorized by the Government for the payment of debts.

leg-a-tee, the person to whom property is left by will.

le-git-i-mate, lawful; born of wedded parents; reasonable.

les-see, one to whom a lease is given.

les-sor, one who grants a lease.

let-ter-head, the heading printed or engraved at the top of a sheet of writing paper.

lev-y, *v. t.,* to raise or collect by authority; to seize for unpaid rent, etc.: *n.,* the act of raising troops or collecting taxes; the number or amount raised.

li-a-bil-i-ty, the state of being subject to or responsible for: *pl.,* debts, opposed to assets.

li-a-ble, responsible; exposed to something unpleasant as danger, damage, etc.

li-ai-son, a bond of union; an illicit intimacy between a man and woman.

li-bel, *n.,* defamation; slander, *v. i.,* to lampoon; defame.

li-bel-ous, defamatory.

li-cense, legal permission: *v. t.,* to permit by law; to authorize. Also, LICENCE.

li-cen-ti-ate, one with the authority to preach or practice a profession.

li-en, a legal claim; security held until a claim is settled.

light-er-age, the unloading of a cargo into a lighter for conveyance to or from the shore; cost of such work.

lin-go, language; a contemptuous term for a particular language or dialect.

liq-ui-date, to pay off; clear up; settle.

liq-ui-da-tion, the act of settling or adjusting debts.

lit-i-gant, one engaged in a lawsuit.

lit-i-gate, to contest in law.

lit-i-ga-tion, the act of carrying on a lawsuit; a lawsuit.

Lloyd's, a marine insurance company with central offices in London.

lob-by, to try to influence the members of a legislative body.

lob-by-ist, a politician who tries to influence the members of a legis-

lative body of which he is not a member.

lock-out, the shutting out of workmen from a shop or factory by their employer.

lodge, a place where members of a society hold their meetings; the members themselves: *v. t.,* to shelter temporarily; deposit: *v. i.,* to live in temporarily.

lodg-er, one who lives in a hired room.

lodg-ing, a temporary dwelling place; a room or apartment hired in the house of another.

long-hand, ordinary handwriting.

lot, a portion of something, as land.

lu-cra-tive, profitable.

lu-cre, money; gain.

M

mag-is-trate, a civil officer with public authority.

mag-nate, a man of high rank, distinction, or influence.

mail-a-ble, lawful or suitable to be sent by mail.

main-tain, to support; keep up.

main-te-nance, means of support.

ma-jor-i-ty, the state of being greater; numerical excess; the full legal age.

make-up, the way in which the parts of anything are assembled; arrangement of printed matter in a newspaper, etc.

mal-prac-tice, a wrongful manner of conducting any profession.

mam-mon, greed for worldly wealth: from Mammon, the Syrian god of riches.

man-da-mus, a command or writ from a superior court directing an inferior court or person to perform some public duty or act.

man-date, an order; an official command.

man-da-to-ry, *adj.,* pertaining to, or expressing, an official command; *n.,* one who acts for another; a country chosen to administer or govern a certain colony or territory. Also, MANDATARY.

ma-nip-u-late, to operate or manage skillfully with the hands; to falsify.

man-u-al, *adj.,* pertaining to, or performed by, the hands: *n.,* a handbook.

man-u-fac-to-ry, a place where goods are made from raw materials; a factory.

man-u-fac-ture, *v. t.,* to make from raw materials: *v. i.,* to be occupied in making goods from raw materials: *n.,* the operation of changing raw material into useful articles; the thing made from raw material.

mar-co-ni-gram, a message transmitted by Marconi's system of wireless telegraphy.

mar-gin, a reserve sum or quantity; an excess of time or money over that which is actually needed or used; money or other security given to a broker to guard him from loss in advancing funds on an investment.

mar-i-time, relating to the sea.

mar-ket, *n.,* a trading place; the state of trade; the region where there is a demand for a certain commodity: *v. t.,* to offer for sale in a market; to sell: *v. i.,* to deal in a market; to buy or sell provisions or goods.

mar-ket-a-ble, salable.

ma-tu-ri-ty, a coming due, as a note or other obligation.

max-i-mum, *n.,* the utmost: *adj.,* highest or greatest possible.

mean, *adj.,* average as, *mean tem-*

perature: *n.,* the middle point between two extremes; *pl.,* resources.

me-di-ate, to interpose between parties to bring about a reconciliation; to bring about by friendly interposition.

me-di-a-tion, the act of trying to reconcile.

me-di-a-tor, one who seeks to bring about friendly relations.

mem-o-ran-dum, a note to help the memory; a brief entry in a diary.

men-su-ra-tion, the art or practice of measuring.

me-nu, a list of dishes to be served at a meal; bill of fare.

mer-can-tile, commercial, pertaining to merchandise or trade.

mer-can-tile a-gen-cy, an organization which ascertains and furnishes to those interested the financial standing, business reputation, or credit ratings of individuals, or firms engaged in mercantile or commercial enterprises.

mer-can-tile pa-per, commercial paper.

mer-chan-dise, goods, wares, etc., bought and sold.

mer-chant, *n.,* a trader; retailer: *adj.,* relating to trade or commerce; mercantile.

mer-chant-man, a trading vessel, as distinguished from a warship.

mer-chant .ma-rine, a nation's facilities for carrying on trade on the ocean.

merg-er, the legal combinaton of two estates, corporatons, or interests.

me-rid-i-an, the highest point reached, as by a heavenly body; the height of prosperity, etc.

mes-sieurs, *n. pl.,* of *monsieur* or *Mister*: *abbr. Messrs.*

me-ter, *n.,* an instrument for measuring and recording; the unit of linear measure in the metric system, 39.37 inches. Also, METRE.

met-ric sys-tem, a system of weights and measures first adopted in France, by which things are measured or numbered by tens or fractions of tens.

mid-dle-man, the dealer between producer and consumer; a broker.

mile, 5,280 feet.

mile-age, aggregate miles; an allowance for traveling expenses at the rate per mile; the charge per mile on railroads.

mil-len-ni-um, a period of 1,000 years, especially the thousand years during which it is supposed that Christ will reign on earth.

mil-li-gram, ⅟₁₀₀₀ of a gram.

mil-li-li-ter, ⅟₁₀₀₀ of a liter.

mil-li-me-ter, ⅟₁₀₀₀ of a meter.

mil-li-ner, one who makes women's hats.

mil-li-ner-y, the articles made or sold by milliners; the occupation of one who makes women's hats.

mim-e-o-graph, *n.,* a stencil device for copying written or typewritten letters: *v. t.,* to copy with such a machine.

min-i-mum, the least possible quantity or degree.

mi-nor, a person not yet twenty-one.

mi-nor-i-ty, the smaller of two numbers; opposed to *majority;* the state of being under age.

mi-nu-ti-ae, minor or unimportant details.

mis-cel-la-ne-ous, varied; consisting of several kinds.

mis-cel-la-ny, a mixture.

mis-de-mean-or, a crime inferior to felony.

mis-rep-re-sent, to represent falsely either through intention or ignorance.

mis-tri-al, a trial in court which comes to nothing because of some error in the course of it.

mit-ti-mus, a warrant for committing to prison.

mod-el, a pattern; standard; one who poses for an artist; one who tries on costumes to display them to customers.

mon-e-ta-ry, pertaining to money.

mon-e-tize, to convert into money.

mon-ey, coin; medium of exchange; currency.

mon-ey mar-ket, the market for the exchange of loanable money or capital; the sphere of financial operations.

mon-ey or-der, an order demanding the payment of money.

mon-o-met-al-lism, the use of only one metal as the standard value of currency.

mo-nop-o-ly, control of any industry; the person or group of persons exercising exclusive control of any industry.

mon-sieur, a French title of courtesy equal to Sir or Mr.

month-ly, *adj.,* happening once a month; continuing for a month: *adv.,* once a month: *n.,* a periodical published once a month.

mort-gage, a conveyance of property as security for debts; the legal paper by which the conveyance is made: *v. t.,* to pledge, as property as security.

mort-ga-gee, the person to whom property is given as security.

mort-ga-gor, the person who gives property as security.

mort-main, possession of lands or tenements by an organized body, ecclesiastical or otherwise.

mulct, *v. t.,* to fine: *n.,* a fine.

mu-nic-i-pal, pertaining to a city or town.

mu-nic-i-pal-i-ty, a town or city having local self-government.

mu-tu-al, interchanged; joint; common.

N

na-tion-al bank, an institution organized under a special act of Congress, for lending or caring for money.

na-tion-al debt, the aggregate of obligations of the United States Government.

nat-u-ral-ize, to grant to (a foreigner) the rights and privileges of citizenship.

nav-i-ga-ble, capable of being traveled over by a boat, etc.

nav-i-ga-tion, the act of traveling on the water in ships; the art or science of managing ships.

nav-i-ga-tor, one who travels in ships; one who manages a ship.

née, born. *Fr.*

ne-go-ti-a-ble, capable of being transferred or exchanged.

ne-go-ti-a-ble pa-per, bills of exchange, notes, drafts, checks, etc., which are made payable to bearer or order.

ne-go-ti-ate, *v. t.,* to trade; sell: *v. i.,* to treat with others on political or business affairs.

nest egg, money laid away to be added to.

night let-ter, a telegram sent at reduced rates at night, to be delivered the next morning.

nom-i-nal, in name only.

nonun-ion, not belonging to, or not favoring, trade unions.

nor-mal, natural; usual.

no-ta be-ne, note well: *abbr.,* N. B.

no-ta-ry, an official who attests deeds, contracts, etc. Also NOTARY PUBLIC.

no-ti-fi-ca-tion, a written or printed document by which warning, announcement, or information is sent.

no-ti-fy, to make known; inform.

nou-veau riche, one who has recently become rich. *Fr.*

nov-ice, a beginner.

null, of no legal value.

nul-li-fi-ca-tion, the act of making invalid.

nul-li-fy, to annul; cancel.

O

o-bit-u-ary, a notice of death; a brief account of a person or persons deceased.

ob-li-gate, to hold under legal or moral obligation.

ob-li-ga-tion, the binding power of a contract, promise, or sense of duty; a written document by which one binds himself under penalty to do anything.

ob-li-ga-to-ry, binding.

oc-cu-pan-cy, the act of having in possession, as a house.

oc-cu-pant, one who has possession of, or lives in.

oc-cu-pa-tion, the act or state of having in possession or dwelling in; business.

oc-cu-py, to take or have possession of.

of-fer, *n.,* a proffer: *v. t.,* to present for acceptance or refusal; bid.

of-fi-cial, *n.,* one invested with a public office: *adj.,* pertaining to a public duty or an office; authorized.

of-fi-ci-ate, to act in a public service or duty.

o-mis-sion, something left out.

o-pen, *adj.,* free; public; unsealed:

v. t., to reveal; begin: *v. i.,* to un-close itself; lead into.

o-pen ac-count, a running or un-settled account.

o-pen pol-i-cy, an insurance policy in which the insurer has to prove the value in case of loss.

op-er-ate, *v. i.,* to work; *v. t.,* to cause to work.

op-er-at-ing ex-pen-ses, the costs of conducting business exclusive of fixed charges.

op-er-a-tion, action; execution.

op-por-tune, well-timed.

op-por-tu-nism, a quickness in tak-ing advantage of chances.

op-ti-mism, the belief that all is for the best.

op-ti-mist, one who looks on the bright side of things.

op-tion, a privilege, given to one of the parties to a time contract, which may be taken advantage of on any day within a certain speci-fied time limit.

op-tion-al, left to one's choice.

op-u-lent, rich.

or-der, instruction to buy or sell.

or-gan, house organ, a paper pub-lished by an organization for cir-culation among its own members.

or-gan-i-za-tion, a body of persons united for some common end.

or-gan-ize, to set in working order; regulate.

out-fit, *n.,* equipment: *v. t.,* and *v. i.,* to furnish with everything neces-sary for any undertaking.

out-lay, expenditure in money, energy, etc.

o-va-tion, a hearty demonstration of popular approval.

o-ver-cap-i-tal-ize, to place a nom-inal or "face" value on the capital of a corporation above that of the cost or market value; to capital-ize more heavily than is war-ranted by the business or by probable profits.

o-ver-draw, to make bank drafts, checks, etc., greater than the amount on deposit.

o-ver-due, past the time for pay-ment.

o-ver-head, or OVERHEAD CHARGES, the expenses not included in the actual running of a business, as rent, insurance, etc.

o-ver-pro-duc-tion, supply over the demand.

o-ver-se-er, a superintendent; an inspector.

o-ver-time, time during which one works beyond the regular hours.

P

par-a-mount, superior to all others.

par-cel post, the system of the gov-ernment of carrying packages by mail.

par ex-cel-lence, beyond compari-son. *Fr.*

par-lia-men-ta-ry, pertaining to, or according to, the rules and usages of public assemblies.

part-ner, an associate; a sharer.

part-ner-ship, the state of being associated in a common under-taking; a fellowship.

pass, permission to go and come, as on a railroad.

pass-book, a depositor's bank book; a book listing articles bought on credit.

pass-key, a master key.

pass-port, an official paper giving one permission to travel in a for-eign country.

pass the buck, to shift the responsi-bility to some one else.

pat-ent, *n.,* a grant of exclusive privilege by the Government: *v. t.,* to grant or secure the exclusive

right to: *adj.*, secured by government protection.

pat-ent-ee, one who has secured from the Government the sole right to make, use, or sell an invention for a certain number of years.

pa-tron, regular customer.

pa-tron-age, guardianship; support.

pa-tron-ize, to support; favor; act as guardian towards.

pawn, *v. t.*, to pledge as security for a loan: *n.*, something given as a security for the payment of a debt.

pawn-bro-ker, a person legally licensed to lend money on goods left with him.

pawn-shop, a place where money is lent on goods deposited.

pay, *v. t.*, to give money, etc., for goods delivered or services rendered; reward; recompense; discharge: *v. i.*, to make recompense; discharge; be worth-while: *n.*, money, etc., given for goods or services rendered.

pay-a-ble, that may or should be paid; justly due.

pay-ee, one to whom money is paid.

pay-mas-ter, one who gives out money for wages.

pay-ment, the act of giving money, etc., for service done; reward.

pec-u-late, to embezzle.

pec-u-la-tion, embezzlement.

ped-dler, one who goes about selling small wares.

pe-nal, pertaining to punishment.

pe-nal-ize, to punish.

pen-al-ty, punishment.

pen-ny, in Eng., 1.16 cents; in United States, one cent.

pen-ny-weight, 24 grains troy weight.

pen-ny-wise, saving small sums at the hazard of larger.

pen-sion, *n.*, an allowance for past services: *v. t.*, to grant a pension to.

pen-sion-er, one who receives a regular allowance, because of past services or present disability.

pe-on-age, the hiring of gangs of laborers to employers, often in bondage, as for debt.

per cap-i-ta, by heads; for each individual.

per cent, by the hundred.

per-cent-age, the rate per hundred; a part or proportion.

per-en-ni-al, enduring; lasting, as a plant that lives through the year.

per-func-to-ry, done mechanically; without interest.

pe-ri-od-ic, occurring regularly.

per-jure, to swear falsely.

per-ju-ry, willful swearing to what is false.

per-mit, a written permission or authorization to do something.

per-pe-tu-i-ty, the state of lasting forever; that to which there is no end: IN PERPETUITY, forever.

per-qui-site, an extra profit or allowance.

per se, by itself.

per-son-al, pertaining to an individual; peculiar to an individual.

per-son-al-i-ty, the sum of one's qualities and characteristics; that which makes one different from all others; an offensive remark made about one's person or private affairs.

per-son-al-ty, personal belongings; movable property.

per-son-nel, a body of persons, especially, a body engaged in a certain business.

per-son-nel man-ag-er, one whose

business it is to take on employees and see that they are properly placed.

pes-si-mist, one who believes that the world is bad rather than good.

pet-it, petty; insignificant; used only in law. Also, PETTY.

pe-ti-tion, *n.,* a supplication; a formal request: *v. t.,* to entreat, supplicate.

pet-it ju-ry, a trial jury, as distinct from a grand jury.

pet-ti-fog-ger, a petty lawyer, often one who uses dishonest methods.

pet-ty cash, money received or paid out in small amounts.

pet-ty cash book, a book in which a record is kept of money received or paid out in small amounts.

pidg-in Eng-lish, the broken English used by the Chinese in their commerce with foreigners.

piece-work, work done by the job: opposite to time-work, or work paid by the hour, etc.

pi-geon-hole, *n.,* a small compartment in a desk: *v. t.,* to lay aside; shelve.

pin mon-ey, money settled on a wife by her husband for her private expenses; money for small personal expenses.

pit-tance, a small allowance.

plain-tiff, one who begins a lawsuit.

pledge, *n.,* anything placed as a security; guarantee; pawn; promise: *v. t.,* to give as security; promise; toast.

plu-ral-i-ty, the majority; excess of votes over those of any other candidate for an office.

plu-to-crat, one powerful on account of his wealth.

pock-et, to take unlawfully; to accept without protest.

pock-et-book, a small case for car-

rying money, papers, etc., in the pocket.

pock-et mon-ey, money for occasional expenses; spending money.

pol-i-cy, course of action or conduct; a certificate of insurance.

poll, *n.,* the casting or recording of votes; *pl.,* the place where voting is done; the number of votes cast: *v. t.* to deposit or call forth a vote.

poll tax, a tax on each person, literally, a head tax.

pool, putting together of the interests of various persons for the purpose of promoting a joint undertaking; the persons themselves; a combination of interests in a common fund for the purpose of manipulating the prices of grain, cotton, securities, etc.

por-tage, a carrying of goods, etc., from one waterway to another; the cost of such carriage.

port-fo-li-o, a case for papers, etc.

post, *n.,* a station; mail; writing or printing paper 18 x 15 inches: *v. t.,* to affix to a wall, etc.; mail; inform fully; transfer an entry from the first to the final record, as from a journal to a ledger.

post-age, the cost of sending letters, packages, etc., by mail.

post-al, pertaining to the post office.

post-al card, a card with a postage stamp officially printed on it.

post card, a private card, as a picture, etc., which may be sent through the mail.

post-date, to date after the actual time of writing.

post-me-rid-i-em, after noon: *abbr., P. M.* or *p. m.*

post-mor-tem, an examination of a dead body.

post-pran-di-al, after-dinner.

post-script, an addition to a letter, book, etc. See *codicil.*

po-ten-tial, capable of being; possible but not actual.

pow-er of at-tor-ney, legal written authority from one person to another to act for him.

prac-ti-cal, pertaining to, or derived from, actual use and experience; useful; not merely theoretical.

prac-ti-tion-er, one who pursues any profession.

pran-di-al, pertaining to a meal.

pre-am-ble, a preface or short introduction.

pre-cau-tion-a-ry, intended to prevent damage or loss.

prec-e-dent, something done or said that may serve as a model in similar cases; an example.

pre-cinct, a district; a place marked by boundaries: *pl.*, surrounding regions.

pre-empt, to establish a prior claim.

pre-emp-tion, the act or right of buying before others.

pre-ferred stock, generally speaking, stock which gives its holders a right to receive dividends before the holders of common stock can share them.

pre-mi-um, reward; bonus; money paid on an insurance policy; a sum above face value.

pre-pay, to pay in advance.

pre-side, to direct or control, as the proceedings of a meeting; have the place of authority.

pres-tige, influence derived from past reputation, achievements, etc.

pri-ma fa-ci-e, at first view.

pri-mo-gen-i-ture, the right of the first-born to inheritance.

prin-ci-pal, one who employs another to act as agent; one primarily liable for an obligation; a capital sum drawing interest.

pri-or, previous; former.

pri-or-i-ty, the state of going before in time, place, or rank.

pro-bate, a document constituting legal proof of a will.

pro-ba-tion, proof; trial; test.

pro-ce-dure, course of action; manner of conducting a legal case.

pro bo-no pu-bli-co, for the public good.

pro-ceed-ings, a published record of the actions of a society or other organization.

proc-ess, a proceeding; legal writ.

proc-la-ma-tion, an official public announcement.

prod-uce, that which is brought forth, especially farm products.

pro-duc-er, one who manufactures goods or raises farm products.

prod-uct, the result; that which is yielded, brought forth, or produced.

pro-fes-sion-al, *adj.*, pertaining to an occupation which requires superior education: *n.*, one who makes his living by arts, sports, etc., as distinct from an amateur.

prof-it, gain.

prof-it-a-ble, bringing benefit or gain.

prof-it-eer, one who takes advantage of an abnormal economic situation such as that produced by war to make undue profits on necessities.

pro-gram, a brief outline of the features that make up a public entertainment, etc.; a regular plan of action.

prom-i-sor, one who makes a legal agreement.

prom-is-so-ry, containing an agreement.

prom-is-so-ry note, a written agreement to pay a certain sum of money at a certain time to a certain person or bearer.

pro-mo-ter, one who forwards new undertakings.

prop-a-gan-da, any organization or method for propagating a doctrine; the doctrine itself.

prop-er-ty, a thing owned: PERSONAL PROPERTY, movable property, REAL PROPERTY, land, houses, etc.

prop-o-si-tion, an offer; formal statement of a topic to be debated.

pro-pri-e-ta-ry, *adj.,* pertaining to an owner: *n.,* an owner; a body of owners.

pro-pri-e-tor, owner.

pro ra-ta, in proportion.

pros-e-cute, *v. t.,* to pursue; bring legal suit against: *v. i.,* to sue; carry on a lawsuit.

pros-e-cu-tion, the act of persisting in or carrying on; the party starting a lawsuit.

pros-e-cu-tor, one who takes legal action against another.

pro-spec-tus, a sketch or plan of a proposed undertaking; a yearly catalog.

pro-test (prō-tĕst′), *v. i.,* to remonstrate; *v. t.,* to assert; to declare that payment of a bill has been refused: (pro′-test), a solemn declaration of opposition; a formal declaration of nonpayment or nonacceptance of a bill.

prov-i-den-tial, effected by divine care or foresight; fortunate.

pro-vi-sion-al, temporary.

pro-vi-so, a conditional clause in a will, etc.

pro-vi-so-ry, conditional.

prox-i-mo, next month.

prox-y, an agent; substitute.

pru-den-tial, proceeding from, or characterized by, careful thought.

pub-li-cist, one who writes on current political topics.

pub-lic-i-ty, state of being known to the public; notoriety.

pub-lic spir-it-ed, interested in the general welfare of the community.

punc-til-i-o, formality; exactness in conduct or ceremony.

punc-tu-al, prompt; exact.

pur-chase, *n.,* buying; the thing bought; leverage: *v. t.,* to buy; to move by mechanical power.

pur-lieus, outskirts; environs.

pur-port, meaning.

purs-er, a ship's clerk; paymaster.

pur-su-ant, according.

pur-vey-ance, the act of supplying provisions.

pur-vey-or, one who supplies provisions.

Q

quar-an-tine, *n.,* the time of stoppage of travel or intercourse on account of disease: *v. t.,* to place under restraint on account of disease.

quar-ter-ly, once every three months.

ques-tion-naire, a series of questions asked of a large number of people.

quire, twenty-four sheets of paper.

quit-claim, a full release of claim: QUITCLAIM DEED, an instrument for the conveyance of property without warranty of title.

quit-rent, a fixed rent paid by a tenant which releases him from other obligations.

quit-tance, a release; acquittance; repayment.

quon-dam, former; sometime.

quo-rum, a sufficient number of any organization to transact business.

quo-ta, a share or proportion from

each to make up a certain quantity.

quo-ta-tion, the current price of merchandise, securities, or other commodities.

quo-tid-i-an, daily.

quo-tient, the result of division.

quo war-ran-to, a judicial writ commanding a person to show by what authority he exercises an office or power.

R

ral-ly, *n.,* a mass meeting: *v. i.,* to recover.

rate, *n.,* amount, degree, value, grade, etc., estimated according to a fixed standard; price: *v. t.,* to estimate.

rat-i-fi-ca-tion, confirmation.

ra-ti-o, the relation of one number or quantity to another; rate.

read-y-made, made beforehand; kept in stock.

re-al es-tate, lands, houses, etc.; immovable property.

re-al-ty, real estate.

ream, twenty quires of paper.

re-bate, *n.,* a discount; deduction: *v. t.,* to allow a discount to; give back a part of a sum already paid.

re-ceipt, *n.,* a written acknowledgment that something has been received: *pl.,* that which is taken in: *v. t.,* to sign in acknowledgment of receipt or payment: *v. i.,* to give a written acknowledgment of something paid.

re-ceipt book, a book of printed forms for receipts; a book in which receipts are kept.

re-ceiv-a-ble, capable of, or suitable for, reception when offered.

re-ceiv-er, one appointed by a court to manage property or funds pending judicial decision on

them; a trustee; a creditor's representative.

re-cip-ro-cal, mutual.

re-cip-ro-cate, *v. t.,* to give and take from one another; exchange: *v. i.,* to move backward and forward; interchange.

rec-i-proc-i-ty, equal commercial rights or benefits mutually enjoyed; free interchange.

reck-on-ing, a calculation; settlement; statement of accounts with another.

re-claim, to recover.

re-com-men-da-tion, that which brings one into favorable notice; a favorable introduction.

re-com-mit, to send back.

rec-om-pense, *n.,* reward: *v. t.,* to compensate; repay.

rec-ord (rĕk′-ŏrd), *n.,* a register; a written or printed report of facts or proceedings: *v. t.,* (rē-kôrd′), to register; chronicle; enroll.

re-cord-er, one who keeps official public records.

re-coup, to counterbalance loss; make good.

re-course, an application for aid or protection.

re-cov-er, *v. t.,* to win back; make good; restore: *v. i.,* to succeed in a lawsuit.

re-cov-er-y, the obtaining of one's right to something by legal procedure.

re-crim-i-nate, to return a charge with another.

re-crim-i-na-tion, the act of accusing in return.

rec-ti-fy, to correct.

re-cur-rent, coming back at intervals.

re-deem, to buy back; make good.

red-let-ter day, a memorable or happy day.

red tape, official formality causing delay.

re-duce, to make lower; lessen.

re-duc-tion, the act of decreasing, degrading, or changing.

re-duc-ti-o ad ab-sur-dum, reduction to an absurdity.

re-fer, *v. t.,* to assign; appeal: *v. i.,* direct attention.

ref-er-ee, an umpire; an arbitrator.

ref-er-ence, *n.,* the act of submitting a matter to another; a written statement of the qualifications of a person; the one who gives such statement.

ref-er-en-dum, the submitting of a law to the decision of a vote by the people.

reg-is-ter, *n.,* an official list or record; that which records: *v. t.,* to enroll; record; show clearly: *v. i.,* to write one's name in a record.

reg-is-ter and re-cord-er, an officer authorized by law to record business transactions.

reg-is-trar, one who keeps lists or records.

reg-is-tra-tion, enrollment.

reg-is-try, a record; the place where an official record is kept.

re-im-burse, to pay back; refund.

re-in-sur-ance, a second insurance on something already insured; an insurance on the insurer's risk.

re-join-der, an answer to a reply; in law, the defendant's answer to the plaintiff's statements.

re-lease, *n.,* a deed by which one person who owns with another a piece of property releases to the second all of his claims; a news item set free for publication: *v. t.,* to set free; deliver from penalty, debt, sorrow, etc.

rel-e-vant, pertinent to the case in hand; appropriate; applicable.

re-li-a-ble, trustworthy; dependable.

rel-ict, a widow or widower.

re-lief, help.

re-miss, neglectful; careless.

re-mis-sion, a canceling of a debt; pardon.

re-mit, to forgive; send, as money, etc.; lessen; relax.

re-mit-tal, a canceling; discharge.

re-mit-tance, the sending of money, etc., in payment; the money sent.

rem-nant, a remainder; fragment.

re-mu-ner-ate, to recompense; compensate; reward.

re-mu-ner-a-tion, a compensation; salary; reward.

re-mu-ner-a-tive, profitable.

ren-dez-vous, a place of meeting; a meeting by appointment.

re-new-al, the giving of a new note for an old.

rent, *n.,* a tear; periodical payment for the use of property: *v. t.,* to use in consideration for periodical payments: *v. i.,* to be leased.

rent-al, money paid periodically for the use of property.

re-plev-in, *n.,* a writ to recover goods; the act of recovering goods wrongfully seized: *v. t.,* to recover by writ or order of court.

re-plev-y, to get through an order issued by a court.

rep-li-ca, a copy.

re-ply, an answer; response: *v. i.,* rejoin; respond.

re-port, *n.,* an official statement: *v. t.,* to relate, make a statement of: *v. i.,* to present or prepare a statement.

re-port-er, one who gathers news and writes an account of public events for a newspaper.

re-pos-i-to-ry, a depository; storehouse.

rep-re-hen-si-ble, deserving reproof.

rep-re-sen-ta-tive, *adj.,* acting for others; typical: *n.,* one with power to act for others; a delegate.

re-prieve, *n.,* a temporary suspension of the sentence of a criminal: *v. t.,* to delay the punishment of; free temporarily from pain or danger.

rep-ri-mand, a severe reproof.

re-pris-al, a repayment of injury with injury; retaliation.

re-pu-di-ate, to cast off; disclaim.

re-pu-di-a-tion, refusal to pay.

rep-u-ta-ble, creditable; honorable.

rep-u-ta-tion, character attributed; honor; credit.

re-pute, *n.,* reputation: *v. t.,* to hold in estimation.

req-ui-site, *adj.,* necessary: *n.,* a necessity.

req-ui-si-tion, *n.,* an authoritative demand or claim: *v. t.,* to demand or claim by authority.

re-scind, to recall; annul.

re-search, a careful investigation of sources.

re-serve, that which is kept in store.

re-sid-u-al, remaining after part has been taken away.

re-sid-u-a-ry, pertaining to the part remaining.

res-i-due, that which remains; dregs.

re-sign, *v. t.,* to give up; *v. i.,* to withdraw from.

re-source, *n.,* that on which one relies in an emergency or difficulty: *pl.,* money, etc., means.

ré-su-mé, a summary.

re-sume, to take up again.

re-sump-tion, the act of taking up again.

re-tail, *n.,* the sale of goods in small quantities: *v. t.,* to sell in small quantities; to tell again: *v. i.,* to sell goods in small quantities.

re-tain, to keep; hire.

re-tain-er, a paid adherent; fee paid to a lawyer.

re-un-ion, a meeting of those who have been separated.

re-vamp, to make over.

rev-e-nue, income; proceeds.

re-voke, *v. t.,* to annul; repeal.

rid-er, a section added to a legislative bill.

ri-pa-ri-an, pertaining to the banks of a river.

rod, sixteen and a half feet.

Ro-ta-ri-an, a member of any one of a number of clubs having the same constitution and affiliated under the International Association of Rotary Clubs.

ro-ta-tion, the act of turning around, as on an axis; recurrence.

rote, mere repetition with little attention to the meaning.

ro-to-gra-vure, the process by which photographs are rapidly printed from copper cylinders; a picture so produced.

round rob-in, a letter or petition signed in a circle.

route, *n.,* way; journey: *v. t.,* to send by a certain way.

rou-tine, regular practice.

S

sab-o-tage, malicious injury of property by workmen during labor troubles; destruction of property during war.

sal-a-ry, regular payment for services rendered.

sales-man, one who sells commodities.

sales-man-ship, the art or practice of selling.

sal-vage, the saving of a ship or goods from a wreck or other danger; property thus saved; payment for saving it.

sam-ple, a specimen: *v. t.,* to test by a specimen.

sat-is-fac-tion, payment; redress.

sat-is-fac-to-ry, leaving no room for complaint.

sat-is-fy, to pay in full.

sav-ings, small sums of money laid by.

sav-ings bank, an institution where small sums may be deposited at interest.

scab, a nonunion worker; a strike-breaker.

sched-ule, a list or inventory.

scru-ple, *n.,* twenty grains; a minute quantity; hesitation for fear of doing wrong: *v. t.,* and *v. i.,* to hesitate from a sense of right and wrong.

sea-far-ing, traveling by sea; following the sea.

sea lev-el, the level of the surface of the sea at mean tide.

sea-port, a town or harbor on the coast.

search war-rant, a warrant giving a police officer the right of search.

sea-son-able, opportune; in good time.

sea-son-al, pertaining to one of the four divisions of the year.

se-cure, *v. t.,* to make safe; protect; obtain: *adj.* safe.

se-cu-ri-ty, a pledge; guarantee; collateral.

sed-en-ta-ry, accustomed to sitting a large part of the time.

sem-i-week-ly, occurring twice a week.

sen-ior, *n.,* one before others in age, rank, etc.; *adj.,* older in name or office; superior in rank, etc.

se-quent, *adj.,* following: *n.,* a result.

se-ri-al, *n.,* a tale, etc., issued in

successive parts: *adj.,* periodical; occurring in regular succession.

se-ri-a-tim, in regular order.

se-ries, a regular succession, sequence.

serv-ice, employment; duty; the operation of a system which supplies a public need.

serv-ice-a-ble, useful.

ses-sion, the time during which a body holds its meetings.

set-tle-ment, a payment or adjustment of an account.

shad-y, questionable.

share, a portion: *v. t.,* to divide; partake of: *v. i.,* to have a part in.

share-hold-er, one who owns one or more parts of a property.

sharp-er, a swindler.

shek-el, an ancient Jewish coin.

ship-ment, a consignment of goods for transportation.

ship-ping, the act or business of transporting goods.

ship-shape, in good order.

shod-dy, material made from refuse woolen or cotton fabrics.

shop, *n.,* a store: *v. i.,* to visit shops for the purpose of looking over and buying goods.

shop-keep-er, a storekeeper; tradesman.

shop-lift-er, one who steals goods from a shop under pretense of buying.

shop-worn, worn or mussed from having been in a shop for a long time.

short, in finance, of, or concerning, the sale of securities or commodities which the seller does not own.

short-age, a deficit.

short-hand, stenography.

show-case, a case, usually glass, in which goods are placed for display.

show-room, an apartment where goods to be sold are displayed.

sig-na-ture, the name of a person written by himself.

si-lo, a pit or tower for preserving green fodder.

sil-ver-ware, vessels, dishes, knives, spoons, etc., made of silver.

si-mul-ta-ne-ous, happening or existing at the same time.

si-ne-cure, a position having a salary but little duty or responsibility.

si-ne di-e, without day; without definite day for reassembling.

sink-ing fund, a money reserve to be used, with its accumulated interest, to pay off a debt.

sit-ting, time during which a body sits.

sit-u-a-tion, location; condition; employment.

skip-stop, the plan of reducing the number of stopping places of street cars, etc.

slo-gan, formerly, a rallying cry or a battle cry; today, a compelling phrase, used in advertising, etc.

slot ma-chine, a machine in which a coin may be inserted for candy, gum, etc.

slump, *n.,* a sudden dropping off: *v. i.,* to fall suddenly, as a price.

so-ci-e-ty, people in general considered as a united body; an association.

so-lic-it, *v. t.,* to ask for earnestly: *v. i.,* to seek, as votes, orders, etc.

so-lic-i-tor, an attorney; a legal agent.

sol-ven-cy, ability to pay debts; capability of being dissolved.

sol-vent, able to pay debts.

so-vi-et, a Russian political organization in which the working class only have a vote, merchants, bankers, landowners, etc., being disfranchised.

spe-cial-ty, a special pursuit, product, or characteristic.

spe-cie, coined money.

spe-cif-ic, definite: SPECIFIC DUTY, a tax definitely fixed; opposite to *ad valorem* duty.

spec-i-fi-ca-tion, a detailed statement; one item in the statement; an item.

spec-i-fy, to state explicitly.

spec-i-men, a sample.

spe-cious, apparently true but not sound or fair.

spec-u-late, to gamble in stocks, etc.

spec-u-la-tion, any hazardous business enterprise.

spec-u-la-tive, theoretical; reflective.

spu-ri-ous, not genuine.

square, *n.,* a figure with four equal sides and four right angles; the result of multiplying a number by itself: *v. t.,* to multiply by itself; balance; *v. i.,* to accord: *adj.,* true; balanced.

square root, the number or quantity which when multiplied by itself produces a given number or quantity.

sta-bi-lize, to make steady.

stag-ger hours, the system whereby one group of people goes to business earlier than another to relieve congested traffic.

stake, *n.,* a hazard: *v. t.,* to wager.

stand-ard, *n.,* a rule; model: *adj.,* established.

stand-ard-ize, to make conform to rule, model, etc.

stand-ing, reputation.

sta-ple, the principal product or industry; raw material.

stat-ed, fixed; regular.

state-ment, a narrative; an account.

state's ev-i-dence, testimony presented by the government or prosecution in a criminal case, especially that presented by an accomplice to the crime.

sta-tion-er-y, paper, pen, ink, and other writing materials.

sta-tis-tics, *n. pl.,* a classified collection of facts pertaining to a nation, industry, etc.; the science of collecting facts and tabulating them numerically.

sta-tus, legal condition of a person; rank.

sta-tus quo, a condition in which a person or thing has been, is, or may be.

stat-ute, a law.

stat-u-to-ry, enacted by law.

ste-nog-ra-pher, one who writes shorthand.

ste-nog-ra-phy, shorthand.

ster-ling, genuine; of high value; standard.

stet, let it stand: used in proofreading to indicate that something marked for omission is to remain.

ste-ve-dore, a dock laborer who loads and unloads vessels.

sti-pend, a settled salary.

stip-u-late, *v. i.,* and *v. t.,* to settle definitely.

stip-u-la-tion, a contract; an item in an agreement.

stock, *n.,* capital; cattle; store; supply: *v. t.,* to fill; supply.

stock-bro-ker, one who buys and sells shares and stocks for others.

stock com-pa-ny, a corporation whose capital is represented by shares held by various persons.

stock ex-change, a place where stocks are bought and sold.

stock-hold-er, one who holds shares in a corporation, etc.

stock-job-ber, one who speculates in stocks.

stop-gap, a temporary expedient.

stop watch, a watch which can be stopped instantly, used in timing races, etc.

stor-age, the act of putting goods away for safekeeping; charge for storing goods.

stor-age bat-ter-y, a device for storing electrical energy.

store, *n.,* stock; shop: *pl.,* food, ammunition, etc.: *v. t.,* to put away.

store-house, a warehouse.

store-room, a room in which things are put away until needed.

stow, to put away; arrange compactly.

stow-age, the act of packing away; room in which things may be packed; charge for packing.

strike, *v. t.,* to hit; dash against; affect suddenly: *v. i.,* to hit; cease work for higher wages, etc.: *n.,* a ceasing of work for higher wages, etc.

strike-break-er, one who takes the place of a man who has stopped work for higher wages or better working conditions.

strik-er, one who stops work to get higher wages or better working conditions.

strin-gent, severe.

sub-com-mit-tee, an under committee.

sub-let, to let to another (property that has been let to oneself).

sub-poe-na, *n.,* a writ summoning a witness into court under penalty: *v. t.,* to serve with a writ of subpœna. Also, SUBPENA.

sub-scribe, *v. t.,* to sign; assent to; promise: *v. i.,* to sign one's name to; approve or promise something by affixing one's name.

sub-scrip-tion, a signature; a formal attestation; amount pledged.

sub-sid-i-a-ry, *adj.,* aiding; tributory: *n.,* a helper; an assistant.

sub-si-dize, to grant financial aid to.

sub-si-dy, money granted by one government to another or to a private enterprise; a grant; bonus.

sub-stan-ti-ate, to prove.

sub-sti-tute, *n.,* a person or thing in the place of another: *v. t.,* to put in the place of another person or thing.

sum-ma-ry, *n.,* an abridgment: *adj.,* concise; done quickly.

sump-tu-a-ry, pertaining to the spending of money.

sump-tu-a-ry laws, laws regulating the amount of money spent on luxuries.

sun-dries, *n. pl.,* various small articles.

sun-dry, several; various.

su-per, a prefix meaning over, above, beyond.

su-per-a-bun-dance, excess.

su-per-an-nu-ate, to impair by age; retire on a pension on account of old age.

su-per-car-go, an official who has charge of the cargo and business affairs of a merchant ship during a voyage.

su-per-in-tend, to oversee; supervise.

su-per-in-tend-ent, an overseer; supervisor.

su-pe-ri-or, *adj.,* preferable; finer: *n.,* one of higher rank or position.

su-per-nu-mer-a-ry, *n.,* a person or thing beyond the regular number to be used in emergency: *adj.,* beyond the required number.

su-per-scribe, to write above or upon; place an inscription on.

su-per-scrip-tion, that which is written on the outside, as of an envelope.

su-per-sede, to set aside; take the place of.

su-per-struc-ture, something built above something else.

su-per-vise, to oversee.

su-per-vi-sion, the act of overseeing.

su-per-vi-sor, an overseer.

sup-ple-ment, *n.,* an addition to a book, paper, etc.: *v. t.,* to add something to.

sup-ply, *v. t.,* to furnish; *n.,* the act of furnishing or providing; store; one who serves for another: *pl.,* reserve stores.

sur-charge, an excessive charge or burden.

sure-ty, security bail; one who becomes responsible for another for debt, etc.

sur-plus, excess.

sur-tax, an extra tax.

sweat-shop, a workroom where people work for starvation wages.

sweat-ing sys-tem, the system of employing poor people to do piece work for very low wages.

swin-dle, *v. t.,* to defraud: *n.,* a cheat.

swin-dler, a cheat.

syn-di-cate (sĭn′-dĭ-kăt), *n.,* an association or combination of persons: *v. t.* (sĭn-dĭ-kāt′), to form into an association or company; offer for sale to a number of periodicals.

sys-tem, an orderly arrangement or assemblage; method.

sys-tem-at-ic, orderly.

sys-tem-a-tize, to reduce to a system or regular method.

T

ta-ble d'hôte, a plan by which fixed meals are served: opposite to à la carte, *Fr.*

tab-u-lar, arranged systematically or in the form of a table.

tales-man, a person summoned to fill a deficiency in a jury.

tal-ly, a score kept by notches, etc.

task-mas-ter, one who imposes a piece of work upon another.

tax, *n.,* an assessment; money paid to a government: *v. t.,* to impose a duty upon.

tax-a-ble, liable to be taxed.

tax-a-tion, the act of levying taxes on persons or property; taxes collectively.

tax-i-cab, a cab with a device for measuring time and distance traveled.

tech-ni-cal, relating to the mechanical arts, any art or science, or to the mechanical side of any branch of learning.

tech-ni-cal-i-ty, something relating to the mechanical part of any art or science; formal or trifling nicety.

tel-e-gram, a message transmitted over wires by means of an electric current.

tel-e-graph, an instrument for transmitting messages to a distance by means of wires charged with an electric current: *v. t.,* to send a message or signal by means of electricity passing over wires.

tell-er, a bank clerk who receives and pays money.

tem-po-ral, worldly; not eternal.

tem-po-ra-ry, not permanent.

tem-po-rize, to delay.

ten-a-ble, capable of being defended or maintained.

ten-an-cy, a holding property as a tenant; in law, ownership by title.

ten-ant, one who rents or leases real property; an occupant.

tend-er, *n.,* an offer; money offered in payment: *v. t.,* to proffer.

ten-e-ment, a house or apartment for renting.

ten-e-ment house, a large building occupied by many families.

ten-ure, a holding; the conditions under which real estate is held.

ter-cen-ten-a-ry, the 300th anniversary.

ter-mi-nal, *adj.,* pertaining to, or forming, the end: *n.,* a limit; an end.

ter-mi-nate, *v. t.,* to end: *v. i.,* to come to an end.

ter-mi-nus, an end, as of a railroad.

ter-ra fir-ma, dry land; solid earth.

ter-ri-to-ry, a region of land; district.

tes-tate, having left a will.

tes-ta-tor, one who has died leaving a will.

tes-ti-fy, *v. i.,* to bear witness; give evidence: *v. t.,* to bear witness to; declare upon oath.

tes-ti-mo-ni-al, a certificate of one's ability; a gift in token of appreciation.

tes-ti-mo-ny, evidence; witness; affirmation; proof.

tex-tile, *adj.,* pertaining to weaving: *n.,* goods manufactured by weaving.

tex-tile fab-rics, woven goods.

thrift, frugality; economical management.

tick-er, a telegraphic instrument which receives news and prints it on a strip of paper or "tape"; a similar instrument in a broker's office to receive and record the reports from the stock market.

tide-wait-er, an officer who watches the landing of goods to secure the payment of duties.

till, a money drawer or tray in a counter or desk.

time bar-gain, an agreement to be carried out at a certain time.

time bill, a bill payable at some future date.

time clock, a clock by means of which employees record their time of arrival, etc.

time draft, a draft payable at some future time.

time-ly, seasonable; opportune.

time note, a note payable at some future time.

time-piece, a watch, clock, etc.

time-serv-er, one who adapts himself to the occasion without regard to principle.

time-ta-ble, a list of dates and hours for events, as of the arrival and departure of trains.

time-work, work paid by the hour: opposite to *piecework*.

tithe, a tenth.

ti-tle, right to the possession of property; evidence of such right.

ti-tle deed, the written evidence of one's right to a piece of property.

toll, a tax on vehicles passing along a public road.

to-pog-ra-pher, one versed in the scientific description of a place.

to-pog-ra-phy, the scientific description of a place.

tort, in law, wrong or injury not growing out of breach of contract for which damages may be obtained.

to-tal, the whole sum or amount: *v. t.,* to add: *v. i.,* to amount to a certain number, etc.

tout en-sem-ble, the general effect; the whole taken together. *Fr.*

town hall, a public building belonging to a community, used for public meetings.

town-ship, the district of a town.

trace, to copy exactly, as a drawing; follow the course of.

trac-er, one who tries to locate lost letters, packages, etc.

trade, *n.,* commerce; business: *v. i.,* to carry on business or commerce: *v. t.,* to exchange.

trade ac-cept-ance, a draft drawn by the seller on the buyer of goods, and accepted by the latter for payment at a definite time.

trade dis-count, an allowance made by dealers to others in the same business.

trade-mark, the distinguishing mark of a merchant or manufacturer.

trade name, the commercial name of a commodity; the business name of a firm.

trade price, the reduced price charged by wholesale to retail dealers.

trad-er, one carrying on commerce; a merchant.

trade school, a school where trades are taught.

trades-man, a shopkeeper.

trade-un-ion, an organization of workmen in a trade to secure favorable working conditions.

trade-un-ion-ism, the principles or practice of organized bodies of workmen.

traf-fic, *n.,* commerce; congestion of vehicles: *v. i.,* to barter; bargain.

trans-act, *v. t.,* and *v. i.,* to perform; manage.

trans-ac-tion, *n.,* the carrying on of any business; negotiation: *pl.,* the reports of the proceedings of a society, etc.

trans-at-lan-tic, beyond or crossing the Atlantic.

trans-fer, *v. t.,* to convey; copy: *n.,* conveyance of something from one person or place to another.

trans-fer-a-ble, capable of being

carried over from one person or place to another.

tran-sient, temporary.

trans-it, a passage through or over. *In transit,* on the way.

trans-mit, to send; allow to pass through.

trans-port (trăns-pōrt′), *v. t.,* to carry across from one place to another: *n.,* (trăns′-pōrt), a vessel or other conveyance for carrying troops, supplies, etc., from one place to another.

trans-ship-ment, the removal of goods or merchandise from one means of transportation to another.

treas-ur-er, one who has charge of funds.

treas-u-ry, a place where money or treasure is kept; the department of a government, which has charge of the funds.

treas-u-ry notes, notes issued by the Government and received in payment for all dues except those on imported goods.

trea-ty, an agreement between nations.

tres-pass, to intrude, as on another's property.

tri-al bal-ance, in double-entry bookkeeping, a statement of the footings of the debit and credit accounts to show whether the two sides of the ledger balance.

tri-al ju-ry, a jury called to try a case: opposite to *grand jury.*

trib-u-ta-ry, subordinate.

tri-cen-te-na-ry, the 300th anniversary.

tri-week-ly, coming three times a week.

tro-ver, legal action to regain goods found and not delivered.

truck, *n.,* a vehicle for carrying heavy goods; vegetables raised for

the market: *v. i.,* to barter; exchange.

truck-age, freight.

truck-man, the driver of a truck; one who sells goods from door to door.

trust, *n.,* confidence; responsibility; a combination of business organizations; property held for another: *v. t.,* to believe; entrust: *v. i.,* to have confidence: *adj.,* held in charge for another.

trust com-pa-ny, a corporation empowered by its charter to receive money and other property in trust, and to lend money on real and personal property.

trust deed, a deed giving power to a body of creditors to foreclose mortgages in the event of nonfulfilment of obligation on the part of the debtor.

trus-tee, one appointed to hold or manage property for another.

tur-bine, a wheel driven by water or steam.

turn-o-ver, that part of the capital of a business available for the purchase of merchandise or other commodities.

two-ply, having two thicknesses.

type-writ-er, a machine for writing in letters similar to those of print; one who writes on such a machine.

ty-pog-ra-pher, a printer.

ty-po-graph-i-cal, pertaining to the art of printing.

ty-pog-ra-phy, the art of printing.

ty-ro, a beginner.

U

ul-te-ri-or, beyond what is expressed; more distant.

ul-ti-ma, the last syllable of a word.

ul-ti-mate, the last; final; utmost.

ul-ti-ma-tum, (*pl.,* **ultimata, ulti-matums**), the final statement or proposition.

ul-ti-mo, *adv.,* in the preceding month. *Abbr., ult.*

ul-tra, extreme.

un-a-bridged, complete; having nothing omitted.

un-al-loyed, pure; unmixed.

u-nan-i-mous, of one opinion; agreeing.

un-der seal, a term, commonly indicated by *seal* or *L. S.,* in addition to the signatures of a contract to show lawful consideration for the agreement made in the contract.

un-der-sell, to sell below the trade price.

un-der-sign, to subscribe; write one's name under.

un-der-val-ue, to underestimate.

un-der-write, to write beneath; insure; subscribe.

un-der-writ-er, one who insures, issues stock, etc.

un-earned in-cre-ment, the increase in the value of property without effort on the part of the owner.

un-i, a prefix meaning *one.*

un-ion, a combination; association.

un-ion-ism, belief in a union; the belief that trade-unions will solve the labor problem.

u-nit, one; a single group in an organization; a standard of measure.

un-war-rant-ed, unjustifiable; not authoritative.

un-writ-ten, not recorded in writing; understood though not expressed.

up-hol-ster, to furnish with cushions, draperies, etc.

up-hol-ster-y, the business of furnishing cushions, draperies, etc.

up-keep, maintenance.

up-to-date, in the latest style.

u-su-fruct, the temporary right of use.

u-su-rer, one who lends money at exorbitant or illegal interest.

u-su-ry, a high or unlawful rate of interest.

u-til-i-ta-ri-an, *adj.,* pertaining to utility or usefulness: *n.,* one who believes that utility should be the sole standard of moral conduct.

u-til-i-ty, usefulness; something serviceable.

u-ti-lize, to make use of.

u-to-pi-an, impractical; ideal.

V

va-de me-cum, a Latin expression meaning, *Go with me;* a constant companion, as a manual or handbook.

val-id, sound; legal.

val-i-date, to make sound or legal; confirm.

va-lid-i-ty, soundness; legality.

val-u-a-ble, *adj.,* of great worth: *n. pl.,* costly personal property.

val-u-a-tion, appraisement; estimation.

val-ue, *n.,* worth: *v. t.,* to estimate the worth of; appreciate.

val-ued, highly prized.

val-ue re-ceived, a phrase used to denote that a note has been made or a bill accepted for a consideration and not for accommodation.

val-ued pol-i-cy, an insurance policy in which the value is agreed on and inserted as liquidated damages.

van, the front; a heavy truck.

van-tage, a superior position; advantage.

van-tage ground, a superior position.

vault, a place for safekeeping, as jewels, etc.

ve-nal, mercenary; open to bribery.

ve-nal-i-ty, a mercenary spirit; prostitution of talents, etc., for money.

vend, to sell; peddle.

vend-ee, a legal term designating the person to whom a thing is sold.

vend-er, one who sells or peddles goods.

ven-di-ble, salable.

ven-due, a public auction.

ve-neer, *v. t.,* to overlay with a thin surface of finer wood; to hide behind superficial show: *n.,* a thin layer of wood overlaid above a less valuable wood; a surface polish.

ve-ni-re, a legal writ summoning a jury.

ven-ti-late, to supply with fresh air; utter publicly.

ven-ue, the place of action in a crime, etc.; the place where the trial is held.

ver-ba-tim, word for word.

ver-dict, the decision of a jury; an opinion.

ver-nac-u-lar, one's native tongue; vocabulary peculiar to a locality, business, profession, etc.

ver-sion, a translation; account.

ver-sus, against. *Abbr., v.* or *vs.*

vest-ed, clothed; fixed; established by law and subject to no contingencies, such as vested interests.

ve-to, *n.,* the power of prohibiting; a refusal from one in authority: *v. t.,* to prohibit by authority.

vi-ce ver-sa, in reverse order; conversely.

vic-i-nage, neighborhood.

vi-cin-i-ty, nearness; neighborhood.

vi-cis-si-tude, a change in circumstances; an unforeseen event.

vi-de, a Latin term meaning *see.*

vi-del-i-cet, *adv.,* to wit; namely. *Abbr., viz.*

vin-tage, the gathering of the grape crop; a year's harvest of grapes; the wine made from it.

vis-à-vis, face to face.

vi-sé, *v. t.,* to examine and endorse: *n.,* an official signature approving a passport or other document.

vi-va vo-ce, by word of mouth; orally.

viz., namely; *Abbr.* for *videlicet.*

vo-li-tion, will; decision; intention.

volt, the standard unit for measuring electric force.

volt-age, the amount of electromotive force in terms of volts.

vol-ume, a book; mass; compass.

vouch, to guarantee; bear witness; answer for.

vouch-er, one who or that which bears witness; a receipt; certificate.

W

wages, payment for services rendered.

waive, to give up; relinquish.

waiv-er, the voluntary surrender of a right.

walk-out, a labor strike.

Wall Street, a narrow street in the lower part of New York City where the most important financial transactions of the country take place.

wares, goods; merchandise.

ware-house, a storehouse.

ware-house re-ceipt, a receipt, sometimes negotiable, given for goods in storage in a warehouse.

warp, the lengthwise threads in a fabric.

war-rant, *n.,* an official paper giving authority to arrest, etc.; a guaranty: *v. t.,* to guarantee; authorize; justify.

war-rant-a-ble, justifiable.

war-rant of-fi-cer, a noncommissioned army or naval officer.

war-ran-ty, a legal guaranty; authority.

war-ran-ty deed, a deed in which the grantor guarantees that his title to the property is as represented.

wast-age, loss due to handling, leakage, etc.

waste, to spend recklessly.

waste-ful, extravagant.

wa-tered stock, stock, the par value of which has been added to without a corresponding addition to the assets for which it stands.

wa-ter-mark, a record indicating the rise and fall of water; a faint trade mark made in paper during its manufacture.

wa-ter-works, the system by which water is supplied to communities; a pumping station.

watt, the unit of electrical power.

way-bill, a list of goods or passengers carried by a train or other conveyance.

way sta-tion, a small station on a railroad on the way to an important place.

week-day, any day but Sunday.

week-ly, *adj.,* happening in or continuing for, seven days; coming every seven days: *n.,* a periodical issued every seven days.

weigh, *v. t.,* to find the heaviness of by weight or balance; ponder: *v. i.,* to have weight.

weight, heaviness, load; importance: *v. t.,* to add to the weight of.

wel-fare, prosperity; well-being.

wharf, a pier.

wharf-age, the fee for the use of a wharf; wharf accommodation.

where-as, considering that.

where-with-al, *adv.,* with which or what: *n. pl.,* means or money by which anything can be done or bought.

whole-sale, a sale of goods in a large quantity: opposite to *retail.*

wild-cat, risky; hazardous.

wind-fall, a piece of unexpected good fortune.

wind-ward, the direction from which the wind blows.

win-now, *v. t.,* to sift; separate: *v. i.,* to separate the chaff from the wheat.

wire-less, without wires: said especially of messages sent through the air by means of electric waves.

wire-less te-leg-ra-phy, telegraphic messages sent through the air by means of electric waves without wires.

wire-less tel-e-phone, a telephonic means of receiving messages without the aid of wires.

wire-pull-ing, the act of using unseen means to gain one's end, as in politics.

wire tap-ping, the making of connection with another's wires so as to gain information.

with-out re-course, words added to the endorsement of a note, etc., to exempt the endorser from liability.

wit-ness, *n.,* testimony; evidence; one who testifies: *v. t.,* to look at; see; testify.

woof, the crosswise threads of a woven fabric.

work-day, a day on which labor is performed.

work-ing day, a day on which work is done.

work-ing-man, a laborer.

work-man, a common or skilled laborer.

work-man-like, worthy of a skilled laborer; careful.

work-man-ship, the manner in which a piece of work is done; style of performance.

work-shop, a room where manufacturing is carried on.

worth, *n.,* merit; price: *adj.,* equal in value to.

Y

ya-hoo, a savage, degraded person.

year-book, a book issued once a year, usually a report or summary.

Z

ze-nith, the point directly overhead; the greatest height.

ze-ro, a cipher; nothing; the neutral point on a scale, as of temperature.

INDEX